Get Into Medical School!

A Guide for the Perplexed

Second Edition

Get Into Medical School!

A Guide for the Perplexed

Second Edition

Kenneth V. Iserson
M.D., MBA, FACEP

Galen Press, Ltd. • Tucson, Arizona

Copyright © 1997, 2004 by Kenneth V. Iserson.
Cover illustrations © 2003 by Brand X Pictures. Used with permission.
All Rights Reserved.

No part of this book may be reproduced or transmitted in any form or by any means, electronic or mechanical, including photocopying, recording, or by any information storage and retrieval system, without permission in writing from the Publisher.

ISBN: 1-883620-31-7

GALEN PRESS, LTD.
P.O. BOX 64400
TUCSON, AZ 85728-4400
PHONE (520) 577-8363 FAX (520) 529-6459
Orders (U.S. & Canada) 1-800-442-5369
www.galenpress.com
Bulk purchase terms are available. Please contact our special sales department.

KENNETH V. ISERSON, M.D., MBA, FACEP
Professor of Emergency Medicine
University of Arizona College of Medicine
1501 N. Campbell Avenue
Tucson, AZ 85724

Library of Congress Cataloging-in-Publication Data

Iserson, Kenneth V.
Get into medical school! : a guide for the perplexed / Kenneth V. Iserson. — 2nd ed.
p. ; cm.
Rev. ed. of Get into medical school / Kenneth V. Iserson. 1996.
Includes bibliographical references and index.
ISBN 1-883620-31-7 (pbk.)
1. Medical colleges—United States—Admission. 2. Medical colleges—United States—Entrance requirements. I. Title: Get into medical school. II. Iserson, Kenneth V. Get into medical school.
R838.4.184 2004
610 ' 71 ' 173—dc20 04-

Printed in the United States of America.
10 9 8 7 6 5 4 3 2 1

— Table of Contents —

— List of Figures —

— Acknowledgements —

This book would not exist but for the significant help I received from others. First and foremost is the fantastic assistance and support from my wife, Mary Lou Iserson, C.P.A. Acting as both a skilled and persistent editor, and the resident computer whiz, she midwifed both the first and second editions.

I greatly appreciate the help of the many students and physicians who graciously provided feedback on the first edition and, in many cases, materials for both.

As always, I owe a debt of gratitude to my friends at the University of Arizona Health Sciences Library, who find sources of information in inscrutable ways. I owe special thanks to my colleagues in the reference section, Ms. Hannah Fisher, R.N., M.L.S., AHIP and Ms. Nga T. Nguyen, B.A., B.S., Senior Library Specialist, who helped assure the accuracy of much of the book's information.

Special thanks goes to Donald B. Witzke, Ph.D., Associate Professor, Department of Pathology & Laboratory Medicine, University of Kentucky, Lexington, KY, who has strongly supported this book's concept and has acted as a superb and knowledgeable content reviewer. Likewise, James W. Tysinger, Ph.D., Deputy Chair for Education, Department of Family and Community Medicine, University of Texas Medical School at San Antonio, who is an expert on résumés, personal statements, and medical career planning, was invaluable in updating those sections of the book.

Ensuring that specific parts of this book would be accurate, clear, and current required the help of individuals intimately involved with those areas. Without their assistance, this book would have failed in its primary mission: to provide the information premeds really need to prepare for and apply to medical schools. Among those who graciously assisted are:

Robert F. Ruiz, M.A., Vice President for Application Services, American Association of Colleges of Osteopathic Medicine; Barbara J. Gordon, Assistant Vice President, Medical School Application Services, Association of American Medical Colleges; Christopher A. Leadem, Ph.D., Senior Associate Dean for Admissions and Student Affairs, University of Arizona College of Medicine, Tucson, AZ; Maggie Gumble, Senior Financial Counselor, University of Arizona College of Medicine, Tucson, AZ; Linda K. Don, Director of the Healthcare Workforce Development, Diversity and Community Outreach for the University of Arizona Health Sciences Center, Tucson, AZ; and several other individuals at the Association of American Medical Colleges.

Many of the questions I have tried to answer in this book were raised by members of a wonderful organization, the National Association of Advisors for the Health Professions. Among my colleagues in that organization, I must doff my hat to the Dean of Advisors, Dr. Daniel Marien, who, although formally retired, still provides wonderful insights into, and an amazing depth of knowledge about, the premed process. Another member, Stan Eisen, Ph.D., Biology Professor and Director of Preprofessional Health Programs, Christian Brothers University, Memphis, TN, has kindly allowed me to use a figure from his website.

Finally, the quality of this book is due, in large measure, to the folks at Galen Press, Ltd., Tucson, AZ. Jennifer Gilbert, M.A., my editor and friend, meticulously edited the entire work, page by page—and eventually chapter by chapter. Chris McNellis, B.S., struggled through the often arcane and user-unfriendly medical school websites to help gather some of the extensive data in the book's charts.

My thanks also to Lynn Bishop of Lynn Bishop Design for producing the wonderful cover and to Anne Olson-Scribner, Casa Cold Type, for redesigning the interior pages using her magic desktop skills.

Of course, Mary Lou Sherk, the publisher, made this all possible with her belief in the project.

My hope is that this updated book will help the next generation of physicians make an easier transition into medical school.

— Kenneth V. Iserson, M.D.

Feedback Form*

Medical schools and other agencies: Please use this form to update or correct your contact information.

I would like to pass on the following information or personal experience for inclusion in the next edition of *Get Into Medical School! A Guide for the Perplexed*. Or, I have a suggestion about what to add to the next edition.

Name (please print)

Address

Phone E-mail

***Please return to:**

Kenneth V. Iserson, M.D., Galen Press, Ltd.
P.O. Box 64400, Tucson AZ 85728-4400 USA
or e-mail: sales@galenpress.com

Thank you for your feedback

1

A Medical Career

Do all the good you can,
By all the means you can,
In all the ways you can,
In all the places you can,
At all the times you can,
To all the people you can,
As long as ever you can.

— John Wesley, *Rules of Conduct*

You want to be a physician? First, ask yourself why you want to put yourself through the following ordeal:

- A prolonged and arduous premedical education
- A highly competitive medical school admissions process
- A demanding medical school education
- An exhausting postgraduate (residency and fellowship) training
- Tough licensing examinations
- Specialty certification examinations, with recertification exams throughout your career

If you are willing to go through all this, you end up in a career with long hours, increasing governmental and insurance company interference, and lots of stress. Clearly, only those individuals who are very dedicated (or foolish) would put themselves into this situation. If you have spoken to practicing physicians who question whether "any sane person should go into medicine," you might reflect on why these individuals went into medicine in the first place. Have they lost their real motivation amidst a flurry of bad career choices? Did they go into medicine for the wrong reasons?

A recent Kaiser Family Foundation survey (see the *Annotated Bibliography*) found that only 53% of physicians would recommend that you enter the profession—findings relatively unchanged from their 1981 survey. The 45% of physicians surveyed who would not recommend entering the profession (8% seemed to be waffling) cited several reasons:

- Excessive professional demands (31%)
- Less respect for the medical profession (31%)
- Inadequate financial rewards (31%)
- Difficulties in starting or operating a practice (22%)
- An overly long, difficult, or expensive medical education process (16%)
- A lack of personal satisfaction in their professional work (15%)

Given all that, why do *you* want to be a physician? Examine your answer carefully. If you can't come up with a good reason, then forget it—the sacrifices are not going to be worth it to you. If, however, you think you have good reasons and the dedication needed to enter the field, research medical careers in depth. Learn what opportunities are available and what physicians' lives and practices are really like. Then, if you still want to become a physician, become familiar with the rules needed to get through the system successfully. This book is designed to guide you through this process.

Remember, however, that the goal is not to get into medical school. No matter how difficult it is to get into (and through) medical school, it is only an interim, short-term objective. The real goal is to be a practicing physician. Is that the goal for which you are willing to work and sacrifice? Think about it very hard. There is a lot of work; there will be many sacrifices.

— Should You Become a Physician? —

Deciding why you want to commit your life to a medical career is the most important step on the road to getting into and through medical school (and then residency and practicing medicine)—and the one most people omit. The beginning of any path offers the most opportunities for changing course. Later, as you travel down the road, you may not have as many options. Before you start your own journey, whether you are a high school, an undergraduate, or a postgraduate student, take the time to study your motives for choosing this career. No one else can peek into your mind, so be honest with yourself.

Most physicians love their work (at least most of the time) and wouldn't trade what they do for anything else. Unfortunately, a significant percentage of physicians hates their career and dreams of doing something else. They didn't spend enough time assessing their own wants, needs, and motivations. It is better to do a self-assessment now, and to make your own well-considered decision to enter or bypass a medical career. That way, you will not become one of those patient-unfriendly doctors who, 15 or 20 years down the road, feels hemmed in by a career and a life that they neither expected nor really wanted.

A well-known general practitioner from Georgia, upon nearing the end of his career, wrote:

> I have not advised anybody to go into medicine. And I have not advised anybody *not* to go into medicine. I personally feel like "what else is there?" Coming to the end . . . of a career as a general practitioner, I still feel that this is The Queen of all professions. That this is something that is so much greater than the sum of all its parts. That you can serve medicine but you can never conquer medicine, and all you can be is a walking disciple. And I wouldn't do anything else if I could.

Another physician put it succinctly, answering her own question:

> Are you sorry you went to medical school? Yes, I would still do this . . . and, NO, I'm not sorry I went to medical school. I thank God for the privilege of having a chance to experience those rare sweet natural highs. Just one or two of those in a lifetime make the strenuous battle worthwhile.

Frequently, bright high school and college students tell me that they would not consider a medical career because they "can't stand the sight of blood." Actually, it is an unusual individual who is not initially made uncomfortable by the sight of someone's blood (especially his own). As a high school senior, I joined our local volunteer rescue (ambulance) squad, although I was somewhat concerned about how I might react when I saw lots of blood or someone badly hurt. A wise officer told me that it was all right if I felt queasy when I saw some of the horrible sights. It was okay to be sick—after I had helped the patient in any way I could. As an example, he pointed out that the biggest, loudest, and strongest person in our organization, after a recent call, had gotten sick from what he had seen. However, this was after he had done his job.

Many people react badly to the sight of injuries because they are uncertain about what they will see when the skin opens up. Part of a physician's training, especially in anatomy and surgery, is to learn exactly what to expect when different parts of the body are exposed in different ways. It's simply a matter of knowledge and experience. If you decide you really want a medical career, you will be able to get through the rough spots. You will also be a physician who loves his or her work.

What Are Your Motivations?

Most people want jobs that provide excitement and give meaning to their lives. Medicine gives its practitioners:

- Respect
- An opportunity to help people
- An action-oriented, rather than a desk-bound, job
- An exciting job (just how exciting depends upon the specialty)
- The chance to change locations, since physicians are in demand almost everywhere
- The flexibility to follow many paths at different career stages
- A good income with a secure future

Most people who want to be a physician are idealistic. They want to help others. Perhaps this idealism is necessary to carry aspiring physicians through their many years of often-grueling education and residency training. Unfortunately, students (and residents) can become disheartened when medical "educators" try to demolish their idealism. In many cases, sadly, they succeed. Others get disillusioned later when they discover that they cannot save the world or even a large part of it. While physicians are an important cog in the health care delivery system, they can relieve pain and suffering for only a small number of people.

Individuals who seek medical careers because of the lure of a substantial income should do some simple calculations. For those who have the aptitude and interest, getting an MBA degree from a good school may be easier and may result in a better income. An MBA degree takes only two years and, for the first decade after they graduate, these business graduates often have higher incomes than those who pursue medicine. One analysis showed that, based on what it costs for a medical education, the "hours-adjusted net present value" of the money invested in education is $10.73 for attorneys, $10.40 for procedure-based physicians, $8.90 for dentists, $8.27 for businessmen, and $5.97 for primary care physicians. After their mid-20s, lawyers, businessmen, and dentists also work fewer hours than do physicians.

Self-test

If you are thinking about a career in medicine, but are not sure if it is right for you, ask yourself the following questions developed by the Association of American Medical Colleges (AAMC):

- Do I care deeply about other people, their problems, and their pain?
- Do I enjoy using my skills and knowledge to help people?
- Do I enjoy learning and gaining new understanding?
- Do I often dig deeper into a subject than my teacher requires?
- Do I enjoy and value learning, not just making good grades?
- Am I interested in how the human body functions?
- Am I intrigued by the ways medicine can be used to improve life?

If you answered "yes" to most of these questions, your interests and personality are most likely similar to those of practicing physicians. Now you must ask yourself whether you are motivated to pursue the studies necessary to achieve that goal.

Premedical advisers suggest that if you don't know whether you want to be a physician or whether you "have what it takes," do two things: Take some required premed science courses and get some clinical experience. The science courses will demonstrate whether you have the interest, aptitude, and ability necessary to learn and understand material that is similar to the basic science courses in medical school. The clinical experiences will show you whether you have a real interest in a medical career.

Formal Tests

Career counselors have tests available to help you decide what career direction to take. While these tests are far from perfect, they provide you with a mirror in which to see your current likes and dislikes related to a career choice. If you are uncertain about whether you really want to go into medicine, you may want to take one or more of these tests. You may not believe what they tell you, but they are among the most objective tools available.

Such a test experience certainly sticks with me. As a ninth-grade student, my classmates and I took the Kuder Preference Record-Occupational Test. It was supposed to give us an idea of what career best suited each of us. I took it, although I already knew I was going to be an attorney. When we got the results, I knew the test was a ridiculous waste of time. It said that I should be a fireman, a forest ranger, or—of all crazy things—a physician. As it turned out, I later spent five years as a volunteer fireman, have spent the last 20 years as a member of a wilderness search and rescue team, and, of course, practice medicine.

Sometimes these tests can tell you things about yourself that you either don't know or don't yet recognize. If you're in doubt, give them a try.

— Why You May *Not* Want to Be a Physician —

Nearly two-thirds (61%) of those applying to medical school decide to pursue medical careers while still in high school, and another 11% decide while they are college freshmen. Many of their peers also consider medical careers but decide not to pursue them. While all groups seek job satisfaction, medical school applicants differ from their peers in that they are more altruistic; desire constant challenges in their job; want time for friends, family, and other interests; and do not want to move frequently because of their job.

Students who seriously consider a medical career take the MCAT examination, do well on it, and plan to apply to medical school. Of these students, about 10% change their mind and never apply. It is instructive to look at the reasons this group gives for not applying to medical school:

- Physicians must give up too much time and freedom.
- Another career seems more satisfying.
- Another field will better fulfill my interest in science.
- The future of medicine is bleak, according to physicians.
- I can help others better in another field.
- The financial rewards do not justify the time and money invested.
- Medical education is too stressful.
- Physicians have too many legal liabilities, and malpractice insurance costs too much.
- Changes in the health care delivery system have impaired physicians' independence.

As you consider a medical career, ponder the statements above. If you agree with two or more of them, you should seriously reconsider whether you really do want to become a physician. If you have doubts, now would be a good time to find an alternative career path, as the route to medicine is long, tortuous, and demanding.

Also, be wary of going into medicine because of family pressures. The premed adviser at a large Midwestern school tells this story:

> I had a student who came in to get the MCAT application materials. "Why?" I asked, since I had never seen this student before.
>
> "To prove to my parents (his mother is a physician) that I shouldn't be a doctor. I plan on being a computer scientist." He explained that he had started undergraduate school as a premed, but while taking a computer course in his first semester, he knew he had found his niche. His physician mother, however, couldn't understand that. He subsequently got appropriately dismal scores on the MCAT and went on to follow his own dream, rather than that of his mother.

Experienced admission officers view applicants whose parents are physicians with a wary eye, and are careful to question their motives for entering medicine. If these students have their *own* reasons for pursuing medicine, there is no problem. If they are following this course to fulfill their parents' dreams, it's a danger signal.

— What Are the Steps to Become a Doctor? —

You have undoubtedly had contact with physicians. They often seem wise, unflappable, and able to work magical feats with their medicines, scalpels, and other devices. You can hardly imagine them struggling though the rigors of medical school and residency, let alone high school and college. Don't let yourself be intimidated by the image. They were once in your situation—just hoping to get into medical school. If you are motivated to be a physician, you can do it. It just takes a lot of time and effort.

Figure 1.1 is a flow chart listing the sequence of events for premed students. Few people follow this course exactly, but, wherever you "jump in," it provides a rough guide to the process. (See Appendix A: *Abbreviations and Acronyms.*)

The Challenge

Although entering medical school is now quite difficult, before World War I, medical schools accepted nearly anyone who could pay the entry fees. Moreover, the quality of U.S. medical schools was inconsistent and, for the most part, not highly regarded. One of the major reforms in medical education was to institute minimum entrance requirements. The following description of 1934 Nobel Prize winner George Minot's entry into Harvard Medical School illustrates how your predecessors could enter medical school nearly by accident:

> **The two cousins felt little urgency to make a decision, and so they separated for the summer of 1908, with George sailing for Europe. When he returned at the end of the summer, he and his cousin talked more about going to the medical school. In their world there was only one medical school to be considered. So they decided to go to medical school on Monday in late September. On that day, they ran some errands and watched football practice; the next day, they picked up their college credentials in Cambridge and on Thursday, 1 October 1908, were among the 65 men who began their medical studies in the Harvard Medical School Class of 1912. (Brieger GH. Getting into medical school in the good old days: good for whom? *Ann Int Med.* 1993;119:1138-43.)**

Initially, changes in medical school curricula and the institution of accreditation led to a decrease in the number of medical students who graduated. Many failed the more difficult courses. Today, nearly all students who enter medical school will graduate—which is to be expected, since they are so highly qualified. Medical schools have also added numerous support systems, both academic and emotional, to assist students through their medical education.

Number of Applicants

The number of individuals that apply to U.S. medical schools waxes and wanes (see Figure 1.2). In the 1970s, large numbers of students applied for about 2,000 fewer positions than are offered today. The number of applicants hit a low in 1988–89. There were about 35,000 applicants for 2003–04.

Medicine may have become less attractive to students due to major changes in health care delivery systems, the effect malpractice suits have had on the profession, or media hype that has both glamorized the medical profession and made it look too difficult to pursue.

If you want to look on the bright side, be thankful that you are not applying to medical school in many European countries, where the ratios of first-year medical students to applicants is extraordinarily high (e.g., Norway 1:20; Greece 1:16; Turkey 1:12; France 1:8; Portugal 1:8; Sweden 1:7).

Number of Positions

It is important to know the reality of the application process so that you can accurately assess your chance of being accepted to medical school. There are approximately 22,000 first-year positions available at U.S. and Canadian M.D. and U.S. Osteopathic medical schools annually (Figure 1.3). This number has remained relatively constant over the past two decades. In the 1990s, several groups tried to decrease the number of medical students and medical schools, saying that a "physician glut" was imminent. Yet, a shortage of physicians—especially in primary care—occurred, and some medical schools recently have increased the number of students they accept. Since 1990, one M.D.-granting

FIGURE 1.1

Typical Premed Activities

High School

- ❑ Get good grades
- ❑ Take biology (1-year minimum)
- ❑ Take advanced science course (1-year minimum)
- ❑ Take foreign language (3-year minimum)
- ❑ Take English (4 years)
- ❑ Take speech
- ❑ Do volunteer community service
- ❑ Do Must/Want Analysis for schools you consider
- ❑ Get medical school Accelerated Program information
- ❑ Apply to Accelerated Program (if you want to)
- ❑ Get college/university information
- ❑ Take chemistry (1-year minimum)
- ❑ Take physics (1-year minimum)
- ❑ Take mathematics (4 years)
- ❑ Take computer science
- ❑ Take psychology/sociology
- ❑ Participate in premed club
- ❑ Shadow a physician
- ❑ Take SAT or ACT exam
- ❑ Apply to colleges

College: Freshman Year

- ❑ Meet with premed adviser/learn premed requirements
- ❑ Think about a major and minor courses of study
- ❑ Plan a tentative schedule for the next 3½ years
- ❑ Develop study skills
- ❑ Maintain excellent GPA
- ❑ Begin extracurricular activities
- ❑ Participate in premed club
- ❑ Work/volunteer in medical area
- ❑ Get AAMC's *MCAT Student Manual* for subject outlines
- ❑ Subscribe to medical student journals (see *Bibliography*)
- ❑ Read interesting books about medicine (see *Bibliography*)
- ❑ Review medical school admission requirements
- ❑ Develop a premed course of study
- ❑ Consider what you will do this summer
- ❑ Apply to MMEP (minorities only)
- ❑ Apply to Accelerated Program (if desired)
- ❑ Talk to premed upperclassman to get a reality check
- ❑ Contact senior medical students or residents and ask if you can "shadow" them for a shift

FIGURE 1.1 (continued)

Typical Premed Activities

College: Sophomore Year

- ❑ Work/volunteer in medical area
- ❑ Read some interesting books about medicine
- ❑ Meet with premed adviser to discuss your program
- ❑ Select your major and minor courses of study
- ❑ Maintain excellent GPA
- ❑ Check medical schools' entry requirements
- ❑ Fine-tune your college schedule
- ❑ Consider participating in research
- ❑ Consider what you will do this summer
- ❑ Apply to MMEP (minorities only)
- ❑ Study for MCAT (summer before junior year if you will take it early)
- ❑ Apply for MCAT (if you will take it early)
- ❑ Plan for any special junior-year program (e.g., junior year abroad)

College: Junior Year

- ❑ Study for MCAT (if not yet taken)
- ❑ Apply for MCAT (if not yet taken)
- ❑ Take MCAT:
    1. August before junior year
    2. April of junior year
    3. August after junior year
- ❑ Meet with premed adviser
- ❑ Meet with minority premed counselor, if applicable
- ❑ Maintain the best GPA you can
- ❑ Gather information about medical schools
- ❑ Complete Must/Want Analysis forms for schools that interest you
- ❑ Get AMCAS/AACOMAS/other applications (February)
- ❑ Begin preparing AMCAS/AACOMAS essay
- ❑ Work/volunteer in medical area
- ❑ Meet with premed committee
- ❑ Request and send reference letters
- ❑ Obtain, review, and send transcripts
- ❑ Complete AMCAS/AACOMAS/other applications
- ❑ Visit nearby schools that interest you
- ❑ Apply for Early Acceptance Program (optional)
- ❑ Submit applications (June)
- ❑ Consider what you will do this summer

FIGURE 1.1 (continued)

Typical Premed Activities

College: Senior Year

- ❑ Work/volunteer in medical area
- ❑ Take MCAT in August to improve scores or if not yet taken
- ❑ Confirm that schools have received your application materials and letters
- ❑ Maintain the best GPA you can
- ❑ Complete secondary medical school applications
- ❑ Interview at medical schools
- ❑ Revise Must/Want Analyses for schools visited
- ❑ Complete GAPSFAS financial aid form
- ❑ If wait-listed, send letter confirming interest
- ❑ Consider what you will do this summer (keep options open)
- ❑ ACCEPT OFFER (by May 15)
- ❑ Accept additional offers if higher on your "Must/Want" Analysis list; withdraw previous acceptances
- ❑ Write to thank references and tell them of your success
- ❑ *Thank your premed adviser for all his/her help*

school has closed (Oral Roberts University), two (Medical College of Pennsylvania and Hahnemann University) have merged, and one has started (Florida State). During the same period, five new D.O.-granting medical schools have opened (Arizona, Lake Erie, Pikesville, Touro, and Edward Via Virginia).

— Medicine: The Potential Future —

It is difficult to predict either the need for or the supply of U.S. physicians in the future—either in total or by specialty. Physician oversupply and maldistribution has been an issue in the United States at least since an 1895 *Journal of the American Medical Association* discussion of the topic, which concluded, "our 'excess of doctors' would disappear at once" if the physician population was equitably distributed. In the early 1990s, experts predicted an oversupply of as many as 165,000 physicians by the year 2000. Yet these dire predictions have not come to pass. *Anticipating future physician and specialty supply and demand is a very inexact science.*

It is now thought that there will be an increasing physician shortage, becoming serious around the year 2011, with a shortage of about 200,000 physicians by 2020. Facts that support this are:

1. A faster-than-expected population growth rate
2. An aging physician population
3. Decreasing resident workloads
4. An increasing supply of women in medicine (who are expected to work 20% fewer hours over their professional lives)
5. A rapidly aging population
6. Shorter working hours for all physicians due to the increase in alternative health plans, legislative requirements, and changing lifestyles

FIGURE 1.2

Applicants to and Acceptance Ratios for U.S. (M.D.) Medical Schools

	Number of Applicants	Number of Applications Submitted	Avg. Number Applications per Person	Number of Accepted Applicants*	Applicant: Acceptance Ratio
1974–75	42,624	362,376	8.5	15,066	2.8
1984–85	35,944	331,937	9.2	17,194	2.1
1985–86	32,893	307,427	9.3	17,228	1.9
1986–87	31,323	295,744	9.4	17,092	1.8
1987–88	28,123	266,900	9.5	17,027	1.7
1988–89	26,721	258,442	9.7	17,108	1.6
1989–90	26,915	262,426	9.7	16,975	1.6
1990–91	29,243	290,489	9.9	17,206	1.7
1991–92	33,301	354,017	10.6	17,436	1.9
1992–93	37,410	405,720	10.8	17,464	2.1
1993–94	42,808	482,788	11.0	17,362	2.5
1994–95	45,365	561,593	12.4	17,317	2.6
1995–96	46,591	595,975	12.8	17,357	2.7
1997–98	43,020	512,878	11.9	17,313	2.5
1998–99	41,004	481,336	11.7	17,379	2.4
1999–2000	38,529	454,380	11.8	17,445	2.2
2000–2001	37,092	433,978	11.7	17,538	2.1
2001–2002	34,859	403,609	11.6	17,456	2.0
2002–2003	33,625	373,686	11.1	17,592	1.9
2003–2004	34,785	N/A	N/A	N/A	N/A

*Some accepted applicants decide not to enter medical school.

N/A: Data not available at time of publication.

Adapted from: Barzansky B, Etzel SI: Educational programs in U.S. medical schools, 2002–2003. *JAMA*. 2003;290(9):1190-96; and other sources.

Physicians may also continue to retire, reduce their workload, or move into nonclinical positions earlier. In recent years, physician retirement rates have increased significantly. The probability of a physician retiring between the ages of 55 and 74 increased by 60% in the past decade. Nearly one-half of practicing physicians aged 50 and above say they will retire or change to a nonclinical position within three years. It's no wonder that the American Medical Association (AMA) estimates that the increasing retirement rates may absorb as much as one-third of the projected growth in physician supply by the year 2020.

Figure 1.4 shows the estimated number of physicians in the major specialties over the next 20 years. Note that the number of most nonprimary care specialists will peak around 2010, after which it is projected to decrease. Since these are only estimates, based somewhat on projected future needs, they are highly speculative.

While a decreasing birth rate may suggest a need for fewer pediatricians, for example, a new health care system allowing children greater access may increase the need. No one knows whether advances in the treatment of coronary artery disease will favor a need for more invasive cardiologists (those who pass catheters under x-ray guidance) rather than for more thoracic surgeons. Changes in both the treatment of chronic renal disease and the government's and the public's attitude toward

FIGURE 1.3

Number of Schools and First-Year Positions at U.S. and Canadian Medical Schools, 2003

Type of School	Number of Schools	Number of 1st-Year Positions[1]
U.S.-M.D.	124+1[2]	16,933
U.S.-Osteopathic	20	3,077
Canadian	16	1,940
TOTAL	**157+1**	**21,950**

1: Available first-year positions for new entrants. There are approximately 800 positions for those repeating the first year.

2: University of Minnesota–Duluth School of Medicine offers only a 2-year curriculum. Students then transfer to University of Minnesota–Minneapolis to complete their degrees.

chronic renal dialysis programs will profoundly affect the need for nephrologists. Finding an organic basis for more major psychoses may reduce the need for psychiatrists, while increasing the need for (and effectiveness of) neurologists. And, if history is any guide, AIDS will be only one of many epidemics requiring more family physicians, Internists, and infectious diseases specialists. Primary care physicians will clearly increase in numbers. Whether that will result in too many primary care physicians is uncertain.

Medicine does not remain static. Rather, it is an ocean of care with many storms and currents. The storms are the major new medical discoveries, new diseases, and changes in the demographics of the population. The currents are the changes in attitudes, within both the medical community and the public, concerning the popularity of various medical practices. (Yes, medicine is guided by more than pure science.) Your ship will sail this ocean. Care, foresight, and a willingness to occasionally alter course slightly will keep you afloat.

Length of Training

The majority of medical students do not make specialty choices based on the length of required training. The pleasure they get out of practicing a specialty in which they are interested generally pays them back for the added preparation.

The length of training does seem to influence some medical students, however, particularly those selecting generalist or support specialties. This influence increases as the student's debt rises, with one-third of graduating medical students admitting that their educational debt influenced their specialty choice. While this may be understandable, it is sad that after so much effort, a lifelong career decision might be made on such a flimsy basis.

One point worth noting, however, is that longer training does not always yield higher income. In the medical subspecialties, for example, because gastroenterologists spend some time specializing, they have large incomes, mainly from well-reimbursed procedures such as endoscopy, while rheumatologists make scarcely more than general internists. This doesn't mean that those who have a calling in rheumatology should not pursue this specialty, only that extra education does not always equal extra income.

Hours Worked

Work hours and lifestyle may also affect your decision whether to become a physician and, later, about which specialty to enter. Medical students often work very long hours during their clinical (third and fourth) years of school. The hours worked during the intern year (now officially called the "first year of residency") can be unbelievably horrible. This varies depending upon the specialty (psychiatry, radiology, and pathology can be pretty easy) and the institution (public hospitals usually have the

FIGURE 1.4

Change in Number and Percentage of M.D. Physician Specialists, 2000, 2010, and 2020

Specialty	Number of (Percent of All) Physicians		
	2000	2010	2020
PRIMARY CARE	**249,406 (34.6%)**	**300,590 (37.3%)**	**339,038 (40.1%)**
Gen/Family Practice	87,803 (12.2)	107,052 (13.3)	123,339 (14.6)
Gen Internal Medicine	109,264 (15.2)	128,938 (16.0)	142,047 (16.8)
Gen Pediatrics	52,339 (7.3)	64,601 (8.0)	73,652 (8.7)
NONPRIMARY CARE	**470,435 (65.4)**	**504,702 (62.7)**	**505,454 (59.9)**
Medical Subspecialties	76,751 (10.7)	91,823 (11.4)	98,734 (11.7)
Pediatric Subspecialties	10,115 (1.4)	13,519 (1.7)	15,854 (1.9)
Obstetrics/Gynecology	41,759 (5.8)	46,088 (5.7)	48,009 (5.7)
General Surgery	34,229 (4.8)	34,452 (4.3)	33,739 (4.0)
Surgical Subspecialties	83,185 (11.6)	84,214 (10.5)	80,515 (9.5)
Emergency Medicine	21,755 (3.0)	23,497 (2.9)	22,644 (2.7)
Psychiatry	47,452 (6.6)	49,275 (6.1)	48;183 (5.7)
Radiology	34,866 (4.8)	35,057 (4.4)	32,972 (3.9)
Anesthesiology	37,073 (5.2)	41,949 (5.2)	43,120 (5.1)
Pathology	20,013 (2.8)	20,483 (2.5)	19,686 (2.3)
Other Specialties	63,238 (8.8)	64,344 (8.0)	61,997 (7.3)

Data supplied by the Center for Health Policy Research, American Medical Association, Chicago, IL: December 1999.

toughest schedules). During residency, the hours spent in a specialty often mimic the hours practitioners work in that specialty. Although official rules (effective July 1, 2003) limit the amount of time most residents can work to a maximum of 80 hours a week and every third night on call, many programs bend the rules.

The number of hours physicians work markedly influences their family life and extracurricular activities. Figure 1.5 shows the weekly hours worked by different specialists, but remember that how hard they work during those hours varies tremendously. If you expect to have any life outside of medicine, consider this carefully. Note that much of the time a surgeon or obstetrician spends at work may be "down time" while waiting (usually in the middle of the night, on weekends and holidays) for an available operating room or for a woman in labor.

Many specialists now join group practices to decrease their work hours and on-call (available in the hospital or on pager for patient care) time. This has resulted in a large variation in work hours, not only among specialties, but also within each individual specialty. Therefore, work hours should not be your only consideration when choosing a medical career—but do not totally ignore this factor.

Stressors

Life and career stresses require many physicians to stop clinical practice, if only for a while. Women, more frequently than men, decrease or stop practicing medicine due to their family responsibilities—especially caring for small children or elderly parents. Both men and women physicians may be plagued by personal illnesses, including substance abuse disorders, mental health ailments, and physical illness. They also experience stress, burnout, and career dissatisfaction. This leads some to permanently abandon their medical careers, while others only pause (but they may face significant difficulties when they try to return to work).

FIGURE 1.5

Average Weekly Work Hours of Different Specialists

Specialty	Patient Care*	All Professional Activities**
Orthopedic Surgery	61	61
General Surgery	60	62
Cardiovascular Diseases	58	61
Anesthesiology	55	58
Gastroenterology	52	60
Radiology	50	59
Obstetrics/Gynecology	49	64
Gen Internal Medicine	49	58
Family Practice	46	55
Pediatrics	44	54
Pathology	44	45
Psychiatry	40	47
Dermatology	40	49
Emergency Medicine	39	48

*Adapted from: American Medical Association. *Socioeconomic Characteristics of Medical Practice, 2000–2002.* Chicago, IL: AMA, 2002.

**Adapted from: American Medical Association. *AMA Workforce Data, 2002.* Chicago, IL: AMA, 2002.

— Basic Rules for Success —

If you decide to pursue a medical career, you can anticipate setbacks and obstacles along the way. To mentally prepare yourself for the grind, consider the rules that military officers use to survive when in hostile territory:

- Get control of your mind before panic sets in
- Mentally motivate yourself
- Think about what you already know about solving the problem
- Break the problem down into a set of smaller, prioritized steps
- Don't dwell on past mistakes; concentrate on solving the current problem
- Mentally prepare yourself for the long haul
- Negative thinking is a dead end

The world is generally hostile to premed students. You must have the personal motivation and be willing to repeatedly overcome personal, academic, and bureaucratic obstacles to succeed. If you are willing to do that, you can become a physician.

2

Medicine's Scope

Medicine is the most difficult art to acquire.
All the college can do is teach the student principles,
based on facts . . . they simply start him in the right direction;
they do not make him a good practitioner.
That is his own affair.

— Sir William Osler

The medical profession is divided into numerous areas of expertise, known as "specialties" and "subspecialties." Each requires that physicians complete special training. As you can see from Figures 2.2 and 2.3, the array of medical specialties and subspecialties is vast. The list would be even longer if some specialties, such as trauma surgery, were officially approved. The various specialties are often grouped as: primary care specialties, hospital-based specialties, and the medical and surgical specialties.

Primary care (sometimes called "continuous care") specialties officially include general internal medicine, family practice, general pediatrics, and obstetrics and gynecology. These physicians are supposed to provide first-contact care to patients and then continue that care over time. Federal and state financial support flows to medical schools and residency programs that train these specialists. Figure 2.1 lists the factors that indicate if a medical student is likely to enter a primary care specialty.

Hospital-based (sometimes called "support") specialties are those which are primarily practiced in hospitals and which often assist other physicians. They include anesthesiology, emergency medicine, pathology, and radiology. At large institutions, this category also includes critical care, neonatology, hospitalist, and nuclear medicine.

Most physicians are in *medical* or *surgical* specialties or in a combination of the two. Surgical specialties include all areas in which physicians do surgery on an inpatient or outpatient basis (all surgical subspecialties) and neurosurgery, orthopedic surgery, otolaryngology, and urology. Medical specialties include pediatrics and internal medicine, with all their subspecialties, plus neurology, dermatology, anesthesiology, physical medicine & rehabilitation, psychiatry, and radiation oncology. Emergency medicine and, sometimes, family practice combine the two areas of practice. (See Figures 2.2 to 2.4 for listings of the approved specialties and subspecialties, as well as the number of physicians practicing in many of these areas.)

Medical students often determine which specialty to enter by deciding whether they want to do a medical specialty, a surgical specialty, neither, or both. Once they graduate from medical school, most medical students do a one-year internship (officially called the first year of residency), either in a specialty or rotating among several specialties (called a transitional internship). If they want to be qualified in a specialty area, this first year is followed by between two and four more years of residency in that specialty. Following their residency training, they may elect to enter a fellowship to get subspecialty training. These fellowships last between one and three years.

FIGURE 2.1

Characteristics Associated with Entering a Primary Care Specialty

- Behavioral science/liberal arts major
- Married
- Older
- Preference on admission
- Attended public school
- Received federal scholarship
- Self or spouse comes from a small town
- "Sensing, feeling, judging" type on Meyers-Briggs Type Indicator Test
- Tolerance for ambiguity

— Jobs: The Ultimate Goal —

Completing medical school and residency seems pointless if you cannot ultimately get a position in your specialty. You will have to take a realistic look at the specialties. Some fields are already crowded; others, according to the best estimates, soon will be. In recent years, graduates in such specialties as anesthesiology, plastic surgery, and pathology have had trouble finding jobs, although in the current health care market, the situation seems to change annually. In response, many residency programs have reduced the number of training positions.

Those programs that have lost the most positions include family medicine, internal medicine, pathology, and pediatrics. Twice as many residency directors in university-based programs anticipate losing positions as do those in university-affiliated and community-based programs. This will dramatically increase the competition for university-based positions. However, positions recently have been added at many residencies in anesthesiology, emergency medicine, and radiation oncology.

Residency directors foresee an increase in job opportunities for residency graduates in anesthesiology (due to decreasing numbers of graduates to fill the positions opened by retiring anesthesiologists), family medicine, internal medicine, and pediatrics. They believe fewer jobs will be available for new ophthalmologists, orthopedic surgeons, radiologists, and pathologists. Despite these predictions, any specialty that you find that you really like, whether it is likely to be populated by a horde of other physicians or not, will most likely suit you the best.

So where do all these physicians practice? The U.S. regions with the most physicians per capita are New England (CT, ME, MA, NH, RI, VT) with one physician for every 252 people and the Middle Atlantic (PA, NJ, NY) with one physician for every 269 people. The regions with the fewest physicians per capita are the West South Central (AR, LA, OK, TX) with only one physician per 441 people, East South Central (KY, AL, MS, TN) with one physician per 426 people, and Mountain (AZ, CO, ID, MT, NV, NM, UT, WY) with one physician per 418 people. The states with the highest physician-to-population ratios are listed in Figure 2.5.

FIGURE 2.2

American Board of Medical Specialties (M.D.)-Approved Specialty Boards, Certifications, and Special Qualification Categories

American Board	Certification	Subspecialty
Allergy & Immunology	Allergy & Immunology	Clinical & Lab Immunology
Anesthesiology	Anesthesiology	Critical Care Medicine Pain Medicine
Colon & Rectal Surgery	Colon & Rectal Surgery	
Dermatology	Dermatology	Dermatopathology Clinical & Lab Derm Immunology Pediatric Dermatology
Emergency Medicine	Emergency Medicine	Medical Toxicology Pediatric Emergency Medicine Sports Medicine Undersea & Hyperbaric Medicine
Family Practice	Family Practice	Geriatric Medicine Sports Medicine
Internal Medicine	Internal Medicine	Adolescent Medicine Cardiovascular Disease Clin Cardiac Electrophysiology Clin & Lab Immunology Critical Care Medicine Endocrinology, Diabetes & Metabolism Gastroenterology Geriatric Medicine Hematology Infectious Diseases Interventional Cardiology Medical Oncology Nephrology Pulmonary Disease Rheumatology Sports Medicine
Medical Genetics	Clinical Biochemical Genetics Clinical Cytogenetics Clinical Genetics (M.D. only) Clinical Molecular Genetics Medical Genetics (Ph.D. only)	Molecular Genetic Pathology
Neurological Surgery	Neurological Surgery	
Nuclear Medicine	Nuclear Medicine	
Obstetrics & Gynecology	Obstetrics & Gynecology	Critical Care Medicine Gynecologic Oncology Maternal & Fetal Medicine Reproductive Endocrinology
Ophthalmology	Ophthalmology	
Orthopedic Surgery	Orthopedic Surgery	Hand Surgery
Otolaryngology	Otolaryngology	Otology/Neurotology Pediatric Otolaryngology Plastic Surgery within the Head & Neck
Pathology	Anatomic & Clinical Pathology Anatomic Pathology Clinical Pathology	Blood Bank/Transfusion Medicine Chemical Pathology Cytopathology Dermatopathology

(continued)

FIGURE 2.2 (continued)

American Board	Certification	Subspecialty
Pathology, cont'd.		Forensic Pathology Hematology Immunopathology Medical Microbiology Medical Genetic Pathology Neuropathology Pediatric Pathology
Pediatrics	Pediatrics	Adolescent Medicine Clinical & Lab Immunology Developmental-Behavioral Pediatrics Medical Toxicology Neonatal-Perinatal Medicine Neurodevelopmental Disabilities Pediatric Cardiology Pediatric Critical Care Medicine Pediatric Emergency Medicine Pediatric Endocrinology Pediatric Gastroenterology Pediatric Hematology-Oncology Pediatric Infectious Diseases Pediatric Nephrology Pediatric Pulmonology Pediatric Rheumatology Sports Medicine
Physical Medicine & Rehabilitation	Physical Medicine & Rehabilitation	Pain Medicine Pediatric Rehabilitation Medicine Spinal Cord Injury Medicine
Plastic Surgery	Plastic Surgery	Plastic Surgery within the Head & Neck Surgery of the Hand
Preventive Medicine	Aerospace Medicine Occupational Medicine Public Health & General Preventive Medicine	Medical Toxicology Undersea & Hyperbaric Medicine
Psychiatry & Neurology	Neurology Neurology with Special Qualifications in Child Neurology Psychiatry	Addiction Psychiatry Child & Adolescent Psychiatry Clinical Neurophysiology Forensic Psychiatry Geriatric Psychiatry Neurodevelopmental Disabilities Pain Medicine Vascular Neurology
Radiology	Diagnostic Radiology Radiation Oncology Radiological Physics	Cardiothoracic Radiology Neuroradiology Nuclear Radiology Pediatric Radiology Vascular/Interventional Radiology
Surgery	Surgery	Pediatric Surgery Surgery of the Hand Surgical Critical Care Vascular Surgery
Thoracic Surgery	Thoracic Surgery	
Urology	Urology	

Information from: American Board of Medical Specialties, 2002.

FIGURE 2.3

American Osteopathic Association (D.O)-Approved Specialty Boards, Certification, and Special Qualification Categories[#]

American Osteopathic Board	General Certification	Certification of Special Qualifications[†]	Certification of Added Qualifications[††]
Anesthesiology	Anesthesiology		Addiction Med Critical Care Med Pain Management
Dermatology	Dermatology		Dermatopathology MOHS-Micrographic Surg
Emergency Medicine	Emergency Med		Emergency Med Services Medical Toxicology* Sports Med
Family Practice	Family Practice & Osteopathic Manipulative Treatment		Addiction Med Adol/Young Adult Med Geriatric Med Sports Med
Internal Medicine	Internal Med	Allergy/Immunology Cardiology Endocrinology Gastroenterology Hematology Infectious Diseases Nephrology Oncology Pulmonary Diseases Rheumatology	Addiction Med Critical Care Med Clinical Cardiac Electrophysiology Geriatric Med Interventional Cardiology Sports Med
Neurology & Psychiatry	Neurology Psychiatry	Child Neurology Child & Adolescent Psychiatry	Addiction Med Neuromuscular Med Sports Med
Neuromuscular Medicine	Neuromuscular Med & Osteopathic Manipulative Med		Sports Med
Nuclear Medicine	Nuclear Med		In Vivo & In Vitro Nuclear Med Nuclear Cardiology Nuclear Imaging & Therapy
Obstetrics & Gynecology	Obstetrics & Gynecology Obstetrics & Gynecologic Surg	Gynecologic Oncology Maternal & Fetal Med Reproductive Endocrinology	
Ophthalmology & Otolaryngology–Head & Neck Surg	Facial Plastic Surg Ophthalmology Otolaryngology Otolaryngology/ Facial Plastic Surg		Otolaryngologic Allergy
Orthopedic Surgery	Orthopedic Surg		Hand Surg
Pathology	Anatomic Pathology Anatomic Pathology & Lab Med Laboratory Med	Forensic Pathology	Blood Bank/Transfus Med Chemical Pathology Cytopathology Dermatopathology Hematology Immunopathology Medical Microbiology Neuropathology

(continued)

FIGURE 2.3 (continued)

American Osteopathic Board	General Certification	Certification of Special Qualifications†	Certification of Added Qualifications††
Pediatrics	Pediatrics	Adolescent/Young Adult Med Neonatology Ped Allergy/Immunology Ped Cardiology Ped Endocrinology Ped Hematology/Oncology Ped Infectious Diseases Ped Intensive Care Ped Nephrology Ped Pulmonary	Sports Med
Physical Medicine & Rehabilitation	Rehabilitation Med		Sports Med
Preventive Medicine	Preventive Med/ Aerospace Med Preventive Med/ Occupational-Environmental Med Preventive Med/ Public Health		Occupational/Environmental Med**
Proctology	Proctology		
Radiology	Diagnostic Radiology Radiation Oncology		Neuroradiology Nuclear Radiology Pediatric Radiology Vascular & Interventional Radiology
Surgery	Gen Vascular Surg Neurological Surg Plastic & Reconstructive Surg Surgery (General) Thoracic Cardiovascular Surg Urological Surg	Gen Vascular Surg	Gen Vascular Surg Surgical Critical Care

ᵃOsteopathic training programs may not exist in all approved specialties and subspecialties.
*Also available to diplomates of other AOA Boards.
**Available only to diplomates from other AOA Boards.
†Requires General Certification—Equivalent to "Subspecialty."
††Requires General Certification or Certification of Special Qualifications—Equivalent to "Subspecialty."
Adapted from: AOA-net (www.aoa-net.org), June 2002.

FIGURE 2.4

M.D. and D.O. Physicians in Practice by Specialty

Specialty	Total Physicians*	Osteopathic Physicians**	% of All Practicing Physicians***
Allergy & Immunology	3,998	77	0.5
Anesthesiology	35,788	1,448	4.8
Cardiovascular Disease	21,031	573	2.8
Colon & Rectal Surgery	1,127	1	0.1
Dermatology	9,675	305	1.3
Emergency Medicine	23,016	2,669	3.3
Family Practice	71,635	19,656	11.8
Gastroenterology	10,627	285	1.4
General Practice	15,210	65	2.0
General Surgery	36,709	922	4.9
Internal Medicine	134,430	3,244	17.7
Medical Genetics	361	N/A	< 0.1
Neurological Surgery	5,007	78	0.7
Neurology	12,357	397	1.6
Nuclear Medicine	1,448	22	0.2
Obstetrics & Gynecology	40,241	1,369	5.4
Ophthalmology	18,126	349	2.4
Orthopedic Surgery	22,289	972	3.0
Osteo. Manipulative Medicine	N/A	418	< 0.1
Otolaryngology	9,294	392	1.2
Pathology-Anat/Clin	18,870	279	2.4
Pediatrics	51,066	1,020	6.7
Pediatric Subspecialties	12,663	N/A	1.6
Plastic Surgery	6,200	65	0.8
Psychiatry	45,737	966	6.0
Pulmonary Diseases	8,706	254	1.2
Radiology (All)	33,659	940	4.5
Thoracic Surgery	4,953	80	0.6
Urology	10,302	194	1.4
Other Specialties	27,843	1,090	3.7
Others in Practice	45,136	N/A	5.8

*Adapted from: Association of American Medical Colleges. *AAMC Data Book*. Washington, DC: AAMC, July 2001.

**Adapted from: American Osteopathic Association. *1999 Yearbook and Directory of Osteopathic Physicians, 90th ed.* Chicago, IL: AOA, 1999, pp. 630-31.

***Does not add up to 100% due to rounding.

N/A = Information not available.

FIGURE 2.5

States with the Most Physicians per Capita (ratio of persons per each physician)

District of Columbia	139	Vermont	267
Massachusetts	223	Rhode Island	280
New York	245	New Jersey	310
Maryland	246	Pennsylvania	314
Connecticut	260	Hawaii	333

Adapted from: American Medical Association. *Physician Characteristics and Distribution in the U.S., 2002–2003.* Chicago, IL: American Medical Association, 2002, p. 327, Table 18.

— Medicine's Future —

I hope you will have a long career in medicine. This means that you will see many changes, not only in the science and art of medicine, but also in health care delivery systems. Your choice of specialty will, in part, determine how well you weather these changes. At present, three factors appear to be influencing the course of health care delivery: The role of primary care versus specialist physicians, the role of managed care delivery systems, and the number of physicians in each specialty compared to those that are needed to provide adequate care for the population.

It is vital to remember that everything, including the need for most specialties, will change. Your future should not be based solely on what is happening now. Rather, you must also anticipate what may happen in the future. Since this is not an easy task, your ultimate specialty selection will most likely be influenced both by changes in health care delivery and by which parts of medical practice you like the most.

3

Specialty Descriptions

The specialist learns more and more about less and less
until, finally, he knows everything about nothing;
while the generalist learns less and less about more and more
until, finally, he knows nothing about everything.

— Donsen's Law

This chapter offers you a look at the wide range of medical specialties that are available. There are probably many specialties listed here that you have never heard of. Read these descriptions to open your mind to the scope of your career choices. Entering medical school is, unbelievably, an easier decision than choosing which specialty you want to practice.

The ease of acquiring a residency position in each specialty varies. This can be expressed by assigning each specialty a relative difficulty factor, just as in competitive diving. While it is impossible to give exact numbers, it is possible to approximate this difficulty. Beside each specialty's name in the descriptions below, I have indicated this factor by using a one (*) to five (*****) asterisk scale. *In specialties with one asterisk, you should have the least difficulty getting a residency position (or into the field, if there is no residency); in those with five asterisks, the most difficulty*. Because of many uncertainties and the constantly changing nature of medical practice, the asterisk system is only a general guide, not an absolute truth.

The specialties designated by "(F)" can be entered only after having completed a prerequisite residency followed by the fellowship training. The terminology PGY-1, PGY-2, etc. (or occasionally R-1, R-2, etc., for Osteopathic residencies) indicates the specified "postgraduate year."

Figure 2.4 lists the total number of physicians currently practicing in each specialty. A visual description of the length of specialty training for both M.D. and Osteopathic (D.O.) physicians can be found in Figures 3.1 and 3.2, following the verbal descriptions of the specialties. Figure 3.3 ranks most specialties and subspecialties by how well they meet current practitioners' expectations of what they were seeking when they entered the specialty.

Legend for Specialty Descriptions

*	Entry into a training program is **Very Easy**
**	Entry into a training program is **Easy**
***	Entry into a training program is **Difficult**
****	Entry into a training program is **Very Difficult**
*****	Entry into a training program is **Extremely Difficult**

(F) Fellowship training following completion of an initial residency.

AEROSPACE MEDICINE ****

Specialty Overview: Aerospace medicine is a specialty within preventive medicine. Practitioners are responsible for the medical care and safety of individuals involved in military and civilian aviation and space travel. This includes crew members and ground personnel. The Federal Aviation Administration, NASA, the military, and the aerospace industry employs most flight surgeons or aviation medical examiners. They are usually engaged in clinical medicine, research and development, or administration. Medical certification of pilots for flight duty often constitutes a large part of their clinical practice, and most physicians in this field are pilots themselves.

Training: Two years of training are required after internship. One year must be spent obtaining an advanced degree in a relevant area, usually a Master of Public Health. The second residency year devotes more time to clinical aerospace medicine. A fourth year of training, teaching, practice, and/or research is required to take the Board examination. There are two military aerospace medicine programs (Brooks Air Force Base, Texas, and Pensacola Naval Air Station, Florida) and two civilian programs (Wright State University, Ohio, and University of Texas at Galveston–NASA, Texas).

For more information, contact:

- Aerospace Medical Association, 320 S. Henry St., Alexandria, VA 22314-3579; (703) 739-2240; www.asma.org.
- American College of Preventive Medicine, 1307 New York Ave. NW, Ste. 200, Washington, DC 20005; (202) 466-2044; www.acpm.org/residency.htm.
- American Osteopathic College of Occupational and Preventive Medicine, P.O. Box 2606, Leesburg, VA 20177; (800) 558-8686; www.aocopm.org.

ALLERGY AND IMMUNOLOGY (F) *

Specialty Overview: Allergy and immunology is a subspecialty of both internal medicine and pediatrics devoted to the diagnosis and treatment of allergic, asthmatic, and immunologic diseases. There is a great deal of art, as well as science, in the practice of the allergist–immunologist. Most patients have asthma and chronic or seasonal allergies. Practitioners get most of their patients through referrals. There is usually very little emergency or night call. Practice opportunities are more restricted than in the past, due to an increasing number of physicians who do allergy testing and treatment. Allergists–immunologists are mainly office-based and are concentrated in metropolitan areas. Research opportunities in this field are increasing. Allergists–immunologists average 41 hours per week doing patient care.

Training: Training is two years after either a pediatric or an internal medicine residency. It includes experiences in both pediatric and adult diseases. A special qualification in clinical & laboratory immunology requires an extra year of training.

For more information, contact:

- American Academy of Allergy, Asthma, & Immunology, 611 E. Wells St., Milwaukee, WI 53202; (414) 272-6071; www.aaaai.org.
- American Association of Immunologists, 9650 Rockville Pike, Bethesda, MD 20814; (301) 530-7178; http://mercury.faseb.org/aai.
- American College of Allergy, Asthma, & Immunology, 85 W. Algonquin Rd., Ste. 550, Arlington Heights, IL 60005; www.allergy.mcg.edu.
- American Osteopathic College of Allergy and Immunology, 7025 E. McDowell Rd., Ste. 1B, Scottsdale, AZ 85257; (480) 585-1580.

ANESTHESIOLOGY ****

Specialty Overview: Anesthesiologists give general and regional anesthesia during surgical, obstetric, diagnostic, and therapeutic procedures; function as critical care physicians; and give anesthetic blocks in conjunction with pain clinics. They often specialize in pediatric, neurosurgical, obstetric, cardiothoracic, or ambulatory anesthesia, although critical care (*see* Critical Care) and pain medicine (*see* Pain Medicine) are the only formal subspecialties. Anesthesiology is hospital based with frequent night call for most practitioners. The growing use of less-expensive nurse–anesthetists and a declining number of surgeries has decreased the need for anesthesiologists. Anesthesiology's popularity as a specialty selection has varied tremendously; at present, it is very popular.

Training: Training consists of an internship in a clinical specialty, followed by three years of training in clinical anesthesiology and critical care. The training is essentially the same for Osteopathic physicians. Training in the subspecialties of anesthesia critical care medicine, anesthesia pain medicine, or pediatric anesthesiology adds a minimum of one year after completing an anesthesiology residency.

For more information, contact:

- American Academy of Pain Medicine, 4700 W. Lake Ave., Glenview, IL 60025-1485; (847) 375-4731; www.painmed.org.
- American Osteopathic College of Anesthesiologists, 17201 E. Highway 40, Independence, MO 64055-6427; (816) 373-4700.
- American Society of Anesthesiologists, 520 N. Northwest Highway, Park Ridge, IL 60068-2573; (847) 825-5586; www.asahq.org.

CARDIOLOGY (F) ***

Specialty Overview: Cardiologists (the specialty is officially known as "cardiovascular disease") primarily deal with adult patients who have diseases of the heart and circulatory system. They are involved in the diagnosis and medical treatment of these diseases. The core of the specialty is the medical history and physical diagnosis augmented by the latest medical technology and medications. Cardiologists are divided by the nature of their practices into invasive and noninvasive specialists. Invasive cardiologists perform angiography (catheters in arteries) to visualize and treat obstructions of vessels, primarily the coronary arteries. This is an expanding and quite lucrative area of the specialty. Cardiologists are generally office-based, but spend about one-third of their professional time in hospitals. This frequently includes long hours and significant night call.

Between 1965 and 2000, there was more than an eight-fold increase in the number of cardiologists; at this rate, the number will nearly double by 2010. However, cardiology has been targeted as having too many practitioners, especially invasive cardiologists, so the number of available training positions will decrease. Cardiologists average 58 hours per week doing patient care.

Training: Training is currently a three-year fellowship following an internal medicine or a pediatric residency. One year (or, in a few four-year programs, two years) is devoted to research. Specialty certification in cardiology is time-limited, and requires periodic recertification. Additional training is available in cardiac electrophysiology, interventional cardiology, and nuclear cardiology. For Osteopathic physicians, training follows internship and two years of internal medicine residency.

For more information, contact:

- American College of Cardiology, 9111 Old Georgetown Rd., Bethesda, MD 20814-1699; (800) 253-4636, ext. 694 or (301) 897-5400; www.acc.org.
- American College of Osteopathic Internists, 3 Bethesda Metro Center, Ste. 508, Bethesda, MD 20814; (301) 656-8877; www.acoi.org.
- American Academy of Pediatrics, 141 Northwest Point Blvd., Elk Grove Village, IL 60007-1098; (847) 434-4000; www.aap.org.

CHILD AND ADOLESCENT PSYCHIATRY (F) *

Specialty Overview: Child and adolescent psychiatrists diagnose and treat mental, emotional, and behavioral disorders in children, adolescents, and their families. Child psychiatrists work with pediatricians, courts, schools, and social service agencies. They often have both in- and outpatient practices, and frequently work as part of a multidisciplinary team. Child psychiatrists average 42 hours per week doing patient care.

Training: Fellowships for both M.D.'s and D.O.'s consist of two years of child and adolescent psychiatry in addition to at least two years (following internship) of general psychiatry. Child and adolescent psychiatry training can start any time after the internship year, but generally begins after the PGY-2 year in psychiatry. There are also nine programs with five years of training combining pediatrics, psychiatry, and child and adolescent psychiatry. These programs consist of two years of pediatrics, one-and-a-half years of adult psychiatry, and one-and-a-half years of child and adolescent psychiatry, making trainees eligible for Board certification in all three specialties. These programs are more difficult to match with than programs in either pediatrics or psychiatry.

For more information, contact:

- American Academy of Child & Adolescent Psychiatry, 3615 Wisconsin Ave. NW, Washington, DC 20016; (202) 966-7399; www.aacap.org.
- American College of Osteopathic Neurologists and Psychiatrists, 28595 Orchard Lake Rd., Ste. 200, Farmington Hills, MI 48334; (248) 553-0010, ext. 295.

CHILD NEUROLOGY (F) *

Specialty Overview: Child neurologists diagnose and manage neurological disorders of the infant, child, and adolescent. They treat diseases of the brain, spinal cord, and neuromuscular system. Many such problems are congenital or developmental in nature. Practitioners, most often based at academic medical centers, usually see patients in consultation for primary care physicians. Child neurologists average 40 hours per week doing patient care.

Training: Applicants must have completed at least two years of an approved pediatric residency before entering the program. Training in child neurology is an additional three years: one year in clinical adult neurology and one year in clinical child neurology. The third year is devoted to studying electrodiagnostic neurology, neuropathology, neuroradiology, neuro-ophthalmology, child & adolescent psychiatry, and the basic neurosciences. Trainees are eligible to take the American Board of Pediatrics examination after their second year of child neurology training.

For more information, contact:

- American Academy of Neurology, 1080 Montreal St., Saint Paul, MN 55116; (651) 695-1940; www.aan.com.
- American College of Osteopathic Neurologists and Psychiatrists, 28595 Orchard Lake Rd., Ste. 200, Farmington Hills, MI 48334; (248) 553-0010, ext. 295.
- The Child Neurology Society, 1000 West County Rd. East, Ste. 126, St. Paul, MN 55126; (651) 486-9447; www.childneurologysociety.org.

COLON AND RECTAL SURGERY (F) ***

Specialty Overview: Colon and rectal surgeons diagnose and treat disorders of the intestinal tract, rectum, anal canal, and perianal areas that are amenable to surgical treatment. They are involved not only in operative treatment but also in diagnostic procedures, including colonoscopy. Patients are usually referred by other physicians. Most practitioners in this specialty are located in medium to large cities. Colon and rectal surgeons average 54 hours per week doing patient care.

Training: The training consists of a complete residency in general surgery followed by a one-year fellowship in colon and rectal surgery. While there are no Osteopathic training programs in this specialty, the more limited specialty of proctology, consisting of two years of training after internship, is available.

For more information, contact:

- American Osteopathic College of Proctology, 9948 State Route 682, Athens, OH 45701-9105; (740) 594-7979.
- American Society of Colon & Rectal Surgeons, 85 Algonquin Rd., Ste. 550, Arlington Heights, IL 60005; (847) 290-9184; www.fascrs.org.

CRITICAL CARE (F) *

Specialty Overview: Critical care physicians work in hospital intensive care units managing the overall care of critically ill medical and surgical patients. The practice requires both a broad knowledge of the medical and surgical conditions that cause patients to be in the intensive care unit and a specialized knowledge of the respiratory, fluid, and cardiovascular management needed to maintain these patients. Many critical care physicians alternate their duties in the critical care unit with practice in their primary specialty. The majority of critical care physicians in adult units are internists, most commonly specialists in pulmonary diseases. Night call or night duty in the intensive care unit is common. Most individuals in this specialty are located in large cities. Critical care physicians average 66 hours (anesthesia), 64 hours (surgery), 51 hours (pediatrics), and 48 hours (internal medicine) per week doing patient care.

Training: At present, positions leading to certificates of special competence are offered in critical care from the American Boards of Internal Medicine (1 to 3 years after residency), anesthesiology (1 year), and surgery (1 year). Pediatrics offers critical care as a subspecialty (3 years after residency). Other Boards may offer a similar certification in the future.

For more information, contact:

- American College of Osteopathic Internists, 3 Bethesda Metro Center, Ste. 508, Bethesda, MD 20814; (301) 656-8877; www.acoi.org.
- Society of Critical Care Medicine, 701 Lee St., Ste. 200; Des Plaines, IL 60016; (847) 827-6869; www.sccm.org.

DERMATOLOGY ****

Specialty Overview: Dermatologists deal with patients who have both acute and chronic disorders of the skin. They diagnose skin lesions and use both chemotherapeutic agents and surgery to effect cures. Dermatologists get referrals from other physicians and from patients who refer themselves. There is little night call and rarely an inpatient service associated with a dermatology practice. With the increase in managed care, many patients who once would have been referred to dermatologists are now being treated by primary care practitioners, decreasing the need for dermatologists. Dermatologists average 40 hours per week doing patient care.

Fellowships are available in clinical & laboratory dermatological immunology and in dermatopathology. Dermatopathology is a subspecialty of both pathology and dermatology. Emphasis is placed on the diagnosis of skin disorders using appropriate microscopic techniques including light and electron microscopy, immunopathology, histochemistry, and aspects of cutaneous mycology, bacteriology, and entomology. Dermatopathologists average 52 hours per week doing patient care.

Training: Dermatology residencies are three years following initial training. Dermatopathology training consists of a one-year fellowship, and is designed for either a research or a clinical practice.

For more information, contact:

- American Academy of Dermatology, P.O. Box 4014, Schaumburg, IL 60168-4014; (847) 330-0230; www.aad.org.
- American Osteopathic College of Dermatology, P.O. Box 7525, Kirksville, MO 63501; (800) 449-2623; www.aocd.org.

EMERGENCY MEDICINE ****

Specialty Overview: Emergency physicians are mainly hospital-based and deal with the entire spectrum of acute illness and injury in all age groups. Hands-on physical diagnosis and the use of both medical and surgical therapeutic modalities are an integral part of the practice. Emergency physicians are trained to stabilize patients with acute injuries and deal with life-threatening conditions. Hours are long, but schedules are fixed in advance. There is rarely a call schedule outside of assigned working hours. Most practitioners in the specialty work in medium to large cities. Many new emergency medicine opportunities are available at academic centers and in research. All sources agree that there will still be a shortage of emergency physicians in the year 2025. Less than 1% of emergency physicians leave the field each year. Emergency physicians average 39 hours per week doing patient care.

Training: Training is three to four years in length. Programs also exist combining emergency medicine with either internal medicine or pediatrics. These are five years long and lead to dual certification. Osteopathic physicians have the option of combining emergency medicine with training in family practice.

Fellowships following residency leading to subspecialty certification are offered in medical toxicology, pediatric emergency medicine—through both emergency medicine (7 programs) and pediatrics (35 programs) departments, and sports medicine. Some critical care programs accept emergency medicine residency graduates. Fellowships are also available in research, hyperbaric medicine, medical education, medical information services, and emergency medical service administration.

For more information, contact:

- American College of Emergency Physicians, P.O. Box 619911, Dallas, TX 75261-9911; (800) 798-1822; www.acep.org.
- American College of Osteopathic Emergency Physicians, 142 E. Ontario St., Ste. 550, Chicago, IL 60611; (800) 521-3709; www.acoep.org.
- Emergency Medicine Residents Association, 1125 Executive Circle, Irving, TX 75038; (800) 798-1822; www.emra.org.
- Society for Academic Emergency Medicine, 901 N. Washington, Lansing, MI 48906-5137; (517) 485-5484; www.saem.org.

ENDOCRINOLOGY, DIABETES, AND METABOLISM (F) *

Specialty Overview: Endocrinologists treat patients with diseases of the endocrine (glandular) system and with a wide variety of hormonal abnormalities. The most common endocrine diseases include diabetes mellitus, high lipid (blood fats or cholesterol) levels, and thyroid disorders. Patients are often referred to endocrinologists for failure to grow, early or late puberty, excess hair growth, high calcium levels, osteoporosis, pituitary tumors, or reproductive problems. Endocrinologists also consult in the rapidly growing areas of nutrition and metabolism, and help manage postoperative and chronic-disease patients needing extra nutritional support. Many endocrinologists also participate in clinical or basic-science research. Endocrinologists average 45 hours (internists) and 35 hours (pediatricians) per week doing patient care.

Training: Training is two years following an internal medicine residency or three years following a pediatric residency. For Osteopathic physicians, training follows internship and two years of internal medicine residency.

For more information, contact:

- American College of Osteopathic Internists, 3 Bethesda Metro Center, Ste. 508, Bethesda, MD 20814; (301) 656-8877; www.acoi.org.
- Endocrine Society, 4350 East-West Highway, Ste. 500, Bethesda, MD 20814-1098; (301) 941-0200; www.endo-society.org.
- American Academy of Pediatrics, 141 Northwest Point Blvd., Elk Grove Village, IL 60007-1098; (847) 434-4000; www.aap.org.

FAMILY PRACTICE *

Specialty Overview: Family physicians treat entire families, as did the general practitioners of the past. They spend more than 90% of their time on direct patient care. The spectrum of their practice varies with the extent of their training, their interests, the area of the country, the number of other medical practitioners in the local area, and the rules of their local hospitals. Family physicians practice mostly in an outpatient setting, and provide primary care to a diverse population, unlimited by the patient's age, sex, organ system affected, or disease. They usually have a significant number of pediatric and geriatric patients. Delivering babies, although always a part of the training, is not always a part of the practice. Due to the rising cost of professional liability insurance, the irregular hours involved, and other factors, many family physicians severely limit this aspect of their practice. Dealing with the behavioral aspects of medicine, including family life-cycle events (birth, stress, grief), and delivering other psychological services are a large part of family practice.

Most family physicians enter group practices, and most participate in some type of managed health care delivery system (HMO, PPO, IPA). Many have assumed the often-uncomfortable role of "gatekeeper" or "case manager" within these systems and end up allocating services to patients. The average family physician works 46 hours per week, with two-thirds of the time spent on office visits and the balance spent on hospital rounds, on other patient visits, and doing surgical/manipulative procedures.

There is a shortage of family physicians, aggravated by an increased demand in managed care systems and in rural areas. Part of the reason for this shortage is that the specialty suffers from a lack of recognition, both publicly and professionally, which discourages new physicians from entering this field. And, while many family physicians work longer hours than their colleagues and often must know how to treat a broader range of medical problems, their remuneration is lower. Physicians in this field get satisfaction from providing continuity of care to patients, within the context of their entire family, throughout the various stages of life.

Training: Training is three years in length. Residencies combining family practice and internal medicine last four years; those combining family practice and psychiatry are five years long. Osteopathic residencies are generally two years in length following internship, and one program exists combining family practice with Osteopathic manipulative medicine. About 10% of family practitioners specialize. Family practice graduates (M.D.'s) can take one-year geriatric medicine or sports medicine fellowships. Osteopathic graduates can take a two-year geriatrics fellowship after their first year of family practice residency, or a two-year Osteopathic manipulative medicine fellowship after completing residency.

For more information, contact:

- American Academy of Family Physicians, 11400 Tomahawk Creek Parkway, Leawood, KS 66211-2672; (913) 906-6000; www.aafp.org.
- American College of Osteopathic Family Physicians, 330 E. Algonquin Rd., Arlington Heights, IL 60005; (800) 323-0794; www.acofp.org.

GASTROENTEROLOGY (F) **

Specialty Overview: Gastroenterologists are internists and pediatricians who specifically deal with diseases of the esophagus, stomach, small and large intestines, liver, pancreas, and gallbladder. A large number of their patients have ulcer disease or chronic diseases of the liver, intestinal tract, or pancreas. Recent advances in endoscopy (esophagogastroduodenoscopy, colonoscopy, and endoscopic retrograde cholangiopancreatography) have increased the number of procedures that gastroenterologists perform. Gastroenterologists are predominantly office-based. They do take some night call and many have active inpatient services. The field of gastroenterology is growing rapidly and has been targeted as an overpopulated specialty. The specialty's leaders are considering a 50% decrease in available training positions. Gastroenterologists average 52 hours (internists) and 50 hours (pediatricians) per week doing patient care.

Training: As a subspecialty of internal medicine, training consists of a two-year fellowship following an internal medicine residency. Pediatric gastroenterology fellowships last three years after a pediatric residency. For Osteopathic physicians, training follows internship and two years of internal medicine residency.

For more information, contact:

- American College of Gastroenterology, 4900-B South 31st St., Arlington, VA 22206-1656; (703) 820-7400; www.acg.gi.org.
- American College of Osteopathic Internists, 3 Bethesda Metro Center, Ste. 508, Bethesda, MD 20814; (301) 656-8877; www.acoi.org.

- American Gastroenterological Association, 7910 Woodmont Ave., Seventh Floor, Bethesda, MD 20814; (301) 654-2055; www.gastro.org.
- American Academy of Pediatrics, 141 Northwest Point Blvd., Elk Grove Village, IL 60007-1098; (847) 434-4000; www.aap.org.

GERIATRIC MEDICINE (F) *

Specialty Overview: Geriatric medicine is a primary care subspecialty that deals with the complex medical and psychosocial problems of older adults. About 20,000 geriatric clinicians are currently needed and the demand for physicians with special skills in geriatric medicine is rapidly increasing. By 2030, 20% of all Americans will be older than 65 and the United States will need more than 36,000 geriatricians. Currently, there are just over 9,000 certified geriatricians, and this number is expected to decline dramatically in the next few years as practicing geriatricians retire.

While one-third of all patients seen by internists are over 65 years old, nearly half of geriatricians' patients are over 75 years old. Geriatricians average 48 hours per week doing patient care.

Opportunities exist in academic medicine and research, corporate (HMO) medicine, community medicine, long-term care, and private practice. At present, most graduates of geriatric medicine and geriatric psychiatry fellowships hold academic faculty appointments, although relatively few do research or publish. Geriatricians must be able to work within a multispecialty team of both medical and nonmedical personnel.

Training: Most geriatricians begin from a base of training in family practice, internal medicine, or psychiatry. Some programs operate jointly, with both internal medicine and family practice participating. Psychiatry has its own programs. All fellowships are one year long. Osteopathic fellowships are available after completion of one or two years of any other residency.

For more information, contact:

- American Academy of Family Physicians, 11400 Tomahawk Creek Parkway, Leawood, KS 66211-2672; (913) 906-6000; www.aafp.org.
- American College of Osteopathic Internists, 3 Bethesda Metro Center, Ste. 508, Bethesda, MD 20814; (301) 656-8877; www.acoi.org.
- American Geriatrics Society, The Empire State Building, 350 Fifth Ave., Ste. 801, New York, NY 10118; (212) 308-1414; www.americangeriatrics.org.
- American Association for Geriatric Psychiatry, 7910 Woodmont Ave., Ste. 1350, Bethesda, MD 20814-3004; (301) 654-7850; www.aagpgpa.org.

HAND SURGERY (F) ***

Specialty Overview: Hand surgeons primarily treat diseases of and injuries to the hand and forearm. Nearly all have training in either orthopedic or plastic surgery, and utilize new microsurgical techniques. Some hand surgeons do reimplantation surgery after traumatic amputations, which normally requires a specialized center. One benefit to hand surgery is that it is usually done sitting down. Much of the surgery is now done on outpatients. Hand surgeons average 59 hours per week doing patient care.

Training: Fellowship training in hand surgery lasts one year after a residency in orthopedic surgery, plastic surgery, or general surgery.

For more information, contact:

- American Academy of Orthopaedic Surgeons, 6300 N. River Rd., Rosemont, IL 60018-4262; (800) 346-2267; www.aaos.org.
- American Osteopathic Academy of Orthopedics, P.O. Box 291690, Davie, FL 33329-1690; (800) 741-2626; www.aoao.org.
- American Association for Hand Surgery, 20 N. Michigan Ave., Ste. 700, Chicago, IL 60602; (312) 236-3307; www.handsurgery.org.

- American Society for Surgery of the Hand, 6300 N. River Rd., Ste. 600, Rosemont, IL 60018; (847) 384-8300; www.hand-surg.org.

HEMATOLOGY–ONCOLOGY (F) *

Specialty Overview: Although separate specialties, hematology (the diagnosis and treatment of diseases of the blood) and oncology (the diagnosis and treatment of cancer) are often combined in both training and practice. This specialty's patients, once seen as victims of hopeless diseases, frequently can now be offered significant life-extending treatments.

The specialty is predominantly office-based, but practitioners often have a large primary or consultative inpatient service. Night call and emergencies can be frequent, and most specialists work in medium to large cities. Hematologists and oncologists are drawn from the specialties of pediatrics and internal medicine. Hematologist–oncologists average 47 hours (internists) and 39 hours (pediatricians) per week doing patient care. Hematologist–pathologists average 57 hours and oncologist–internists average 45 hours.

Training: Training in either hematology or oncology is usually a two-year fellowship, but many programs combine the two specialties into three-year fellowships. Training follows an internal medicine or pediatric residency, or three years of a pathology residency for a one-year fellowship in hematology. For Osteopathic physicians, training follows internship and two years of internal medicine residency.

For more information, contact:

- American College of Osteopathic Internists, 3 Bethesda Metro Center, Ste. 508, Bethesda, MD 20814; (301) 656-8877; www.acoi.org.
- American Society of Clinical Oncology, 1900 Duke St., Ste. 200, Alexandria, VA 22314; (703) 299-0150; www.asco.org.
- American Society of Hematology, 1900 M St. NW, Ste. 200, Washington, DC 20036; (202) 776-0544; www.hematology.org.

HOSPITALISTS *

Specialty Overview: Hospitalists care for inpatients. Under current definitions, physicians are hospitalists if they spend 25% or more of their time caring for patients admitted or transferred to the hospital by their primary doctor. Their practice has been described as "caring for horizontal patients"; when patients are discharged, office-based physicians take over their care. This specialty's growth has been encouraged by managed care organizations that want their office-based physicians to primarily see outpatients while streamlining the treatment given to inpatients, i.e., reduce lengths of stay and reduce costs. Having hospitalists see all inpatients saves the time required for the other physicians to do rounds. In some cases, hospitalists also compensate for the reduction in resident physicians at some hospitals. However, some managed care organizations require the use of their hospitalist, rather than allowing the primary physician to provide patient care. This has raised serious, and organized, opposition to their presence.

Although the original description of hospitalists raised the question of whether these physicians would suffer "burnout" more than others, studies demonstrate that their burnout rate is no greater than that of physicians in emergency medicine or critical care. Hospitalists must balance the demands of patients, families, primary physicians, hospitals, and insurers. They seem to be doing that well, with more hospitals and medical groups employing them. Standard residency training, however, does not seem to prepare them well for this role.

Of the current 5,000 hospitalists, about 90% are internists, 5% are pediatricians, and 5% are family physicians. It is estimated that there will be about 19,000 hospitalists by 2010. At some academic centers, hospitalists do most of the inpatient teaching to residents and students. A benefit of being a hospitalist is having set hours to work. The pay is 20% higher than that of general internists.

It is unlikely that hospitalists will become an official specialty in the near future, since that may mean managed care groups and hospitals will require such certification for all primary care physicians to care for hospitalized patients—a situation no one wants.

Training: Currently, training consists of completing an internal medicine or family practice residency. Some residency programs have special tracks to train hospitalists, although they are not well publicized. There are currently about 10 hospitalist fellowships, one or two years in duration. Most of these programs have special training in end-of-life care, interacting with other specialists, dealing with managed care, and improving business and communication skills.

For more information, contact:

- National Association of Inpatient Physicians, 190 N. Independence Mall West, Philadelphia, PA 19106; (800) 843-3360; www.naiponline.org.

INFECTIOUS DISEASE (F) **

Specialty Overview: Infectious disease specialists diagnose and treat contagious diseases. At the onset of the antibiotic era, the specialty was thought to be on the edge of extinction. It is now making a comeback due to drug-resistant bacteria, the AIDS epidemic, and the fear of bioterrorism. Infectious disease specialists act as consultants to other physicians. Many are also involved in research, and most work in major medical centers. With the increased importance of nosocomial infections, many infectious disease specialists work part-time as hospital infection control officers. Physicians in this subspecialty generally receive lower salaries than specialists who are more procedure-oriented. Many infectious disease specialists also practice general internal medicine. Infectious disease internists average 43 hours per week doing patient care.

Training: Training consists of either a two-year fellowship following an internal medicine residency or a three-year fellowship after a pediatric residency. For Osteopathic physicians, training follows internship and two years of an internal medicine residency.

For more information, contact:

- American College of Osteopathic Internists, 3 Bethesda Metro Center, Ste. 508, Bethesda, MD 20814; (301) 656-8877; www.acoi.org.
- Infectious Diseases Society of America, 66 Canal Center Plaza, Ste. 600, Alexandria, VA 22314; (703) 299-0200; www.idsociety.org.

INTERNAL MEDICINE **

Specialty Overview: Internists (specialists in internal medicine, not to be confused with "interns") are divided into general internists and subspecialists in internal medicine (see listing under "Internal Medicine" in Figure 2.2). The general internist provides care to adult patients with both acute and chronic diseases. In rural areas, the general internist often acts as a consultant to other practitioners on complex medical cases. In suburban and urban areas, however, other primary care practitioners usually consult with internal medicine subspecialists; surgical specialists consult with both general and subspecialty internists. Urban general internists provide primary health care and treat nonsurgical diseases such as diabetes, hypertension, and congestive heart failure on both an inpatient and an outpatient basis. They also work in managed care plans such as HMOs.

Students attracted to general internal medicine seek an intellectual challenge, have an interest in primary care, and often had a positive experience during their third-year internal medicine rotation. General internal medicine, however, has been less popular in recent years. This may be due to several factors, including: the lower income, low prestige, the perception that caring for chronically ill patients is burdensome, and the increasing hassles of practice. Studies show that general internists are less satisfied with their jobs than are either family physicians or internal medicine subspecialists. However, the growth of managed care plans and societal pressure to enhance primary care have led to increased job opportunities for general internists.

Internal medicine is often described as "less procedural and more cerebral" than other specialties. While this may be true for general internists, it is not true of the procedurally oriented subspecialists in gastroenterology, critical care, pulmonary diseases, and cardiology. The average internist (general and subspecialists) has a 59-hour work week, with 47% of the time spent in office visits, 18% on hospital rounds, 27% on other patient care activities, and 3% doing surgical/manipulative procedures. In some areas, the amount of hospital time is decreasing as hospitalists assume inpatient tasks. Internists average 49 hours per week doing patient care.

Training: Training in internal medicine is three years in length. Programs that combine internal medicine with family practice (*see* family practice–internal medicine), pediatrics (*see* below), preventive medicine, or nuclear medicine are four years. Programs combining internal medicine with emergency medicine (*see* emergency medicine–internal medicine), neurology, physical medicine and rehabilitation, or psychiatry are each five years. These combined programs qualify graduates for Board examinations in both specialties. If an Osteopathic graduate enters an internal medicine "specialty-track" internship, the internal medicine training time is shortened by one year.

One of the advantages of internal medicine training is the number of options available following residency. More than half of all internal medicine residency graduates go on to subspecialize. Following residency, fellowships are available in: cardiovascular disease; clinical cardiac electrophysiology; critical care medicine; endocrinology, diabetes & metabolism; gastroenterology; geriatric medicine; hematology; infectious diseases; interventional cardiology; oncology; nephrology; pulmonary diseases; rheumatology; and sports medicine.

For more information, contact:

- American College of Osteopathic Internists, 3 Bethesda Metro Center, Ste. 508, Bethesda, MD 20814; (301) 656-8877; www.acoi.org.
- American College of Physicians–American Society of Internal Medicine, 190 Independence Mall West, Philadelphia, PA 19106-1572; (800) 523-1546; www.acponline.org.
- Society of General Internal Medicine, 2501 M St. NW, Ste. 575, Washington, DC 20037; (800) 822-3060; www.sgim.org.

INTERNAL MEDICINE–PEDIATRICS ***

Specialty Overview: Combined internal medicine–pediatrics training programs are designed for the individual who wishes to have a primary care practice for families without offering obstetric and surgical services.

Graduates of these combined training programs report that they feel as comfortable as other pediatricians handling infant, child, and adolescent cases, but less comfortable than family practitioners treating adolescent health problems. Although they are more comfortable than family practitioners dealing with complex internal medicine patients, they report being less comfortable than other internists treating intensive care and geriatric patients. Internist–pediatricians average 51 hours per week doing patient care. Completion of combined programs makes the individual eligible to take the specialty Board examination in both pediatrics and internal medicine.

Training: Training lasts four years, with a minimum of 20 months of internal medicine. The programs are, for the most part, integrated. Trainees take blocks of internal medicine and then blocks of pediatrics. This often leads to spending nearly two years at the intern level of training. Most graduates feel that they needed to spend more time in the ambulatory setting and less in intensive care.

For more information, contact:

- American College of Physicians–American Society of Internal Medicine, 190 Independence Mall West, Philadelphia, PA 19106-1572; (800) 523-1546; www.acponline.org.
- American Academy of Pediatrics, 141 Northwest Point Blvd., Elk Grove Village, IL 60007-1098; (847) 434-4000; www.aap.org.

MEDICAL GENETICS *

Specialty Overview: Medical genetics is the newest medical specialty. Currently, more than 1,000 physicians have been certified in M.D. clinical genetics. Most of them come from the specialties of pediatrics, obstetrics and gynecology, or internal medicine. While the field is still quite small, the rapid changes occurring in clinical genetics with the deciphering of the human genome and the application of that knowledge suggest that there may be a much greater need in the future for practitioners in the specialty for both diagnosis and treatment.

Training: Two years of training in another medical specialty is required before admission. Training in medical genetics lasts two or more additional years. Some programs offer all four years of training. Eight programs combine training in medical genetics with pediatrics.

For more information, contact:

- American College of Medical Genetics–American Society for Human Genetics, 9650 Rockville Pike, Bethesda, MD 20814-3998; (301) 571-1825; www.faseb.org/genetics.

MEDICAL MANAGEMENT *

Specialty Overview: Medical managers have existed almost as long as the profession. (As soon as there were two physicians, one was assuredly the administrator.) Recently, medical management has come into its own with the increasing complexity of Byzantine government rules, the web of managed care organizations, and the constantly changing patient and payer demands. Also called "medical administration," this specialty competes with nonphysicians who also manage health care systems.

Since managing physicians is somewhat like herding cats, it is often a thankless job. Yet many physicians try it at various stages of their career—especially in the decade before retirement. Positions are available in hospitals, group practices, clinics, insurance companies, and corporations.

Closely linked to medical management is "managed care medicine." Those taking courses in this area also intend to manage other physicians, but often with the more defined goal of working within managed care. According to the *New England Journal of Medicine* (1999;341(25):1945-8), the inherent conflicts in the medical directors' role are "satisfying the desires of patients and physicians, on the one hand, and the financial profit or survival of the organization, on the other, and between the unlimited demands of individual patients and the limited resources of society."

Training: Courses are available through the American College of Physician Executives, the American College of Managed Care medicine, and through various MBA and MPH programs.

For more information, contact:

- American College of Managed Care Medicine, 4435 Waterfront Dr., Ste. 101, Glen Allen, VA 23060; (804) 527-1906; www.acmcm.org.
- American College of Physician Executives, 4890 W. Kennedy Blvd., Tampa, FL 33609; (800) 562-8088; www.acpe.org.
- American Medical Directors Association, 10480 Little Patuxent Parkway, Ste. 760, Columbia, MD 21044; (800) 876-2632; www.amda.com.

MEDICAL TOXICOLOGY (F) *

Specialty Overview: Medical toxicologists diagnose, treat, and consult on a wide variety of intentional, accidental, and industrial poisonings. Toxicology is a subspecialty of emergency medicine, pediatrics, and preventive medicine.

Training: Programs are usually two years following the primary residency. A list of current training programs is on *FREIDA*.

For more information, contact:

- American Academy of Pediatrics, 141 Northwest Point Blvd., Elk Grove Village, IL 60007-1098; (847) 434-4000; www.aap.org.

- American College of Emergency Physicians, P.O. Box 619911, Dallas, TX 75261-9911; (800) 798-1822; www.acep.org.
- American College of Occupational and Environmental Medicine, 1114 N. Arlington Heights Rd., Arlington Heights, IL 60004-4770; (847) 818-1800; www.acoem.org.
- Society for Academic Emergency Medicine, 901 N. Washington, Lansing, MI 48906-5137; (517) 485-5484; www.saem.org.
- Society of Toxicology, 1767 Business Center Dr., Ste. 302, Reston, VA 20190-5332; (703) 438-3115; www.toxicology.org.

NEONATAL–PERINATAL MEDICINE (F) *

Specialty Overview: Neonatologists treat the problems associated with premature births. Their practice centers on the neonatal intensive care unit. They are pediatricians who do critical care on those neonates who do not yet have the capacity to live without medical assistance. As with other critical care specialists, they must be able to skillfully perform procedures—but on *very* small babies. The size of the infants they work with has progressively decreased. Neonatologists work closely with a specialized team of nurses, social workers, and respiratory therapists. They also work with families to sort out both medical and ethical issues of care. Neonatologists average 53 hours per week doing patient care.

Training: These fellowships are two years in length following a pediatric residency.

For more information, contact:

- American Academy of Pediatrics, 141 Northwest Point Blvd., Elk Grove Village, IL 60007-1098; (847) 434-4000; www.aap.org.
- American College of Osteopathic Pediatricians, 142 E. Ontario St., Chicago, IL 60611; (312) 202-8188; www.acopeds.org.

NEPHROLOGY (F) *

Specialty Overview: Nephrologists diagnose and (nonsurgically) treat diseases of the kidney and the urinary system. Most of their patients have chronic diseases requiring long-term care. Managing dialysis and treating dialysis and renal transplant patients are large parts of most nephrologists' practices. The specialty is predominantly office-based. However, practitioners may have large primary or consultative inpatient services. Night call can be frequent. Nephrologists average 55 hours (internists) and 42 hours (pediatricians) per week doing patient care.

Training: Training is generally a two-year fellowship following an internal medicine residency or three years after a pediatric residency. For Osteopathic physicians, training follows internship and two years of an internal medicine residency.

For more information, contact:

- American College of Osteopathic Internists, 3 Bethesda Metro Center, Ste. 508, Bethesda, MD 20814; (301) 656-8877; www.acoi.org.
- American Society of Nephrology, 1725 I St. NW, Ste. 510, Washington, DC 20006; (202) 659-0599; www.asn-online.org.
- Renal Physicians Association, 4701 Randolph Rd., Ste. 102, Rockville, MD 20852; www.renalmd.org.

NEUROLOGICAL SURGERY ****

Specialty Overview: Neurosurgeons provide operative and nonoperative management of lesions of the brain, spinal cord, peripheral nerves, and their supporting structures (skull, spine, meninges, central nervous system blood supply). Many are also involved in pain management. This requires much manual dexterity and a willingness to accept both dramatic successes and long-term failures in patient care. Developments in autologous and fetal tissue transplantation and in stereotactic surgery for epilepsy, Parkinson's disease, and tumors may increase the need for neurosurgeons during the next decade. Patients range in age from neonates to the elderly. Night call and emergency surgery are frequent parts of neurosurgical practice. Neurosurgeons average 62 hours per week doing patient care.

Training: Residency training lasts five years following one year of general surgery. A minimum of 36 months must be spent in clinical neurosurgery and three months in clinical neurology. The balance of time can be spent in the study of relevant basic sciences, such as neuropathology and neuroradiology, or other related fields, such as pediatric neurosurgery or spinal surgery. The areas covered during these extra months are the key differences among this specialty's training programs.

For more information, contact:

- American Association of Neurological Surgeons, 5550 Meadowbrook Dr., Rolling Meadows, IL 60008; www.aans.org.
- American College of Osteopathic Surgeons, 123 N. Henry St., Alexandria, VA 22314-2903; (800) 888-1312; www.facos.org.

NEUROLOGY *

Specialty Overview: Neurologists diagnose and treat patients with diseases of the brain, spinal cord, peripheral nerves, and neuromuscular system. Much of the practice deals with the diagnosis and, more and more often, the treatment of patients seen in consultation. Many of these patients have headaches, strokes, or seizure disorders. Neurologists follow not only these patients but also those with chronic neuromuscular diseases. It is anticipated that the need for neurologists will increase as the population ages. The specialty is predominantly office-based. Neurologists may, however, have large primary or consultative inpatient services. Night call can be frequent, especially in solo or small group practices. Neurologists average 48 hours per week doing patient care.

Training: Training is three years after a general first-year residency, most often in internal medicine, pediatrics, family practice, or a transitional program. Some neurology programs have their own PGY-1 year, and so are four years long. Combined programs, which take five years to complete, exist in internal medicine–neurology (*see* internal medicine), neurology–nuclear medicine, and neurology–physical medicine & rehabilitation. Four programs, which are seven years long, combine neurology, diagnostic radiology, and neuroradiology. Nine programs also exist combining neurology and psychiatry. Basic neurology training programs are similar for Osteopathic physicians.

For more information, contact:

- American Academy of Neurology, 1080 Montreal St., St. Paul, MN 55116; (651) 695-1940; www.aan.com.
- American Association of Electrodiagnostic Medicine, 421 First Ave. SW, Ste. 300 East, Rochester, MN 55902; (507) 288-0100; www.aaem.net.
- American College of Osteopathic Neurologists and Psychiatrists, 28595 Orchard Lake Rd., Ste. 200, Farmington Hills, MI 48334; (248) 553-0010, ext. 295.
- American Neurological Association, 5841 Cedar Lake Rd., Ste. 204, Minneapolis, MN 55416; (952) 545-6284; www.aneuroa.org.

NUCLEAR MEDICINE *

Specialty Overview: Specialists in nuclear medicine use radioactive materials both to diagnose and to treat diseases by imaging the body's physiologic function. The field combines medical practice with certain aspects of the physical sciences, including physics, mathematics, statistics, computer science, chemistry, and radiation biology. Specialists in nuclear medicine, unlike those in radiation oncology, use radioactive materials that are "unsealed," i.e., free in the bloodstream, for their diagnostic studies and treatments. At some institutions, they also perform radioimmunoassay tests. Practitioners in the specialty have no primary patient-care responsibility and little night call. Many individuals who are currently practicing nuclear medicine have been neither formally trained nor certified in the specialty. However, anyone entering the field is expected to have been fully trained. The future of the specialty may either be very dynamic or rather static, depending upon how rapidly some currently innovative techniques become available. Nuclear medicine physicians average 52 hours per week doing patient care.

Training: Training consists of two years of nuclear medicine following, interspersed with, or, in a few cases, preceding two years of initial training in another clinical specialty, most commonly radiology, internal medicine, or pathology. Other fields of clinical training have also been rather freely accepted. Osteopathic programs also accept two years of initial training in family practice. Note that nuclear medicine is a specialty distinct from nuclear radiology.

For more information, contact:

- American College of Nuclear Medicine, P.O. Box 175, Landisville, PA 17538; (717) 898-5008; www.acnucmed.org.
- American College of Nuclear Physicians, 1850 Samuel Morse Dr., Reston, VA 20190-5316; (703) 326-1190, ext. 1216; www.acnponline.org.
- American Osteopathic Board of Nuclear Medicine, 1000 E. 53rd St., Chicago, IL 60615.

OBSTETRICS AND GYNECOLOGY ****

Specialty Overview: Obstetrician–gynecologists manage pregnancies and treat disorders of the female reproductive tract. Obstetricians deal with pregnancy in women. Gynecologists deal with medical and surgical diseases of the female reproductive tract and infertility. While some specialists in this field work primarily in one or the other area, most work in both. This is the only surgical specialty that is considered "primary care." Obstetrics has been greatly affected by the rising cost of medical liability insurance and the increasing propensity to sue physicians. Because of this, obstetricians are eliminating deliveries from their practice or are reducing the provision of care to patients who have or are likely to have high-risk pregnancies. As the population ages and there is a greater awareness of women's health care needs, there will be a need for more gynecologists.

The specialty combines both surgical and nonsurgical approaches to disease, and is increasingly using endoscopic surgical techniques (minimally invasive surgery). The average obstetrician–gynecologist, in a 49-hour work week, spends about 50% of the time in the office and about 33% in surgery or the delivery room. Obstetrics and gynecology is primarily office-based, but may have a sizable inpatient load. A busy obstetric practice consists of considerable emergency and night call. An increasing number of women are entering this field.

Training: The basic training program in obstetrics and gynecology consists of four years of training following medical school. If Osteopathic graduates enter an obstetrics/gynecology "specialty-track" internship, their obstetrics and gynecology training time is shortened by one year. Following residency, physicians can take subspecialty fellowships in reproductive endocrinology (more commonly known as infertility) or gynecologic oncology, which requires extra surgical training. The two newest subspecialties are maternal and fetal medicine, in which physicians treat the developing child *in utero,* and urogynecology/reconstructive pelvic surgery.

For more information, contact:

- American College of Obstetricians & Gynecologists, 409 12th St. SW, P.O. Box 96920, Washington, DC 20090-6920; www.acog.org.
- American College of Osteopathic Obstetricians & Gynecologists, 900 Auburn Rd., Pontiac, MI 48342; (800) 875-6360; www.acoog.com.
- American Society for Reproductive Medicine, 1209 Montgomery Highway, Birmingham, AL 35216-2809; (205) 978-5000; www.asrm.org.

OCCUPATIONAL MEDICINE *

Specialty Overview: Occupational medicine is one of the specialties of preventive medicine. It focuses on the effects of specific occupations on health. Occupational physicians work in industry, teaching hospitals, government, or occupational health clinics. As the positions in industry decrease, private practice within occupational health clinics has become a burgeoning area, and specialists rarely take night call or have inpatient responsibilities.

Training: Training consists of two or three years following internship. Part of the time is used to get a graduate degree in an appropriate area, usually a Master of Public Health. A fourth year of training, teaching, practice, and/or research is required to take the Board examination. Osteopathic physicians can specialize in the specialty of preventive medicine–occupational medicine–environmental medicine.

For more information, contact:

- American College of Occupational and Environmental Medicine, 1114 N. Arlington Heights Rd., Arlington Heights, IL 60004-4770; (847) 818-1800, www.acoem.org.
- American College of Preventive Medicine, 1307 New York Ave. NW, Ste. 200, Washington, DC 20005; (202) 466-2044; www.acpm.org.
- American Osteopathic College of Occupational and Preventive Medicine, P.O. Box 2606, Leesburg, VA 20177; (800) 558-8686; www.aocopm.org.

OPHTHALMOLOGY ***

Specialty Overview: Ophthalmologists prevent, diagnose, and treat the diseases and abnormalities of the eye and periocular structures. A combination of office-based medical practice and surgical treatment of eye diseases makes this one of the most popular and competitive of specialties. Ophthalmologists treat patients of all ages, often using high-technology equipment in both diagnosis and therapy. Patients are usually seen as outpatients. Many ophthalmologists take some night call, but they rarely have to go into the hospital after-hours. Inpatient services represent a small proportion of the care they deliver. With optometrists performing many of the functions once reserved for ophthalmologists, the field is rapidly becoming overstaffed. Ophthalmologists average 43 hours per week doing patient care.

Training: The training consists of three years following an internship. Residency programs place great emphasis on high class-standing and research experience. Students must do an "audition elective" at the residency program they are considering.

For more information, contact:

- American Academy of Ophthalmology, P.O. Box 7424, San Francisco, CA 94109; (415) 561-8500; www.aao.org.
- American Osteopathic Colleges of Ophthalmology, Otorhinolaryngology–Head & Neck Surgery, 405 W. Grand Ave., Dayton, OH 45405; (800) 455-9404; www.aocoohns.org.

ORTHOPEDIC SURGERY *****

Specialty Overview: Orthopedic surgeons treat diseases and injuries of the spine and the extremities. Using surgery, medications, and physical therapy, their goal is to preserve maximal function of the musculoskeletal system. Much orthopedic surgery is now done as ambulatory surgery. Individuals who go into this specialty like to work with their hands. Many have hobbies such as woodworking that emphasize this, and the majority are sports-oriented. Many orthopedic surgeons continue to take night and emergency call during their entire career.

Orthopedic surgeons average 61 hours per week doing patient care. Among subspecialists, adult reconstructive orthopedic surgeons average 48 hours, orthopedic spinal surgeons average 53 hours, orthopedic sports medicine physicians average 55 hours, and pediatric orthopedic surgeons average 56 hours per week doing patient care.

Training: Training consists of one year in a broad medical specialty followed by four years of orthopedics. Orthopedic surgery is one of the most competitive specialties. Programs look for high USMLE scores, research experience, election to AOA (honorary), and successful "audition clerkships."

Both subspecialty training and certification are available in hand surgery *(see* Hand Surgery). One-year fellowship positions also exist in musculoskeletal oncology, adult reconstructive orthopedics, foot and ankle orthopedics (13 programs), orthopedic sports medicine *(see* Sports Medicine), pediatric orthopedics, orthopedic trauma (25 programs), and surgery of the spine (12 programs).

For more information, contact:

- American Academy of Orthopaedic Surgeons, 6300 N. River Rd., Rosemont, IL 60018-4262; (800) 346-2267; www.aaos.org.
- American Osteopathic Academy of Orthopedics, P.O. Box 291690, Davie, FL 33329-1690; (800) 741-2626; www.aoao.org.

OTOLARYNGOLOGY ****

Specialty Overview: Otolaryngologists, or head and neck surgeons, specialize in the evaluation and treatment of medical and surgical problems of the head and neck region, including disorders of the ears, upper respiratory tract, and upper GI tract. The specialty is frequently referred to as ENT (Ear, Nose, & Throat). Practitioners have a substantial office practice with varying amounts of surgery, which is usually performed in an ambulatory setting. Most practitioners have few inpatients. Since managed care organizations have targeted some of this specialty's common procedures, such as tympanotomies, for decreased use, this field may quickly become overstaffed. Otolaryngologists average 52 hours per week doing patient care.

Training: Training consists of one or two years of general surgery followed by three or four years of ENT training. Two-year fellowships and certification are available in otology/neurotology (8 programs) and pediatric otolaryngology (4 programs). Additional fellowships are available in facial plastic & reconstructive surgery and in head & neck cancer surgery. About one-fourth of all residency graduates take additional fellowship training. Most Osteopathic programs combine otolaryngology with facial plastic surgery. Osteopathic residents who take a "specialty-track" internship in the specialty can shorten their training by one year.

For more information, contact:

- American Academy of Otolaryngology–Head and Neck Surgery, 1 Prince St., Alexandria, VA 22314-3357; (703) 836-4444; www.entnet.org.
- American Osteopathic Colleges of Ophthalmology, Otorhinolaryngology–Head & Neck Surgery, 405 W. Grand Ave., Dayton, OH 45405; (800) 455-9404; www.aocoohns.org.

PAIN MEDICINE (F) *

Specialty Overview: Pain medicine, previously called "pain management," is concerned with the study of pain, the prevention of pain, and the evaluation, treatment, and rehabilitation of persons in pain. A pain medicine physician serves as a consultant to other physicians but is often the principal treating physician and may provide care at various levels. A relatively new subspecialty of anesthesiology, neurology, physical medicine & rehabilitation, and psychiatry, it has expanded rapidly with the recognition that chronic pain control has often been poorly managed in the past. Specialists work in hospitals and independent pain control clinics, and use a variety of pain management techniques. Pain medicine physicians average 55 hours per week doing patient care.

Training: Pain medicine fellowships are one year following completion of a core residency in one of the sponsoring specialties. Anesthesiology departments run nearly all the programs.

For more information, contact:

- American Academy of Pain Medicine, 4700 W. Lake Ave., Glenview, IL 60025; (847) 375-4731; fax: (877) 734-8750; www.painmed.org.
- American College of Osteopathic Pain Management & Sclerotherapy, Inc., 303 S. Ingram Ct., Middletown, DE 19709; (800) 471-6114; www.acopms.com.

PATHOLOGY **

Specialty Overview: Pathologists are laboratory-based physicians who are often said to be the "doctor's doctor." They act as consultants for other physicians, helping them to determine the nature of disease in tissue, body fluids, or the entire organism. They apply the methods of basic sciences to the detection of disease, but generally have little or no direct contact with (live) patients; they interact with other physicians. Pathologists' lives are generally low-key and there is little or no in-hospital night call.

The field is divided into two areas: (1) *anatomic pathology*, i.e., autopsies, cytopathology, surgical pathology (gross and microscopic pathology); and (2) *clinical pathology*, i.e., hematology, microbiology, clinical chemistry, and blood banking/transfusion medicine. Most pathologists, especially the anatomic pathologists, are hospital-based. Many also function as researchers and teachers in university medical centers/medical schools, frequently while also maintaining an active pathology practice. In the past, the income has been very generous—especially for clinical pathology. However, changes in reimbursement have decreased pathologists' income. Many recent pathology residency graduates have had difficulty finding desirable positions. Pathologists average 44 hours per week doing clinical work. Among subspecialists, blood banking/transfusion pathologists average 40 hours, cytopathologists average 44 hours, and forensic pathologists average 47 hours per week doing clinical work.

Training: A residency can be taken separately in either clinical pathology or anatomic pathology (3 years), or the two can be combined (4 years). A "credentialing year" is required prior to taking the Board examination. This is usually taken before beginning a pathology residency. It can consist of a clinical year, clinical experience, or clinically related research. Positions available for subspecialty training following the initial residency include: neuropathology, requiring two years; forensic pathology, dermatopathology *(see* Dermatopathology), blood banking/transfusion medicine, chemical pathology, pediatric pathology, hematology *(see* Hematology), selective pathology, cytopathology, and medical microbiology, each requiring one year.

For more information, contact:

- American Osteopathic College of Pathologists, 12368 NW 13th Court, Pembroke Pines, FL 33026-3817; (954) 432-9640; www.aocp-net.org.
- American Society of Clinical Pathologists, 2100 W. Harrison St., Chicago, IL 60612; (312) 738-1336; www.ascp.org.
- College of American Pathologists, 325 Waukegan Rd., Northfield, IL 60093-2750; (800) 323-4040; www.cap.org.

PEDIATRIC SURGERY (F) ****

Specialty Overview: Pediatric surgeons diagnose and treat surgical diseases in children. Depending upon their training, they deal with abdominal, urologic, and thoracic problems, as well as multiple trauma. Because a high volume of patients is needed to support their practice, most pediatric surgeons live in moderate- or large-size cities and are associated with major medical centers. Pediatric surgeons average 73 hours per week doing patient care.

Training: Since this is a subspecialty of general surgery, applicants for training must first complete a general surgery residency. Training in pediatric surgery is an additional two years in length.

For more information, contact:

- American Pediatric Surgical Association, 60 Revere Dr., Ste. 500, Northbrook, IL 60062; (847) 480-9576; www.eapsa.org.

PEDIATRICS **

Specialty Overview: Pediatricians take care of pediatric patients. While that may sound circular, it is the only way to describe many pediatric practices. Pediatricians may at one time have dealt primarily with children, but they have expanded the scope of their practice to include adolescents and young adults. Twenty-two percent of the average pediatrician's patients are from 12 to 21 years old. Pediatricians may continue to care for some patients into adulthood, especially those with illnesses like cystic fibrosis that used to be uniformly fatal during childhood. Pediatricians do a great deal of well-child and preventive care. More recently, they are being asked to fill the often-uncomfortable role of "gatekeeper" or "case manager" for prepaid health plans. In this position, they determine patients' access to care.

Progressively fewer pediatricians are opting for private practice; two-thirds work in group practices. Much of the intensive exposure to ill children seen by residents and medical students during their training does not exist for the practicing pediatrician. Office-based for the most part, pediatricians rarely utilize surgical techniques such as suturing or fracture reduction. More women and fewer IMGs are entering this field. The average pediatrician, in a 44-hour work week, spends more than half of the time on office visits and the rest on nonclinical care activities, hospital rounds, and additional clinical activities. Pediatrics is one of the lowest paying specialties. Most pediatricians choose this field because they love working with children.

Training: Initial pediatric residency training is three years. There are also four-year residencies combining pediatrics with internal medicine, and five-year programs combining pediatrics with emergency medicine, psychiatry/child psychiatry, medical genetics, or physical medicine & rehabilitation. Osteopathic residents who take a "specialty-track" internship in pediatrics can shorten their training by one year.

Following initial pediatric residency training, about one-third of all graduates specialize, although this number appears to be steadily decreasing. Subspecialty training (each two to three years long) is available in neonatal–perinatal medicine, pediatric cardiology, pediatric critical care, pediatric emergency medicine, pediatric endocrinology, pediatric gastroenterology, pediatric hematology–oncology, pediatric nephrology, pediatric pulmonology, and sports medicine.

Fellowships are also possible in adolescent medicine, allergy–immunology, pediatric infectious diseases, and pediatric rheumatology. Child neurology training can be started after two years of pediatrics residency.

For more information, contact:

- American Academy of Pediatrics, 141 Northwest Point Blvd., Elk Grove Village, IL 60007-1098; (847) 434-4000; www.aap.org.
- American College of Osteopathic Pediatricians, 142 E. Ontario St., Chicago, IL 60611; (312) 202-8188; www.acopeds.org.

PHYSICAL MEDICINE AND REHABILITATION **

Specialty Overview: Physiatrists (specialists in physical medicine and rehabilitation, or PM&R) deal with the diagnosis, evaluation, and treatment of patients with impairments or disabilities that involve musculoskeletal, neurologic, cardiovascular, or other body systems. Physiatrists diagnose and treat patients of all ages with: (1) musculoskeletal pain syndromes, industrial and sports injuries, degenerative arthritis, or lower back pain; (2) severe impairments amenable to rehabilitation from strokes, spinal cord and brain injuries, amputations, and multiple trauma; and (3) electrodiagnosis (i.e., EMG, nerve conduction, somatosensory evoked potentials). The physiatrist's goal is to maximize the patient's physical, psychosocial, and job-related recovery, as well as to alleviate pain. Depending upon their practice, they may have frequent or no night call. Physiatrists average 48 hours per week doing patient care.

Training: Residency training is four years. This can either be three years following at least one year of prior training or a straight four-year program. There are combined programs in internal medicine–PM&R (6 programs), pediatrics–PM&R (5 programs), and neurology–PM&R. Following residency, fellowship training is available in pain medicine, pediatric rehabilitation medicine, and spinal cord injury medicine.

Osteopathic physicians can also take training in neuromuscular medicine combined with Osteopathic manipulative treatment (OMT) or take an extra year (+1) of Osteopathic manipulative medicine (OMM) after an AOA-approved residency. Many D.O.'s with advanced training in these techniques have the "problem" of having too many patients seeking their services. Some programs allow M.D.'s to apply.

For more information, contact:

- American Academy of Physical Medicine and Rehabilitation, One IBM Plaza, Ste. 2500, Chicago, IL 60611-3604; (312) 464-9700; www.aapmr.org.
- American Osteopathic Board of Neuromusculoskeletal Medicine, 3500 DePauw Blvd., Ste. 1080, Indianapolis, IN 46268-1136; (317) 879-1881; www.academyofosteopathy.org.
- American Osteopathic College of Physical Medicine and Rehabilitation, 314 S. Knight Ave., Park Ridge, IL 60068-3804; (847) 825-2515; www.aocpmr.org.
- Association of Academic Physiatrists, 1106 N. Charles St., Ste. 201, Baltimore, MD 21201; (410) 637-8300; www.physiatry.org.

PLASTIC SURGERY (F) *****

Specialty Overview: Plastic surgeons operatively treat disfigurements of the body, whether they are congenitally or traumatically induced or are caused by aging. This area of surgery is as much an art as a science, and an artist's vision is said to be necessary to excel in the field. Microsurgery and liposuction are two techniques being used in both reconstructive and cosmetic surgery. There is a large amount of night call to the emergency room, especially early in a practitioner's career. Much of plastic surgery is done on an ambulatory basis. While the field is quite lucrative at present, plastic surgery is expected to have many more practitioners than necessary in the near future. Plastic surgeons average 56 hours per week doing patient care.

Training: Plastic surgery offers two routes for training. The "integrated" route is aimed at senior medical students who match at the PGY-1 level. These programs accept medical students into five- or six-year plastic surgery programs. The "independent" route is for those who first complete at least three years of general surgery or an entire otolaryngology or orthopedic surgery residency. They then have at least two, and often three, years of plastic surgery training.

Applicants must ascertain the minimum requirements by contacting each program and obtaining the "Preliminary Evaluation of Training" form from the American Board of Plastic Surgery (www.abplsurg.org). For more details, visit the website of the Association of Academic Chairmen of Plastic Surgery.

Postgraduate fellowships and certification are available in hand surgery. Additional training in plastic surgery, and fellowships in craniofacial surgery, microsurgery, and burn surgery are also available. Osteopathic physicians can also train in otolaryngology–facial plastic surgery (*see* Otolaryngology).

For more information, contact:

- American Academy of Facial & Reconstructive Surgery, 310 S. Henry St., Alexandria, VA 22314; (800) 332-3223; www.aafprs.org.
- American College of Osteopathic Surgeons, 123 N. Henry St., Alexandria, VA 22314-2903; (800) 888-1312; www.facos.org.
- American Society of Plastic & Reconstructive Surgeons, 444 E. Algonquin Rd., Arlington Heights, IL 60005-4664; (800) 766-4955; www.plasticsurgery.org.
- Association of Academic Chairmen of Plastic Surgery, 4900 B South 31st St., Arlington, VA 22206, (703) 820-7400; www.aacplasticsurgery.org.

PREVENTIVE MEDICINE, GENERAL *

Specialty Overview: Preventive medicine requires that those entering the field enter through one of its four subspecialties; general preventive medicine is one of these. Physicians in this field are committed to population-based approaches to disease prevention and health promotion. Training includes both clinical preventive medicine and education in epidemiology, biostatistics, informatics, environmental health, health promotion and disease prevention, and research. These physicians work in primary care settings, managed care organizations, public health, government agencies, industry, and academia.

In some cases, family practice programs have made arrangements so that training in both specialties can take place concurrently. Two subspecialty certifications are now available in preventive medicine: medical toxicology and undersea & hyperbaric medicine. Preventive medicine specialists average 30 hours per week in clinical work.

Training: At least one year of clinical training and a Master of Public Health or equivalent degree is needed to complete the program and to be eligible to take the specialty examination.

For more information, contact:

- American College of Preventive Medicine, 1307 New York Ave. NW, Ste. 200, Washington, DC 20005; (202) 466-2044; www.acpm.org.
- American Osteopathic College of Occupational and Preventive Medicine, P.O. Box 2606, Leesburg, VA 20177; (800) 558-8686; www.aocopm.org.

PSYCHIATRY **

Specialty Overview: Psychiatrists diagnose and treat disorders of the mind. They deal with the entire spectrum of mental illness, from mild situational problems to severe, incapacitating psychotic illnesses. Psychiatrists practice in private offices, community mental health centers, psychiatric hospitals, prisons, and substance abuse programs. The majority are office-based. While there may be night call, it is easier than it might otherwise be, since many psychiatrists use other health care workers to screen their calls. The wide diversity of potent psychotropic medications has given the psychiatrist a powerful pharmacological armamentarium. Treatment results can often be obtained that would have been unbelievable a few years ago, and many more disease-specific drugs are anticipated. This may increase the ties between psychiatry and other types of clinical practice. There are many job openings for psychiatry residency graduates.

Only about 3% of medical students choose to specialize in psychiatry, primarily due to their perceptions that the treatments have little efficacy, that the ability to treat patients will be limited due to health care "reform," and that the specialty lacks status within the profession. Those who go into psychiatry, do so because of the intellectual challenge, the desire to return to a humanities/social science background, the novel and unique problems, or because they want to treat the "whole person." Psychiatrists average 40 hours per week doing patient care.

Training: Training is three years following a clinical internship that is usually very similar in structure to a transitional year. The residency consists of training not only in psychiatry but also a significant amount in neurology. Subspecialty fellowships and certification are available in addiction psychiatry, child & adolescent psychiatry, forensic psychiatry, geriatric psychiatry, and pain medicine. Twenty-four programs combine psychiatry with internal medicine, 11 combine psychiatry with family practice, and 9 combine neurology and psychiatry. There are also 9 programs with 5 years of training combining pediatrics, psychiatry, and child psychiatry.

For more information, contact:

- American College of Osteopathic Neurologists and Psychiatrists, 28595 Orchard Lake Rd., Ste. 200, Farmington Hills, MI 48334; (248) 553-0010, ext. 295.
- American Psychiatric Association, 1400 K St. NW, Washington, DC 20005; (888) 357-7924; www.psych.org.
- American Society of Addiction Medicine, 4601 N. Park Ave, Arcade Ste. 101, Chevy Chase, MD 20815; (301) 656-3920; www.asam.org.

PUBLIC HEALTH *

Specialty Overview: Specialists in public health, an area of preventive medicine, work in governmental and private health agencies, academic institutions, and health service research organizations. They deal with the health problems of entire communities and countries, as well as individual patients. Their goals are to promote health and to understand the risks of disease, injury, disability, and death. They (1) assess information about the community's health; (2) develop comprehensive public health policies; and (3) assure the provision of services necessary to achieve the public health goals. This frequently involves dealing with the administrative and political sides of medicine. This specialty usually has no night call and very low (usually government) pay. The dearth of residency programs has made these specialists some of the most sought-after in medicine (although still some of the worst paid).

Training: Training consists of two years following a clinical internship. One of these years is spent obtaining an advanced degree, usually a Master of Public Health. A fourth year of training, teaching, practice, and/or research is required to take the Board examination. Some programs in family practice, internal medicine, and pediatrics have dual training with public health.

For more information, contact:

- American Association of Public Health Physicians, PMB #1720, P.O. Box 2430, Pensacola, FL 32513; (678) 458-1795; www.aaphp.org.
- American College of Preventive Medicine, 1307 New York Ave. NW, Ste. 200, Washington, DC 20005; (202) 466-2044; www.acpm.org.
- American Osteopathic College of Occupational and Preventive Medicine, P.O. Box 2606, Leesburg, VA 20177; (800) 558-8686; www.aocopm.org.

PULMONARY DISEASES (F) **

Specialty Overview: Pulmonologists diagnose and treat patients with diseases of the lungs in both in- and outpatient settings. Their patients have lung cancer, asthma, and many types of chronic lung disease. In many cases, pulmonologists act as full- or part-time critical care physicians. The specialty combines patient care and manipulative procedures with a strong underlying base of physiology. The major manipulative procedures performed are bronchoscopy, endotracheal intubation, management of mechanical ventilators, and placement of pulmonary artery catheters. Night call depends upon the type of practice. Pulmonologists average 51 hours per week (internists) and 33 hours per week (pediatricians) doing patient care. Pulmonology–critical care physicians average 64 hours per week doing patient care.

Training: Training consists of a two- or three-year fellowship following completion of an internal medicine residency or three years following a pediatric residency. Adult programs that are three years in length may fulfill the requirements for certification in critical care as well as pulmonary diseases. For Osteopathic physicians, training follows internship and two years of an internal medicine residency.

For more information, contact:

- American College of Chest Physicians, 3300 Dundee Rd., Northbrook, IL 60062-2348; (847) 498-1400; www.chestnet.org.
- Society of Critical Care Medicine, 701 Lee St., Ste. 200, Des Plaines, IL 60016; (847) 827-6869; www.sccm.org.

RADIATION ONCOLOGY ****

Specialty Overview: Radiation oncologists use radiation therapy in the treatment of malignancies and other diseases. A flood of new information about radiation and cancer biology has made radiation oncology a rapidly changing field. While there has previously been a scarcity of radiation oncologists, the specialty is now close to equilibrium. Radiation oncologists have relatively little night call. Radiation oncologists average 50 hours per week doing patient care.

Training: Training lasts four years after internship.

For more information, contact:

- American Osteopathic College of Radiology, 119 E. Second St., Milan, MO 63556-1331; (800) 258-AOCR; www.aocr.org.
- American Society for Therapeutic Radiology & Oncology, 12500 Fair Lakes Circle, Ste. 375, Fairfax, VA 22033-3882; (800) 962-7876; www.astro.org.

RADIOLOGY, DIAGNOSTIC ****

Specialty Overview: Diagnostic radiologists use x-rays, ultrasound, magnetic fields, and other forms of energy to make diagnoses. While they still learn to read basic radiographs, diagnostic radiologists must now also learn how to interpret nuclear scans, PET scans, ultrasonography images, CT scans, and MR images. Additionally, they are trained to perform diagnostic and interventional procedures, such as angiography, guided biopsy and drainage procedures, and noncoronary angioplasty. This is an enormous body of knowledge to learn during a residency.

Most practitioners are hospital-based, although there is a movement for radiologists to practice out of freestanding diagnostic facilities. Diagnostic radiology night call has become very active in many hospitals, although many studies now are being read at home via teleradiology. Radiology has also joined obstetrics and gynecology as one of the most frequently sued specialties.

Diagnostic radiologists average 50 hours per week doing clinical work. Among subspecialists, neuroradiologists average 52 hours per week, pediatric radiologists average 53 hours, and vascular and interventional radiologists average 54 hours.

Training: Diagnostic radiology programs generally require four years of training following internship. Some programs now require completion of a clinical first year before starting the residency. Osteopathic training is four years after internship. Some M.D. residencies in diagnostic radiology provide special competence in nuclear radiology after an additional formal year of training. This should not be confused with a residency in nuclear medicine—a distinct specialty with training only in that area.

For more information, contact:

- American College of Radiology, 1891 Preston White Dr., Reston, VA 22091-4397; 800) 227-5463; www.acr.org.
- American Osteopathic College of Radiology, 119 E. Second St., Milan, MO 63556-1331; (800) 258-AOCR; www.aocr.org.
- American Roentgen Ray Society, 44211 Slatestone Ct., Leesburg, VA 20176-5109; (800) 438-2777; www.arrs.org.

RHEUMATOLOGY (F) *

Specialty Overview: Rheumatologists diagnose and treat patients with a wide variety of diseases of the joints, soft tissues, and blood vessels. These include the various types of arthritides, both acute and chronic, which can affect individuals. The field has grown in recent years with the increased interest in the autoimmune diseases underlying many rheumatologic conditions. Rheumatology is one of the quieter subspecialties of internal medicine and pediatrics. Yet rheumatologists often care for very ill patients with various autoimmune and acute joint diseases. There is usually little night call and small primary or consultative inpatient services for those not mixing their rheumatology practice with general internal medicine or pediatrics. Internist–rheumatologists average 49 hours per week doing patient care.

Training: Training consists of a two-year fellowship following completion of an internal medicine residency or three years following a pediatric residency. For Osteopathic physicians, training follows internship and two years of an internal medicine residency.

For more information, contact:

- American College of Rheumatology, 1800 Century Place, Ste. 250, Atlanta, GA 30345; (404) 633-3777; www.rheumatology.org.
- American Osteopathic College of Rheumatology, Inc., 193 Monroe Ave., Edison, NJ 08820-3755; (732) 494-6688.

SPORTS MEDICINE (F) ***

Specialty Overview: sports medicine fellowships are available under the auspices of emergency medicine, family practice, internal medicine, and pediatrics. This specialty is sometimes called "primary care sports medicine" (by the NRMP as well as others) to distinguish it from orthopedic surgery's sports medicine subspecialty. Specialists in this area diagnose and treat nonoperative sports-related injuries. They also emphasize prevention and rehabilitation. Some perform epidemiological studies to determine the best preventive methods. Many practitioners incorporate sports medicine into their existing practices by offering fitness evaluations, acting as team physicians, and working with recreational athletes.

Orthopedic sports medicine is a subspecialty of orthopedic surgery. These practitioners perform many of the same preventive and therapeutic measures as other sports medicine physicians; in addition, they treat injuries surgically when necessary. Primary care sports medicine physicians average 41 hours per week doing patient care. Orthopedic sports medicine physicians average 55 hours per week doing patient care.

Training: Primary care sports medicine (primarily in family practice) is one year after the initial residency. Orthopedic sports medicine is a one-year fellowship following the completion of an orthopedic surgery residency.

For more information, contact:

- American College of Sports Medicine, 401 W. Michigan St., Indianapolis, IN 46202-3233; (317) 637-9200; www.acsm.org.
- American Orthopaedic Society for Sports Medicine, 6300 N. River Rd., Ste. 200, Rosemont, IL 60018; www.sportsmed.org.
- American Osteopathic Academy of Sports Medicine, 7600 Terrace Ave., Ste. 203, Middletown, WI 53562; (608) 831-4400; www.aoasm.org.

SURGERY, GENERAL ****

Specialty Overview: General surgeons primarily diagnose and treat diseases and injuries of the abdominal organs and to the soft tissues and vasculature of the neck and trunk. They are also usually called in to manage, often in concert with other surgical specialists, patients suffering injuries to more than one body area. In rural settings, the general surgeon may still be "general," doing orthopedic, urologic, and, occasionally, thoracic or neurosurgical procedures. Increasingly, endoscopic, laparoscopic, and other minimally invasive surgical techniques are being used.

During their average 60-hour work week in private practice, surgeons spend about half their time on office visits, a third in surgery, and the rest on hospital rounds and other patient care activities. Nearly all surgical specialties are oversupplied with practitioners for the perceived need in the population. Yet there are still many areas of the country that are underserved by surgeons.

Training: Training in general surgery is usually five years after medical school. It is four years after internship for Osteopathic physicians. "Categorical" general surgery residency positions, designed for those interested in completing an entire general surgery residency, have become relatively difficult to obtain. About one-third of the available surgery PGY-1 positions are "preliminary," which only guarantees training for one or two years; they are designed for those wishing to enter other fields, particularly other surgical specialties. Subspecialty fellowships and certification are available in surgery of the hand, pediatric surgery, surgical critical care, and vascular surgery.

For more information, contact:

- American College of Surgeons, 633 N. Saint Clair St., Chicago, IL 60611-3211; (312) 202-5000; www.facs.org.
- American College of Osteopathic Surgeons, 123 N. Henry St., Alexandria, VA 22314-2903; (800) 888-1312; www.facos.org.
- Society of American Gastrointestinal Endoscopic Surgeons (SAGES); www.sages.org.

THORACIC SURGERY (F) **

Specialty Overview: Thoracic, or cardiothoracic, surgeons operatively treat diseases and injuries of the heart, lungs, mediastinum, esophagus, chest wall, diaphragm, and great vessels. The most common surgery they perform is coronary artery bypass grafting. The other common procedures include cardiac surgery for acquired valvular disease or congenital cardiac defects, pulmonary surgery for malignancies, and surgery for trauma to intrathoracic organs. Postoperative care for these patients is usually the responsibility of the thoracic surgeon. As might be expected from the nature of the diseases treated, very long and erratic hours are often necessary; thus, thoracic surgery is one of the most time-consuming and stressful of all the specialties. Those in the field, though, generally feel that the rewards are worth the price. Thoracic surgeons average 67 hours per week doing patient care.

Training: Thoracic surgery is a subspecialty of general surgery, and certification in general surgery is required to take the thoracic surgery Boards. Training lasts two to three years after completion of a general surgery residency. Since the process of going through a general surgery residency is itself grueling, this acts as a major deterrent to many individuals who might otherwise enter this field. Osteopathic programs in thoracic–cardiovascular surgery are two years in length after three years of general surgery and one year of internship.

For more information, contact:

- American College of Osteopathic Surgeons, 123 N. Henry St., Alexandria, VA 22314-2903; (800) 888-1312; www.facos.org.
- Society of Thoracic Surgeons, 633 N. St. Clair St., Ste. 2320, Chicago, IL 60611-3658; (312) 202-5800; www.sts.org.

TRAUMA SURGERY (F) **

Specialty Overview: While not yet an official subspecialty, trauma surgery is one of the fastest growing areas in surgery. With the wide institution of trauma centers, there is an increasing need for surgeons with training in the treatment of patients with multiple-injuries. Trauma surgeons are generally the operating surgeon for patients with major injuries. They also oversee and coordinate the large team responsible for both the initial and the postoperative care. In-hospital call is usually required on a frequent basis. As with firefighters, there is often the need to immediately go to full speed from a dead stop. Long hours are required, and family life can be difficult. Most trauma surgeons are in medium- to large-sized cities.

Training: Training normally consists of a one- or two-year fellowship at a major trauma center following a general surgery residency. Many trauma surgery fellowships are combined with training in critical care or with research. At the present time, most practicing trauma surgeons have not completed such a fellowship. The necessity for such a fellowship in the future is currently unknown.

For more information, contact:

- American Association for the Surgery of Trauma at: www.aast.org/fellowships.

UROLOGY *****

Specialty Overview: Urologists diagnose and treat diseases of and injuries to the kidney, ureters, bladder, and urethra. In males, they also treat disorders of the prostate and genitals. Often they work in concert with nephrologists and have both a surgical and nonsurgical practice. Investigations into fertility and male sexuality, and the use of noninvasive techniques, such as lithotripsy, are expanding areas within the field. Urologists have a moderate amount of night call and often have small inpatient services, since much of urologic surgery is now done in an ambulatory setting. Urologists average 56 hours per week doing patient care.

Training: Urology training generally consists of two years of general surgery followed by at least three years of urology. The preliminary (first two) surgical years are at the same institution as the urology training in about half of the programs. Fifteen programs offer pediatric urology fellowships. Osteopathic residents who take a "specialty-track" internship in urology can shorten their training by one year.

For more information, contact:

- American College of Osteopathic Surgeons, 123 N. Henry St., Alexandria, VA 22314-2903; (800) 888-1312; www.facos.org.

- American Urological Association, 1120 N. Charles St., Baltimore, MD 21201; (410) 727-1100; www.auanet.org.

VASCULAR SURGERY (F) **

Specialty Overview: As subspecialists of general surgery, vascular surgeons diagnose and treat diseases of the arterial, venous, and lymphatic systems. Unless they are associated with very large medical centers, specialists in this field often have to perform general surgery in order to make a living. This is partly because so many general surgeons perform vascular surgery as a routine part of their practice. Vascular surgeons average 62 hours per week doing patient care.

Training: Training for M.D.'s is one or two years following completion of a general surgery residency. There are currently no Osteopathic programs.

For more information, contact:

- American College of Osteopathic Surgeons, 123 N. Henry St., Alexandria, VA 22314-2903; (800) 888-1312; www.facos.org.
- American Association for Vascular Surgery, 13 Elm St., Manchester, MA 01944-0314; www.vascsurg.org.

WOMEN'S HEALTH

Specialty Overview: Female patients are treated by all medical specialists. This new area's goal, according to some advocates, is "to produce physicians with an expertise in clinical, teaching, and research aspects of women's health, and to produce physicians capable of leadership roles in the expanding field of women's health." Another program says it exists to help physicians "provide optimal care for all patients. We were clearly deficient in caring for a major sector of the population, necessitating the establishment of specific women's health activities." Hopefully, women's health programs will raise primary care physicians' awareness of those women's health care issues that are not directly related to obstetrics and gynecology. Whether the extra training will prove worthwhile remains to be seen.

Training: Training in women's health is available either combined with an internal medicine or a family practice residency (3 years total), or as a two-year fellowship following the completion of residency training in family practice, internal medicine, neurology, obstetrics and gynecology, psychiatry, or surgery. Various groups sponsor these fellowships, and each program's content depends on their specialty orientation. There is no subspecialty certification in women's health.

For more information, contact:

- American Medical Women's Association, 801 N. Fairfax St., Ste. 400, Alexandria, VA 22314, (703) 838-0500; www.amwa-doc.org.
- Office on Women's Health, U.S. Dept. of Health & Human Services, 200 Independence Ave. SW, Room 730-B, Washington, DC 20201; (202) 690-7650; www.4women.gov/owh.

FIGURE 3.1

Length of Postgraduate Training for M.D. Physicians*

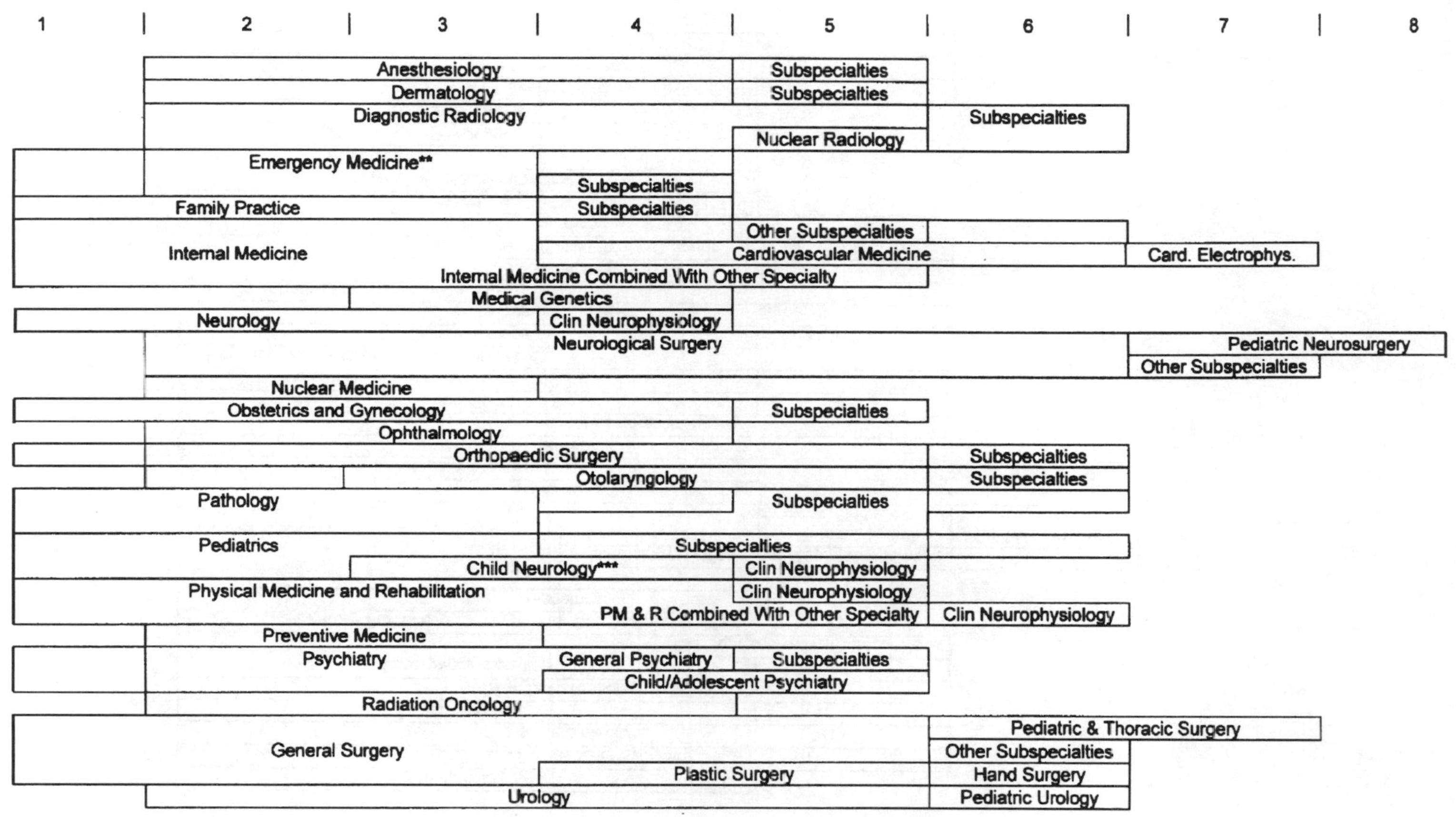

*Many programs offer a broad-based GY-1 and GY-2 years as part of their residencies.

**Emergency Medicine programs may include GY-1 through GY-3, GY-1 through GY-4, or GY-2 through GY-4.

***One broader, adult medicine year may be substituted for one year in Pediatrics.

FIGURE 3.2

Length of Postgraduate Training for Osteopathic (D.O.) Physicians

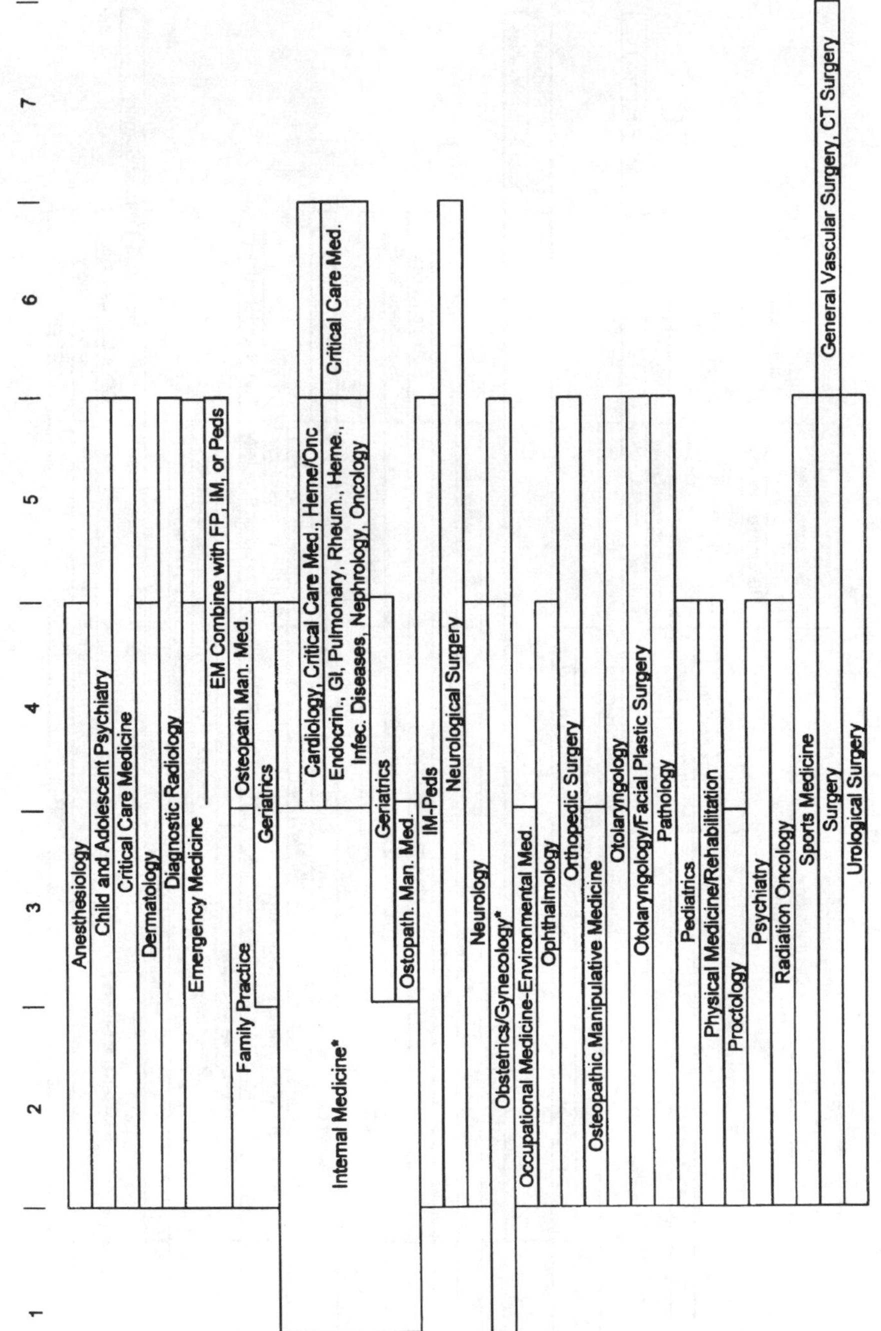

*Nearly all Internal Medicine and OB/Gyn residents take AOA-approved "specialty track" internships to shorten their training by one year.

FIGURE 3.3

Is This Specialty for You?

	% Practitioners saying that they are "Very Satisfied" with their specialty	% Practitioners saying that they are "Dissatisfied" with their their specialty	How satisfied with *current* practice position (1=unsatisfied to 5=very satisfied)	Hours per week doing patient care
Geriatric Medicine (IM	59.6%	7.0%	3.5	49.3
Geriatric Psychiatry	*	*	4.5	47.7
Neonatal–Perinatal Medicine	58.7	13.0	3.7	52.6
Dermatology	56.1	10.8	3.7	39.6
Thoracic Surgery	53.4	17.8	3.4	66.6
Oncology (IM)	50.5	11.3	3.8	44.7
Infectious Diseases (IM)	50.0	6.3	3.6	42.7
Allergy & Immunology	48.2	10.7	4.1	41.3
Pediatrics	48.1	12.6	3.7	44.0
Urology	48.0	13.8	3.8	55.8
Orthopedic Surgery	47.1	19.3	3.7	60.5
Neurological Surgery	47.0	15.2	3.7	61.7
Nephrology (IM)	46.2	9.0	3.6	55.2
Endocrine, Diabetes, & Metabolism	44.9	10.2	3.5	44.8
Emergency Medicine	44.4	13.3	3.8	38.7
Occupational Medicine	43.8	15.1	#	#
Cardiology	43.8	16.5	3.7	58.0
Pediatric Surgery	*	*	3.4	73.1
Plastic Surgery	43.3	23.1	3.3	55.7
General Surgery	43.0	20.4	3.5	59.9
Family Practice	42.8	16.9	3.6	45.5
Pediatric Cardiology	*	*	3.6	43.7
Internal Medicine–Pediatrics	*	*	3.3	50.7
Rheumatology	42.6	18.0	3.7	48.6
Ophthalmology	41.4	21.0	3.5	43.4
Vascular/Interventional Rad.	*	*	3.8	53.5
Hand Surgery (Ortho)	*	*	3.8	59.1
Obstetrics & Gynecology	34.4	24.2	3.7	48.7
Child & Adolescent Psychiatry	40.6	19.8	3.5	41.8
Pathology	*	*	3.8	44.1
Child Neurology	*	*	3.7	40.4
Physical Medicine & Rehabilitation	39.1	12.6	3.7	47.9
Neurology	39.0	16.2	3.6	48.4
Radiology, Diagnostic	*	*	3.8	50.2
Otolaryngology	38.8	25.2	3.8	51.9
Radiation Oncology	*	*	3.6	49.5
Gastroenterology	38.5	19.5	3.8	51.7
Pulmonology–Critical Care	*	*	3.8	63.6
Pediatric Gastroenterology	*	*	4.0	50.0
Psychiatry	38.6	38.6	3.6	40.1
Vascular Surgery	*	*	3.8	61.9
Internal Medicine	36.5	20.3	3.4	49.3
Anesthesiology	*	*	3.7	54.7

(continued)

FIGURE 3.3 (continued)

	% Practitioners saying that they are "Very Satisfied" with their specialty	% Practitioners saying that they are "Dissatisfied" with their their specialty	How satisfied with *current* practice position (1=unsatisfied to 5=very satisfied)	Hours per week doing patient care
Colon & Rectal Surgery	*	*	4.0	54.0
Hematology–Oncology	*	*	3.6	46.6
Pulmonary Diseases	33.3	17.9	3.6	51.2
Preventive Medicine	*	*	4.2	29.8
Hand Surgery (Non-Ortho)	*	*	3.0	56.7
Critical Care (All)	*	*	3.4	65.8
Nuclear Medicine	*	*	3.7	51.9
Pain Medicine	*	*	3.5	54.5
Pediatric Pulmonology	*	*	3.5	33.2
Pediatric Hematology–Oncology	*	*	3.4	39.0
Gynecology	27.3	25.0	#	#
Medical Genetics	#	#	2.0	28.0

(To order specialties, numbers were not rounded, as they were in the specialty descriptions.)
*Position based on 2000 AMA survey data.
#No information available.
Adapted from: *AMA Statistics, 2002*; and Leigh JP, Kravitz RL, Schembri M, Samuels SJ, Mobley S: Physician career satisfaction across specialties. *Arch Intern Med.* 2002;162:1577-84.

FIGURE 3.4

Effect of Lifestyle, Income, Work Hours, and Years of Training on Specialty Selection

Specialty	Students Selecting This Specialty as 1st Choice*	Lifestyle**	Avg. Annual Income: Thousands $	Avg. Hours Worked per Week	Req. Years of Residency
Internal Medicine	25%	U	158	57	3
Pediatrics	11%	U	138	54	3
Family Practice	10%	U	132	53	3
General Surgery	8%	U	238	60	5
Emergency Medicine	7%	C	183	46	3
Anesthesiology	6%	C	225	61	4
Radiology (Diag)	6%	C	263	58	4
Ob/Gyn	6%	U	224	61	4
Orthopedic Surgery	5%	U	323	58	5
Psychiatry	4%	C	134	48	4
Ophthalmology	3%	C	225	47	4
Dermatology	2%	C	221	46	4
Neurology	2%	C	172	56	4
Otolaryngology	2%	C	242	54	5
Urology	2%	U	245	61	5
Pathology	1%	C	202	46	4
AVERAGE	—	—	**208**	**54**	**4**

*U.S. senior medical students from M.D.-granting medical schools, 2002. Numbers do not add to 100% due to rounding.
**C = Controllable lifestyle (relatively predictable schedule); U = Uncontrollable lifestyle (on-call frequently, unanticipated long hours).
Adapted from: Dorsey ER, Jarjoura D, Rutecki GW: Influence of controllable lifestyle on recent trends in specialty choice by medical students. *JAMA.* 2003;290(9):1173-78, Tables 1 and 2.

4

Osteopathic Medicine: The Other Degree

What's in a name? That which we call a rose
By any other name would smell as sweet.

— Shakespeare, *Romeo and Juliet*, II, 2

A Doctor of Osteopathic Medicine, or D.O., is a physician, although this degree is less familiar to most people than the M.D. degree. As Gertrude Stein said, however, a "rose is a rose is a rose." Both D.O.'s and M.D.'s are licensed to practice medicine and surgery, may prescribe drugs, usually hold appointments on hospital staffs, and legitimately use the title "Doctor," as in "Is there a doctor in the house?" (Ph.D.'s may consider themselves the only "real" doctors, but they often get squeamish when they see sick people.) About 45,000, or 5%, of U.S. physicians have D.O. degrees. About half of Osteopathic physicians practice in primary care fields, in contrast to about 15% of M.D.'s.

— Why Are There Two Different Degrees? —

In nineteenth-century America, many types of medical practitioners existed. These included homeopaths, eclectics, hydropaths, magnetic healers, allopaths (a term often incorrectly applied to M.D.'s), Osteopaths (D.O.'s), and M.D.'s. None of these different disciplines tolerated each other, leading to bitter professional rivalries. The outcome of this internecine warfare is that M.D.'s dominate American medicine, and D.O.'s are the only other type of physician that still exists in any appreciable number. The bitterness and misunderstanding between these two physician groups has continued, however, and is only slowly subsiding as new generations of M.D.'s and D.O.'s work side by side.

In the late 1800s, Andrew Taylor Still, M.D., founded "Osteopathy," now called Osteopathic Medicine, after a family medical tragedy led him to promote the body's innate healing ability rather than the use of dangerous medications. The medications he decried as dangerous, which enjoyed widespread popularity at the time, included arsenic, cyanide, and mercury,

Originally, Osteopathic physicians concentrated on curing patients by manipulating their spines and other joints. Later, they adopted many techniques used by M.D.'s, although they continue to use spinal manipulation, now known as Osteopathic Manipulative Treatment (OMT) or Osteopathic Manipulative Medicine (OMM). In the mid-twentieth century, D.O.'s began emphasizing their role as general practitioners, especially to smaller communities. They naturally grew into this role when, after World War II, smaller communities could find no other physicians to serve their needs. Their expansion into primary care was enhanced when D.O.'s were banned from virtually all M.D. residency (graduate) training programs. (This total ban no longer exists.)

Today, most colleges of Osteopathic medicine still emphasize treating the whole patient and encourage their graduates to enter family practice. About half of all Osteopathic physicians are in generalist/primary care practices, which include family practice, internal medicine, obstetrics and gynecology, Osteopathic manipulative treatment, and pediatrics.

— Why Choose a D.O.-Granting Medical School? —

Students may have any of four reasons for applying to D.O.-granting medical schools: a D.O. role model, the Osteopathic philosophy/primary care orientation, ease of entry into the school, and the desire to learn Osteopathic manipulative treatment.

D.O. Role Model

Role models strongly influence students' career decisions. Many Osteopathic physicians applied to D.O. schools due to the memorable contacts they had with one or more Osteopathic physicians as they grew up. These "Marcus Welby-like" physicians demonstrated a caring, as well as a curing, attitude that these students wanted to emulate. Many of these D.O.'s also acted as the students' mentors as they progressed through undergraduate and medical school.

If you have such a mentor, it will be important to get a letter from him or her when applying to Osteopathic medical school. Most schools require or strongly suggest that applicants send a letter from an Osteopathic physician. In part, this is so that they can be assured that the applicant really knows something about Osteopathic medicine. Aside from premed advisers, you can find local Osteopathic physicians through your state's Osteopathic Association or the American Osteopathic Association's Web directory (http://directory.aoa-net.org).

Philosophy/Primary Care Orientation

Osteopathic medicine has always concentrated on the entire patient rather than just the disease process. While this is now considered the basis of modern medical practice, especially family practice, D.O.'s have held this attitude from the beginning. Osteopathic medical schools try to instill this attitude in their students. This is in contrast to M.D. medical schools, where they may "talk the talk" about the "whole patient," but they don't "walk the walk" where it counts—in the clinical setting.

Andrew Taylor Still, M.D., used the following principles as a foundation for Osteopathic medicine:

- The body is an integral unit, a whole. The structure of the body and its functions work together, interdependently.
- The body systems have built-in repair processes that are self-regulating and self-healing in the face of disease.
- The circulatory system or distributing channels of the body, along with the nervous system, provide the integrating functions for the rest of the body.
- The contribution of the musculoskeletal system to a person's health is much more than providing framework and support. Improper musculoskeletal functioning can impede essential blood and nerve supplies.
- While disease may be manifested in specific parts of the body, other parts may contribute to a restoration or a correction of the disease.

The Osteopathic profession is currently struggling with the once deeply held belief that the musculoskeletal system is central to disease processes. Many Osteopathic residencies, especially in non-primary care specialties, barely mention manipulative techniques, and many Osteopathic physicians complete M.D. residencies that, of course, do not include these procedures. Some within Osteopathic medicine believe that losing this touchstone of their professional heritage will eventually dissolve any remaining differences between M.D.'s and D.O.'s.

Ease of Entry

About 30% of applicants to Osteopathic medical schools first hear about the profession from their premed advisers. That is because Osteopathic medical schools have often admitted students that M.D. schools rejected, such as students who are older and who have lower GPAs (3.5 in 2001), lower science GPAs (3.36 in 2001), or lower MCAT scores (8.54 Biological Sciences; 8.08 Physical Sciences; 8.10 Verbal Reasoning in 2001). As evidence of the vagaries of medical schools' admission procedures, some D.O.'s who were rejected from M.D. medical schools are now on their faculties. Many Osteopathic medical schools will admit applicants with an interest in primary care in preference to those with higher grades and scores who do not express such an interest. As the qualifications (if not the quality) of applicants to medical school increase, entering Osteopathic medical school will become more difficult. (For additional information about Osteopathic medical schools, see Figures 15.4 through 15.7.)

Unlike M.D.-granting schools, which have been combining, the number of Osteopathic medical schools has increased. In 1996, the Arizona College of Osteopathic Medicine held its first classes, and both Pikesville College School of Osteopathic Medicine (PCSOM) and Touro University College of Osteopathic Medicine opened in 1997. The Edward Via Virginia College of Osteopathic Medicine in Virginia received provisional accreditation from the AOA and admitted its first class in 2003, becoming the twentieth Osteopathic medical school.

The number of applicants to D.O. schools has slightly decreased in recent years: there are now about 2.3 applicants for each first-year position. The percentage of women applying to D.O. schools has increased. The number of women in Osteopathic medical schools varies markedly by school, from PCSOM, at which only about a third of students are women, to the University of Medicine and Dentistry of New Jersey School of Osteopathic Medicine (UMDNJ-SOM) and University of New England College of Osteopathic Medicine (UNECOM), where women account for at least half of the student body. On average, 43% of all Osteopathic students in 2002 were women.

All underrepresented minorities composed only 8.6% of first-year Osteopathic students in 2001. The number of underrepresented minority students also varies markedly among schools, from less than 10% of the students at PCSOM, UNECOM, and West Virginia School of Osteopathic Medicine, to nearly half of the enrollment at NYCOM, UMDNJ-SOM, and Western University of Health Sciences/College of Osteopathic Medicine of the Pacific (WesternU/COMP). Historically, both women and underrepresented minorities have had a lower-than-average record of acceptance.

Some Osteopathic medical schools serve mostly state residents, while others draw from the entire country. Those that take primarily in-state students are:

- Univ. of North Texas Health Science Center/TCOM (96.7%)
- Michigan State Univ. COM (89.6%)
- Oklahoma State Univ. COM (86.8%)
- Univ. of Medicine and Dentistry of New Jersey–SOM (84.3%)
- Ohio Univ. COM (83.9%)
- Western Univ. of Health Sciences/COMP (78.6%)
- New York COM (69.6%)
- West Virginia SOM (67.5%)
- Touro Univ. COM (64.0%)
- Pikesville College SOM (60.9%)
- Philadelphia COM (60.6%)

Just as with M.D.-granting schools, you can maximize your chance of being accepted to an Osteopathic medical school by applying to your state's school or to schools that give no preference to state residents.

Osteopathic Manipulative Treatment

A unique part of Osteopathic medical schools' curricula is Osteopathic Manipulative Treatment (OMT), also called Osteopathic Manipulative Medicine (OMM)). This is the manipulation of the spine to relieve painful conditions. Medical school applicants with a background in physical therapy or related fields have often seen for themselves the extraordinary relief that patients can obtain with OMM, and they want to learn to use it in their own practice.

However, most D.O.'s rarely use OMT, especially if they are in nongeneralist specialties, graduated in the past few decades, practice with HMOs or a group, or took an M.D. residency. Others, especially older family physicians who did D.O residencies and are in solo practice, use it to supplement standard medical treatments. A few D.O.'s specialize in OMT after completing an OMT residency or fellowship. In fact, some M.D.'s now take special courses to learn the simpler OMT techniques.

Less than 4% of Osteopathic medical school faculty specialize in OMT. And while, on average, more than one-fourth of students' clinical experiences in their "preclinical" years (usually years one and two) involve learning OMT, students only spend an average of one week doing OMT during their clinical (usually third and fourth) years.

— The Osteopathic Curriculum —

Osteopathic medical schools have essentially the same curricula (Figures 4.1 and 4.2) as do M.D. medical schools, although the curricula and teaching methods vary among schools. Osteopathic students may take the same licensing examination (USMLE) as M.D. students, although most take the Comprehensive Osteopathic Medical Licensing Examination (COMLEX), which covers the same material and is administered by the National Board of Osteopathic Medical Examiners.

While most Osteopathic medical schools have strong basic science courses, some schools' clinical training is weaker than that of comparable M.D. schools. Such Osteopathic medical schools do not have their own teaching hospitals nor do they have strong ties with large, busy teaching hospitals at which their students can do clinical rotations. This is partly because M.D.'s have long controlled the teaching hospitals in many large communities, and have often been reluctant to allow Osteopathic students to do clinical rotations alongside M.D. students.

Even with this caveat, students at any Osteopathic medical school should be able to get as good a medical education (or better) as do students at comparable M.D. schools. As in M.D. schools, success depends upon the student's ability to assertively seek out clinical opportunities and to get the best possible rotations.

— Impact of an Osteopathic Degree on a Medical Career —

Osteopathic physicians face four obstacles during their careers, which may or may not be of importance to you:

- Confusion about what a D.O. is.
- Hostility and discrimination within the physician community.
- Insufficient residency positions, especially in surgical specialties.
- Potential problems in obtaining an international medical license.

First, many individuals, both within the medical profession and among the lay community, do not know that D.O.'s are physicians, albeit with a different degree. Many confuse Osteopathic physicians with chiropractors. To avoid this confusion, some Osteopathic physicians wear nametags with "Dr. S. Victory" rather than "S. Victory, D.O."

Second, Osteopathic physicians still face hostility from segments of the M.D. community. They feel it the most when applying to residencies. Even though many Osteopathic physicians are warmly welcomed into undersubscribed M.D.-run primary care specialty residency programs, they are less

FIGURE 4.1

Average Osteopathic Curriculum: Basic Sciences (Preclinical)

Subject	Average Number of Hours	Percent of Time
Clinical Medicine	279 hours	15%
Gross Anatomy	173	9
Pathology	149	8
Osteopathic Manipulative Medicine/Treatment	143	8
Physiology	120	6
Pharmacology	102	5
Microbiology	98	5
Biochemistry	96	5
Ambulatory Medicine	85	5
Physician Skills	81	4
Osteopathic Principles/Practice	80	4
Histology/Microanatomy	71	4
Neuroanatomy	55	3
Cardiovascular System	54	3
Epidemiology	40	2
Miscellaneous Basic Sciences	40	2
Behavioral Medicine	35	2
Psychiatry	29	2
Miscellaneous Clinical Sciences	23	1
Immunology	19	1
Nutrition	17	1
Genetics	16	1
Radiology	16	1
Ethics/Policy/Law	14	1
Embryology	13	1
Geriatrics	11	1
TOTAL	1,859 hours	100%

Adapted from: American Association of Colleges of Osteopathic Medicine. *2002 Annual Report on Osteopathic Medical Education*. Chevy Chase, MD: AACOM, 2003, Tables 17 and 18, p. 38.

commonly accepted into difficult-to-match-with specialties, such as emergency medicine and dermatology. Because of long-standing animosity at the national level, few D.O.'s are accepted into M.D.-run surgery programs.

Third, Osteopathic residency training in many specialties is currently difficult to obtain due to a lack of available positions, as described below.

Finally, if you want to practice international medicine, it may be difficult to obtain a medical license—or a medical license other than solely for manipulative medicine—in many foreign countries. Each country establishes rules for medical licensure, and many do not recognize the D.O. degree. This may limit your opportunity to practice with international aid groups and medical missions, as well as to establish a practice outside the United States. Figure 4.3 lists the countries that allow the unrestricted medical licensure of Osteopathic physicians.

FIGURE 4.2

Average Osteopathic Curriculum: Clinical Years

Subject	Average Number of Weeks	Percent of Time
Electives	16.1 weeks	14%
Family/Community Medicine	14.1	13
Internal Medicine	13.4	12
Selectives*	8.9	8
Pediatrics	7.0	6
General Surgery	6.9	6
Obstetrics & Gynecology	5.6	5
Psychiatry	5.2	5
Emergency Medicine	4.9	4
Osteopathic Manipulative Treatment	3.9	4
Surgical Subspecialties	3.8	3
Radiology	2.8	3
Anesthesiology	2.4	2
Orthopedics/Orthopedic Surgery	2.3	2
Geriatrics	2.1	2
Otolaryngology	2.0	2
Neurology	1.9	2
Ophthalmology	1.7	2
Critical Care	1.4	1
Other	5.1	5
TOTAL	112 weeks	100%**

*Selective courses, unlike electives, are chosen from limited options.

**Total does not equal 100% due to rounding.

Adapted from: American Association of Colleges of Osteopathic Medicine. *2002 Annual Report on Osteopathic Medical Education.* Chevy Chase, MD: AACOM, 2003, Table 19, p. 39.

D.O.-Run Residency Training

The increase in Osteopathic medical students far outpaces the increase in students at M.D. schools. Between 1970 and 2003, the number of D.O. graduates increased by nearly 600%, severely straining the Osteopathic graduate education system (i.e., residency programs). During that same period, the number of Osteopathic medical schools increased from 9 to 20. There are now over 2,500 Osteopathic graduates annually. Both the 1,165 funded Osteopathic transitional internships and the 1,078 funded entry-level (first-year) residency positions are insufficient to meet the needs of Osteopathic graduates if they all entered D.O. training programs (Figure 4.4). And those programs that do exist cannot accommodate the increasing number of new D.O.'s who want to pursue specialties other than primary care. This means that many Osteopathic graduates must look to the M.D. side of the profession for their training.

One detail about residency programs still seems to elude the Osteopathic community. While most M.D.-run residency programs and their applicants use a national matching program, applicants to D.O.-run residency programs must scramble around trying to match themselves with training sites. Just recently, Osteopathic medicine established a matching program (more than 40 years after M.D. students began using matching programs), but it is only for their internship program.

FIGURE 4.3

Countries That Allow Unrestricted Medical Licensure of D.O.'s[1]

Argentina	Columbia	Italy	Saudi Arabia
Australia[2]	Costa Rica	Lebanon	Sierra Leone
Austria	Dominican Republic	Liberia	Sweden
Bahamas	Ecuador	Luxembourg	Taiwan
Bermuda	Finland	Micronesia	Tanzania
Brazil	Germany	Nepal	United Arab Emirates
Canada[2]	Greece	New Zealand[4]	Vietnam
Cayman Islands	Guyana	Nigeria	Zambia
Central African Republic	Honduras	Panama	
Chile	Hong Kong	Papua New Guinea	
China	Indonesia[3]	Russia/CIS	
	Israel (?)	St. Lucia	

1: Some countries allow D.O. licensure only for OMT (Osteopathic Manipulative Therapy). Many other countries have never been asked to grant medical licensure to D.O.'s.

2: Varies by state or province

3: Unrestricted if with a university or mission

4: Unrestricted on an "exceptions" basis

Adapted from Mascheri L: AOA *International Licensure Summary*. Chicago, IL: AOA, August 2002.

D.O.'s in M.D.-Run Training

Osteopathic graduates say they "jump ship" to M.D. programs because they believe these programs provide better training, pay higher salaries, and include specialty training unavailable in Osteopathic programs. That is not surprising, since there are only 13 Osteopathic teaching hospitals with more than 300 beds in the United States. Osteopathic educators now see AOA-approved residency programs as a haven for D.O.'s interested in surgical and other noninternal medicine or non-family practice specialties. As one said in defense of students who do M.D. residencies, "students do not see anything distinctive in what Osteopathic graduate medical education training programs have that would differentiate them from [M.D.] programs . . . these choices may be the result of enlightened decision making and not necessarily an indication of disloyalty."

Over the past 15 years, increasing numbers of ACGME (M.D.-approved) internal medicine and family practice programs have also become accredited by the American Osteopathic Association (AOA), ensuring that both M.D.'s and D.O.'s trained in their programs will be eligible for Board certification and licensure. This cooperation grew out of a need for more primary care residents, and was influenced by several factors, including the increased number of D.O. students without a corresponding increase in Osteopathic residency positions and the M.D. programs' only two alternatives: to take international medical graduates or have unfilled positions. In recent years, 60 ACGME-accredited institutions had such dual-accredited programs, opening an additional 705 positions for Osteopathic graduates. This represents nearly one-third of all AOA internship positions. About 11% of Osteopathic medical students plan to enter one of these positions. Another 47% plan to do an M.D. residency program. Another 10% plan to enter a federal government-sponsored residency (that both M.D. and D.O. groups must recognize). Only about 32% plan to enter a residency approved only by the AOA.

FIGURE 4.4

Osteopathic Specialties, Programs, and Number of Positions

Specialty	Number of Programs	Number of Approved Positions[1]	Number of Funded Positions[2]	Number of Funded First-Year Positions[3]	Number of All Residency Positions Filled[4]
Anesthesiology	10	45	30	10	6
Cardiology	10	48	36	12	13
Child Psychiatry	1	2	1	1	0
Critical Care Medicine	3	6	3	1	1
Critical Care Surgery	1	2	0	0	0
Dermatology	16	76	38	13	24
Diagnostic Radiology	11	90	70	14	36
Emergency Medicine	32	549	409	93	126
Emerg Med–Family Prac	3	20	15	2	15
Emerg Med–Internal Med	11	100	69	11	15
Family Practice	121	1,474	1,092	544	334
Fam Prac–Neuromuscular Med	1	9	6	2	0
Fam Prac–OMM	2	6	3	1	0
Fam Prac–OMT	3	8	0	0	0
Gastroenterology	5	16	12	4	3
Geriatric Med–Family Prac	5	15	8	2	1
Geriatric Med–Internal Med	2	4	3	1	0
Hematology/Oncology	1	2	2	1	0
Infectious Diseases	2	8	3	2	0
Internal Medicine[3]	50	567	426	142	85
Internal Med–Pediatrics[3]	1	4	2	2	0
Maternal–Fetal Medicine	1	3	3	1	0
Nephrology	2	4	3	2	1
Neurological Surgery	11	51	29	5	9
Neurology	5	32	28	6	7
Neuromuscular Med+1	4	12	9	2	5
Neuromuscular Med–OMT	7	32	24	10	1
Obstetrics/Gynecology[3]	32	292	240	60	72
Ophthalmology	9	40	38	13	6
Orthopedic Surgery	29	274	241	48	114
Otolaryngology	1	2	1	<1	1
Otolaryngology/Facial Plastics[3]	18	81	74	15	19
Otolaryngic Allergy	1	3	0	0	0
Pediatrics[3]	13	144	97	28	21
Pediatric Emergency Med	1	4	2	1	0
Physical Med/Rehabilitation	1	9	8	2	0
Plastic & Reconstructive Surg	2	9	3	1	0
Preventive Med–Public Health	1	3	0	0	0
Preventive Med–Occupational Med–Environmental Med	1	3	3	0	2

(continued)

FIGURE 4.4 (continued)

Specialty	Number of Programs	Number of Approved Positions[1]	Number of Funded Positions[2]	Number of Funded First-Year Positions[3]	Number of All Residency Positions Filled[4]
Proctology	1	2	2	1	1
Psychiatry	3	33	27	7	9
Pulmonary Medicine	3	8	4	2	1
Pulmonary Med–Critical Care	1	2	1	<1	0
Radiation Oncology	0	0	0	0	0
Sports Medicine	6	13	8	5	2
Sports Med–Family Prac	3	9	3	3	0
Surgery, General	35	297	240	54	79
Thoracic–Cardiovascular Surg	2	11	9	3	1
Urological Surgery[3]	4	34	13	2	4
Vascular Surgery	8	19	15	5	2
Transitional Internship	150	481	1,165	1,165	686

1: Number of residency positions, in all years of training, that the AOA has officially approved.

2: Many programs list positions for which they do not have funding. This column lists only funded (real) positions available for Osteopathic physicians or students.

3: Annual number of funded entry-level positions, which may be at the first year of residency ("R-1" after an AOA-approved internship) or a *specialty track* internship available to Osteopathic medical students. Specialty-track internships can shorten the total residency length by one year and are available in Internal Medicine, Obstetrics/Gynecology, Otolaryngology/Facial Plastic Surgery, Pediatrics, and Urological Surgery.

4: Number of all Osteopathic residents training in that specialty (at all levels of residency) during the 2002-2003 academic year.

Information from: American Osteopathic Association, July 2002.

If you enter Osteopathic medical school intending to pursue M.D. training, you will have to deal with both the American Osteopathic Association (AOA) and the programs. If you change your mind after you have completed an M.D. internship and want to do an Osteopathic residency, they will not accept you. Also, even though you will generally be eligible to take the AMA's specialty Board examination upon successful completion of an M.D. training program, you will not be allowed to take the AOA's specialty examination in the same field unless you pay the AOA to site-visit your residency program. Even after you pay the high fee, they may not approve the program. This may mean that you will not be eligible for specialty staff privileges at some Osteopathic hospitals. (You may also be unable to obtain a license in some states. See below.)

More Osteopathic graduates are entering ACGME-approved training programs each year. Between 1986 and 2002, the number of D.O.'s entering PGY-1 positions in M.D. residency programs grew 250%. However, for whatever reason, ACGME-approved training in some specialties is almost completely off-limits to Osteopaths (Figure 4.5). Chief among these are general surgery and various surgical specialties, such as colon and rectal surgery, neurosurgery, orthopedic surgery, otolaryngology, pediatric surgery, thoracic surgery, and urology. Even in the military, it is nearly impossible for an Osteopathic medical school graduate to obtain a position in, and be allowed to finish, a surgical residency program. This decision is controlled by the "powers" granting accreditation to residency programs. It may change in the future, but don't hold your breath.

Finally, there is the Osteopathic hierarchy itself to contend with. While bureaucracy exists throughout medicine, the often-justified paranoia of Osteopathic medicine's leadership places great strains on young practitioners. First is the problem of getting a medical license. In some states (such as Florida and Michigan), D.O.'s cannot get a medical license unless they complete an internship approved by the

FIGURE 4.5

Osteopathic Graduates in ACGME-Approved Programs

Specialty	Number in Training	% of all Available M.D. Positions
Allergy/Immunology	6	3%
Anesthesiology	259	6
Cardiovascular Disease	45	2
Child/Adolescent Psychiatry	28	5
Colon & Rectal Surgery	0	0
Critical Care Medicine (All)	47	3
Dermatology	10	1
Emergency Medicine	258	7
Endocrinology	3	1
Family Practice	1,096	11
Gastroenterology (IM)	35	4
Geriatrics (IM & FP)	9	2
Hand Surgery (All)	5	7
Hematology/Oncology (IM)	23	3
Infectious Diseases (IM)	10	2
Internal Medicine	1,011	5
Internal Med–Pediatrics	56	4
Nephrology (IM)	30	5
Neurological Surgery	1	<1
Neurology	58	5
Nuclear Medicine	4	4
Obstetrics & Gynecology	258	6
Ophthalmology	26	2
Orthopedic Surgery	17	1
Otolaryngology	9	1
Pathology	56	3
Pediatrics	377	5
Pediatric Surgery	0	0
Physical Med/Rehabilitation	153	15
Plastic Surgery	3	1
Preventive Med/Pub Hlth (All)	22	8
Psychiatry	203	5
Pulmonary Diseases (IM)	5	5
Radiation Oncology	12	3
Radiology, Diagnostic	153	4
Rheumatology (IM)	18	6
Surgery, General	136	2
Thoracic Surgery	4	1
Transitional Year	9	7
Urology	10	1

Adapted from: Appendix II, Table 1. *JAMA*. 2002;288(9):1051-53.

American Osteopathic Association. (Osteopathic medical boards change these rules without notice.) Unfortunately, these internships do not count toward any M.D.-run specialty training, and they count as a specialty-training year only for selected D.O. specialties. Most individuals who want to enter a D.O.-run residency, and all who want to enter an M.D.-run residency, must repeat the year. The duration of Osteopathic-run residencies is usually the same as M.D.-run residencies.

While I was in the military, I first experienced the M.D. establishment's often-shabby treatment of Osteopathic physicians. In one incident, a very competent physician was booted out of a general surgery residency when the program director was told that they could lose their accreditation if they graduated an Osteopathic physician. This physician went on to become an excellent flight surgeon (although these "surgeons" do not do surgery).

In another case, an excellent Osteopathic student of mine, who wanted to do an internal medicine residency at the premier military hospital, was originally told that they would not take any D.O.'s. Only after several M.D.'s intervened did they, very reluctantly, agree to take him. (He was so good that he was later appointed Chief Resident; some years later he became head of the department.) More recently, a well-trained (one D.O. and two M.D. residencies) Osteopathic physician was told by the director of an M.D. school's residency program, who was seeking faculty members, that they "would never accept a D.O. on our school's faculty." She is on the faculty at another prestigious (M.D.) medical school in the same specialty.

Some areas of the country, such as the Midwest, have large numbers of Osteopathic physicians and Osteopathic training facilities, so these problems may be somewhat lessened.

Osteopathic Medical Practice

The states with the largest numbers of practicing Osteopathic physicians are Pennsylvania and Michigan (about 4,500 each). Other states with large numbers of Osteopathic physicians are California, Florida, New Jersey, New York, Ohio, and Texas (each with more than 2,000). Arizona, Illinois, Missouri, and Oklahoma each have more than 1,000 practicing D.O.'s.

Where to Get More Information

More information and current application materials can be obtained from the American Association of Colleges of Osteopathic Medicine (AACOM), 5550 Friendship Blvd., Suite 310, Chevy Chase MD 20815-7231, (301) 968-4100, fax: (301) 968-4101, or online. Publications you may want to read are:

- *Osteopathic Medical College Information Book*
  www.aacom.org/data/cib/index.html
  Describes Osteopathic medicine and lists each Osteopathic medical school, giving their contact information, curricula, entrance requirements, application procedures selection factors, class sizes, deadlines, and tuition.
- *Annual Report on Osteopathic Medical Education*
  www.aacom.org/data/annualreport/index.html
  AACOM's comprehensive overview of Osteopathic medical education presented in table and chart form.
- *Debts and Career Plans of Osteopathic Medical Students*
  www.aacom.org/data/studentreport/index.html
  A periodic publication that provides another perspective on Osteopathic medical education.

5

Preparation In High School

When I was a child, I spake as a child,
I understood as a child, I thought as a child;
but when I became a man, I put away childish things.

— I Corinthians, XIII, 11

— High School Academics —

Ideally, potential physicians should take enough high school math and science courses to be able to "test out" of them in college. If you do this, you will have the advantage of taking advanced science courses earlier in your curriculum. In addition, if you decide to major in a nonscience area, it gives you more leeway to pursue studies in that area and still complete the required premed courses.

The most important thing you can learn in high school is *proper study skills*. Many students who consider becoming physicians have not had to study very hard throughout their schooling. Because of this, they do not develop the discipline or the time-management skills necessary to learn the vast amount of material required to get good grades in college, let alone in medical school.

When you get to college, you will probably work twice as hard as you did in high school to achieve the same or lower grades. Studying in medical school is harder than in college, particularly because there is no such thing as asking "What's on the test?" The answer, at least for a medical career, is that everything is on the test. This is the nature of medical practice. Therefore, it pays to develop the discipline needed to set time aside every day to study the required (or extra) course material.

The following are study habits that successful students use:

- Study *at least* one hour outside of class for every hour spent in an academic class. The time you spend on each subject will vary from day to day.
- Plan your daily study schedule based on the class requirements and how well you are doing in various courses. Don't skimp on those courses in which you are doing poorly.
- Study your least-favorite subject first. That way you can't keep putting it off, and the rest of your studying becomes easier.
- Spend time reviewing your notes from previous classes in each subject during the term. The midterm and final exams are usually comprehensive.
- Study alone, unless you are working on a group project. Studying with friends provides an excellent way to waste time. (The exception may be if you are specifically trying to improve your problem-solving skills, where group interaction often helps.)
- Study in a quiet, well-lit place. Turn off the stereo, radio, and television.
- When in the library, face a wall or use a study cubicle. The library's distractions are noise and people (especially friends).
- If you have any breaks between classes, use them to study.

Over time, you will undoubtedly discover your own techniques to improve your studying. By developing these study habits now, you will have a much easier time in both college and medical school. Both are far less structured than high school, have many more distractions, and require you to learn much more in much less time.

— A Taste of Medicine: Volunteer and Work Opportunities —

Once you think you have decided on medicine as a career, why don't you give it a try? Would you buy a car without taking it for a test drive? Of course not! Then why consider investing time, effort, money, and the risk of disappointment to pursue a medical career without first testing your decision?

If you can get any type of clinical experience, it will help you to determine whether you really want to pursue a medical career. If your parents or your parents' friends are physicians, ask to "shadow" them as they work. Your high school counselor may be able to arrange the opportunity for you as well. Watching a physician at work in an office, in the operating room, or on hospital rounds allows you to see both the exciting and the routine sides of medical practice. It also dispels some of the myths perpetuated by medical television shows and movies.

Another way to get a small taste of what practicing medicine is like is to take an Emergency Medical Technician (EMT) course. These are often given through local junior colleges, and part of the training is actual observation in emergency departments and on ambulances. In smaller communities, local volunteer ambulance squads may allow high school students with EMT training to participate.

Although you may not be able to practice medicine, you can certainly observe what physicians do, talk to them about their careers, and see how happy they are with their decision to enter medicine. Over the years, I have met a number of medical students who claimed that they had not been in a hospital since birth. And, while hospitals are not the only arena where medicine is practiced, so much physician training and medical practice occurs in them that I had to assume that these individuals had not made the effort to become familiar with the career they were entering. This is not a very intelligent way to proceed with your life. Be smart. Test your career choice before you invest too much of yourself in it. (For more information about volunteering, see "Extracurricular Activities" in Chapter 7.)

Special Programs

Some high schools have special programs for potential physicians. Many medical schools offer summer programs that give underrepresented minority and disadvantaged high school students who are interested in medicine a chance to learn about the science and practice of medicine. To find this type of program, search Google, www.google.com, with the terms: "summer program" "high school" medicine. (Put the phrases in quotation marks.)

A key to using these programs effectively is to not only attend and complete the course, but also maintain contact with the faculty you meet in the program. As Linda Don, the University of Arizona's minority premed counselor, says, "Once a MedStarter [their program], always a MedStarter." Maintaining these contacts allows you to learn about additional programs that become available to you as you progress through your undergraduate schooling.

— Information about Medicine: Realism versus Reality —

Many sources describe medical careers. Unfortunately, many of these are wrong and also overglamorize a physician's life. You may want to check some of the sources listed in the *Annotated Bibliography* to get a more realistic and vivid picture of the medical profession.

Physicians go through different stages during their careers. For the majority, these are education, residency training, practice, and retirement. Many modify their career at some stage to enter medical management (part- or full-time), switch into other medical areas, or, occasionally, change careers entirely. Some of the alternative paths physicians have taken (either before or after their "official" retirement) include:

- Administering hospitals, nursing homes, hospices, or other health care institutions
- Returning to school for degrees in law, business, the arts, or sciences
- Working with disabled physicians
- Reviewing malpractice cases
- Processing Peer Review Organization claims
- Creating medical computer applications
- Doing utilization review or quality assurance for hospitals, insurance agencies, or the government
- Publishing medical material
- Teaching in high school or college
- Entering the ministry
- Working with home health agencies
- Performing aeromedical examinations
- Doing locum tenens for other physicians (replacing them when they are away on vacation or at meetings)
- Working with pharmaceutical companies
- Counseling alcoholics and drug abusers
- Going into a medically related business
- Entering politics (medical or nonmedical)
- Writing fiction, nonfiction, and technical pieces

It must be obvious by now that medicine offers an enormous number of opportunities, and physicians have many options when they want to slow down or stop their clinical practices.

— Getting into College —

Experts say that you have a better chance of getting into the college of your choice if you follow these rules:

Have a solid senior-year schedule. Since you already did well in your prior three years, have nearly enough credits to graduate, and are tired of high school (a description of many good high school students), you may be tempted to opt for easier courses and essentially "blow off" the senior year. Don't. Good colleges look at how seriously you take your last high school year, how difficult your courses are, and how willing you are to accept additional academic challenges. International Baccalaureate (IB) and Advanced Placement (AP) courses on a transcript signal that you enrolled in programs much tougher than the standard high school honors courses. This impresses colleges.

Follow your passions. If you enjoy specific activities, participate fully. Whether it is the yearbook, a sports team, the French club, playing an instrument, Scouts, or a community-related beneficent group, take an active role, show your commitment, and stay excited. You don't have to kill yourself doing every possible activity. Follow your interests; being exceptional in one area is even better than being well-rounded.

Major–Shmajor. So you don't know what you want to major in yet. No big deal! Many excellent students go through their first two college years trying to figure that out. They enjoy so many things that it is a difficult choice. Colleges also know that many students who "know" their major will change it one or more times before they graduate.

Descriptive reference letters. You want reference letters from someone who can describe your character, your energy, and your intelligence. That comes from working with you and observing you—preferably outside class. The colleges already know what kind of student you are from your grades and SAT scores. They use the reference letters to tell what kind of a person you are.

Brag a little. Use every opportunity to describe your best qualities, including every part of the college application—essay, activity list, and any question that permits you the opportunity to shine. Try to give them a picture of who you are rather than what you think they want to hear.

If possible, speak with the college admission officer, even though it is not required. This gives you another opportunity to highlight your strongest qualities and to make a positive impression.

You Haven't Blown It Yet

If you did poorly in high school, you can still get into medical school. It will just take more effort than if you were an academic star. Since you are reading this book, you probably didn't do well due to a lack of effort and motivation, and possibly a lack of encouragement from your teachers. As one student wrote:

> A student in my high school class performed dismally, barely squeaking by to graduate. Her perpetual expression was one of boredom. She drifted off to a small college—probably getting in purely by chance. Yet, once she reached college, she found a goal (medicine) and teachers who could inspire her to achieve her real potential. It gave me quite a start to see her in the crowd of new medical students on my first day at school. She had found a goal, decided to aggressively pursue it, and didn't let her marginal high school performance weigh her down. (She is now a general surgeon.)

If you now have the motivation and are willing to put out the effort, you still can make the grade.

6

Undergraduate–Medical Degree Programs

Audentis Fortuna juvat.
[Fortune favors the bold]

— Virgil, *The Aeneid, X*

If you are a mature, stellar high school student who is aiming for a career in medicine, you may want to investigate programs that combine undergraduate and medical degrees; some "accelerated" programs can even shorten the process by a year or two. About 2% of medical students enter these programs, which have been in existence for nearly 50 years.

Such programs accept high school seniors or college freshmen and sophomores into a combined Bachelor of Science/Arts–medical school curriculum. The undergraduate portion can last between two and five years (usually for engineering students). Students take their "premed" courses at the medical school's undergraduate campus or at an affiliated school. If they do well in these courses, they then enter the medical school as regular students. Some programs, such as the Wilkes Premedical Program, include a one-semester clinical research component with the undergraduate experience.

The benefit of most of these programs is that, as long as the student meets minimal requirements, admission to medical school is guaranteed. A few programs still require their students to take the MCAT, which defeats their purpose somewhat. The downside is that students must attend specific undergraduate schools that, considering their stellar high school records, the students might not otherwise have attended. Be sure to read the programs' written and online descriptions carefully, since each is unique.

— Accelerated Programs —

Some of these programs are "accelerated," that is, they reduce the amount of formal schooling needed to become a physician by one to three years. They are, of course, heavily weighted with the premed requirements. Some students in these programs find that they do not have time either to complete enough credits to graduate or to take other courses they find interesting. However, most programs allow students to defer entrance into medical school for one or two years to spend more time on undergraduate studies if they desire. If a student in such a program does not acquire enough credits to get an undergraduate degree before entering medical school, the school normally awards a Bachelor of Medical Sciences after the student's first year of medical school.

Studies suggest that for students with equivalent records before college, accelerated students do as well in medical school and in postgraduate (residency) training as do those who completed a traditional premedical course. However, a greater percentage of accelerated students take more than four years to graduate from medical school. (Does this mean they become "decelerated"?)

Although they may appear to be the best way to pursue a medical education, accelerated programs are not perfect. Before you leap into one of these programs, consider the pros and cons.

Positive Aspects

1. Greater chance of completing the program than "normal" premed students. Studies have shown that students in combined bachelor's–medical degree programs are eight times as likely to become physicians as other premed students, even when the SAT scores for the groups were controlled. For underrepresented minority students, the differences are a little less dramatic but still impressive.
2. Stress reduction. As long as participants do well in the undergraduate program (and, for some programs, also on the MCAT), they are guaranteed a slot in medical school.
3. As long as they complete the premed requirements, students can choose any major they want, unlike other students who must gear their major toward possible employment alternatives in case they don't get into medical school.
4. Some programs offer accelerated students summer courses or research opportunities at the medical school. Since these students are (almost) in the profession, the medical school faculty takes a kinder view of their participation in the school's activities.
5. Since they have had prior experience at the medical school, accelerated students have an easier time adjusting. Unlike many new medical students, they usually know other students in their own and upper classes, as well as some of the faculty.

Negative Aspects

1. Entering an accelerated program weds you to a medical career, often well before you have had many other life experiences. (You can, of course, always divorce yourself from this decision, but, like all divorces, it can be a soul-wrenching process.) A major concern should be *who* made your decision to enter medicine and *why* it was made. Think hard before you commit yourself.
2. Each program has minimum requirements during the undergraduate years. These may include a specific GPA (or subsets, such as a minimum GPA in science or humanities courses), a minimum grade in any course (for example, nothing less than a "C"), and, in some cases, minimum scores on the MCAT. Each program has different requirements; it is important to check to see if you are willing and able to meet them.
3. You will probably have a different undergraduate experience than most of your peers. First, you may have less time to participate in extracurricular activities, since you will take a very heavy load of science classes, usually with extended laboratory time. Second, you may live with other students in the accelerated program, which could reduce your interaction with other undergraduates. In some cases, there is friction between accelerated students and other premed students who aren't getting the "free ride" into medical school.
4. Accelerated students often feel that they have missed the wider life perspective that a liberal arts education offers. While they may attempt to compensate for this with self-study or other courses later on, few physicians have the time for this. (In fairness, however, many regular-curriculum "gunner" premed students also miss these opportunities.)
5. Since students in accelerated programs have proven that they have the intelligence and motivation to be physicians (at least up to this point in their schooling), they can apply to and probably get into more than one medical school. Yet, in many of these programs, students lose their guaranteed place in medical school if they apply to other schools. In addition, since these students often do not yet have bachelor's degrees when they are ready to enter medical school, they are at a competitive disadvantage when applying to other schools.

To mangle an old expression, if you have seen one accelerated program, you have seen *one* accelerated program. The programs vary considerably: Some are rigid, others are highly flexible. In some, the students form a distinct and isolated group within the college; in others, they are fully integrated into the school and student body. There are programs at small colleges and at large universities. Few are linked to the most prestigious (not necessarily the best) medical schools. Since there are so many variations among the accelerated programs, be sure to investigate the details thoroughly.

The American Association of Medical College's annual book, *Medical School Admission Requirements*, also has a section describing schools with these programs. The listings include each school's entrance requirements; selection factors; curriculum; expenses; available financial aid; application policies; and the number of in-state and out-of-state applicants, interviewees, and matriculants during the prior year.

Note that Accelerated Programs and Early Admission Programs (described in Chapter 7) are two different animals.

— Schools with Combined Undergraduate–M.D. Programs —

Programs marked with an asterisk (*) have programs combined with undergraduate schools at other institutions. The medical school (MD) and the undergraduate campus (UG) are both listed.

Note: Information was correct at time of publication. However, these programs are subject to change, so always check directly with the schools.

ALABAMA

University of Alabama School of Medicine
(B.A./B.S., 8 years)
UAB Office of Undergraduate Admissions
1530 3rd Avenue South, HUC 260
Birmingham, AL 35297-1150
(800) 421-8743; (205) 934-8743
UndergradAdmit@uab.edu
http://main.uab.edu/show.asp?durki=27435
www.uab.edu/emsap

University of South Alabama
(B.A./B.S., 8 years)
Office of Admissions
Administrative Bldg., Room 182
Mobile, AL 36688-0002
(251) 460-7176; (251) 460-6878
admiss@usamail.usouthal.edu
www.southalabama.edu/admissions/comeap.html

CALIFORNIA

UCLA School of Medicine (M.D.)*
(B.S., 7 years)
University of California, Riverside (UG)
Thomas Haider Program in Biomedical Sciences
UC Riverside, Office of Student Affairs
B600 Statistics/Computer Building
Riverside, CA 92521
(909) 787-4334
www.biomed.ucr.edu/bsmd/prospective
[Apply during first college year]

University of California, San Diego
(B.A./B.S., 8 years)
Admissions Office, 0621
Medical Teaching Facility, UCSD School of Medicine
9500 Gilman Drive
La Jolla, CA 92093-0621
(858) 534-5282; fax: (858) 534 3880
somadmissions@ucsd.edu
http://meded.ucsd.edu/admissions/med_scholar.html
[State residents only]

University of Southern California
(B.A., 8 Years)
USC College Admission
3454 Trousdale Parkway
Los Angeles, CA 90089-0152
http://college.usc.edu/bamd

CONNECTICUT

University of Connecticut School of Medicine
(B.A./B.S., 8 years)
Office of Undergraduate Admissions
Special Programs in Medicine and Dental Medicine
University of Connecticut
2131 Hillside Road, U-88
Storrs, CT 06269-3088
(860) 486-3137; fax: 860-486-1476
www.uconn.edu

DISTRICT OF COLUMBIA

George Washington University
(B.A., 7 years; Engineering, 8 years)
Undergraduate Admissions, Rice Hall
2121 I Street NW
Washington, DC 20052
www.gwumc.edu/smhs/academic/medicine/degrees/joint.html#bamd

Howard University School of Medicine
(B.S., 6 years)
Director, Center for Preprofessional Education
The Howard Center, Room 518
2225 Georgia Avenue NW
Washington, DC 20059
(202) 238-2363
www.hucmlrc.howard.edu/hucm/admissions

FLORIDA

Univ. of Florida College of Medicine (M.D.)*
(B.S., 7 years)
Admissions Coordinator, Junior Honors Program
Box 100216, Health Science Center
Gainesville, FL 32610
(352) 392-4569
www.med.ufl.edu/oea/admiss/#UE
[Apply during second college year]
Affiliated institutions:
Florida A&M University (UG)
University of Florida (UG)

University of Miami
(B.S., 6 to 7 years)
Office of Admissions
P.O. Box 016059
Miami, FL 33101-R-159
(305) 284-4323
www.miami.edu/medical-admissions

ILLINOIS

Finch University of Health Sciences/Chicago Medical School (M.D.)*
(B.S., 8 years)
Illinois Institute of Technology (UG)
Office of Undergraduate Admissions
3300 South Federal Street
Chicago, IL 60616-3793
(800) 448-2329
admission@vax1.ais.iit.edu
www.iit.edu/~premed/med3.html

Northwestern University
(B.S., 7 years)
Office of Undergraduate Admissions
P.O. Box 3060
Evanston, IL 60204-3060
(847) 491-7271
ug-admission@nwu.edu; www.ugadm.nwu.edu

Rush Medical School
(B.A./B.S., 8 years)
Illinois Institute of Technology (UG)
Office of Undergraduate Admissions
3300 South Federal Street
Chicago, IL 60616-3793
(800) 448-2329
admission@vax1.ais.iit.edu
www.iit.edu/~premed/med3.html
[Apply during second college year]

Univ. of Illinois–Chicago, College of Medicine
Guaranteed Professional Program Admissions Initiative
UIL–Chicago, Undergraduate GPPA Coordinator
Office of Admissions and Records (MC 018)
Box 5220
Chicago, IL 60680-5220
(312) 355-2477
www.uic.edu/depts/oaa/spec_prog/gppa [UG]
www.uic.edu/depts/mcam [MS]

MASSACHUSETTS

Boston University
(B.A., 7 years)
Office of Admissions
121 Bay State Road
Boston, MA 02215
(617) 353-2300
http://web.bu.edu/bulletins/und/item14.html#anchor02

MICHIGAN

Michigan State University
(B.A./B.S., 7 to 9 years)
MSU College of Human Medicine
CHM Office of Admissions
A-239 Life Sciences Bldg.
East Lansing, MI 48824-1317
MDAdmissions@msu.edu
(517) 353-9620; fax: (517) 432-0021
www.chm.msu.edu/chmhome/admissions

MISSOURI

St. Louis University College of Human Medicine (M.D.)*
(B.A./B.S., 8 years)
Office of Admissions, DuBourg Hall, Room 221
North Grand Boulevard
St. Louis, MO 63103
medadmis@slu.edu
http://medschool.slu.edu/admissions/process
Affiliated institutions:
Drury College (UG), www.drury.edu
Rockhurst University (UG), www.rockhurst.edu

University of Missouri–Columbia, School of Medicine*
(B.A./B.S., 8 years)
Coordinator of Admissions and Recruitment
UMO School of Medicine, Office of Admissions
Room MA213-215
Columbia, MO 65212
(573) 882-9219; nolkej@health.missouri.edu
www.hsc.missouri.edu/~ahec/bryantscholars.shtml
[State residents only]
Affiliated institutions:
- **Drury College** (UG), www.drury.edu
- **Southeast Missouri State University** (UG), www.semo.edu
- **Southwest Missouri State University** (UG), www.smsu.edu
- **Truman State University** (UG), www.truman.edu
- **UMO–Columbia** (UG), www.missouri.edu/index.cfm
- **UMO–Rolla** (UG), www.umr.edu

University of Missouri–Kansas City, School of Medicine
(B.S., 6 years)
Admissions Office/Enrollment Services
120 Administrative Center
5100 Rockhill Road
Kansas City, MO 64110-2499
(816) 235-1000
medicine@umkc.edu; www.umkc.edu

NEW JERSEY

UMDNJ–New Jersey Medical School*
(B.A./B.S., 7 to 8 years)
Office of Admissions
185 South Orange Avenue
Newark, NJ 07103-2714
(973) 972-4631; fax: (973) 972-7986
NJMSADMISS@UMDNJ.ED
http://njmsa.umdnj.edu/umdnj.html
Affiliated institutions:
- **Boston University** (UG), www.bu.edu
- **College of New Jersey** (UG), www.tcnj.edu
- **Drew University** (UG), www.drew.edu
- **Montclair State University** (UG), www.montclair.edu
- **New Jersey Institute of Technology** (UG), www.njit.edu
- **Richard Stockton** (UG), http://loki.stockton.edu
- **Rutgers University–Newark Campus** (UG), http://lifesci.rutgers.edu/%7Ehpo/BAMD.htm
- **Stevens Institute of Technology** (UG), www.stevens-tech.edu

UMDNJ–Robert Wood Johnson Medical School*
(B.A., 8 years)
Admission Officer, BA/MD Program
Rutgers University (UG)
249 University Avenue
Newark, NJ 07102
http://rwjms.umdnj.edu/admissions
http://lifesci.rutgers.edu/%7Ehpo/BAMD.htm
[Apply during sophomore year at Rutgers]

NEW YORK

Albany Medical College*
www.amc.edu/academic/college
Affiliated Institutions:

Rensselaer Polytechnic Institute (UG)
(B.S., 7 years)
Admissions Office
Troy, NY 12180-3590
(518) 276-6216; (518) 276-4072
admissions@rpi.edu; http://admissions.rpi.edu

Siena College (UG)
(B.A., 8 years)
Office of Admissions
Loudonville, NY 12211-1462
(888) 287-4362
admissions@siena.edu, www.siena.edu

Union College (UG)
(B.S., 8 years)
Associate Dean of Admissions
Schenectady, NY 12308-9968
(888) 843-6688
admissions@union.edu
www.medicine.union.edu

New York College of Osteopathic Medicine/NYIT*
(B.S., 7 years)
Admission Office
P.O. Box 8000
Old Westbury, NY 11568
(516) 686-3831; mschaefe@iris.nyit.edu
http://iris.nyit.edu/nycom/future/fut_BSDO.htm
Affiliated institutions:
- **Marist College** (UG), www.marist.edu/science/apply.html#two
- **New York Institute of Technology** (UG), www.nyit.edu
- **SUNY–Genesco** (UG), http://admissions.geneseo.edu
- **SUNY–New Paltz** (UG), www.newpaltz.edu/admissions/index.html

New York University
Admission Office, College of Arts & Science
Room 904, Main Building
22 Washington Square North
New York, NY 10003
(212) 998-4500
www.med.nyu.edu/som/medsch

Sophie Davis School of Biomedical Education
(B.S., 7 years)
City University of New York Medical School
Office of Admissions, Room H-101
138th Street and Convent Avenue
New York, NY 10031
(212) 650-7711; (212) 650-7712
http://med.cuny.edu
Affiliated medical schools:
Albany Medical College, www.amc.edu
New York Medical College, www.nymc.edu
New York University School of Medicine, www.med.nyu.edu
SUNY Health Science Center at Brooklyn, http://sls.downstate.edu/admissions/medicine/index.html
SUNY at Stony Brook School of Medicine, www.hsc.stonybrook.edu
SUNY Health Science Center at Syracuse, www.upstate.edu/com/options.shtml

SUNY–Brooklyn College of Medicine*
(B.A., 8 years)
http://sls.downstate.edu/admissions/medicine/index.html
Brooklyn College, Office of Admissions (UG)
1201 Plaza Building
Brooklyn, NY 11210
(718) 951-5001
www.brooklyn.cuny.edu/bc/offices/admit

SUNY at Stony Brook
(B.S./B.A., 6 to 8 years)
Honors College
Stony Brook, NY 11794-3357
prehealth@notes.cc.sunysb.edu
www.sunysb.edu/healthed/bamd.html

SUNY–Syracuse College of Medicine*
(B.S., 8 years)
www.upstate.edu/com/options.shtml
Affiliated institution:
Wilkes University Premedical Scholars Program (UG)
SLC 141-142
Wilkes-Barre, PA 18766
(800) 945-5377, ext. 4823; fax: (570) 408-7812
sharpe@wilkes.edu
www.wilkes.edu/academics/lifesci/hlthsci
[Regional residents only]

University of Rochester School of Medicine and Dentistry
(B.S./B.A., 8 years)
REMS Program Coordinator
Undergraduate Admissions
P.O. Box 270251
Rochester, NY 14627
(888) 822-2256; fax: (585) 461-4595
admit@admissions.rochester.edu
www.urmc.rochester.edu (Search for REMS)

OHIO

Case Western Reserve University
(B.S./B.A., 8 years)
www.meds.cwru.edu/admissions/admiss_f.htm
Prehealth Professions Scholars Program
Undergraduate Admission, 103 Tomlinson Hall
10900 Euclid Avenue
Cleveland, OH 44106-7055
(216) 368-4450; fax: (216) 368-5111
admission@po.cwru.edu
www.cwru.edu/provost/ugadmiss/ppsp.html

Northeastern Ohio Universities College of Medicine*
(B.S., 6 or 7 years)
Admissions
NEOUCOM
P.O. Box 95, State Route 44
Rootstown, OH 44272-0095
admission@neoucom.edu
Affiliated institutions:
Kent State University (UG), www.kent.edu
University of Akron (UG), www.akron.edu
Youngstown State University (UG), www.ysu.edu

Ohio State University College of Medicine and Public Health
(B.S., 7 to 8 years)
Admissions, OSU College of Medicine
209 Meiling Hall
370 West 9th Avenue
Columbus, OH 43210
(614) 292-7137; medicine@osu.edu
http://medicine.osu.edu/admissions/eap.cfm

University of Cincinnati College of Medicine*
(B.S., 8 to 9 [engineering] years)
Admissions, College of Medicine
P.O. Box 670552
Cincinnati, OH 45267-0552
COMADMIS@ucmail.uc.edu
www.med.uc.edu/admissions

Affiliated institutions:
Miami University of Ohio (UG), http://zoology.muohio.edu/premed/dual.htm
University of Cincinnati (UG), www.uc.edu/pre_pro_advising/dualadmission.aspx
Xavier University (UG), www.xu.edu/health_advising/Dual_Admission.html

PENNSYLVANIA

Drexel University College of Medicine*
(B.A./B.S., 7 years)
Office of Admissions
2900 Queen Lane
Philadelphia, PA 19129
215 991-8202; fax: (215) 843-1766
www.drexel.edu/ecm/ugsite/undergrad/preprofeshealth/accelerated_degrees.html
Affiliated institutions:
Drexel University (UG), www.drexel.edu/ecm/ugsite
Lehigh University (UG), www3.lehigh.edu/arts-sciences/cashealth.asp
Rosemont College (UG), www.rosemont.edu
Villanova University (UG), www.healthprofessions .villanova.edu/medicine
Wilkes University (UG), www.wilkes.edu/academics/lifesci/hlthsci/default.asp

Jefferson Medical College*
(B.S., 6 to 7 years)
Pennsylvania State University (UG)
Undergraduate Admissions
201 Shields Building–Box 3000
University Park, PA 16804-3000
(814) 865-7620
www.tju.edu/jmc/admissions/home
www.psu.edu/admissions/academics/majors/bacc/pmm.htm

Lake Erie College of Osteopathic Medicine*
(B.S., 7 years)
Duquesne University (UG)
Suite B101, Bayer Learning Center
600 Forbes Avenue
Pittsburgh, PA 15282
(412) 396-6335; fax: (412) 396-5587
prehealth@duq.edu
www.duq.edu/PHPP/affiliations.html

Penn. State Univ. School of Medicine*
(B.S., 8 years)
www.hmc.psu.edu/md/admissions/contact.html
Affiliated institution:
Wilkes Univ. Premedical Scholars Prog. (UG)
SLC 141-142
Wilkes-Barre, PA 18766
(800) 945-5377, ext. 4823; fax: (570) 408-7812
sharpe@wilkes.edu
www.wilkes.edu/academics/lifesci/hlthsci
[Regional residents only]

Philadelphia College of Osteopathic Medicine*
(B.S., 7 years)
www.pcom.edu
Affiliated institution:
Wilkes Univ. Premedical Scholars Prog. (UG)
SLC 141-142
Wilkes-Barre, PA 18766
(800) 945-5377, ext. 4823; fax: (570) 408-7812
sharpe@wilkes.edu
www.wilkes.edu/academics/lifesci/hlthsci
[Regional residents only]

Temple University School of Medicine*
(B.A./B.S., 8 years)
www.medschool.temple.edu/Main/index.html
Affiliated institutions:
Duquesne University (UG), www.duq.edu/PHPP/affiliations.html
Temple University (UG), www.temple.edu/healthadvising/medschol.html
Widener University (UG), www.science.widener .edu/pre/premedscholars.html

RHODE ISLAND

Brown Medical School
(Sc.B/A.B., 8 years)
Office of Admissions and Financial Aid
97 Waterman Street, Box G-A212
Providence, RI 02912-9706
(401) 863-2149; fax: (401) 863-3801
MedSchool_Admissions@brown.edu
www.brown.edu/admissions/index.html
[Primary entrance method to medical school]

TENNESSEE

James H. Quillen College of Medicine–East Tennessee State University
(B.A./B.S., 8 years)
Director, Premedical–Medical Program
Office of Medical Professions Advisement
P.O. Box 70592
Johnson City, TN 37614-0592
(423) 439-5602; fax: (423) 439-6905
premed@etsu.edu; http://qcom.etsu.edu

Meharry Medical College*
(B.S., 7 years)
www.mmc.edu/medschool/Admin/Admission.htm
Affiliated institution:
Fisk University (UG)
Office of Admission
1000 17th Avenue North
Nashville, TN 37208-3051
(800) 443-3475; (615) 329-8666
admit@fisk.edu; www.fisk.edu/index.asp
[Apply during first year at Fisk]

TEXAS

Baylor College of Medicine*
http://public.bcm.tmc.edu/admissions
Affiliated institutions:
Baylor University, Waco (UG), www.baylor.edu
Rice University (UG), http://futureowls.rice.edu
University of Texas–Pan Am (UG), www.panam.edu
University of Houston (UG), www.uh.edu/enroll/admis

University of North Texas Health Science Center
(B.S., 7 years; B.S./M.P.H., 8 years)
Texas College of Osteopathic Medicine
Office of Medical Student Admissions
3500 Camp Bowie Boulevard
Ft. Worth, TX 76107-2699
(817) 735-2204; (800) 535-8266

VIRGINIA

Eastern Virginia Medical School*
(B.S., 8 years)
Office of Admissions
721 Fairfax Avenue
Norfolk, VA 23507-2000
(804) 446-5812
Affiliated institutions:
ET/MD Program Coordinator (Engineering)
Old Dominion University (UG)
College of Engineering & Technology
Norfolk, VA 23529-0236
(757) 683-3789
www.eng.odu.edu
engineer@odu.edu

BS/MD Program Coordinator (Other undergraduate degrees)
Old Dominion University
4541 Hampton Boulevard
Department of Chemistry and Biochemistry
Norfolk VA 23529-0050
(757) 683-4078

Virginia Commonwealth University School of Medicine
(B.S./B.A., 8 years)
Guaranteed Admission Programs
University Honors Program
701 W. Grace Street, Box 843010
Richmond, VA 23284-3010
jfberglu@vcu.edu
www.vcu.edu/honors/honors/guaranteed.html

WISCONSIN

University of Wisconsin–Madison, Medical School
(B.A./B.S., 8 years)
Medical Scholars Program
Room 1140A, Medical Sciences Center
1300 University Avenue
Madison, WI 53706-1532
(608) 263-7561; fax: (608) 262-2327
www.med.wisc.edu/Education/Programs/MS
[State residents only]

7

Undergraduate Preparation

We promise according to our hopes
and perform according to our fears.

— La Rochefoucauld, *Maxims*, 38

Medical educators don't have a high opinion of most medical school applicants' undergraduate experiences. Robert Petersdorf, president emeritus of the Association of American Medical Colleges, expressed this when he said,

> **We must face the fact that the U.S. medical education system has in fact, if not by design, been guilty of stifling intellectual growth and exploration. All too often a career in medicine is launched in the rigid premedical educational environment that prevails in colleges and universities. Students become study machines, characterized as hypercompetitive and narrow-minded at best, and greedy and dishonest at worst. They are thought to be interested only in courses they believe will help ensure their admission to medical school. Students in college should be broadening their educational background, exploring various disciplines, and broadening their minds to new intellectual horizons. Instead, we hear too often of students who will not consider an intellectually challenging course for fear of getting a poor grade and hurting their chances of admission to medical school.** [Petersdorf RG, Turner KS. Medical education in the 1990s—and beyond: A view from the United States. *Acad Med.* 1995;70(7)Supp:S41-7.]

Being motivated, disciplined, goal-oriented, and getting good grades are positive attributes. However, don't let the negatives of "premed syndrome" overwhelm you and obscure the positive aspects of your undergraduate education. As you peruse this section of the book, decide what type of premed student you want to be: grade greedy or educationally enlightened.

— "Best" Preparation for Medical School —

Students always ask about the "best" preparation for medical school. "Is this college the best?" they ask. Or, "What major is best?" There is no universal "best" answer, since each student is unique. Nevertheless, there are some guidelines to follow. In the end, each of you must choose what is right ("best," if you must) for yourself—whether you are choosing an undergraduate school, a medical school, or a major course of study.

Choosing a Major

A lot of scuttlebutt exists about which major to choose. As you ponder your selection, think about this: if you like a subject area, you will be happy taking in-depth courses in it. Consequently, you will do better than you would if you did not enjoy the subject. Remember that you will spend a lot of time, over four or five years, studying in your major field. If you decide to major in a field that interests you, learning will be enjoyable, and you will be less stressed as an undergraduate. The best answer is to major in an area that you would choose even if you did not want to go to medical school.

What if you either don't get into medical school or change your mind about going? Will your major be something that was worthwhile studying? Will it prepare you for anything else you might want to do? Is it something that will help you with the rest of your life? Also (but least important), if you have a nonscience major, you will stand out from the crowd of biochemistry and molecular biology majors when you apply to medical school. It might just give you an edge in being accepted.

When choosing a major, make sure you will have enough time to complete your basic premed requirements. Some premeds have difficulty completing their major and fulfilling premed requirements. This occurs most frequently in those majors with few electives, such as engineering or architecture. If you wish to pursue either of these majors, you will need an understanding adviser and a superb knowledge of your school's systems (e.g., registration, administration) so that you can complete all the courses you need in a timely manner. (Note also that students majoring in "difficult" areas, especially engineering, may be near the top of their class even though they have a "B" average. Medical school admission officers do consider this if the reference letters confirm this situation.)

Most premeds play it safe by majoring in the biological sciences. (This must really bore most medical school admission officers. All majors, however, are evaluated equally.) Less than 20% of all medical students had majors in the physical sciences as undergraduates; more than half of these were in chemistry or biochemistry. Sadly, fewer than 17% of medical students majored in nonscience subjects, with only a negligible number in the humanities. In contrast, only 20% of non-premed students major in the natural sciences; most major in the social sciences, business, or the humanities.

One of the top students in my medical school class majored in French literature. It amazed everyone that a premed would pick this major. He explained that he actually had an easier time as an undergraduate than many of his compatriots. Since he really enjoyed his major subject area, he did not feel stressed when studying for those courses. Therefore, he found it much easier to put in the "drudge time" studying organic chemistry than did other premed students.

A survey of medical students that asked about their undergraduate experiences yielded this "top five" list of recommendations about premed education:

1. You don't have to major in science.
2. Take classes dealing with people, society, communication, ethics, and life—they are all helpful in clinical medicine.
3. Biochemistry and upper-level biology are the science courses that help you the most in medical school. (A recent study suggests that taking biochemistry as an undergraduate provides the most help to first-year medical students.)
4. Concentrate on developing your skills in critical thinking, scientific thinking, and problem solving.
5. Realize that courses such as physics and organic chemistry help you prepare for the MCAT but are of little or no use to you during medical school.

Other comments they made about their majors were:

> I majored in chemistry. While I'm not sure if it helped or hurt getting into medical school, and while I loved chemistry, I think it's totally useless. If I had it to do it over, I would major in something pertinent to medicine and health such as medical anthropology, health education, political science, or economics. (She got an MPH while in medical school.) The liberal arts classes I did take gave me the skills and perspectives that have been useful in medicine.
>
> As a theology major, it's hard to say—maybe God was on my side.
>
> My major was history and, at first, I was afraid that it would hinder my chances of being accepted. But it was actually kind of an advantage. I was different from the average applicant and it really helped in interviews because we could discuss a variety of topics. Admissions personnel seemed glad not to see another biology/chemistry major.

Two caveats: First, even if you choose not to major in the sciences, it is still important to take more than one laboratory course during some semesters. If you don't do this, you may extend your undergraduate career interminably. Medical schools specifically look at performance during these semesters to determine how well you will do in medical school. Second, studies suggest that, on average, students with a broad-based (nonscience) undergraduate education don't initially do as well in medical school as those with science majors. However, the performance for both groups evens out during their clinical years.

Keep Your Options Open

Not everyone who enters college as a "premed" goes to medical school. (And some who enter college without any expectation of going to medical school eventually "see the light" and become physicians. I am one of those.) In any case, plan several alternative routes as you progress through school. If you do not like the courses in your major, are you prepared to switch fields without losing too much time or too many credits? If the courses you need are not open when you go through registration, do you have alternatives to take? Finally, if you find that your goals have changed and you don't want to go to medical school, have you considered other options? If so, do you know how to get there from here?

Life is uncertain. Your life plan is just a guide. These facts won't change after you graduate, when you go to medical school, or once you are a practicing physician. It's always an excellent idea to have alternative plans at every stage of your life. As the Scouts say, "Be prepared."

Length of Premedical Education

Most premeds now take five years to complete their undergraduate degrees. They often choose this longer course so that they can pursue a nonscience major or minor, work to pay for school, or pursue extracurricular activities. At some schools, it is difficult to get the necessary classes at the right time and that hinders students from advancing through their program.

Choosing an Undergraduate College

After you have given at least some thought to your major field of study, it's time to choose your undergraduate college. If you know your major, you can look for schools known for their expertise in that field. If you are still unsure of your major, look for schools that allow you a wide range of areas to study while you complete premed requirements.

Choosing a college is tough. Choosing a college based on whether you can get into medical school after graduation is even tougher.

In the past, men had the best chance of entering medical school if they attended the private universities with associated medical schools, previously all-male colleges that had recently become coeducational, or traditionally coeducational colleges. Women's entry rates were highest for students from women's colleges, distantly followed by those from private universities with associated medical schools. However, these rates are changing due to the increasing numbers of women entering medical schools and the decreasing number of all-women colleges.

Medical schools reportedly give preference to applicants from "top name" colleges and universities. Medical schools have offered some of these students interviews before they submitted secondary applications. Yet, attractive as this sounds, it is not reason enough to pick such a school for your undergraduate work. Students get into medical schools from all U.S. undergraduate schools. You can too.

Undergraduate schools can be very expensive. In the United States, the annual tuition at community colleges averages less than half the cost of tuition at public four-year colleges, and only about 10% of that at private four-year colleges (Figure 7.1). Since you will probably incur large debts for your medical school education, you may want to limit the amount you owe for undergraduate school.

Although community colleges are relatively inexpensive, medical schools want applicants to have taken at least their upper-level science courses at a four-year college. They believe that four-year schools have more rigorous standards, have less "grade inflation," and better measure a student's ability to perform well in medical school. This means that if you start out at a community college, you should immediately begin planning your transfer to a four-year school.

Your primary goal when selecting an undergraduate school is to get a good education. Hopefully, while you complete your course of study, you will also mature as an individual, enjoy your experience,

FIGURE 7.1

Average Annual Undergraduate School Tuition

State	Community College	Public 4-Yr. School	State	Community College	Public 4-Yr. School
AL	$2,099	$3,488	MT	$1,891	$3,707
AK	2,208	3,595	NE	1,536	3,199
AZ	977	2,583	NV	1,365	2,370
AR	1,752	3,725	NH	4,429	5,995
CA	330	1,993	NJ	2,524	6,533
CO	2,117	2,704	NM	768	2,222
CT	2,034	4,556	NY	2,855	4,153
DE	1,806	5,640	NC	1,096	2,677
FL	1,576	2,691	ND	2,263	3,307
GA	1,550	2,605	OH	2,300	5,920
HI	1,323	3,349	OK	1,613	2,377
ID	1,547	3,060	OR	2,059	3,773
IL	1,684	4,606	PA	2,285	5,532
IN	2,957	4,468	RI	2,014	3,761
IA	2,670	4,118	SC	2,343	4,340
KS	1,554	2,593	SD	NA	3,987
KY	1,536	3,205	TN	1,740	3,491
LA	1,485	2,587	TX	977	3,259
ME	2,040	3,860	UT	1,770	2,427
MD	2,564	5,148	VT	3,312	5,374
MA	2,861	4,075	VA	1,304	4,195
MI	1,752	4,891	WA	1,982	3,471
MN	3,049	3,970	WV	1,708	2,856
MS	1,396	3,531	WI	2,902	3,526
MO	2,437	4,127	WY	1,575	2,997
Average Annual Cost				$1,957	$3,718

Adapted from: Trombley W: College affordability in jeopardy. *National Crosstalk.* Winter 2003.

and not go broke doing it. To meet all these goals, you should consider many factors as you try to find the "best" school to attend.

College Ranking Guides

Several groups publish annual rankings of the "top" U.S. undergraduate schools. As tempting as it may be to take these rankings seriously and, when the option is available, to go to a "top" school, these lists have many problems: They definitely will not tell you which is the best school for you.

Technical problems of these lists begin with the incomplete data they use to determine their rankings, and include the elements they choose to rank (e.g., Do you care whether they get lots of grants for interstellar astrophysics research?), the failure to verify the information they receive, and the weight given to many schools' outdated reputations. After considering this, they don't seem like the type of list you want to base your life decisions on. A better decision path is to determine *what elements of an undergraduate education are important to you* and then to do your own evaluations. The next section shows you how to do just that.

— "Must/Want" Analysis: Undergraduate School —

One way to determine which undergraduate (and, later, which medical) school to attend is to use the "Must/Want" Analysis (see also Chapter 16). This method allows you to analyze which factors are important to you and to determine which schools meet your needs. By forcing you to examine what you really need and want in a school, it helps you to see beyond a school's reputation and the "best college" pronouncements of your advisers, family, and friends.

To use the "Must/Want" Analysis, first make a list of all the factors that could possibly influence your decision about which undergraduate school you would like to attend. (See Figure 7.2 for an example.) Read the instructions below and look at the examples to see how you will use the list.

Once you have your list, you will assign a "Weight" to each factor based on its importance to you. (Refer to Figures 7.3 and 7.4 to see how a sample student assigned the "Weight" to the factors important to her.) In giving a "Weight" to each factor, remember that the total of the "Weights" must equal "100." Therefore, apportion each item's importance in relation to its importance to all the other factors you are considering.

How to assign "Weights":

1. Select those factors that are not at all important to you and rate them "0." Eliminate them from your list later.
2. Find those items that are absolute necessities for you, such as a special premed curriculum. *If an item is an absolute necessity, a "Must," you have decided that the factor is so important that it must be present or else you will eliminate a school from consideration, regardless of its other qualities.* If a factor is a "Must," put the word "Must" in the "Weight" column.
3. Decide the relative importance of the remaining factors by assigning each factor a "Weight." Choose factors of minimal importance and rate them "1." Then choose those with more importance and rate them a "2." Continue in this fashion until all the items have been assigned a "Weight." The total for all assigned weights should equal "100." *You will use your same weighting of the same factors to rate all the schools that you consider*. For example, you might want to live in the Midwest, if possible, and might rate "geography" a "1." However, you are much more interested in schools' academic programs than their locations, so you would rate that factor a "4."
4. You will use one "Must/Want" form for each school you consider. As you find information about the school, assign a "Score" (on a 1–10 scale; 10 is "perfect") to each factor on the form, based on your estimate of how well each school fulfills your expectation for that factor. The Score will allow you to rank schools in the order that they meet your needs. If an element that you have rated as a "Must" is not present at the school, you should drop that school from consideration.
5. Multiply the "Weight" by the "Score" to give the factor "Total" for that school.
6. Add the factor "Totals" to give your "School Evaluation Score."

Figures 7.3 and 7.4 are examples of one student's "Must/Want" Analyses for two schools she was considering. As you look at these examples, notice several things. First, the student has deleted from the list any factor that was not important to her ("Weight" = 0). This considerably shortened the list. Second, notice that even though the school in Figure 7.4 got high marks in some factors the student considered important, two of her "Must" factors (concerning a strong computer science department) were not present. Therefore, she did not continue completing the form and eliminated that school from consideration. Even if this school offers her admission, she will not accept. When making factors a "Must," be sure that they are so important that you are willing not to go to an otherwise excellent school if it lacks that factor.

Finally, look at Figure 7.3. This student will use Hometown University's "School Evaluation Score" of 613 to compare this school with other schools in which she is interested. If there is no change in her situation, she will go to the school with the highest score that accepts her.

— Medical School Requirements —

The requirements to enter medical school have changed since the Association of American Medical Colleges (AAMC) first standardized them in 1894. At that time, they listed the application requirements as:

1. An English composition in the handwriting of the applicant of not less than 200 words, said composition to include construction, punctuation, and spelling.
2. Arithmetic—fundamental rules, decimal fractions, and ratio and proportion.
3. Algebra—including quadratics.
4. Physics—elementary.
5. Latin—an amount equal to one year of study as indicated in *Harkness's Latin Reader*.

It wasn't until 1900 that medical schools required a high school diploma or the equivalent as demonstrated by examination.

Medical school admission requirements vary from school to school. *Medical School Admission Requirements—United States and Canada (MSAR),* published annually by the AAMC, lists the specific requirements for each (M.D.) medical school in the United States and Canada. The Association of Canadian Medical Colleges also occasionally publishes a more detailed description of the Canadian schools in its *Admission Requirements to Canadian Faculties of Medicine and Their Selection Policies*. The American Association of Colleges of Osteopathic Medicine issues a similar annual book, *Osteopathic Medical College Information*. These books are vital for everyone considering applying to medical school, so that they can plan their undergraduate course of study. Most college libraries have a copy of at least the AAMC book, usually in the reference section; all college bookstores carry this book. For the Canadian and Osteopathic books, write to the respective association or go to their website (see Appendix B: *Contact Information*).

Most medical schools expect applicants to take the Medical College Admission Test (MCAT) and to have completed *at least* the following course work:

- Biology (1 year)
- Physics (1 year)
- English (1 year)
- Chemistry—through Organic Chemistry (2 years)

Since you don't know where you will apply to medical school, the safest course is to meet at least these minimum requirements. These requirements represent about one-third of the credits needed to graduate from college; what you do with the rest of your time is up to you. No medical school requires you to major in a specific area.

Some medical schools will not accept advanced placement (AP) or College Level Examination Placement (CLEP) credits in lieu of their required courses (Figure 15.8). They will expect students to take the same amount of the subject in college, even though they may begin their college studies with higher-level courses. For example, if you get AP credit for chemistry, you may need to take not only organic chemistry in college, but also another year of chemistry courses, such as biochemistry. Although having AP credits may not decrease the number of classes you need to meet premed requirements, it is still worth taking AP classes in high school, since they will better prepare you for college-level work.

Also, consider taking a foreign language in college. Although a language may not be explicitly required (except for Puerto Rican and French Canadian schools), students who can converse in another language (especially Spanish) are given preference at medical schools where many patients speak that language.

FIGURE 7.2
"Must/Want" Analysis: Undergraduate School

SCHOOL ____________________

PROGRAMS	WEIGHT X	SCORE =	TOTAL
Broad Range of Courses			
Special Premed Curriculum			
Strong in Your Major & Minor			
Has All Required Premed Courses			
Strong Science Department			
Flexibility (Times, Year-Round)			
Enough Positions in Courses			
Class Size			
GEOGRAPHIC LOCATION			
Inner City, Suburb, Rural			
Part of Country			
Specific City			
Spouse/Family/Dependent Needs			
REPUTATION			
School's Reputation			
High Academic Standards			
School's Age and Stability			
Percentage On-Time Graduation			
Attitude Toward Women, Minorities			
Success Getting Into Medical School			
FACULTY			
Availability			
Teach Introductory Courses			
Teach Advanced Courses			
CURRICULUM			
Curriculum Structure			
Innovative Curriculum			
Time to Degree			
Combined Degrees			
Self-Paced Learning			
Computer Education			
Orientation Prior to Start of School			
Major/Specialty-Selection Counseling			
Case-Based Teaching			
Small-Group Learning			
Large/Small Classes			
Student-Teacher Ratio			
Types of Examinations			
ESPRIT DE CORPS			
RESEARCH OPPORTUNITIES/TRAINING			
Knowledge			
Materials			
Time			
Funding			

(continued)

FIGURE 7.2 (continued)

	WEIGHT	X SCORE	= TOTAL
LOCAL JOB PROSPECTS			
FACILITIES			
Easy Registration Process			
Campus Size			
Student-Body Size			
Strong Computer Use/Orientation			
Up-To-Date Lecture Facilities			
Good Laboratory Facilities			
Library/Media			
Parking			
Bookstore			
Safety/Security			
HEALTH CARE			
Medical Insurance			
Student Health Service			
Psychiatric Counseling			
MISCELLANEOUS			
Child Care			
Premed Counseling			
Mentoring			
Available Housing			
Available/Affordable Food			
Student-Learning Center			
EXTRACURRICULAR ACTIVITIES			
Social Life			
Medically-Related Activities			
General Atmosphere			
FINANCIAL			
Tuition Costs			
Housing Costs			
Other Costs			
Scholarships			
Loans			
Jobs			

TOTAL OF ALL WEIGHTS = *100*

SCHOOL EVALUATION SCORE = ______

FIGURE 7.3

Undergraduate School "Must/Want" Analysis—Example A

SCHOOL *HOMETOWN UNIVERSITY*

	WEIGHT X	SCORE =	TOTAL
PROGRAMS			
Broad Range of Courses	8	5	40
Strong in Your Major & Minor	6	9	54
Has All Required Premed Courses	10	10	100
Strong Science Department	5	4	20
Flexibility (Times, Year-Round)	1	7	7
Enough Positions in Courses	7	3	21
REPUTATION			
School's Reputation	1	4	4
High Academic Standards	8	7	56
Percentage On-Time Graduation	1	5	5
Attitude Toward Women, Minorities	3	7	21
Success Getting Into Medical School	2	6	12
FACULTY			
Availability	7	3	21
Teach Introductory Courses	1	1	1
Teach Advanced Courses	3	8	24
CURRICULUM			
Curriculum Structure	3	2	6
Time to Degree	1	4	4
Self-Paced Learning	1	2	2
Computer Education	MUST	YES	✓
ESPRIT DE CORPS	2	7	14
FACILITIES			
Easy Registration Process	2	1	2
Strong Computer Use/Orientation	MUST	YES	✓
Good Laboratory Facilities	1	4	4
Library/Media	3	9	27
Safety/Security	2	6	12
HEALTH CARE			
Student Health Service	1	1	1
MISCELLANEOUS			
Premed Counseling	1	5	5
Available Housing	3	9	27
EXTRACURRICULAR ACTIVITIES			
Social Life	1	4	4
Medically Related Activities	3	7	21
General Atmosphere	2	5	10
FINANCIAL			
Tuition Costs	5	9	45
Other Costs	1	7	7
Scholarships	2	9	18
Jobs	3	6	18

TOTAL OF ALL WEIGHTS = 100

SCHOOL EVALUATION SCORE = 613

FIGURE 7.4
Undergraduate School "Must/Want" Analysis—Example B

SCHOOL NEVERMORE COLLEGE

PROGRAMS	WEIGHT X	SCORE =	TOTAL
Broad Range of Courses	8	8	64
Strong in Your Major & Minor	6	1	6
Has All Required Premed Courses	10	10	100
Strong Science Department	5	9	45
Flexibility (Times, Year-Round)	1	6	6
Enough Positions in Courses	7	8	56
REPUTATION			
School's Reputation	1	8	8
High Academic Standards	8	9	72
Percentage On-Time Graduation	1	5	5
Attitude Toward Women, Minorities	3	7	21
Success Getting Into Medical School	2	7	14
FACULTY			
Availability	7	6	42
Teach Introductory Courses	1	5	5
Teach Advanced Courses	3	10	30
CURRICULUM			
Curriculum Structure	3	5	15
Time to Degree	1	6	6
Self-Paced Learning	1	3	3
Computer Education	MUST	NO	STOP!!
ESPRIT DE CORPS	2	—	—
FACILITIES			
Easy Registration Process	2	—	—
Strong Computer Use/Orientation	MUST	NO	STOP!!
Good Laboratory Facilities	1	—	—
Library/Media	3	—	—
Safety/Security	2	—	—
HEALTH CARE			
Student Health Service	1	—	—
MISCELLANEOUS			
Premed Counseling	1	—	—
Available Housing	3	—	—
EXTRACURRICULAR ACTIVITIES			
Social Life	1	—	—
Medically Related Activities	3	—	—
General Atmosphere	2	—	—
FINANCIAL			
Tuition Costs	5	—	—
Other Costs	1	—	—
Scholarships	2	—	—
Jobs	3	—	—

TOTAL OF ALL WEIGHTS = 100

SCHOOL EVALUATION SCORE = NO SCORE (Does not have a "MUST" Requirement

How Much Science and Math Must (Should) You Take?

Science majors will need to take lots of math and science courses to complete their course requirements. For them, this question is moot. How about nonscience majors? While you can get by with only the basic premed courses, most medical schools recommend that you also take some upper-level science courses to prepare you for the preclinical basic science courses. These science courses should be the same courses taken by students majoring in that area. ("Physics for Dummies 101," for example, won't cut it.)

If possible, take physiology, biochemistry, and molecular biology (Figure 7.5). Taking these courses as an undergraduate allows you time to grasp the basics so that you can better assimilate additional information during medical school. Unlike many other parts of the premed curriculum, these courses are relevant to medicine and are, on the first pass, often difficult to learn. (Learning this material now may also allow you more time to study anatomy!)

For those who do not need math courses for their major (or minor), note that many medical schools suggest or require calculus. And, while not specifically required, computer skills and statistics are an integral part of medical education and medical practice. Try to acquire at least basic knowledge in these areas. (See Figure 15.4 for each school's specific requirements.)

Most medical schools encourage students to take honors courses, complete independent study, and do research. All of these allow students to explore specific subject areas in-depth. Even if the subjects are not related to the sciences or medicine, these types of independent learning are vital to a physician's continuing education.

What GPA Do I Need?

Medical schools vary in the minimum GPA they require of applicants and in the mean GPA of those they accept (Figure 15.7). Each also evaluates transcripts differently. While some schools have rigid and

FIGURE 7.5

Usefulness of Premed Courses as Medical School Preparation

Subject	Rated "Very" Important*
Physiology	69%
Biology	56
Biochemistry	46
Comparative Anatomy	36
Genetics	35
Ethics	22
English Composition	20
General Chemistry	17
Other Humanities	16
Statistics	14
Organic Chemistry	13
Psychology	12
Physics	9
English Literature	7
Zoology	6
Calculus	2

*Percentage of graduating medical students who believed the course was "very important" in preparing them for medical school.

Adapted from: Association of American Medical Colleges. *2002 Medical School Graduation Questionnaire—All School Report.* Washington, DC: AAMC, 2002.

high GPA requirements, others will overlook earlier marginal performance if there is an improvement in upper-division, graduate, or postbaccalaureate course work.

When evaluating GPAs, admission committees realize that in some majors, such as engineering, few students can maintain "B" averages, and that others, such as biology, "A" and "B" are the norm. In addition, admission committees usually recognize that some undergraduate schools require more work from their students to get good grades than do others. As you review the mean GPAs from different medical schools, realize it is only a mean: About half their students are admitted with lower GPAs—often much lower.

— Extracurricular Activities —

You will never have as much free time to try new activities and explore your world as you do during undergraduate school. Take advantage of this time. Use extracurricular activities to unwind from class work, to stretch your mind, and, perhaps, to make money. Getting involved in activities and sticking with them throughout college shows others that you have the maturity and commitment needed to succeed in a medical career. It is important to try to have fun, but don't sacrifice your schoolwork to extracurricular activities.

A big mistake some budding premedical students make is to think that their summer "vacation" is really a vacation. Admission committees often closely scrutinize an applicant's summer activities. Did the student use the time to earn money for school, to do new and interesting things, to take additional course work, or to just "goof off"? Students' choices during these free periods offer excellent insights into their personality.

What extracurricular activities "look best" on your application? While there are no particular activities that stand out, those you engage in should encourage your personal growth and show that you are both altruistic and people-oriented. These activities should also demonstrate that you are a well-rounded individual. Any activities in which you spend time helping others will be beneficial to your application. More importantly, however, such activities correlate with the life of service to others that epitomizes the medical profession.

When seeking out activities, find something you like to do, not just something that will enhance your résumé. For the activities to "count," you need to do them over a prolonged period. If you don't like doing something, you won't be able to stick it out. What are some examples? If you like teaching, mentor high school students. If you like community service, help at a food or clothing bank. If you are more organization-oriented, work with your campus premed group, student government, or first-responder team, or join the service-oriented fraternity or sorority (αφΩ; ΓΣΣ).

Even if you must work to finance your schooling, try to engage in some other activity. Can you help your church, synagogue, temple, or mosque with their fund-raising events? How about becoming a student guide for incoming freshmen? There are many opportunities, you just need to be open to new experiences.

Clinical Experiences

Currently, nearly all applicants admitted to medical school have some experience with the medical profession. They may have been health care workers (nurse, PA, EMT, nurses aide, orderly, technologist), volunteers (on an ambulance; in a hospital, hospice, or nursing home), or ancillary workers in a health facility (clerk, housekeeper). All of these put you in close contact with physicians and patients. Such health-related experiences are carefully scrutinized by both premed committees and medical school admission officers. They want to know how intense the experience was and when you had it. As one medical student said, "It's not how much experience you have that matters, but the quality of it. If you've never experienced anything clinical, saying 'I know I want to do medicine' during your interview isn't going to cut it."

If there has been too much time (e.g., three years) between a less-than-intense experience (e.g., a short stint as a part-time volunteer) and your medical school application, evaluators may wonder if you have had enough clinical experience to know what you are getting into and whether you have a real interest in medicine. With more intense experiences (such as several years working as a clinical nurse), the timing may be less important.

Sometimes working in clinical settings also solidifies an individual's desire to become a physician, as the following story illustrates:

> I really decided to go to medical school in my sophomore year of college when I tried out all of the "easier" careers that combine science and service. I say "easier" meaning better hours, less stress, more conducive to having a family, less time for training. I volunteered in a state hospital working with occupational therapists, shadowed physical therapists, and took an education class (to see if I wanted to be a biology teacher). After trying these and considering nursing, I decided that training as a physician would teach me about all the illnesses that these specialists look at incompletely. Basically, I wanted to know it all. I decided to pursue what I considered the ultimate in education and service. And if I didn't get in, I would fall back on one of the other professions I had considered.

Volunteering

This is an excellent time to volunteer your services in a medical area. You generally have time to spare. If you are asking yourself, "When?" the answer is that you have time to do anything that is important to you. *And this is important*. Certainly you can arrange to spend a couple of hours a week to learn about the field you wish to enter. How about Saturday mornings? *This experience can help you determine if you really want to become a physician*. After all, this must be *your* choice, not your parents', teachers', or friends' choice for you. Also, in volunteering, you will be able to see the amount of dedication, hard work, and commitment to continued learning that the profession requires. If a medical career is really what you want, this experience will renew your motivation. If not, it may save you a lot of frustration and help you to redirect your energies.

How do you volunteer? First, determine what you are interested in and what you are willing to do. Ask yourself the following questions:

- What am I seeking in a volunteer experience?
- What do I want to accomplish through volunteering?
- Who (patients, clinicians, others) do I want to work with?
- What setting would be ideal?
- How much time am I willing to commit?
- What skills do I have?

Volunteers can work either through an organization or with an individual physician, or both. Most premeds volunteer through organizations, such as hospitals, nursing homes, hospices, and ambulance services. When choosing an organization, you may want to consider the following:

- What is the organization's purpose?
- Who does it serve?
- What time commitment does it require? (This may vary depending upon the specific activity you choose.)
- Will you have patient contact?
- Will you have any responsibility?
- Does the organization provide training? If so, how much and of what quality?
- Does it provide the type of volunteer activity you are seeking?
- How will this activity improve you as an individual?

Another option is to volunteer with an individual practitioner. Since you may have few contacts in the medical field, your best bet is to first approach your own family's doctor or a physician at your college's health center. Tell him or her of your interest in the medical profession and of your desire to experience medicine firsthand by "tagging along and helping out." Usually the clinician will be flattered that you asked, and will let you participate in at least a limited fashion. After a few months of this (stick it out, you are learning vital information on which to base lifelong decisions), it may become obvious that you have experienced most of what this practitioner is willing to offer you. If he does not spontaneously suggest it, you should inquire as to whether a colleague can offer you more in-depth (read "active") medical experiences. If you know him really well, you might even address the possibility in your first meeting. In many cases, of course, working with the practitioner will be interesting and intriguing. If that is true for you, stick with it.

Working in Medicine

If you have the opportunity and the time, you might consider seeking employment in a medical setting. Paid positions for individuals with little or no health care experience are often available in hospitals, hospices, nursing homes, and physicians' offices. These jobs are usually not very glamorous. They may involve being a housekeeper, nurse's aide, patient "sitter" (people who watch patients who may harm themselves), or clerical worker. The positions, however, have three advantages: they give you an excellent inside view of medical practice, they offer you a "bottoms-up" look at physicians, and they give you a paycheck. (And they introduce you to those who can help you in your future career.)

As a real part of the team, you will often interact with clinicians, patients, and their families. You will be able to observe physicians at work—warts and all. If you have an idea that medicine is all glamour and kudos, this should disabuse you quickly. Additionally, students who have worked their way up from one of these jobs to eventually go through medical school have been, in my experience, among the finest physicians. They interact well with nurses and patients, and generally are sensitized to patient's concerns. Being paid for this learning experience is just an added bonus.

The Emergency Medical System

Since many medical schools now expect applicants to have medically related experience, paid positions on ambulances have become much more difficult to get than they once were. Also, the requirements for even volunteer ambulance personnel now often include at least Emergency Medical Technician (EMT) certification, if not training at a higher level. If you can get such a position, however, it provides one of the best clinical experiences available to nonlicensed individuals. It also allows you to interact with physicians in a variety of settings, and may itself be an entrée into a paid part-time hospital job. I am particularly fond of the Emergency Medical System (EMS), since that is how I began my medical career, and I still practice medicine "in the field" as part of the Southern Arizona Rescue Association (wilderness search and rescue).

My own introduction to medicine was through a volunteer ambulance service, the Wheaton Rescue Squad in Maryland. At the time, the training requirements were Advanced Red Cross First Aid, the "new-fangled" American Heart Association CPR course (not yet approved by the Red Cross), and an emergency childbirth class. This limited training was considered the best in the country at that time (1967). Most ambulance crews had far less first-aid training. My experiences on the ambulance enamored me with the practice of medicine, and especially Emergency Medicine. It also demonstrated that you don't have to have a heart of stone or a cast-iron stomach to deal with many of the terrible events physicians must witness. Based on these experiences, I quietly switched from prelaw to a premed curriculum. Because I went into medicine with firsthand knowledge of the field, I have never regretted the decision.

Some undergraduate schools now have their own first-responder teams to provide first aid for on-campus accidents and illnesses. These groups provide care at campus gatherings, including sporting and large social events, until ambulances arrive. While it usually provides a somewhat lightweight medical experience, this activity may be a desirable introduction to the world of medicine.

Other Work

Some students need to work at the best-paying job they can get, just to pay for tuition or other essentials. Medical schools understand that. Even if this is your situation, try to find some time for medically related activities. Also, take a hard look at the amount of money you really need (maybe you could eliminate a few incidental luxuries) to determine how much you need to work.

Older students may have family responsibilities, requiring that they provide for and spend time with dependents. This may hamper their participation in other outside activities, but it will demonstrate a level of commitment and altruism that is an essential part of being a physician.

Reflect on what you are learning from your job, talk to your premed adviser about its relationship to your future medical career, and make the most of your opportunities to interact with people having various backgrounds and a variety of life goals. Such people, rather than your college friends, better represent the world in which you will eventually practice medicine.

Research

Opportunities exist for undergraduates to do summer research, either in the laboratory or elsewhere. Research need not be in the "hard" sciences, and may simply be an independent investigation supervised by a professor. Medical schools look for individuals who can work independently to expand their interests, abilities, and work habits. When considering a project, ask yourself if it accomplishes these goals.

Special research programs are also available through national research organizations, such as the National Institutes of Health and the Howard Hughes Foundation. Some medical schools also offer a limited number of research opportunities to undergraduates. See Chapter 9 for additional opportunities available to minority and disadvantaged premed students.

Relaxation

Okay, so you are a good citizen. You have served mankind through research and clinical and community service. What do you do to relax? This is a very individual decision, and it reveals a lot about your personality.

Medical schools are interested in how you relax because a medical career is often stressful. (Medical school and residency are definitely stressful!) If you don't know how to relax now, what will you be like when you are a medical student or physician? Will you be prone to abuse drugs or alcohol? Will you decompensate? If you engage in relaxing pastimes, you will be less likely to have these problems. So, they want to know, can you relax?

There is absolutely no optimal relaxation method, but whatever yours is, you should do it regularly. If you are sports-oriented, do you like a particular sport, especially one you will still be able to play in five or ten years? (Tackle football is probably out, although many physicians now play rugby.) If you have a more sedate hobby, such as woodcarving or yoga, do you make time to do it regularly? Do you enjoy it? Do you have goals for yourself within the discipline? If you do, you have an avocation that may last a lifetime, or at least give you something to do when you need stress reduction.

Is your family your avocation? Excellent! Just ask yourself if you make enough time for yourself, and what do you do with that time. Watch television? Not a good answer. Read mystery novels or go hiking? Okay.

— Interacting with Your Professors —

As a premed student, you will take some very challenging courses. Think of your premed curriculum as a triathlon. In this three-event race (swimming, running, biking), not all competitors excel in every event. Nevertheless, to succeed, they must finish every event in a reasonable manner. Similarly, not every student excels in every course. You may have difficulty with a science course, a nonscience course, or a lab. Where do you turn for help?

Believe it or not, you should go to your professor. All professors have office hours, but few students know how to use their expertise.

Here are some tips to effectively use your time with a professor:

- Visit your professors during office hours if you are having difficulty with a course or need other assistance.
- Go as soon as you begin having trouble, even if it is early in the course. Do not wait until the situation seems to be beyond help.
- Few situations are actually beyond help—again, ask for it.
- Write out your questions ahead of time in case you have trouble thinking or speaking when you are there.
- Ask the professor to watch you work a problem or to listen while you answer a question, so he or she can spot and help correct your errors.
- Don't simply accept a hard-to-understand answer to your question and plan to read more later. That's what got you into this situation in the first place. If you don't understand, ask for clarification. Keep asking until both you and the professor know that you really understand.
- Be assertive. (This might not be in your nature, but do it for your own good.)
- Make frequent (not constant) eye contact. Although it may not be culturally correct for you, this shows the professor that you are interested and alert.
- If you want a recommendation letter from this professor, meet with him or her early in the course to ask for it. The professor can then pay more attention to how you do—and possibly help you sooner if you have trouble in the course.

While many undergraduates complain that they don't see their professors enough, it is often their own fault. Professors are there to help you—let them do their job.

— Premedical Advisers: The Good, The Bad, and The Ugly —

Premed advisers are available at most U.S. and Canadian four-year undergraduate schools, although some smaller colleges have recently dropped the position to save money. Few exist at junior colleges, and many junior college students often first learn the specifics about premed requirements when they transfer to four-year schools. Nationally, about 30% of all undergraduate students who begin the premedical curriculum and who receive advice from their premedical education offices eventually go to medical school.

Premed (or prehealth careers) advisers are either volunteers or draftees. Volunteers are often individuals whose sole responsibility is advising (professional advisers), although some very committed volunteers balance this job with teaching and research responsibilities. Draftees get their advising job due to their administrative position, because they were unlucky in the faculty lottery, or simply because it was their turn to accept it. They are generally not too happy about being premed advisers, and often view this as an additional chore for which they are not rewarded either professionally or financially. More than half of them get no time off from their other duties to advise students. Premeds who believe that their adviser does not have his or her "heart" in the job must rely on other sources of information, such as knowledgeable faculty members or, if available, medical school faculty.

Volunteers, of course, are preferable as premed advisers, but only larger schools can generally afford to fund them. Nationally, the premed advisers are 67% tenure-track faculty, 31% professional advisers, 1% full-time hourly staff, and 1% part-time hourly staff. The numbers are the same for public and private schools. The chance of getting a professional premed adviser increases when the school has more than 100 medical school applicants each year.

Although there are no standard training or background requirements for premed advisers, they usually do have unique information about the medical school application process, and few other college advisers are willing to substitute for them when they are absent. This means that, early on, you should develop a close working relationship with your school's premed adviser. Depending upon the individual, he or she can be extremely helpful, can hurt good applicants' chances of getting into medical school, or can simply be an annoyance to students.

The average premed adviser counsels nearly 300 students a year; those at the larger schools or at schools with a high percentage of premed students, often counsel 500 to 600 students each year. This includes premed students who seek advice during their freshman (about 34%), sophomore (22%), junior (25%), and senior (20%) years, as well as alumni. Forty-five percent of students counseled by premed advisers at public colleges, and nearly 60% at private schools, eventually apply to medical school. Many premed advisers also act as liaisons to high schools, junior colleges, and some medical schools. In some cases, university premed offices have calendars of interesting events for premed students. Many have webpages for campus' premed students.

Premed advisers typically:

- Provide initial contact with and orientation of students at freshman registration.
- Counsel students about the course work needed to satisfy premed requirements.
- Advise students and alumni on an individual basis before, during, and after the application and acceptance processes.
- Hold group meetings several times a year to disseminate updated information.
- Organize premed clubs and bring in speakers.
- Provide a conduit for students to obtain clinical and research experiences.
- Supply information on special awards, summer jobs and fellowships, minority intern programs, non-U.S. medical schools, Medical Scientist Training Programs, and alternative career pathways.
- Maintain a library of relevant information.
- Coordinate the distribution of application materials.
- Help students to prepare for interviews and the MCAT.
- Distribute recommendation letters and produce a composite/premed committee letter.
- Advise rejected students and alumni about their options.

A premed adviser's role is to inject common sense, realism, and information into the process of getting into medical school. The best premed advisers do not tell students whether they will get into medical school. Instead, they show students the average achievement levels of those accepted by medical schools, determine the level of each advisee's achievements, and then let the student decide if the goal is worth the effort. If the student decides to pursue this goal, the adviser can then help him or her go through the necessary steps without being delayed, discouraged, or dismayed by the details. As Josephine Gin, the University of Arizona's former premed adviser, said, "Each student is unique. They all have different paths to achieve their goals. My job is to help them."

Premed advisers are in a very powerful position. One former premed student relates that, after taking some chemistry classes, she told her premed adviser that she had decided to major in chemistry. "You don't want to do that," said the adviser. So she didn't. Subsequently, after doing well in school and on the MCAT, this student decided to choose another career. Her adviser said to her, "Go ahead and apply to medical school anyway. You are certain to get in." This time, however, she didn't listen to this (bad) advice. That student is now the premed adviser at a large university—and has not forgotten the damage that an adviser's ill-timed words can cause.

Medical school admission deans loathe the "screening out" of potentially excellent doctors done by premed advisers and premed committees. Studies show that about 60% of premed advisers try to discourage some potential medical school applicants. In part, this may be because more than half of premed advisers believe that medical education is rigid, physically demanding, and excessively costly, and that the subsequent medical career requires too much of a time commitment. In addition, discouraging marginal applicants makes their undergraduate school look better to prospective students (and their parents) by increasing the percentage of their students that applied to medical schools who are accepted. *Good advisers don't dissuade qualified students from applying to medical school.*

The ideal premed adviser has the following qualities:

- Flexible when working with various types of students
- Presents information nonjudgmentally
- Imparts accurate and verifiable information about their school, medical schools, and medicine
- Genuinely cares about students
- Provides options for school and career
- Stays attuned to students' attitudes, interests, and activities
- Remains open to new ideas, including retrying old ideas
- *Doesn't serve as a prescreener for medical schools!*

As the following anecdotes demonstrate, premed advisers vary greatly in their skill and willingness to help students. The first story is from a physician who graduated from a University of California school and now practices emergency medicine. The second is from a physician who graduated from a large state school in the East and is now a medical school professor. The others are from medical students from a wide spectrum of undergraduate schools.

> I met my premed adviser my first week of school. She was wonderful! She helped me to develop an appropriate course of study, assisted me over some rough spots, and showed me the best way to use the application system for medical schools. She knew a great deal about medicine and medical schools. In my senior year, I helped her out by orienting new premeds.
>
> We had one premed adviser for a student body of about 35,000. He was a chemistry professor who had failed to get into medical school as an undergraduate. He was very clear about detesting medicine as a career and physicians as a group. He met with most premeds. The story was that he always gave one of two speeches. If you were an excellent science student, he tried to convince you to go into something intellectual, particularly the "hard" sciences. If you were majoring in anything other than science or you were not the top student in the class, he would say that you had no chance of ever becoming a physician and you were wasting his time. I was in the latter group. Fortunately, I had enough self-confidence to ignore his "advice."
>
> My premedical advisor was very valuable to me when I applied after being out of school five years. Without him, I would not have had a clue how to pursue this goal, since I'm the first person in my entire family to go to medical school. I saw him each semester when making up my schedule, and knew him fairly well from being around the Chemistry Department and being active in the school's premedical club.
>
> Looking back on it, I feel that my premedical advisor didn't have a clue. I made my decision to pursue medicine late, and the advisor didn't give me good advice, didn't take me seriously, and basically left me completely on my own.
>
> My premedical advisor gave me great advice, great preparation, and great follow-up after graduation. She helped dissuade me from some rather crazy plans.

One suggestion about advisers: Even if the system insists that you keep a "formal" premed adviser who is inadequate, nothing prevents you from securing your own "informal" adviser who better meets the criteria above. As one hematologist–oncologist says about her undergraduate experience:

> This was such a large school, with so many premeds, they used almost anyone as a premed adviser. None of them seemed to have any interest in our career goals or any real knowledge of the process. The premed adviser assigned to me was called "the drill sergeant." She was nasty to all premeds, told all of us we wouldn't get into medical school, and really didn't have a clue about the entire process. After she told me that I couldn't ever get into medical school, I didn't even bother asking her to write the "official" premed adviser's letter. I simply got recommendation letters from other faculty who knew me well.

She was not the only one who used other advisers. As these comments from two medical students demonstrate, sometimes this strategy works and sometimes it doesn't.

> **The "official" premedical advisor at my school was a dinosaur with outdated information. He had little information about or experience with minority admissions. He was full of stereotypes and myths about medical school, but you had to work with him to get a cover letter. I had lots of "surrogate" advisors.**
>
> **My school had no premedical advisor, so I sought out an instructor who I thought could help. He did give me information about a summer research fellowship I took, but misinformed me about when to take the MCAT (in the Senior Year!). That set me back an entire year.**

The national organization for premed advisers is the National Association of Advisors for the Health Professions (NAAHP). If you do not have a premed adviser, they can try to help you locate one. Contact them at: NAAHP, P.O. Box 1518, Champaign, IL 61824-1518; (217) 355-0063; fax: (217) 355-1287; staff@naahp.org.

Peer Advisers

Some schools use students as the first advisers other premed students encounter when they have questions. Most often these are the best of a school's junior and senior premed students and are personally selected by the official premed adviser. They answer many of the routine questions, give other students pointers gained from personal experience, run special programs (such as stress reduction, women in medicine, and awareness of Osteopathic medicine) for other premed students, maintain the premed library, and talk to high school students and incoming freshman premeds. Some schools have only a few paid peer advisers; at others, this is a volunteer activity spread among a larger group, and some schools have both. Peer advisers' training and knowledge varies. If you have doubts about their information, ask to see the official adviser.

One premed adviser offered to fix any trouble that resulted when premed students followed incorrect advice from his office—whether it was from him or a peer adviser. This is a great (although not always doable) offer. Although he found that such problems rarely occurred, not many advisers offer to correct the damage their bad information causes. In the future, the use of peer advisers will probably increase dramatically, since they cost much less than professional advisers.

For information about special advisers or counselors for minority students, see Chapter 9.

Mentors

You may be able to discover a path through the premed jungle on your own, but it will be much easier if you have help and support. This is where a mentor comes in. Selecting a mentor is one of your most important career decisions. Most students, however, don't have one—they only have "advisers." These faculty members are usually officially designated and often have multiple advisees—and little time for any of them. They may not even be interested in actually helping students advance their careers in the right direction. *You need a mentor!*

Selecting a mentor is serious business. When Odysseus went on his travels, Mentor was the person he entrusted with caring for his house and son. He looked for a wise and faithful counselor. That is also what you seek.

Ideally, the qualities to look for in a mentor are:

Experience. Has the individual helped other premeds get through the system and enter medical school? Can he or she give you advice that is sound, valid, and verifiable? (Ask the individual or find out from your peers.)

Knowledge. Does the individual know the current rules of "the game"? If not, is he or she willing to learn them (just as you will) so that you don't make a mistake? (Ask the individual what the MCAT, AMCAS, or AACOMAS is all about. Anyone who knows the answers or is willing to find out is fine; if they just shrug their shoulders, watch out.)

Empathy. You will probably experience insecurity at various points in your journey. Will this individual take enough interest in you to encourage you during these tenuous times? (Your first meeting should give you a good idea.)

Compatible personality. Will you enjoy working with this individual? Is he or she warm and open, or rigid and standoffish? The better you interact with your mentor, the more you will gain from the relationship. (Both her reputation and a brief meeting should confirm this.)

Role model. Is this someone you can use as an example of how to live your life (at least in some areas)? Does he or she exemplify some of the characteristics that you admire in people? Role models are useful, since you can see excellent characteristics demonstrated "in the flesh." (Reputations can sometimes be misleading. Check for yourself.)

When you were born, you could not choose your parents. You do, however, have a choice of mentors. At best, your mentor can simplify the whole process of deciding upon a medical career; selecting an appropriate curriculum; locating appropriate summer work, awards, and clinical opportunities; identifying the best study plan for your classes and for the MCAT; choosing appropriate medical schools; and, then, applying to these schools. At worst, a mentor can obstruct your path by lowering your self-confidence, providing erroneous or incomplete information, sitting on your paperwork, and generally putting roadblocks in your way.

An optimal mentor helps you make the most of your education. He or she gets you over the rough spots, shows you opportunities that you otherwise might miss, guides your career, and generally thinks of your interests above those of other students. Your mentor is your guide, your teacher, and your role model. But finding one is up to you. It takes effort, initiative, and assertiveness to locate the right individual. The choice is yours—you can either find a mentor or resign yourself to struggling through on your own.

Choose Early

You should select your mentor early to have the widest possible selection and to fully use his or her expertise. "I'm only a freshman," you say. "I'll wait until I have had some clinical experience." Baloney! The longer you wait, the less likely it is that your mentor will be: (1) your first choice; (2) a mentor, rather than a standard "adviser"; and (3) able to actually help you very much.

What Type of Person?

How do you find a mentor? This will take some effort on your part. Generally, you should choose a faculty member at your school. (Even if your professional mentor is a physician with whom you have worked, a parent, or your family physician, you also need someone on your school's faculty.) These individuals know not only "the system" at the school but also how to help you if you have difficulties with the system (getting necessary classes, avoiding administrative hassles).

Start by making contacts with upper-level (junior, senior, and graduate) students. You may find them in the premed club, in your dorm, or acting as teaching assistants for a laboratory course. Introduce yourself as a fellow premed student and tell them that you need some advice. They will generally be honored that you have asked them for advice, and will probably give you honest answers since you will not be competing with them for a medical school position. Ask them whom they consider the best teachers at the school. Ask several students for their opinions. This will get you started.

Pick a Known Teacher

Now you have a list of teachers that other students consider excellent. Why did they choose these people? Being an excellent teacher takes effort. This effort stems from an interest in helping students to learn. It is also based on a deep and abiding interest in student welfare. Doesn't this sound like the type of person you want for a mentor? Of course, since other students consider them excellent, some of them may already be counseling many students. If they cannot add another student, ask if they can recommend someone else to be your adviser. These people can usually spot the gems among their colleagues, so take their suggestions seriously. If one of them feels that she can add you to her group, go for it. You already stand out by showing initiative so early.

You can now do several other things to enhance that positive image:

- ***Be visible.*** This means showing up with some regularity at your adviser's doorstep. The best and most productive way to accomplish this is to spend time with him or her. This could mean working together in the laboratory or on a project. This will provide you with the opportunity to learn potentially valuable skills, interact with people on a professional level, and demonstrate your personality to someone who will eventually write you a letter of recommendation for medical school.
- ***Develop an image*** in your mentor's mind of a likable, courteous, and considerate individual. It is always pleasant to have a cheerful person around. However, fawning and flattery generally have a negative effect. Mentors can see through these false actions in a minute.
- ***Be respectful of your mentor's time.*** Once a professor has agreed to be your adviser/mentor, make an appointment to see that individual whenever necessary. This is the professional thing to do and your mentor will appreciate your consideration of his or her valuable time. Ask if you should use their scheduled office hours or make appointments at a different time so you and their other students aren't short-changed.
- ***Be clear about what you desire*** from your mentor (advice) and what your mentor can expect from you (hard work and dedication). Don't push for anything else. If you demonstrate the hard work and dedication, all else will follow.

— Transferring from a Junior/Community College —

Students often go to junior or community colleges to save money, to avoid enormous class sizes in the introductory or survey courses, or to see if they are able to do college-level work. If you plan, or have already begun, to study at a junior college, you can do several things to smooth your passage into a university and, subsequently, into medical school.

As early as possible, contact the premed adviser at the college to which you plan to transfer (if you already know) or at the local four-year college. Find out which courses will transfer, what the college requires for various degree programs, and what they recommend as their premed curriculum. Also, find out what grades, courses, and paperwork are required to transfer to their school.

In general, medical schools want students to take upper-level science courses at four-year institutions, because the competition is generally much stiffer and the grading scale less inflated than at junior colleges.

— Accelerated and Early-Assurance Programs —

Accelerated programs take both high school seniors and those in their first or second year of undergraduate school. These programs provide one way to shorten the time it takes to complete undergraduate and medical school curricula. Chapter 6 more fully describes these programs.

Early-assurance programs guarantee students admission to a particular medical school (usually the school associated with the undergraduate school) if they do well in their course work. They may accept students during either their first or second year of undergraduate school. One interesting aspect of the early-assurance programs is that while they require accepted students to maintain their GPAs, they often don't require the MCAT—so these students don't take it. Some cynics have suggested that the reason these schools don't require the MCAT is so that their students will not be able to apply to other medical schools. (Medical school admission officers wouldn't think that way, would they?)

— Early Admission —

If you are a stellar sophomore student with a clear and convincing desire to become a physician, you may qualify for early admission to certain medical schools. Not all schools are willing to admit students without a bachelor's degree. (See Figure 15.5 for schools that do not require bachelor's degrees.)

Fewer than 10% of all first-year medical students lack an undergraduate degree, so the odds are not favorable. However, you should certainly try for early admission if you have the qualifications, want to shorten your undergraduate career, and are willing to expend the time and energy to go through the application process.

Applying for early admission and failing to get in does not harm your chance of later being accepted as a regular admission by a medical school. The major downside to the process is the amount of work it takes along with the possible deleterious effect this effort will have on your class work. In addition, many students are disappointed when they are rejected. If it does work for you, however, it will be worth the effort.

The process of applying for early admission varies with each school. If this appeals to you, contact the schools that interest you to find out if they have this program.

Undergraduate school can provide students with many educational opportunities. Most premeds, however, mistakenly see their undergraduate training as simply a barrier to cross on their way into medical school. This diminishes the quality of what can be learned and makes the work much more difficult than it should be. The best course is to view undergraduate school as an opportunity to expand your horizons. You may never have this chance again.

8

Women In Medicine

If men cannot cope with women in the medical profession, let them take a humble occupation in which they can.

— Emma Hart Willard,
Godey's Lady Book (1853)

In 2003–04, women made up 50.8% of all medical school applicants, and 49.7% of those who began medical school (Figures 8.1 and 8.2). These numbers represent a steady rise in medical schools' acceptance rates for women: In 1960–61, women formed only about 7% of all applicants and accepted M.D. students and, in the late 1960s, less than 3% of Osteopathic medical students.

In 2002–03, women comprised 47.7% of all first-year M.D. medical students, 45.7% of all medical students, and 44.1% of all new medical school graduates. Women were about 42% of first-year Osteopathic medical students and 39% of new graduates. (The difference between the first-year and graduating percentages reflects the increasing number of women entering, rather than any difficulty completing, medical school.) More than half of all underrepresented minority medical students are women.

It is now common for women to constitute the majority of a medical school class; in 2003, more than half the entering class at 48 U.S. medical schools was women. Not all schools admit women equally, however. Figure 8.3 lists the schools where women comprise 50% or more of the first-year class and the schools with entering classes of between 27% and 40% women. In 1970, about 1 in 13 U.S. physicians (7.7%) was female; in 2003, it had become nearly 1 in 4. It is estimated that by 2010, almost a third of all U.S. physicians will be women. Clearly, women will be among the next generation of physician leaders—nearly 62% of all women physicians in the United States are now less than 44 years old.

The first woman to graduate from a U.S. medical school, Dr. Elizabeth Blackwell, graduated from the Geneva Medical College in upstate New York in 1849. Despite many obstacles, she graduated first in her class. In the latter half of the nineteenth century, about 5% of all physicians in the United States were women, and the country had at least 17 women's medical schools.

Most medical schools, however, did not tolerate women students. But, in 1893, the new Johns Hopkins Medical School, because it needed the funds that women were raising, agreed (under duress) to accept qualified women as medical students. Sir William Osler wrote of this, "It is always pleasant to be bought, when the purchase price does not involve the sacrifice of an essential—as was the case in the happy purchase of us [Johns Hopkins School of Medicine] by the Women's Education Association."

By 1910, all but three of the women's medical schools had either closed, become co-educational, or merged with other schools, thus severely limiting women's access to a medical education. Boston University and the Medical College of Pennsylvania both began as women's medical schools. The attitude toward women physicians within the profession was generally negative, typified by Osler's statement, "There are three classes of human beings: men, women, and women physicians." At the

FIGURE 8.1

Students Accepted into M.D.-granting U.S. Medical Schools, by Gender

	Number of Men Accepted	% of Male Applicants Accepted	Number of Women Accepted	% of Female Applicants Accepted
1975–76	11,699	35.8%	3,666	38.1%
1981–82	11,953	47.7	5,333	45.7
1985–86	11,370	53.3	5,858	50.7
1991–92	10,493	53.5	6,943	50.7
1995–96	9,920	37.0	7,437	37.6
2000–01	9,509	48.0	8,027	46.5
2001–02	9,160	50.5	8,294	49.6
2002–03	8,962	52.5	8,630	52.1

Adapted from: Table B8, Women Applicants, Accepted Students, and Matriculants to U.S. Medical Schools. *AAMC Data Book*. January 2003 update. Washington, DC: AAMC, 2003.

FIGURE 8.2

Women Enrolled in Osteopathic Medical Schools

	Women Enrolled in First-Year	Women as % of First-Year Students	Total Women Enrolled	Women as % of All Students
1970	17	2.7%	61	2.8%
1975	140	13.5	362	10.5
1980	329	22.0	971	19.7
1985	480	28.2	1,799	27.2
1990	667	34.2	2,221	32.7
1995	850	37.4	3,075	36.3
2000	1,240	42.4	3,402	44.1

Adapted from: American Association of Colleges of Osteopathic Medicine. *2001 Annual Report on Osteopathic Medical Education*. Chevy Chase, MD: AACOM, 2002, p. 22.

beginning of the twentieth century, medical schools imposed quotas on the number of women they accepted—usually no more than four women per year. By 1921, only 8% of U.S. hospital internships accepted women. These quotas remained in effect (except during World War II, when there was a shortage of male applicants) until at least the 1960s.

At graduation, nearly one-third of women physicians plan to go into generalist practices, as compared to less than one-fifth of the men. Women tend to enter pediatrics, obstetrics and gynecology, family practice, psychiatry, dermatology, pathology, and preventive medicine, while men tend to enter the other hospital-based specialties and surgical specialties (Figures 8.4 and 8.5). This may be one reason that women earn one-fourth to one-third less than their male counterparts once they enter practice. An equal proportion of men and women plan academic careers. Although in 1977 there were female residents in fewer than two-thirds of all the specialties, by 2003, women were training in every accredited specialty area.

All medical schools and many teaching hospitals have a designated "Women's Liaison Officer" to address the concerns of women in medicine. To identify the Women's Liaison Officer at a particular institution, contact: Staff, Women in Medicine, Association of American Medical Colleges, 2540 N Street NW, Washington, DC 20037-1126; (202) 828-0521; www.aamc.org/members/wim/start.htm. Liaison officers may be able to answer women's questions during the applicant interview better than some of their colleagues. Other medical women's organizations are listed in Appendix B.

FIGURE 8.3

Percentage of Women in First-Year Class at Selected Medical Schools

50% or More of First-Year Class

Medical School	% Women in First-Year Class	Medical School	% Women in First-Year Class
Morehouse	69%	Southern Illinois U.	54%
U. New Mexico	67	U. Calif.–San Francisco	54
Mayo	62	Yale	54
Rush	62	Colorado	53
U. Puerto Rico	62	Mt. Sinai	53
George Washington	61	SUNY–Stony Brook	53
Michigan State U.	60	U. Buffalo	53
Wright State	60	U. North Carolina	53
Oregon Health Sciences U.	59	U. Missouri–Columbia	53
U. Vermont	59	U. Calif.–Davis	52
Northeastern Ohio U.	58	UCLA	52
Penn State U.	58	U. Massachusetts	52
U. Miami	58	Dartmouth	51
U. Rochester	58	Drexel U.	51
U. Missouri–Kansas City	57	Eastern Virginia	51
U. Washington	57	Harvard	51
U. Wisconsin	57	Howard	51
Brown U.	56	Washington U.	51
E. Tennessee State	56	Marshall U.	50
U. Maryland	56	Texas A&M	50
Stanford	55	U. Connecticut	50
U. Arizona	55	UMDNJ–SOM*	50
U. Louisville	55	U. North Dakota	50
Meharry	54	U. South Carolina	50

40% or Less of First-Year Class

Medical School	% Women in First-Year Class	Medical School	% Women in First-Year Class
Boston U.	40%	U. Cincinnati	35%
Lake Erie COM*	39	Arizona COM*	35
Johns Hopkins	39	U. Minnesota–Duluth	34
OSU COM*	38	U. Mississippi	33
Wake Forest U.	37	Finch U./Chicago Med	33
Uniform Services U.	37	Pikesville College SOM*	28
Nova Southeastern U. COM*	37	Kirksville COM*	27

*Percentage of women in entire student body in 2001. (First-year class percentages are not available for Osteopathic medical schools.)

COM = College of Osteopathic Medicine; SOM = School of Osteopathic Medicine.

Adapted from: Appendix IA, Table 2. *JAMA.* 2002;288(9):1142-45; and American Association of Osteopathic Medical Colleges: *2001 Annual Report on Osteopathic Medical Education.* Chevy Chase, MD: AACOM, 2002, Figure 8, p. 23.

FIGURE 8.4

Percentage of Women Residents and Fellows in Selected Specialties*

Specialty	% Women	Specialty	% Women
Obstetrics & Gynecology	71%	Nephrology	32%
Pediatrics	66	Ophthalmology	32
Dermatology	56	Critical Care Medicine	30
Neonatology	54	Emergency Medicine	29
Endocrinology	52	Radiation Oncology	29
Child/Adolescent Psychiatry	51	Anesthesiology	28
Child Neurology	51	Radiology	25
Psychiatry	51	General Surgery	24
Geriatrics	50	Nuclear Medicine	24
Family Practice	49	Plastic Surgery	23
Rheumatology	49	Colon & Rectal Surgery	21
Allergy & Immunology	48	Pediatric Surgery	20
Pathology	48	Cardiology	19
Infectious Diseases	44	Gastroenterology	19
Pulmonary Diseases	44	Otolaryngology	19
Preventive Medicine	42	Urology	13
Hematology/Oncology	40	Neurosurgery	11
Internal Medicine	40	Vascular Surgery	10
Neurology	38	Orthopaedic Surgery	9
Physical Medicine/Rehab	38	Thoracic Surgery	7

*Many include the numbers from both the adult and pediatric specialties.
Adapted from: Appendix II, Table 1. *JAMA*. 2002;288(9):1151-64.

FIGURE 8.5

Women's Representation in Selected Specialties

Specialty	% of All Physicians in This Specialty	% of Physicians in the Specialty That are Women	% of Residents in the Specialty That are Women
Internal Medicine	18%	28%	40%
Family Practice	10	28	49
Pediatrics	9	48	66
Psychiatry	6	31	51
General Surgery	5	11	24
Obstetrics/Gynecology	5	35	71
Anesthesiology	5	21	28
Radiology	5	18	25
Emergency Medicine	3	19	28
Orthopedic Surgery	3	3	7

Association of American Medical Colleges. *AAMC Data Book*. Washington, DC: AAMC, 2001; American Medical Association. *AMA Workforce Data*. Chicago: AMA, 2002; and *JAMA*. 2002;288(9):1151-3.

— Women as Premeds and Applicants —

The large number of women premedical students and medical school applicants represents a wide and diverse group. Characterizing any such group is difficult, but at least one study suggests that there are some common motivating factors among women who pursue a medical career, including:

- One or both parents emphasized intellectual success
- Parental support for traditional feminine values (helping, nurturing, marriage)
- A positive maternal attitude toward female employment
- An interest in science
- A desire to work with people
- An emphasis on vocational flexibility or autonomy
- A need for intellectual stimulation
- The encouragement of parents, teachers, and peers

While at least as many women as men begin premed studies, more men complete the programs and apply to medical school. This has been termed the "premed persistence gap." Why does it occur? What happens to the women who fall by the wayside?

One explanation, now shown to be too simplistic, is that sex discrimination keeps women out of medical school. (Since the early 1980s this has not been true at most schools, and such discrimination is now virtually nonexistent.) Another oft-cited reason is that women have lower expectations for their own achievements, especially in science-related areas. They don't, although women are slightly more likely to attribute failure to "bad luck" than are men. And, while women have, on average, not done as well as men on many measures of scientific accomplishment, this difference cannot explain the large number of women who do not continue to pursue medical careers: Women with the highest GPAs (3.5 to 4.0) have equally good or better science grades than do comparable men.

Some have suggested that women receive less encouragement to pursue medical careers, yet they actually receive as much or more support from parents, friends, lovers, and professors than do men. It is also claimed that women have difficulty seeing themselves in the potentially conflicting roles of physician, wife, and mother. While role conflicts are a part of all professional women's lives, women who continue and those who drop out of premed curricula plan to marry in nearly equal numbers and plan to have an equal number of children, although those who persist in a medical career plan to marry and have children slightly later in life.

The gap between men and women applicants begins in high school. While women students with "A" averages are as likely as their male counterparts to continue to pursue their career goals, women with lower grades are from 1½ to 2 times less likely to continue than are men with the same grades.

In college, women seem to drop out of premed curricula because they are not as persistent as their male peers. Men are more likely to pursue medical careers until they either succeed or unequivocally fail (and sometimes beyond this point), but women tend to pursue the goal only until they see that they *might not succeed*. The result is that many marginally competitive women who might not get into medical school on the first pass (or who think they might not) abandon their dream of becoming a physician. The men stick it out and many get accepted.

Why do women have this attitude? One theory that has gained credence over the years is that women, because of their socialization (how they were raised), view pursuing a high-status career as transgressing cultural norms. Normative barriers may exist, but not in the way most people expect. While women are no longer barred from medical school through quotas, sociologists actually believe that there is no societal mandate (norm) for women to strive for career success. They are permitted, but not required, to pursue lucrative or prestigious careers.

— Women in Medical School and Beyond —

The last U.S. medical school to begin admitting women students was Jefferson Medical College in Philadelphia in 1960. The last U.S. medical school to become co-educational was the Women's Medical College of Philadelphia, which first admitted men in 1970. Its name was then changed to the Medical College of Pennsylvania. In 1994, it merged with Hahnemann University Medical School to form

Allegheny University of the Health Sciences, which is now known as Drexel University College of Medicine.

Once in medical school, women do not do as well as men of the same racial/ethnic background on the first part of the national licensing examination, which primarily tests basic science knowledge. Not surprisingly, this seems to parallel performance on the MCAT examination. It appears, however, that this difference does not persist into the second and third (clinical) parts of the licensing examination.

Perhaps because of their multiple life roles, sexism, and difficulty resolving issues of intimacy and career, women medical students experience more distress than their male cohorts. Medical school counselors see this manifested in an increased incidence of stress, depression, daily alcohol use, and personal problems among women students.

Discrimination against women trying to get residency positions has slowly diminished as the specialties find that, without women, their programs will not have sufficient residents. The sheer numbers of young women physicians have resulted in many more opportunities opening up for them than were available only a few years ago.

Nearly 60% of female physicians under 35 years old are in primary care (general internal medicine, general pediatrics, family practice and obstetrics and gynecology). About 60% of male physicians in this age group are in nonprimary care specialties. This gender disparity is similar for physicians 35 to 54 years old. Nearly half of all women physicians (46%) specialize in a primary care specialty. One of the biggest discrepancies is in general surgery; more than 5% of male physicians enter this specialty, but only 2% of female physicians do so. Only 57% of all women physicians are Board-certified in their specialty, as opposed to 67% of men. Most well-paying positions and nearly all academic appointments require physicians to be certified by their specialty's Board after completing residencies, taking specialty-specific examinations, and fulfilling additional requirements.

Greater awareness of federal laws prohibiting discrimination against women in hiring and during employment, as well as a change in social attitudes toward professional women, have made discriminatory practices more complex and subtle. These practices are often based upon the irrational fears of potential employers, who are frequently disturbed by the idea of working with women as equals. One possible result is the underrepresentation of women on medical school faculties.

The percentage of women faculty members varies greatly by specialty, and their academic ranks are lower than those of their male colleagues (Figure 8.6). This disparity had become so egregious that, in mid-1996, the AAMC launched its "Increasing Women's Leadership in Academic Medicine" initiative. Their initial report showed that the percentage of women full professors at medical schools had remained stable since 1980, despite the marked increase in the number of women physicians. Women constituted only 5% of medical school department heads and fewer than 10% of major teaching hospital CEOs. Only four women were medical school deans. A follow-up report in 2002 showed that not much had changed.

One example of widespread discrimination is seen in the discrepancy between the average male and female physicians' incomes. Women physicians in practice (who do not work for the federal government) receive an average of 40%, or about $75,000, less annual net income than their male counterparts. Differences in specialty, practice setting, age, and productivity only partially explain this discrepancy. The exact amount varies by specialty, but this trend pervades medical practice.

Sexual Harassment

Nearly half of women physicians report having been harassed on the basis of gender, and more than a third report having been sexually harassed by patients, peers, or attending physicians. The frequency of both is about the same during medical school and training; it decreases somewhat when the physicians enter practice. (During medical school interviews, women are often asked sexist, blatantly illegal questions. See "Illegal Questions" in Chapter 25 for more information.)

The United States Equal Employment Opportunity Commission defines sexual harassment as:

> Unwelcome sexual advances, requests for sexual favors, and other verbal or physical conduct of a sexual nature constitute sexual harassment when:

FIGURE 8.6
Women M.D. Faculty in Various Specialties

Specialty	% of All M.D. Faculty in Each Specialty Who are Women	% of Women M.D. Faculty in Each Specialty Who are Full Professors
Pediatrics	40%	18%
Physical Medicine	37	15
Obstetrics/Gynecology	36	11
Family Practice	36	15
Dermatology	34	12
Psychiatry	29	13
Pathology (All)	29	14
Public Health	27	64
Anesthesiology	27	11
Radiology	26	9
Emergency Medicine	25	7
Internal Medicine	24	8
Neurology	21	9
Ophthalmology	21	8
Otolaryngology	13	9
Surgery, General	10	3
Orthopedic Surgery	7	2

From: Association of American Medical Colleges Faculty Roster System, 2002.

1. submission to such conduct is made either explicitly or implicitly a term or condition of an individual's employment;
2. submission to or rejection of such conduct by an individual is used as the basis for employment decisions affecting such individual; or
3. such conduct has the purpose or effect of unreasonably interfering with an individual's work performance or creating an intimidating, hostile, or offensive working environment.

Sexual harassment, including physical harassment, sexual slurs, and sexual advances, is not uncommon. It is more common among women than men and, in residency, varies by specialty. Married women and those with children suffered less harassment than single women. Most women say they do not report harassment because they fear the negative impact and they believe that no action would be taken anyway, even though virtually all teaching hospitals have policies regarding the sexual harassment of residents. Those who harass them generally have a higher professional status than the harassed woman. One study showed that while lesbian physicians suffer no more harassment than their heterosexual peers, they report these offenses four times as often.

Even without discrimination, women in medicine face unique personal challenges. For example, medical school and residency cut directly across the childbearing years. This results in women physicians having fewer children, and at a later age, than nonphysician women. Only 60 to 70% of married women physicians have children, compared to 90% of their married male counterparts.

Information for and about women in medicine can be obtained from the American Medical Women's Association. This organization provides student members with educational loans, scholarships, awards, a bed-and-breakfast program, and a bimonthly journal. The AMA's Women Physicians Section serves as an information resource on issues relating to women physicians. Many individual specialties also have separate societies for women physicians. You can locate them through the main specialty society, AMWA, or the AMA. (See Appendix B: "Women in Medicine.")

— Marriage, Pregnancy, and Children —

The problems associated with adjusting to marriage and having children during medical training were once thought to be solely a woman's concern. Not any longer. While women do have unique biological concerns regarding pregnancy, both male and female physicians frequently base career decisions on how they will affect their family. The major concerns include maintaining the family relationship, pregnancy, and child-care. [Even though this section appears in this chapter, it applies to anyone pursuing a medical career.]

Studies show that women and men seek different attributes in potential mates. This impacts on the available partners for both. Women generally seek an intelligent partner whose ambitions and achievements they can respect, and whose occupational status is equal to or higher than their own. They generally want to get married during their last year of medical school or during residency because they are concerned either about fertility or about their chances of marrying if they wait much later. Men generally seek mates with equal or lower occupational status and income who are physically attractive. They prefer to marry during or after residency training. Women medical students overwhelmingly believe that as their status increases, the pool of acceptable partners decreases, while men believe exactly the opposite. In general, unmarried women and men medical students have equivalent support from their significant others.

Marriage

Upon entering medical school, only 13% of women students and 15% of men are married, while at graduation, 30% of the women and 34% of the men have achieved "wedded bliss."

Nearly half (48%) of all married women physicians are married to other physicians, and nearly all the rest are married to nonhealth professionals (22%), those in business or creative areas (17%), or other health professionals (6%). Nearly 82% of women physicians' spouses have graduated from college or graduate school.

Three times as many married women medical students as men report stress in their personal relationships. It has been suggested that this may be due to the fact that women do not necessarily have the "work first" attitude that men generally take.

Marriages and relationships take effort to maintain, and up to 70% of medical marriages are dysfunctional. In part, it is because physicians often hold positions of unquestioned authority at work and it can be difficult to relinquish this role at home. Medical students and residents don't have much personal time, and those in relationships wage a constant tug-of-war between their personal and professional lives. Does this mean that your partnership is doomed? No! All new professionals have the same stresses. The relationships that work are those in which both partners give each other emotional support for their careers. The key is to lend your partner as much support for his or her career as you desire for your own.

Balancing personal and professional goals can be a major challenge for both men and women—although women have more stressors. Significant social expectations for women physicians, apart from their medical careers, can create tension between their private and professional lives. This contributes to the fact that only 66% of women physicians marry, compared to 90% of both nonphysician women and male physicians. In addition, since up to 70% of married women physicians are married to other physicians, the complications mount.

Compared to women physicians partnered with nonphysicians (usually other professionals), the women in physician-physician relationships are more likely to bear the primary responsibility of caring for their children and home. Many do this by working fewer hours and subordinating their career to that of their partners. As many as half of all women physicians change their career plans because of marriage or family responsibilities. The best partnerships, regardless of the individuals' professions, are those that are mutually supportive.

Male physicians' marriages (including those to other physicians) are often dysfunctional because of the average male physician's compulsive personality. While the divorce rate for physicians is less than that of the general public, physicians are generally unhappier in their marriages. The (mostly male) physician's compulsive personality limits emotional intimacy or avoids it altogether. In marriages to women physicians, many male physicians assume that their spouses have fewer emotional needs than other, "regular" women. Several traits are related to this compulsive personality: perfectionism, a susceptibility to self-doubt and feelings of guilt, a chronic sense of emotional impoverishment, difficulties managing dependency and aggression, and a limited capacity for emotional expression. While these traits may be useful in medical practice, the resulting rigid and emotionally flat method of relating to others helps destroy relationships. Physicians often blame their lack of emotional commitment on their time commitments.

In spite of everything, studies show that marriage enhances well-being. Married men and women are generally happier and less stressed than single people. Men benefit more from marriage than do women. However, both show decreased stress, which can help to enhance their lives.

Pregnancy

Two of the most stressful personal situations that medical students must deal with are pregnancy and child rearing. On entry to medical school, 6% of women and 7% of men have children. By graduation, however, 11% of women and 16% of men have at least one child. Approximately 7,500 women currently in residency have at least one dependent—usually a child. *Most medical schools do not have formal policies dealing with parental leave*. Despite this, some are quite flexible when dealing with the situation, while others are not. One proposal for a family leave policy for medical school is shown in Figure 8.7.

With ingenuity and foresight, successful pregnancies can take place at any time during medical school, although there will be unavoidable stresses and compromises. Some students who are pregnant during their preclinical years find that the classroom seats are too small to accommodate them, and they need special chairs. (This may also be true during USMLE examinations, so special arrangements must be made in advance.) Many medical schools now allow any student, on a case-by-case basis, to take a leave of absence of from one term to an entire year. While many students take a leave of absence to do research or pursue other studies, such as for an MPH degree, women have also used this opportunity for childbearing. (Some have pursued research or other studies while pregnant.)

FIGURE 8.7

Model Family Leave Policy for Medical Schools

- Family leave is available for all medical students for birth, adoption, or a child's severe illness.
- An independent-learning option is available for pregnant students during the basic science years.
- Pregnant students may be allowed to postpone their education or take a leave of absence, with the option of making up the work during the summer if such courses are available.
- Vacation time during the clinical years can to be lumped together to permit adequate family leave time.
- During family leave, students are considered enrolled in school and receive the same benefits students normally receive.
- Following family leave, students must return on a full-time basis. If in their preclinical years, they need not attend lectures, but they must attend laboratory sessions and take all examinations. If in their clinical years, returning students may take elective clerkships or research, postponing their required clerkships.
- All students will fulfill all school requirements prior to graduation.

Adapted from: Justin I. Parental leave policies. *Colorado Med.* 1994;91(1):22-3.

The advice from women physicians who have had children during their training varies. Most who have been pregnant during their clinical school years or during residency training report receiving inequitable treatment, ranging from unconscious slights to actual harassment. Most suggest avoiding (if possible) having children during the third year of medical school and the intern year, since these are the most time-intensive and stressful training periods. To lessen stress, some women physicians suggest planning pregnancies for the time between the second and third year of medical school, during the fourth year of medical school when they can schedule electives to accommodate the pregnancy, during the senior year of residency (not a surgical residency), during a year off, or after residency. (Of course, pregnancies often are not planned.) In addition, it helps to give your (hopefully supportive) colleagues adequate notice that you will be on leave. Women medical students (and residents) have survived having children at all stages of training. This illustrates their tenacity, strength, and motivation.

Pregnant medical students, and residents, usually have lifestyles that they would not recommend to their patients—long hours, rigorous physical activity, poor eating and sleeping habits, and, during the clinical years, exposure to disease. Fortunately, studies have shown that these stressors have had little effect on the success of their pregnancies, although there appears to be a higher-than-expected incidence of preeclampsia and preterm labor, but not preterm delivery. Additionally, female residents (and presumably medical students in their clinical years) have the same rate of induced abortions as their nonphysician counterparts. (Figure 8.8)

Policies for family leave (previously called maternity leave or parental leave) have been problematic for at least two reasons. First, women residents who have been pregnant feel that less than six weeks of leave is inadequate. Second, since these policies only apply to a subset of medical students (parents, usually mothers), extended leave can wreak havoc on schedules and on the baseline educational requirements that they must meet to graduate. The Federal Family and Medical Leave Act, which took effect in August 1993, applies to most residents but not to medical students (since they are not yet employees).

Children

Child-care can be an enormous burden for medical students, especially if both parents are either in school or work. Child-care facilities, although relatively common in the business world, have yet to routinely exist in the medical field. Even hospitals that offer child-care rarely include medical students' children.

Women carry most of the burdens of child rearing in our society. They cannot be both medical students and parents without some help. Whether they enter school with children or have them while in school, they must arrange for help in caring for their children to successfully continue their careers. Some resources containing helpful tips for parents are listed under "Pregnancy and Parenting" in the *Annotated Bibliography*.

Once they finish residency, most women physicians plan to work part time for at least the first two to three years after their children are born. Some take part-time or "shared-schedule" residency programs to spend more time with their children during residency training.

FIGURE 8.8

Women Physicians' Complications during Pregnancy

Complication	Women Physicians	Physicians' Wives
Preterm labor requiring bed rest	11.3%	6.0%
Preeclampsia or eclampsia	8.8	3.5
Premature ruptured membranes	6.4	6.7
Placenta previa	0.8	1.2
Placental abruption	0.4	0.7
Miscarriages	13.8	11.8

Adapted from: Klebanoff MA, Shiono PH, Rhoads GG. Outcomes of pregnancy in a national sample of resident physicians. *N Engl J Med.* 1990;323(15):1040-45. (This is the most recent valid study available!)

9

Minority Applicants

It is never too late to give up your prejudices.

— Thoreau, *Walden*

The night is beautiful
So the faces of my people.
The stars are beautiful
So the eyes of my people.
Beautiful also is the sun.
Beautiful also are the souls of my people.

— Langston Hughes, *My People*

Minority recruitment by medical schools focuses on four groups that are underrepresented in the medical field (11% of new medical students) when compared with their percentage (about 25%) of the general U.S. population: Mexican-Americans (Chicanos), African-Americans (blacks), Puerto Ricans (in mainland United States), and Native Americans (American Indians, Alaskan Natives, Native Hawaiians). By 2030, these groups will make up more than one-third of the U.S. population. While other groups, such as non-Chicano Hispanics, are also minorities, only these four groups (officially called "underrepresented minorities") get preference for programs that recruit and retain premed and medical school students.

One of the benefits of increasing the number of underrepresented minority (URM) physicians is that they are 2.5 times more likely than other physicians to plan to practice in underserved areas, with nearly half of them planning to enter a primary care specialty. Between 1974 and 2001, the number of URM applicants to medical schools increased 50%. However, the number of applicants from all these groups has decreased since 1996. According to a 2002 report by the Association of American Medical Colleges (AAMC):

> Between 1996 and 2001, the ability for schools in several states to use race/ethnicity as one element in the admissions process was limited by public referenda or court challenges. This had a negative effect on URM matriculation rates. In 1996, schools in California, Louisiana, Mississippi, Texas, and Washington matriculated 22% of all underrepresented minorities. In 1997, when laws took effect in all the affected states (except Washington), these same schools accounted for 18.5% of URM matriculants. Since 1997 (when Proposition 209 and the Hopwood legal decision took effect), through other means Texas and California schools have increased their numbers of URM matriculants.
>
> While only schools in five states are affected by anti-affirmative action rulings, the attention focused on using race/ethnicity as part of the admissions process—not only in medical school, but also in undergraduate admissions, and even in pipeline programs—had a chilling effect at many medical schools. The proportion of URM matriculants now has dropped to just under 11%. [*Minority Students in Medical Education: Facts and Figures XII*. AAMC, 2002, pp. 25, 28.]

Another reason for the dearth of URM applicants to medical schools may be that they do not want to pursue a medical career. These students earn only 13% of all bachelor's degrees awarded in the biological sciences (the most common entry path into medical school)—7% by blacks, 6% by Hispanics.

Underrepresented minorities now account for about 10% of the applicants to Osteopathic medical school, but less than 8% of their medical students. The Osteopathic medical schools with the most URM students are the University of Medicine and Dentistry of New Jersey, Western University of Health Sciences, Oklahoma State University, Ohio University, New York/NIT, and Nova Southeastern University.

Well-funded conservative groups continue to erect barriers to race-conscious admissions. Some institutions, however, have found ways around those already erected. For example, medical schools in Texas use a variety of criteria to help balance the disparity between URM and non-URM applicants. By law, they may consider:

- High school and college academic records
- Socioeconomic background during elementary, secondary, and college years
- Proficiency in more than one language
- Responsibilities (e.g., working, raising children) during school years
- Region in which applicant lived during high school
- Community activities
- Whether hometown has a shortage of physicians
- Interview
- Standard test scores compared to those of individuals from similar socioeconomic backgrounds
- Admission to college under state rule requiring admission of those in top 10% of high school class (without regard to the school's quality)

More than half of underrepresented minority applicants to U.S. M.D.-granting schools now come from seven states: California, New York, Texas, Florida, Georgia, Illinois, and Maryland. In 2001, medical schools accepted 46% of the applicants from underrepresented minorities, compared to 51.2% of all other applicants.

Many medical schools have minority admission offices that seek out qualified students, help them through the admission process, and provide assistance to them during medical school. They often identify qualified candidates through the Medical Minority Applicant Registry (Med-MAR; see below for more information). You can identify these individuals either from the school's website (see *Appendix E)* or from their listing in the AAMC's *Medical School Admission Requirements* (M.D. schools only).

Medical admission officers generally look at a minority applicant's entire history rather than simply their grades and scores. This does not mean that good grades and high MCAT scores are not important, but that admission officers are more likely to make allowances for merely adequate grades and test scores if an applicant demonstrates other personal factors that are associated with success in medical school. Schools understand that minorities, as a group, may not perform as well as others on standardized examinations and that such applicants, for many reasons, may have spotty academic records. They seek applicants who have demonstrated the capability to succeed academically, even if they have not been consistently successful in their attempts.

Admission officers look for minority applicants who demonstrate leadership and who have strong culturally based support systems. They also seek individuals who have a realistic view of their own capabilities. Specifically, they look for the determination and motivation to be a physician, social interest, maturity, the ability to cope with adversity, and good communication skills.

The AAMC runs an annual three-hour Expanded Minority Admissions Exercise (EMAE) at member schools to explain these factors to admission officers and committee members, as well as other faculty members who participate in the admission process. Individual schools then use the EMAE for their admission committee staff and interviewers. The program is designed to teach faculty how to look beyond a student's GPA and MCAT scores to evaluate how well a minority applicant will do in medical school. To do this, they are taught to evaluate "noncognitive" factors, such as the individual's realistic self-appraisal, ability to communicate, leadership, determination, maturity, emotional support, and social commitment.

The reasons that minority students give for choosing a medical career differ only slightly from those of other students. However, minority medical students often have a greater desire to serve their community and to educate patients about health issues. They generally put less value on working independently.

Don't let financial worries keep you from medical school. Minority students often feel that they can enter medical school only if they can afford to pay the fees. Few students can afford the ever-increasing tuition and fees that medical schools charge (and don't forget about living expenses). (See Chapter 18: *Paying for Medical School*.) Rest assured that medical schools work closely with the students they accept to ensure that they get the necessary funds to see them through.

— Minority Applicants and Acceptance Rates —

Between 1992 and 1998, URM applicants had a statistically better chance of being accepted to medical school than did their cohorts. Since 1999, however, the situation has reversed for black, but not other, URM applicants. In 2003, for example, while 50.4% of the 34,785 applicants were accepted to medical schools, 40.9% of the 2,736 black (African-American) applicants were accepted. At the same time, 40.2% of the 107 Native American applicants, 46.7% of the 773 Mexican-American (Chicano) applicants, and 55.7% of the 522 Puerto Rican applicants were accepted. As a result, URM minority students composed less than 11% of the first-year class.

The typical URM applicant to M.D.-granting schools has the following characteristics:

- Black female, 22 years old
- Biological Sciences major
- First-time applicant
- Average GPA
  - Science GPA: 2.95
  - Other GPA: 3.37
  - Total GPA: 3.13
- Applications submitted: 10.4
- Average MCAT scores
  - Verbal: 6.6
  - Physical Sciences: 6.8
  - Biological Sciences: 6.9
  - Writing Sample: N
- Median parental income: $50,000
- Both parents have business or professional/managerial occupation and some college or post-high school training

How do other ethnic groups compare? Approximately 53% of all white applicants (20,194), 51.7% of all Asian-American applicants (6,126), and 42% of all other Hispanic applicants (1,032) were accepted to medical school. Thus, whites composed 61% of first-year medical students; Asian-Americans, 18.4%; URM students nearly 11%; and other Hispanics, 2.5%. (The ethnic background of 3.5% is either "foreign students" or unknown.)

Are You a "Minority" Student?

This is not as unusual a question as you might imagine. If you have always identified yourself with a minority culture, there is no problem. However, many students who come from underrepresented minority populations don't consider themselves to be minorities. They have been "mainstreamed" their entire lives and thus don't identify with a minority culture. According to several minority premed advisers, many such students "find" their cultural heritage only after discovering that it gives them an advantage when applying to medical school. These students are often called "check-box" minorities, in reference to the boxes on forms where they designate themselves as minority students.

These advisers suggest that minority applicants should ask themselves whether they feel comfortable identifying with the culture and as a "minority" student—many don't. Some struggle with the decision about whether to classify themselves as minorities. Minority affairs counselors suggest that you examine your family-derived values to see how strongly you have been influenced by the culture, even if you have not consciously thought of yourself as a minority. Although they considered themselves "mainstream," some Native American students, for example, return to family gatherings for traditional ceremonies or are strongly influenced by stories of how the government treated their parents or grandparents. This may indicate a strong cultural identity. Talking with a medical school's minority affairs office can help clarify this issue.

With the increasing diversity of the American population, some applicants have trouble deciding which box to check. About 1.5% of Americans, approximately four million people, consider themselves "multiracial." Of the 2003 medical school applicants, 3.8% described themselves as "multiracial" (51% of them were accepted). One student who is part Native American, part Mexican, part Scot, and part Puerto Rican said, "Okay, so I'm an underrepresented minority—which one?" The Association for Multi-Ethnic Americans (AMEA) reports that many people now confront this problem when they must complete forms, such as MCAT or medical school applications. If you have not ever truly identified with a particular culture, you may find yourself in a bind when asked to "check a box." If so, you may want to consult with your minority affairs office for advice or contact AMEA, P.O. Box 31402, Tucson, AZ 85751; (877) 954-AMEA; www.ameasite.org.

At some medical schools, the minority affairs office has the unenviable task of determining which students really do qualify as minorities. Most schools have wisely avoided this no-win trap by allowing applicants' self-designations to prevail. Of course, that too can lead to problems, as in the case of Rommel Nobay. Mr. Nobay, a Princeton graduate, listed himself as black when applying to prestigious medical schools, including Vanderbilt, Georgetown, Tufts, and Dartmouth. When Princeton notified the schools that it did not consider Mr. Nobay to be black, the medical schools either withdrew their acceptance offer or pressured him to withdraw his application. Nobay sued Princeton! (The judge eventually dismissed the suit.)

For these reasons, among others, the AAMC is struggling with the definition of "underrepresented minority." Their most interesting idea is to replace it with the more inclusive term of "Underrepresented in Medicine," defined as "those racial and ethnic populations that are underrepresented in the medical profession relative to their numbers in the general population." For more information, go to the webpage: www.aamc.org/meded/urm/start.htm.

Culture as a Strength

Minority applicants have unique cross-cultural insights that they can contribute to medical schools and, eventually, to what has been described as "culturally competent" health care. (Nonminority students with intense cross-cultural experiences, such as from working with the Peace Corps, also have insights that may help them when applying to medical school.) Minority applicants do best if they view their cultural heritage as an asset that other applicants may not have, rather than as a crutch to lean on to excuse poor motivation or performance.

Many individuals from underrepresented minorities, however, have felt marginalized. If they voice their desire to become physicians, they often receive negative feedback not only from advisers but also from their peers and families. For many of these students, the response only serves to confirm their belief that they will never attain this goal. When nonminority students receive similar feedback, such as "you lack what it takes," they more often see it as an affront (the "Oh yeah? I'll show them!" or "Says who?" response) and try even harder to reach their goals.

Many minority applicants avoid announcing their intention to apply to medical school because they fear a negative response. They wait until the last possible moment to meet with premed or minority advisers, to apply for or take the MCAT, and to submit applications. These are big mistakes. Most minority (and many premed) advisers will be supportive. In fact, they can actually ease the way for students progressing through the complex system of applying to medical school. They can also offer specific assistance with special programs, such as the Minority Medical Education Program (MMEP). Minority applicants, students, and residents often view minority affairs offices as "safe havens" in the midst of a relatively unfriendly environment.

It is never too early to contact a medical school minority adviser, even if you are still in high school. Call a nearby or state medical school for their adviser's contact information. The earlier you make contact, the more information you can obtain about the rules of the medical school application "game" and how to improve the quality of your application packet. Once you contact the minority adviser, you may be put on mailing lists and receive useful information concerning academic opportunities at every stage of your education. This is especially true if you participate in some of the special programs put on by the minority affairs office.

In those cultures in which extended families are important, minority advisers often are willing to speak to applicants' families. Advisers can explain the importance of family support throughout the stressful years of premed, medical, and graduate medical (residency) education. An applicant's (and a medical student's) family must be flexible and understanding for the individual to succeed. Early input from a knowledgeable source, such as a minority adviser, can ease the way for both the student and his family. Medical students often find it useful for an influential family member to spend a day with them to observe the time constraints and other stresses they must handle.

The "I'm Not a Minority" Attitude

A schism often exists between minority premed and medical students who identify with other minority students and those who don't. Some students do not want to be identified with other minority students because they want to "make it on their own," because they don't want to be stigmatized and stereotyped, or because they are tired of being outside the mainstream student culture. They may distance themselves from other minority students implicitly (for example, by sitting or socializing with nonminority students) or explicitly (openly stating that they do not want a "minority medical school experience").

Medical schools' minority affairs offices adopt differing attitudes toward these students. Some are openly hostile, believing that those who don't identify with their own culture have abandoned them. Others are more tolerant, offering their help while accepting that people may choose different paths and have different goals. Many minority affairs counselors, however, feel that those who remain committed to their heritage usually tread an easier road and have happier and more peaceful lives. This sometimes leads to stress when individuals from multiethnic backgrounds feel that they are being forced to identify more with one part of their heritage than with another.

— Successful Minority Applicants —

Those who work with minority medical school applicants (and students) say that the one quality that most distinguishes those who succeed from those who don't is *persistence*. Even though the students themselves may be the only ones who believe that they can get into or succeed in medical school, those who are successful search for resources to get help and stick to their goal. Persistence is vital, since more minority medical students choose their career before or during high school (62%) than do other medical students (42%). For students to be successful, they must be adaptable when pursuing their goal. If one route doesn't work, they should try another.

According to the AAMC, the typical *successful* underrepresented minority applicant to medical school has the following characteristics:

- Black female
- First-time applicant
- Average GPA
  Science GPA: 3.21
  Other GPA: 3.61
  Total GPA: 3.34
- Applications submitted: 11.7
- Acceptances received: 2.3
- Average MCAT scores
  Verbal: 7.9
  Physical Sciences: 7.9
  Biological Sciences: 8.4
  Writing Sample: N
- Median parental income: $55,000
- Both parents have business or professional/managerial occupation and some college or post-high school training

The median parental income of first-year medical students of all ethnicities is higher than that of similar families in the United States. For example, in 2001, the median family incomes of blacks

($30,000) and of all Hispanics ($33,000) were significantly lower than the median incomes of those families with students accepted to medical school that were black ($55,000), "Other Hispanic" ($70,000), mainland Puerto Rican ($60,000), or Mexican-American ($50,000). Similarly, the median incomes for all white ($46,000) and Asian-American ($56,000) families were below the median incomes of the families of white and Asian-American first-year medical students ($90,000).

One predictor of how well minority students will do on the MCAT is the Developing Cognitive Abilities Test (DCAT), a measure of scholastic aptitude. Some premed advisers, university teaching offices, and summer minority premed programs use this test to help students assess their own abilities. The MCAT scores and GPAs of applicants from various ethnic groups accepted to medical school in recent years are shown in Figure 9.1. In contrast, Figure 9.2 shows ethnicity, age, GPA, MCAT scores, and number of applications submitted for students who were *not accepted* by medical schools.

A significant percentage of minority students (including Asians and Pacific Islanders) don't apply to medical school even though their MCAT scores are high enough to make them competitive candidates. Many of these students believe (incorrectly) that their MCAT scores are too low. If you have questions about this, ask your minority affairs counselor or a medical school admission officer.

Office Hours and Getting Help

Many minority students earn lower grades than other students and thus are thought to be less intelligent. Often the lower grades are due to culturally related behavior, such as deferring to professors or not asking questions because of a respect for elders or more learned people. Sometimes, students don't think they should ask for help. When they do, perhaps during a professor's office hours, they

FIGURE 9.1

Average MCAT Scores and GPAs of Accepted Applicants by Race/Ethnicity

	Black	Native American	Mexican American	Mainland Puerto Rican	Asian/ Pacific Islander	Other Hispanic	C'wealth Puerto Rican	White
Women								
MCAT								
Verbal Reasoning	7.9	8.6	8.6	8.3	9.5	9.0	8.8	9.8
Physical Sciences	7.7	7.9	8.1	8.4	10.3	8.9	6.5	9.6
Biological Sciences	8.2	8.7	8.7	8.9	10.4	9.4	7.5	10.1
Writing Sample*	N	O	O	O	P	O	K	P
GPA								
Science	3.23	3.25	3.18	3.18	3.56	3.46	3.44	3.59
Other	3.56	3.56	3.51	3.54	3.74	3.69	3.76	3.74
Total	3.37	3.39	3.33	3.33	3.6	3.57	3.58	3.66
Men								
MCAT								
Verbal Reasoning	7.9	8.9	8.2	8.1	9.5	9.1	6.4	9.7
Physical Sciences	8.4	8.9	9.0	8.7	11.1	9.8	7.15	10.5
Biological Sciences	8.7	9.2	9.4	9.4	10.8	10.0	7.6	10.5
Writing Sample*	N	O	O	O	P	O	K	P
GPA								
Science	3.19	3.39	3.29	3.24	3.58	3.43	3.38	3.58
Other	3.45	3.57	3.45	3.44	3.68	3.57	3.59	3.67
Total	3.30	3.47	3.35	3.32	3.62	3.49	3.47	3.62

*Median score

Adapted from: Association of American Medical Colleges. *Minority Students in Medical Education: Facts and Figures XII.* Washington, DC: AAMC, 2002, p. 99.

FIGURE 9.2

Attributes of Students Who Were Not Accepted by Medical Schools[1]

	Black	Native American	Mexican American	Mainland Puerto Rican	Asian/ Pacific Islander	Other Hispanic	C'wealth Puerto Rican	White
Men	34%	52%	51%	42%	53%	51%	40%	54.5%
Women	66%	48%	49%	58%	47%	49%	60%	45.5%
Age[2]								
Under 21	1%	0%	0%	0%	2%	<1%	2%	1%
21-23	39%	27%	35%	41%	53%	53%	74%	46%
24-27	34%	39%	43%	37%	34%	34%	18%	34%
28-31	14%	12%	14%	14%	8%	8%	5%	11%
32 and over	12%	22%	9%	8%	4%	4%	1%	9%
Avg. Number of Applications	9.5	7.5	10.3	10.0	15.8	11.8	3.9	9.7
Repeat Applicants	35%	37%	43%	31%	44%	34%	17%	32%
MCAT								
Verbal Reasoning	5.7	7.0	6.3	6.3	7.7	7.2	4.7	8.3
Physical Sciences	5.9	7.1	6.5	6.4	8.8	7.5	5.4	8.2
Biological Sciences	5.9	7.1	6.8	6.3	8.8	7.8	5.3	8.6
Writing Sample*	M	M	N	M	O	N	K	O
GPA								
Science	2.75	2.90	2.77	2.82	3.18	3.02	2.87	3.25
Other	3.25	3.32	3.24	3.35	3.49	3.40	3.46	3.51
Total	2.97	3.09	2.96	3.06	3.31	3.18	3.14	3.35

1: Social characteristics of these applicants' families are similar to those of accepted applicants.

2: Percentages may not total 100 due to rounding.

* Median score

Adapted from: Association of American Medical Colleges. *Minority Students in Medical Education: Facts and Figures XII.* Washington, DC: AAMC, 2002, p. 102.

often don't know how to interact effectively to get the most out of these sessions. See Chapter 7: *Undergraduate Preparation* for some helpful tips.

Other help with your course work is also available. Tutors can often be arranged through your minority counselor or premed adviser. If you need a tutor, get one early to establish rapport and to keep from falling behind in your classes. Switch tutors if the one you have isn't helping you.

— Information for Different Minorities —

Black (African-American)

In 2002, M.D.-granting schools in the United States had 4,779 black students. While this is 605 fewer students than in 1997, it is a marked increase since 1969, when only 783 blacks were enrolled in U.S. medical schools. Blacks now constitute only 7% of all medical students. Fifty-five percent of black applicants came from seven states: California, New York, Texas, Florida, Georgia, Illinois, and Maryland. Women account for 66% of black applicants. In 2003, 40.9% of black applicants were accepted into medical school. Figure 9.3 lists the undergraduate schools that produced the most black medical school applicants in 2002.

A number of historically black undergraduate schools were analyzed to determine why their graduates have been so successful. Undergraduate schools with active premed programs, a broad range of externally sponsored enrichment activities, and a high proportion of premeds majoring in biology or

FIGURE 9.3

Undergraduate Schools that Produced the Most Black Medical School Applicants (2002)

Undergraduate School	Number
Xavier University of Louisiana, New Orleans, LA	165
Howard University, Washington, DC	79
Hampton University, Hampton, VA	54
Morehouse College, Atlanta, GA	53
Spelman College, Atlanta, GA	47
University of Michigan, Ann Arbor, MI	43
University of Maryland, College Park, MD	37
FL Agricultural & Mechanical Univ., Tallahassee, FL	36
University of Virginia, Charlottesville, VA	36
Tennessee State University, Nashville, TN	34
Oakwood College, Huntsville, AL	33
University of California, Los Angeles, CA	33
Johns Hopkins University, Baltimore, MD	31
University of Florida, Gainesville, FL	31
Duke University, Durham, NC	30

Adapted from: Applicant Matriculant File as of April 18, 2003. Washington, DC: Association of American Medical Colleges.

chemistry produced the strongest applicants. The most successful premed programs provided offices and clubs, active premed advisers, early career planning assistance, and curriculum development to their students. Undoubtedly, the presence of all these factors increases the chance of medical school acceptance for all applicants, regardless of their undergraduate school.

The 11 M.D.-granting schools with 20 or more black graduates in 2001 were: Finch–Chicago, Drexel, Howard, Meharry, Morehouse, SUNY–Brooklyn, Temple, University of Illinois, University of Maryland, University of North Carolina, and Wayne State.

Studies show that once they enter medical school, black medical students' performance (at least on the USMLE) is strongly related to their perception of the amount of control they have over their lives. Those who believe that they control their own destiny do better than those who believe that external forces control them. To encourage self-esteem among black students, some schools pair black students with black faculty mentors, with excellent outcomes.

For more information, contact: Student National Medical Association, 5113 Georgia Avenue NW, Washington, DC 20011; (202) 882-2881; fax: (202) 882-2886; snmamain@msn.com; www.snma.org/members; or National Medical Association, 1012 Tenth Street NW, Washington, DC 20001; (202) 347-1895; fax: (202) 898-2510; www.nmanet.org.

Native American (American Indian, Alaska Native, Native Hawaiian)

In 2002, U.S. medical schools (M.D.) had 516 Native American students. This is 59 fewer students than in 1999, but is a big increase over the past 25 years: In 1969, only nine Native American students were enrolled in U.S. medical schools. Native Americans constitute 0.8% of all medical students.

Nearly one-half the Native American applicants came from Oklahoma, California, Texas, Arizona, and Hawaii. Women account for 50% of Native American applicants. In 2003, 40.2% of Native American applicants were accepted into medical school. Figure 9.4 lists the undergraduate schools that produced the largest number of Native Americans who applied to medical school in 2002.

FIGURE 9.4

Undergraduate Schools that Produced the Most Native American Medical School Applicants (2002)

Undergraduate School	Number
University of Oklahoma, Norman, OK	13
Oklahoma State University, Stillwater, OK	9
Stanford University, Stanford, CA	9
University of Arizona, Tucson, AZ	9
University of Hawaii at Manoa, Honolulu, HI	9
University of New Mexico, Albuquerque, NM	7
University of Virginia, Charlottesville, VA	6
Auburn University, Auburn, AL	5
Northeastern State University, Tahlequah, OK	5
Texas A&M University, College Station, TX	5
University of California San Diego, La Jolla, CA	5

Adapted from: Applicant Matriculant File as of April 18, 2003. Washington, DC: Association of American Medical Colleges.

Native Hawaiians are officially included in this category, but they apply primarily to Hawaii's medical school. In 1967, when the John A. Burns School of Medicine was established, there were only 10 Native Hawaiian physicians practicing medicine in Hawaii. In 1972, the school developed the *Imi Ho`ola* [*Those who seek to heal*] postbaccalaureate program to channel disadvantaged students of native Hawaiian, Filipino, Samoan, Chamorro, and Micronesian descent into the medical school. The program accepts up to 10 students annually; upon completion of the one-year program, they enter the medical school. More than one-third of the medical school's graduates are Native Hawaiians. In recent years, about 11% of graduates of the John A. Burn School of Medicine have been Native Hawaiian.

The high number of Native American applicants in Oklahoma can be partially attributed to the state's policy of offering preferential treatment to those state residents who had an ancestor listed on the official U.S. rolls and who consider themselves Native Americans. These students can receive scholarship funding for undergraduate and graduate schools in Oklahoma. The University of Oklahoma College of Medicine's Native American Center of Excellence sponsors programs for high school and college students. Some information can be found at: http://w3.uokhsc.edu/nace/main.html.

The University of North Dakota Medical School runs the very successful "Indians into Medicine" (INMED) program for Native American prehealth professionals. Begun in 1973, the program provides academic-year support at all levels; the Indian Health Service or the Health Careers Opportunity Program pays for participants' travel, room, and board, as well as a small stipend for each student. The program draws students primarily from Montana, Wyoming, Nebraska, and North and South Dakota. One hundred twelve graduates of the program have become medical doctors; this is approximately 20% of the country's Native American physicians. For more information, contact: Indians Into Medicine Program, 501 N. Columbia Rd., Grand Forks, ND 58202-9037; (701) 777-3037; www.med.und.edu/depts/inmed/home.htm.

The University of Arizona College of Medicine initiated an INMED program in 2001 with Indian Health Service support. The Arizona INMED hosts an annual preadmissions workshop, cosponsored by the Association of American Indian Physicians in Tucson each summer. For more information, see www.publichealth.arizona,edu/INMED.

Harvard Medical School offers an eight-week "Four Directions" summer research program for Native American premed students. This program includes opportunities not only to participate in research but also to gain clinical exposure. For information, contact: Four Directions Summer Research

Program, Harvard Medical School/Division of Medical Sciences, 260 Longwood Ave., MEC 432, Boston, MA 02115; (800) 367-9019, ext. 2; www.hms.harvard.edu/dms/diversity/application/images/fdsrpapp.pdf.

The five M.D.-granting schools with four or more Native American medical graduates in 2001 were: Brody–East Carolina, Hawaii, Minnesota–Minneapolis, Oklahoma, and the University of Washington.

For more information, contact: Association of American Indian Physicians, 1225 Sovereign Row, Suite 103, Oklahoma City, Oklahoma 73108; (405) 946-7072; fax: (405) 946-7651; e-mail: aaip@aaip.com; www.aaip.com.

Mainland Puerto Rican

In 2002, U.S. medical schools (M.D.) had 450 mainland Puerto Rican students. While this is 58 fewer students than in 1998, it is a large increase since 1969, when only three mainland Puerto Ricans were in U.S. medical schools. Mainland Puerto Ricans now constitute only 0.7% of all medical students. Forty percent of mainland Puerto Rican applicants came from New York and Florida. Women make up 53% of mainland Puerto Rican applicants. In 2001, 60.4% of mainland Puerto Rican applicants were accepted into medical school. Figure 9.5 lists the undergraduate schools that produced the largest number of mainland Puerto Rican medical school applicants in 2002.

The six (M.D.) medical schools with five or more mainland Puerto Rican graduates in 2001 were: University of Illinois, Mount Sinai, UMDNJ–NJ Medical, SUNY–Brooklyn, Ponce, and the University of Puerto Rico.

Mexican-American (Chicano)

In 2002, U.S. medical schools (M.D.) had 1,649 Mexican-American students. While this is 194 fewer students than in 1997, it is a marked increase since 1969, when only 59 Mexican-Americans were enrolled in U.S. medical schools. Mexican-Americans now constitute only 2.5% of all medical students. Nearly two-thirds of Mexican-American applicants came from California and Texas. Women make up 46% of Mexican-American applicants. In 2003, 46.7% of Mexican-American applicants were accepted into medical school. Figure 9.6 lists the undergraduate schools that produced the largest number of Mexican-American medical school applicants in 2002.

The five M.D.-granting schools with 15 or more Mexican-American medical graduates in 2001 were: University of Illinois, UCLA, UT–Galveston, UT–Houston, and UT–San Antonio.

The National Hispanic Mentor Recruitment Network (NHMRN), a cooperative effort of the Interamerican College of Physicians and Surgeons and the National Health Service Corps, establishes links between Hispanic medical students and practicing Hispanic clinicians. This program helps the students develop their own professional networks, provides supportive role models, and provides

FIGURE 9.5

Undergraduate Schools that Produced the Most Mainland Puerto Rican Medical School Applicants (2002)

Undergraduate School	Number
University of Florida, Gainesville, FL	10
Rutgers University, New Brunswick, NJ	7
University of Miami, Coral Gables, FL	7
Harvard University, Cambridge, MA	5
University of Central Florida, Orlando, FL	5
Yale University, New Haven, CT	5

Adapted from: Applicant Matriculant File as of April 18, 2003. Washington, DC: Association of American Medical Colleges.

FIGURE 9.6

Undergraduate Schools that Produced the Most Mexican-American Medical School Applicants (2002)

Undergraduate School	Number of Mexican-American Applicants
University of California, Los Angeles, CA	39
University of Texas, Austin, TX	30
Stanford University at Stanford, CA	28
University of Texas-Pan American, Edinburg, TX	25
University of New Mexico, Albuquerque, NM	23
St. Mary's University, San Antonio, TX	22
University of Texas at El Paso, TX	21
University of Arizona, Tucson, AZ	20
University of California at San Diego	19
University of Texas at San Antonio	19
University of Notre Dame, Notre Dame, IN	17
Baylor University, Waco, TX	15
University of California at Berkeley	15

Adapted from: Applicant Matriculant File as of April 18, 2003. Washington, DC: Association of American Medical Colleges.

opportunities for early clinical exposure. For information, contact: National Hispanic Mentor Recruitment Network (NHMRN), Interamerican College of Physicians and Surgeons (ICPS), 1101 Pennsylvania Avenue NW, Suite 820, Washington, DC 20004; (202) 467-4756; fax: (202) 467-4758; nhmrn@icps.org; www.icps.org.

Medical schools that are associated with or have federally funded Hispanic Centers of Excellence (HCOE) offer comprehensive support programs for Hispanic medical students. These HCOEs assist the institutions in their efforts to recruit and retain Hispanic medical students and faculty. For more information, visit the website: http://bhpr.hrsa.gov/diversity/coe.

For general information, write: National Hispanic Medical Association, 1411 K Street NW, Suite 200, Washington, DC 20005; (202) 628-5895; fax: (202) 628-5898; http://home.earthlink.net/~nhma.

Other Minorities

Other Hispanic

Other Hispanics, including Cuban-Americans and those of Central and South American heritage, constitute 2% (1,330) of all medical students. These numbers represent a major increase since 1978 when there were 426 "other Hispanics" in U.S. medical schools. Forty-seven percent of the applicants from this group are women. In 2001, 42.6% of other Hispanic applicants were accepted into medical school. Figure 9.7 lists the undergraduate schools that produced the largest number of "Other Hispanic" medical school applicants in 2002.

Asian-American

Asian-Americans are not an underrepresented minority in medicine. In 2002, there were 13,204 Asians in U.S. medical schools (M.D.). This represents 19.9% of all students and is a large increase since 1978, when they constituted only 2.4% of medical students. Forty-seven percent of applicants from this group are women. In 2003, 51.7% of Asian-American applicants were accepted into medical school. Figure 9.8 lists the undergraduate schools that produced the largest number of Asian-American medical school applicants in 2002.

FIGURE 9.7

Undergraduate Schools that Produced the Most "Other Hispanic" Medical School Applicants (2002)

Undergraduate School	Number of Hispanic Applicants
University of Puerto Rico, Rio Piedras, PR	186
University of Puerto Rico, Mayaguez, PR	83
University of California, Los Angeles, CA	69
University of Miami, Coral Gables, FL	69
University of Texas, Austin, TX	47
University of Florida, Gainesville, FL	44
University of New Mexico, Albuquerque, NM	39
University of California, Davis, CA	33
Florida International University, Miami, FL	32
University of Texas-Pan American, Edinburg, TX	32
Stanford University, Stanford, CA	31
University of California, Berkeley, CA	31
University of Texas, El Paso, TX	30

Adapted from: Applicant Matriculant File as of April 18, 2003. Washington, DC: Association of American Medical Colleges.

Medical school applicants identifying themselves as Asian further classify themselves as: Indian or Pakistani (37%), Chinese (21.1%), Korean (11.3%), Vietnamese (8.8%), Filipino (7.7%), Japanese (2.5%), or Other (11.6%).

Asian-American applicants traditionally have had high grades in math, physics, and other science courses and have high MCAT scores. Studies suggest that all other things being equal, the main predictor for how well Asian-Americans will perform in medical school is the MCAT Verbal Reasoning section (and probably the Writing Sample, although the studies were done before this section was added). Since many Asian-American students now applying to medical school are first- or second-generation citizens, they may have learned English as a second language. In addition, medical education is very language intensive, so English-language ability plays a large part in a student's performance. Asian-Americans whose first language is not English should keep this in mind and concentrate on honing their English-language skills. Premedical Asian-American and Pacific Islander students can find additional resources by contacting the Asian Pacific American Medical Student Association (APAMSA), www.apamsa.org.

French-Canadian

French-Canadians are often separated from their countrymen by a language barrier. Francophones (those of, having, or belonging to a population using French as its first or, sometimes, second language) comprise a distinct minority within Canada, especially outside Quebec. One Canadian school outside Quebec, the University of Ottawa (www.medicine.uottawa.ca/fra), has a special French-language track designed to provide French-speaking physicians familiar with the French-Canadian community to that population.

— Special Preparation Programs —

Medical Minority Applicant Registry (Med-MAR)

Medical schools (M.D.) often identify qualified candidates from underrepresented groups through the Medical Minority Applicant Registry (Med-MAR). The AAMC compiles this list of financially

FIGURE 9.8

Undergraduate Schools that Produced the Most Asian-American/ Pacific Islander Medical School Applicants (2002)

Undergraduate School	Number
University of California, Berkeley, CA	348
University of California, Los Angeles, CA	292
University of California, San Diego, La Jolla, CA	148
University of Michigan, Ann Arbor, MI	148
Stanford University, Stanford, CA	132
University of California, Irvine, CA	128
University of Texas, Austin, TX	124
Northwestern University, Evanston, IL	123
Johns Hopkins University, Baltimore, MD	119
Harvard University, Cambridge, MA	117
University of California, Davis, CA	100

Adapted from: Applicant Matriculant File as of April 18, 2003. Washington, DC: Association of American Medical Colleges.

disadvantaged and minority applicants from the demographic information provided by those taking the MCAT. When students take the MCAT, they indicate whether they want to be included in the Registry. (This is a free service.) The AAMC circulates the list to medical schools twice a year, usually in July and November.

The Registry provides the following information about each student: name, address, birth date, social security number, undergraduate college and major, racial or ethnic self-description, state of legal residence, and MCAT scores. Schools contact the applicants that interest them. Highly qualified applicants listed in the Registry may expect to receive many phone calls and letters from medical schools throughout the country. After minority students graduate from medical school, the AAMC enters them into the Minority Physicians Database (MPDB) and tracks their practice patterns. For information about Med-MAR, contact: Medical Minority Application Registry, AAMC, 2450 N Street NW, Washington, DC 20037-1126; (202) 828-0573; lmjohnson@aamc.org; www.aamc.org/students/minorities/resources/medmar.htm.

Minority Medical Education Program (MMEP)

Minorities have long been underrepresented in medicine. To help correct this imbalance, the Minority Medical Education Program (MMEP) was developed to identify and assist promising black (African-American), Native American, Mexican-American (Chicano), and mainland Puerto Rican undergraduate students who are interested in medical careers. Although these four groups make up about 26% of the U.S. population, they represent only about 14% of U.S. physicians. Since 1989, when the program began, more than half of the program's participants have applied to medical school and about 63% of those have been accepted. This is the key piece of information you need when you decide whether to participate in this program, so it bears repeating: *Of the students who complete the MMEP and apply to medical school, 63% have been accepted.*

The six-week summer program (supported by the Robert Wood Johnson Foundation and with direction from the AAMC) gives students an intimate understanding of the personal and academic requirements needed to become a physician. It also gives them a chance to associate with other students who share their dreams of a medical career. According to MMEP's director, "The program provides a 'handbook' on how to transform a dream into reality." As one former participant testified,

> An important factor that helped me get into medical school was that I attended the Minority Medical Education Program (MMEP). This program gave me a better understanding of the medical school application process, and helped me to prepare for the MCAT. In addition, this program gave me additional educational and practical experiences to improve my competitiveness in the medical school application process.

MMEP programs differ widely in their design. Each of the MMEP sites has a slightly different curriculum, and some may be better fitted to your needs than others. All MMEP programs contain these four components to some degree: academics, MCAT preparation, clinical or laboratory exposure, and counseling. Specifics for these areas can be found at: www.aamc.org/students/minorities/mmep/progsites/start.htm. MMEP webpages for each program can be accessed at www.aamc.org/students/minorities/mmep/progsites.

All the programs include formal assessments of participants' academic strengths and weaknesses, and have academic reviews of MCAT topics. Many programs also pair students with laboratory or clinical mentors for the duration of their stay. Some sites have "work-shadowing" programs, in which students follow physicians while they work, observing and questioning what they do and participating when possible. Participants have found work-shadowing to be a valuable experience.

Many programs work closely with those who plan to apply to medical school in the coming year. Counselors make certain that students are familiar with the application process and help them complete their paperwork.

Students can apply to a maximum of three programs. Contact the national MMEP office or the individual programs before you finalize your decision. The application packet for MMEP can be found at: www.aamc.org/students/minorities/mmep/apply.htm. Links at that site provide detailed instructions, other useful information, and additional contact information. The application deadline is usually in early April, although if they still have openings, some programs may allow students to apply later. (Programs with open positions can also be found at the MMEP website.)

You can contact MMEP at: Minority Medical Education Program, AAMC, 2450 N Street NW, Suite 201, Washington, DC 20037-1126; (877) 310-MMEP; mmep@aamc.org.

Students must meet all of the following requirements to be eligible for the MMEP, although exceptions can be made on a case-by-case basis:

- Be a U.S. citizen or permanent resident
- Be a member of one of the underserved minorities listed above
- Have completed at least one year of college before starting the program (those with bachelor's degrees may apply)
- Have an overall GPA of 3.0 (on a 4.0 scale) with at least a 2.75 in the sciences
- Have combined scores of at least 950 on the SAT or 20 on the ACT
- Demonstrate a serious interest in a medical career

Think about your summer plans during the fall semester. That will give you enough time to investigate your options, complete the paperwork, and send everything to the programs in a timely manner. Treat the process as if you were applying to medical school; the two are very similar. If you are not constrained by geographic limitations, apply to three programs. This will give you the best chance of being accepted by at least one of them.

Apply early! Programs begin accepting students in early December. Once your application is complete, including all transcripts, the national office simultaneously sends the application to all programs to which you applied. They have 10 business days to notify you about whether you have been accepted. Applicants then have10 days to respond—by e-mail, fax, or mail. For more about the rules, go to: www.aamc.org/students/minorities/mmep/trafficrules.htm.

Individuals may participate in MMEP only once. The application form requires much of the same information you will put on medical school applications (AMCAS, Texas, Ontario, and AACOMAS). Simply having this information readily available will benefit most applicants.

Currently, there are MMEP programs at 14 locations offered by the schools listed below:

Univ. of Alabama School of Medicine
UAB–MMEP Recruitment Coordinator
P-100 Volker Hall
Birmingham, AL 35294-0019
(203) 934-7975; fax: (205) 934-8724
mmep@uasom.meis.uab.edu

Baylor College of Medicine/Rice Univ.
Honors Premedical Academy
(800) 798-8244; fax: (713) 798-6516
hpa@bcm.tmc.edu
mmep@bcm.tmc.edu

Case Western Reserve Univ. School of Medicine
Director, Office of Minority Programs
10900 Euclid Ave., Room E 421
Cleveland, OH 44106
(216) 368-1914; fax: (216) 368-8597

Chicago Summer Science Enrichment Program
Associate Dean for Multicultural Affairs
Univ. of Chicago Pritzker School of Medicine
5841 South Maryland Ave., MC1000
Chicago, IL 60637-1470
(773) 702-1939; fax: (773) 702-2598
mmepchicago@aol.com
Consortium member sites:
Northwestern University
Rush University
Univ. of Chicago/Pritzker

Columbia Univ. College of Physicians and Surgeons
630 West 168th St.
P&S Room 3-413
New York, NY 10032
(212) 305-4157; fax: (212) 305-1049
mmep-ps@columbia.edu

Duke Univ. School of Medicine
3635 DUMC
Durham, NC 27710
(866) 227-3453 [toll free]
mmep@mc.duke.edu

Fisk Univ. and Vanderbilt Univ.
Mary E. McKelvey, Ph.D.
Fisk University
1000 Seventeenth Ave. North
North Nashville, TN 37208-3051
(615) 329-8636; fax: (615) 329-8636
mckelvey@fisk.edu

New Jersey Medical School
Program Director
185 South Orange Ave., MSB C696
Newark, NJ 07103-2714
(973) 972-3762 or 3763; fax: (973) 972-3768
anthondd@umdnj.edu

Univ. of Virginia School of Medicine
MAAP Program Manager
Box 800446, HSC
Charlottesville, VA 22908
(434) 243-6165; fax: (434) 982-1870
jbg8v@virginia.edu; maap@virginia.edu

Western Consortium
Member sites:
Univ. of Washington School of Medicine
MMEP
Box 357430
Seattle, WA 98195
(206) 685-2489; fax: (206) 543-9063
Univ. of Arizona College of Medicine
MMEP
P.O. Box 245140
1501 North Campbell Ave., Rm. 1119-B
Tucson, AZ 85724
(520) 626-4149; fax: (520) 626-2895

Yale Univ. School of Medicine
Office of Multicultural Affairs
MMEP Program Coordinator
P.O. Box 208036
New Haven, CT 06520-8036
(203) 785-2129; fax: (203) 737-5507
omca@yale.edu

Laboratory Internships

The National Institutes of Health (NIH) have a number of research programs for minority undergraduate and medical students. Some can be based at local institutions. For more information, see their website: http://grants1.nih.gov/training/careerdev/colopportindex.html.

NIH also sponsors and provides funding for minority and disadvantaged undergraduate and graduate students to engage in research projects to help prepare them for biomedical careers. Under the NIH Undergraduate Scholarship Program, a limited number of students can receive scholarships of up to $20,000 per academic year. Awardees spend10 weeks during the summer as paid employees in NIH research laboratories, where they work with mentors and attend various programs. After graduation or after finishing medical or postgraduate education, each awardee must work in an NIH research laboratory one year for each year of scholarship support received. For more information, contact: National Institutes of Health, Office of Loan Repayment and Scholarship, 2 Center Drive, MSC 0230, Bethesda, MD 20892-0230; http://ugsp.info.nih.gov/default.htm.

Several other national programs exist to encourage underrepresented minority medical students to choose careers in biomedical research. The Deans of Students and minority advisers at medical schools can assist you in locating such programs and funding.

Individual Medical School Programs

More than three-fourths of medical schools, and some undergraduate schools, have their own summer enrichment programs for minority and disadvantaged students interested in medical careers. These programs provide a wide variety of experiences, including laboratory and clinical work, and are designed for different groups—from elementary/junior high school through postbaccalaureates and those already accepted into medical school. See *Appendix D* for the types of programs at each school.

One example of such a course is the Health Careers Opportunities Program. Check on the Web to see which schools have this available. See also the AAMC's *Minority Student Opportunities in United States Medical Schools* (in *Bibliography*). For Osteopathic schools, check each individual school's website.

Many undergraduate schools have similar programs. To find out about them, contact your high school counselor, your premed adviser, or the local medical school's minority affairs office.

Design Your Own Summer Program

If you cannot travel to an MMEP program site, were not accepted, or have already gone through the program but feel that you want or need more exposure to medicine, you can still use the summer to improve your chance of entering medical school. Work with your counselor or premed adviser to develop a combination of classes, self-study programs, and clinical experiences that will improve your academic performance and enhance the other factors that medical school admission committees seek.

Medical Association Programs

Native Americans may go to the annual premedical advisory workshops sponsored by the Association of American Indian Physicians. At these conferences, Native American premed students meet with practicing American Indian physicians to learn about the medical school application and interview processes. The Association pays the expenses for students' to attend this conference.

Nearly all local, state, and national medical organizations have annual conferences. Most of these organizations, especially the ethnic physician groups, will allow you to attend. In some cases (but only if you ask), they may even be willing to pay some of your expenses.

Many large undergraduate campuses have minority premed organizations that sponsor their own special programs. The minority or premed adviser will know about whether such organizations exist on your campus.

— Applying to Medical School —

Choosing a Medical School

Minority applicants prioritize their criteria for choosing medical schools differently than do other applicants (Figure 9.9). A school's friendliness, teaching methods, and curriculum are typically more important to minorities than to other applicants. Minority applicants are more interested in the community experiences provided by the school, and whether they have been offered financial support. The cost of medical education is a more important factor for URM applicants; more than 67% of URM students have debts exceeding $75,000 upon graduation from medical school, compared to 55% of non-URM medical school graduates.

In addition, minority applicants pay close attention to the student diversity at a school. Minority applicants say that they evaluate the quality of a school's minority programs and services, and half consider faculty mentor programs when they choose schools.

FIGURE 9.9
*Criteria for Selecting a Medical School**

Underrepresented Minority Students		Other Students	
Factor	Rated Very Important	Factor	Rated Very Important
Friendliness	59%	Location	48%
Teaching methods	54	Friendliness	47
Curriculum	51	Teaching methods	41
Cost to attend	48	Reputation	39
Ability to place residents	48	Ability to place residents	39
Location	48	Cost to attend	39
Community experiences	46	Curriculum	38
Offered financial support	46	In-state school	37
Reputation	45	Community experiences	30
Student diversity	39	Medical ethics	24

*Percent of entering medical students who said that the factor was "very important" when choosing the medical school they were entering.

Association of American Medical Colleges. *Minority Students in Medical Education: Facts and Figures XII.* Washington, DC: AAMC, 2002, p. 34.

Two Admission Strategies

Applicants from underrepresented minorities may want to consider applying to medical schools that have not recently admitted many applicants from their ethnic group. If you are willing to brave it as an "ethnic rebel," this may provide your best chance for admission to medical school. How do you find out which schools these are? The AAMC includes a list, by school, of the numbers of "new entrants," "first-year students," and "total students" from the four underrepresented groups in their book *Medical School Admission Requirements*. (By comparing the "new entrant" and "first-year student" categories you can determine if any of the minority students from the previous year's class were held back.) Be aware, however, that some medical schools (those in Puerto Rico, for example) see themselves as having a special mission (in their case, educating physicians for Puerto Rico), and thus have less interest in other students.

Another strategy, which is just as valid for minority as for nonminority applicants, is to apply to Osteopathic medical schools. Although, traditionally, minorities have not "gone the D.O. route," increasing numbers are doing just that. In 2001, for example, 78% of all Osteopathic medical students were minority students. Given that the number of positions at Osteopathic medical schools is increasing and the number at M.D. schools is decreasing, you may want to seriously consider this option.

— Once You Get Into Medical School —

More than half of all U.S. medical schools offer optional summer enrichment programs for newly admitted students from underrepresented minorities and nontraditional backgrounds. Most programs are solely for students accepted to that school (see *Appendix D*).

These programs provide information and help develop skills that are valuable for first-year medical students. While they vary in structure and content, they usually include academic material, study-skills enhancement, familiarization with available support resources (personal, academic, and financial), and early clinical exposure. The programs help students succeed in medical school. Studies show that most students who complete these summer "prematriculation" programs do significantly better in their first- (and often their second-) year course work than they would have done without the program. Performance in these sessions has also been used to identify participants' academic weaknesses, so that they can get additional assistance as they need it. Participants usually adjust to the medical school environment much better than do similar students who do not participate.

Some schools also offer special tutorial, counseling, and advising sessions throughout the first and second years of medical school for students who participated in the prematriculation program. Again, these are generally optional, but are worth investigating.

Take all the help that the school offers if you think you may need it—and the statistics suggest that you may. While 93% of nonminority medical students and 91% of other minority medical students graduate in *five* years or less, only 82% of underrepresented minority students graduate within this time period. Of those underrepresented minority students who don't graduate within five years, 4.2% withdraw, 3.4% are academically dismissed, and about 8% are still in medical school.

An even larger difference exists for *four*-year graduations. At the end of four years, about 85% of nonminority, 79% of other minority, and 66% of underrepresented minority medical students graduate. Among *all* medical students after five years, 3.7% are still in school, 0.8% have been dismissed, 1.9% are on official leave, 2.3% withdrew, and 91.2% graduated.

Once you have begun medical school, you want to think about residency programs. Some medical schools offer special summer clinical fellowships in an attempt to attract additional minority residents to their programs. The minority counselor at your school will know of such programs, as will the national organization for each underrepresented minority. Many of these fellowships offer stipends and special clinical opportunities. They are worth investigating.

Many minorities will, for the foreseeable future, remain underrepresented among practicing physicians and physician-researchers. These individuals often need additional support to overcome the social, financial, and educational barriers to entering the medical profession. The keys to success are to look for that help early and to persevere.

10

Unconventional Premed Students

To do easily what is difficult for others is a mark of talent.
To do what is impossible for talent is the mark of genius.

— Amiel, *Journal, Dec. 17, 1856*

— Physically Challenged/Disabled Applicants —

Data on disabled physicians and medical students is sparse and incomplete. Two studies, one in the early 1980s and the other in the late 1990s, showed that about 0.2% of graduating medical students had physical disabilities, and most of them had the disability when they entered medical school. Other information suggests that about 3,000 practicing U.S. physicians have major physical disabilities. Nearly all of them became disabled after entering, and usually after completing, medical school. Of those medical students with a known physical impairment, approximately 59% have neurological or musculoskeletal impairments, 13% have visual disabilities, 9% have auditory disabilities, and the rest have other physical disabilities. (Learning disability remains a highly controversial area and is often not included as a disability, as was the case in the latest study.)

The subgroup of physically impaired medical students is unique. These individuals are singular both among medical students for their tenacity and drive to overcome obstacles and among the physically impaired, since they are able to complete medical school's clinical requirements, albeit often with special accommodations.

Who Is "Disabled"?

Under the Americans with Disabilities Act of 1990, "disability" is defined as a physical or mental impairment that substantially limits one or more major life activities (e.g., limitations in caring for oneself, performing manual tasks, walking, seeing, hearing, speaking, breathing, learning, and working). According to the Act, persons are considered disabled if they have a record of such an impairment or if others regard them as having such an impairment. The Act requires potential employers to make "reasonable accommodations" for the known physical or mental disabilities of an otherwise qualified individual, as long as these accommodations do not impose an "undue burden" on the institution (e.g., cause "significant difficulty or expense" given the circumstances) or the individual does not pose a direct threat to the health or safety of others. If you are a medical school applicant and are disabled, that applies to you. In addition, if you are not currently disabled, but become disabled once you are a medical student or a resident, the school must make reasonable accommodations for you.

Various contagious diseases, such as tuberculosis or HIV, are considered impairments under the Act. However, the Act does not cover the current use of illegal drugs, the excessive use of legal drugs, alcoholism that interferes with performance, sex-related behavior and disorders, and certain behavioral disorders (including pyromania, kleptomania, and compulsive gambling).

Learning Disabilities

Learning disabilities include a wide spectrum of disorders, including dyslexia, dyscalculia, and attention-deficit disorders. Many individuals with recognized learning disabilities are accepted to medical school, including those whose disabilities have not been diagnosed. It is estimated that up to 2% of all medical students have learning disorders. As Charles Bardes, admissions dean at Cornell Medical College, wrote, "Learning disabilities are specific 'glitches' in one or more areas related to learning. They are not related to intelligence." Special programs have been developed for those students who need help to pass their courses and the USMLE.

One of my brightest residents took our specialty's national in-service examination and scored in the lowest 1%. In our faculty's estimation, this did not come close to reflecting his true abilities, since he was an excellent clinician with a vast knowledge base. Upon questioning, he admitted that he could only learn material when he read things aloud to himself—usually two or three times. In classes, he simply memorized everything the professor said. He had not yet taken a licensing examination (since, at that time, physicians could take the one-part FLEX test) and had had trouble taking tests in medical school. In some cases, professors had given him oral, instead of written, examinations without investigating the problem further. When I referred him to our university's learning center for evaluation, they found that he was severely dyslexic, but had developed unique coping mechanisms. After working with specialists for a year, he successfully took and passed both his licensing and specialty board examinations without any special accommodations.

Unfortunately many, if not most, medical schools lack skilled personnel to either diagnose or support learning-disabled students. Those who know they are learning disabled may find it useful to quietly determine whether a medical school has such services. You can do that by writing to the Dean of Students, who is not usually involved in the application process.

A unique program exists to help medical students with learning disabilities—the Medical H.E.L.P. Program at Marshall University in West Virginia. This five-week program is designed for those with learning disabilities and dyslexia. Call (304) 696-6315 or visit their website: www.marshall.edu/medicalhelp.

Physical Disabilities

Physical disabilities are diverse in their scope and severity. Many would appear to preclude individuals from performing a variety of physician-related tasks, while others simply require alternative practice methods. In most cases, it is the individual, rather than the disability, that determines whether that person can become a physician, as the following story illustrates:

> **A gowned patient with cerebral palsy came to a medical school class on a stretcher. The patient had a speech impediment and severe ataxia (inability to coordinate muscle movements). After the instructor took the medical history and did a physical examination, the patient was wheeled out of the room. The class was asked to evaluate the patient's job potential; they thought it was extremely poor. A few minutes later, the "patient" reappeared, now in his suit and white coat, and was recognizable as the physician–director of a large rehabilitation hospital. (From Corbet B, Madorsky JG. Physicians with disabilities. *West J Med*. 1991;154(5):514-21.)**

However, as sometimes needs to be pointed out, the presence of a disability often makes it more difficult to be admitted to many medical schools. A recent study showed that while there was an average of one student per medical school with a significant physical disability, the numbers were highly skewed since more than half the schools had none.

Infectious diseases represent another physical disability. While medical schools in the United States don't discriminate against those individuals with infectious diseases that do not pose a danger to others, nearly all schools require immunization against hepatitis B, and about half the schools have policies regarding students who become HIV- or hepatitis B-positive. Elsewhere in the world, there is discrimination against those with infectious diseases. In Britain, for example, some schools reject applicants if they test positive for specific diseases.

Other Disabilities

Some disabilities may not be obvious, and can be recognized only if you are tested for them. One such disability (or potential disability) is a genetic predisposition to lethal or devastating diseases, such as early-onset cancer or Huntington's Disease. Another more common (at least for the present) set of disorders are unrecognized physical impairments that can prevent medical school graduates from entering certain medical specialties. For example, at least one-third of the Ophthalmology programs, all Aerospace Medicine programs, and a smattering of other programs test applicants for color vision and stereognosis. This is perfectly legal if all applicants are screened and it can be shown that the examination is job-related. Some applicants, especially men who never knew they were "impaired," fail.

Admission Requirements: An Equitable Playing Field

Medical schools have struggled to piece together policies ("technical standards") that meet the requirements of the federal laws governing the disabled (Americans with Disabilities Act of 1990 and Section 504 of the 1973 Rehabilitation Act).

Their first question is whether the scores for the increasing number of applicants taking the MCAT "with special accommodations" are equivalent to those for the MCAT taken under routine conditions. Special accommodations, such as separate rooms or increased time-limits, can be arranged for students with disabilities. If you have special needs due to a documented disability, contact the MCAT administrators as early as possible. They will then supply you with additional information. If applicants request and receive special accommodations, current policy is to report the special testing circumstances to the medical schools. Special accommodations for nonphysical disabilities, such as learning disorders, will be granted only if there is documentation of the disability from a licensed professional. By itself, this can be problematic, since the range of learning disabilities is wide and their definitions are still being debated.

The second, and much tougher, question is: What body of knowledge and skills define a physician's academic qualifications? Put another way, what is essential for every graduating medical student to know and to be able to do, without regard for how these goals are achieved? The key word is "essential." This is where the debate becomes strident.

Must all medical school graduates have the potential to enter any specialty? Must they have the ability to perform, at the least, such lifesaving interventions as CPR, IV placement, and mouth-to-mouth resuscitation? Or can some of the knowledge and techniques be foregone given an agreement by the student to enter only areas where these procedures will not be needed? Some disabled applicants want to use "trained intermediaries" to help them do some tasks they cannot physically accomplish, such as parts of the physical examination. It's unclear how expansive the role of a trained intermediary can be and what part such intermediaries should take. Most schools find that using trained individuals who interpose themselves between the physician and the patient is unacceptable, because it may color the physician's judgment. (However, unskilled intermediaries, such as individuals who talk on the telephone for deaf physicians when they communicate with nondeaf patients and colleagues, seem to be acceptable.)

While medical schools, in general, are willing to make accommodations for students that they feel can complete all of the cognitive and the majority of the procedural parts of a medical curriculum, they take a tough stance against accepting students who cannot do so. As Michael Reichgott, a prominent medical educator, wrote: "Medical schools have traditionally excluded the physically disabled, [with] one reason [being that] physical disability of any kind seems to engender an expectation of total incompetence, even among sophisticated medical professionals."

This reticence is often unwarranted. The most notable exception has been a quadriplegic man who was grudgingly admitted to medical school because of significant outside pressure; he graduated from Einstein Medical School and entered a Neurology residency program. At least two other quadriplegics have graduated from U.S. medical schools in recent years, although they reportedly became disabled while in medical school. Medical schools have admitted numerous deaf applicants, as well as those with visual or other significant disabilities; many are now practicing medicine in a variety of fields.

As the following story illustrates, some very brave and persistent people led the way.

> In 1976, Frank Peter Hochman became the "first American who was born deaf to complete medical training, earn a degree, and become a physician." His road to that achievement was far from easy. For years, counselors tried to steer him into "normal" careers for the deaf: first [into] printing because "he spells well," and then engineering because he was "good at math and science."
>
> His devoted parents sent him to the National School for Speech Disorders where he learned to speak and be easily understood. He was later "mainstreamed," attending top-flight public schools and then entering the City College of New York as a premed. After he graduating in 1958, no medical school would grant him an interview because he was deaf. With what seemed to be an insurmountable roadblock, he entered the applied sciences, working for the City of New York's Food and Drug Laboratory, and eventually becoming supervisor of their Narcotic Detection Unit.
>
> Eventually, Peter left New York and began working as a medical technologist and research biologist. Never having abandoned his dream of becoming a physician, he took the MCAT in 1971, doing very well despite having been out of school 18 years. This time, several medical schools accepted him and he entered Rutgers Medical School in Piscataway, New Jersey, at the ripe old age of 37, describing himself as probably "the oldest medical student in America."
>
> Graduating in 1976, he went on to do his residency in San Francisco and San Jose. He then entered private practice, but also served as the physician for the California School for the Deaf in Fremont from 1979 to 1992. Still practicing in California, about 90% of his patients are hearing. One of the things he teaches is to "beware of the 'Can't Cant's'—experts in deafness who will always tell you things you can't do. Pay no attention to them. They 'can't' help it!"

If applicants disclose their disabilities, medical schools may request further information to determine whether they will require special accommodations. Admission committees must decide on a case-by-case basis whether an applicant is otherwise qualified for admission. They first ask whether, without the disability, the individual's qualifications meet their acceptance criteria. If the answer is yes, the school then determines what accommodations can reasonably be made to provide the student with an education equivalent to that of his or her classmates.

The "reasonable accommodations" medical schools must make for disabled students are alterations in the learning or physical environment that do not fundamentally change the educational program, do not impair public safety, and do not impose an insurmountable financial burden on the school (based on the school's entire budget). Sometimes these accommodations take only minor ingenuity rather than major expense. An interesting example of the special accommodations one school made for colorblind students is to use special stains for the hematology and histology specimens they must examine. Another school uses transparent surgical masks to help hearing-impaired students work in the operating room, delivery suite, and emergency department.

What Barriers Do You Face?

Federal law requires that medical schools "provide an equal opportunity for an individual with a disability to participate in the . . . application process and to be considered [for admission]." This means that applications must not include questions about an applicant's health, medical history, or disability status. If requested, schools must provide materials (applications, forms, brochures, catalogs, and curriculum descriptions) that accommodate a disabled applicant's needs, such as large-print versions. They must also have these materials in locations accessible to disabled applicants. Interviews must be conducted in accessible locations and special accommodations must be made (e.g., sign-language interpreters) upon request. While the law prohibits asking questions about an applicant's disability, expect this rule to be broken.

To test whether you will need special accommodations, get some health-related experience. How you perform in patient-care situations will enable you to determine what, if any, accommodations you may need. Talk to some disabled physicians. If you don't know any, contact your local medical society to find some names. You will be surprised at how many are in successful practices. Finally, try to visit the campuses before you apply to see whether the facilities necessary for your day-to-day activities are currently accessible to you. While the school may fulfill the basic requirements, for example, of having wheelchair-accessible facilities, the parking, living, and geographic (e.g., hills) situations may not be as good.

Medical schools accept students on the condition that they fulfill certain expectations, such as successfully completing current course work. One of these requirements can be to complete a medical history form for the school's records. A school can legally withdraw its acceptance if an applicant's history reveals that he could not fulfill the *essential* requirements for graduation, if accommodating his special needs would cause the school undue hardship, or if he would need *unreasonable* accommodations.

Even though a few blind applicants have been admitted to medical school, and at least one graduated (Temple University in the 1970s), medical schools are now reluctant to repeat this experience. In the mid-1990s, a court ordered Case Western Reserve University Medical School to admit a blind applicant. They refused and appealed the decision, saying that it was "not possible for any blind person to complete medical school unless the curriculum and requirements are significantly altered." The Ohio Supreme Court agreed with the medical school.

Admission Committee Attitudes

Admission committees understand the need to evaluate disabled applicants in a reasonable and thoughtful manner. The question committees face is: How much "reasonable accommodation" can the school make for students and still be assured that they will be qualified to practice medicine when they graduate? Since producing practicing physicians is the ultimate goal, they are concerned about applicants who may not be capable of "going the distance."

The official (and oft-repeated) policy is to "focus on the individual, not the disability." According to several Deans of Admission, many schools remain hesitant to voluntarily enter into situations requiring large financial outlays to accommodate disabled students or to fill a precious medical school position with a student who either will not be able to meet minimum requirements to practice medicine (as set by the school or state licensing boards) or will not even live long enough to finish training. Once accepted, it is the student's responsibility to notify the medical school about special accommodations needed.

Inquiring about the potential problems a disabled medical school applicant might face, a premed adviser wrote:

> I just met with a great premed student who carries a 3.9 GPA, has a great personality and has a great work ethic. Here is the problem. He has a congenitally deformed left hand that has no fingers. Several surgeries have resulted in two small digits on his fist. While I will write a very strong recommendation letter for him, I am not sure how a med school would view this disability. I should add that I had him in two lab courses (micro and cell biology) and he was able to do everything others could, although a little slower. He also works at a hospital emergency department, performing many clinical duties.

My response, which should give heart to any applicant, was:

> If he is an otherwise good applicant, his condition may actually help him—since his interviewers will remember him better than they will remember anyone else. As for any physical disability, if the individual can perform required tasks (even if they need some additional equipment or an aide to assist them), they will normally be treated the same as all other applicants. In addition, my first attending in Orthopedic Surgery when I was a medical student had been born with no hands. She worked at the rehabilitation hospital, primarily with children—and was an excellent surgeon.

Admission committee members, however, often have inaccurate perceptions of disabled applicants' limitations and of what tasks they can really do. As one deaf physician who spent 17 years trying to enter medical school said, "They just assumed that I couldn't do it. I would explain technical advances, I would bring pictures of my instruments, and I would explain how to do it. Even after I answered, they felt uncomfortable. They didn't want to say yes, but they had a hard time saying why not." This applicant also admits that she failed to appreciate her own limitations. Her speech was difficult to understand in interview situations. After several years of trying and failing to be admitted to a medical school, she finally brought an interpreter to the interview and was accepted.

Disabled Medical Students, Residents, and Physicians

Most teaching hospitals have made at least superficial accommodations for disabled residents, faculty, and staff to comply with the Americans with Disabilities Act. While some residency programs may hesitate to take a physically impaired individual, this attitude is normally due to ignorance.

Disable physicians' choice of which medical specialty to enter generally depends upon when their disability occurred. Those who became disabled before or during medical school usually are drawn to physiatry (physical medicine and rehabilitation), psychiatry, pathology, and anesthesiology. Those whose disabilities occurred later tend to remain in their original specialty, but they modify their working environment to accommodate their needs.

For more information about resources and referrals for physically impaired physicians, write: The U.S. Equal Employment Opportunity Commission, 1801 L Street NW, Washington, DC 20507; (202) 663-4900; TTY: (202) 663-4494; www.eeoc.gov.

— Older Applicants —

If you are reading this book, chances are you are probably not too old to begin a medical career. At our medical school, one student began his first year at age 49. (As a joke, his medical-student classmates, all dressed in black, presented him with a black cake for his 50th birthday.) In another case, one of my residents began her internship the same year that her oldest son began college. She not only practiced medicine, but also became the state's medical director for emergency medical services. Older medical students have done very well. Ask yourself whether you *feel* young enough to change your career, to learn a mass of new information, and to radically alter your lifestyle. If so, go for it!

Perhaps the best-known "older medical student" story is that of Albert Schweitzer. He earned a Ph.D. in philosophy at age 24 and then a doctorate in theology at 25. He soon became a world-renowned theologian while simultaneously becoming recognized as an accomplished organist. Not content with this, he graduated medical school when he was 38 years old and traveled to Africa as a medical missionary. Based on his remarkable accomplishments as a physician, he won the 1952 Nobel Peace Prize for his efforts on behalf of "the Brotherhood of Nations." If anyone gives you grief about your age, tell them about Dr. Schweitzer.

You don't have to be a potential Nobel laureate to enter medical school as an older student. A friend and one of my former residents, Jeff Baker (Colorado, Class of '93), describes his experience:

> **I was a "ski bum" until I was 27 years old. I lived from paycheck to paycheck, working at lots of different jobs, including heavy-equipment operator and clinic "gopher" in the off season. I took the clinic job because I thought I might be interested in physical therapy as a career. By that time, I knew I would eventually have to give up the vagabond's life. What I saw there convinced me that I wanted to be a doctor. Then, I simply had to apply to undergraduate school, complete the requirements, get into medical school, and graduate. No problem. (Jeff now practices medicine near the Aspen ski slopes.)**

In 1995, Tufts University School of Medicine graduated a 58-year-old former computer manufacturer. He completed his residency at age 61. He said, "Only perseverance has kept my dream alive." His mother earned her M.D. degree from Tufts in 1927. Another student entered Michigan State University College of Human Medicine in 1991, at age 59.

One out of 50 first-year students at M.D.-medical schools in the United States is at least 36 years old, and 8% of medical students begin their medical education after age 30. Nearly 7% of medical students received their bachelor's degrees seven or more years before entering medical school. No applicant older than 50 was accepted to a U.S. M.D.-granting school in 2002, although there were six applicants 55 years or older, and more between 51 and 54 years old.

You, your inertia, and your fears are the barriers to following your desire to practice medicine. If you really want to do it, go for it now. Four years from now, you will still be four years older—whether or not you will also have a medical degree is your choice. As the saying goes, "It is better to wear out than to rust out."

Why Medical School Now?

You have your own reasons for considering medical school now, but they probably fall into one of the following categories. Each has its challenges.

Mid-life career change. Most often found among lawyers, architects, and engineers, this desire to change represents dissatisfaction with their current career. Having shown that they have talent in an area in which they have not found personal fulfillment, they seek another life path. Admission personnel ask: How do you know you will be happier in medicine? Are you running toward medicine or away from your prior career and lifestyle?

After child-rearing. Rather than suffering from the "empty-nest" syndrome, many women find that their lives improve when they have fewer household-based restrictions. They discover that they can use their talents to achieve personal and professional recognition. Admission personnel ask: Are you just looking for something to do now that your children are out of the home?

Mixing careers. Some individuals seek to introduce a new aspect to their current profession through medical school. These may include lawyers, engineers, artists, and others who may foresee being able to successfully combine their talents in one profession with a physician's skills and knowledge. In a (very) few cases, individuals can continue their old career while pursuing medical studies—but no one should count on being able to do this. Admission personnel ask: How serious are you about medicine? Aren't there much easier ways to pursue your goals? Are you more interested in the degree than in the knowledge?

Retirement. Usually, individuals who retire think that they are too old to enter medical school. Especially for those with some government jobs ("20 years and out"), this is not the case. In any event, an increasing number of older applicants are applying. Some, essentially because of their age, must either abandon their dream of going to medical school or go to a non-U.S. medical school. Admission personnel ask: Do you have the [fill in the blank] to keep up with the younger students? What they really mean is, "Aren't you too old to be applying?"But, of course, they can't legally ask it that way.

Issues to Consider

Older applicants must consider several issues that do not concern younger applicants. Upon reflection, you may decide either that they present insurmountable barriers to attending medical school or that they can be overcome with understanding and patience.

Many older applicants have been away from school so long that their study habits have grown rusty. However, your study habits can be honed while preparing to take the MCAT. If you did (or do) well on the MCAT, don't worry about your study habits. (As shown in Figure 15.8, many schools require that applicants take the MCAT within two to three years of applying. As Figure 10.1 shows, this is not beneficial to older applicants.) Part of developing good study habits is having good time-management skills. If life and work experiences have helped you in this area, you have little to worry about.

If you return to school to finish your bachelor's degree, you may want to consider applying for acceptance to medical school after completing only 90 semester hours (or the equivalent in quarter hours). Of course, you must do well in school and complete both the MCAT and the required science courses. While many medical schools have a provision to accept students without a bachelor's degree, they do not generally accept younger students under this rule. Older students, however, sometimes can shave a year off the process through this mechanism.

Part of your identity is the job you do now. Very few people can deftly and successfully manage to continue in their present career while going to medical school. Medical school is not a part-time

FIGURE 10.1

MCAT Scores by Examinee's Age

Age (years)	Verbal Reasoning	Physical Sciences	Biological Sciences	Writing Sample
<21	8.2	8.7	8.8	P
21-22	7.8	8.0	8.3	O
23-27	7.5	7.7	8.1	O
28-31	7.2	7.4	7.7	O
>31	6.7	6.8	7.0	O

Adapted from: "Table of April/August 2002 MCAT performance" on AAMC website: www.aamc.org/mcat.

experience; it is difficult enough going full time. Consider whether you are willing to give up your current position to take the leap into medicine.

Attending medical school will place a double financial burden on you. Not only will you incur the same large debt as other medical students, but you will also lose the income you receive from your current job. Unless you are among the lucky few who are independently wealthy, this will probably lead to a radical change in your lifestyle for at least seven years (residents make about $30,000 to $40,000 a year). Think about that while you eat pâté de foie gras. (It isn't good for you anyway.)

If you are determined to go to medical school, you may have to relocate. This can wreak havoc on you, your family, and your friendships. You may even have to move out of the country if you are not accepted to a U.S. school and decide to go the foreign route. A number of older applicants have done just that. Are you ready for such a significant readjustment? Is your family?

Speaking of family, you probably have more people depending upon you than do younger applicants. Do they support your decision? Are they willing to subsist at a much lower standard of living (and work harder) to help you reach your dream? If so, you can probably do it. If not, you will have a very rough time. Personal problems in addition to the rigors of medical school (and residency) make awfully tough sledding.

Since you are "older," who do you think will be your bosses on the clinical services when you are a medical student and resident? That's right! The "kids." In one extreme case, an older medical student was supervised by his own son, who was the attending during one of his medical school rotations. Now that's a real role reversal. Is your ego strong enough to take it? If not, quit now.

Finally, there is the question of stamina. Will you be able to keep up with the younger folks? While this concern is undoubtedly at the forefront of most interviewers' minds, they won't voice it. But ask yourself, "Can I pull 'all-nighters' to study for exams if necessary? Can I work 36-hour shifts?" And, while you probably can do anything that younger students can do, the real question is: Do you want to? If you do, go forth and pursue your dream.

You and the Premed Adviser

Even though you may have graduated from college many years ago, you are still welcome at your undergraduate school's premed office. They will feel that they still have a connection to you, since you have now decided to pursue a medical career. The premed adviser has materials and information that may prove invaluable to you. Most will not charge you for their services, although some will if you did not graduate within the past five to seven years. If you are too far away to interact in person with your alma mater's premed adviser, write or e-mail the office. Also, contact the premed adviser at a nearby college for information and advice.

Of course, if you are still an undergraduate or have returned to school for premed courses, simply seek out the adviser at your current school.

Some Different Criteria

You may be nervous about competing against younger applicants, but, as an older and, presumably, more experienced applicant, you are expected to excel in certain areas, especially the interview. Interviewers expect older applicants to be more self-assured, poised, and articulate than their younger compatriots. Because of this, excelling in the interview may not score you as many points as a youngster's equivalent performance, but being only mediocre can be devastating. One technique to use, not only to excel but also to make a positive impression, is to draw the interviewer into interesting discussions about what you have done when you weren't in school.

Admission officers can be sticklers about grades. They want to know if you can "hack it" in competition with kids with sharp study skills who are right out of undergraduate school. Excellent grades in postbaccalaureate programs or graduate school may not be a big help, but mediocre grades will hurt you badly, as one applicant found out but overcame:

> **An interviewer told me my numbers weren't good enough to get in, blah, blah, blah. I finally got mad and told him to ask me what I *could* do instead of telling me what I couldn't do. By the end of the interview, he was president of my fan club and was off to the Dean of Admissions to tell her to take me. [She related this story after graduating from medical school and entering residency training.]**

Studies have shown that while older medical students had slightly lower GPAs than did their younger cohorts, they had equivalent MCAT scores—and ultimately did nearly as well in medical school. The biggest difference in medical school performance was in the first year basic science courses, as might be expected.

As their age increases, there is a gradual decrease in the percentage of students accepted to medical school. This is true for both men and women (Figure 10.2). The really dramatic difference is after the age of 20! Of course, 98% of all medical school applicants have already passed over that hill.

While only one U.S. medical school explicitly discriminates against older applicants (the Uniformed Services University, which takes civilians up to age 30 and military personnel up to age 35), admission officers want to know whether you still have the neurons and the drive to go the distance in medical school and to complete residency training. Show them you've got it! Remember, as Bernard Baruch said, "Old age is always fifteen years older than I am."

— Postbaccalaureate Premed Students —

Postbaccalaureate premed programs are courses taken by individuals who already have at least a bachelor's degree to prepare them to apply to medical school. They take them either to complete premed requirements or to improve their scholastic record. Many students decide to pursue medical careers after they have received their bachelor's degree—some many years afterward. These individuals may not have taken the required preparatory courses, or have taken them too long ago to

FIGURE 10.2

Acceptance Rates for Medical School Applicants by Age*

Age (years)	% of All Applicants	% of Those Accepted
<21	0.6%	0.7%
21-23	53.8	61.0
24-27	30.9	28.0
28-31	8.8	6.7
>32	6.0	3.5

*These numbers are for white applicants. Among non-white groups, there are only slightly more applicants accepted who are younger than 21 years old (blacks, Native Americans, Asian/Americans, and Other Hispanics) and who are 32 years and older (blacks, Native Americans, Mainland Puerto Ricans, and Other Hispanics).

Adapted from AAMC. *Minority Students in Medical Education: Facts and Figures*. Washington, DC: AAMC, 2002. Tables 4a, 8a, and 9a.

remember much, and must complete them before taking the MCAT or applying to medical school. Other students have done badly in undergraduate school and use postbaccalaureate programs as a method of "academic renewal," knowing that admission committees often give more weight to the most recent courses.

If you are interested in postbaccalaureate education, there are three ways to proceed. First, simply take the necessary premed courses at your local college. Second, you may enroll in a graduate degree program that will improve your GPA or give you the required course work. Finally, you may go to one of the increasing number of special premed programs designed for those who already have their bachelor's degree. Usually, individuals enter these programs because they have been out of school awhile, they originally were nonscience majors, or they have already tried and failed to enter medical school.

Students seeking a postbaccalaureate premed program (see list in *Appendix C*) should realize that these programs differ markedly in their entry requirements, length, curricula, and costs. They also vary in what they promise students—and in what they deliver. Selecting a postbaccalaureate program is much like selecting a medical or an undergraduate school. Therefore, the "Must/Want" Analysis (Figures 7.2 and 16.1) will be useful. Some additional questions to ask are:

- Will the premed adviser actively work with me? Is that person easily accessible?
- Does the program guarantee that there will be space in the classes and labs I need?
- Will the program provide a recommendation letter for medical schools?
- Does this program have links with specific medical schools? What is their "track record" of getting graduates into medical school?
- Does the program provide tutoring and other academic aids?
- Is the medical school application process built into the program?
- How much does this program cost? Is financial aid available?
- Will this program help me even if I don't get accepted into medical school?

Some programs accept only minorities, women, or state residents, while others accept only graduates of specific schools. There are programs that take only science majors and others which accept only nonscience majors. Some require minimum GPAs or MCAT scores, while others are less rigid. A number of programs are only for students who have tried and failed to enter medical school, while others are for those who have not yet applied. Carefully review the entry requirements before applying to a program.

Postbaccalaureate premed programs vary in length from one to more than two years. The curricula range from basic premed courses to the entire course load of a first-year medical student. The costs range from nothing (scholarships are provided) to well above the normal cost for a year at most medical schools. Most programs offer assistance in obtaining loans and other financial aid. Special programs for underrepresented minority students may provide not only free tuition but also a stipend. (For more information about these, contact: Director, NIH Academy, 2 Center Drive, Bldg. 2, Bethesda, MD 20892-0240; www.training.nih.gov.)

Most schools promise only to give students a good premed education, although a few guarantee medical school admission if students do well in the program.

One benefit of these programs is the immediate close tie students have with the premed (and often a separate minority premed) adviser. Postbaccalaureate students who take premed classes on their own should contact the premed advising system on campus before classes begin. This will give them a support system, including an experienced individual to guide them through the medical school application process.

Postbaccalaureate students generally have the following qualities that, for better or worse, you may recognize in yourself:

- Feel pressured by significant personal and financial responsibilities
- See themselves in a win-lose situation, with this program being their last chance at reaching their goal
- Are focused and goal-oriented

- Have employers who may not be sympathetic to their goals
- Need both moral and practical support to succeed
- Have high anxiety when they move from a comfortable and known situation to an uncomfortable and unknown situation and future
- Waiver between confidence and self-doubt
- Have high expectations for themselves, the faculty, and their advisers
- Have little tolerance for glitches in the program

In general, postbaccalaureate students act like "adult learners": They want to know what they need to know without any extraneous garbage thrown in, they want to receive positive feedback for good work, and they want to get through as quickly as possible. Does that describe you correctly? In many ways, it also describes many medical students.

Studies suggest that while postbaccalaureate students who enter medical school do a little worse in their first year (as do older students in general), their overall medical school performance is on a par with traditionally prepared students.

— Other Unconventional Students —

Special Programs for Ph.D.'s

In the 1970s and 1980s, special programs existed at the University of Miami and at Washington University for entering medical students who already had Ph.D.'s. These programs shortened the length of medical school training. Although the faculty seemed pleased with graduates of these programs, both have been discontinued. Some medical schools, especially those with active M.D.–Ph.D. programs, say that they will give applicants with Ph.D. degrees advanced standing on a case-by-case basis. This, unfortunately, means you must contact each medical school, determine which ones are willing to give you advanced standing if accepted, and then apply to those schools. Since each applicant has a unique background, this onerous process seems to be the only way to shorten your medical education by getting credit for your Ph.D. experiences.

Special Programs for Dentists

Some medical schools allow a few dentists or dental students to transfer into their school, usually with "advanced standing," meaning that they enter at the second- or third-year level. No more than about 30 such transfers take place each year, with most transferring into the third-year medical school class. Currently, only five medical schools accept such transfers (Finch–UHS Chicago Med, UMDNJ–NJ Med, UNC–Chapel Hill, Oregon Health Sciences University, and Drexel).

More commonly, top dental school graduates apply to medical schools that have combined M.D./Oral and Maxillofacial Surgery (OMS) programs. These programs are about six years in length, and combine didactics with an OMS residency, meaning that graduates can begin practice as soon as they finish. Some of the schools with this program are: Loma Linda, Louisiana State University, Mayo Medical School, University of Maryland, University of Rochester, and UT–Southwestern. Fourteen medical schools will also accept oral surgeons into their programs as second- or third-year students. See Figure 15.8 and the website: http://services.aamc.org/tsp_reports.

Teenagers

The average age for students entering medical school is nearly 24 years old. Yet a few brave, extremely smart boys and girls try to follow Doogie Howser's example. According to *Guinness World Records*, the youngest person to graduate from any medical school was a 17-year-old who graduated from a New York medical school in 1995.

Sho Yano, a shy spectacle-wearing 12-year-old boy with an IQ of over 200, began classes in the Fall of 2003 on a full scholarship at the University of Chicago's medical school. Clearly a prodigy, he scored 1,500 out of 1,600 possible points on the SAT and enrolled at Loyola University at age nine, graduating summa cum laude in three years. When applying to medical schools, Sho was often told that he was too young; someone even commented that his patients "would be shocked." Yet, University of Chicago admission officers found that the shy young man "answered tough questions with maturity and thoughtfulness." Sho, who is also a gifted pianist, shrugs off the "genius" tag, saying, "I am not a genius. I am gifted." While at the University of Chicago, he will be working on both his M.D. and Ph.D. degrees. Classmates have been telling him to "grow a beard and a mustache as soon as you can to look older."

Another youngster is Dr. Santosh Nandi, who, in 2003, had nearly completed his general surgery residency at Akron City Hospital—at the age of 24. He started college at 11 and medical school at 16 and says that he still lies about his age to some patients, although by fewer years than previously. Born in Virginia to Indian immigrants, he entered a program at California State University that would let him skip high school and start college, where he majored in biology and biochemistry. He entered medical school at the University of California–Irvine, where, not sharing the sentiments of many students, he said, "Medical school was a blast."

Despite these cases, medical schools are hesitant to accept very young students. No matter how bright these students are, the question arises: Are they mature enough to deal with matters of life and death? Not many are.

Rural Americans

If you grew up in a rural area, you probably needed to overcome quite a few educational and social obstacles to complete college and apply to medical school. You are an (unofficial) underrepresented minority. Since medical schools are being pushed to increase the number of their graduates who enter primary care, especially in inner-city and rural areas, they may see you as a "diamond in the rough." Since you came from a rural area, they believe that you will return to a similar area to practice. They're generally wrong about this, though.

Most medical students come from large cities or their suburbs; less than 10% come from rural areas. To take full advantage of your background, make it clear to the admission committees that you are from America's hinterlands. Some schools specifically ask if you are from a rural area, and then give special consideration to such applicants if they complete the appropriate forms and supply details about their background.

In some states, special programs exist that pay the medical school expenses for students who agree to practice medicine in a rural part of the state for a specific period of time once they finish residency. In some cases, these students leave medical school with little or no debt. Medical schools with these programs are constantly seeking applicants who are willing to participate. If you are, let them know it. A 2002 study by Baco et al., showed that there has been a marked reduction in the proportion of rural applicants offered admission interviews if the schools do not give them special consideration. Rural students should apply to those who do give them special consideration (look in school materials and on their websites).

Transfer Students

Some M.D.-granting schools will accept students from "other" graduate or professional degree programs as transfer students. Individual school policies can be found online at: http://services .aamc .org/tsp_reports. Students should contact the Osteopathic schools directly. No Canadian schools accept such transfers.

About 28 U.S. medical schools accept current students from non-U.S. medical schools as transfers. These students comprise the bulk of those admitted to M.D.-granting U.S. schools from graduate or professional degree programs. They represent only a tiny portion of the U.S. citizens who are training at non-U.S./Canadian medical schools, since transferring from a non-U.S. medical school to a U.S. medical school is extremely difficult. (See Chapter 17 for more details.)

Most medical schools do accept transfers from other U.S. medical schools, especially for "compassionate reasons," such as a family member being at the school as a student or resident. Even those who don't officially allow these transfers usually permit such students to do many of their clinical rotations—especially in the fourth year—at the school.

Non-Native English Speakers

This category encompasses anyone who spent much of his life speaking a language other than American English. This includes our English-speaking cohorts in Britain and the countries that once made up the British Empire. You may speak and write excellent English, but it is not American English, and that may be your downfall.

American English is full of colloquial expressions that make no sense unless you memorize them. Use one of the books listing these expressions to build your vocabulary, such as Spears' *Essential American Idioms* (see *Annotated Bibliography*), and then practice on your friends.

Your accent may also be problematic. Speaking with a mild British or Australian accent may be considered very fashionable. But if your accent is too difficult for Americans to understand, you will be at a disadvantage during your interviews—as well as in class, on the wards, and when applying to residency programs. Many colleagues have said that they improved their American English accent by attending special classes where, rather than teaching English grammar, they concentrated on the students' accents and being understood. Many colleges offer such courses at night or on weekends. Audiotapes are also useful (if you actually listen to them) since you can use them whenever it's convenient, but you don't get any feedback.

Foreign Nationals

Permanent U.S. residents who hold "Green Cards" (actually, they are pink) may apply to U.S. medical schools on the same basis and through the same mechanisms as any U.S. citizen. In Canada, "landed immigrants" may apply on the same basis as Canadian citizens.

Although they may apply, U.S. medical schools admit very few foreign nationals, since qualified U.S. citizens receive preference. However, about 40 U.S. medical schools will accept foreign nationals who otherwise meet admission requirements. Another 25 will accept such students if they pay for their schooling in advance.

Foreign nationals must be ready to supply medical schools with complete visa information, and they must have a visa that allows them to complete their studies at a U.S. graduate school under current Naturalization Service rules. Since medical schools are not generally able to provide foreign nationals with scholarships or loans, these applicants must arrange to finance their own medical school education—and demonstrate, to the school's satisfaction, how they will do it. Some schools require that a portion of these monies be placed in an escrow account before the student begins classes.

Foreign nationals applying to transfer with advanced standing to U.S. medical schools should contact individual schools directly. They should also contact the ECFMG for information about taking the USMLE Step 1. The chances of non-U.S. citizens/permanent residents getting advanced standing at U.S. medical schools is very small. (For additional information, see Figure 15.8.)

Gay, Lesbian, Bisexual, and Transgender Applicants

Gay, lesbian, bisexual, and transgender medical students and physicians are a largely invisible minority, although they are becoming more visible within the medical profession as our society becomes more accepting of diversity. Maturing societal attitudes now recognize diverse sexual orientations and many individuals feel more comfortable identifying themselves as gay, lesbian, or bisexual. Medical organizations of gay, lesbian, and bisexual physicians have thousands of dues-paying members, and membership is growing at the rate of 10% annually. Great strides have recently occurred within organized medicine, with the AMA now recognizing the Gay and Lesbian Medical Association as one of their specialty committees. These groups' unique health concerns, including AIDS, have gained the profession's attention. Yet, as mentioned in other sections, medical practitioners generally have conservative attitudes toward their life and work.

Organized medicine has not felt comfortable accepting gay, lesbian, and bisexual physicians, as exemplified by the difficulty that many national physician organizations have in approving resolutions banning discrimination on the basis of sexual orientation. A 1996 study showed that about 10% of physicians would oppose openly gay and lesbian physicians seeking residency training in Obstetrics and

Gynecology, Urology, and Pediatrics, and about 10% would not refer patients to them no matter what their specialty. About 4% would refuse gays' and lesbians' admission to medical school.

While these numbers are an improvement over prior surveys (in which 30% of physicians would refuse medical school admission based solely on an applicant being gay or lesbian and 40% would discourage individuals from entering Pediatric or Psychiatric residencies on that basis alone), these numbers still indicate a great deal of prejudice and fear among this highly educated population. This suggests that gay, lesbian, bisexual, and transgender medical students may not want to broadcast their sexual orientation when applying for residency positions. As one medical student, Lydia Vaias, wrote in *JAMA*, "Interviews are uncomfortable, scary processes for everyone. They are particularly terrifying for lesbian and gay people, because we must grapple with telling who we are, without revealing an integral aspect of ourselves."

Gay, lesbian, bisexual, and transgender medical school applicants may also encounter admission committees' fears that they will add to the estimated 5,000 HIV-infected physicians. This fear represents more than mere homophobia; it denotes concerns about having medical students who need prolonged absences, have a disability, and have other problems with which medical school administrators do not want to deal if they can avoid them.

Transgender (transsexuals and transvestites) applicants may face additional problems. According to those working closely with these medical students, transgender applicants may not be able to use the institutional acceptance of lesbian, gay, and bisexual students and residents as a guide to whether they will be accepted. Respect for diversity sometimes stops before reaching this group.

As with any applicant, demonstrating to interviewers that you are not "mainstream" may doom your application. Wearing triangle or rainbow jewelry or any other any other symbolic reference to gay culture will most likely decrease the probability of your acceptance into medical school. If you feel, however, as some people do, that it is essential to demonstrate your sexual orientation to interviewers, be forewarned that it may cost you the medical school position you desire. On the other hand, if this is the reason you don't get in, you may not want to be there anyway.

Two national groups now lend assistance and support to gays, lesbians, and bisexuals in medicine: Gay and Lesbian Medical Association, 459 Fulton Street, Suite 107, San Francisco, CA 94102; (415) 255-4547; fax: 415-255-4784; e-mail: info@glma.org; www.glma.org; and for medical students: Lesbian, Gay, Bisexual, and Transgender People in Medicine (LGBTPM), an advocacy group within the American Medical Student Association, (800) 767-2266; fax: (703) 620-5873; e-mail: lgbtpm@ www.amsa.org; www.amsa.org/adv/lgbtpm. There are also a number of local groups in larger cities, and specific groups within some medical specialties.

Summary

There are many paths into medical school and many types of individuals within the medical profession. The keys for any successful applicant are to persist, know your own strengths and weaknesses, and improve yourself however possible. Many individuals get into medical school because others have fallen by the wayside and don't pursue their dream. It's up to you.

11

The Medical College Admission Test

Genius is one percent inspiration and ninety-nine percent perspiration.

— Thomas A. Edison

The Medical College Admission Test, commonly referred to as the "MCAT," represents a major hurdle for most medical school applicants. The nine-hour (longer, if you include breaks, registration, etc.) multiple-choice examination, sponsored by the Association of American Medical Colleges (AAMC), measures your knowledge of the biological and physical sciences, your ability to read and interpret information, and your ability to write coherently. Nearly all U.S. medical schools require applicants to take the MCAT before applying for admission (Figure 15.5), although how much weight they give the exam varies widely. Many Canadian medical schools either do not require the MCAT or do not weigh it heavily. Most schools suggest or require that applicants take the test within two to three years of applying (Figure 15.8), and, if applicants have taken the test multiple times, they will look for progressive improvement.

The MCAT is designed to put applicants with different backgrounds and from different schools with disparate grading systems and grading stringency on an "even playing field" for comparison. The test supposedly measures how well students will do in medical school. In fact, it primarily indicates who will be outstanding medical students (the top MCAT performers) and who will do miserably (the worst MCAT performers). Those scoring in the middle can go either way. The MCAT repeatedly has been shown to be a reasonably good predictor of performance both in medical school and on Step 1 of the USMLE, although combining MCAT scores with undergraduate GPAs slightly improved these correlations. The MCAT Verbal Reasoning score combined with the undergraduate nonscience GPA is most closely associated with performance in the clinical years and on Steps 2 and 3 (clinical) of the USMLE. Above all, the MCAT is an endurance test, leading one student to suggest that medical schools might do just as well having students run a marathon, with those who finish first having the first pick of schools to attend.

Although you need to do well on the MCAT, good scores on this test will not substitute for a poor GPA. For those with borderline grades that have improved over time, however, excellent MCAT scores can suggest to medical schools that you have enough potential for them to take a chance on admitting you.

Your premed adviser and the AAMC's MCAT webpage (www.aamc.org/mcat) have detailed information about MCAT schedules, as well as samples of useful study materials.

When to Take the MCAT

The MCAT is administered twice a year, on a Saturday in mid-April and in mid-August. For an additional $10 fee and with advance notification, special Sunday administrations (on the same weekend as the Saturday administration) can be arranged for those with religious or other unavoidable conflicts.

Many undergraduates take the test either in April of their junior year or in August of their senior year. Most medical schools and the AAMC suggest that students take the MCAT in April, about 18 months before they plan to enter medical school. This makes sense for several reasons. Taking the test in April allows you, if you wish, to participate in the Early Decision Program (see Chapter 26). If you don't do well in April, you then have a chance to retake it in August. Finally, since few students benefit from the additional course work taken between the April and August administrations, why not take the test in April and get it over with? The exceptions are those students who use the summer to take science courses or MCAT prep courses.

Still, more people continue to take the MCAT in the "fall" (actually August). In 2002, for example, out of 57,539 examinees, 25,629 (45%) took the test in April and 31,910 (55%) took it in August. Many of the August examinees, however, are repeating the test that they first took in April. The major problem with taking the April administration is that you will have to prepare for the exam while you are also studying for your regular classes. Even if you lighten your class schedule during that time period, this is not an easy endeavor and can be quite stressful.

Another option, which is not frequently mentioned, is to take the MCAT in August after your sophomore year. The advantages of this strategy are that you will probably have completed the basic science courses covered on the test and you will have an entire summer to study (assuming you don't have to work) or to take an MCAT prep course. If you entered college with advanced standing in some of your premed courses, you may even have taken upper-level science courses by the time you take the MCAT. Taking the test in your sophomore year also gives you the opportunity to apply to an early-decision program if you do well, or to retake the test if you do poorly. The main reason not to take the MCAT at this time is that you have not yet completed the course work covered on the exam.

Some postbaccalaureates take the MCAT before they have completed the required premed subjects covered on the exam. In that case, they have to find alternative ways of studying, as one student did:

> **The only courses I needed for medical school were my science requirements. I realized that if I took the MCAT before taking all the classes, I could shave a whole year off the admissions process. I learned organic chemistry and physics in the Test & Tape library of the Kaplan course and did very well on the MCAT.**

Another student in a similar situation tried the same tactic but, in the end, barely made it to the exam:

> **I used a prep course, since I hadn't taken physics or organic chemistry when I took the MCAT. When I took the MCAT, I was an active duty military officer and for a month prior to the exam had been playing war games in a remote area of Washington State. I had to be helicoptered out of the mountains to take the test and then flown back. A bit stressful. [I'll bet!]**

— Description of the MCAT —

The MCAT is a grueling, multiple-choice examination developed by medical school admission officers, premed instructors, medical educators, practicing physicians, AAMC staff, and testing experts, all working under the auspices of the Association of American Medical Colleges. While the test's format was revised in 1991 to emphasize a broader knowledge of the humanities and the natural and social sciences, it still concentrates on subjects near and dear to the premed curriculum.

Rather than simply asking for a regurgitation of memorized facts, the MCAT is designed to test how well you can scan information, synthesize data, and solve problems. It tests information processing, rather than information collecting.

The Test Day

A typical test-day schedule (Figure 11.1) includes 5¾ hours of testing plus time for breaks. The day of the test, *you must arrive on time*; you will not be allowed to take the test if you are late. Normally, you must be there no later than 8 a.m. What time the test actually begins will depend upon the number of registrants at that site and the amount of time needed to check in all of them. Therefore, when you arrive to take the test, realize that there will be delays while proctors check individuals against their registration photos and complete other preliminary paperwork. Stay calm! You will normally be able to leave by about 5:30 p.m.

Physical Sciences Section

The Physical Sciences section lasts 100 minutes and covers information, divided equally, from the introductory undergraduate courses in general chemistry and general noncalculus physics. Questions consist entirely of science problems and may include data presented in graphs, tables, or charts. The questions test examinees' knowledge of basic concepts and their ability to interpret data and solve problems. There are 10 or 11 long, medically relevant passages to read (each about 250 words), each with 4 to 8 multiple-choice questions. In addition, there are 15 standalone multiple-choice questions not based on a written passage.

Passages may include descriptive information with diagrams, problems to solve, or persuasive arguments. They may describe experiments, instruments (often with diagrams), or study designs. Passages in this section are presented in one of four formats:

1. ***Information*** passages present problems from previously published material. A good place to find this type of passage, with the turgid writing style, is *The New England Journal of Medicine*. It is available online, and in most public and all medical libraries.
2. ***Problem-solving*** passages are similar to the word problems found in science texts.
3. ***Research study*** passages describe all or part of a scientific experiment.
4. ***Persuasive argument*** passages attempt to convince the reader that particular results are correct or that specific methods, evidence, or conclusions are appropriate.

The answers to some questions, especially those dealing with organic chemistry or physics, may require multiple mathematical calculations or the understanding of abstract and integrated concepts. However, knowledge of calculus is not needed, nor is memorization of unusual constants, formulas, and conversion factors; these are all provided if needed. (A periodic table is provided in the test booklet.) The questions in this section often resemble those in textbooks.

FIGURE 11.1

Typical MCAT Schedule

Section	Number of Questions	Time (minutes)
Morning Session		
Physical Sciences	77	100
(Break)		10
Verbal Reasoning	60	85
(Lunch Break)		60
Afternoon Session		
Writing Sample	2	60
(Break)		10
Biological Sciences	77	100

A detailed list of the topics that will be covered on this section can be found in a file called "Topics for Biological and Physical Sciences Section of the MCAT," accessed through the AAMC's "About the MCAT" webpage at www.aamc.org/students/mcat/about/start.htm.

As a group, math and statistics majors score the best on this section. Physical science majors also do well on this section.

Verbal Reasoning Section

The Verbal Reasoning section tests examinees' ability to read and comprehend information while under pressure and to critically reason and assess the material. There are 9 or 10 long passages (each 500 to 600 words), each associated with 5 to 10 multiple-choice questions. All information necessary to answer the questions is presented in the passages. The passages are drawn from the humanities, natural sciences, and social sciences, but the subject content itself is not tested. These passages are "arguments," in which the author presents and defends a controversial position to try to persuade the reader to accept his viewpoint. The passages are taken from previously published material, so they are often truncated versions of the originals. This can make them sound somewhat awkward, but the questions can still be answered based on the material presented.

Four types of questions generally accompany these passages.

1. ***Comprehension*** questions require examinees to identify, justify, and synthesize the central concept of the passage. For example, what is the writer saying, how is the position justified, what assumptions are made, and what conclusions are drawn? They may also ask for comparisons of information or the definitions of terminology contained in the passage. If the question begins "According to the author," the answer should be in the passage.
2. ***Evaluation*** questions ask whether the author's reasoning, information sources, claims, and conclusions can be supported by the evidence presented in the passage.
3. ***Application*** questions ask examinees to apply the information contained in the passage to hypothetical or real-world situations.
4. ***Incorporation*** questions require examinees to decide how the writer's argument is affected by new information supplied in the question.

Although MCAT study materials break down these question types even further, independent experts suggest that doing so is not particularly useful.

One way to prepare for this section is to critically read newspaper editorials, since they are about the same length as the passages. (It is useful to get into this habit, since medical school interviewers will ask you about current events.) Others suggest taking college courses that use argument and reasoning skills, such as rhetoric, logic, and composition. In fact, many medical schools require or recommend that applicants take these courses (Figure 15.4). These courses also will help to improve your score on the MCAT Writing Sample.

When taking the Verbal Reasoning section, don't leave any questions blank expecting to return to them later. Answer each question when you get to it. You won't have enough time to reread the long passage and answer the question. You can, of course, skip an entire item (a passage and its questions) and return to it later, since that does not take any more time than it would have initially. Also, while reading the passage, systematically highlight important words or phrases. (Highlighters are not permitted.) Some examinees use a double line under the passage's main theme, a single line under principal details supporting the theme, and brackets around [secondary details].

As a group, Humanities majors do the best on this section. Everyone else trails behind. Note that being a native English speaker (i.e., having learned English at age 10 or earlier) markedly helps examinees in this section. While native English speakers have average scores of 8.0, those who learned English at age 11 or older scored a mean of between 4.9 (native Spanish speakers) to 5.9 (native speakers of all other languages).

Writing Sample Section

The Writing Sample section comes at the start of the afternoon session. Examinees have one hour to complete two essays on different topics (30 minutes for each essay). This portion of the test examines critical thinking, the ability to organize ideas, and writing skills. A real danger lies in the fact that this section comes just after lunch. Overeating may make you sleepy (i.e., ineffective, sloppy), so don't have a big meal.

In the past, the topics have been related to architecture, art criticism, astronomy, economics, ecology, evolutionary biology, language development, literature, literary criticism, patients' rights, and sociology. The topics do *not* include: the technical content of biology, chemistry, physics, or mathematics; the medical school application process; why you chose medicine as a career; social or cultural issues that are not within the general experience of MCAT examinees; and religious or other emotionally charged issues.

The "topic" provided for each essay consists of a statement that expresses an opinion, discusses a philosophy, or describes a policy. It is usually a quotation (see examples below). You must accomplish three basic tasks in each essay.

1. You must explain or interpret the quotation. Your explanation should be as complete as possible. The statements are not straight facts or self-evident, so they cannot generally be explained in a single sentence.
2. You must oppose the concept by finding an instance in which it might be contradicted or in which it might not be applicable. Here, it is useful to provide a specific example supporting the topic, as well as one opposing it, along with further exploration of the statement's meaning.
3. You must resolve the conflict between the initial statement and the contradiction that you have described. In doing this, you should attempt to apply your understanding of the topic to more general issues raised by the conflict between the opposing views.

Two graders independently score each essay. (A third is used if there is a discrepancy.) They expect an essay to flow logically from one point to the next. The score is determined by the depth, cohesiveness, and clarity with which each task is addressed and by the extent to which ideas are developed. The essay should be written using acceptable grammar, syntax, and punctuation, but at "first-draft" level. Don't waste valuable time polishing your writing and thereby ending up with incomplete essays. Do take the time to *make your handwriting legible*, since real people have to read it. If they cannot decipher your scratchings, the essay will be graded "X" for "Not Ratable."

The following examples are typical of the essay questions (and are the examples the AAMC has used in seminars to explain this test section):

> Consider this statement: **Architecture in general is frozen music.**
>
> Write a unified essay in which you perform the following tasks: Explain what you think the above statement means. Describe a specific situation in which architecture could be compared to music. Discuss the relationship between the arts that this phrase suggests.
>
> ---
>
> Consider this statement: **In matters of principle, stand like a rock; in matters of taste, swim with the current.**
>
> Write a unified essay in which you perform the following tasks: Explain what you think the above statement means. Describe a specific situation in which it is hard to distinguish between principle and taste. Discuss what criteria one should use to distinguish between principle and matters of taste.

The key to answering these questions appropriately is to first read them carefully and note what they are asking you to do. Successful essay writers will quickly jot down an outline covering the points requested and then write them in prose. They (1) develop the central idea for their essay, (2) synthesize their concepts and ideas, and (3) present their ideas cohesively and logically.

Those who begin to write without these few minutes of advance planning doom themselves to sloppy, disorganized essays. Remember, an essay's quality, not its length, determines the score. You can see sample essays, along with descriptions about how they are graded, on the MCAT practice tests (www.aamc.org/students/mcat/practicetests.htm). These samples were developed by the people who will grade you.

As a group, humanities and social sciences majors do the best on this section. Also note that being a native English speaker (i.e., having learned English at age 10 or earlier) markedly helps examinees in this section. While native English speakers had average scores of "O" on this section, those who learned English at age 11 or later had mean scores of "M" (native Spanish and Asian-language speakers) or "N" (native speakers of all other languages).

Biological Sciences Section

The Biological Sciences section lasts 100 minutes and has 77 questions that cover information contained in undergraduate first-year introductory general biology (~75%) and organic chemistry (~25%) courses. It consists entirely of science problems and may include data presented in graphs, tables, or charts. The questions test examinees' knowledge of basic biological concepts and their ability to interpret data and solve problems. A detailed list of the topics covered in this section can be found in a file called "Topics for Biological and Physical Sciences Section of the MCAT," accessed through the AAMC's "About the MCAT" webpage.

There are 10 or 11 long, medically relevant passages (each about 250 words), each with 4 to 8 multiple-choice questions. Passages may include descriptive information with diagrams, problems to solve, and persuasive arguments. They may describe experiments, instruments (often with diagrams), or study designs. The problem-based questions often require an advanced understanding of research methods and the interpretation of results in biology or organic chemistry. Passages in this section are the same formats as those described above in the "Physical Sciences Section."

In addition, there are 15 standalone multiple-choice questions which are not based on the descriptive passages.

As a group, humanities, math, statistics, and physical science majors do the best on this section. Biological science majors trail behind them.

MCAT Test Items

To reassure you that the MCAT is assembled with considerable care, the following is an outline of how each test item is prepared.

1. Undergraduate and medical school faculty, at an MCAT editor's request, write test items for a specific content area.
2. MCAT's editors review and revise these items for technical accuracy and clarity. They often request up to three times the number of items they will finally need, since so many are rejected.
3. MCAT technical editors, who are content experts in the tested areas, review the questions for technical accuracy. "Bias editors," who represent various racial and ethnic groups, also review the questions for potentially objectionable or inaccessible material. (Examples of item bias include a question about facial flushing that was considered biased against blacks, and an item about air pressure and scuba diving that was thought to favor men, as they might have more experience with the sport.) Both groups suggest improvements.
4. MCAT test editors review the suggestions and revise the items.
5. Acceptable items are field-tested during actual MCAT administrations. (There is no way to tell which are the "real" questions and which are not.)

6. Field-test results are examined for validity and bias. Acceptable items are added to subsequent tests.
7. Following each MCAT administration, the staff usually gets more than 150 letters from examinees describing items they consider flawed. These letters are evaluated before the tests are scored. If the staff finds that any of these individuals have detected previously unnoticed flaws in a test item, then an individual question, or even all of the questions associated with a passage, will not be scored.

— Preparing for the MCAT —

Almost anybody can do well on the MCAT as long as he or she develops a sound study plan and begins preparing for the exam as early as possible. Start by downloading the AAMC's "Topics for Biological and Physical Sciences Section of the MCAT," accessed through the AAMC's "About the MCAT" webpage, during your freshman year. As you take your course work, you can compare each class syllabus with the "Topics," and highlight the areas that are important to learn well the first time. That makes it easier to review the material before the MCAT.

Then, get into the mindset that you plan to take the test only once. That way, you will give it the preparation it deserves. If you entered college determined to become a physician, you should have included those courses necessary to do well on the exam. It's best to complete at least the minimum premed curriculum (including biochemistry even if it isn't part of the curriculum) before you take the test. Then you will at least recognize the questions, even if you do not know all the answers. Beginning your preparation early will also allow you the freedom to choose the time when you want to take the exam, rather than having it thrust upon you.

Most students know the study techniques that work best for them. Use this knowledge to determine how you will prepare for the MCAT. Draw up your plan of action, and decide if you are going to study alone, with a study group, or enroll in a commercial prep course. Then, obtain all available MCAT materials from the AAMC. Sometimes it's hard to fit the studying in, but if you're serious about it, you can do it, as this student showed:

> **I had a seven-month old daughter at the time I was preparing for the MCAT and was working about 50 hours a week as an engineer (as was my wife). I was also taking two premedical courses and an MCAT prep course on the weekends. The only time I had free to study was from 3 a.m. to 6 a.m. I did that every morning for three months. [Now, that's dedication!]**

Keep all your textbooks, laboratory manuals, and laboratory notebooks for the courses that cover any topics included in the MCAT outline. Use these books not only to review for the MCAT, but also to help you link topics between various courses. For example, if you encounter the Krebs cycle in your biochemistry course, see how it was discussed in the biology course you already completed. This provides a better insight into various topics and gives you the necessary cross-linkage of concepts between the subject areas.

Since the test heavily favors those who read quickly with good comprehension, and since it relies so heavily on problem-solving ability, taking courses to improve these skills will help you as much as learning the specific test content will. For example, many of the basic-science principles with which you should be thoroughly familiar will be buried within complex paragraphs to make them harder to recognize.

You should take a writing course. Most premed students concentrate on the science portions of the MCAT and then do poorly on the writing section. Most physicians (and presumably premeds) can write a coherent sentence. Therefore, it does not take much skill to do well on the MCAT writing section. You simply have to prepare for it as you do for the science sections.

The best preparation for the Writing Sample section is to write essays. Write at least one essay each week under the same time constraints (30 minutes) as on the test. Use prompts from the *MCAT Writing Sample Prompts* webpage, accessed through the AAMC's "About the MCAT" website. Other sources include commercial MCAT books and books with provocative quotations, such as *Bartlett's Familiar Quotations.* These are available in all libraries.

Although mathematics is not a separate MCAT section, you will need to know basic math, including algebra and trigonometry, to solve some questions. In addition, many of the questions incorporate tables, graphs, or diagrams, which you will have to interpret.

Since the MCAT is a long series of examinations, consider it a "test marathon." Runners train for a marathon by progressively running longer distances. When training for the MCAT, take as many "Practice Tests" (old or simulated tests) as you possibly can. Take the tests under the same time constraints as you will have during the real test. This will give you a feel for how you should deal with different types of test questions.

A national survey of medical students found that 90% felt that individual study was important to their success on the MCAT. Nearly two-thirds felt that studying old MCATs and preparatory books benefited them the most. One-fourth believed that formal preparatory courses were important to their success. Of course, everyone learns a little differently. Those who seemed to benefit from structured courses included students who had been out of school for a while, nonscience majors, and those who had not yet taken some of the required premed courses (usually postbaccalaureate students).

Materials for Self-Study

A wide variety of materials are available to help students prepare for the MCAT. The most important ones to get are those produced by the Association of American Medical Colleges, the folks who run the MCAT. (Good source, right?) These include the following:

- ***MCAT Essentials*** (Online; free). This annual publication is available through the MCAT webpage (www.aamc.org/students/mcat/start.htm). It contains all the information you need to know about registering, what to bring with you, who to contact with problems or for additional information, how to obtain and send scores, the basic exam design, and changes to the exam from prior years. It can be downloaded to your computer or printed.
- ***MCAT Discussion Board*** (Online; free). Enrolling in either of the AAMC's free or paid MCAT practice tests allows students to participate in this discussion board. It includes discussions on general topics, test content, and Web resources for the MCAT. The AAMC's MCAT staff also answers questions. You should take advantage of this extremely valuable resource, which is less publicized than it should be.
- ***MCAT Practice Test*** (Online; free). Accessed from the MCAT "Practice Tests" webpage, the test requires online registration (no charge) before you can use it. It contains questions used on recent MCATs that can be taken timed, and provides feedback. Even without signing up for the entire free practice test, you can see representative questions at "MCAT sample" on the MCAT homepage.
- ***MCAT Practice Tests Online*** ($40 each or $80 for three tests in 2003). Updated versions of the online free Practice Test. This is the best way to test your readiness for the MCAT and to determine your weaknesses, so you can concentrate your studying in those areas. The tests, based on prior MCAT questions, allow the examinee to select items by content area, skill, or item difficulty. It provides automated scoring and diagnostic reports to help you focus your studying. These tests can be ordered through the "MCAT Shopping Cart" on the MCAT "Practice Tests" webpage.
- ***MCAT Practice Tests***—Paper versions ($40 each + postage/handling for two tests and solutions in 2003—the tests are the same as two of the online tests). These tests are also used by some commercial review courses. They can be ordered through the "MCAT Shopping Cart" on the MCAT "Practice Tests" webpage.

There are many books describing the MCAT that are prepared by commercial sources, but the formats vary and not all are up-to-date. Ask your premed adviser which ones the other students have found most helpful.

If you plan to study on your own, you also need reference materials containing the subject matter that the MCAT tests. Textbooks, especially ones you've used, are excellent. Highlight the important parts of your books when you take your courses, so you can more effectively review them. Lecture notes may be less helpful, because they are often too detailed for MCAT preparation. It is important to methodically review the following texts:

- Biology text and laboratory manuals
- General chemistry text and laboratory manuals
- Physics (without calculus)
- Mathematics (without calculus)

Use your texts along with the outlines provided in the "Topics for Biological and Physical Sciences Section of the MCAT." Using an MCAT practice test, do at least 20 problems in each of the Verbal Reasoning, Physical Sciences, and Biological Sciences sections every day.

When reviewing for the MCAT, remember that you need not recall specific facts, but you must be familiar with how to apply various concepts. (When necessary, specific facts are provided in the questions.) Even so, one medical student claims that his success on the MCAT came from watching *Jeopardy* for three months prior to the test.

Commercial Preparation Courses

Commercial prep courses do not replace personal study plans. They only help structure and supplement such plans. Even if you use a prep course's study guides, you still must review other reference materials on relevant MCAT topics. The best use of such courses, if you use them, is to map out your study schedule and to supplement your weak subjects. Always keep commercial courses and aids in perspective. *You are the key ingredient in doing well on the MCAT.* Unless you put forth the effort, no course or study aid will help you.

Aside from their exorbitant cost (from more than $1,000 for a classroom course to about $4,000 for private tutoring), a problem with commercial courses is that, because they must cater to large audiences, their course schedules are rigid. For example, the Kaplan (www.kaplan.com), Princeton Review (www.princetonreview.com), and similar classroom-based courses are usually designed in 5- or 10-week periods. Such time frames may not work for you. Premed advisers have also complained that some commercial course instructors have given attendees bad advice concerning the entire medical school application strategy, including when to take the MCAT.

A prep course only succeeds for those who are willing to put in the time to do the assigned work. It is important not only to attend all their classes, but also to visit their "Test Center" as often as possible to work on practice tests and review the correct answers. These courses aren't cheap—so get your money's worth.

According to at least one study, taking commercial prep courses makes only a negligible difference in MCAT scores: 0.2 points or less if taken before taking the MCAT or 0.2 to 0.4 points if taken before retesting. The Writing Sample score was unchanged. If you develop a good study plan and follow that plan closely, you have an excellent chance of scoring well on the MCAT.

— Test-Taking Hints —

These hints have been gathered from successful MCAT examinees (those who got into medical school). Use them to good advantage.

- Bring your admission card, a passport-type photo, at least three *presharpened* number 2 pencils, a good eraser, and some high-carbohydrate snacks to eat during the breaks. Also, remember to bring a watch—without a calculator, timer, camera, or other built-in advanced device—to help pace yourself (you may not use the alarm since it will disturb others), and two ballpoint pens with black ink for the essays. You need two, because Murphy's Law says that if you bring only one, it won't work.

- Calculators, computers, a timer (other than an unenhanced watch), and, of course, notes may *not* be taken into the exam room. Other banned items include beeping or calculator watches, pagers, cell phones, slide rules (does anyone still use them?), cameras, radios, tape recorders, highlighters, colored pencils, scrap paper, lapboards/deskboards, and other aids. If you bring any of these, the proctors will hold them during the test. Earplugs are also forbidden during the test.
- Get a good night's sleep before the exam. If necessary, find someplace other than the dorm, fraternity, or sorority house to sleep. (Remember, it will be a Friday night.)
- Don't study the morning of the exam, or even the night before. Do something relaxing (but not mind-altering). Reducing stress will help you on the test.
- Eat a low-carbohydrate, high-protein breakfast.
- Some examinees feel better if they visit the examination room before the test. You can generally do this until the exam day, but understand that the room may be changed to accommodate additional examinees or for other reasons. You will not be able to select your seat; the proctors will assign one to you.
- Dress very comfortably. Bring a sweater, sweatshirt, or jacket in case the room gets too cold—a common problem. The AAMC says that it gets more complaints that the rooms are too hot, so be prepared.
- Allow enough time to transfer your answers from the test booklet to the answer sheet, since if answers aren't on the answer sheet, they won't be scored. This must be done within the time allotted for each section, because no additional time is allowed to transfer answers.
- Don't discuss the test during breaks—it will only serve to distract and depress you. Do stretching exercises, meditate, and check out the bathroom.
- After the test, go out and celebrate with people who have *not* taken it. You don't want to rehash the test or go over the "right" answers with anyone.

— Test Disruptions —

Premed advisers report that there are disruptions at about 100 MCAT testing sites each year. While many of these are minor and affect relatively few test-takers, others have literally been disasters. In recent years, marching bands practiced and athletic events occurred just outside of the testing rooms, fire alarms required the rooms to be evacuated, and tornadoes blew through the area, panicking everyone. My own story is somewhat dated, but certainly sticks with me.

> **The night before the MCAT, civil unrest (a riot) took place on campus. Although Vietnam protests were occurring regularly, this was somewhat unexpected. What began with a rather unruly protest march quickly gave way to a massive police presence, including the widespread use of tear gas. The tear gas was liberally deposited not only among the protesters, but also in the dorms, the chapel, and in the large lecture hall where the MCAT was to be given the next day. Since my dorm was one of those tear-gassed, I spent a very uncomfortable night in a classroom building far enough away from the melee so that only some of the tear gas seeped in. The next morning when I showed up for the test, I was understandably depressed, since I felt my performance would suffer due to my lack of rest. Only when I arrived did I discover that my limited exposure to the tear gas had built up my tolerance enough so that I wasn't bothered by the residual tear gas in the room. Most of my fellow test-takers weren't so fortunate. No adjustments to anyone's scores were made.**

Other, more recent, test-takers have also endured disruptions during the MCAT.

> **At an April MCAT, having just read a passage on the nutritional value of fast foods, the examinee was geared up to answer the eight questions in the Verbal Reasoning section that followed. The questions were about astrophysics! She panicked. Unfortunately, the printers had made a mistake on some test booklets. Test proctors were in a quandary about what to**

> do, and the hubbub disturbed many others taking the exam. (Since each exam site has multiple forms of the exam, only some of the examinees were directly affected.) Eventually, the printing error forced the AAMC to rethink their quality-control procedures. All examinees at the affected sites were given the option of retaking the exam in August at no charge, and could have their test either voided or scored and sent with an explanatory letter to any score recipient.
>
> The night before one MCAT administration, a huge storm shut down the air conditioning at a test site in the desert Southwest. As the test began, the temperature hovered at over 100°F. Water from a burst pipe flooded the front row where examinees were sitting. They reported that it was so hot that they could see steam rising from the pooled water. Vapor curled their test booklets and answer sheets. Just outside of the exam room, workers used chain saws to dismember trees felled in the storm. Nevertheless, the exam continued. However, this was not the end of the saga for these hapless examinees. About a month later, they were notified that their Writing Sample essays had been lost and they would have to retake that portion of the test. Unfortunately, some students were not notified (they were out of the country) and their entire tests were voided. The AAMC sent an explanatory letter with all these students' scores. No one knows if medical schools considered these letters, but at least some of these students are now in medical school.
>
> During one MCAT administration, a gunman burst into a San Francisco test center just before the last MCAT section began. Waving his gun, he screamed, "I want the test. I want the test." Many examinees ducked on the floor, fearful for their lives. After a violent struggle, proctors and test-takers subdued the would-be robber, who supposedly wanted the test to sell on the black market. "After I saw blood around his head and on the floor, it was hard to finish the test," said one man, who nevertheless completed the exam. Some examinees did not complete the test. All were offered an opportunity to take a different version of the test the following weekend. Very few people took them up on their offer.

If there is a disruption at your test site, immediately write a letter to the MCAT Program Office (P.O. Box 4056, Iowa City, IA 52243-4056). Detail the disruption and specifically ask that a letter describing the incident be included with your scores. Have your friends who took the test do the same thing. Also, immediately contact your adviser, describe the incident, and give her a copy of the letter you sent.

The response from the AAMC has varied depending on the nature of the incident and the number of people who complained. In some instances, especially where it was "an act of God," they included a letter explaining the circumstances with the scores they send from that site. In some cases, however, they have not responded at all. The best that can be said is that their policy for dealing with disruptions is inconsistent.

— MCAT Scores —

You cannot "pass" or "fail" the MCAT, although you can do relatively well or "bottom out." Examinees score points for correct answers. There is no penalty for incorrect answers. Once you take the MCAT, the scores remain on your record; you may not cancel or delete them.

Four separate scores are reported: Verbal Reasoning, Physical Sciences, Writing Sample, and Biological Sciences. Examinees receive both a "raw score," which is the number of correct answers, and a "scaled score" for each test section. Scaled scores are graded using a 1 (worst) to 15 (best) scale for all sections except the Writing Sample. The Writing Sample is graded from "J" (worst) through "T" (best), with scores of "L" and lower designating the bottom 14% and those of "R" or higher the top 11%. Most people's scores are scattered in the "M" through "P" range, with the 50th percentile being "P."

Medical schools and the American Medical College Application Service (AMCAS) receive the scaled scores and the Writing Sample letter score. They also receive a Combined Score that is the total of all three numerical scores plus the letter, e.g., "31R" for someone who scored 9 on Physical Sciences, 9 on Biological Sciences, 12 on Verbal Reasoning, and "R" on the Written Sample.

What's a Good Score?

The average MCAT scaled scores are about "8" for Verbal Reasoning, Physical Sciences, and Biological Sciences and "P" for the Writing Sample.

Figure 11.2 shows the approximate number of correct answers needed to get a particular scaled score on each of the three numerically scored sections. It also shows the percentage of test-takers who get that score and how many did better and worse than that score. The exact distribution will vary slightly with each test administration, but the chart roughly approximates what your scores mean. (A similar chart for your MCAT administration will come with your scores.)

Figure 11.3 gives an overall view of how all applicants and those who were accepted scored on the MCAT (for M.D.-granting schools only). Note, however, that students' average MCAT scores (Figure 15.7) vary widely among individual schools. MCAT scores for applicants and matriculants to D.O.-granting schools are slightly lower than those for M.D.-granting schools.

Some medical schools use a formula that combines applicants' GPAs with their MCAT scores. If you ask, the school may tell you how much weight they apply to each figure. This will will help you evaluate your chances of acceptance.

Only about two-thirds of those who take the MCAT actually apply to medical school. Some apply to other health-related schools. Many, however, do not score well and thus never apply. This self-screening increases the average scores of all applicants and, subsequently, matriculants.

FIGURE 11.2

Percentages Correlating to MCAT Raw and Scaled Scores

	Verbal Reasoning			Physical Sciences			Biological Sciences		
Score	Number Correct[1]	Examinee Percentile Rank	% Examinees with Score[2]	Number Correct[1]	Examinee Percentile Rank	% Examinees with Score[2]	Number Correct[1]	Examinee Percentile Rank	% Examinees with Score[2]
15	59–60	99.9+	0.1%	76–77	99.9+	0.1%	76–77	99.9+	0.1%
14	57–58	99.7–99.8	0.2	74–75	98.7–99.8	1.2	73–75	99.4–99.8	0.5
13	54–56	97.9–99.6	1.8	70–73	96.2–98.6	2.5	70–72	96.0–99.3	3.4
12	51–53	94.3–97.8	3.6	65–69	91.1–96.1	5.1	66–69	91.0–95.9	5.0
11	48–50	83.8–94.2	10.5	62–64	83.9–91.0	7.2	62–65	81.2–90.9	9.8
10	44–47	68.2–83.7	15.6	58–61	71.8–83.8	12.1	58–61	64.0–81.1	17.2
9	41–43	51.0–68.1	17.2	54–57	58.9–71.7	12.9	53–57	47.1–63.9	16.9
8	37–40	35.6–50.9	15.4	48–53	42.4–58.8	16.5	48–52	30.4–47.0	16.7
7	34–36	25.3–35.5	10.3	42–47	25.7–42.3	16.7	44–47	21.2–30.3	9.2
6	30–33	14.4–25.2	10.9	36–41	12.7–25.6	13.0	39–43	13.5–21.1	7.7
5	27–29	7.5–14.3	6.9	30–35	4.8–12.6	7.9	34–38	6.8–13.4	6.7
<4	0–26	0–7.4	7.4	0–29	0–4.7	4.7	0–33	0–6.7	6.7
Mean Score[3]		8.2			8.1			8.5	
Std. Dev.		2.4			2.3			2.4	

1: The "Number Correct" will vary widely among the various forms of the test. There is no specific number of correct answers that can assure an examinee of getting a particular score. These numbers are used as generalized examples.

2: The "% Examinees with Score" will vary with each group to whom the MCAT is administered. These numbers reflect the April 2003 MCAT.

3: Mean scores for the August 2003 MCAT administration were unchanged, except for Verbal Reasoning, which dropped to 8.1.

Adapted from: Association of American Medical Colleges. *MCAT Practice Test 3R*, www.e-mcat.com/mcat2/HelpScoring.asp, accessed July 5, 2003; and AAMC MCAT examinee information for the April 2003 administration.

FIGURE 11.3

Average MCAT Scores of Applicants and Matriculants

		1998*	1999	2000	2001	2002	2003
Biological Sciences	Applicants	9.2	9.3	9.5	9.2	9.3	8.5
	Matriculants	10.2	10.2	10.2	10.1	10.2	—
Physical Sciences	Applicants	8.9	9.0	8.9	9.0	9.1	8.1
	Matriculants	9.9	10.0	10.0	10.0	10.0	—
Verbal Reasoning	Applicants	8.6	8.7	8.7	8.6	8.7	8.1
	Matriculants	9.5	9.5	9.5	9.5	9.5	—
Writing Sample	Applicants	O	P	P	P	P	O
	Matriculants	P	P	P	P	P	O

*The year medical schools first used the "new" MCAT test results.

Reporting Scores

MCAT scores are sent to examinees, AMCAS, and anyone else designated to receive them, such as premed advisers, about two months after the exam by first-class mail—scores are never released over the phone. As one recipient noted, it's "a bit like waiting for the death notice of a terminally ill relative. Even though you expect to hear at any time, you are always unprepared when word actually comes."

At the same time, MCAT scores are posted on the AAMC's "THx" (Testing History) webpage that is part of the MCAT site (www.aamc.org/mcat). Examinees can access their own scores by using their User Name and Password. (MCAT THx, AMCAS, and the AAMC's Fee Assistance Program all use the same User Name and Password.) At this time, students can designate who, other than AMCAS, should receive the scores. There is no additional charge to send MCAT scores.

In 2003, the AAMC implemented a "full disclosure" policy, meaning that when they report your scores, they will automatically send the scores from every time you took the MCAT. AMCAS will also receive all older (1991 to 2002) scores that applicants released to them. The THx reports will show *only* those older scores that you have chosen to send; you may "unselect" specific scores, if you wish. To send unreleased scores to an AMCAS school, you may either release them to AMCAS or have a THx report sent to that individual school.

Paper requests for MCAT scores earned after 1990 will not be honored. The online THx system is now the *only* way to send these MCAT scores. Paper requests will be honored only for pre-1991 MCAT scores. Note, however, that some schools and application services require your entire MCAT history as part of your application. They are in a different list on the THx system. If you elect to send scores to one of these schools, your entire THx report will be sent; you are not able to withhold any older scores.

There are only two ways to avoid having your MCAT scored—and both must occur on the day you take the test. The first is simply to leave before the test is over. This automatically voids your test, even if you had a good reason for leaving. The second is to personally ask the proctor to void your test. Once you take the entire MCAT and leave the test center, the test cannot be voided.

— Registering for the MCAT —

Registration materials are available online at the MCAT website: www.aamc.org/mcat. Materials are also available from: MCAT Program Office, P.O. Box 4056, Iowa City, IA 52243-4056; (319) 337-1357; e-mail: mcat_reg@act.org. You can also contact the program office for answers to questions and to voice any complaints. If using a courier service, send the materials to: MCAT Program Office, Tyler Building, 2255 N. Dubuque Road, Iowa City, IA 52243-0168. Deaf applicants can call (319) 337-1701 via TDD (Mon-Fri, 8:30 a.m. to 4:30 p.m. Central Time).

Examinees must preregister for the MCAT. There is no walk-in registration. You must register on time and, preferably, as early as possible. There may be limited space available at the test site nearest to you, and spots are assigned on a first-come, first-served basis. The MCAT is administered in the United States, Guam, Puerto Rico, Virgin Islands, and Canada, and at "international" sites in Australia, England, France, Germany, India, Japan, Lebanon, Qatar, and Singapore.

If you miss the "Final" registration deadline, tough luck—there are no extensions, no matter how good your sob story. The MCAT Program Office begins mailing Admission Tickets for specific test locations and MCAT Identification Cards about five weeks before the test date. Those applicants with the earliest registrations get their materials first.

If you must change test centers, send a written request, your unused Admission Ticket, and a check or money order for $20 to the MCAT Program Office at the address above. Include the code, name, and city of the test center to which you wish to go. The MCAT office must receive such requests by the late-registration deadline, and they are processed on a first-come, first-served basis.

If you have taken the MCAT three or more times, you will also need to submit evidence that you really are applying to medical schools. This evidence can be in the form of a rejection letter, a current completed application, or a letter from a medical school or premed adviser. Special permission is also needed to take the test if you are not applying for a health professions school or if you are already enrolled as a medical student.

Computer-Based Testing

MCAT administrators are gradually switching to computer-based examinations, starting with the international sites. *Computer-based MCAT testing may be introduced in the United States as early as 2005.* Those who have taken the computer-based MCAT appreciate that:

1. You can register up to two days before the test. Several wealthy procrastinators flew from the United States to London to take advantage of this.
2. You do not have to wait for others to complete a section to begin the next section. Test-takers proceed at their own pace.

Special Testing Accommodations

You may request special testing accommodations due to a disability, but you will need to provide the MCAT Program Office with a substantial amount of additional information. A 10-page description can be accessed through the MCAT webpage, www.aamc.org/students/mcat/registration.htm. Follow the "General Guidelines for All Disabilities," as well as special guidelines if your problem is "Learning Disabilities" or "Attention-Deficit/Hyperactivity (ADHD)."

In 1998, the AAMC tightened its requirements for special testing accommodation requests to match the standards of both the Association for Higher Education and Disability and the National Board of Medical Examiners. Applicants must first register for the MCAT online and state that they will be requesting special test accommodations. They then must provide written documentation, including a cover letter, to the AAMC before the late-registration deadline. The documentation can be submitted by mail/courier, or fax to the MCAT Program Office at the address above. Or submit it by e-mail to mcat_ada@act.org.

Submit your requests as early as possible, since it may take three to four weeks to process. If the MCAT office needs additional information, it can take even longer. Every test center may not be equipped to provide the special testing accommodations you need, so you may have to take the test at a center other than the one you preferred.

Cost

Taking the MCAT cost $185 in 2003. Additional fees include: $10 to take the examination on Sunday, $60 for testing at "international" sites, $50 for registering after the first deadline, $20 to change test centers, and $20 for bounced checks. All payments must be in U.S. funds and be paid by using MasterCard, VISA, or E-Payment.

Applicants with "extreme" financial hardships who are U.S. citizens or permanent residents are eligible for the AAMC's MCAT Fee Assistance Program. Be sure to apply early. If approved, applicants pay only $80 to take the test (in 2003), and pay reduced fees for the AMCAS application and the next MCAT administration, if they take take the test again. For information and application materials, go to www.aamc.org/students/applying/fap/start.htm. You can also contact: Fee Assistance Program (FAP), AAMC, 2450 N Street NW, Washington, DC 20037-1123; (202) 828-0600; fax: (202) 828-1120; e-mail: fap@aamc.org.

Partial refunds, up to $100, are available if you decide not to take the test after you have registered. Write "Refund" across your unused Admission Ticket and return it to the MCAT Program Office, P.O. Box 4056, Iowa City, IA 52243-4056. No refunds are available if you have opened the MCAT test booklet or for Sunday fees, late registration penalties, or international testing site fees. If you tell your credit card company not to pay the AAMC, they hold your scores and you cannot take the test again until you have paid your bill.

— Test Security —

How carefully does AAMC protect the exam? *Very* carefully. For example:

- During each MCAT administration, several forms of the test, each with different questions, are issued. Each of these forms has several versions with the questions in different order.
- Photographs, photo IDs, and thumbprints are used to detect impersonators. Obvious impersonators are not admitted, and suspicious cases are investigated after the test, often by using handwriting analysis.
- Proctors assign examinees to widely scattered seats, and adjacent examinees receive different forms of the test.
- Prior test-takers will not be issued the same form of the test they previously took.
- The tests are transported by bonded courier, and two people must always be present when the tests are out of secure storage. These individuals may not break the test seals or examine the test contents.
- If there are test violations, the episodes are investigated. If fraud is proven, the scores are voided and all medical schools are notified.

The MCAT is well protected, ensuring that all those who invest the time, money, and grief to take the test are likewise protected.

— How Many Times Should You Take the MCAT? —

Since the MCAT is so important, some students think that they should take the test once for practice and then again "for real." Bad move. Depending on the medical school, the MCAT report may include not only your most recent MCAT scores, but also *all previous scores*. So, which scores do medical schools use to evaluate candidates for admission? A survey by the AAMC showed that about 37% use only the most recent scores, 25% use all scores, 21% use only the highest scores, and 17% use an average of all scores.

Medical schools don't normally like to see students take the MCAT more than three times. Unless you really do miserably on your first try, don't retake the test unless you have to reapply to medical schools.

You should retake the test, however, if: (1) there is a marked discrepancy between your undergraduate performance and MCAT scores, (2) you took the test before you were prepared for it (meaning that you *will* be prepared when you take it again), (3) you were ill or had a distracting personal situation when you took the test, or (4) a medical school's admission committee recommended that you retake the test.

Figure 11.4 shows the percentage of students whose scores increased and decreased upon retaking the MCAT. On average, MCAT retesters gain 0.6 in Verbal Reasoning, 0.7 in Biological Sciences, 0.4 in Physical Sciences, and less than a letter grade on the Writing Sample.

If you score a "10" on most numerically scored sections or an "O" on the Writing Sample and retake the examination, you are as likely to get a worse score on the retake as to get a better one—except for the Physical Sciences section, where there is a much greater chance of doing worse. (The score was unchanged for just under one-third of repeaters who had initially scored at these levels.) In general, the lower your score the better your chance of improving with reexamination, although even with the lowest scores, some people don't improve upon retesting. Also, while you may improve in one section, you may do worse in others. The higher your score, the better the chance that you will score lower if you retake the MCAT.

If you retake the MCAT, you must complete the entire registration process again.

FIGURE 11.4

Percent of MCAT Retakers Changing Their Scores

Verbal Reasoning			Biological Sciences		
% with Decreased Score	Original Score	% with Increased Score	% with Decreased Score	Original Score	% with Increased Score
16%	6	60%	18%	6	73%
22	7	55	18	7	62
30	8	48	18	8	57
32	9	37	23	9	50
40	10	32	32	10	36
50	11	17	50	11	24
72	12	12	70	12	14
79	13	0	73	13	9
			99	14	0

Physical Sciences			Writing Sample		
% with Decreased Score	Original Score	% with Increased Score	% with Decreased Score	Original Score	% with Increased Score
10%	4	65%	0%	J	56%
15	5	56	11	K	66
20	6	51	18	L	61
23	7	48	23	M	43
27	8	41	41	N	45
37	9	38	41	O	41
48	10	27	48	P	35
54	11	25	21	Q	22
64	12	15	60	R	13
76	13	10	65	S	7
79	14	4	71	T	0

Adapted from: "Percent MCAT Retesters Attaining Specified Scores." www.aamc.org/students/mcat/examineedata/tables.htm, accessed June 2, 2003.

12

Applying To Medical School

For the want of a nail the shoe was lost,
For the want of a shoe the horse was lost,
For the want of a horse the rider was lost,
For the want of a rider the battle was lost,
For the want of a battle the kingdom was lost—
And all for the want of a horseshoe-nail.

— Benjamin Franklin,
Poor Richard's Almanac, 1758

The medical school application process can be daunting. Knowing how it works is the key to alleviating anxiety and doing well. If you are like most premed students, you are, in the words of one adviser, "wound so tight that I have to unscrew them from the ceiling." You can reduce your stress by learning the steps in the application process and developing an effective strategy to complete all of them on, or ahead of, time. To learn about the process, read the information below and then talk with your premed adviser.

Think of the admission process as a series of screens with progressively smaller holes. Premed students, potential applicants, and applicants are filtered out at every step. As you will see below, just how small the holes get will depend partly upon whether you can "get your act together" in a timely manner.

Timing: It's Your Future

The American Medical College Application Service (AMCAS) and the American Association of Colleges of Osteopathic Medicine Application Service (AACOMAS®) begin accepting applications on June 1, and the Texas Medical and Dental Schools Application Service (TMDSAS) begins accepting applications on May 1. It is wise to submit your materials to them as close to these dates as possible. Even though it is very advantageous for applicants, especially those who are marginal, to submit their applications early, these services receive very few applications in the first few weeks after they begin accepting them.

Many schools use "rolling admissions" systems, in which applicants who submit their materials first get the first interviews. These schools then select acceptable candidates for admission from those interviewed, and continue this process until they fill their class. Many of these individuals are admitted to medical school before other applicants are even interviewed. Therefore, it is to your advantage to get your application materials in early. Don't diminish your chances (or delude yourself into thinking that you are on track) by waiting to submit your applications until just before a medical school's official deadline. That is often too late.

One of the most common reasons that good applicants don't get into medical school is because they fail to submit the required materials on time. Medical schools have, in the past, allowed applicants some leeway with their deadlines, but since the more recent overwhelming crush of applications, most now rigidly stick to their rules. One school reported that one year they received 50 completed secondary applications after their deadline; the school wouldn't even consider those applications.

Late applications usually come from students whose credentials will barely get them through the interview screen. Such students have a habit of tardiness, and often sloppiness, in all their work. As one admission officer said, "They can't seem to get *anything* done on time." People in this group don't make the best physicians. If you want to get into medical school, send your materials in early or on time—and check to make certain that they have been received.

Keep a copy of *everything* you submit to the schools, including your applications, transcripts, and reference letters (if you can get copies). File them in a safe place, using a system that allows you to easily retrieve any document. Even if you have them on a disc or on your computer, make "hard copy" backups. Computers fail—and always at the most crucial moments, corrupting the most vital information. A sturdy cardboard file box (sometimes called a "bankers box") is inexpensive and doesn't take up too much room. A 12" x 15" x 10" box can hold about 35 files. Since medical school admission staff, college records offices, MCAT staff, and national application service staff, as well as their systems, are fallible, some of your vital materials may go astray. If you have duplicates, you can quickly mail, fax, or e-mail them another copy. And, since nearly two out of three applicants do not get accepted to medical school the first time they apply, these materials are useful if you must reapply.

Keep track of any material you receive (and when you received it) from schools. Likewise, keep track of what materials you send (and when) to each school or service bureau. Figure 12.1 is an example of one tracking system. Modify Figure 12.1 to fit your needs.

Using a Résumé

Although you don't need a résumé to apply to medical school, spending the time to prepare a good one does three things: First, it forces you to gather the facts, names, and dates you will need to complete your applications. Second, it helps you organize your thoughts about what is and is not important in your history. Third, and most important, it will be the basis of the ongoing résumé that you will keep and update throughout your career. You will soon be using it to apply for residency positions and postresidency jobs.

FIGURE 12.1

Application Record

	Schools				
Event	**U of A**	**B Med**	**UC Med**	**D School**	**U of E**
Application Deadline!!	Nov 1	Nov 15	Nov 15	Oct 15	Oct 15
Receive Catalog	Feb 20	April 8	March 6	May 16	May 3
Receive Application	May 12	May 10	May 12	May 16	May 12
Application to Typist	NA	May 15	NA	May 22	NA
Application Mailed	May 30*	June 3	May 30*	June 5	May 30*
Receipt Confirmed	June 8	June 9	June 8	June 18	June 8
Receive 2° Materials	None	None	Rejected	Aug 7	July 14
Returned 2° Materials	NA	NA	NA	Aug 10	July 17
Receipt Confirmed	NA	NA	NA	Aug 14	July 22
School Got Rec. Letters	June 20	June 12	NA	Aug 14	July 28
Interview Date	Oct 22	Dec 12	N	Jan 12	Sept 6
Accepted?	Y	W	N	N	Y
	Mar 3	Feb 15	July 30	Feb 20	Oct 15

*Designates a uniform application.

NA = Not Applicable; Y = Yes; W = Waiting List; N = No.

Putting together your first résumé can be an onerous project. If you prepare one before you complete your medical school applications, it will make completing these applications easier and faster. A résumé also allows premed committees, mock interviewers, reference-letter writers, and, occasionally, medical school interviewers, to quickly see who you are and what you have accomplished. For help preparing your résumé, see Tysinger's *Résumés and Personal Statements for Health Professionals* (see *Annotated Bibliography*).

— Medical School Applications —

Medical schools use three types of applications: *uniform applications* (AMCAS; AACOMAS; TMDSAS; Ontario Medical School Application Service), *school-specific primary applications*, and *school-specific secondary applications*. An applicant applying to 12 medical schools could conceivably need to complete *28* applications! (This, of course, doesn't include the forms used to apply for financial aid.)

About half of all medical schools require that applicants submit both a uniform application and a school-specific application. Another 20% use a uniform application as a screen and then send their own secondary application to students meeting their screening criteria (Figure 15.8). Just over 10% require only a uniform application or only their school-specific primary application. A few schools require that students who apply to special programs or declare minority status submit a supplemental form. Nearly all applicants for combined-degree curricula (e.g., medical degree plus Ph.D., M.P.H., or J.D.) must submit a separate application for entry into the additional program.

Online applications can be confusing, and some of them periodically have glitches in their systems. If you encounter any problems, see your premed adviser. They will, in all probability, have already dealt with the problem or are in contact with other advisers or the system's managers to find a solution. *Don't panic! And don't use the glitch as a reason to procrastinate!*

The AMCAS Application (M.D. Schools)

AMCAS (American Medical College Application Service) is a centralized application service that coordinates the application process for 116 medical schools and one program (this includes all but 13 U.S. M.D.-granting schools). These schools recommend and approve AMCAS's policies and procedures. In recent years, about 95% of all medical school applicants used AMCAS to apply to at least one school.

Applicants for first-year positions at AMCAS-participating schools may apply only through AMCAS. AMCAS processes and sends your application and MCAT scores to the participating medical schools to which you apply. Those applying to such schools for "admission with advanced standing" or who are transferring from other schools should contact each school directly. The primary benefit of AMCAS to applicants is the reduction of paperwork, because it allows students to send out a single initial application to most medical schools. AMCAS does not make admission decisions and does not advise applicants where to apply.

The AMCAS online application becomes available each spring, and is used to apply for medical school positions that begin the following year (about 16 months after the form is issued). The application is detailed and requires several hours to complete. It consists of the following sections:

- Biographical Information (name, birth information, contact information, residency/citizenship, race/ethnicity, languages, disadvantaged status)
- Essay (For help completing the Personal Statement portion, consult Tysinger's *Résumés and Personal Statements for Health Professionals,* listed in the *Annotated Bibliography*.)
- Postsecondary Experiences (work, volunteering, etc.)
- Schools Attended
- Transcript Requests
- Course Work (grades, specific course information)
- Grade Point Average

- Designation of medical schools to receive AMCAS application
- Application Audit (automatic notification if you have omitted any required information)
- Certification and Submission (This is where you will electronically "sign" your application. You will also certify whether you have been the subject of institutional action due to unacceptable academic performance or conduct violations, if you have ever been convicted of a felony, and if you have ever been a medical student in any country.)

Download the form so that you can answer the questions in a word processor with a spell checker and, possibly (for the essay), a grammar checker. If you save this in a text-only format, you can then cut-and-paste the result directly into the AMCAS application. Be certain to type everything just as you want the medical schools to see it. DO NOT USE ALL CAPS or all lower case. The essay limit is 5,300 characters, or about one page.

For help with any of the questions, especially the arduous task of listing your courses and grades, download and carefully read the *AMCAS Instruction Booklet*, available from the AMCAS website (www.aamc.org/students/amcas). If you have difficulty interpreting the instructions or completing the form, contact your premed office.

Transcripts

In order for your application to be processed, you must have your official transcripts sent to AMCAS. Official transcripts are required from any junior or community college, college, university, graduate school, U.S. medical school, trade school, or professional school that you have attended in the United States, Canada, or U.S. Territories, whether or not you earned any credits and whether or not the courses appear on another transcript as transfer credit.

AMCAS compares the course work information you entered against the official transcripts. After this verification process is complete, a final AMCAS GPA is calculated and your application is forwarded to the schools you indicated. AMCAS does not forward your application materials until all course work is verified. You must repeat this process each year that you apply, even if you have sent transcripts to AMCAS for prior application cycles. You should also ask each school to send you a copy of your transcript, since you will need them to complete the AMCAS application. The *Instruction Booklet* contains detailed instructions for nearly all the exceptions you can imagine (transcripts don't exist, foreign grades, noncredit courses, etc.).

Deadlines

The online AMCAS application opens in early May. Applicants may begin submitting applications in early June. This gives you a full month to work on the application prior to submitting it for processing. Apply as close to this date as possible, and you may begin receiving secondary applications from some schools during the summer and start interviewing in early October. As mentioned previously, applying early gives you an advantage at schools with a "rolling" admission policy.

AMCAS application deadlines vary depending on the schools to which you apply. They can be found under each school's listing in the AAMC's annual publication, *Medical School Admission Requirements*. These are the dates by which AMCAS must receive all of an applicant's materials except transcripts. AMCAS accepts transcripts from May 1 until two weeks after the deadline provided by each school for submitting your AMCAS application. The AMCAS deadline for all materials pertaining to the Early Decision Program, including the transcript, is August 1. Special instructions for completing the AMCAS form apply to students who have deferred entering a medical school where they have been accepted and to reapplicants from the prior year. See the *Instruction Booklet* for the instructions that meet your specific situation.

Problems that frequently delay the application processing include:

- Receipt of official transcripts without an accompanying *AMCAS Transcript Request Form* (available in the AMCAS application). This makes it difficult to match the transcript with the appropriate AMCAS application.

- Returned e-mail messages. Because e-mails are often sent to many applicants at once, they may automatically be labeled "spam" and deleted by spam filters. Turn off your spam filter or set up a separate e-mail account to use only to communicate with AMCAS, medical schools, and other medical school application services.
- Failure to complete all required AMCAS fields. Required fields are marked with a red asterisk (*) in the form.
- Improper submission of changes to an application. If you make one of the few allowable changes to the application (e.g., contact information, applying to additional schools) after submitting it, you must go through the steps to recertify and resubmit your application before the changes can be entered into the system.
- Payment problems, such as insufficient funds in a checking account or using a credit card that is "maxed out."

Cost

As of 2003–04, AMCAS charged $150 for the first application to a school and $30 for each additional school. The fee is calculated when you complete the AMCAS application, based on the number of schools receiving your application. This fee must be paid electronically by credit card or check in U.S. funds. Your AMCAS application will be placed on hold if you owe the AAMC money for any reason. They notify you if this happens, but it does delay processing your application. Individual schools charge additional fees, normally in conjunction with submission of a secondary application.

If you have "extreme financial limitations," the Fee Assistance Program (FAP) significantly reduces the cost of both the MCAT and the AMCAS application process. This program allows applicants who cannot afford the fee to have it waived for up to ten schools. You must submit your fee assistance request no later than December 1, prior to submitting your AMCAS application. It is best to apply three to four weeks before the earliest medical school deadline you have to meet. Even better, apply two months before you need to take the MCAT, since the same request (if approved) grants you a fee reduction for the test. Students must contact medical schools directly to have supplemental fees waived, although some will automatically waive their fees if the applicant has an AMCAS fee waiver. To see if you qualify and what benefits the FAP provides, go to their website at: www.aamc.org/students/applying/fap/start.htm.

Application Status

Once you initiate your online application, you can check your status by logging back on to your application welcome page, which will display your status. After you certify and submit your application, continue to check your status online or via the 24-hour automated phone system at (202) 828-0600. If you prefer to speak with an information specialist, call the AMCAS number during regular business hours. Alternatively, you can e-mail AMCAS at amcas@aamc.org or write to: AMCAS, AAMC, 2450 N Street NW, Washington DC 20037-1123.

The AACOMAS Application (D.O. Schools)

The AACOMAS (American Association of Colleges of Osteopathic Medicine Application Service) application is a single form used by 19 of the 20 D.O.-granting U.S. medical schools. (UNTHSC–Texas Osteopathic uses the TMDSAS application described below.) *Students applying for first-year positions at Osteopathic medical schools must use AACOMAS*. Those applying for "admission with advanced standing" or who want to transfer from another school should contact each school directly. The benefit of using AACOMAS is that it reduces paperwork, since students send only one set of material for their initial applications.

AACOMAS does not make admission decisions. Its only responsibility is to process, duplicate, and send your application, MCAT scores, and transcripts to the participating medical schools you have selected.

While most AACOMAS applications are filed online because it is easier and provides faster processing, the application can still be filed by submitting a paper form. The form can either be downloaded from their website (https://aacomas.aacom.org) or be requested from: AACOMAS, 5550 Friendship Blvd., Ste. 310, Chevy Chase, MD 20815; e-mail: aacomas@aacom.org.

AACOMAS, which becomes available in early spring, is used to apply for medical school positions for the following year (about 16 months after the form is issued). Most of the information requested is the same as that for AMCAS.

The application consists of the following parts:

- Biographic Information
- Parental Data
- Personal Data
- Additional Data (Military experience; Felony convictions; Relative who is a D.O. or M.D.; Volunteer experiences; Contact with D.O. profession; Prior careers; Employment; Personal statements; Honors and awards; Summer study programs)
- MCAT Data
- Colleges Attended
- Undergraduate Education
- Graduate Education
- Academic Courses
- Professional Courses
- College Designation Form

A "Personal Statement/Additional Comments" section provides space for a short essay (about 500 words), but must also be used to provide additional information for specific questions in other sections. Unless you have to use part of this space to explain prior questions, you may use it to "provide your motivation for applying to the field of Osteopathic medicine." For help with this personal statement, consult Tysinger's *Résumés and Personal Statements for Health Professionals* (see *Annotated Bibliography*).

For help listing your courses and grades, carefully read the *AACOMAS Instruction Booklet*. If you have difficulty interpreting the instructions or completing the form, get help from your premed adviser's office.

The "College Designation Form" allows you to designate which Osteopathic medical schools should receive your information. AACOMAS will then send your application materials to them. This part of the application also contains the fee schedule.

If you plan to submit the form online, first print a copy to complete in advance. If you plan to submit the paper form, give your final copy to a professional typist to complete. Your submitted application must look professional, without any errors, stains, or sloppiness.

AACOMAS accepts applications beginning June 1. Apply as close to this date as possible. If you do so, you may begin receiving secondary applications from some schools in the summer and be able to interview in early October. This gives you an advantage at schools with "rolling" admissions policies, which accept students from each group as they are interviewed until they fill their class.

Transcripts

Before you send your application to AACOMAS, arrange for them to receive your transcripts. They must receive an official transcript directly from the registrar at each of the following schools that you attended in the United States, Canada, and U.S. Territories, whether or not you earned any college credits: junior or community college, college, university, graduate school, U.S. medical school, trade school, and professional school. Also ask each school to send you a copy of your transcript, since you will need them to complete the AACOMAS application. (You must repeat the process each year that you apply, even if you have sent transcripts to AACOMAS for prior application cycles.) If AACOMAS does not receive all your transcripts, they will not be able to process your application.

Undergraduate course work taken at foreign institutions can be evaluated for U.S.-institution equivalence. If you want to include foreign course work on your Applicant Profile, the AACOMAS website has a list with contact information for the organizations approved to do this evaluation.

Be careful when you complete the application! If AACOMAS finds *major* discrepancies between your data and the information contained in your transcripts, they may either return your application to you or file an "AACOMAS Report" with the colleges you selected and with the AAMC (which also files similar reports with AACOMAS).

If an official transcript is unavailable, AACOMAS requires a letter of explanation from the school. If transfer credits are noted on a transcript, you also must supply AACOMAS with the original transcript for these courses. Grade 13 and Canadian college-level courses are not included on the AACOMAS Applicant Profile, but if a transcript for this work is provided, it will be sent to the designated medical schools. List any summer-study programs that you have attended, such as a Health Careers Opportunity Program, in the Personal Comments section. Have a copy of your Certificate of Completion sent to AACOMAS for distribution to the schools.

MCAT Scores

You must supply your MCAT scores to complete the AACOMAS application. Indicate that you wish to have your MCAT scores sent to AACOMAS when you take the test. If you failed to do this, use MCAT's online THx system (www.aamc.org/students/mcat) to obtain an Additional Score Report (ASR) form. When you return the completed form and the fee, the AAMC will forward your scores to AACOMAS. AACOMAS keeps MCAT scores on file for three years. If you have previously submitted these scores and have not retaken the test, you do not need to resubmit them.

Deadlines

The deadlines for receiving your AACOMAS application and all transcripts range from December 15 to February 15, depending upon the schools you selected. Check the AACOMAS website for the date for each school. When AACOMAS receives your completed materials, they will only forward them to the schools whose deadlines have not passed. *AACOMAS will not forward your materials after the deadline for a school has passed.*

Some Osteopathic medical schools offer Early Decision programs. Contact each school to determine their deadline for Early Decisions. Then apply to AACOMAS no later than six weeks before that date. Apply as early as you can; if things can go wrong, they will. You don't want to be denied a position because of a glitch in the process.

It takes AACOMAS from four to six weeks to process applications; applications submitted via AACOMAS online are processed slightly faster than paper applications. If you cannot view your Applicant Profile on the AACOMAS website by four weeks after submitting it, contact AACOMAS to make sure that your materials have been received.

After you submit your application, you must notify AACOMAS, in writing, if you want them to stop processing it or to change the information. If there are new or updated grades to enter, you must also send a transcript reflecting these grades.

Cost

AACOMAS charges applicants based on the number of Osteopathic medical schools to which they apply. The fees for 2003–04 ranged from $155 for one school to $630 for all 19 schools. Individual schools charge additional fees, normally for submitting secondary applications. AACOMAS accepts payment only by credit card or money orders.

The AACOMAS Fee Waiver Program allows applicants who cannot afford the fee to have it waived for applications to the first three schools. If you apply to more than three schools, you must pay the standard additional fee. To apply for a fee waiver, submit the Student Aid Report you received from the Department of Education after filing the FAFSA form to AACOMAS. (See Chapter 18: *Paying for Medical School.*) See their website for specific application information. Wait to submit your application until you receive a notice about your Fee Waiver. Those granted fee waivers, and those who qualify for them but who do not receive them only because funding no longer exists, have their names forwarded to Osteopathic medical schools to be considered for waivers of the schools' supplemental application fees.

U.S./Canadian Medical Schools Not Using AMCAS or AACOMAS

Thirteen M.D.-granting U.S. schools, all foreign medical schools, and all Osteopathic medical schools do not participate in AMCAS. One Osteopathic school does not participate in AACOMAS. The application procedures for non-AMCAS, non-AACOMAS schools are described below.

Texas Application/Matching System

Texas, as usual, goes its own way. Six M.D-granting schools (UT–Southwestern, UT– Galveston, UT–Houston, UT–San Antonio, Texas Tech, and Texas A&M) and the state's lone Osteopathic medical school (UNTHSC–Texas Osteopathic) use their own uniform application for first-year students: Texas Medical and Dental Schools Application Service (TMDSAS). (However, applicants to the M.D.–Ph.D. program at UT–Southwestern must use AMCAS.) Students applying for advanced standing or for transfers should apply directly to the medical schools.

TMDSAS functions as both an application and a matching service. Through the service, each of the seven schools receives applications, ranks applicants in order of their desirability, and matches with corresponding applicants who have ranked them highest. There are, of course, exceptions. Most often these are either non-Texas residents applying only to one school or applicants to combined-degree programs (e.g., M.D.–M.B.A., D.O.–Ph.D.), who generally apply directly to the school or through AMCAS.

Applicants must access TMDSAS online (www.utsystem.edu/tmdsas); there is no paper version of the application. The computer must support Java script and have a laser or ink-jet printer attached. You will want to print the instructions, a preview copy of your application (to see how it will look to TMDSAS), and a copy of your completed application. The computer can be either a PC or a Macintosh Power PC. For updated system and browser requirements, see the TMDSAS website. Note that some common browsers do not always work, so read this section carefully before starting.

TMADAS normally contacts applicants via e-mail. If you use a free e-mail service that quickly fills with spam, TMDSAS messages may not reach you if your in-box is full. In addition, many applicants have accidentally deleted their messages, thinking that they were spam. It may be worthwhile to pay for an e-mail account to use only for medical school and application service correspondence.

Start the TMDSAS process by requesting two transcripts from *every* junior college, college, or university you have attended: One for you to use when completing the TMDSAS form and an "official transcript" to be sent directly to TMDSAS. If you are a current student, you must wait until your spring semester grades are posted before sending the transcript. (This also means that you cannot submit your application until you have put those grades on the TMDSAS application.)

Next print and carefully review the "General Instructions," "General Instructions for Record of College Work," and "Detailed Instructions for Record of College Work" from the TMDSAS website. Apply for a personal ID (PIN) number and supply a case-sensitive password. Keep them safe, since they are your key into the system.

Answer the questions on the application in the provided text boxes. These boxes will accommodate only a limited amount of text. Although the program does not stop you from typing as much as you want, it will print only the permitted amount of text. Print a preview copy of the application to see if you need to delete or compress the text in some boxes. You may find it easier to type answers in a word processor, such as MS Word, and use the spell checking program, and then cut and paste the answer onto the application. This also is a good method for answering the essay question (see Chapter 13: *Essays, Recommendations, and Secondary Applications*).

The TMDSAS application asks all the usual questions. In addition, they want to know specifics about your Texas residency. They have an entire webpage devoted to the topic, with links to a questionnaire to help you decide if you are a Texan and to the official rules governing Texas residency. They also want a list of your reference-letter writers.

After submitting the application, send the signed "Certification Page," the nonrefundable application fee (check or money order; the amount varies with the number of schools), and photos (approximately 2 x 3 inches; one for each school). Expect TMDSAS to process your application within about two weeks. During the heaviest application periods, or if there are questions about your Texas residency, it will take longer. TMDSAS will attempt to contact you by e-mail regarding any problems and, failing a response from you, will send their query by mail, considerably delaying the process. Also, have your Health Professions Evaluation Committee send their evaluation packet to TMDSAS. If you have no committee, have two individual's letters sent there.

The TMDSAS deadlines are:

- August 1 for the Early Decision programs at Texas Tech and UNTHSC–Texas Osteopathic. August 15 for all supporting information.
- November 1 for all regular medical school applications and supporting documents (transcripts, letters, MCAT scores). November 10 for the fees, photos, and Certification pages.

Once TMDSAS distributes the applications to the medical schools, most applicants will receive secondary applications from individual schools. These must be completed and returned quickly to get an interview slot.

Applicants enter (or rearrange) the order in which they would prefer to attend University of Texas schools after completing interviews at each school. Go to the TMDSAS website and enter the ranking of the schools you want to attend under "Applicant Preference." This must be completed by January 15.

TMDSAS then runs a computer match to determine who gets initial acceptances to each UT medical school. The results of the TMDSAS medical school match are posted on their website around February 1. Applicants are matched with the school they ranked the highest among those willing to admit them. This offer is not official until applicants receive a letter from the school offering them a position, which they can accept or decline.

After accepting an offer, applicants may receive an acceptance from another school that they prefer. If so, they are responsible for withdrawing their initial acceptance and accepting the second offer.

Ontario [Canada] Medical Schools Application Service

The six medical schools in Ontario, Canada (McMaster University, University of Ottawa, Queen's University, University of Toronto, University of Western Ontario, and, beginning in 2005, Northern Ontario Medical School), use the Ontario Medical Schools Application Service (OMSAS). It can be accessed at www.ouac.on.ca/omsas. *Applicants for first-year positions may apply only through OMSAS*. The primary benefit of applying through OMSAS is the reduction of paperwork, since students send only one set of material to OMSAS for these medical schools.

The OMSAS form becomes available each summer (usually in July). It is used to apply for medical school positions that begin the following year (about 14 months after the form is issued). The application is detailed and difficult to complete. OMSAS estimates that applicants will need between 10 and 50 hours to complete the application. There is a detailed, 33-page booklet describing the OMSAS process and the Ontario medical schools at http://compass.ouac.on.ca/shopouac/omsas_english/pdf/b_omsas_e.pdf.

Applications must be completed in English. However, if you are applying to the University of Ottawa, you may use French. It is important to provide OMSAS with a valid e-mail address, so that they can notify you of any problems with your application.

Applicants must arrange to have official transcripts for *all* postsecondary education sent to OMSAS, 170 Research Lane, Guelph, ON, N1G 5E2, Canada. Transcripts must be received between August 1 and October 15. Individuals currently attending Ontario universities must use the Transcript Request Form (www.ouac.on.ca/omsas) to order their final transcripts. Those with non-Canadian/non-U.S. education course work must have their grades assessed and a GPA calculated by World Education Services ((416) 972-0070; (886) 343-0070; www.wes.org/ca).

Three "Confidential Assessment Forms" (found in the application) must be sent directly to OMSAS by referees, one of whom should be a nonacademic character reference. OMSAS will not forward more than three of these forms to medical schools. However, applicants at U.S. schools with premed advisory committees can submit the committee's recommendation along with the three required forms.

Premed committees should *not* also submit Confidential Assessment Forms. All forms must be received by October 15. OMSAS must also receive your MCAT scores by this date.

OMSAS charges a basic fee ($175 Canadian in 2003) plus a fee for each medical school receiving your materials. There is another small fee for applicants with mailing addresses outside Canada. OMSAS must receive the fees (in Canadian funds) by October 31 as a check, money order, credit card payment, or through selected internet/telephone bill payment services. All fees are nonrefundable.

Once OMSAS receives your application, they will send an acknowledgment within three weeks. If you haven't heard by then, contact them. Once they receive your transcripts, they send a Verification Report that details any missing transcripts or Confidential Assessments.

OMSAS does not make admission decisions. Its only responsibility is to process, duplicate, and send your application, MCAT scores, premed committee recommendation letter or Confidential Assessment Forms, and transcripts to the participating medical schools you select. There is a place on the application to indicate which schools should receive your information.

Ontario medical schools begin notifying applicants who are accepted on May 31. Applicants must respond to OMSAS by June 14. While students can hold only one acceptance to an OMSAS-participating school at a time, they may provisionally accept an offer pending their acceptance to a school they prefer.

Other M.D.-granting Schools

There are 17 U.S./Canadian medical schools that do not participate in AMCAS, AACOMAS, TMDSAS, or OMSAS. They are (C=Canadian school):

- Alberta (C)
- Baylor
- British Columbia(C)
- Brown
- Calgary (C)
- Columbia
- Dalhousie (C)
- Laval (C)
- McGill (C)
- Montréal (C)
- Newfoundland (C)
- New York Univ.
- Saskatchewan (C)
- Sherbrooke (C)
- U. MO–Kansas City
- U. North Dakota
- Univ. Rochester

Contact the individual schools to obtain an application. Each has a different deadline, so read their instructions carefully. If you expect them to seriously consider your application, do not simply send a copy of your AMCAS Application!

Many of these schools' applications for the next school year are not available until after July 1. The state-supported schools on this list require out-of-state applicants to send a second request for an application after they have received the school's initial information.

— Bad Options: The Desperate Application —

Some people fail to get accepted into medical school and then try some pretty bizarre things to get in. One desperate applicant posted this classified ad under the heading "In search of" in *USA Today* (sounds like a good candidate for medical school!):

> Looking for U.S. Medical School to accept me! BSN, St. Louis Univ. 4 yrs exper. in telemetry, ICU, ER, L&D. 3.7 GPA (cum), 3.80 Science GPA, 30 MCAT. Excellent letters of recomm., Alpha Sigma Nu honor society. U.S. Army Reserve Nurse. [Telephone number]

However, this is not the way to get accepted to a U.S. or Canadian medical school. Follow the rules, get your application materials, complete them, and send them in early. That's how to have the best chance of being accepted into a medical school.

13

Essays, Recommendations, And Secondary Applications

"The time has come," the Walrus said,
"To talk of many things:
Of shoes—and ships and sealing wax—
Of cabbages and kings—
And why the sea is boiling hot—
And whether pigs have wings."

— Lewis Carroll, *Through the Looking Glass*

— Personal Statements and Essays —

Personal statements and essays cause more anguish among applicants than almost anything else in the application process. Many applicants spend a great deal of time and effort polishing these epistles—and their work often pays off in interviews and acceptances, since admission officers carefully scrutinize personal statements and supplementary essays.

If admission committee members read your essay, they have already determined that you can handle medical school academics. They look at your essay to decide if you will make a good physician. So think about what qualities a good physician should have (e.g., motivation, confidence, altruism, leadership, ability to work well with others). Then show them that you possess these traits with stories from your life.

Committee members also use personal statements to eliminate those individuals who clearly stand out as being: (1) relatively illiterate, (2) pompous or tactless, or (3) outside the reasonable norm for medical students and physicians. The key to writing a good personal statement is to *be honest, but not shy* about your virtues. Describe why you are motivated to be a physician. Rather than simply repeating your résumé in prose, *describe yourself as a person*, using personal anecdotes wherever possible. Many students find this hard to do.

The application forms for AMCAS, AACOMAS, TMDSAS, and OMSAS contain fairly straightforward questions. You only need to find and transcribe your information. However, one page (half a page on AACOMAS) labeled "For Personal Comments" is blank. This is your opportunity to speak directly to the admission committee in your own words. Many schools also have "secondary" applications that contain blank pages for essays, but these often must discuss specific topics (see "Secondary Application" below).

The task of writing these compositions can be daunting, so plan ahead to produce essays that represent you well. Begin to write them early, so you have time to think about them and write several drafts. Be sure to have them competently proofread for content, spelling, and grammar. For additional hints, see Chapter 12: *Applying to Medical School*.

While there is no "ideal" essay, some of the best personal statements and essays are interesting stories about the applicant that reveal his personality, thought processes, and motivations. If you have a story, perhaps about how you became interested in medicine or why you want to pursue this career, then tell it. If it catches the eye of a jaded admission officer and conveys your message about why you want to enter medical school, it is a good personal statement. The sample essays contained in this chapter were used by applicants who are now medical students or physicians. They illustrate the following elements of "safe and sane" personal statements:

1. **Who are you?** Give a brief (two or three sentences) sketch of yourself and where you are in life.
2. **How did you get where you are?** Briefly explain what has drawn you to a medical career. If you have a noteworthy story to tell, tell it. Describe any particular event or person that stands out as markedly influencing your career decision. If you are a minority applicant, you may want to indicate that here, as in "I want to provide care to my fellow (fill in the minority)." Do not state that you are interested in medicine because of the influence of pop culture (e.g., current movies or television shows), the prestige of the profession, or the monetary rewards you anticipate. These reasons are usually considered evidence of a shallow personality. You may mention other elements of your life, such as family, sports, and community activities, if they fit into your story. Admission officers look for applicants who have enough time, interest, and academic skills to take their nose out of their books and spend quality (i.e., helpful) time with their compatriots. Medicine is a helping profession, and most physicians spend lots of time with people. Are you a "people" person?
3. **What do you intend to do during your medical career?** Be general. It is always safe to say that you plan to pursue a primarily clinical career with some clinical research and teaching. Many schools now actively seek individuals who want to enter primary care specialties, such as general internal medicine, family practice, general pediatrics, or obstetrics and gynecology. It is unrealistic and patronizing for you to say that you are sure you want to go into a particular specialty unless you can back this up with reasons grounded in experience. It is safe, however, to say that you are interested in caring for the same patients over a long period. Try to demonstrate that you like to work with people. If you have any reason to honestly say that working in inner cities or rural areas also interests you, this comes across very positively. *If possible, tell a personal story that explains why you want your medical career to take this path.*
4. **Ideals.** How do your values fit into a medical career, and vice versa? Wrap up your essay by briefly mentioning how some of the experiences you have already discussed illustrate these values or motivations. Talk is cheap, so admission committees are interested in seeing evidence that you really have these ideals and have acted on them.

Additional points that you may want to address in the statement include explanations of any major problems or deficiencies that appear in your application or transcript. You might want to mention something particularly outstanding from your undergraduate career or your life outside school. *Avoid discussing politics or religion.* Neither has any place in your application materials. In addition, do not say, "I want to relieve the world's suffering," or anything similar. Admission committees do not seriously consider applicants who have lost touch with reality.

Whether writing your personal statement or the essays on secondary applications, think carefully about the *content*. *Organize* it logically, even the best content will be ignored if the ideas are presented in a jumbled, incoherent manner. Choose anecdotes that *demonstrate your character*, especially those qualities that will make you an outstanding physician.

Even if your essays have superb content and structure, poor grammar, spelling and typographical errors can ruin the effect. Do not rely on your word processor alone to proofread your essays. Set the word processor to the "formal" or "business" setting to catch the most errors possible. After you think that you have a perfect document, ask a literate person whom you trust to review it. If you pick the right person, you will be surprised at what you have missed. Figure 13.1 contains a checklist to use when reviewing your statement. As a final check, have someone else read your statement aloud to you. If it makes sense, use it; otherwise, try again.

Occasionally, applicants ask whether they should make their personal statements bizarre enough to stand out. This is not a good idea and you take a big risk in doing so. Remember that physicians, in general, are conservative. Anything odd or unusual is seen as a negative. Those who read personal statements normally interpret "unusual" as something that is cute, flippant, or crass. These are not the qualities that medical school admission committees look for in applicants.

While some applicants have gotten interviews and even positions based, in part, on unusual personal statements, it is very rare. Unless your life story by itself is unusual, stick with using personal anecdotes to illustrate your points. The question you should ask yourself when you have completed your personal statement is, "If I were on an admission committee, would I be interested in meeting the person who wrote this essay?" If not, perhaps you need to rewrite it.

An additional point: Before you submit your personal statement to your prehealth committee, ask if they will allow revisions, if necessary, before they forward it to medical schools. Such revisions, of course, should only be made if you have pertinent new experiences to add.

Sample Personal Statements

The following personal statements were used by students who were accepted to medical school. Each essay shows aspects of the individual's personality, motivation, and background that suggest why they were accepted. Further examples and a detailed method for writing personal statements and essays can be found in *Résumés and Personal Statements for Health Professionals* by James W. Tysinger (see *Annotated Bibliography*).

Alternative Style

Although not suitable for everyone, occasionally an applicant may decide to use an alternative form of personal statement rather than the typical prose style. The advantage of using a unique format is that it will stand out from other essays; this is also its primary drawback. The example of such a format, *Personal Statement #10,* was written by a medical school applicant with an unusual educational background. While his premed adviser encouraged him to use this format, his school's premed committee discouraged him from submitting it. He did submit it, completed medical school, and is now practicing medicine.

FIGURE 13.1

Personal Statement/Essay Writer's Checklist

Content

Provide a word picture of yourself with one or more stories. Ask yourself:

- Does the essay say something about me as a person and future physician?
- Does it have elements that will stick with the reader?
- Do the action words accurately describe me?
- Are there specific, personal examples to back up my statements and illustrate my qualities?
- If this is a secondary application, have I answered the question posed?

Organization

Even the best content will be lost if the ideas are presented in a jumbled, incoherent manner.

- What is your message? Write that first.
- How will your ideas logically progress to get to that conclusion?
- Write your key sentences. These may be parts of your larger story, but should lead to the message.
- Provide a framework for your essay, with the first and last sentences referring to the same topic.
- Do the key sentences flow in a logical order? Does the entire thing make sense?
- Can you "flesh out" each of the key sentences with interesting paragraphs that complete the sentence's idea?
- Does the final essay say what you wanted in a logical and compelling way?

Uniqueness

Demonstrate the qualities that will make you an outstanding physician. Your essay should:

- Sound interesting. After you have written and rewritten it, it may bore you. Ask others what they think about it.
- Read like a story that ends in a logical conclusion.
- Start with a personal anecdote that will entice readers to continue reading.
- Continue to show, by example, your finest traits.
- Avoid clichés, redundancies, and $25 words.
- Sound like you.

Edit

Poor grammar, spelling, and typographical errors can ruin your statement. Review your essay. Did you:

- Size it to fit in the available space?
- Use varied sentence structures? Do not start every sentence with "I."
- Use standard punctuation, capitalization, and spelling? (American for U.S. schools; Canadian for schools in Canada.)
- Use no exclamation points? (Except in dialogue!!!)
- Use the more interesting active, rather than the passive, voice when possible (e.g., "I found the book" rather than "The book was found by me")?
- Write sentences no longer than about 30 words? Some should be much shorter.
- Shorten paragraphs so that the page doesn't look like a gray wall of type?
- Avoid contractions?
- Maintain agreement between subjects and verbs?
- Use large enough type (at least 10-point)?

Personal Statement #1

I was raised in a low-income, bilingual family (Spanish and English). My parents did everything possible to expose me to all the things that make a well-educated, well-rounded individual. Because of their limited income, one of the most valuable lessons they taught me was to be resourceful in obtaining those opportunities. I sought what they could not offer. I began violin lessons at the age of eight and by the time I started high school I had performed as soloist with both the Mesa and Phoenix Symphonies. I performed at various social functions as Concert Master for my high school's chamber orchestra. I enjoyed the traveling and the opportunities to meet new people that my musical pursuits offered. It was during a music tour to Egypt, where I was exposed to Arabic, that I learned of my affinity for languages.

After high school, I joined the Air Force to pursue language studies and to earn money for college. On my own, I learned some basic Arabic from a self-paced program. The Air Force sent me to the Defense Language Institute (DLI) to learn Hungarian. After completing the DLI course, I was assigned to a special airborne unit attached to the National Security Agency in Maryland. There I traveled in high-performance aircraft to different parts of the world translating and transcribing various languages. During the six years I served in the Air Force, I also learned Italian and a limited amount of Russian. I also competed as the Air Force's representative in the triathlon at national and international levels. I thoroughly enjoyed learning and using the languages, meeting new people, and learning about their cultures. However, something was missing: A complete education.

I took evening college courses while in the Air Force. In many instances though, I was ordered on missions out of the country with little advance notice. This forced me to withdraw from many classes. During my first psychology class at Anne Arundel, I was unable to return until after the class had ended and I received an irreconcilable grade of F. I later repeated the class and earned an A. Eventually, I realized the only way to complete my undergraduate degree was to leave the Air Force and attend school full-time. At first I intended to continue my linguistic studies, but during my secondary jobs as a Medical Records clerk and a CPR/First Aid instructor, I realized my interest in health and human physiology.

My first year out of the Air Force was difficult. I encountered many financial difficulties, which required me to work part-time. I chose to work as a Resident Assistant representing the nontraditional student body, including hearing-impaired students. To better assist the hearing-impaired students, I learned sign language and translated at sporting events and social functions. I derived great satisfaction in bridging the gap between the hearing and the hearing-impaired students. Also, while at Western Maryland College (WMC), I founded a CPR training program for Resident Assistants that still exists. Teaching CPR and First Aid, and knowing that there are now many more people with the basic skills to save a life, is very rewarding to me. It became even more personal when, toward the end of my first semester at WMC, my father suffered a heart attack. I flew home a few weeks before finals and returned to school just after the beginning of the January term. I was allowed to take the finals when I returned, which accounts for the grades I earned that year.

To gain exposure to the field of human physiology, I completed a January-term internship in the Sports Medicine Clinic at Union Memorial Hospital in Baltimore. However, instead of working with the clinic's physiologists, I ended up working with its orthopedic surgeons. I scrubbed in and observed the surgeons during the operations. I administered stress tests, drew blood, and assisted patients undergoing neuromuscular assessment and rehabilitation. I enjoyed being directly involved with the patients and watching their progress. It was then that I connected my interest in science and physiology, my ability to work well with people, my desire for promoting a healthy lifestyle, and my experience working alongside surgeons, and realized that I should become a physician.

I knew that I had some catching up to do academically and that my financial troubles would not go away. I earned an Army ROTC scholarship, which helped my financial situation and I continued to work as a Resident Assistant. My grades improved, and I ended my senior year on the Dean's List with a 4.0. I earned a commission as an officer in the Army's Medical Service Corps. I currently manage a health clinic that supports 595 people. Besides my administrative duties in managing the clinic, I also conduct the initial patient assessment and screening. My work has only increased my interest in becoming a primary health care provider. I am focused and confident in my commitment to study medicine and become a physician.

— Benjamin Gonzalez

Personal Statement #2

My interest in medicine was sparked by a high school anatomy class in which the semester project involved dissecting fetal pigs. I wasn't too enthusiastic about cutting up pigs in the first place, so when I discovered that our field trip to see a human dissection was mandatory, you can imagine my enthusiasm. Unsure how I would react to the ordeal, I waited as they wheeled in the first cadaver. Upon seeing the body, I took a deep breath and, after the initial shock, opened my eyes to the world of medicine. The body before me seemed a pure miracle, a work of art, and it thoroughly fascinated me. That night at dinner, I excitedly told my parents what I had witnessed. Although their reaction didn't match my excitement, they were glad to see my newfound enthusiasm.

No one in my family has ever gone into medicine, so when I decided to major in biochemistry, my mother lovingly suggested that I shoot myself instead, a much faster way to the same end. Yet, I have never taken the easy road and have constantly searched for new and exciting things to do. Early in high school, I began volunteering in the community. I started in a hospital's transportation department. Soon I was staffing city carnivals with the Parks and Recreation division, helping at the Special Olympics' tennis match, demonstrating dissections of the eye at an elementary school, and working with the Mayor's Youth Committee in a homeless shelter during the winter holidays.

My volunteering continued when I came to college. I got involved with several clubs and found myself Christmas caroling in the children's ward of University Medical Center, tutoring fellow students, staffing an annual university carnival, helping with a Halloween party for a retirement home, serving as a peer mentor in the honor's college, volunteering in a child crisis center, and taking groups of children on camping trips with Camp Wildcat while working as the Donations Coordinator for the club.

My interest in volunteering is partially selfish, for I receive an unexplainable satisfaction in helping someone in need. For example, during my senior year in high school, I was with a group delivering Christmas food baskets and a man in his upper 80s was the last delivery of the day. His only family consisted of three very large dogs that roamed his tiny, barren home. Although we brought the basket of food, he still needed something more. We were the first people to visit him in a long time, and he desperately wanted to talk to someone. We stayed until late in the evening while this man poured out his life story, including the fact that he had bone cancer. If I had ever needed a goal for my life, it was clarified while talking to that lonely man. Volunteering has allowed me to mature in ways that ordinary school life could not possibly have done.

At the University of Arizona, I continue to excel in my studies and participate in a variety of activities. It must be dedication when you find yourself attending 8 a.m. meetings on Monday mornings! I joined honors clubs such as the Honors Student Association, Phi Eta Sigma, and Golden Key National Honor Society; medically-oriented clubs such as HIV Advisory Committee and the Student Health Advisory Committee; and interest clubs such as Camp Wildcat, Relate Crew (a freshman orientation organization), Manzi-Mo Funhouse (a theater group), and even the Kazzoo Band (the volleyball pep club)! In addition, I continued to pursue personal interests in piano, tennis, and private aviation.

I have been involved in research since my freshman year. My first research experience was in an entomology lab where I studied the mechanisms of olfactory reception in *Triatoma rubida*, commonly known as the Kissing Bug. I spent most of my time gathering data on the insects, tracking pathways in response to various odors. The following year, I entered a chemistry laboratory where I had the challenge of synthesizing butadiene-iron-tricarbonyl, an uncharacterized chemical. After several experiments, I was the first in our group to obtain the pure compound. I then presented my work at the 1992 Honors Mini-Symposium. The next summer, I worked full-time in the neuro-oncology laboratory at the Barrow Neurological Institute in Phoenix. There I was exposed to the demands of a fast-paced research lab where I studied bFGE signal-transmission pathway mechanisms in neuroblastomas (basically, how a cancerous brain cell imports a growth hormone) using immunochemistry and tissue culture techniques. In addition, I studied the effects of chemicals secreted by cancerous cells on normal tissues. I presented my work during the 1993 Summer Cancer Biology Seminar series. The director of the lab invited me back the following summer to conduct research involving cell migration of malignant gliomas by the use of immunoflourescence. After conducting this cancer research, I wanted to see the clinical aspect of cancer, so I observed in the Oncology Radiation Center of Desert Samaritan Hospital. I interacted with patients and learned how to read MRIs and bone and CT scans. This clinical experience reaffirmed my interest in medicine. This past fall, I worked as a research assistant in a neuroanatomy laboratory at University Medical Center, where I studied the developmental organization of glycine receptors in embryonic rat neurons. I compared various aged neurons using fluorescent microscopy techniques.

After spending two full summers working in an oncology lab, I have two interests: medical research and clinical medicine. For this reason, I am applying to M.D.–Ph.D. programs. I am confident that I will excel in both worlds. As a physician and a scientist, I will bridge the gap between the two disciplines and help people help themselves while teaching them to stay healthy. I want this more than anything and, with determination like mine, I know I am going to enter an M.D.–Ph.D. program and succeed.

— Tracy L. Davis

Personal Statement #3

I want to provide medical care for the financially indigent. For years I have worked with low-income people, those who struggle with haunting memories of past abuse, and those who live with fear—one emotion which overrides all others. My interest in medicine started when I was an EMT. Working on an ambulance let me observe difficult situations in people's lives. Reared with unusual privilege, I was shocked by the conditions under which some people live. Later, as a Parent/Counselor/Aide, I visited mothers in their homes, listened to their problems, and helped them meet their families' physical and emotional needs. I interviewed more than 100 women, reporting their stories of many types of abuse, neglect, and just plain bad luck.

For two years, I volunteered as a crisis counselor for the H.E.L.P. child-abuse hotline. This work did not tire me, as it did some. Instead, it energized me to find out more to change things. I had had an abusive marriage where I lost all hope in the future and all interest in my self-worth. I had been through bankruptcy and the loss of my home and possessions, and inevitably, my pride. The fact that over a ten-year period I was able to struggle out of that way of life leaves me with no less compassion for those still in it.

My children have given me a perspective on life beyond academia or personal satisfaction. I would not have understood so many of the hardships families face without having experienced motherhood. Perhaps it is this that causes me to be consistently drawn to helping those who do not know how to overcome their struggles. Over the years, I have learned to leave the emotional residue from my sometimes-frustrating occupations at work.

Three years ago, I returned to school with the express desire to become a physician. I had seen that the service I could provide as a layperson was limited. Continuing to work in those areas of need was important to me, even as a premedical student, because I wanted to keep my perspective. I have organized three women's resource fairs on campus and volunteered much time to community efforts for women. Presently, I still visit families as a genetics counselor for the Sickle Cell Anemia Society.

My past experiences have helped me discover the type of work I wish to pursue as a physician. I have seen that there is a definite and increasing need for medical care in rural and low-income areas. As a physician, I plan to do much more to serve and teach those with limited resources.

— Gina M. Jansheski

Personal Statement #4

I am truly blessed. My husband, a physician, is my soul mate and partner in all things. I have three wonderful children who I have the great honor of rearing. My parents' love has always been there, and they are two of my closest friends. I have much to be thankful for. So, with all these blessings, why do I want to put myself through the long, grueling task of becoming a physician? Instead of seeing this as something I am putting myself through, I view this as a process toward fully becoming who I am.

I have wanted to be a physician for as long as I can remember. As a little girl, I bought first aid books and watched all the medical shows on TV. I took First Aid and CPR courses at the Red Cross. I also had a very special woman doctor during my childhood with whom I always identified, because "I was going to be doctor, too." As a teenager, I volunteered as a candy striper at the local hospital. In high school, I majored in math and science, took all the advanced classes, and won both the National Honor Society's Award and the Harvard Award for all-around excellence during my junior year. I enrolled in two college courses during my senior year through a merit scholarship and graduated a semester early with a Regents' diploma.

I began college as a premed major on two academic scholarships and did very well in my first semester. However, three traumatic events changed my life path. First, my brother, who had been the "genius" of the family, was diagnosed with acute paranoid schizophrenia. He was hospitalized for six months and was ill for another two years. At the time, the biochemical causes of schizophrenia were not understood and a Freudian approach was taken in which our family was repeatedly blamed for my brother's illness. This greatly heightened the pain our family experienced. I now realize the doctors were doing their best with the knowledge available at that time. However, it is clear to me that healing involves more than knowledge and that knowledge increases. The caring and support of the physician are essential ingredients that must remain constant. My brother's experience sparked my interest in the psychiatric aspects of both physical and mental illnesses and profoundly impacted my sense of priorities and values. (Fortunately, my brother recovered completely and is now a happily married tax attorney.)

In the next event, I was injured in a car accident. This made me contemplate my own mortality. Did I really want to spend the next ten years in medical school and training? The final blow came when I contracted mononucleosis. I missed a third of that semester, and I contracted multiple infections during the next year because of my weakened immune system. Despite all this, I always took more than a full load of classes, worked from 30 to 40 hours a week as a waitress, fit in time for socializing, and graduated a year early. My grades, however, had suffered. I ended up with a 3.4 GPA and felt that my grades were inadequate to fulfill my dream of attending medical school. I worked for a year after college to replenish my financial reserves, which had been put toward the family's basic needs during my brother's illness.

I then completed my Master of Science a semester early, with a double major in Rehabilitation Counseling and Vocational Evaluation, at the University of Arizona. I worked 30 to 40 hours a week during this time as a Rehabilitation Counselor, helping clients who had been injured on the job to find alternative employment or retraining. My internship and subsequent year in San Diego turned out to be one of the most important periods of my life. Being alone and in an unsupportive environment, I learned a great deal about creating my own happiness and sense of self-worth.

I next took a transition job in insurance and financial investments, where I had the highest sales of any "rookie" in that office's history.

As time passed, I realized that only a job in the medical profession would fulfill me. I returned to the University of Arizona for a Ph.D. in Rehabilitation Psychology. I also worked as a Psychiatric Crisis Worker at Kino Community Hospital. This job involved evaluating and treating suicidal, homicidal, and psychotic patients, both in the emergency department and with police officers in the field. I felt totally at home working with the patients, medical staff, and police, and felt a great sense of fulfillment.

During this time, I married and put my academic work on hold to start a family. I debated about what to do with my education. I only had a few more classes to complete before my internship and dissertation. However, I had three children in three years and was unsure how to incorporate my school work with my duty to my children. After some false starts, I decided to finish my degree. However, during this three-year absence, the Rehabilitation Department had changed the course requirements. Instead of a few classes, it would now take five more years of study to complete my Ph.D. This change led me to evaluate my options. My husband, a psychiatrist, asked me where my passion truly lay and I immediately knew that I had to become a doctor. Since this confirmed his suspicions, we began together to determine how I could "have it all."

I soon returned to the University of Arizona to compete my premedical requirements and have maintained a 4.0 GPA. (In evaluating my MCAT scores, it may be helpful to know that I had not yet taken the second semester of organic chemistry and physics when I took the test.) After this circuitous route, I have returned to the path I know is mine. In my heart, I am a physician, a healer. I have no regrets about the time or the energy I spent in other pursuits. Each experience provided learning and growth, and I know that I will make a much better physician now than if I had followed the more conventional path.

— Molly Roberts

Personal Statement #5

Growing up in a small town, I have always felt the support of the families in my community. As neighbors and friends, they offered emotional support. As professionals, they offered services, including those of a small but vital medical community. As a child, I watched our town's physicians resolve situations with what seemed to be an almost mystical knowledge of the sciences. I envied physicians for their mastery of that knowledge and their ability to use it to positively change others. That introduction, along with my growing love for science and my community, has committed me to become a physician. I want to affect other's lives with the same substantial, positive influence these physicians had on my life. I want to be like them, the very foundation of a small rural community.

This firm commitment developed over time. In the early seventies, a personal situation adversely affected my grades. After my first year in college, my adviser informed me that my grades would keep me out of medical school, so I temporarily discontinued my studies. I also married and started a family. Determined to regain control of the situation, I returned to school and changed majors to make a fresh start. I earned a Bachelor of Business Administration in 1978.

I secured a sales position with a large corporation and established myself professionally. Then, ready for a challenge and more confident of my own skills, I returned to school for postbaccalaureate work in 1980–81 and earned a second degree, Bachelor of Science, with a GPA of 3.92.

I spent the next seven years working as a commercial insurance underwriter and a marketing representative. As an underwriter leading a team of four, I learned the importance of interpersonal communication skills in reaching defined objectives. As a marketing representative, I mediated contract negotiations, which were frequently antagonistic, between outside brokers and company underwriters. This experience further developed my interpersonal skills by teaching me how to negotiate a common agreement through compromise. These skills will prove invaluable to my future work with patients and colleagues.

Although I had learned a great deal in business, I was not fully satisfied with my professional life. I still wanted to become a physician. I knew I had to push myself, not only for self-enrichment, but also for the benefit of my family and community. Over the past two years, I have completed my medical school prerequisites and earned a 3.92 GPA.

While fulfilling these prerequisites, I enrolled in a course entitled Student Pre-Med Internship (HES 394) in which I observed and assisted emergency physicians at a level-one trauma center. This work, coupled with my volunteer work in the emergency department of my neighborhood hospital, allowed me to witness how of physicians apply their knowledge to practical, vital work. This experience reinforced my original impressions of the challenges and rewards of being a physician and confirmed my decision to pursue medicine.

Observing physicians has let me see the pressures of being a physician. Life-support technology demands answers to the right-to-die question. Assisting patients who have AIDS tests the wills of even the strongest physicians. Litigation threatens medical careers as it moves toward becoming a form of social insurance against accidental outcomes. Government intervention threatens to reduce the physician's role from that of patient advocate to industrial technician. These pressures have not deterred me from my career goals. Instead, they have reinforced my desire to be among those physicians who determine the eventual solutions and compromises.

In all my assessments, my conclusion remains the same as it was when I was a small child watching our family physician work. Fifteen years have passed since my earlier attempt to study medicine. Today, as a more mature person, I am totally dedicated to becoming a physician.

— Brian D. Fitch

Personal Statement #6

Throughout my life, I have been most rewarded by helping others. Whether it was sharing a meal with a small boy in a Rwandan village or playing a game of chess with a lonely rehabilitation patient, the satisfaction of helping someone fulfills me. In this essay I highlight those experiences that have solidified my desire to become a physician.

My love of science and personal desire to improve the quality of medical care led me to leave the security of a well-paying profession to enter the medical field. A physicist, I saw the vital role of technology in medicine while earning my B.S. from the Institute of Optics at the University of Rochester. Soon after graduation, when my uncle was diagnosed with macular degeneration, I learned that technology, with its limitations, must complement compassion and never just substitute for it. The ophthalmologist told my uncle that no treatment could stop the rapid deterioration of his vision. My uncle was devastated. Upon hearing this, I did a comprehensive literature review at UCLA's medical library. I learned that laser treatment offered the only hope of preventing my uncle's blindness. The laser treatment that he subsequently received slowed, but did not halt, the disease's progression. The doctor was correct, but I believe my efforts gave my uncle time to come to terms with his loss of sight. The feeling of having made a difference in someone's life was tremendous. I recall thinking that a physician probably enjoys that feeling often. However, it wasn't until five years later, upon returning from a trip to central Africa, that I earnestly began to pursue a medical career.

While backpacking through central Africa, I met a young French doctor from the organization Doctors Without Borders. He invited me to his clinic—a thatched-roof hut in a remote Rwandan village. Many of his patients were children who suffered from dehydration caused by dysentery. The antibiotics and rehydration therapy that this doctor administered helped many of these children survive. That evening, while sharing my rice and beans with a small boy, I reflected on what I had witnessed that day. I had seen how primary care—a physician's skills, medication, and rehydration solution—saved the lives of five children just like the one eating with me. At that moment I decided to become a physician.

When I returned to the United States, I began taking medical school prerequisites while maintaining my full-time engineering responsibilities. I combined my MCAT preparations with my duties as an engineer and a new father, making use of the quiet time between 3 a.m. to 6 a.m.! My efforts paid off for me and for coffee bean growers around the world.

Three years ago, I turned my desire to help into action and began my first volunteer position. The Harbor–UCLA Medical Center's emergency department and intensive care unit taught me the importance of comforting patients in stressful environments. This usually meant lending an attentive ear while the staff was busy. The chief trauma surgeon befriended me and, upon hearing of my plans to attend medical school, invited me to observe his activities. In time, I witnessed the entire acute care process, from examination to postoperative recovery. I also saw that the emergency department has become a costly bottleneck of care, the default method many people use to obtain medical attention for minor ailments. This immersion in emergency medicine and the acute care setting strongly reinforced my decision to pursue medicine as a career.

One year ago, I began another volunteer position, which I continue to this day, at the Rehabilitation Institute of Tucson. At the Institute, I really began to understand and appreciate the patient's perspective of day-to-day care. As a volunteer, I have time to listen. Because of this, patients have shared their unique insight into medical care with me. Frequently, patients, who at first are quiet and withdrawn, talk for hours about their homes, grandchildren, or youth. Sometimes, as I listen to their stories, I know that they are not sitting in those wheelchairs, but are at home or with their grandchildren. When I am a part of this, I am happy.

Most recently, I have also started a research project at the Arizona Health Sciences Center's Department of Radiology. The project involves evaluating spiral CT technology in the area of cervical spine trauma. The study's objective is to minimize patient discomfort, handling, and exposure to multiple costly procedures without compromising the effectiveness of the current means of establishing diagnoses and prescribing courses of action.

I am aware of the commitment and responsibility required to become a physician. I look forward to the day when I will combine my knowledge and my compassion to help others. I want to make a difference to the medical community and to the people it serves.

— Steve Hochader

Personal Statement #7

In February 1992, I was accepted into the College of Medicine class beginning that fall. Shortly afterward, I failed my human neuroscience course at the University of Arizona. The College of Medicine withdrew my acceptance. I was devastated and humiliated. However, I accepted full responsibility for my choice to prioritize my full-time research position as a Research Technician in Anesthesiology over the class.

I missed class when there was an eligible patient for one of the protocols. I also remained at the hospital late at night for heart transplants and postsurgical blood draws for the drug study protocols. These choices compromised my academic performance. I simply did not spend enough time studying the course material and preparing for the exams. Since the withdrawal of my application, I have learned much about responsibility. I reduced the hours for my job and took considerable time off from work prior to the September 1992 MCAT. I have retaken the MCAT and enrolled in two upper-level biology courses to demonstrate my academic ability in science.

I became interested in medicine years ago when, as a child, doctors appeared to me as a source of immediate comfort and trust. As a teenager, I watched my grandfather succumb to emphysema and wished I could have helped him. At the same time, my high school anatomy and physiology class sparked my interest in the complexities of the human body. I tried to understand, through this new knowledge, the reasons behind my grandfather's death. These experiences began my desire for an active role in health care.

I enrolled at the University of Arizona as a premed student, with a history major and a biochemistry minor to obtain a broad liberal arts education. My work in history has served me far better than I had anticipated, particularly as it relates the development of individuals and their communities to the expanding field of health care. To gain practical knowledge of medicine, I volunteered in the Department of Anesthesiology at the U of A College of Medicine, and two months later took a job as a student investigator. This exposed me to the clinical aspects of medicine with the first project: Evaluation of implicit memory during general anesthesia. I discussed the study with surgical patients, played them a tape during their operation, and tested their recall postoperatively. I learned that patients with confidence and trust in their physician were relaxed and confident going into surgery.

Our research team became involved in studies of cardiac surgery and anesthesia, and this work gave me my first quantifiable contribution to the field of medicine. We examined the effect of altered hemoglobin-oxygen affinity during cardiopulmonary bypass. We also tested the effectiveness of the beta-blocker esmolol to lower cellular oxygen demand and protect cardiac tissue from damage caused by oxygen debt during cardiopulmonary bypass. I recorded numerous surgical parameters and drew blood for blood gases, drug concentrations, and various plasma levels. I was an active part of a research project designed to improve the quality and duration of cardiac patients' lives. Our research expanded into the investigation of human heart tissue, and I was responsible for obtaining samples of the left atrium from transplant recipients' hearts. Seeing a successful heart transplant gave me an even deeper appreciation for life and the advances of medicine.

In sharp contrast, I witnessed the death of a cardiac patient during a seemingly routine procedure. As the O.R. team frantically attempted to sustain the patient's life, I could only wait and watch. The pressures dropped, the heart ceased, and a thick silence replaced the commotion. As with my grandfather, I was frustrated by my inability to help, and questioned how and why the death occurred. I wondered what could have been done to improve the outcome and what new therapies the future will provide.

At that point in my senior year, I was so eager to enter medical school that I took another job to finance the MCAT and the application process. Ironically, my performance in bio-chemistry suffered as a result. Unexpected reconstructive knee surgery and rehabilitation the following spring further complicated my academic efforts while I maintained my research position to support myself. After graduation, I was promoted to Research Technician and my duties were expanded to include study development and design, the drafting of grant applications, and supervision of the research team. Our team has continued the esmolol and memory during anesthesia projects, and has also studied the narcotic mirfentanil for conscious sedation, the anti-nausea drug ondansetron for use in the postoperative setting, and the narcotic agonist-antagonist dezocine for use during gall bladder removal and conscious sedation during endoscopic colonoscopy.

In the last four years of work in clinical research, I have had patient, physician, and staff interactions that have shown me the reality of medicine. However, no greater lesson has slapped me in the face than my failure last spring. I have learned that my research position is a transitional role, and that my responsibilities in the lab must never interfere with my goal of becoming a physician. I have proved my academic potential and removed any doubts about my dedication to my career goal. Temporary setbacks, rejections, and detours are all a part of being human. My goal to become a physician remains strong, and I will succeed.

— Steve Behr

Personal Statement #8

I have wanted to be a doctor since I was a senior in high school. I worked for a doctor to pay my tuition to a private church school, and observing her sparked my interest in medicine. To pay for my medical school tuition, I became an Emergency Medical Technician. Being an EMT gave me a first-hand look at the medical profession and allowed me to decide exactly what career I wanted. During EMT school, I really found my niche and, when I began working in the ambulance, I knew that I belonged in medicine. I enjoyed patient care, and I enjoyed explaining medical conditions to people even more than I enjoyed the adrenaline rush of responding to calls. Two years later, I was the valedictorian of my paramedic class.

I knew when I finished paramedic school that I had only tasted medicine and I wanted more. I began training to be a flight medic on a helicopter. Two years later, I was flying for Flight for Life, based at Mother Francis Hospital in Tyler, Texas. Even though many people view aeromedical transport as the pinnacle of EMS, it was still not enough for me. One day as we were flying a critical patient to the hospital and I was giving my report to the doctor over the radio, it struck me that I was on the wrong side of the radio. It was time to return to school and continue my education.

That day on the radio, I realized that I wanted the leadership role in medicine that physicians have. Physicians have more autonomy and the depth of care that they can provide is much greater than any other member of the health care team. Most of all, physicians are involved in the doctor-patient relationship, and I believe that this relationship has a greater effect on people's lives. I want to be a part of that.

I have pursued my education while working as a paramedic at Life Star Ambulance. These last ten years on an ambulance have been highly educational for me. I have become ACLS certified, a BTLS instructor, EMD-certified, and am currently working on becoming a pediatric prehospital life-support instructor. More importantly, however, I have learned to talk with patients, listen to them, and care for them and their families.

In 1989, I attended a class on pediatric prehospital trauma. I watched videotapes of a physician from the University of Florida talking about the number of pediatric trauma-related deaths that could have been prevented by the caregivers at the hospital. These talks sparked my interest in pediatric critical care. A few years later, I began volunteering at Cook–Fort Worth Children's Medical Center holding sick babies in the Special Care Unit. I now want to work with critical pediatric patients, either in an emergency department or in oncology. I want to spend the rest of my life caring for sick children and, when possible, making them better.

I should be accepted into medical school for many different reasons. I have worked on an ambulance for ten years and I know what I am getting into. I have worked full time while obtaining my medical school prerequisites, maintained a high GPA, and scored well on my MCAT. I am a highly motivated, goal-oriented, altruistic person who can make a difference in my patients' lives. I have the intangible qualities of a good doctor: The desire to educate, to serve, and to heal.

— Priscilla Madsen

Personal Statement #9

With changes in the field of medicine, many people wonder what medicine will be like in the future. For example, will we still live in fear of contracting an incurable and deadly disease like AIDS? Or will medicine have the capability to handle such threats to our lives? Answering these questions and having the proper education and training to help prevent such threats has been my major ambition. I can best fulfill this ambition by becoming a physician. I never really thought of attending college until the tenth grade. Just like my father, I had always thought I would be a mechanic and own my own shop because I enjoyed the challenges of diagnosing problems in cars. It wasn't until I was at my doctor's office one day that I realized the similarities between the work of physicians and mechanics. Both require one to diagnose and solve problems. That was when I became interested in medicine. As time went by, I became fascinated with the anatomy, physiology, and biochemistry of the human body. Furthermore, I was amazed with how physicians used medications to alleviate pain and heal individuals. These attractions to the workings of the human body and the physician's roles led me to pursue a career in medicine.

During my first semester at the University of Arizona, my interest in medicine was further intensified by attending the Minority Premed Club meetings and hearing physicians speak about their paths to medical school and their current positions. The following semester, I accepted an offer to help organize and implement community service projects and special events for the Club. This role let me use my skills and interests to help the community and my fellow premed students.

During the spring of 1993, I started tutoring in mathematics and chemistry for the Minority Student Services Math & Science Learning Center at the U of A. I honed my interpersonal skills and knowledge of the concepts and procedures gained from previous courses to help students in their classes. Not only was this a valuable learning experience for the students I tutored, but it was also a learning experience for me. In particular, working with students from different cultural backgrounds was very broadening and personally rewarding.

In the summer of 1993, I volunteered in the transportation department at St. Mary's Hospital in Tucson. This position allowed me to communicate with many patients and observe many physicians. I will never forget the faces of those severely ill patients. The importance of medicine and physicians in our society became even clearer and more compelling.

The following summer I participated in the first Minority Medical Education Program (MMEP) held at the University of Arizona College of Medicine. This program helped me understand the demands of medical school and the responsibilities and characteristics of a commendable physician. Through my involvement with MMEP, I have shadowed an orthopedic surgeon at University Medical Center. For more than 12 months, I observed his special skills with his patients and fellow physicians. In one case, as a scrubbed observer in the O.R., I helped as the medical team gave an infant with deformities the chance to walk. It was the climax of my premedical experiences. I will never forget the trust and confidence this physician had in my ability to give him a helping hand in surgery. More importantly, I was part of a team that made a significant difference in the patient's life. This is a feeling nobody can take from me. I absolutely knew after this that I wanted to be a physician.

I know that one day when I am a physician, I will provide the same type of help to a premed student. Without mentors, premed students do not get the proper experiences to be certain that medicine is the career for them.

I am the first in my family to attend college. Luckily, my family has supported and encouraged my success in college. I have also made it this far with the help of my premed adviser, premed programs (MMEP), and my mentor. With their continued support, I will become a physician. I know that the road to a medical degree will be difficult and long, but I will never give up my dream of becoming a physician. I am determined to help fight the war against life-threatening diseases like AIDS and, by becoming a physician, I can be on that special team that will make a difference in a patient's life.

— Robert G. Bonillas

Personal Statement #10

What can I offer to medicine?

I have a passion for life, my own as well as others'. I also bring to medicine an analytical mind attached to a compassionate heart.

What does medicine offer me?

The simple smile of a 9-year-old when his sister signs his cast. The swell of warmth as I guide a patient to health. These rewards are indescribable. There is something magical in working with people to better their health. It is the interaction with people intertwined with the pursuit of science in a way that will bring a common goal: A healthier and happier lifestyle.

What kind of person am I?

Eclectic. I am a student-athlete graduating with a degree in Electrical Engineering and a Philosophy minor. To me, life is engaging. Throughout my education and career, I hope to never stop growing. I have always struck a natural balance of mind, body, and spirit when striving for academic excellence, when competing in sports, or in understanding my place in this universe.

Why Electrical Engineering?

Electronics have amazed me since I first played with a 30-in-1 Heath Kit at age eight. Although I found my career direction (medicine) early in college, I still wanted to study engineering in school. I have learned to critically analyze a situation and solve problems efficiently, and discovered that health care can be improved with electronics. For my senior project, I am designing a hearing aid that shifts spoken sounds to lower frequencies where the ear is usually less damaged. While practicing medicine, I will find further applications of electronics to health care.

Why a Philosophy minor?

I'm a reflective person, and philosophy examines the "whys" and "hows" that underlie everyday life. I can think critically and logically, yet I can be creative while conjuring abstract notions. My philosophical background has opened my mind to countless ways of thinking.

Have I experienced health care?

My motivations have been reinforced by my experiences in health care. As a volunteer, I help admit and discharge patients. I see the change in patients' expressions as they go from sick to well. I see nervous families waiting for their loved ones in surgery. When the physician comes out, there is a wave of relief. I see the caring, knowledgeable way in which physicians interact with patients, and I aspire to be in that position.

I am also prepared for the other side of health care: The embittered patient, the terminal case of cancer. As a volunteer in General Hospital Emergency Department, I see how difficult it can be to deal with the patients who are physically and/or mentally ill. I have learned to face life's harshness with patience, perseverance, and love.

Will I be a good physician?

Yes. My strength lies in the balance of qualities of a complete physician: An intelligent person who evaluates a situation effectively; a human with the humility and compassion to relate with patients; a health advocate asserting that healthiness and happiness are really the same word.

— William Segalla

Essays for School-Specific Applications

The essays that applicants must submit with their "secondary" or "supplemental" applications usually are mixtures of the following themes:

- What experiences led you to pursue a medical career?
- What personal goals do you have?
- What motivates you?
- Other personal topics that demonstrate your values and attitudes.

Many of the essay questions parallel the questions that you may be asked during medical school interviews (see Chapter 25: *The Questions—The Answers).*

While mulling over ideas for your personal statement, jot down ideas for parallel essays. If you can, write a few standard essays in advance, so you can polish them before they are due. Since you should return your secondary applications as soon as possible, prewriting some essays will markedly speed the process. Even if the schools ask for something different in their essays, you can probably cut-and-paste material from your essays to answer most questions.

If possible, tailor part of your essay to the specific school. You can get a sense of what they seek from viewing their website (see Appendix E: *Medical Schools*). For example, most schools with a specific primary care mission ask questions that correlate with a primary care career, such as:

- To what extent have your past experiences, goals, or accomplishments demonstrated your understanding of and commitment to this school's mission?
- Discuss the type of medical practice in which you see yourself.
- What other career possibilities have you considered?

Studies suggest that, aside from discussing their prior contact with a specialty, the content of applicants' essays has little to do with their final specialty choice.

— Reference Letters —

The reference letters sent to medical schools describe you from other people's perspectives. They play an important part in determining whether a school asks you to interview. Obtaining good reference letters takes advance planning, hard work, and initiative. The steps outlined below will help you to get the best possible reference letters. They will also help you make the most of the ones you do get.

Medical schools generally expect to see letters from: (1) a science professor (or, for graduate students, your major adviser); (2) a responsible person who can comment on your clinical or research experience; and (3) your premed committee or adviser. If you are currently employed, some schools also want a letter from your supervisor. In general, they want letters from individuals who know you well enough to comment specifically on the elements of your character that will make you a great physician. Some schools request specific letters and others limit the number of letters they wish to see. (Figure 15.8 gives an approximation of each school's preferences.) Carefully read all the information you receive from the schools and that comes with the uniform applications. Unless you follow their rules to the letter, schools may deny you an interview.

You also need reference letters when you apply for scholarships. You may ask the same individuals who wrote letters for your application for these letters, or even use the same reference letters. This makes obtaining strong reference letters doubly important.

Letters from Premed Advisers and Committees

About 94% of premed advisers at private undergraduate schools and 75% at public schools write reference letters for their students applying to medical school. While most write these letters for all premed students, about 15% require students to meet minimal standards (such as a prehealth committee recommendation, specific faculty support for their application, or a minimum GPA) before they will write such letters. About 1% require all students to pay for such letters, even though this seems to produce a major conflict of interest and diminishes the letters' significance to medical school admission committees.

To prepare for writing the letters, premed advisers normally ask students to submit a résumé and an essay, after which they interview them. Premed advisers' letters usually present the student in the best possible light, and stress the student's positive aspects rather than trying to balance strengths and weaknesses. Medical school admission officers say that advisers' letters are often used to determine which applicants are interviewed, and that these letters play a major part in the admission committees' decisions. (Given their importance, it is odd that medical schools rarely contact the advisers about their letters.) If the premed adviser does not write a recommendation, it is often written by the school's premedical committee.

Most colleges and universities also have premedical committees that will produce composite reference letters if students request them. Typically, the committee is comprised of faculty members representing both the sciences and the nonsciences. Before writing the letters, they review students' records and a résumé the student submits, and then, as a group, they interview each student. (At some schools, the committees do not interview students; instead, they write letters that highlight accomplishments using comments taken from other reference letters and the school's records.) In general, committee members evaluate the student's undergraduate performance and activities to see if he or she has realistic goals, has considered alternatives to medical school, and has obtained clinical experience. For most students, the committee's interview will be the first "live" part of the application process. Prepare for this interview the same way you would for an interview at a medical school. (See Chapter 22: *Preparing For The Interview;* Chapter 23: *The Interview;* and Chapter 25: *The Questions—The Answers*.)

Medical schools take premedical committees' recommendations very seriously. Admission committees know that these are objective evaluations from individuals who are experienced in judging undergraduates applying to medical school. Although students can choose their individual references, they cannot choose committee members. Moreover, since individual students cannot pressure committee members, they are more willing to write critical letters if it is appropriate. Many premed committees use standard language to summarize their evaluations, such as "Highly Recommended," "Recommended," or "Recommended With Reservations." *Take these interviews very seriously*. They can either help you immensely or hurt you badly.

Premedical committee interviews have one additional benefit: Committee members often provide feedback to students about qualities to emphasize, how to act, and what deficiencies should be explained during medical school interviews. Of course, to even get to a medical school interview, you usually have to do well at the committee's interview.

Many medical schools accept a premed committee's recommendations in lieu of additional reference letters (Figure 15.8). In fact, most prefer to see these recommendations, and a school may even contact an applicant's undergraduate school if their premed committee did not send a letter. Experience has shown that most applicants also benefit from excellent reference letters from individuals who know them well. (Some schools, however, instruct you not to add them. Follow their instructions.) If your committee gives you a less-than-enthusiastic evaluation, these additional letters may still help you get a medical school interview.

Medical schools may require the committee's or adviser's letter to state that the applicant is "in good standing" at their school. If this is the case, tell your committee or adviser that this statement should be included. Letter writers will also need to know if you waive your right to see the letter. Medical schools prefer that applicants waive that right.

Some committees do not actually send letters; they may send forms that rate each student on a variety of factors. In some cases, medical schools do not even accept recommendation letters, but rather send a form to any individual who sends such a letter. Figure 13.2 is an example of such a form used by the University of Southern Mississippi's Premedical and Health Professions Office. They have several faculty members rate a student, and send a composite of the ratings to the medical schools.

FIGURE 13.2

Rating Sheet for Medical School Applicants

Applicant ____________________

FACTORS

Please indicate with a check mark (✓) your opinion of this applicant's rating on each factor relative to other students you have observed.

RANKING STANDARDS

1. Exceptional, top 5%
2. Excellent, next 10%
3. Good, next 20%
4. Average, middle 30%
5. Reservation, next 30%
6. Poor, low 5%
7. No basis for judgment

FACTORS	1	2	3	4	5	6	7
EMOTIONAL STABILITY Performs under pressure; mood stability; constancy in ability to relate to others							
INTERPERSONAL RELATIONS Ability to get along with others; rapport; cooperation; attitude toward supervision							
JUDGMENT Ability to analyze problems; common sense; decisiveness							
RESOURCEFULNESS Originality; skillful management of available resources and time; initiative							
RELIABILITY Dependability; sense of responsibility; promptness; conscientiousness							
PERSEVERANCE Stamina; endurance (physical and psychological)							
COMMUNICATION SKILLS Clarity in writing and speech; articulation							
SELF-CONFIDENCE Assuredness; capacity to achieve with awareness of own strengths and weaknesses							
EMPATHY Consideration; tact; sensitivity to the needs of others							
MATURITY Personal development; social consciousness; ability to cope with life situations							
INTELLECTUAL CURIOSITY Realness and intensity of desire to learn and extend beyond course expectations							
SCHOLARSHIP Ability to learn (quality of study habits plus native intellectual ability)							
MOTIVATION Genuineness and depth of commitment; intensity, reality, and maturity of expressed reasons to enter medicine							

EVALUATION SUMMARY

Compare with other premed students you (have) know(n) and provide an overall evaluation.

( ) Exceptional Candidate, top
( ) Excellent Candidate, next 10%
( ) Good Candidate, next 20%
( ) Average Candidate, middle 30%
( ) Weak Candidate, bottom 35%
( ) No basis for judgment

Adapted, with permission, from the form used by the University of Southern Mississippi.

Other Reference Letters

Whom to Ask?

Most of the reference letters you send to medical schools will be written by individuals you have personally asked. It is essential for you to know whom to ask. Select people who know you well, who can comment on your character using specific examples, and who are credible. You also want the letters to complement and reinforce what you say about yourself in your personal statement.

The *ideal reference letter* is written by an individual who is well-known to members of the admission committees. This is usually a nationally recognized physician, researcher, or scholar who (1) has worked closely with you in school or elsewhere, (2) thinks you are a "star," and (3) graduated from the medical school to which you are applying. If the individual is on a medical school's faculty, it is best if the letter says that you have been strongly encouraged to apply to his or her school. All this may be difficult—or impossible—to achieve in one letter, but think of such a reference as the "gold standard."

Faculty

Faculty members, especially senior faculty, are good references. Choose someone with whom you have worked closely in some capacity and who thought you did a great job. For example, you may have worked with a professor in the laboratory or on extracurricular activities, or have participated in his or her seminar. If these activities are in a "medically related" area, such as molecular biology, so much the better. Get one letter from a faculty member outside your major area. For example, if you are a science major, get a letter from a faculty member in the humanities. This helps to demonstrate that you are the well-rounded person many medical schools seek. The letter should not just say "she was a good student." The admission committee can see that from your transcript.

If you have cultivated a mentor, whether or not they are in a health care field, have them write a letter for you. If your mentor has worked closely with you (and, if not, it is *your* fault), their opinion will carry a great deal of weight. Letters, even from prominent faculty members, hold much less weight if the writer cannot show that they know you well.

Nonacademic References

You may have played an active role in nonschool activities, such as being a Scout leader, Little League coach, or volunteer firefighter. The supervisor for the activity (such as the fire chief) can write a reference letter detailing your selfless effort, explaining how well you get along with people, and citing specific outstanding events that he or she has witnessed. If chosen wisely, such references add spice to your application and make you a memorable, and often desirable, applicant.

If you have worked in a medical setting, ask a physician with whom you have worked closely to write a letter. Such an individual is qualified to assess your behavior in a medical setting. Admission committees look for this type of information, as well as details about an applicant's work style, personality, and stamina. Most Osteopathic schools require or strongly suggest that you get a letter from an Osteopathic physician. You can locate one through your local or state Osteopathic medical society or through the American Osteopathic Association's website: http://directory.aoa-net.org/cfm/PublicSearch.cfm.

Your supervisor at work can also be an excellent reference. Hopefully, he or she will say that you are a diligent, hard-working employee, or that you are innovative and demonstrate common sense, honesty, or other positive attributes.

Counterproductive References

Do not get letters from teaching assistants, friends or school alumni (other than those in a category above), relatives, clergymen, politicians, or people who just don't like you. You think I'm being funny? Not at all. Medical schools often receive reference letters from individuals in all these categories. Letters from these sources do not normally help your application. Why do people request letters from such references, especially from individuals who don't like them? Usually, students feel obligated to ask such individuals for letters because they have worked with them or mentioned them in their résumé or personal statement. Don't fall into this trap!

Many students ask teaching assistants for letters. Even though they may know you better than your professors do, they are very weak references and may even be detrimental. (If they are so inclined, ask them to write the letter for the professor's signature.) Admission officers are interested in how well you will do in school *and* the profession. They want consistent information from reputable, knowledgeable sources. That means your professors. "If she can't get these letters, there must be something wrong with her," they say. Don't make the admission committee think that!

As for letters from the clergy or a politician, use them only with great care. If a clergyman can speak to your qualities as a leader and person without discussing their church's doctrine, then a letter from them might be beneficial. (Loma Linda Medical School is the exception. They specifically seek applicants who are members of the Seventh-day Adventist Church or "nonchurch-related applicants who have demonstrated a strong commitment to Christian principles.") As for politicians, unless they know you well, their prestigious (or infamous?) name is not likely to help you, as the following story from one admission committee shows:

> **One of our applicants had the U.S. Secretary of Health and Human Services send a recommendation letter. His mother had once worked for him as a secretary, so he was glad to do it. However, not knowing the applicant, he could only write, "I firmly support his application to your medical school. He will undoubtedly be a fine physician."**

Great! The applicant wasted one of his valuable reference letters on one that didn't help him at all.

When to Ask

Don't be a wimp! If you want a letter from a particular individual, ask for it. But, ask at the right time and in the right way. When is the right time? If you do a great job in a class and you want the professor to write a reference letter, ask near the end of the term or soon afterward. Don't wait until six months or a year later. Even if the faculty member's memory of you does not fade with time, he or she may move away, be on sabbatical, or be otherwise unavailable. Ask if the letter can be drafted immediately, explaining that you will tell him where to send it later.

Ask your mentor or adviser during a counseling session. If your adviser has been arbitrarily selected by another person, for example by the Dean of Students, first think about whether he or she knows you well enough to write a good reference letter.

If you want a letter from someone with whom you have worked, such as on a job, as a volunteer, or in the laboratory, just ask if he or she can "write me an excellent reference letter." If you will be working with several individuals over an extended period of time, ask each of them in advance if they will write you a letter when you are ready to apply. Then provide the final information needed to write it to those individuals whose letters you think will be the strongest.

Be certain to ask for your reference letters no later than the spring before you submit your AMCAS application. If you wait longer than that, some of the faculty you have asked to write letters will be busy giving final exams; afterward, they may be away from campus until the fall. Ask for these letters early.

How to Ask

When asking for a reference letter, don't send coded messages. Ask for it directly, but phrase your request in such a way that neither you nor the faculty member will be saddled with either a negative or a neutral (read "negative") letter.

One way of doing this is to ask if the faculty member "would feel comfortable writing me a *strong* letter of support?" If you note any hesitation, forget it and try elsewhere. Avoid getting a letter from someone who may be uncomfortable writing you a superior reference letter. Be thankful that this person did not just say "yes," and then send a lukewarm or even a negative reference. Such letters can demolish your chance of getting into medical school. One of our wisest and most experienced faculty members, Douglas Lindsey, M.D., D.P.H. (unfortunately, now retired), offered to write letters for every student. He wrote them honestly, then showed the student the letter. It was up to the student to decide whether to send it. This was an excellent policy of a great teacher; unfortunately, it is probably unique.

If someone agrees to write a reference letter for you, assist him or her (and yourself) by supplying the information needed to make it an outstanding letter. Give the writer a copy of your résumé, your personal statement, your "goals" statement if you have one, and perhaps a picture. A picture? Sure! Remember, your professor may have from 300 to 500 students each term. Remind him of who you are—give him a picture.

One way to circumvent the problem of a poor reference letter is to ask for a copy of the letter for your files. This gambit is somewhat tricky. If you firmly believe that the individual will write a superlative letter but will not give you a copy, go ahead—at some risk. If the individual agrees to give you a copy of the letter, then you stand a good chance of at least marginally upgrading the letter's quality; people often write a more positive letter if they know you will see it. Only a few people in academia make it a policy to send copies of the reference letters they write to the individuals for whom they write them. In the business world, this is standard practice and common courtesy. Too bad the practice isn't yet widespread in academia.

Many medical school admission committees prefer "confidential letters," which means that you have waived your right to ask the prehealth adviser's office to show them to you. However, this doesn't prevent your letter writers from sending you a copy. If possible, you want to see those letters before they go out, so ask your references to send you a copy, explaining (if it is true, as it is in most cases) that the prehealth committee will not give you access to your file.

The Format

While letters from your premed adviser are usually professionally typed or printed on the school's stationary, the same may not be true for other reference letters. It may seem unbelievable, but faculty and other professionals often send out reference letters that are not on letterhead, are handwritten, or both. This is a negative reflection not only on these individuals, but also on you. Other references, such as the coordinator of the Little League team you coach, may not use letterhead or a computer. Physicians working for some branches of the federal government and those in solo or rural practice also seem to have difficulty producing professional reference letters. If you believe that any of your references will not submit a professional-looking document, either offer to have the letter typed for them or just ask someone else. The best format to use is a laser- or inkjet-printed letter on letterhead stationery with a handwritten note from the writer. That gets attention.

Few people know what goes into a good reference letter. They might find it useful if you give them a copy of Figure 13.3, Elements of a Reference Letter, when you ask them to write one for you. Older or more experienced individuals may prefer that you first ask if they would like you to send them a copy of the figure. Whether or not you send this to them, do provide them with the materials mentioned above to help them when they write the letter.

Be sure to tell them where to send the letters. Also, tell them, and include prominently in the materials you give them, the deadline for the letter's receipt. (You might want to provide preaddressed and stamped envelopes in which to send the letters.) Use one or more copies of Figure 13.4 if your premedical committee does not collect and send out your letters.

Follow-up

Once an individual says a reference letter has been sent on your behalf, you have two more jobs—ensuring that the letter arrives and thanking the letter writer. Your first duty is to ensure that the letters actually arrived where they needed to go—either to the medical schools or to the premed office. It's surprising how many reference letters get lost in the mail, in an office, or, most commonly, on the letter writer's desk. About two weeks after the writer says the letter was sent (or after you received a copy), call the offices that were to receive the letter and ask if it has arrived. If it hasn't, contact your reference, explain the situation, and ask him or her to send another copy.

Your second duty is to send a thank-you note to each person who wrote a letter on your behalf. This is the professional and courteous thing to do. It also increases the probability that this person will write letters for future medical school applicants. That's a gift you can give to those students who are behind you in the process.

FIGURE 13.3

Elements of a Reference Letter

You have been asked to write a reference letter for medical school. Medical schools heavily weigh these letters when considering applicants. If possible, please consider including the following items in your letter:

Please address the letter to: "Dear Admission Committee"

A. How and How Long You Have Known the Individual?

B. Who are You? (Brief, one sentence description.)

C. Individual's Scholastic Record
1. Standing in graduating class
2. Honors/commendations in courses
3. Other honors
4. Any extenuating circumstances that should be considered when interpreting the individual's grades

D. Individual's Personal Characteristics
(List strongest points first. Give specific examples.)
1. Relations with peers, faculty, ancillary staff
2. Willingness to assume responsibility
3. Ability and methods for handling stressful situations
4. Consistency of working up to potential
5. Dependability
6. Integrity; moral and ethical qualities
7. Industriousness
8. Initiative
9. Motivation
10. Interest in medicine and learning
11. Emotional maturity
12. Flexibility
13. Sense of humor

E. Summary
1. Of all premedical students with whom you have dealt, how would you rate this applicant on the basis of his or her personal characteristics (e.g., Top 1%, 5%, 50%)?
2. Are there any personal characteristics that might interfere with this individual's career in medicine?
3. May the admission committee contact you about your letter?

— Secondary Applications —

About five weeks after you submit your AMCAS, AACOMAS, or other application materials, you should begin receiving secondary applications from schools (Figure 15.8). Each medical school has its own forms. Read the cover letters accompanying the secondary applications very carefully.

While most schools actively screen applicants by eliminating individuals whose uniform application clearly indicates they are not competitive, some send secondary applications either to all applicants or to all in-state applicants. (Why do so many students apply to schools that clearly state that they do not take out-of-state students? Carefully read a school's information before applying.)

FIGURE 13.4

Request for Reference Letter

[Type or neatly print all information]

NAME ______________________________ DATE ______________

ADDRESS ____

____

PHONE ________________________

Schools must receive these letters by __________________________

SCHOOL	ADDRESS
________________________	________________________
	________________________
	________________________
________________________	________________________
	________________________
	________________________
________________________	________________________
	________________________
	________________________
________________________	________________________
	________________________
	________________________
________________________	________________________
	________________________
	________________________
________________________	________________________
	________________________
	________________________
________________________	________________________
	________________________
	________________________
________________________	________________________
	________________________
	________________________

Schools may send different cover letters depending on how competitive an applicant appears. The cover letter will say either that you "still merit consideration" but must first complete the secondary application or that "Your credentials are not competitive with other applicants." If you get the second message, you may still complete the secondary application but it is probably not worth your effort.

Secondary applications are now available on some school websites. Schools may allow applicants to either submit them online or to download, print, and then mail the forms. In some cases, part of the form can be submitted online, while the remainder (e.g., photograph, check) must be mailed.

In most cases, secondary applications request the same material you included on your uniform application plus some additional details, essays, and, usually, an additional fee of from $25 to $100 or more. It doesn't take long for these sums to add up—often to over $1,000. If the school asks for one or more additional essays, they will provide you with specific topics to write about. (Hopefully, you have written all or some of these essays in advance.)

Since your uniform application is sent to all the schools at the same time, your secondary applications may arrive in batches. *The worst possible move is to procrastinate in generating any requested materials and completing them.* Set a time limit for submitting each one, for example, two days after its arrival. Write this deadline on the envelope in which you received the material and try very hard to meet it. To spur you on, note that some schools will not consider secondary applications that are returned more than three weeks after they were sent to the applicant.

If you cannot submit the secondary application online, use a fast delivery method with a tracking method (U.S. Priority or Express Mail or an overnight service) to return the application materials to the school. (Send "return-requested" if by U.S. mail. Overnight services automatically track packages and most allow you to check the package's status online.)

Letter-file Services

Your reference letters are sent to schools only with the secondary applications (not with the uniform application). About 77% of undergraduate schools have a "letter-file service," often through their premed offices, which keeps your reference letters on file and mails them when you provide your list of medical schools. The larger the school, the more likely they are to offer this service. About 12% of schools charge a fee for this service; schools with more than 100 medical school applicants per year are most likely to charge. The cost ranges from $20 to $160 for those with a one-time charge; for schools that charge per letter, the average is $5 per letter. (Some services only charge individuals who are not current undergraduates.)

Most (about 72%) of these services have no maximum number of letters that they will file for a student. If an applicant needs to reapply in a subsequent year, nearly all permit additional reference letters to be added. Most services automatically send all letters in a student's file, although about 29% allow the student to select which letters from their file they want sent. Nearly half of these services store students' letter files permanently. The rest destroy the letters sometime after the student's graduation.

If you do not have such a service available or you elect not to use it, inform your letter writers of the addresses for your schools. If possible, give them adhesive labels to put on their envelopes to speed the process. Many secondary applications also include special forms for your letter writers to complete. Make sure that they receive these. *Check back within two weeks to be sure that they have sent the letters or forms.*

Although secondary applications are painful to complete, they indicate that you have cleared the first obstacle in your pursuit of a medical education.

— Photographs —

About half of the school-specific applications and the University of Texas System's uniform application either require or give the applicant the option of including a passport-size photograph. Because photos reveal race, gender, and age and schools cannot discriminate against individuals based on race, sex, age, or national background, requesting or requiring such pictures may be illegal under civil rights legislation. If pictures are optional, don't include one. Let your application materials speak for you.

Once you have been granted an interview, however, you should have a photograph for the school to include with your application materials. Why should you do this? For a very obvious reason: You want to be remembered. Do you really think that an interviewer will remember anything specific about Jerry Glover or Mary Smythe after seeing 40 applicants? Probably not. But with a photograph to jog their memory during final selection, the good impressions that you left with the interviewers will come flooding back.

What kind of photograph do you give them? As with everything else you do in the application process, your photograph must look professional. Don't sit in the drugstore photo machine that gives you five pictures for one dollar (as I foolishly did as a destitute undergraduate). Your career is at stake! Go to a professional photographer and explain that you need a portrait photo. Unless you are specifically asked for a black and white picture, get it in color. The benefit of using a skilled photographer is that no matter what you look like, you will appear much better in the picture. Shop around to get the best price. The differences, especially if you are in a large city, can be enormous.

Finally, before handing the picture to the admission secretary for your file, put a gummed label on the back with your name, address, telephone number, and the date that you are interviewing. Oh yes, remember to say "cheese."

— Assessing Your Chance for Acceptance —

There is a rather simple formula that seems to be a good barometer for measuring each student's chance of being accepted to medical school, although its validity is based only on anecdotal evidence. Developed by Dr. William Hussey at Brooklyn College, that formula is:

(Total GPA x 10) + (Science GPA x 10) + MCAT Score = Admission Score

Using the admission score, applicants can be divided into three groups according to their chance of admission to medical school. Applicants with scores of 100 or greater have an excellent chance of acceptance to medical school. Those with scores in the high 90s have a reasonable chance of acceptance, and those scoring in the low 90s probably will not be accepted. Note that this scale is shifted down by 15 points for minority and disadvantaged applicants, by 5 to 10 points for Osteopathic medical schools, and by varying amounts for selected medical schools.

> ***Example:*** Jane Smith has a GPA of 3.6, a Science GPA of 3.5, and a total MCAT score (excluding the essay) of 29. Her "admission score" is: (3.6 X 10) + (3.5 X 10) + 29 = 100. Based on her admission score, Jane Smith has an excellent chance of getting into medical school.

When the number of applicants increases, those in the high-acceptance group still get in and those in the low-acceptance group generally do not. Students in the middle category, with scores in the high 90s, are the "swing" group; they are eliminated as the number of applicants in the high-acceptance group increases.

There are several problems with this formula. One is that many medical schools say they give more weight to MCAT scores than to GPAs, while other schools don't require MCAT scores or else barely consider the scores. So there is a great deal of variation among the schools.

As for MCAT scores, you may be delighted (or saddened) to learn that in 2002, applicants with scores as low as 2.8 on the Verbal Reasoning section, 4.3 on the Physical Science section, 4.9 on the Physical Science section, or "K" on the Writing Sample were accepted to M.D.-granting schools; many applicants scoring much higher in each section were rejected. (The Writing Sample is the portion of the MCAT most frequently ignored or downplayed by medical school admission committees.)

In terms of GPAs, in 2002, some applicants who were accepted to M.D.-granting schools had an overall GPA of 2.6, a science GPA of 2.27, or a nonscience GPA of 2.78, while many applicants with much higher GPAs were rejected.

— Communicating with the Schools —

Once you submit your initial application packet, you will communicate with the schools primarily by e-mail, and occasionally by telephone. The first time you should contact a school is about one month after you have requested that all your material be sent to them. Find out if everything has arrived. If not, what is missing? It is your responsibility, not theirs, to make sure that they have received all your paperwork. If they don't answer your e-mail within three working days, call them.

How you communicate with schools is very important. Amazingly, the nicest, most sophisticated individuals often have terrible e-mail etiquette—and an even worse telephone "presence." Make it a practice to think before you write and to reread everything you plan to send by e-mail. Only hit the "send" button if:

1. You are sure you are sending it to the right place. You will be more than embarrassed if you accidentally send the question about Podunk U Medical School to Harvard.
2. The message is exactly what you want to say, asks understandable questions, and does not contain overblown syntax, e-mail jargon or abbreviations, or misspellings.
3. The message is courteous and professional.

If you phone the school, your voice and attitude will make a big impression on the admission staff. Don't think that you can be brusque or rude because you are *only* talking to the secretary! As in many businesses, a secretary who interacts with applicants usually has a major impact on who is selected for both interviews and final positions. Many admission officers ask their secretaries for input, and most take this input very seriously. Refine your telephone technique and be very pleasant to those secretaries. They can be either your allies or your enemies. Make them think of you as a nice person, someone they want as a student at *their* medical school.

Once you are in a medical school's admission system, stay in touch with the Dean of Admissions or the admission committee. Unless your premed adviser or the school's application materials tell you that they do not want additional information from you, write to tell them about anything interesting or relevant to your future medical career that you have done since you submitted your application. Continue to do this even after your interview. If something particularly noteworthy happens, give them a call. Some schools keep track of these "interest communications." Your message to them is that you are the right choice for their medical school!

14

Admission Committees And Procedures

Though this be madness, yet there is method in't.

— *Shakespeare,* Hamlet, II,

Admission committees and admission procedures vary among medical schools. General information is provided below, but each school's system has individual quirks.

The average admission committee consists of about 15 people, usually including the Dean of Admissions and both basic science and clinical faculty. About two-thirds of the schools also have at least one medical student on the committee, in either a voting or nonvoting capacity. About one-fourth include alumni or members of the admission staff, and one in eight schools has residents (physicians in postgraduate training) serving as committee members.

As Randall Zielinski writes in *The Medical School Interview,* "The committee must compare apples with oranges, and predict which, when fed to the cow, will make the tastiest steak four years down the road." It's not an easy task, and, being human, they do it imperfectly.

— The Screening Process —

The admission committee sets the criteria that its members use to screen applications. These criteria often differ, even at some private schools, for in-state (in-Territory, in-Province) and out-of-state residents. In addition, their criteria usually vary for underrepresented minority candidates. A small subcommittee, often just two or three committee members, usually screens the initial applications and supporting materials to decide which applicants will be interviewed. They generally place applicants into one of four categories: interview, possible later interview (depending upon the quality of other applicants), re-review (often by a larger subcommittee or the entire committee), and reject. At some schools, the subcommittee alone makes this determination, while at others the entire admission committee makes all these decisions or just those decisions that are difficult or borderline. Most take this task very seriously, since they understand that applicants must spend a lot of money for travel and lodging, in addition to taking time off from work or school to interview at their school. Therefore, they try to offer interviews only to those applicants whom they are seriously considering.

At some schools, applicants who rate high enough after the initial screening are sent a secondary application. Otherwise, they can be rejected at this stage. (Schools that use a "passive screen" send cover letters stating that an applicant is not competitive, but also include a secondary application.) Some schools, especially state-supported medical schools, are quite liberal in sending secondary applications, while others skip this step altogether. Members of the admission committee also screen the secondary applications and place applicants into one of the aforementioned categories.

After the interviews, the entire admission committee reviews each applicant's admission packet. While only one or two members of the committee may have interviewed the applicant, the other committee members review the application materials and the interviewer's comments. Normally, all members vote on each applicant's acceptability. Applicants with the highest number of votes (in any admission cycle) are accepted to the medical school, while those with a lower number are either put on a waiting list or rejected. If an applicant is rejected, no appeals mechanism exists (except for the courts, which is a long, costly, and usually fruitless process). The only options are to be accepted at another medical school or to reapply in a subsequent year.

Figure 14.1 is a flowchart of one medical school's selection process. Keep in mind that each school has different criteria.

— Selection Criteria —

Lots of scuttlebutt exists about what information medical school admission committees consider important. When these committees were actually surveyed, they divided the information into three categories: Very Important, Moderately Important, and (by implication) Not Important.

The VERY IMPORTANT factors are:

- Ratings from medical school interviews
- Undergraduate, postbaccalaureate, and graduate school GPAs
- MCAT scores
- Recommendation letters from premedical committees, undergraduate advisers, or faculty members
- Knowledge about health care issues
- Commitment to a health care career

The MODERATELY IMPORTANT factors are:

- Number of incompletes, withdrawals, or repeated undergraduate or graduate courses
- Community and campus citizenship
- Health-related (volunteer or paid) work experience
- Extracurricular activities
- Recency of relevant course work
- Quality of the school(s) attended
- Number and quality of science courses
- Compatibility between candidate's characteristics or professional goals and the school's mission
- Personal statement(s) on centralized and institution-specific applications

Since these are the factors they do consider important, other factors, by implication, are not important. Note that although admission committees do use these criteria and sources of information, exactly how they evaluate each piece of information may differ among applicant categories.

How Good Are the Selection Criteria?

While this question may seem obvious and easily tested, the real question is: What are the committees looking for? As Drs. Coombs and Paulson wrote in the *Journal of Medical Humanities*,

> **The typical recruitment process favors applicants who are emotionally inexpressive, grade-conscious, competitive and narrowly specialized in science. They are . . . self-sacrificing and bookish rather than broadly experienced, and trust in a hard science quantifying approach that disregards less readily measurable psychosocial factors, such as feelings.**

Although the current criteria seem to favor such individuals, most admission committees specifically *don't* want this type of person. They want to select those applicants who will be excellent clinicians, and, sometimes, clinical researchers and educators.

So, what type of individual do they seek? Is it someone who will do best in the first two (preclinical/basic science) years of medical school? Is it someone who will pass the USMLE, the test

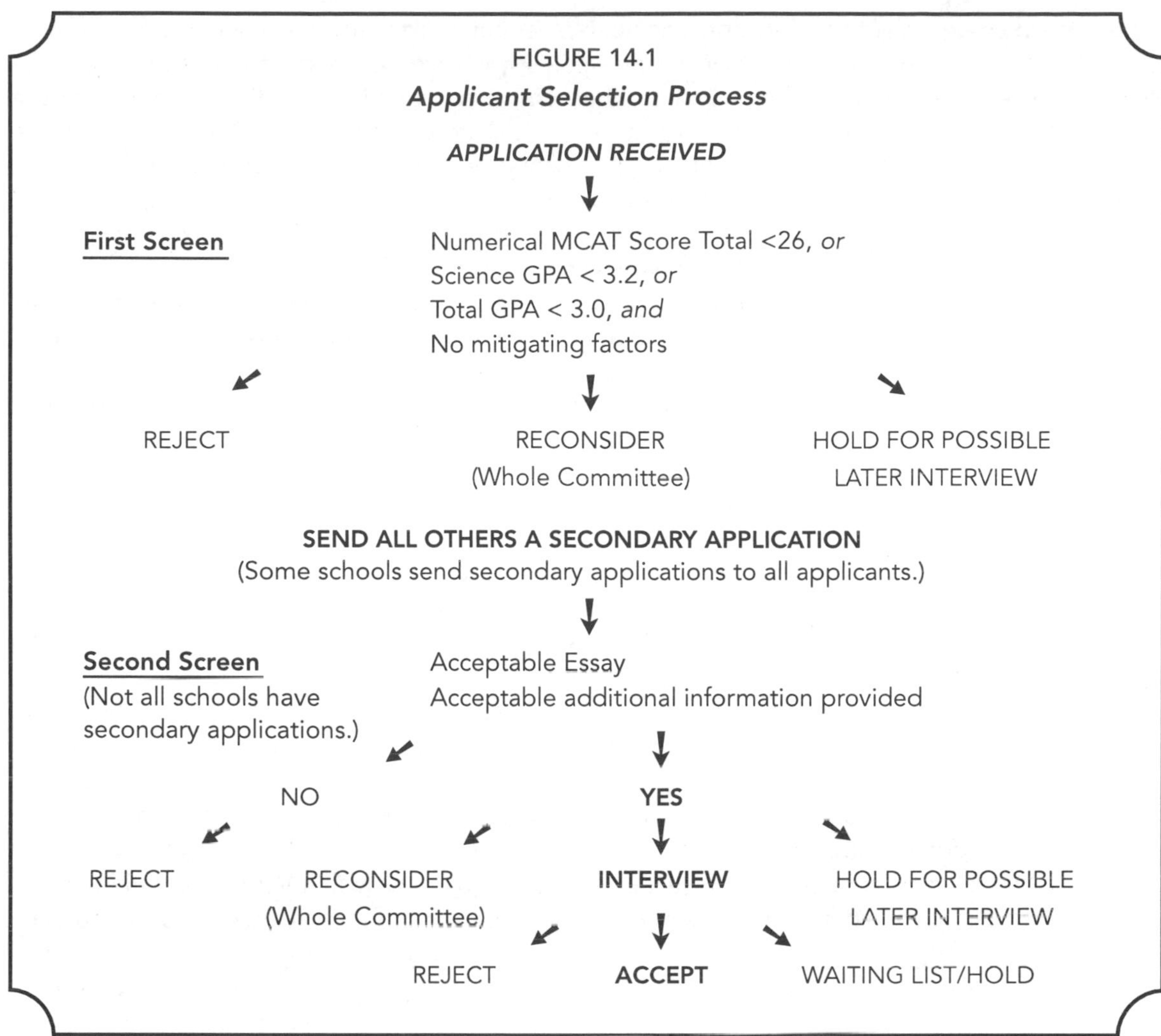

FIGURE 14.1
Applicant Selection Process

everyone must pass (D.O.'s have an equivalent test) to practice medicine? Is it an individual who will be accepted into the most competitive residency? Or is it, in the end, someone who will make the "best" physician—who is intelligent, has compassion for patients, and has the ability to survive the stresses of medical practice?

This last is what medical schools would *like* to test for in their applicants. Unfortunately, the qualities of the "best" physicians are still unquantifiable. What we do know is that some measurements correlate with performance in medical school, passing the USMLE, and subsequent performance in residency. We also know that some measures that are commonly thought to be indicators of performance actually correlate poorly or not at all. Applicants' MCAT scores, their science and overall GPAs, and the selectivity of their undergraduate schools (based on the mean SAT scores for entering students) are good predictors of how well students will perform in their preclinical years. This seems to be true for both traditional and less-traditional medical school curricula. Students' MCAT scores and GPAs also appear to correlate, although not as strongly, with how well students do on the first two USMLE Steps and in their clinical rotations.

Special Applicants: School Ties

At many schools, applicants with special ties to the school receive preference for interviews and, sometimes, for acceptance. Some schools say that they waive residency (state or country) requirements for such applicants. Others give these applicants preference for interviews and, if they are "borderline" or on the waiting list, special preference for admission.

Being in this applicant category offers no guarantees but, since every advantage helps, it would be wise to apply to schools where you have a connection. If you have a connection to a medical school, it is worthwhile noting that fact on your application or in a separate letter to the school's admission office. What is considered a "tie" varies among schools. Categories include the children, grandchildren, spouses or significant others of: current medical students, medical school and resident alumni, faculty, staff, volunteers, former employees, any Osteopathic physician, "friends of the school," or current applicants to the medical school. Some schools also designate a number of medical school positions each year for graduates of their undergraduate school.

In most instances, however, applicants with these special ties receive only a "courtesy interview" or "counseling session" if their file is not competitive. If you have a connection to a medical school that invites you for an interview, you may want to verify that it is a regular interview before you go. While the courtesy interview or counseling session may prove useful to you, you may not want to spend the money unless it is a "real" interview and you have a bona fide chance of being admitted.

Selecting Applicants to Be Generalist Physicians

Educators have tried to determine which characteristics lead to physicians who will become generalists (general internal medicine, family practice, and general pediatrics), rather than specialists. Some schools have a mission, often designated by their primary funding sources (the legislatures), to produce a large number of generalists, so they take this goal very seriously. They have found that many of the current admission criteria select for specialists, rather than for general physicians.

Medical students who subsequently have subspecialty or research careers usually have high MCAT Science scores, an extensive science background, and an interest in intellectual achievement. They also have higher "Machiavellian scores," that is, they prize devious behavior and flattery as a means of getting ahead and devalue homosexuals, people with low IQs, patients with self-inflicted problems, and individuals who don't contribute to society.

Individuals who enter general medicine usually score high on the MCAT Verbal Reasoning section, are more tolerant of ambiguity, are primarily interested in patient problems related to social issues and psychology, are nonscience majors, have a more acute sense of social responsibility, and are women. They usually have taken a wide variety of undergraduate courses and have shown a strong commitment to community service in their prior activities and in their essays. The likelihood of an applicant entering a generalist specialty also seems to be directly related to taking strong leadership roles, inversely related to his or her socioeconomic status, and not related to the type or number of nonservice extracurricular activities.

About one-fourth of those who eventually enter a generalist specialty envision that career path at the time they take the MCAT, while only about 1 in 12 of those who think they will be specialists eventually enter a generalist specialty. Medical school applicants, savvy to what admission committees want to hear, tend to answer questions about career choice in a "politically correct" manner. To counteract this, some schools train their interviewers to ask about applicants' medically related experiences to determine whether they are oriented toward generalist specialties. To increase the number of their graduates entering generalist specialties, some medical schools accept students specifically for a primary care track, even if though they may have lower test scores or GPAs than the average medical student.

Some medical schools have tried recruiting students from rural areas with the hope that they will return to practice in these medically underserved regions. However, these students generally don't return, preferring instead to follow the same path as their classmates. (As the 1918 song goes, "How You Gonna Keep 'Em Down on the Farm After They've Seen Paree?")

— A More Perfect Application System? —

You don't look so great on paper, but you have all the personal qualities needed to be a great physician. "Why don't they look at me as a person?" you ask. Some leading medical educators and policy makers are asking the same thing. They know that the majority of the applicants they reject from medical schools would make good physicians, perhaps better than many of those that they currently accept.

With that in mind, they would like to see medical schools select students who have a tolerance for ambiguity and an ability to function with uncertainty, individuals who want to care for and not just cure their patients, those who can tolerate the increasing oversight and regulation within medicine, those with interpersonal skills, and those who are comfortable with cultural diversity. They would, of course, like to see these qualities in those who have also demonstrated intellectual achievement, diverse academic interests (demonstrated by taking courses in humanities, ethics, and social sciences), computer literacy, a capacity for self-education, and critical thinking skills. Figure 14.2 lists some of the positive and negative personal qualities that admission committees look for—usually in interviews, personal essays, and recommendation letters.

Admission officers repeatedly say that they could replace admission committees with computers if all they had to do was "crunch the numbers." The recent deluge of applications combined with the limited time committee members have to devote to the process (rarely, if ever, are they thanked or

FIGURE 14.2

Positive and Negative Personal Attributes in Medical School Applicants

Positive Attributes

- Self-motivation
  - Positive attitude toward self-education
  - Spirit of inquiry and curiosity
  - Imagination and creativity
- Compassion, tolerance, empathy, and patience
- An appropriate view of the physician's changing roles
  - Realistic expectations
  - Tolerance of others' beliefs
  - Ability to work as part of a team
  - Willingness to subordinate one's own needs to those of patients
  - Flexible outlook
- Social responsibility
  - Self-confidence
  - Altruism
- Intellectual honesty
- Optimism
- Maturity
- Verbal communication ability

Negative Attributes

- Neurotic
- Rigid and intolerant of other ideas and people
- Dishonest
- Extreme traits
  - Introvert/Extrovert
  - Compulsive/Disorganized
  - Obsessed/Poorly motivated
  - Manic/Apathetic

Adapted from: Powis DA. Selecting medical students. *Medical Education.* 1994;28:443-69.

compensated for this work) does not let them really assess applicants' subjective qualities—especially in the first cut, when they decide whom to interview. As Dr. John Bruhn wrote in the *Journal of Medical Education*, "The admission committee often bows to the following rationale: Why belabor noncognitive factors in the biography of an academically borderline applicant when there are so many applicants with strong academic credentials (grades and MCAT scores) irrespective of noncognitive factors?"

If committees begin to use subjective criteria more heavily, though, rejected students with higher grades and MCAT scores will have cause for legal action under the U.S. Constitution's 5th Amendment guarantees of due process and the 14th Amendment's guarantees of equal protection under the law. (Schools are aware of the cases, especially in California and Texas, where rejected students have successfully sued on these bases.) Schools violate these constitutional rights if they publish their admission criteria in their brochures and in the AAMC's *Medical School Admission Requirements* but then do not apply those criteria equally to all applicants. If they use extended, personality-related criteria, they must explicitly say this in the information that all applicants receive.

The bottom line for applicants, then, is to strive to improve your "numbers" and demonstrate your other qualities in your essays and interviews.

— The "Perfect" Applicant —

Everyone wants to know who is the "perfect" applicant. That is neither the right question to ask nor a question with a unique answer. Why shouldn't you ask this question? First, because it is demoralizing. No one is perfect, and striving for perfection can only produce headaches.

Second, the person you compete against is nearly always yourself. Have you done the best you could? Are you doing it now? Since you can only do your best, it really doesn't matter that much what others do. Contrary to popular belief, it does not take a genius to be a physician; it takes the willingness to work hard over the long haul. Nearly anyone who can graduate from college has the ability to become a physician. The question is whether an individual has the necessary motivation to put forth the effort.

Third, you really don't compete against "perfect" applicants. If anyone comes close to these criteria, they have no difficulty getting into medical school. It is the other 99% of applicants, imperfect like you and me, who compete for the remaining slots.

FIGURE 14.3

The "Imperfect" (Real) Medical School Matriculant

Grade Point Average	• 3.6 on a 4.0 scale (mean)
MCAT Score	• 9.9 scores (<30 total); "P" on Writing Sample (mean)
Experience	• Clinical: Recent • Research: Minimal or none (except those applying to combined Ph.D. programs)
Reference Letters	• Excellent, from premed committee or adviser, undergraduate/graduate faculty, or clinicians • Say that applicant is personable, insightful, and understands what a medical career entails
Interview	• Articulate and outgoing • Demonstrates understanding of medical profession
Abilities	• Walks on land, swims through water, and falls through the air (will float gently over land after medical school and fall through the air a little slower after residency)

The question of what constitutes the "perfect" applicant also has no universal answer. Each medical school has different criteria for choosing medical students. Figure 14.3 offers a composite of the typical "imperfect" student who *does* get into medical school.

Having said that, I'll succumb to the temptation and list the criteria for the "perfect" applicant, knowing that such individuals exist in remarkably small numbers. See Figure 14.4 for the qualities of those who "walk on water." In the end, the question is: "Do your qualities match those selection factors sought by the schools to which you apply?" The key is to carefully read the schools' materials and then apply to the schools that want people like you.

FIGURE 14.4

The "Perfect" Medical School Matriculant

Grade Point Average	• 3.9+ on a 4.0 scale
MCAT Score	• 13+ scores; "T" on Writing Sample
Experience	• Clinical: Recent and significant • Research: Published research related to medicine
Reference Letters	• From dynamic, well-known people • Say that applicant is personable, insightful, and understands what a medical career entails
Interview	• Articulate and personable • Demonstrates compassion and understanding
Abilities	• Walks on water, flies through the air, catches bullets with hands (will catch them in teeth after medical school and stop them by using telepathy after residency)

15

Picking The Right Schools

See one promontory, one mountain,
one sea, one river, and see all.

— Socrates

— Differences Among Medical Schools —

Most applicants, for better or for worse, use a school's general reputation and its geographic location as their two most important selection factors. Women are more concerned about a school's teaching methods and curriculum than are men. Women are also more frequently dissatisfied with the course of study upon graduation.

Size

Many people compare medical schools by citing differences in their sizes. You can measure medical school sizes in two ways: The number of students in each year of the curriculum and the total number of students in the school. Class size varies greatly (Figure 15.6), from the minuscule 20 students per year at Drew/UCLA to a gargantuan 300 students per year at both the University of Illinois and Indiana University. One can approximate the total number of medical students at a school by multiplying the class size by the number of years for the typical curriculum. The University of Illinois, for example, has about 1,200 students in all four years (give or take some to account for decelerated, dismissed, combined-degree, and transfer students).

There are three reasons why these numbers may not be very helpful. First, some schools, such as Indiana University and the University of Nevada, have more than one preclinical campus. Preclinical students at such schools rarely, if ever, see their compatriots on the other campuses. Second, at some schools, such as Texas A&M, their preclinical campus is far away from their clinical campus, so preclinical students rarely see the upperclassmen. Third, most schools have many clinical sites where medical students train. The number of sites is usually in direct proportion to the number of medical students at the school. Therefore, the total number of students, in itself, should not prevent you from applying to a medical school. It is much more important to know about the faculty-to-student ratio for the preclinical years and whether adequate positions are available for training during the clinical years.

Curriculum

How the faculty imparts the information necessary to practice medicine, and what information the faculty deems "necessary," varies among schools. If you are a self-directed learner, you will likely prefer schools that predominantly use independent-study or problem-based learning, rather than schools using the rigid curriculum/lecture method. The evaluation methods used by each school (and departments within the school) also differ significantly. Find medical schools with curricula, teaching philosophies, and evaluation methods that mesh with your needs. Many applicants do not consider this, and they suffer the consequences.

Nearly one in 20 medical school graduates is dissatisfied with the quality of his or her medical education. Worse (and this is sort of scary), about one in six graduating medical students are not confident that they have learned the clinical skills required to begin a residency program! This, however, may have more to do with individual students than with the schools they attended.

Time to Complete Medical School

The typical medical school curriculum lasts four years, although the actual time varies from 129 to 177 weeks. (Note that, according to the LCME, the official minimum is 130 weeks, preferably spread over four years.) The average length of study at U.S. M.D.-granting schools is 38 weeks in the first year, 36 weeks in the second year, 47 weeks in the third year, and 35 weeks in the fourth year. These numbers do not include the time devoted to studying for midterm and final examinations, or the time set aside to study for the licensing examinations. While the amount of scheduled teaching time has gradually increased over the past decade, the average number of hours that first- and second-year medical students meet with their instructors has decreased by about 10%, in part due to the introduction of computer-assisted instruction.

Between 15% and 19% of medical students enrolled in four-year programs take five years to graduate. Students most likely to take more than four years to graduate are women, those 28 years or older when they apply, those with undergraduate GPAs of 2.5 or less, and those with MCAT Science Composite Scores less than 8. The last two factors are the most significant predictors. Minority students are least likely to graduate in four years. By ethnicity, the percent of medical students who graduate in four years are: nonminority students (85%), underrepresented minorities (65%), and other minority students (79%).

Medical School Courses

Medical students spend their first two years primarily studying the basic sciences. The first year, they concentrate on learning normal or healthy conditions in anatomy, histology, neuroanatomy, physiology, and biochemistry. The second year courses, which focus on abnormal conditions and medical treatment, are: pathology, microbiology, and pharmacology. During the first two years, students also take other courses, including behavioral sciences, medicolegal topics, introductory physical diagnosis, and public health/epidemiology. About 25% of medical schools include time for electives in the first and second years.

At most schools, students spend their second two years on the clinical services. Third-year students normally "rotate" through pediatrics, surgery, internal medicine, obstetrics and gynecology, psychiatry (and sometimes neurology) and, in an increasing number of schools, family practice. Their clinical time is usually divided between hospitals and clinics. Students are given varying amounts of responsibility for evaluating patients, devising courses of further evaluation and of treatment, and performing procedures. They go on "rounds" from one to three times a day, attend lectures, and participate in the operating room. The amount of time spent in ambulatory settings—where most physicians really practice—is increasing (Figure 15.1). Students are supervised by residents, with a varying amount of faculty input. These rotations always have final written examinations and, often, an oral examination. One-third of medical schools allow their third-year students to take electives, although the available options may be very limited.

At most medical schools, there are few, if any, required rotations during the fourth year. Most students spend their fourth year doing elective rotations, taking vacation, and looking for a residency position. On average, schools allow 25 weeks of elective time. Some schools limit the amount of time (averaging 15 weeks) that students may spend away from the school and its affiliated facilities. While students are required to successfully complete a certain number of rotations, they usually get to select where, when, and what rotations they take. The quality of each student's fourth-year curriculum depends, therefore, on his or her willingness to be challenged by new experiences and on the insight of his advisers.

FIGURE 15.1

Length of Required Third- and Fourth-Year Rotations

Specialty (Number of schools requiring)	Average Weeks	% of Time in Ambulatory Care (Average)
Internal Medicine (all schools)	2	23
General Surgery (all schools)	8	20
Obstetrics & Gynecology (all schools)	7	32
Pediatrics (all schools)	7	41
Family Practice (113 schools)	6	94
Psychiatry (all schools)	6	27
Surgical Subspecialties (64 schools)	4	32
Neurology (94 schools)	4	27
Ambulatory Care (46 schools)	5	100

Data derived from: Barzansky B, Etzel SI. Educational programs in U.S. medical schools, 2001-2002. *JAMA*. 2002; 288(9):1067-72.

Special Tracks

In an effort to produce more primary care practitioners, some medical schools have added family practice to their required curricula, often increasing the time spent on these rotations to six weeks. Others have developed special primary care "tracks" that allow participants to substitute an extended rural family practice experience for the usual third-year rotations. A few schools condense medical school and family practice (FP) or an internal medicine (IM) residency into a total of six, rather than seven, years.

Medical schools will probably continue to experiment with similar programs in an attempt to maintain the increased interest in primary care specialties. However, graduates of internal medicine residencies mostly enter subspecialty training instead of practicing primary care.

Teaching Methods

When assessing medical schools, ask yourself which schools use teaching methods that work for you?

Problem-based learning (PBL), small-group sessions, integrated learning, and computer-assisted instruction are the newest buzzwords in medical education. Except for computer instruction, most schools only pay lip service to these methods and continue to use traditional teaching methods. In part, this is because no one has convincingly demonstrated that using the new methods leads to better physicians. (Some educators suggest that medical schools have not implemented these methods correctly, saying that if they did so, they would produce better physicians.)

Problem-based Learning (PBL)

This method (also described in Chapter 24) makes students work through problems, which are usually clinical, using all the resources at their disposal. To solve the problem, students must integrate basic sciences and clinical knowledge, just as practicing physicians do. By doing this with adequate faculty leadership, they are supposed to learn both the factual knowledge and the problem-solving skills necessary for clinical practice. Many schools that have tried PBL are uncertain whether students really do "get" the information they need, so they supplement these sessions with formal lectures.

The push nationally is to make most medical education follow the PBL model. Early studies suggest that students taking only PBL courses do worse on the first two parts of their licensing examination, which are basic science oriented, than their cohorts who take "standard" courses. However, PBL-trained students do better on the last, clinical practice-oriented part of these exams.

Small-group Sessions

Similar to PBL, these sessions hone students' communication, teamwork, and learning skills. However, small-group sessions require an enormous amount of faculty time, which has become scarce as funding for medical schools shrinks. During the first year of medical school, students spend about 50% of their class time in traditional lectures and only about 13% in any type of small-group session. Unfortunately, many of these sessions deteriorate into formal lectures, defeating the purpose of small-group teaching. Most small-group learning occurs on the clinical services, since only a small number of medical students and residents are on a service at any one time.

Integrated Teaching/Learning

Ideally, medical students should simultaneously learn normal anatomy, pathology, and physiology with the associated pharmacology, ethical and legal dilemmas, and epidemiology for the same body areas or systems. This, however, would require an enormous restructuring of the curriculum, as well as extraordinary cooperation among faculty from the disciplines involved. Even with the best intentions, this is almost impossible to accomplish. In addition, a fail-safe mechanism for medical students may be lost in the process. While there is an enormous amount of information thrown at medical students, the truism is that anything that is really important will be taught at least three times in various parts of the curriculum (or on the wards or during residency). Integrating the curriculum may lessen this effect. Since it is so difficult to do, even at the medical schools that attempt to do it, only a minuscule part of students' instruction involves integrated learning.

Computer-assisted Instruction

Nearly all medical schools now use computer-based instructional programs in one or more courses. Most often, they are part of the basic science courses. Computer programs may be used as the primary instructional method, as supplementary study aids, and for students to self-test their understanding of previously presented material. More than half of all medical schools use computer-based simulations to teach or evaluate students' diagnostic or therapeutic decision-making skills. Nearly all medical students now use computer-based programs as study aids, and most use them as a formal part of their courses.

Other Methods and Programs

Many medical schools offer unique programs. They are usually used in parallel with the "regular" program, with some students electing to follow the "special" program. Many schools also have experimented with different teaching methods. Read schools' materials carefully to locate programs that interest you.

Evaluation Methods

Medical schools primarily use five testing methods: multiple-choice examinations, oral examinations, structured patient examinations, computer-based simulations, and direct observation. The most stringent of these are the multiple-choice United States Medical Licensing Examination (USMLE) and the Objective Structured Clinical Examination (OSCE).

To advance from the preclinical to the clinical portion of medical school, 106 (of 128 total) U.S. M.D.-granting schools require their students to pass Step 1 of the USMLE. Another 74 schools require students to pass Step 2 before either advancing to their third year or graduating. The USMLE is a national, standardized, multiple-choice test given in three separate parts, called "Steps." Step 1 primarily tests basic science information. Step 2 tests information necessary to begin practicing medicine as a first-year resident, and requires students to integrate basic sciences with clinical medicine. Step 3 is taken during or after internship.

Relatively new in medical schools, the OSCE tests a student's clinical abilities over a wide range of patient problems commonly seen in primary care. The OSCE uses "standardized patients"—either patients with stable physical findings (e.g., arthritis, heart murmurs), who describe disease symptoms, or staff members trained to describe such symptoms and to simulate the relevant physical signs. The standardized, six- to eight-hour-long test evaluates how well students apply their knowledge to deal with real patients' problems. Ideally, the OSCE tests whether a student can:

- Perform a focused history and physical examination
- Recognize pathological processes
- Interpret laboratory data
- Establish a relevant differential diagnosis
- Develop a treatment plan
- Clearly document these clinical findings and plans

More than 80% of medical schools now use the OSCE either for specific clinical courses (27%), as part of a comprehensive final assessment of a student's clinical skills (10%), or for both (44%). Several schools require students to pass it before graduation. In the future, more schools will undoubtedly use this test.

In the preclinical years, USMLE-style multiple-choice examinations are common. Computer-based testing is also becoming more common, often using the multiple-choice format.

During the clinical years, the testing modalities most frequently encountered are school-generated multiple-choice examinations or USMLE-type "Subject Exams," oral examinations, OSCE or standardized patients, observed history-taking and physical examinations, and computerized case simulations.

Grading Systems

Medical schools primarily use one of two grading systems: Pass/Fail or numeric/letter grades. Some schools mix the two systems, depending upon the courses. When they do this, the least-significant courses are usually graded using the Pass/Fail system. In the 1960s and 1970s, there was a big push toward placing less emphasis on grades, resulting in the use of Pass/Fail grading systems at most medical schools.

Gradually, however, schools succumbed to using a three-grade system (Honors/Pass/Fail) as faculty and students found that the Pass/Fail system was too simple: Students who had been conditioned to the "carrot" of better grades had little motivation to work harder. In addition, residency directors began relying heavily on scores from licensing examinations to compare applicants, since usable grades and class rankings were no longer available.

Today, most medical schools use the Honors/Pass/Fail grading system. "Honors" grades have become very important for students applying to the most competitive residencies. Everyone realizes this system is simply a modification of the old numeric/letter grading system—essentially reduced to A, C, and F. Only a few schools still use a true Pass/Fail system and their graduates are at a disadvantage when they apply to highly competitive residencies.

Costs

The charges for medical school tuition and fees vary markedly among schools, and, especially at public schools, may be different for state and out-of-state residents (Figure 15.6). The average yearly cost to attend medical school from 1960 to 2003 is shown in Figure 15.2. If you compare the cost for each year to the adjusted "real" dollars amount shown in the column labeled "1960 $," you can see that it is not your imagination—the costs really have increased dramatically over time.

Location

There are medical schools throughout the United States, its Territories, Canada, and in most other countries. How do you decide where, geographically speaking, to go? Students normally consider five factors when choosing geographic locations: Their "state-residency" status, where they want to live and practice permanently, the location of their "support system," personal or family requirements, and their "gestalt" for that locale.

The first factor you should consider is your "state of residence." Being an "in-state" student is one of the few ways to get an inexpensive medical education. You don't necessarily have to live in the state where the medical school is located to be considered "in-state." Several states have made special arrangements so that their citizens can be treated as in-state applicants at specific medical schools

FIGURE 15.2

Median Annual Medical School Tuition and Fees

	Private Schools		Public Schools			
			Resident		Non-Resident	
	Cost	1960 $*	Cost	1960 $*	Cost	1960 $*
1960–61	$ 1,050	$ 1,050	$ 498	$ 498	$ 830	$ 830
1970–71	2,000	1,526	683	521	1,300	922
1980–81	7,910	2,841	2,079	747	4,118	1,479
1990–91	18,930	4,287	6,115	1,385	13,839	3,134
1995–96	23,695	4,583	8,715	1,686	20,133	3,894
2002–03**	29,122	5,213	10,056	1,800	27,954	5,004

*Indicates cost in 1960-adjusted "real" dollars.

**Includes M.D. and D.O schools in the United States. Figures do not include those schools not charging tuition for in-state residents and those schools not accepting out-of-state residents (see Figure 15.6).

Adapted from: Association of American Medical Colleges. *AAMC Data Book: Statistical Information Related to Medical Education.* Washington, DC: AAMC, 1996, Table E1, and other sources.

located in other states. (See Chapter 16 for more information.) You also have a better chance of acceptance at your state school(s) than at most other medical schools. Note that many private schools also give some preference to in-state residents. (See Figure 15.7 for school-specific information.) About two-thirds of all medical students attend medical school in the state where they are legal residents; nearly 90% of those at public medical schools and more than 40% of those at private schools are residents of the state where they are attending medical school.

Some students pick a medical school based on where they want to live permanently. This is a mistake. Most physicians do not ultimately practice in the city where they attended medical school. Rather, physicians tend to settle near the city where they complete their residencies. It is often more important for medical students to be near their personal "support system." Your support system may include your family, friends, co-religionists, mentors, or teachers. If you are married, you can usually take your support system with you wherever you go. If not, it is very helpful to have people close by who can bolster your spirits during the difficult times you will inevitably encounter while in medical school. You or your family members may also have special circumstances that require you to be in a certain place during school. Among these are your spouse's job, children's medical needs, or parents who need special attention.

Finally, you should feel comfortable at the medical school. Would you feel safe and "at home" in that area of the country, that city, or that part of the city? Just because you are not familiar with a particular locale, however, is no reason to dismiss it out of hand. Locations often "grow on you."

For some schools, actual physical safety may be a concern. The federal Campus Security Act requires all U.S. colleges and universities to publish an annual security report containing campus security policies and procedures, campus crime statistics, campus programs to prevent sexual assault, and procedures to report sex offenses. Schools must distribute these reports to current and prospective students. Few medical schools spontaneously send out such information, but they will if you ask for it.

Success in "Competitive" Residencies/Specialties

A school's reputation does play a role in how easily its graduates obtain competitive residency positions. How much of a factor it is remains unclear and varies with the specialty. Students from schools known for graduating excellent clinicians, for example, often have an easier time than those from "big-name" schools in obtaining the most competitive primary care residencies. To see how graduates of a particular school have done in getting residencies, ask the Dean of Students to show you a list of the residency sites and specialties for students from the last one or two classes. While many graduates, especially from state schools, opt for in-state residencies, look to see if some graduates matched in the competitive specialties (even if you don't think you will want to) and whether some went to competitive training sites. (You may have to rely on physician mentors to help you decipher these lists.)

However, when schools tell you how many of their students "got their first or second residency choice," ignore it. That is a bogus figure. Many students who do not believe they are competitive erroneously put their "sure bet" programs high on their list so that they will be certain to get a position in the Match. This can vastly inflate the number of students who get the programs "they wanted."

The Faculty

Medical school faculties are comprised of full-time, part-time, and volunteer instructors in both the preclinical and clinical areas. How a school's faculty compares to the average faculty may give you an idea of their orientation: teaching, clinical work, or research (see Figure 15.3).

At the average medical school, about 10% of the school's faculty, and more than 18% of full-time faculty, are in the preclinical (basic) sciences. About 5% of the preclinical faculty are part-time and 26% are volunteers (unpaid). Roughly 90% of medical school faculty and about 82% of full-time faculty are clinicians, while about 6% of the clinical faculty are part-time and 58% are volunteers.

The ratio of full-time faculty members to medical students is about 1.6 to 1.0. This represents a marked increase over the past two decades. In 1984–85, for example, the ratio was only 0.88 to 1.0. Most of this increase stems from the need for more clinicians to generate income to keep the schools financially viable.

Only 26% of preclinical faculty and only 30% of clinical faculty are women, with very few full professors among them. Only 23% of women preclinical faculty are full professors versus 65% of men. Among the clinical faculty, only 9% of women are full professors, while nearly 28% of men hold that rank. (See Figures 8.4 and 8.5.)

FIGURE 15.3

Average Percentage of Full-Time Medical School Faculty in Various Areas*

	Percent of Faculty		Percent of Faculty
Preclinical			
Anatomy/Cell Biology	1.9%	Pathology**	4.5%
Biochemistry	1.9	Pharmacology	1.9
Biomedical Engineering	0.2	Physiology/Biophysics	1.7
Genetics	0.7	Neuroscience	0.6
Microbiology	1.7	Other	2.7
Clinical			
Anesthesiology	4.9%	Otolaryngology	1.2%
Dermatology	0.8	Pediatrics	11.3
Emergency Medicine	1.5	Physical Med/Rehab	1.1
Family Practice	3.9	Plastic Surgery	0.1
Internal Medicine	24.0	Psychiatry	8.0
Neurology	3.2	Public Health/Prev Med	0.9
Neurosurgery	0.8	Radiation Oncology	1.1
Obstetrics & Gynecology	3.9	Radiology	7.1
Ophthalmology	1.8	Surgery	6.9
Orthopedic Surgery	1.8	Urology	0.7
		Other	2.0

*Percentages do not add up to 100% due to rounding.

**Many Pathologists work both as preclinical and as clinical faculty.

Adapted from: Association of American Medical Colleges: *AAMC Data Book 2003*, Table C2.

Type of Physicians Produced

Key questions to ask that reveal both the school's curricular strengths and the opportunities that will be available to you are: What type of physicians does the school produce? Do most graduates enter primary care, or do they enter other specialties? What is the school's mission? You can find current answers to these questions in the annual AAMC's *Medical School Admission Requirements*, from the school's website (Internet addresses are in *Appendix E*), or from the material they send you. Many have a specific mission to produce primary care providers. Some even have special primary care "tracks," which may also allow students to shorten their residency training by one year if they enter the track.

There are two other questions you may want to consider: Does the school have a reputation for producing researchers or clinicians? Are their graduates educators or in nonteaching practices? You often can get this information from the school's published materials, but, if it is unclear, ask these questions during interviews. Most medical school graduates are nonteaching clinicians (even those from the "big name" schools), but you may want to know if the school is known for producing either researchers or educators in case you decide to follow one of these paths. If you are interested in research, you should probably investigate combined Ph.D. or M.P.H. programs. If you want to be an educator, it does not matter that much which medical school you attend, only that you get a good education, pattern yourself after the best role models, and pick up good teaching techniques along the way.

Attrition Rates

The common wisdom has been, for at least four decades, that once you enter medical school, you graduate. In this case, conventional wisdom is as close to the truth as it ever gets.

For example, of all U.S. (M.D.) medical students expected to graduate in 2000, only 2.8% (347 of 15,749) students had withdrawn from school or been academically dismissed by the time their class graduated. Of those, schools dismissed only 117 for academic deficiencies. Others withdrew for personal, financial, or health reasons. Some left to pursue other careers or because they became disenchanted with medicine. About 40% of those who left medical school were first-year students.

Nearly 5% of all medical students take official leaves of absence during medical school, most commonly to pursue research or another degree, but also for personal, financial, or health reasons; academic deficiencies; and other reasons. Students most often take leaves of absence during their second and third years of school.

Instructional Language

Nearly all U.S. and Canadian medical schools teach their classes in English. There are, however, some exceptions. Three LCME-accredited schools teach their courses in French: Université Laval, Université de Montréal, and University of Sherbrooke—all located in Quebec, Canada. These schools require fluency in French. Students at the University of Ottawa may write their examinations in French, although instruction is in English.

Some or all of the teaching is conducted in Spanish at the three Puerto Rican medical schools: Universidad Central de Caribe, Ponce, and University of Puerto Rico. Students must be fluent in Spanish and in English. Most Caribbean medical schools that cater to U.S. students teach in English, as do, of course, medical schools in Britain, Ireland, New Zealand, and Australia. Other non-U.S./non-Canadian medical schools may teach their classroom work in English, but clinical work will generally be in the host country's language.

Bricks and Mortar?

Entrepreneurs have recently touted the establishment of "virtual" medical schools that would allow students to take their classes on-line and, therefore, from anywhere in the world. The idea sounds innovative, exciting, potentially inexpensive—and dangerous. No U.S. or Canadian licensing body has approved this type of medical education. If you spend your time, effort, and money on such a venture, *caveat emptor*! Do not expect anyone to allow you to practice medicine, at least in this hemisphere.

— Comparison Charts for U.S. and Canadian M.D. and D.O Medical Schools —

Medical schools differ in their teaching methods, facilities, ambiance, costs, faculty, curricula, admission processes and requirements, reputations, special programs, locations, and the types of students they take. There are, however, more similarities than differences among them. Some factors you may want to consider before applying to specific schools are found in Figures 15.4 through 15.8.

Read Me First!

Considerable effort has gone into confirming the information in these Figures. However, schools may change their requirements, fees, tuition, and structure. Always confirm this information directly with the schools. Contact information for each school is listed in *Appendix E*.

FIGURE 15.4

Medical School Admission Requirements—Courses

(The amount of each subject varies among the individual schools.)

School	Biol.	Gen. Chem.	Org. Chem.	Physics	Math	English	Other
Alabama	B,L	L	L	L	•	C,Lit	—
Alabama, South	L	L	L	L	Cl*	C/Lit	H
Albany	B,L	L	L	L	—	—	—
Albert Einstein	L	L	L	L	St,Cl	•	H*,Ss*,Cm*,AB*
Alberta[1]	•	•	•	•	St	•	Bc
Arizona	B	•	•	•	—	C,Lit	—
Arizona Osteo.[2]	•	•	•	•	—	•	—
Arkansas	•	•	•	•	•	•	G*,Q*,Psy*
Baylor	L	L	L	L	—	•	—
Boston	L	L	L	•	Cl*	C/Lit	H
British Columbia[1]	L	L	•	*	St*,Bm*	C	Bc,Psy*
Brown[3]	•	•	•	•	Cl,St	—	Ss,Psy,Bc
Calgary[1]	*	*	*	*	Cl*	*	Bc*,Phy*,Ss/Psy*
Calif.–Davis	L	L	•	•	Cl	•	—
Calif.–Irvine	B,G*	•	•	•	Cl,St*	•	Bc,H,Ss,Psy,P*
Calif.–San Diego	•	•	•	•	Cl/Cm/St	—	—
Calif.–San Francisco	B,Z,L	L	•	L	*	C*	AB*,H*
Calif.–UCLA	L,AB	L	L	L	Cl,St	C	Q,Bc*,Sp*,H*,Cm*
Calif., Southern (Keck)	L	L	L	L	Cl*,St*	C	M,Ss,H,Cm*
Caribe[S]	B	•	•	•	•	•	Ss/Psy,Sp
Case Western Res.	•	•	•	•	—	C	Bc*
Chicago–Pritzker	L	L	L	L	—	—	Bc*
Chicago Medical	B,L	L	L	L	Cl/St	Rh/C	O*
Chicago Osteo.[2]	•	•	•	•	—	•	—
Cincinnati	*	*	*	*	St	—	Cm*,Psy*,Ss*
Colorado	B,L	L	L	L	•,Cl*	C,Lit	—
Columbia	•	•	•	•	—	—	—
Connecticut	B,L	L	L	L	—	—	—
Cornell	B	•	•	•	—	C/Lit	AB*
Creighton	L	L	L	L	—	•	—
Dalhousie[1]	*	*	*	*	—	—	Ss*,H*
Dartmouth	•	•	•	•	Cl	—	—
Des Moines Osteo.[2]	B,L	L	L	L	—	C/Lit/CS	Bc*,AB*
Drew/UCLA	L,G*	L,Bc*	*	L	Al,Cl*,St*	C/Lit	Sp*,Cm*,Psy*,O*
Drexel[X]	L	L	L	L	—	•	Bc*
Duke	B	•	•	•	Cl	•	Bc*
East Carolina (Brody)	B,L	L	L	L	—	•	H*,Ss*
E.V. Virginia Osteo.[2]	L,A*	L	L	L	—	•	Bc*,G*,Phy*
Emory	L,G*	L	L	L	—	•	H,Ss/Psy,Bc*
Florida State	L	L	L	L	—	—	Bc
Florida, South	L,G*,A*	L	L	L	•,Cl*,St*	•,CS*	E*,Bc*,P*,M*,H*,Cm*
Florida, Univ. of	L,G*	L	L	L	—	—	Bc,Phy*,M*
Geo. Washington	B,L	L	L	L	—	C,Lit	—
Georgetown	L,G*	L	L	L	•	•	Bc*,H*,Cm*,E*,Q*,P*

(continued)

FIGURE 15.4 (continued)

School	Biol.	Gen. Chem.	Org. Chem.	Physics	Math	English	Other
Georgia, Med. Coll.	B,L	L	L	L	—	•	Bc*
Harvard	L	L	L	•	Cl	C*	Bc*,M*
Hawaii	L,G*	L	—	L	—	—	M,H*,Ss*,Psy*,Bc
Howard	L	L	L	L	•	•	Bc*,M*,E*
Illinois, Southern	B*	*	*	*	St*	C*	Bc*
Illinois, Univ.	B,L	L	L	•	Cl*	—	Psy,Ss,Bc*,O*
Indiana	L	L	L	L	—	—	H,Ss,Psy
Iowa	L,B,Bt	L	L	L	•	Rh*,Lit*	H*,AB*,Ss*,Psy*
Jefferson	L	L	L	L	*	—	—
Johns Hopkins	L	L	L	L	Cl	—	H,Ss
Kansas	L	L	L	L	Al,St*	•	Bc*,Ss*,AB*
Kentucky	—	L	L	L	—	•	—
Kirksville Osteo.[2]	L	L	L	L	—	•	Bc*,A*
Lake Erie Osteo.[2]	Bt,B,L	L	L	L	—	C,Lit	Psy,Bc*,Phy*,A*
Laval[1,F]	L	L	•	L	Cl	—	H,Ss,Psy,Fr
Loma Linda	B,L	L	L	L	—	•	—
Louisville	L	L	L	L	•	•	—
Loyola–Stritch	L	L	L	L	—	—	Bc*
LSU–New Orleans	B,L,G*	L,Bc*	L	L	—	•	AB*,O*,Ph*,Ss*
LSU–Shreveport	B,L	L	L	L	—	•	—
Manitoba[1]	—	—	—	—	—	Lit	Bc,H,Ss
Marshall	B,L	L	L	L	—	C,Rh	Ss/Psy
Maryland	L	L	L	L	—	•	—
Massachusetts	L	L	L	L	Cl*,St*	•	Bc*,Ss*,Psy*
Mayo	B	•	•	L	—	—	Bc
McGill[1]	L	L	L	L	—	—	M*,Bc*
McMaster[1]	+	+	+	+	+	+	+
Meharry	B,L	L	L	L	—	C,Lit	H*,Ss*
Mercer	L	L	L	•	—	—	Bc,H*,Ss*
Miami	L,G*	L	L	L	—	•	Bc*,M*,Phy*, AB*
Michigan Osteo.[2]	L,G*	L	L	L	—	•	Psy,Bc*,A*,M*
Michigan State	L	L	L	L	—	C,Lit	Ss/Psy
Michigan, Univ.	L	L	L	L	—	C,Lit	Bc,H
Minnesota–Duluth	B,L	L	L	L	Cl/St	C	H,Psy,Bc
Minnesota–Minneap.	B,L	L	L	L	Cl,St*	C,Lit	Bc,Psy*,G*,H*
Mississippi	B,L	L	L	L	•	•	AS,H*,Psy*
Missouri–Columbia	L	L	—	L	•	C,CS*	Bc*,H*,Ss*
Missouri–KS City	+	+	+	+	+	+	—
Montréal[1,F]	•	•	•	•	Cl	•	Fr,Ss,Psy,Ph
Morehouse	L	L	L	L	•	C	Psy*
Mount Sinai	•	•	•	•	•	•	—
Nebraska	L,G	L	L	L	Cl/St	C	H/Ss/Bc
Nevada	L,AB	L	L	L	—	C,Lit*	Psy,H*,Ph*,Cm*
New England Osteo.[2]	L,G*	L	L	L	Cl*	C,Lit	Bc,A*,Phy*,P*
New Mexico	L	L	L	•	Cl*	—	Bc,Sp*
New York Osteo.[2]	B,L	L	L	L	—	C	—

(continued)

FIGURE 15.4 (continued)

School	Biol.	Gen. Chem.	Org. Chem.	Physics	Math	English	Other
New York Medical	L	L	L	L	—	C,Lit	—
New York Univ.	L	L	L	L	—	•	Bc*,AB*
Newfoundland[1]	—	—	—	—	—	•	—
North Carolina	B,L	L	L	L	*	•	M*,G*,Bc*,H*,Ss*
North Dakota	B	•	•	•	•	C,Lit	Ss/Psy,Cm*
Northwestern	•	•	•	•	—	•	—
Nova Univ. Osteo.[2]	L,G*	L	L	L	—	C,Lit	E*,Psy*,H*
Ohio Osteo.[2]	•	•	•	•	—	•	Psy,AB*
Ohio State	•	L	L	•	—	—	—
Ohio, Med. Coll.	•	•	•	•	•	•	AB*
Ohio, Northeast[3]	—	—	•	•	—	—	—
Oklahoma	B,L	•	•	•	•	•	Ss/Psy/H,AB
Oklahoma Osteo.[2]	•	•	•	•	—	•	Bc*,M*,A*
Ontario, Western[1]	L	—	L	—	*	C	Bc*,O
Oregon	•	L	L	L	—	C	G*,H,Ss,Bc*
Ottawa[1]	B,L	L	L	—	*	—	Bc,H/Ss
Pacific Osteo.[2]	•	L	L	•	—	•	Psy
Pennsylvania State	L,G*	L	L	L	•,Cl*,St*	*	H,Psy,Ss*
Pennsylvania, Univ.	*	*	*	*	*	CS*	Psy*,H*,Ss*
Philadelphia Osteo.[2]	L	L	L	L	—	C,Lit	Bc*
Pikeville Osteo.[2]	•	•	•	•	—	•	—
Pittsburgh	L	L	L	L	*	C,Lit	H*,Psy*,Ss*
Ponce[S]	•	•	•	•	•	•	Sp
Puerto Rico[S]	•	L	L	L	—	•	Ss/Psy,Sp
Queen's Univ.[1]	Bc	PS	PS	PS	—	—	H/Ss
Rochester	L	L	L	L	Cl*,St*	C	Bc*,H/Ss/Psy
Rush	B,L	L	L	L	—	—	Bc*,H*
Saint Louis	B,L	L	L	L	Cl*	•	H
Saskatchewan[1]	L	L	L	L	—	Lit,C	Bc,H/Ss
Sherbrooke[1,F]	L	L	L	L	Cl	L	H,Ph,Ss,Psy,Fr
South Carol., Med. U.	+	+	+	+	+	+	+
South Carol., Univ.	B,L	L	L	L	•,Cl*	C,Lit	—
South Dakota	B,L,G*	L	L	L	•,Cl*,St*	—	AB*,Cm*,Bc*,Phy*
Stanford	L	L	L	L	Cl*	—	Bc*,P*,Psy*,FL
SUNY–Brooklyn	B,L	L	L	L	Cl*	•	AS*,Bc*,M*,A*
SUNY–Buffalo	L	L	L	•	—	•	Ss*,H*
SUNY–Stony Brook	L	L	L	L	—	•	Bc*
SUNY–Syracuse	B,L	L	L	L	—	•	—
Temple	L	L	L	L	—	*	H
Tennessee State, E.	L	L	L	L	—	CS	—
Tennessee, Univ.	L	L	L	L	—	C,Lit	—
Texas A&M	L	L	L	L	Cl/St	•	AB
Texas Coll. Osteo.[2]	L	L	L	L	Cl/St	C	—
Texas Tech	B,L	L	L	L	•	•	—
Texas–Galveston	AB/B,L	L	L	L	—	•	H*,O,AS
Texas–Houston	L	L	L	L	Cl	•	H*

(continued)

FIGURE 15.4 (continued)

School	Biol.	Gen. Chem.	Org. Chem.	Physics	Math	English	Other
Texas–San Antonio	L/Bc	L	L	L	Cl/St	●	H*
Texas–Southwest	L	L	L	L	Cl/St	●	H*
Toronto[1]	●	—	—	—	St/Bm*	—	H/Ss/FL
Touro Osteo.[2]	B,L	L	L	L	—	●	—
Tufts	L	L	L	L	Cl*,St*	—	G*,Bc*
Tulane	B,L	L	L	L	—	●	—
UMDNJ–Osteo.[2]	L	L	L	L	●	C	Psy/Ss,H*,Ph*
UMDNJ–NJ Med.	B,L	L	L	L	*	●	—
UMDNJ–RWJ	B,L	L	L	L	●	C	—
Uniformed Serv. U.	L	L	L	L	Cl	●	—
U. Health Sci. Osteo.[2]	L,G	L	L	L	*	C,Lit	Bc,A*,Ss*,Ph*,Psy*
Utah	●	L	L	L	—	C/CS	H,Ss,M/Bc
Vanderbilt	B,L	L	L	L	—	C	—
Vermont	B,L	L	L	L	—	—	—
Virginia, Eastern	L	L	L	L	—	—	—
Virginia, Med. Coll.	L	L	L	L	●	●	—
Virginia, Univ. of	L	L	L	L	—	—	—
Wake Forest (B. Gray)	B,L*	L	L	●	—	—	—
Washington U. (MO)	●	●	●	●	Cl	—	—
Washington, Univ. of	●	●	●	●	*	*	O
Wayne State	B,L	L	L	L	—	●	H*,Ss*
West Virginia	L	L	L	L	—	●	Ss/Psy,Bc*,M*
West Virginia Osteo.[2]	B,L	L	L	L	—	●	Bc*,M*,A*,AB*
Wisconsin, Med. Coll.	L	L	L	●	●	C	—
Wisconsin, Univ. of	L,AB	L	L	L	Cl*,St*	●	Bc*,H*,Ss*,Q*,G
Wright State	●	●	●	●	●	●	—
Yale	B,L	L	L	L	—	—	—

●: Required
*: Recommended
/: Alternative courses (e.g., H/Ss= Humanities or Social Sciences)
+: No specific prerequisite courses for admission
1: Canadian medical school (most require first-aid certificate)
2: College of Osteopathic Medicine
3: Most students admitted directly from high school
A: Anatomy
AB: Advanced Biology course
Al: Algebra
AS: Advanced Science course
B: Biology or Zoology
Bc: Biochemistry
Bm: Biometrics
Bt: Botany
C: Composition
Cl: Calculus
Cm: Computer-literate or courses
CS: Communication Skills
E: Embryology
F: Classes taught in French
FL: Foreign language
Fr: French language
G: Genetics
H: Humanities
L: Required with laboratory
Lit: Literature
M: Molecular & Cellular Biology
O: Other sciences (Biology, Chemistry, or Physics)
P: Physical Chemistry
Ph: Philosophy
Phy: Physiology
PS: Any combination of Physical Sciences
Psy: Psychology/Behavioral Sciences
Q: Quantitative Analysis
Rh: Rhetoric
S: Classes taught in Spanish
Ss: Social Sciences
Sp: Spanish language
St: Statistics
X: Formerly Medical College of Pennsylvania/Hahnemann/Allegheny Univ. Health Sciences
Z: Zoology

Information obtained from: Association of American Medical Colleges. *Medical School Admission Requirements United States and Canada 2004-2005*; American Association of Colleges of Osteopathic Medicine. *2002 Annual Report on Osteopathic Medical Education*. Rockville, MD: AACOM, 2003; and other sources.

FIGURE 15.5

Medical School Admission Requirements—Other

School	AMCAS	Applic. Deadline[1]	Early Decision Program	Applic. Fee ($)	% Out-of-State Students	MCAT[2]	Bach. Degree Req.[3]
Alabama	•	Nov 1	•	65[4]	14	•	—
Alabama, South	•	Nov 15	•	25[4]	11	•	•
Albany	•	Nov 15	—	75	61	•	—
Albert Einstein	•	Nov 1	•	95	54	•	—
Alberta[5]	—	Nov 1	•	60	15	•	—
Arizona	•	Nov 1	—	75	0[6]	•	3ac
Arizona Osteo.[7]	A	Jan 1	—	40[4]	70	•	—
Arkansas	•	Nov 15	—	10[4]	2	•	—
Baylor	—	Nov 1	•	—	25	•	•
Boston	•	Nov 15	•	100	80	•	—
British Columbia[5]	—	Oct 1	—	105/185[8]	18	•	—
Brown[9]	—	Mar 1	—	65	NA	—	—
Calgary[5]	—	Nov 15	—	85	15	•	—
Calif.–Davis	•	Nov 1	—	60	3	•	3ac
Calif.–Irvine	•	Nov 1	—	60	0	•	3ac
Calif.–San Diego	•	Nov 1	—	60	6	•	—
Calif.–San Francisco	•	Nov 1	—	60	20	•	—
Calif.–UCLA	•	Nov 1	—	60	15	•	3ac
Calif., Southern (Keck)	•	Nov 1	•	70	NA	•	—
Caribe[S]	•	Dec 15	•	50	15	•	—
Case Western Res.	•	Dec 15	•	85	39	•	•
Chicago–Pritzker	•	Oct 15	•	75	73	•	3ac
Chicago Medical	•	Nov 15	•	90	76	•	•
Chicago Osteo.[7]	A	Jan 1	—	50[4]	51	•	—
Cincinnati	•	Nov 15	•	25	28	•	3ac
Colorado	•	Nov 15	•	70	20	•	120 hrs
Columbia	—	Oct 15	—	85	76	•	3ac
Connecticut	•	Dec 15	•	75	20-30	•	•
Cornell	•	Oct 15	•	75	5	•	•
Creighton	•	Dec 1	•	75	87	•	•
Dalhousie[5]	—	Oct 31	—	65	10	•	•
Dartmouth	•	Nov 1	—	75	5	P	3ac
Des Moines Osteo.[7]	A	Feb 1	—	50[4]	75	•	•
Drew/UCLA	•	Nov 15	—	50	NA	•	—
Drexel[X]	•	Dec 1	•	75	25-30	•	—
Duke	•	Oct 15	—	75	86	•	3ac
East Carolina (Brody)	•	Nov 15	•	50	0	•	•
E.V. Virginia Osteo.[7]	A	Mar 1	—	75	NA	•	•
Emory	•	Oct 15	—	80	59	•	—
Florida State	•	Dec 13	•	—	—	•	•
Florida, South	•	Dec 1	•	30	0	•	•
Florida, Univ. of	•	Dec 1	—	30	0	•	•
Geo. Washington	•	Dec 1	•	80	95	—	•
Georgetown	•	Nov 1	—	100	96	•	—

(continued)

FIGURE 15.5 (continued)

School	AMCAS	Applic. Deadline[1]	Early Decision Program	Applic. Fee ($)	% Out-of-State Students	MCAT[2]	Bach. Degree Req.[3]
Georgia, Med. Coll.	•	Nov 1	•	—	2	•	—
Harvard	•	Oct 15	—	75	92	•	•
Hawaii	•	Dec 1	•	50	10	•	—
Howard	•	Dec 15	—	45[4]	91	•	—
Illinois, Southern	•	Nov 15	—	50[4]	0	•	—
Illinois, Univ.	•	Dec 15	•	60[4]	16	•	•
Indiana	•	Dec 15	•	45	11	•	3ac
Iowa	•	Nov 1	•	30[4]	32	•	•
Jefferson	•	Nov 15	•	75	65	•	•
Johns Hopkins	•	Oct 15	•	75	0	—	•
Kansas	•	Oct 15	•	40[8]	10	•	•
Kentucky	•	Nov 1	•	30[4]	5	•	•
Kirksville Osteo.[7]	A	Feb 1	•	50[4]	89	•	—
Lake Erie Osteo.[7]	A	Feb 1	—	50[4]	57	•	•
Laval[5,F]	—	Feb 1	—	55	8	—	•
Loma Linda	•	Nov 1	•	75	47	•	•
Louisville	•	Nov 1	•	75	10	•	•
Loyola–Stritch	•	Nov 15	—	60[4]	50	•	•
LSU–New Orleans	•	Nov 15	•	50[4]	2[11]	•	3ac
LSU–Shreveport	•	Nov 15	•	50	0	•	3ac
Manitoba[5]	—	Nov 15	—	60	4	•	•
Marshall	•	Nov 15	—	50/80[8]	10	•	—
Maryland	•	Nov 1	•	50[4]	13	•	3ac
Massachusetts	•	Nov 1	•	75	0	•	•
Mayo	•	Nov 1	•	75	64[12]	•	•
McGill[5]	—	Nov 15	•	60	21	•	•
McMaster[5]	O	Oct 1	—	175	8	—	3ac
Meharry	•	Dec 15	•	60	78	•	3ac
Mercer	•	Nov 1	•	40	0	•	3ac
Miami	•	Dec 15	—	65	14	•	3ac
Michigan Osteo.[7]	A	Dec 6	•	30+75[4]	20	•	—
Michigan State	•	Nov 15	•	50	24	•	•
Michigan, Univ.	•	Nov 15	—	60	50	•	—
Minnesota–Duluth	•	Nov 15	•	75[4]	13	•	•
Minnesota–Minneap.	•	Nov 15	•	75[4]	15	•	•
Mississippi	•	Oct 15	•	—	0	•	•
Missouri–Columbia	•	Nov 1	•	50	1	•	—
Missouri–KS City	—	Dec 1	—	25/50[8]	16	—	—
Montréal[5,F]	—	Mar 1	•	50/30[10]	2	—	—
Morehouse	•	Dec 1	•	50	48	•	3ac
Mount Sinai	•	Nov 1	•	100	37	•	•
Nebraska	•	Nov 15	•	40	9	•	—
Nevada	•	Nov 1	•	45[4]	10	•	3ac
New England Osteo.[7]	A	Jan 2	—	55[4]	60	•	3ac
New Mexico	•	Nov 15	•	55	4	•	—
New York Osteo.[7]	A	Feb 1	—	60[4]	10	•	•

(continued)

FIGURE 15.5 (continued)

School	AMCAS	Applic. Deadline[1]	Early Decision Program	Applic. Fee ($)	% Out-of-State Students	MCAT[2]	Bach. Degree Req.[3]
New York Medical	●	Dec 15	●	100[4]	65	●	●
New York Univ.	—	Nov 15	—	75	52	●	●
Newfoundland[5]	—	Oct 15	—	75	27	●	P
North Carolina	●	Nov 15	●	65	11	●	96 hrs
North Dakota	—	Nov 1	—	50	20	●	P
Northwestern	●	Nov 1	●	70[4]	71	●	3ac
Nova Univ. Osteo.[7]	A	Jan 15	—	50[4]	55	●	P
Ohio Osteo.[7]	A	Jan 2	—	30[4]	15	●	—
Ohio State	●	Nov 1	●	30	24	●	●
Ohio, Med. Coll.	●	Nov 1	●	50	20	—	—
Ohio, Northeast[9]	●	Nov 1	●	30	NA	●	●
Oklahoma	●	Oct 15	●	50	15	●	—
Oklahoma Osteo.[7]	A	Feb 1	—	25[4]	20	●	—
Ontario, Western[5]	O	Oct 15	—	175	19	●	—
Oregon	●	Oct 15	—	75	24	●	●
Ottawa[5]	O	Oct 15	—	175	10	—	3ac
Pacific Osteo.[7]	A	Jan 15	—	60[4]	28	●	3ac
Pennsylvania State	●	Nov 15	●	60	56	●	3ac
Pennsylvania, Univ.	●	Oct 15	—	65	76	●	—
Philadelphia Osteo.[7]	A	Feb 1	—	50[4,8]	35	●	—
Pikeville Osteo.[7]	A	Feb 1	—	75	38	●	—
Pittsburgh	●	Nov 1	—	60	71	●	●
Ponce[S]	●	Dec 15	●	100	17	●	—
Puerto Rico[S]	●	Dec 1	—	15	0	●	—
Queen's Univ.[5]	O	Oct 15	—	250	29	●	—
Rochester	—	Oct 15	—	75	60	●	●
Rush	●	Nov 15	●	65	83	●	3ac
Saint Louis	●	Dec 15	●	100	75	●	●
Saskatchewan[5]	—	Dec 1	—	40/75[8]	8	●	—
Sherbrooke[5,F]	—	Mar 1	—	30	10	—	—
South Carol. Med. U.	●	Dec 1	●	45	9	●	●
South Carol. Univ.	●	Dec 1	●	45	11	●	●
South Dakota	●	Nov 15	—	35	8	●	●
Stanford	●	Nov 1	●	75[4]	55	●	●
SUNY–Brooklyn	●	Dec 15	●	65	7	●	3ac
SUNY–Buffalo	●	Nov 1	●	65	6	●	60 hrs
SUNY–Stony Brook	●	Nov 15	●	75	0	●	—
SUNY–Syracuse	●	Nov 1	●	100	—	●	●
Temple	●	Dec 15	●	65	23	●	●
Tennessee State, E.	●	Dec 1	●	50	10	●	—
Tennessee, Univ.	●	Nov 15	—	50	10	●	—
Texas A&M	T	Nov 1	—	55/100[8]	9	●	3ac
Texas Coll. Osteo.[7]	A	Nov 1	●	NA	8	●	●
Texas Tech	T	Nov 1	●	55/100[8]	7	●	P
Texas–Galveston	T	Nov 1	—	55/100[8]	7.5	●	3ac
Texas–Houston	T	Nov 1	—	55/100[8]	≥10	●	—

(continued)

FIGURE 15.5 (continued)

School	AMCAS	Applic. Deadline[1]	Early Decision Program	Applic. Fee ($)	% Out-of-State Students	MCAT[2]	Bach. Degree Req.[3]
Texas–San Antonio	T	Nov 1	—	55/100[8]	6	●	3ac
Texas–Southwest	T	Nov 1	—	65	10	●	—
Toronto[5]	O	Oct 15	—	175/75	NA	●	●
Touro Osteo.[7]	A	Feb 15	●	NA	36	●	●
Tufts	●	Nov 1	●	75	71	●	3ac
Tulane	●	Dec 15	●	95	74	●	—
UMDNJ–Osteo.[7]	A	Feb 1	—	75[4]	33	●	●
UMDNJ–New Jersey	●	Dec 1	●	75	94	●	3ac
UMDNJ–RWJ	●	Dec 1	●	50	13	●	●
Uniformed Serv. U.	●	Nov 1	—	—	NA	●	●
U. Health Sci. Osteo.[7]	A	Feb 1	—	50	88	●	P
Utah	●	Oct 15	—	100[4]	24	●	●
Vanderbilt	●	Oct 15	●	50	93	—	●
Vermont	●	Nov 1	●	80	72	●	●
Virginia, Eastern	●	Nov 15	●	90[4]	30	●	100 hrs
Virginia, Med. Coll.	●	Nov 15	●	80	3	—	●
Virginia, Univ. of	●	Nov 1	—	60	35	●	●
Wake Forest (B. Gray)	●	Nov 1	●	55	44	●	●
Washington U. (MO)	●	Dec 1	—	50	96	●	—
Washington, Univ. of	●	Nov 1	—	35	2	●	●
Wayne State	●	Dec 15	●	40[4]	9	●	●
West Virginia	●	Nov 15	●	50	3	●	—
West Virginia Osteo.[7]	A	Feb 15	—	35/75[4,8]	33	●	3ac
Wisconsin, Med. Coll.	●	Nov 1	●	60	52	●	—
Wisconsin, Univ. of	●	Nov 1	●	45	13	●	●
Wright State	●	Nov 15	●	45	13	●	—
Yale	●	Nov 15	●	75	13	●	3ac

●: Required
1: Latest date for primary application. Some Canadian schools have later dates for in-Province applicants.
2: MCAT not required of students entering accelerated programs
3: At many schools that do not require bachelor's degrees, 95% to 99% of entrants have such a degree (except for students in accelerated programs)
3ac: Attendance for at least three full academic years (90 credits) at an accredited college in the U.S. or Canada
4: Fee requested after application screened
5: Canadian medical school
6: WICHE applicants considered "in-state" (Alaska, Montana, Wyoming)
7: College of Osteopathic Medicine
8: Fee for nonresidents
9: Most students admitted directly from high school
10: Paper application/electronic application
11: Students from special program with Univ. of New Orleans considered "in-state"
12: Minnesota, Arizona, and Florida residents considered "in-state"
A: Application through AACOMAS
F: Classes taught in French
NA: Data not available
O: Application through the Ontario Medical School Application Service (OMSAS)
P: Preferred, not required
S: Classes taught in Spanish
T: Application through the University of Texas System Medical and Dental Application Center
X: Formerly Medical College of Pennsylvania/Hahnemann/Allegheny Univ. Health Sciences

Information obtained from: Association of American Medical Colleges. *Medical School Admission Requirements United States and Canada 2004-2005*; American Association of Colleges of Osteopathic Medicine. *2002 Annual Report on Osteopathic Medical Education*. Rockville, MD: AACOM, 2003; and other sources.

FIGURE 15.6
Medical School Specifics

School	TUITION ($) In-State	TUITION ($) Out-of-State	Fees ($)	Class Size	Start Date	Deferred Accept[1]
Alabama	5,708	17,124	2,159	169	Aug	•
Alabama, South	5,808	11,616	567	64	Aug	6/1-R
Albany	24,074	25,346	—	130	Aug	•
Albert Einstein	34,375	34,375	2,050	180	Aug	6/1-R
Alberta[2,11]	10,066[3]	10,066[3]	465[3]	128	Aug	•
Arizona[6]	10,575	—	85	100	July	Indv
Arizona Osteo.[7]	30,283	30,283	NA	145	Sept	—
Arkansas	11,642	21,168	2,163*	150	Aug	7/15
Baylor	6,550	19,650	1,993	168	Aug	•
Boston	36,530	36,530	450	154	Aug	—
British Columbia[2]	10,272[3]	10,272[3]	594[3]	128	Aug	•
Brown[8]	30,648	30,648	1,876	68	Sept	•
Calgary[2]	6,992[3]	35,000[3,4]	474[3]	100	Aug	6/1
Calif.–Davis	—	11,577	14,295	93	Sept	6/1
Calif.–Irvine	—	11,132	11,635	92	Sept	7/15
Calif.–San Diego	—	11,132	10,642	122	Sept	7/1
Calif.–San Francisco	—	11,132	10,712	141	Sept	5/1
Calif.–UCLA	—	11,132	10,712	121	Aug	5/1
Calif., Southern (Keck)	35,052	35,052	1,132	160	Aug	6/15
Caribe[S]	18,000	25,000	1,300	60	Aug	—
Case Western Res.	35,000	35,000	1,379	177	Aug	5/15
Chicago–Pritzker	28,065	28,065	2,018	104	Sept	6/1
Chicago Medical	36,740	36,740	100	185	July	•-R
Chicago Osteo.[7]	25,878	31,430	NA	165	NA	1/1
Cincinnati	16,986	29,634	1,162	160	Aug	•-R
Colorado	13,286	63,612	1,968	132	Aug	•-R
Columbia	34,016	34,016	1,938	150	Aug	6/15
Connecticut	10,440	23,750	4,430	80	Aug	6/1-R
Cornell	28,500	28,500	1,090	101	Aug	6/1
Creighton	33,520	33,520	682	115	Aug	•
Dalhousie[2]	8,800[3]	12,900[3,4]	489[3]	82	Aug	•
Dartmouth	30,100	30,100	3,900	81	Aug	—
Des Moines Osteo.[7]	26,350	26,350	1,050	200	Aug	Rare
Drew/UCLA	—	11,132	10,712	20	Aug	—
Drexel[X]	32,622	32,622	500	250	Aug	•
Duke	29,706	29,706	3,421	99	Aug	6/1
East Carolina (Brody)	3,437	27,824	1,167	72	Aug	—
E.V. Virginia Osteo.[7]	29,500	29,500	1,200	150	NA	—
Emory	31,025	31,025	1,369	112	July	•
Florida State	12,177	33,473	744	40	May	5/1
Florida, South	13,643[5]	36,159	2,797[9]	100	Aug	•
Florida, Univ. of	13,687[5]	34,936	2,808[9]	108	Aug	•
Geo. Washington	36,192	36,192	1,592	155	Aug	•
Georgetown	31,764	31,764	43	170	Aug	Indv

(continued)

FIGURE 15.6 (continued)

School	TUITION ($) In-State	TUITION ($) Out-of-State	Fees ($)	Class Size	Start Date	Deferred Accept[1]
Georgia, Med. Coll.	8,516	30,064	566	180	Aug	6/1
Harvard	30,500	30,500	2,208	167	Sept	7/1
Hawaii	14,208	27,912	142	62	Aug	Rare
Howard	18,700	18,700	1,293	110	Aug	Indv
Illinois, Southern	14,682	44,046	1,369	72	Aug	8/1
Illinois, Univ.	9,940	23,005	889	300	Aug	7/1
Indiana	17,136	35,073	490	300	Aug	7/1
Iowa	17,188	35,656	1,320	142	Aug	•
Jefferson	31,958	31,958	—	228	Aug	8/1
Johns Hopkins	29,800	29,800	1,500	120	Aug	5/1
Kansas	12,566	26,948	370	175	Aug	7/30
Kentucky	11,405	26,119	—	95	Aug	6/1-R
Kirksville Osteo.[7]	26,450	26,450	690	158	Aug	•-R
Lake Erie Osteo.[7]	23,400	24,400	1,175	212	Aug	Rare
Laval[2,F]	1,964[3]	7,696[3]	200[3]	171	Aug	—
Loma Linda	31,808	31,808	—	159	Aug	•
Louisville	13,342	33,268	500	143	Aug	•
Loyola–Stritch	31,400	31,400	700	130	July	6/1-R
LSU–New Orleans	10,387	24,258	1,306	165	Aug	•
LSU–Shreveport	8,581	22,729	487	100	Aug	•
Manitoba[2]	7,595[3]	7,595[3]	150[3]	90	Aug	•
Marshall	11,080	29,010	516	48	Aug	4/15-R
Maryland	14,717	28,165	2,957	150	Aug	•
Massachusetts[6]	8,352	—	1,720	100	Aug	7/1-R
Mayo	5,625[10]	11,250	—	42	Aug	6/1
McGill[2]	3,559[3]	21,031[3,4]	2,070[3]	150	Aug	8/1
McMaster[2]	13,500[3]	38,970[3,9]	—	128	Sept	•
Meharry	23,208	23,208	3,916	80	June	—
Mercer[6]	25,056	—	—	56	Aug	•
Miami	28,050	36,740	130	150	Aug	—
Michigan Osteo.[7]	17,448	37,248	NA	125	Aug	•
Michigan State	14,556	31,038	856	106	Aug	•
Michigan, Univ.	19,900	30,600	176	170	Aug	•
Minnesota–Duluth	25,073	46,581	1,544	55	Aug	6/1
Minnesota–Minneap.	14,616	29,112	586	165	Aug	•
Mississippi	6,938	13,298	—	100	Aug	•
Missouri–Columbia	17,496	34,430	324	96	Aug	7/1
Missouri-KS City	25,597	51,274	538	122	Aug	—
Montréal[2,F]	2,450[3]	13,810[3]	30[3]	200	Aug	—
Morehouse	29,066	29,066	4,405	44	July	6/1
Mount Sinai	28,250	28,250	1,600	120	Aug	6/15
Nebraska	14,470	33,930	1,572	117	Aug	—
Nevada	9,232	26,810	2,375	52	Aug	•
New England Osteo.[7]	30,990	30,990	365	117	Sept	No

(continued)

FIGURE 15.6 (continued)

School	TUITION ($) In-State	Out-of-State	Fees ($)	Class Size	Start Date	Deferred Accept[1]
New Mexico	9,015	25,843	32	75	Aug	8/1
New York Osteo.[7]	26,755	26,755	—	260	Aug	No
New York Medical	32,730	32,730	700	190	Aug	7/1
New York Univ.	24,950	24,950	5,300	160	Aug	7/1
Newfoundland[2]	6,250[3]	30,000[3]	85[3]	60	Sept	•
North Carolina	7,033	32,501	1,035	160	Aug	6/15
North Dakota	13,446	35,902	1,033	57	Aug	4/15
Northwestern	35,616	35,616	—	171	Sept	•
Nova Univ. Osteo.[7]	22,265	27,955	225	180	Aug	•
Ohio Osteo.[7]	16,452	23,976	1,953	100	Sept	8/1
Ohio State	15,195	20,711	378	210	Aug	6/1
Ohio, Med. Coll.	15,060	31,510	2,100	135	Aug	•
Ohio, Northeast	15,738	31,476	966	25	Aug	Indv
Oklahoma	10,698	26,439	582	150	Aug	—
Oklahoma Osteo.[7]	11,557	30,144	—	88	Aug	No
Ontario, Western[2]	14,280[3]	14,280[3]	800[3]	133	Sept	No
Oregon	20,000	30,000	3,517	102	Aug	—
Ottawa[2]	10,500[3]	17,625[3,4]	449[3]	111	Sept	7/3
Pacific Osteo.[7]	29,410	29,410	630	189	Aug	•
Pennsylvania State	23,910	33,240	40	131	Aug	7/1
Pennsylvania, Univ.	33,316	33,316	2,066	150	Aug	5/1
Philadelphia Osteo.[7]	27,985	27,985	525	250	Aug	No
Pikeville Osteo.[7]	25,000	25,000	—	64	NA	—
Pittsburgh	30,084	35,867	600	148	Aug	4/15
Ponce[S]	17,835	26,590	2,808	60	July	—
Puerto Rico[S]	5,500	10,500	870	115	Aug	—
Queen's Univ.[2]	12,500[3]	NA	751[3]	100	Sept	8/1
Rochester	30,300	30,300	1,850	100	Aug	•
Rush	30,792	30,792	1,500	120	Sept	8/1
Saint Louis	34,800	34,800	1,462	150	Aug	•
Saskatchewan[2]	9,431[3]	9,431[3]	187[3]	60	Aug	6/30
Sherbrooke[2,F]	3,019[3]	15,019[3,4]	—	122	Aug	—
South Carol. Med. U.	13,302	37,622	813	135	Aug	7/1
South Carol. Univ.	12,960	37,552	25	80	Aug	4/1
South Dakota	11,270	26,995	2,835	50	Aug	•
Stanford	33,063	33,063	1,150	86	Sept	7/15
SUNY–Brooklyn	15,185[5]	27,285[5]	—	185	Aug	5/15
SUNY–Buffalo	12,840	23,940	1,150	135	Aug	•
SUNY–Stony Brook	18,840	33,940	3,000	100	Aug	6/15
SUNY–Syracuse	14,840	26,940	1,040	153	Aug	6/1
Temple .	28,056	24,555	460	190	Aug	8/1
Tennessee State, E.	14,390	29,332	553	60	Aug	7/1-R
Tennessee, Univ.	16,048	31,962	858	150	Aug	7/1
Texas A&M	6,550	19,650	1,375	64	July	2/1

(continued)

FIGURE 15.6 (continued)

School	TUITION ($) In-State	Out-of-State	Fees ($)	Class Size	Start Date	Deferred Accept[1]
Texas Coll. Osteo.[7]	6,550	19,650	1,251	125	Aug	6/1
Texas Tech	6,550	19,650	1,626	130	Aug	•-R
Texas–Galveston	6,550	19,650	427	200	Aug	8/15
Texas–Houston	9,242	22,342	250	200	Aug	—
Texas–San Antonio	6,550	19,650	3,231	200	July	Spring
Texas–Southwest	6,550	19,650	1,252	200	Aug	6/1
Toronto[2]	16,482[3,5]	29,165[3,4,5]	—	198	Sept	7/1
Touro Osteo.[7]	28,000	28,000	100	125	Aug	Indv
Tufts	39,579	39,579	525	168	Aug	Indv
Tulane	33,519	33,519	1,730	155	Aug	7/1
UMDNJ–Osteo.[7]	17,362	27,169	—	85	Aug	—
UMDNJ–New Jersey	18,143	28,392	2,151	170	Aug	Rare
UMDNJ–RWJ	17,362	27,169	1,952	142	Aug	7/15
Uniformed Serv. U.	0	0	—	167	June	•
U. Health Sci. Osteo.[7]	29,990	29,990	60	228	Aug	Aug
Utah	13,296	25,172	588	102	Aug	—
Vanderbilt	27,325	27,325	1,766	104	Aug	5/15
Vermont	21,140	36,980	811	97	Aug	7/1
Virginia, Eastern	18,975	35,075	2,966	110	Aug	5/1
Virginia, Med. Coll.	11,725	30,050	1,306	184	Aug	6/15
Virginia, Univ. of	18,298	30,580	—	139	Aug	7/1
Wake Forest (B. Gray)	30,529	30,529	—	108	Aug	•
Washington U. (MO)	25,170	25,170	—	122	Aug	6/15
Washington, Univ. of	10,143	25,668	—	178	Sept	•
Wayne State	15,774	32,372	750	256	Aug	Spring
West Virginia	11,404	28,144	—	98	Aug	•
West Virginia Osteo.[7]	14,206	35,158	—	75	Aug	No
Wisconsin, Med. Coll.	20,197	30,288	35	204	Aug	7/1-R
Wisconsin, Univ. of	21,153	32,277	572	151	Aug	5/1
Wright State	12,244	17,332	672	90	Aug	•-R
Yale	32,300	32,300	375	100	Aug	6/30

•: Deferred acceptance is offered
*: Includes Malpractice Insurance and Health Insurance
1: Date by which deferred acceptance must be requested (month/day)
2: Canadian medical school
3: Canadian dollars
4: Non-Canadians
5: Tuition plus fees
6: Do not accept out-of-state students, so no out-of-state tuition.
7: College of Osteopathic Medicine
8: Most students admitted directly from high school
9: Nonresident
10: Applicants from Arizona, Florida, and Minnesota considered "in-state"
11: Accepts Canadian citizens/permanent residents only
F: Classes taught in French
Indv: Determined on a case-by-case basis
NA: Data not available
S: Classes taught in Spanish
R: Restrictions on reapplication.
X: Formerly Medical College of Pennsylvania/Hahnemann/Allegheny Univ. Health Sciences

Information obtained from: Association of American Medical Colleges. *Medical School Admission Requirements United States and Canada 2004-2005*; American Association of Colleges of Osteopathic Medicine. *2002 Annual Report on Osteopathic Medical Education*. Rockville, MD: AACOM, 2003; and other sources.

FIGURE 15.7

Medical School Applicant Statistics

School	Applicants: In-State	Applicants: Out-of-State	% of Applicants Interviewed: In-State	% of Applicants Interviewed: Out-of-State	Accepted Students: Mean GPA	Accepted Students: Mean MCAT*	Accepted Students: % Women
Alabama	578	1,738	70	9	3.6	29.0	40
Alabama, South	550	957	41	1	3.6	28.4	40
Albany	2,496	7,596	11	8	3.5	29.7	50
Albert Einstein	1,405	4,258	31	21	3.6	31.0	44
Alberta[1]	544	514	36	14	NA	NA	40
Arizona	540	602	95	4[2]	3.6	28.2	53
Arizona Osteo.[3]	500	1,500	30	70	3.4	26.0	62
Arkansas	400	505	94	3	3.5	25.4	40
Baylor	954	2,831	34	10	3.8	33.9	47
Boston	566	8,204	28	10	3.5	29.6	40
British Columbia[1]	705	178	47	12	3.3	31.8	56
Brown[4]			No information available				
Calgary[1]	574	708	31	12	3.7	29.7	56
Calif.–Davis	2,986	515	12	1	3.5	33.0	42
Calif.-Irvine	3,031	369	13	1	3.7	32.0	50
Calif.–San Diego	3,016	1,167	18	6	3.8	33.0	51
Calif.–San Francisco	2,375	1,719	NA	NA	3.7	33.0	57
Calif., Southern (Keck)	2,797	1,649	13	6	3.6	32.0	48
Calif.–UCLA	3,070	2,133	17	9	3.7	31.5	38
Caribe[S]	435	644	43	3	3.1	18.0	47
Case Western Res.	754	3,374	41	14	3.6	31.8	49
Chicago–Pritzker	819	4,961	15	9	3.7	33.3	50
Chicago Medical	919	6,142	11	5	3.4	28.0	47
Chicago Osteo.[3]	605	4,429	34	5	3.3	24.0	40
Cincinnati	884	1,221	47	18	3.5	28.5	45
Colorado	590	1,610	69	15	3.7	30.1	45
Columbia	548	1,840	31	54	3.8	35.6	46
Connecticut	299	1,752	65	10	3.6	31.0	50
Cornell	1,170	4,596	15	12	3.7[5]	33.0	49
Creighton	208	3,612	19	13	3.6	28.6	50
Dalhousie[1]	205	90	100	50	3.7	2.90	67
Dartmouth	52	4,895	32	12	3.7	33.0	47
Des Moines Osteo.[3]	134	4,356	NA	NA	3.5	24.3	45
Drew/UCLA			No information available				
Drexel[X]	780	6,659	26	74	3.5	29.5	48
Duke	294	4,729	22	17	3.6	32.4	46
East Carolina (Brody)	628	464	69	<1	3.5	26.2	51
E.V. Virginia Osteo.[3]			No information available				
Emory	495	4,891	26	13	3.8	32.0	49
Florida State	717	91	100	0	3.6	25.6	35
Florida, South	1,137	355	31	0	3.7	29.4	57
Florida, Univ. of	1,040	930	27	2	3.7	30.7	53
Geo. Washington	50	8,076	2	98	3.5	28.2	54
Georgetown	49	7,038	31	16	3.6	30.6	53

(continued)

FIGURE 15.7 (continued)

School	Applicants		% of Applicants Interviewed		Accepted Students		
	In-State	Out-of-State	In-State	Out-of-State	Mean GPA	Mean MCAT*	% Women
Georgia, Med. Coll.	723	564	58	<1	3.5	28.2	35
Harvard	342	4,979	19	13	3.8	34.1	51
Hawaii	197	978	80	7	3.5	28.0	53
Howard	47	4,430	40	8	3.0	21.0	52
Illinois, Southern	1,439	665	16	<1	3.5	26.4	45
Illinois, Univ.	1,474	2,165	42	7	3.4	27.9	35
Indiana	558	1,146	88	22	3.7	29.1	49
Iowa	324	2,021	76	15	3.7	28.2	45
Jefferson	1,407	10,287	71	58	3.5[5]	10.1	47
Johns Hopkins	470	5,920	17	10	3.8	35.0	53
Kansas	414	929	76	10	3.6	27.7	45
Kentucky	400	483	63	10	3.5	29.0	41
Kirksville Osteo.[3]	NA	2,256	NA	21	3.5	26.0	37
Lake Erie Osteo.[3]	206	1,831	48	52	3.2	23.1	38
Laval[1,F]	1,600	155	35	10	NA	NA	60
Loma Linda	1,530	1,568	12	17	3.8	28.9	41
Louisville	418	845	57	8	3.6	27.0	52
Loyola–Stritch	1,170	5,156	17	7	3.6	29.6	47
LSU–New Orleans	783	363	50	1	3.6	28.2	49
LSU–Shreveport	662	181	31	0	3.6	26.4	45
Manitoba[1]	232	261	90	19	3.6	31.0	52
Marshall	196	491	85	3	3.5	26.9	50
Maryland	692	2,199	43	9	3.7	30.0	60
Massachusetts	612	432	55	0	3.6[5]	30.0	52
Mayo	296	2,129	NA	NA	3.8	30.0	48
McGill[1]	500	400	44	26	3.6	30.5	49
McMaster[1]	2,239	761	15	5	3.5	NA	70
Meharry	219	2,982	25	16	3.1	22.5	56
Mercer	488	371	35	0	3.5	25.8	46
Miami	1,152	911	24	7	3.7	28.0	54
Michigan Osteo.[3]	NA	NA	NA	NA	3.2	24.0	41
Michigan State	1,266	2,453	23	6	3.4	27.9	52
Michigan, Univ.	755	3,933	28	10	3.7	33.1	46
Minnesota–Duluth	332	315	35	4	3.6	28.5	55
Minnesota–Minneap.	504	1,141	70	6	3.7	30.9	55
Mississippi	236	213	64	0	3.7	27.5	39
Missouri–Columbia	354	361	60	9	3.7	29.5	50
Missouri–KS City	277	199	98	22	NA	NA	60
Montréal[1,F]	1,730	211	34	7	3.7	NA	80
Morehouse	281	1,697	31	8	3.0	21.0	55
Mount Sinai	1,747	3,671	25	12	3.7	32.4	51
Nebraska	254	493	100	15	3.7	28.8	38
Nevada	170	275	NA	NA	3.6	28.2	40
New England Osteo.[3]	NA	NA	NA	NA	3.2	22.5	38

(continued)

FIGURE 15.7 (continued)

	Applicants		% of Applicants Interviewed		Accepted Students		
School	**In-State**	**Out-of-State**	**In-State**	**Out-of-State**	**Mean GPA**	**Mean MCAT***	**%**
WomenNew York Medical	1,510	6,126	27	17	3.3	30.0	33
New Mexico	248	564	94	3	3.6	27.6	55
New York Osteo.[3]	1,100	3,500	50	5	3.3	23.6	50
New York Univ.	2,901	NA	30	NA	3.6	32.1	54
Newfoundland[1]	179	445	78	22	NA	27.0	NA
North Carolina	744	2,280	58	5	3.4	27.0	50
North Dakota	121	106	94	43	3.7	27.4	62
Northwestern	879	5,175	13	9	3.7	33.1	45
Nova Univ. Osteo.[3]	330	1,547	45	55	3.4	25.0	41
Ohio Osteo.[3]	334	1,584	44	2	3.5	25.0	62
Ohio State	1,054	1,944	42	13	3.6	31.0	48
Ohio, Med. Coll.	876	1,266	68	32	3.6	28.1	42
Ohio, Northeast[4]	566	338	37	9	3.7	27.3	58
Oklahoma	362	572	62	5	3.7	28.4	38
Oklahoma Osteo.[3]	221	838	68	9	3.5	27.0	43
Ontario, Western[1]	1,690	NA	NA	NA	3.5	25.0	NA
Oregon	394	1,689	57	8	3.7	30.0	61
Ottawa[1]	1,585	517	NA	NA	NA	NA	NA
Pacific Osteo.[3]	NA	2,254	NA	21	3.4	26.0	39
Pennsylvania State	762	4,012	29	13	3.6	28.7	50
Pennsylvania, Univ.	561	4,118	20	18	3.8	33.3	51
Philadelphia Osteo.[3]	476	2,678	63	13	3.4	24.4	48
Pikeville Osteo.[3]	102	1,193	45	8	3.3	23.0	37
Pittsburgh	685	3,596	25	19	3.6	32.0	43
Ponce[S]	444	366	85	14	3.4	21.5	50
Puerto Rico[S]	356	418	41	0	3.7	22.0	61
Queen's Univ.[1]	1,114	527	25	35	3.6[6]	29.0[6]	47
Rochester	934	2,347	24	19	3.6	31.2	58
Rush	1,185	2,509	32	4	3.4	27.3	43
Saint Louis	285	4,123	13	88	3.6	30.0	47
Saskatchewan[1]	100	168	87	20	86.0[7]	NR	58
Sherbrooke[1,F]	1,540	191	5	5	NA	NR	73
South Carol. Med. U.	404	1,334	63	2	3.6	29.0	49
South Carol. Univ.	353	650	60	10	3.5	27.0	49
South Dakota	133	461	100	5	3.7	27.5	50
Stanford	1,939	3,308	46	54	3.8	35.0	55
SUNY–Brooklyn	1,586	1,092	43	21	3.5	27.9	49
SUNY–Buffalo	1,430	389	29	9	3.5	28.5	56
SUNY–Stony Brook	1,820	591	29	3	3.6	31.0	61
SUNY–Syracuse	1,620	771	20	4	3.6	28.7	45
Temple	849	5,809	49	7	3.5[5]	29.0	50
Tennessee State, E.	465	679	14	3	3.7	27.8	55
Tennessee, Univ.	515	841	56	5	3.6	28.0	55
Texas A&M	1,473	137	34	18	3.6	28.5	49
Texas Osteo.[3]	1,045	107	37	28	3.6	26.0	46

(continued)

FIGURE 15.7 (continued)

	Applicants		% of Applicants Interviewed		Accepted Students		
School	**In-State**	**Out-of-State**	**In-State**	**Out-of-State**	**Mean GPA**	**Mean MCAT***	**% Women**
Texas Tech	1,826	159	33	13	3.6	28.6	40
Texas–Galveston	1,295	263	36	23	3.7	27.0	46
Texas–Houston	2,211	302	54	12	3.6	26.7	56
Texas–San Antonio	2,149	286	40	27	3.5	28.0	59
Texas–Southwest	2,040	360	28	23	3.8	32.1	46
Toronto[1]	NA	NA	NA	NA	3.6[6]	24.0[6]	NA
Touro Osteo.[3]	NA	NA	NA	NA	3.5	27.0	52
Tufts	537	6,893	34	9	3.5	29.8	47
Tulane	510	5,993	21	13	3.5	30.0	43
UMDNJ–Osteo.[3]	294	1,268	52	48	3.5	27.0	59
UMDNJ–New Jersey	705	1,543	NA	NA	3.4	28.8	46
UMDNJ–RWJ	894	1,154	52	11	3.6	29.1	46
Uniformed Serv. U.[8]	1,658	—	—	30	3.5	30.0	27
U. Health Sci. Osteo.[3]	115	2,038	47	23	3.5	25.0	50
Utah	390	710	58	18	3.7	29.7	38
Vanderbilt	229	3,198	5	95	3.7	33.3	39
Vermont	60	4,613	65	11	3.5	28.3	58
Virginia, Eastern	640	1,816	41	14	3.4	30.0	51
Virginia, Med. Coll.	723	2,748	44	11	3.5	29.0	51
Virginia, Univ. of	701	2,863	29	10	3.7	31.5	45
Wake Forest (B. Gray)	830	7,457	32	4	3.4	29.1	41
Washington U. (MO)	142	3534	25	27	3.8	36.5	48
Washington, Univ. of[9]	919	1,961	70	5	3.7	30.5	56
Wayne State	960	1,470	55	9	3.6	28.3	49
West Virginia	223	513	75	15	3.7	27.0	36
West Virginia Osteo.[3]	146	1,372	72	9	3.5	22.2	43
Wisconsin, Med. Coll.	469	3,460	44	13	3.7	30.0	46
Wisconsin, Univ. of	549	1,400	82	7	3.7	31.1	49
Wright State	1,341	2,332	29	2	3.5	24.0	52
Yale	132	3,210	31	24	3.6	33.0	55

1: Canadian medical school
2: Certified WICHE applicants from Alaska, Montana, Wyoming
3: College of Osteopathic Medicine
4: Most students admitted directly from high school
5: Science GPA
6: Lowest GPA or MCAT score considered for acceptance
7: Grades calculated on 100-point scale
8: Considers residents of all states and territories equally
9: In-state figures include Washington, Wyoming, Alaska, Montana, and Idaho residents
*: Mean MCAT = total of three numerical scores
F: Classes taught in French
S: Classes taught in Spanish
NA: Not Available
NR: MCAT not required
X: Formerly Medical College of Pennsylvania/Hahnemann/Allegheny Univ. Health Sciences

Information obtained from: Association of American Medical Colleges. *Medical School Admission Requirements United States and Canada 2004-2005*; American Association of Colleges of Osteopathic Medicine. *2002 Annual Report on Osteopathic Medical Education*. Rockville, MD: AACOM, 2003; and other sources.

FIGURE 15.8
Medical School Application Information

School	Percent Secondary Application In-State/ Other	Recom- mendation Letters[7]	AP Credit OK?	Last MCAT Date	Transfers Accepted? Into Which Years?	Admit Non-U.S. Citizen/ Non- Perm. Resident	When Finan- cial Aid Info Sent?
Alabama[1]	90/10	C+2/4L	Yes	2 Yr	M,D,O*→2,3	Rare	April
Alabama, South	•/50	A+5	+/–	3 Yr	I,*M→2,3;D→2	Yes	Accept
Albany	100	C/2L	Yes[2]	3 Yr	Rare	Yes	Jan
Albert Einstein	100	C/2-4L	Yes[2]	3 Yr	No	Yes	Spring
Alberta[3]	No 2°	2L	No	New	M→2,3	Can	Accept
Arizona	•	C+2/3L	Yes	2 Yr	M*→3	No	Jan
Arizona Osteo.[4]	70/70	C+2/3L(D)	Yes	3 Yr	Rare*	Yes	Jan
Arkansas	•	C/3L+3	Yes[2]	3 Yr	Rare	No	Accept
Baylor	100	A or C+3	Yes[2]	5 Yr	M[16]→3	Yes	Jan 1
Boston	100	C/3L	No	3 Yr	No	No	Accept
British Columbia[3]	No 2°	3L	Yes[5,6]	5 Yr	M→3	No	—
Brown[7]	No 2°	A/C+L	Yes	—	M,D,I,O*→3	Yes	Jan
Calgary[3]	No 2°	3L	Yes	New	M→3	Non-Can	Accept
Calif.–Davis	75/5	C/3L	No	3 Yr	M→3	No	Intvw
Calif.–Irvine	25/0	3-6L	Yes	3 Yr	No	No	Intvw
Calif.–San Diego	40	C/3L	Yes[2]	3 Yr	No	No	Accept
Calif.–San Francisco	25	3-5L+C/A	Yes[8]	3 Yr	No	No	May
Calif.–UCLA	50	A+3/C	No	3 Yr	No	Yes	Req
Calif., Southern (Keck)	100	C/2L	Yes	2 Yr	M→3,O	Yes	—
Caribe[S]	100	C/L	Yes	3 Yr	M,D,I→2,3	Yes	Accept
Case Western Res.	•	C/3-5L	Yes[2]	2 Yr	M→3	Yes	Intvw
Chicago–Pritzker	100	C or A/≥3L	Yes[2]	3 Yr	M→2,3	Yes	Intvw
Chicago Medical	100	C/3L	Yes	3 Yr	M,D,I→2/3,O	Yes	Intvw
Chicago Osteo.[4]	100	C/2L	Yes[2]	3 Yr	D→3	Yes	Intvw
Cincinnati[1]	100	C+L	Yes	3 Yr	M*→3	Yes	Accept
Colorado[1]	100	3-5L	Yes[2]	3 Yr	M,D*,I*	Rare	—
Columbia	No 2°	C+L/L	Yes[2]	3 Yr	M→2,3;I→2	Yes	Accept
Connecticut	100	C+4	Yes[2]	3 Yr	M→3	Yes	Accept
Cornell	100	C/2L	Yes[2]	3 Yr	M→3	Yes	March
Creighton[1]	100	C+3	Yes[2]	3 Yr	No	Yes	Accept
Dalhousie[3]	—	—	—	5 Yr	No	—	Accept
Dartmouth[1]	100	C/A+2	Yes	3 Yr	M,D→2,3;I→2	Yes	April
Des Moines Osteo.[1,4]	85	C/A+2/3L	Yes	2 Yr	M,D→3	Yes	Accept
Drew/UCLA	—	3L/C	—	—	—	—	—
Drexel[1,X]	100	C+A+L/L	Yes	2 Yr	M→2,3,O	No	Feb
Duke[1]	75	C+4-5/4-5L	Yes[2]	4 Yr	M,D**	Yes	Intvw
East Carolina (Brody)	•/?	L	Yes	3 Yr	M,D,I	No	Intvw
E.V. Virginia Osteo.	—	C/A+2(D)[9]	Yes[2]	3 Yr	M,D→1,2	No	Intvw
Emory	100	C/A+3	Yes	4 Yr	M→3	Yes	April
Florida State	90/0	C+2/3L	Yes[2]	3 Yr	M→2	No	Feb

(continued)

FIGURE 15.8 (continued)

School	Percent Secondary Application In-State/ Other	Recom- mendation Letters[7]	AP Credit OK?	Last MCAT Date	Transfers Accepted? Into Which Years?	Admit Non-U.S. Citizen/ Non- Perm. Resident	When Finan- cial Aid Info Sent?
Florida, South[1]	90/0	C+3/6L	Yes	3 Yr	M→2,3	No	Jan
Florida, Univ. of	50	C/3L	Yes[2]	2 Yr	M→3	No	Jan
Geo. Washington	100	C+3/3L	Yes[2]	3 Yr	M,D,I→2,3	Yes	Jan
Georgetown	100	C/2L	Yes	3 Yr	M,D,I→2,3,O	Rare	Feb
Georgia, Med. Coll.	•	C+2/3L	Yes[2]	3 Yr	M,I*→2,3	Yes	Jan
Harvard	100	C+3/4L	Yes[2]	3 Yr	No	Yes	Accept
Hawaii	50	C/2L	Yes[2]	3 Yr	M→3	Yes	—
Howard	100	C+≤5/2L	Yes[2]	3 Yr	M→3	Yes	April
Illinois, Southern	40	C/4L	Yes	2 Yr	M→2,3	No	Intvw
Illinois, Univ.	80/30	C/3L	Yes	3 Yr	M,D	No	Dec
Indiana	80/20	4L	Rev	4 Yr	M,D,I	Yes	Accept
Iowa[1]	90	C+2/3L[9]	Yes	5 Yr	No	No	Accept
Jefferson	100	C/L	Yes[2]	3 Yr	M→3	Yes	Accept
Johns Hopkins	100	C+A or 2L	Yes[2]	NR[10]	M→2,3	Yes	Jan
Kansas	100	C+3/3-5L	Yes	3 Yr	M→3	No	April
Kentucky	•/10	C/3L	Yes[2,11]	2 Yr	M→2,3	Yes	Jan
Kirksville Osteo.[1,4]	—	C+L/A+2	Yes	3 Yr	M,D→2,3,4	Yes	Intvw
Lake Erie Osteo.[4]	100	C+2/3L(D)	Yes	3 Yr	No	No	Intvw
Laval[3,F]	No 2°	None	—	NR	No	Yes	Accept
Loma Linda	100	L	No	3 Yr	M→3	Yes	Accept
Louisville	98	C/3L	Yes[2]	2 Yr	M*→2,3	No	Jan
Loyola–Stritch	13/63	C+2L	Yes	4 Yr	M,D→3	No	Apr
LSU–New Orleans[1]	100/0	C+5L	Yes[2]	3 Yr	M→2,3,4	No	Intvw
LSU–Shreveport[1]	100/0	C+L/2-3L	+/–	3 Yr	M→3	No	Feb
Manitoba[3]	60/15	C/3[9]	Yes	3 Yr	M→3	Can	Accept
Marshall[1]	100	3L	Yes[2]	3 Yr	M→2,3;I→3*	No	March
Maryland	100/25	C+L/3L	Yes[2]	3 Yr	M*→3	Yes[17]	Jan
Massachusetts	100	C/3L	Yes[2]	3 Yr	M→3	No	June
Mayo	No 2°	C+L/3L	Yes	2 Yr	O,M→2	No	Accept
McGill[3]	No 2°	C/L[9]	Yes	3 Yr	No	Yes	—
McMaster[3]	No 2°	C/3L[9]	No	NR	No	Yes	Req
Meharry[1]	100	C/3L±A	No	2 Yr	No	Yes	Intvw
Mercer	80/0	C/2L	No	2 Yr	M*→3	No	Accept
Miami[1]	65/25	C/3L	Yes[2,5,6]	3 Yr	M,I*→3	No	Accept
Michigan Osteo.[1,4]	85-90	2L(D)[9]	Yes	2 Yr	No	Yes	Jan
Michigan State[1]	60/40	C/3-5L	Yes	3 Yr	M→3	AC	April
Michigan, Univ.	100	L/C+L	Yes	3 Yr	No	No	Accept
Minnesota–Duluth	75/0	C/3L	Yes	3 Yr	No	CM	Accept
Minnesota–Minneap.	90/80	C+4	Yes[2]	3 Yr	M→3	Yes	Accept
Mississippi	•	L	No	3 Yr	M→2,3*	No	Feb
Missouri–Columbia	100/10	C+L/3L	Yes[2]	1996	M→3*	No	Jan
Missouri–KS City[15]	No 2°	L[9]	Yes	NR	No	No	Accept

(continued)

FIGURE 15.8 (continued)

School	Percent Secondary Application In-State/ Other	Recom-mendation Letters[7]	AP Credit OK?	Last MCAT Date	Transfers Accepted? Into Which Years?	Admit Non-U.S. Citizen/ Non-Perm. Resident	When Finan-cial Aid Info Sent?
Montréal[3,F]	No 2°	—	Yes	NR	No	NCan	—
Morehouse	87	C/3L	+/–	2 Yr	M→2	Yes	Intvw
Mount Sinai	100	C/L	Yes[2]	All	M→3	Yes	Accept
Nebraska[1]	—	2L	No	3 Yr	M→3	No	—
Nevada	•	C/3L	No	3 Yr	M,D*→2,3	No	—
New England Osteo.[1,4]	40/60	C+L/2L(D)	Yes[2]	2 Yr	D→2,O,M,I→1	No	Accept
New Mexico	99/3	C/3L	Yes	4 Yr	M,D,I*→2	No	Accept
New York Osteo.[1,4]	@interv	C/A+3(D)	Yes	3 Yr	D→2,3	No	March
New York Medical[1]	100	C/3L	Yes	3 Yr	M→3	Yes	March
New York Univ.	No 2°	C/2L	Yes	2 Yr	M,D	No	April
Newfoundland[3]	No 2°	A/2L	Yes[2]	5 Yr	M→2,3,4	Yes	Accept
North Carolina	50/10	C+L/A+3	Yes	5 Yr	M*→3	No	Intvw
North Dakota	No 2°	C/4L	Yes	3 Yr	M→3	No	Jan
Northwestern	100	C+L/A+3	Yes	3 Yr	Rare	Yes	Intvw
Nova Univ. Osteo.[4]	80/49	C+2/3L(D)	Yes	3 Yr	D→3	Yes	Intvw
Ohio Osteo.[1,4]	60	C or A+2(D)	Yes	3 Yr	D	No	Jan
Ohio State	100	L	+/–	2 Yr	M→3	Yes	April
Ohio, Med. Coll.[1]	80/70	L	Yes	3 Yr	M→2,3	Yes	Accept
Ohio, Northeast[7]	60	L	Yes[5]	2 Yr	M,D→3	Yes	Intvw
Oklahoma[1]	100	C/L	Yes[2]	New	M*→3	No	Accept
Oklahoma Osteo.[4]	100/?	C+2/3L(D)	Yes[2]	3 Yr	D	No	Accept
Ontario, Western[3]	No 2°	3L[9]	No	5 Yr	M[12]	Can	Accept
Oregon	75/?	C/A+L/L	Yes	3 Yr	M→3	No	Intvw
Ottawa[3]	No 2°	3L[9]	No	—	Rare	Can	Req
Pacific Osteo.[4]	90	C/A+3(D)	Yes[2]	3 Yr	M,D→2,3	Yes	Intvw
Pennsylvania State	100	C/A/4-6L	Yes	2 Yr	M→3	Yes	May
Pennsylvania, Univ.	100	C/2L	Yes[2]	3 Yr	No	Yes	May
Philadelphia Osteo.[4]	100	C/A+(D)/L+(D)	Yes[2]	3 Yr	No	Yes	Accept
Pikeville Osteo.	100	3C/L	Yes	3 Yr	M→3	Yes	Accept
Pittsburgh	—	C+3L	Yes[2]	3 Yr	M→3	Yes	Accept
Ponce[S]	No 2°	C/A+3L	Yes	2 Yr	M,I→2,3	Yes	Accept
Puerto Rico[S]	•/?	C/3L	Yes	3 Yr	M*→3	No	Accept
Queen's Univ.[3]	No 2°	L[9]	Yes	New	No	Can	Aug
Rochester	100	C/3-5L	Yes[2]	3 Yr	No	No	Intvw
Rush	100	3L	Yes[2]	3 Yr	M→3	No	Jan
Saint Louis[1]	100	C/3L	Yes[2]	3 Yr	M→3	Yes	Accept
Saskatchewan[3]	No 2°	3L[9]	Yes	5 Yr	Rare	Can	—
Sherbrooke[3,F]	No 2°	—	—	NR	No	Yes	Req
South Carol., Med. U.	•/?	A+3/C/3L	Yes	5 Yr	No	No	Jan
South Carol., Univ.	90/20	C+6/3-6L	Yes	5 Yr	M→2,3	Yes	Jan
South Dakota	•/?	3L/C	Yes[2]	3 Yr	M*→2,3	No	Accept
Stanford[1]	38/62	A+3/3L	Yes	3 Yr	Yes→2,3	Yes	Accept

(continued)

FIGURE 15.8 (continued)

School	Percent Secondary Application In-State/ Other	Recom-mendation Letters[7]	AP Credit OK?	Last MCAT Date	Transfers Accepted? Into Which Years?	Admit Non-U.S. Citizen/ Non-Perm. Resident	When Finan-cial Aid Info Sent?
SUNY–Brooklyn[1]	100	C/2L	Yes[2]	3 Yr	M→3,O	Yes	March
SUNY–Buffalo	100	C+3-5/3-5	Yes[2]	3 Yr	M,D,FS→3	No	Jan
SUNY–Stony Brook	100	C+L	Yes[2]	1 Yr	M→3	No	Accept
SUNY–Syracuse[1]	100	C/2L	Yes	3 Yr	M,D,FS	Yes	Accept
Temple	100	C/3L	Yes	3 Yr	M,D→2,3	No	Accept
Tennessee State, E.[1]	25/10	C/L	Yes[2]	2 Yr	M→2,3	No	Spring
Tennessee, Univ.	80/20	C/3L	Yes[2]	5 Yr	M	No	April
Texas A&M	100	C+2/A+2	Yes	<5 Yr	M→3	Yes	Accept
Texas Coll Osteo.[4,13]	33/?	C/3L	Yes[2]	3 Yr	D*→3	No	Intvw
Texas Tech	100	A+2/2L	Yes[2]	5 Yr	M	No	Accept
Texas–Galveston[13]	No 2°	C/2L	Yes	5 Yr	M**	Yes	Accept
Texas–Houston[13]	No 2°	C/2L	Yes	5 Yr	No	No	Feb
Texas–San Antonio[13]	100	C/A+2	AB	3 Yr	M→3,O→2	No	Accept
Texas–Southwest[13]	100	C/2L	Yes	5 Yr	M	Yes	Accept
Toronto[3]	No 2°	3L[9]/C	Yes	5 Yr	No	Yes	Accept
Touro Osteo.[4]	—	C/L+(D)	Yes	3 Yr	D→2,3	No	Intvw
Tufts[1]	100	C+L/L	Yes[2]	3 Yr	M→2,3	Yes	May
Tulane	100	C/3L	Yes[2]	3 Yr	M,I**→2,3	Yes	Jan
UMDNJ–Osteo.[4]	100	C/2L	Yes[2]	3 Yr	D→2,3	No	Accept
UMDNJ–New Jersey	100	C+2/3L	Yes[2]	All	No	Yes	Accept
UMDNJ–RWJ	—	C+L/3L	Yes[2]	4 Yr	M,D,I→3	No	Accept
Uniformed Serv. U.[1]	—	C/3L	Yes[2]	3 Yr	No	No	—
U. Health Sci. Osteo.[4]	70	C/3L(D)	Yes[2]	2 Yr	No	Yes	Accept
Utah	90/30	6L	Yes[14]	3 Yr	M**→3	Yes	Intvw
Vanderbilt	100	3L	No	3 Yr	M→3	Yes	April
Vermont[1]	100	C	Yes	3 Yr	M,D,I→1,2	Yes	Feb
Virginia, Eastern	80/50	C/3L	Yes	2 Yr	M→2,3	No	Accept
Virginia, Med. Coll.	75/30	A+L	Yes	3 Yr	M→3	No	Intvw
Virginia, Univ. of[1]	100	2L	+/–	3 Yr	M→3	Yes	May
Wake Forest (B. Gray)	50	C/2L	+/–	3 Yr	M→3	Yes	April
Washington U. (MO)[1]	100	C/3L	Yes	3 Yr	M→3	Yes	April
Washington, Univ. of[1]	—	C/L	Yes[2]	3 Yr	No	No	—
Wayne State	70/25	C/3L	Yes[2]	3 Yr	M,D,O→2,3	AC	Accept
West Virginia	•/?	2L/C+L	Yes[2]	2 Yr	M,D→2	No	Accept
West Virginia Osteo.[4]	72/9	L+A(D)	Yes[2]	3 Yr	M,D→1,2	No	Intvw
Wisconsin, Med. Coll.	100	2L	Yes[2]	3 Yr	M→3	Yes	Intvw
Wisconsin, Univ. of	95/20	A+4	Yes[2]	4 Yr	I*,M→2,3	No	Jan
Wright State	100	C+3/3L	Yes	3 Yr	M,D→2,3	No	Feb
Yale	90/20	A+4	Yes[2]	4 Yr	M**→2/3	Yes	Accept

•: All in-state applicants get secondary application
*: State residents only or preferred
**: Transfer considered if there is a personal relationship with a student or staff at the school
+/–: May grant credit in some circumstances

(continued)

FIGURE 15.8 (continued)

1: School has a "rolling" admission policy
2: Supplement premed courses with advanced courses in same areas
3: Canadian medical school 4: College of Osteopathic Medicine
5: Organic Chemistry not accepted as an Advanced Placement (AP) credit
6: Biochemistry not accepted as an Advanced Placement (AP) credit
7: Information is primarily for those not applying through the eight-year program
8: Biology not accepted as an Advanced Placement (AP) credit
9: School has special forms for letters
10: Does not require MCAT, but requires results of SAT, ACT, GRE, or MCAT
11: Physics not accepted as an Advanced Placement (AP) credit
12: Transfers from other Canadian medical schools only
13: School has a uniform admission date and thereafter uses a "rolling" admission policy
14: Chemistry accepted if AP score is 4 or 5
15: Information is about six-year program for high school students
16: Does not accept Canadian students
17: Non-U.S. citizens/nonpermanent residents on diplomatic visas considered
A: Premed Adviser cover letter
AB: Advanced Biology is the only AP course accepted
AC: Accepts Canadian citizens
Accept: Financial information sent when applicant is accepted or shortly thereafter
C: Premed Committee letters preferred
Can: Only Canadian citizens or landed immigrants admitted
CM: Accepts Canadian citizens from Manitoba
D: Transfers accepted from U.S. D.O.-granting schools
(D): At least one letter must be from a D.O.
F: Classes taught in French
FS: Transfers accepted from foreign schools approved by the NY Dept. of Education
I: Transfers accepted from non-U.S. medical schools
Intvw: Financial information distributed at interview
L: Individual recommendation letters required with/or instead of Premed Committee letter. If no number is specified, it indicates that several letters should be sent.
M: Transfers accepted from U.S. and Canadian M.D.-granting schools
NCan: Non-Canadian citizens/landed immigrants admitted
New: MCAT scores must be from the "New" MCAT, administered since 1991
NR: MCAT not required
O: Oral surgeons or general dentists accepted into second-year class, unless otherwise noted
Req: Financial information distributed on request only
Rev: Reviewed on an individual basis
S: Classes taught in Spanish
X: Formerly Medical College of Pennsylvania/Hahnemann/Allegheny Univ. Health Sciences

Information obtained from: Association of American Medical Colleges. *Medical School Admission Requirements United States and Canada 2004-2005*; American Association of Colleges of Osteopathic Medicine. *2002 Annual Report on Osteopathic Medical Education*. Rockville, MD: AACOM, 2003; and other sources.

16

Which Medical Schools? The "Must/Want" Analysis

Anyone can make a decision given enough facts.
A good manager makes decisions without enough facts.
A perfect manager operates in perfect ignorance.

— Corollary to Murphy's Law

— "Must/Want" Analysis —

One way of deciding which medical school to attend is to use the "Must/Want" Analysis. (See also Chapter 7.) This method allows you to first determine which factors are important to you and then figure out which schools meet your needs. It allows you to look past the glitter (or dullness) of a school's reputation and forces you to examine what you really want (and need) from a school.

To use the "Must/Want" Analysis, first make a list of all the possible factors that could influence your decision about the medical school you would like to attend. (See Figure 16.1 for an example.) Some of the items may be absolute necessities for you, such as a problem-based curriculum or computer instruction. *If an item is an absolute necessity, a "MUST," you have decided that the factor is so important that it must be present or else it will eliminate a school from consideration, regardless of its other qualities.*

Other items will be relatively important. For example, living in the Midwest might be more important to you than living on either coast. In that case, you will rate each item based on its relative importance to you. Use the examples as a guide, and add items that are of particular importance to you. Some factors, of course, will not be important to you at all and can be eliminated from your list.

Once you have made your list, assign "Weights" to each factor based on its importance to you. In giving "Weights" to each factor, remember that the total must equal "100." Therefore, apportion each item's Weight in relation to all the other factors you are considering. It is easiest to first select those factors that are not at all important and rate them "0." Then move on to those of minimal importance, rating them "1." Continue in this fashion until the total for all assigned Weights equals "100." However, if a factor is a "MUST," instead of assigning it a number value, you should assign it the word "Must." *Once you make up your list of factors and their weights, you will use this same list for every medical school you consider. (Make copies of your blank list.)* Refer to Figures 16.2 and 16.3 to see how a one applicant assigned "Weights" to the factors on her list.

When you gather information about each school, you will "Score" each factor for that school. The "Score" is your estimate of how well the specific school fulfills your expectations for that category (use a 1–10 scale; 10 is "perfect"). If an item that you have rated as a "MUST" is not present, you will drop the school from consideration (as in Figure 16.3).

The information for scoring the factors can be obtained from the schools' written materials, the charts in Chapter 15, the AAMC's or AACOM's annual school listings, and each school's website. For additional information, try searching the AAMC's *Curriculum Directory* (http://services.aamc.org/currdir), although it is limited to U.S. M.D.-granting schools. During the interview, you can verify this information and add information (such as an evaluation of faculty interest, esprit de corps, and the quality of the food) that can only be obtained by visiting the school.

Once you have entered all Scores, calculate each Factor's total by multiplying the "Weight" by the "Score." All factor "Totals" are added to give your "School Evaluation Score." Use this score to decide the ranking of the schools on your list.

Figures 16.2 and 16.3 are examples of how one student (married, one child, spouse with transferable job that includes family health benefits) completed her "Must/Want" Analysis for two schools that she was considering. She has shortened the list given in Figure 16.1 to eliminate those factors that are not important to her (and which she gave "0" for the Weight). The factors she eliminated include all the Research Opportunities, most Curriculum factors, and Health Benefits. She also deleted all the Non-Health Benefits except for Meals and Parental Leave, which is a "MUST" for her.

This student will use U. of M.'s "School Evaluation Score" of 546 (Figure 16.2) to compare this school with other schools that interest her. If there is no change in her situation, she will go to the school with the highest "School Evaluation Score" that accepts her.

Although U. of C. Medical School (Figure 16.3) got high marks in some factors this student considered important, the school did not have a formal parental-leave policy. This was her "make or break" factor that she rated "MUST." Since this factor was not present, she eliminated the school from consideration. Therefore, even if this school offers her an interview (or a position if she did not find out this information until she interviewed), she will not accept. When making factors a "MUST," be sure that they are so important to you that you are willing not go to an otherwise excellent school if it lacks that factor.

Medical School Accreditation

One "MUST" factor for every applicant is medical school accreditation by the Liaison Committee on Medical Education (LCME) or the American Osteopathic Association. If the school is in the United States or Canada and is not accredited, then you can *never* practice medicine in the United States. Foreign schools avoid this problem by being listed in a special worldwide index that is not available to schools within the United States or Canada. (See Chapter 17: *Foreign Medical Schools*.)

All medical schools listed in the AAMC's *Medical School Admission Requirements* or on the AOA website are accredited. However, they may also be on probation. To find out the status of M.D.-granting schools, go to www.lcme.org/directry.htm. (Note how "directry" is spelled in this URL.) A few schools may be on "probation." That is bad. Some schools may be "provisionally accredited," meaning that they are too new to have full accreditation.

— Playing the Odds: To How Many Schools Should I Apply? —

If you look at the long list of medical schools, you can be overwhelmed. However, you don't have a real chance of getting into most of those schools. Most medical schools are publicly funded state schools, and take few or no out-of-state applicants, although many people foolishly apply with no hope of getting in. (See Figure 15.5 for the percentage of out-of-state residents accepted by schools.) Therefore, consider applying first to your state's medical schools and to schools that consider you to be an in-state resident through a cooperative program, such as the Western Interstate Commission for Higher Education (WICHE). (See "Interstate Cooperative Programs" later in this chapter.) Next, pick the private schools where you think that you will have the best chance of success. Your preliminary list will have, at most, about 25 schools, and probably fewer.

Once you have a list, look at Figure 15.6 for the tuition and fees for each school and Figure 15.7 for the average GPA and MCAT scores of the students they accept. Put schools on your "short list" that you can afford and to which you have at least a reasonable chance of being admitted.

FIGURE 16.1
"Must/Want" Analysis for Medical School

SCHOOL ________________________________

CLINICAL EXPERIENCE	WEIGHT	X SCORE	= TOTAL
In Preclinical Years			
Patient Population			
Responsibility			
Clinical Settings			
Elective Time			
Range of Local Specialties			
Exposure to Managed Care			
Time in Ambulatory Setting			
GEOGRAPHIC LOCATION			
Inner City, Suburb, Rural			
Part of Country			
Specific City			
Spouse/Family/Dependent Needs			
REPUTATION			
School's Reputation			
School's Age and Stability			
Percent On-Time Graduations			
Success on USMLE Steps 1 and 2			
Attitude Toward Women, Minorities			
Success Getting Desired Residency			
FACULTY			
Availability			
Interest			
Stability			
CURRICULUM			
Curriculum Structure			
Innovative Curriculum (PBL)			
Time to Degree			
Combination Degrees			
Self-Paced Learning			
Computer Education			
Preschool Orientations			
Specialty-Selection Counseling			
Case-Based Teaching			
Small-Group Learning			
Large/Small Classes			
Student-Teacher Ratio			
Types of Examinations			
Grading System			
Amount of Elective Time			
Graduation Requirements			
ESPRIT DE CORPS			
Friendliness			
Cooperation Among Students			

(continued)

FIGURE 16.1 (continued)

RESEARCH OPPORTUNITIES/TRAINING	WEIGHT	X SCORE	= TOTAL
Knowledge			
Materials			
Time			
Funding			
FACILITIES			
Clinical Laboratory Support			
Computerized Records/Lab Results			
Lecture Hall/Lab Age, Atmosphere			
Hospitals' Ages, Atmosphere			
Library/Media			
Parking			
Medical Bookstore			
Safety/Security			
Recreation Facilities			
Easy, Affordable Transportation			
Cafeteria/Food			
HEALTH BENEFITS			
Health Insurance			
Health Promotion			
Psychiatric Counseling			
NONHEALTH BENEFITS			
Child-care			
Educational Counseling			
Residency Application Counseling			
Mentoring			
Family Educational Benefits			
Uniforms/Scrubs			
Parental Leave			
Meals			
Photocopying			
Vacation			
Student-Learning Center			
Dorms/Subsidized Housing			
FINANCIAL COSTS & ASSISTANCE			
Tuition			
Housing			
Other Costs			
Employment for Spouse/Family			
Scholarships			
Loans			
Jobs			

TOTAL OF ALL WEIGHTS = 100

SCHOOL EVALUATION SCORE = ______

(Total of Weights x Scores)

FIGURE 16.2

"Must/Want" Analysis—Example A

SCHOOL U. of M. Medical School

CLINICAL EXPERIENCE	**WEIGHT**	**X SCORE**	**= TOTAL**
In Preclinical Years	6	8	48
Patient Population	1	6	6
Responsibility	4	8	32
Clinical Settings	3	7	21
Elective Time	2	2	4
Range of Local Specialties	1	5	5
Exposure to Managed Care	2	2	4
Time in Ambulatory Setting	3	2	6
GEOGRAPHIC LOCATION			
Part of Country	3	6	18
REPUTATION			
School's Reputation	3	3	9
Percent On-Time Graduations	1	7	7
Success on USMLE Steps 1 and 2	3	8	24
Attitude Toward Women, Minorities	2	7	14
Success Getting Desired Residency	3	6	18
FACULTY			
Availability	6	6	36
Interest	4	3	12
CURRICULUM			
Curriculum Structure	1	3	3
Innovative Curriculum (PBL)	3	2	6
Computer Education	3	2	6
Specialty-Selection Counseling	1	1	1
ESPRIT DE CORPS			
Friendliness	2	3	6
Cooperation Among Students	2	3	6
FACILITIES			
Lecture Hall/Lab Age, Atmosphere	3	4	12
Hospitals' Ages, Atmosphere	1	6	6
Library/Media	3	4	12
Safety/Security	3	3	9
Cafeteria/Food	2	7	14
NONHEALTH BENEFITS			
Parental Leave	MUST	YES	✓
Meals	2	8	16
FINANCIAL COSTS & ASSISTANCE			
Tuition	10	9	90
Other Costs	3	5	15
Scholarships	8	5	40
Loans	4	6	24
Jobs	2	8	16

TOTAL OF ALL WEIGHTS = 100

SCHOOL EVALUATION SCORE = 546

FIGURE 16.3

"Must/Want" Analysis—Example B

SCHOOL U. of C. Medical School

CLINICAL EXPERIENCE	WEIGHT	X SCORE	= TOTAL
In Preclinical Years	6	6	36
Patient Population	1	8	8
Responsibility	4	7	28
Clinical Settings	3	7	21
Elective Time	2	6	12
Range of Local Specialties	1	8	8
Exposure to Managed Care	2	5	10
Time in Ambulatory Setting	3	7	21
GEOGRAPHIC LOCATION			
Part of Country	3	7	21
REPUTATION			
School's Reputation	3	5	15
Percent On-Time Graduations	1	4	4
Success on USMLE Steps 1 and 2	3	7	21
Attitude Toward Women, Minorities	2	6	12
Success Getting Desired Residency	3	8	24
FACULTY			
Availability	6	5	30
Interest	4	5	20
CURRICULUM			
Curriculum Structure	1	6	6
Innovative Curriculum (PBL)	3	3	9
Computer Education	3	3	9
Specialty-Selection Counseling	1	3	3
ESPRIT DE CORPS			
Friendliness	2	6	12
Cooperation Among Students	2	6	12
FACILITIES			
Lecture Hall/Lab Age, Atmosphere	3	7	21
Hospitals' Ages, Atmosphere	1	3	3
Library/Media	3	3	9
Safety/Security	3	5	15
Cafeteria/Food	3	5	15
NONHEALTH BENEFITS			
Parental Leave	MUST	NO	X
Meals	2	—	—
FINANCIAL COSTS & ASSISTANCE			
Tuition	10	—	—
Other Costs	3	—	—
Scholarships	8	—	—
Loans	4	—	—
Jobs	2	—	—

TOTAL OF ALL WEIGHTS = **100**

SCHOOL EVALUATION SCORE = NO SCORE (Does not have a "MUST" Requirement)

Don't be too pessimistic about your personal or financial assessment, however. Professional photographers constantly tell amateurs to go ahead and take lots of pictures. So what if you blow a few shots? You may end up with some beautiful pictures you wouldn't have gotten if you had been more conservative. Remember, they say, the film is the least expensive part of system. Just so with the application process. Applying to a few extra schools, especially those you really want to attend but don't think would accept you, makes good sense for at least two reasons. First, you will never have to say to yourself, as so many physicians do when they meet up with a moronic graduate from a medical school to which they really wanted to go, that "I could have gotten in if only I had applied." Second, you actually may get an interview (and then a position) at that school. It takes very little extra effort to apply to a *few* more carefully selected schools. If the school's tuition is a reason for not applying, see Chapter 18: *Paying for Medical School*. Follow your dreams—they may come true!

One thing to consider when applying to medical schools is that most schools with secondary applications charge between $40 and $100 to file these applications. Also, it takes lots of time (three to eight hours each) to complete the secondary applications, generate the required essays, and send the additional materials. How much time do you have? Perhaps it is wiser to spend more time assessing the answers to the following questions:

1. To which schools do you want to go?
2. At which schools do you have the best chance of admission?
3. Which schools can you afford?

Then, put your efforts toward completing the materials for these schools instead of dithering away (and driving yourself crazy) trying to complete extraneous paperwork.

Medical Schools and In-State Applicants

Although you should try to follow your dreams, be realistic about your chances when applying to out-of-state schools. While medical schools receive an extraordinary number of applications, many seem to be submitted only to kill trees, waste money, bog down the Web, or give the U.S. Postal Service something to do. Most public medical schools accept few or no students who are not official residents of their state. Applying to these schools is like spitting in the wind. Private schools may also give preference to in-state residents, since many receive state funds or support from foundations and endowments within their state.

If your state has one or more medical schools, you should apply to these schools. If your state does not have a medical school, find out which medical schools treat applicants from your state as in-state students. Every state without a medical school has at least one such arrangement. See "Interstate Cooperative Programs," below, and contact your premed adviser for additional information. (See also *Appendix E* for a list of medical schools by state.)

What Defines "In-State" Applicants?

Each state has its own requirements for determining who is an "in-state" applicant. Often these definitions stem from the state's tax code. In general, to be considered an "in-state" resident, an individual must:

1. Have lived in the state at least one year,
2. Have a state driver's license,
3. Be registered to vote in the state,
4. Have a car registered in the state (if a car owner), and
5. Pay (or qualify to pay) income tax as a state resident *OR*
6. Own property, usually a house, in the state, *OR*
7. Live permanently in the state.

If, for example, you move to a new state but are still registered to vote in your old state and complete that state's resident income tax forms, you will probably be considered a resident of your old state. Even if you complete the above requirements, you may not be considered a resident if you were a college student the entire time you lived in the state. This can get very tricky and every state is different, so if you have a question about your residency status, check with the schools in question before applying. (It is so difficult that the University of Texas' application includes a special form to submit so they can determine your residency status.) You may have to demonstrate your in-state eligibility to the school during the selection process.

Residency requirements also extend to medical schools in Canada and Puerto Rico. Few U.S. citizens are accepted to Canadian medical schools, except for McGill University in Montreal and McMaster in Ontario. Similarly, few non-Puerto Ricans are accepted to that island's three accredited medical schools.

Interstate Cooperative Programs

Some states do not have medical schools, but, instead, have contracts with public and private medical schools in other states that require them to treat you as an "in-state" student when they consider your application and tuition. Other states want to provide special medical school opportunities, so they underwrite some students' private medical education costs in their own or other states. Such programs exist throughout the country and are managed by regional agencies. Contracts change from year to year, so it is important to check with your state's Department of Education or regional agency (listed below) to find out which M.D.- or D.O.-granting institutions your state currently uses.

If your state has such a contract, you must fulfill certain residency and academic requirements to be eligible for these programs and for the state to support the nonresident part of your tuition. You must apply to your state or regional agency to be certified as a "qualified" student *before you apply* to medical schools. The Southern Regional Educational Board works mainly with black medical students; WICHE and WWAMI work with a variety of applicants.

- **Southern Regional Education Board (SREB)**
  592 Tenth Street, N.W.
  Atlanta, GA 30318-5790
  (404) 875-9211; www.sreb.org
  Participating States: Alabama, Arkansas, Florida, Georgia, Kentucky, Louisiana, Maryland, Mississippi, North Carolina, Oklahoma, South Carolina, Tennessee, Texas, Virginia, West Virginia
  Participating Schools: Nearly all M.D.- and D.O.-granting medical schools in these states.
- **Western Interstate Commission for Higher Education (WICHE)**
  P.O. Drawer P
  Boulder, CO 80301-9752
  www.wiche.edu
  Participating States: Montana, Wyoming
  Participating Medical Schools:
  Arizona Coll. of Osteopathic Med.
  Coll. Osteopathic Med. of Pacific
  Loma Linda
  Stanford
  Touro Univ. Coll. of Osteopathic Med.
  U. Arizona Coll. of Med.
  U. Calif. Berkeley–UCSF Med. Prog.
  U. Calif.–Davis
  U. Calif.–Los Angeles
  U. Calif.–San Diego
  U. Calif.–San Francisco
  U. of Colorado
  U. of Hawaii
  U. of Nevada
  U. of New Mexico
  U. of Southern Calif.
  U. of Utah
- **Washington, Wyoming, Alaska, Montana, Idaho Program (WWAMI)**
  Basic Medical Sciences Program (WWAMI)
  Washington State University
  Morrill Hall, Room 108
  Pullman, WA 99164-3510
  www.montana.edu/wwwwami/#WAMI
  Participating States: Alaska, Idaho, Montana, Washington, Wyoming
  Participating School: U. of Washington

"Other" Categories

Schools sometimes have intermediate categories for students, such as "state-related." These apply to students who, while not currently in-state residents, have such close ties to the state that they are given consideration after in-state residents, but before other out-of-state residents. Examples of such ties are: Having lived most of one's life in the state, working and paying taxes in the state but not yet establishing residence, or preparing to move to the state because of a firm job offer or for specific personal reasons. Not all schools have this category, but, if your situation is similar to these, investigate whether they do. It may mean that there are additional schools at which you have a good chance of being admitted.

Some schools also give special consideration to their alumni's children (known as "legacies"), and consider them on the same basis as in-state students, even if they live in another state. But, they generally have to pay the out-of-state tuition. (No one will tell you about this.) So, if one of your parents is a physician, have him or her check with their school's alumni office to see if you will get special consideration.

Minorities and Medical School Admissions

Most medical schools admit a significant number of minority students. You may have a better chance of acceptance, however, if you apply to schools in areas where your minority is not well-represented. This may give you a slight advantage.

There is, of course, a caveat to this advice. You must be personally strong enough to survive in a place that you have already defined as lacking cultural supports for you. Think very hard and thoroughly investigate all aspects of the potential cultural life in a community before you apply (or at least before you commit) to its medical school.

Apart from touring the community to observe the setting in which the school is located, contact the school's minority affairs office, the town's chamber of commerce, or look in an almanac or other reference book for statistical information about the city. Then contact any identifiable cultural organizations, such as a church of your denomination.

U.S. News & World Report 2003 Rankings

Each March, *U.S. News & World Report* publishes its evaluation of the "top" U.S. medical schools. These are broken down into several categories. The rankings are based on the school's reputation among medical school deans, senior faculty, and residency directors; how selective they are in taking medical students (average GPA and MCAT scores of entering students); and the ratio of the full-time basic science and clinical faculty to the total number of medical students. When ranking the "primary care schools," they also include the percentage of graduates entering "primary care residencies." For the "Specialties" rankings, they use only the ratings from medical school deans and senior faculty.

Both medical and nonmedical journals have criticized the rankings for their sloppy methodology and the lack of objectivity and scientific integrity. (See Graham A, Thompson N: Broken ranks. *Washington Monthly*. Sept. 2001, p. 9+; and McGaghie WC, Thompson JA: America's best medical schools: critique of the *U.S. News & World Report* rankings. *Acad Med.* 2001;76:985-92.) Amy Graham, who oversaw the publication's ranking process for two years, suggested that the magazine's method of data-gathering and ranking colleges "defies common sense and produces misleading results."

So why list them? These rankings are so well-known and so popular that, if nothing else, your friends and relatives will "ooh" and "ahh" when you tell them that you have applied to a school on the list. (That, of course, is not your goal. Okay, maybe it's a *little* bit of a goal.) While the schools on this list provide an excellent medical education, so do nearly all the other U.S. and Canadian medical schools.

By now, you should know why any list of the "best" medical schools will not do you much good. You need to choose the factors that are important to you and weigh them accordingly. However, since so many people wish to know how others rate medical schools, the 2003 rankings are listed in Figure 16.4.

Acceptance Rates

It would be nice to be able to compare acceptance rates for the various medical schools. But that is extremely difficult, if not impossible. Medical schools actually accept more students than they have room for in their first-year class. Many students receive multiple acceptances and, of course, can go to only one school. The best you can do is to compare each school's percentage of applicants who are interviewed, the number of interviewees, and the size of their first-year class (Figure 15.6). This will give you a rough idea of how competitive the school is.

FIGURE 16.4

U.S. News & World Report 2003 Rankings

Primary Care Medical Schools

1. Univ. of Washington
2. Oregon Health Sciences Univ.
3. Univ. of Calif.–San Francisco
4. Michigan State Univ.–Osteopathic
5. Univ. of Minnesota
6. Univ. of Calif.–San Diego
7. Univ. of New Mexico
8. Univ. of Wisconsin–Madison
9. Univ. of Iowa
10. Univ. of Minnesota–Minneapolis
11. Univ. of Rochester
12. Univ. of Colorado Health Sci. Center
13. Univ. of Massachusetts–Worcester
14. Univ. of Missouri–Columbia
15. Univ. of North Carolina

Specialties

Family Practice

1. Univ. of Washington
2. Univ. of Missouri–Columbia
3. Oregon Health Sciences Univ.

Internal Medicine

1. Harvard Univ.
2. Johns Hopkins Univ.
3. Univ. of Calif.–San Francisco

Pediatrics

1. Harvard Univ.
2. Univ. of Pennsylvania
3. Johns Hopkins Univ.

Geriatrics

1. Johns Hopkins Univ.
2. Univ. of Calif.–Los Angeles
3. Mt. Sinai School of Medicine

Rural Medicine

1. Univ. of Washington
2. Univ. of New Mexico
3. East Tennessee State Univ.

Women's Health

1. Harvard Univ.
2. Univ. of Pennsylvania
3. Univ. of Calif.–San Francisco

Research-Oriented Medical Schools

1. Harvard Univ.
2. Johns Hopkins
3. Washington Univ.
4. Duke Univ.
5. Univ. of Pennsylvania
6. Univ. of Calif.–San Francisco
7. Columbia Univ.
8. Stanford Univ.
9. Univ. of Michigan–Ann Arbor
10. Yale Univ.
11. Univ. of Washington
12. Baylor College of Medicine
13. Cornell Univ.
14. Univ. of Calif.–Los Angeles
15. Vanderbilt Univ.
16. Univ. of Calif.–San Diego
17. Univ. of Texas–Southwestern
18. Univ. of Pittsburgh
19. Emory Univ.
20. Mayo Medical School
21. Northwestern Univ.
22. Univ. of Chicago
23. Univ. of North Carolina–Chapel Hill
24. Case Western Reserve Univ.
25. Univ. of Alabama–Birmingham
26. Univ. of Iowa

17

Foreign Medical Schools

Misery acquaints a man with strange bed-fellows.

— Shakespeare, *The Tempest, II, 2*

'Tis a lesson you should heed:
Try, try, try again.
If at first you don't succeed,
Try, try, try again.

— W. E. Hickson, *Try and Try Again*

The admissions process that U.S. and Canadian medical schools use is not perfect. They routinely reject individuals who would make good (or great) physicians, and accept others who do not belong anywhere near patients. This is unfortunate for both patients and the medical profession, but not unfair—everyone knows the rules. Foreign medical schools that cater to applicants rejected by U.S. and Canadian schools see themselves as "second chance" schools. Whether they do indeed represent a second chance or are the last resort of desperate people depends upon the individual applicant and on the school selected.

How lucky do you feel? Or, perhaps, how desperate are you? You have to be both to succeed at a foreign medical school. My best advice, and the advice from many who are experts in this area, is: DON'T GO!

Since you are continuing to read, you aren't planning on taking this advice. Therefore, here are the specifics; you alone must decide whether this path is right for you.

— Approved/Nonapproved Schools —

The United States (including its Territories), Canada, and Australia are the only countries which have intense, government-sanctioned licensing bodies for medical schools. In the United States, the Liaison Committee on Medical Education (LCME) and the American Osteopathic Association (AOA) accredit medical schools. In Canada, the LCME and the Committee on Accreditation of Canadian Medical Schools (CACMS) jointly accredit the schools. Australia's schools are accredited by the Australian Medical Council, which is similar to the American and Canadian agencies.

None of these bodies accredits schools outside its geographic boundaries. In this book, therefore, "foreign school" means any medical school not accredited by the U.S. and Canadian agencies, generally indicating schools outside the United States, U.S. Territories, and Canada. One foreign school (Ross) claims a home base in New York, although students do not attend preclinical classes there.

Note that one school in the United States, San Juan Bautista, which is located in Puerto Rico, is not LCME-approved. Only Puerto Rico has approved this school. And, because it is located in a U.S. Commonwealth, students are not eligible for an Educational Commission for Foreign Medical Graduates (ECFMG) Certificate. This means that their graduates may be licensed only in Puerto Rico.

— Who Should Consider Going to a Foreign School? —

Most of the foreign medical schools that cater to U.S. students will take nearly anyone who applies. The exceptions are those few schools whose students subsequently do the best on U.S. licensing examinations. Their high standards make it relatively difficult to get into them. If you are like most students, you will either not apply to those schools or apply but not get in.

Therefore, it is not the foreign medical schools—but you—who must be the ruthless decision maker. Do you really have what it takes to succeed *despite* going to a foreign school? Try to be honest with yourself—don't expect these schools to decide for you. Graduates of foreign medical schools are called International Medical Graduates (IMGs). Special rules exist for IMGs to get a U.S. residency training position and, in most states, to get a license to practice medicine.

Dr. Carlos Pestana, an expert on foreign medical schools that admit U.S. citizens, recommends that the only people who should go to these schools are those who are "wealthy, adaptable, a master of the multiple-choice test, very flexible in terms of specialty and location of residency training, capable of becoming an excellent physician and determined to do so, and gracious when confronted with prejudice." I would add: Those who are committed to becoming physicians no matter what hurdles they may face, and those who have no other options.

Those with Money

Foreign medical schools that cater to U.S. students do so for one reason—they want to make money. Tuition and fees at these schools are as high as at the most expensive U.S. schools. Some are private schools that have been specifically set up as for-profit operations. Others are government-run schools that take U.S. students to generate income with which to improve the school for the country's own nationals. (National medical schools have very low tuition and neither expect nor encourage U.S. students to apply; it is nearly impossible for U.S. applicants to get into them.)

There are other costs to consider besides tuition. Travel is one. If you want to return to the United States occasionally, there is the cost of airfare (or of a long drive from some Mexican schools). How about travel to take a Board preparation course or to do clinical rotations? If you are at a Caribbean school and do some clinical rotations in Britain, for example, factor in at least one roundtrip transatlantic airfare. Also, consider basic living expenses, which may be either higher or lower than in the United States. Some of the amenities that Americans take for granted can be astronomically expensive.

In the past, many U.S. students attending foreign schools were eligible for many of the same government loans as U.S. medical students. Now, however, as the AAMC writes, "students attending foreign or unaccredited U.S. medical schools should be aware that they will be ineligible for almost all financial aid and loans. Students in these categories should give careful thought to financial planning before enrollment." Remember, even if you are eligible for Stafford Loans, these provide a maximum of $18,500 per year—and they must be repaid. (See Chapter 18: *Paying for Medical School*.)

However, this situation is fluid, and a few schools have unique financial resources for students. Also, U.S. citizens remain eligible for some government-guaranteed loans while attending some foreign medical schools, such as St. George's University, Ross University, the American University of the Caribbean, and the Autonomous University of Guadalajara. Check with each school about financial aid before accepting or declining a position.

Adequate Preparation

To prepare adequately, you must have completed enough undergraduate courses to eventually be licensed and have average or better MCAT scores. All medical licensing boards require that you complete your medical degree and residency training, and some require completion of specific undergraduate courses. (I don't have a clue why.)

Some foreign schools accept students into the medical curriculum directly out of high school. If those schools don't include at least premed science courses in their curricula, students may be unable to obtain a medical license in many states. Medical boards are obsessively strict about their requirements, as can be seen in the following example: One of my residents, after getting undergraduate and medical school degrees with honors at prestigious U.S. institutions, completing a university residency program, and becoming chief resident, could not initially be licensed in California. Why? He had "tested out" of one undergraduate course rather than taking it, so he did not have the three credit hours in this course that the state board required. He was provisionally licensed only after he enrolled in the undergraduate course; he got his full license when he completed it. And his degrees were from U.S. schools!

So, be sure you have the undergraduate credits you will need to be licensed. The U.S. and Canadian medical schools that accept high school students and undergraduates early in their courses of study usually provide adequate course hours. In some cases, however, such students may also have difficulties.

The other "preparation" is an adequate MCAT score. Presumably, your ultimate goal is to be a licensed and practicing U.S. physician, and to do this you will need to pass the USMLE. Since *fewer than half of all U.S. citizens from foreign medical schools pass both Steps 1 and 2* (Figure 17.1), you need a solid reason to believe that you will be among those who pass these tests. (Note that about 98% of U.S. medical students pass all USMLE Steps.) The only scorecard you have for rating your chances are your MCAT scores. Studies show that there is a high correlation between success on the MCAT and success on the USMLE (especially Steps 1 and 2, which are required for an ECFMG Certificate).

Dr. Pestana recommends going to a foreign medical school only if your individual MCAT scores average 10 or your total (excluding the essay) is at least 30. Students with cumulative MCAT scores of 26 or above seem to do well at LCME- and AOA-approved schools. However, they have much better support, facilities, and instruction than do students at foreign schools. Since students with MCAT

FIGURE 17.1

Recent Pass Rates for USMLE

	Pass Rate STEP 1	Pass Rate STEP 2
U.S. Citizen IMGs*		
Overall average	42%	68%
First-time takers	51	76
Repeaters	31	50
Foreign Citizen IMGs*		
Overall average	59	75
First-time takers	67	81
Repeaters	39	55
U.S. M.D. Medical Students**		
Overall average	88%	95%
First-time takers	92	97
Repeaters	59	70
U.S. D.O. Medical Students**		
Overall average	67	88
First-time takers	70	89
Repeaters	32	50

*2002 Administrations of Step 1 and 2001–02 Administrations of Step 2.

**2002 Administrations.

Adapted from: *Educational Commission for Foreign Medical Graduates Annual Report 2002.* Philadelphia, PA:ECFMG, 2003; and *The National Board Examiner: 2002 USMLE Performance Data*, 2002.

scores in the low 20s are two to three times more likely to fail the USMLE, these students are essentially wasting their time (and money) going to a foreign school. Their chances of ever practicing medicine in the United States are negligible.

Flexibility and Humor

If you go to a foreign school, your living conditions will be at least different, if not inadequate (see "Living Conditions" below), and you may need to alter your residency plans to fit what is available. In addition, throughout your career, colleagues may raise questions about your adequacy as a physician. To overcome these obstacles, you will need flexibility and a sense of humor.

If your goal is to practice medicine in the United States, you will need to obtain and complete a residency there. Even if you succeed in obtaining an ECFMG Certificate, which allows you to apply for residency positions, most residency directors do not want IMGs—especially in the most competitive specialties, such as general surgery, emergency medicine, and orthopedic surgery. Also, you may not be welcome at the most prestigious training institutions (generally those associated with medical schools). Therefore, you may need to alter your goals to get a residency position. If you have always dreamed of being an emergency physician, for example, you may have to rethink your goal.

Just after the NRMP Match one year, several students from Caribbean schools called me to ask what they should do, since they didn't match. They were initially appalled when I suggested looking for positions in psychiatry residencies. In general, these positions were available, provided clinical training, and often closely paralleled the curriculum of transitional internships. This wasn't exactly what they wanted, but at least it gave them a way of entering U.S. medicine.

Some IMGs do get into very competitive residencies, but these are generally the very best students from the very best foreign schools. It's just not something that you can count on.

Lastly, the medical establishment (but usually not patients) sneers at IMGs. Can you take the rebuffs, the snide comments, and the need to constantly "show your worth"? If you can't, don't even start the process.

A Medical Career—No Matter What

Don't consider foreign medical schools until you have exhausted every option within the United States and Canada. You didn't apply to your state's schools and some private schools located in less-than-optimal locations? Why not? If you think that going to these schools will be less prestigious or more difficult than going to a foreign medical school, think again. You didn't apply to Osteopathic medical schools? Why not? If you think many Osteopathic physicians have a difficult time in an M.D.-dominated medical profession, be assured that it is a cakewalk compared to the lot of IMGs. Rethink all your options before you leap into the difficulties posed by going to a foreign medical school.

The other consideration is whether you are so committed to becoming a physician that you are willing to suffer much more angst, turmoil, and uncertainty than medical students at LCME- or AOA-approved schools (who suffer enough). Dr. Robert Marion described his decision process in his classic novel, *Learning to Play God*:

> **At the end of four days of intense despondency after receiving that final rejection, I realized it was time to assess my options. I carefully examined my motivation and my staying power and, after tormenting myself and those around me for nearly a week, I reached a conclusion: I didn't want to be a dentist; I didn't want to be a graduate student in biology and end up teaching; what I most wanted to do was to be a doctor, and the longer I thought about it, the more I was convinced that I could, and would, do anything necessary to reach that goal. That's when I began looking into foreign schools. (p. 9)**

Ask yourself: *Am I that committed?* Through a series of fortuitous circumstances, after doing a "preregistration year" at the Royal College of Surgeons in Ireland, Dr. Marion became one of the lucky few who are able to "transfer" into a U.S. medical school. (Actually, he was simply admitted, since he had not actually started the Royal College's medical curriculum.) It's doubtful that your luck will be as good.

— Who Attends Foreign Schools? —

More than 80% of U.S. citizens who attend foreign medical schools (based on the number of those who eventually get ECFMG Certificates) come from only 11 states. Students from three of those states (New York, California, and New Jersey) make up more than half of all IMGs. The balance come from Illinois, Florida, Pennsylvania, Texas, Maryland, Michigan, Massachusetts, and Ohio.

— Useful Safeguards —

After reading the information provided below and reviewing materials sent by the school, there are three final safeguards to help protect your investment of time and money.

1. **Visit the school before you enroll.** "It costs a lot of money!" you say. It sure does. It will cost you even more to move, pay very high tuition and fees, and then find out that you just cannot tolerate the place. In addition, you may avoid getting scammed by a school that is not well-established—or that doesn't even exist. The Web is a great resource, but anyone can design and post wonderful webpages describing nonexistent facilities, programs, and students.

   When you visit the school, talk with current students and faculty. Get a sense of how the students feel about their education. Also, find out how many of their graduates succeeded in passing the USMLE, transferring to U.S. schools, or obtaining suitable U.S. residencies. If possible, get a student newsletter to see the real "scuttlebutt."
2. **Don't enroll in any school that hasn't graduated at least one class.** Don't be a guinea pig—or worse, a roasted pig.
3. **Don't go to a medical school that won't tell you where you will do your clinical rotations.** Even if they don't put the information in their brochures or on their website, if you are serious enough to visit their school (or their stateside office), they should be willing to share the information with you—in writing—at that time. If they can't or won't give you such a list, go somewhere else. If they do give you the list, call a few of the places to see if this school's students actually rotate at their hospitals or clinics. Yes, some schools have listed numerous clinical sites in the United States that will not and have not taken their students.

Teaching Facilities

Teaching facilities at many foreign medical schools are inadequate or antique, and overcrowded. Many new for-profit schools, especially in the Caribbean, Eastern Europe, and Mexico, have set up "campuses" in a couple of rented rooms, in someone's home, or in a trailer. Even when the facilities are a little "grander," say a couple of buildings, they often have intermittent electricity (read: cooling and lights) and water.

Many schools outside the United States lack adequate libraries, computer facilities, or internet access. These are extremely important for an adequate medical education today. Medical students must learn how to use and access information in medical libraries and online. In addition, many modern teaching methods (and testing methods, including the USMLE) rely on computer literacy. Those schools with large libraries should have modern tomes and current journal subscriptions covering the major specialties and subspecialties. When you visit, check out whether they have these necessary medical education tools.

Even where schools seem to have adequate facilities, you must question whether their facilities are adequate for the number of students enrolled. One way of easily determining this is to ask, "How many students work on each cadaver?" The norm in the United States is four.

Clinical Facilities

The lack of adequate clinical teaching facilities is a major drawback at many foreign medical schools. This is primarily a problem for Caribbean schools, where the medical facilities on the islands are often inadequate for the population, let alone for teaching medical students. It also occurs at small

Mexican schools. To conceal this problem, the schools often coyly say that they "allow" their students to take clinical rotations in the United States or England. What they really mean is that if students can find places to do their clinical rotations, the best of luck to them. (By the way, the schools continue to collect tuition while their students spend time elsewhere.) In addition, many institutions listed by Caribbean schools as "teaching hospitals" either do not currently allow students to do clinical rotations or are not really considered teaching hospitals (having an ACGME-approved residency program) in the specialty areas in which the students will rotate.

In the 1990s, a study by the U.S. Government Accounting Office found that of the clinical training sites in the United States listed by (primarily) Caribbean and Mexican medical schools (plus the non-listed sites U.S.-citizen graduates from these schools claim to have used), 61% had no formal affiliation with the schools, 51% were with hospitals not associated with a U.S. medical school or having only a very limited affiliation, 29% had no residency programs, 10% of the affiliations no longer existed, and 7% of the institutions denied that they had any relationship to the school. In fact, some of the affiliated institutions never even existed!

Adequate clinical teaching facilities are much less of a problem at established schools associated with universities (such as Mexican, Israeli, Australian, or European schools) that have their own teaching hospitals. Also, St. George's University in Grenada currently has adequate affiliations with about 30 U.S. and 17 British teaching hospitals.

Faculty

To mangle an old expression, there are liars, damn liars, and public relations people. Foreign medical schools seem to delight in inflating the number of their faculty. Some do this by double (or triple or quadruple) counting faculty members if they teach multiple courses. Others count faculty who are retired, who are no longer there, or who only visited the school once. (Similar false advertising is also a problem at U.S. and Canadian schools, where many senior faculty are in the laboratory much of the time.)

When evaluating a school, ask current medical students how many faculty really teach them. Also inquire whether those faculty who are on-site are qualified to teach their assigned subjects. If a biochemist is teaching anatomy and pharmacology, watch out! Having a professor who is only one lesson ahead of the students is not the way to really learn—or to have your questions answered.

For schools in non-English-speaking countries that offer "classes in English," find out how well the professors actually speak English. In most cases, while they may read English quite well, their ability to speak it and be understood can be a whole different ball game.

Living Conditions

Students attending foreign medical schools are often astonished by the living conditions. Those at schools in major cities must learn to adjust to different—and sometimes expensive—lifestyles, customs, and diets.

However, these are minor adjustments compared to those experienced by students on some Caribbean islands, who come face-to-face with primitive, third-world conditions. Unlike the paradise of swanky island resorts they may have envisioned, these students live with unaccustomed deprivations and inconveniences. Among these are intermittent and unsafe water supplies, inconsistent electricity, unusual laws and endless bureaucracy, the lack of "normal" conveniences, erratic transportation, slow mail, no telephone service or Web connection, an inability to get spare parts for broken equipment, and the ever-present bugs and lizards.

Such living conditions may severely interfere with a student's ability to study, and medical students often quit in frustration. Not everyone is cut out for an expatriate's life.

— Choosing a School —

U.S. and Canadian citizens who attend medical schools in other countries generally pick schools that teach their classes in English. Many of these are located in the Caribbean. Some are in other English-speaking countries or in Europe or Israel (see *Appendix E*). There are, of course, excellent medical schools in non-English-speaking countries, but usually only students with special ties (such as dual citizenship and fluency in the language) can attend them. No matter where students go to school outside the United States or Canada, they are considered international medical graduates (IMGs) and must go through all the hoops necessary to get a residency and practice medicine in the United States.

Based on the number of U.S. citizens taking the USMLE Step 1 through the ECFMG, apparently most U.S. citizens study abroad (in order of diminishing frequency) in Mexico, Dominica, Grenada, Netherlands Antilles, and the Dominican Republic.

Track Record

Medical schools throughout the world vary widely in their admissions policies—from restrictive, as in the United States and Canada, to "open," as in Argentina. The restrictive model selects a limited number of students with the expectation that all will complete their medical training. U.S., Canadian, English, Israeli, Irish, Australian, and Caribbean schools follow this format. The European/Latin American open model, taken from the French system, accepts nearly all applicants, but quickly winnows down the number of students through a grueling course of study, often by the second year. Nearly all Mexican, Central and South American, and mainland European schools follow this format.

These different policies lead to a disparate percentage of entering students who graduate. Figure 17.2 shows the approximate percentage of entering students who graduate. (These numbers have not changed much over the past several decades.) Note that these statistics often include high school graduates in six- and seven-year programs, so older U.S. citizen-students with good science backgrounds can expect to do much better than these numbers indicate.

Getting Information

Virtually all the schools that cater to U.S. and Canadian students have excellent websites and will send you glossy brochures about their institutions. These ads show smiling students who are often performing laboratory experiments, looking at radiographs, or doing clinical rounds. They generally don't show pictures of the buildings, classrooms, wide-angle views of any laboratory facilities, or student quarters. They also don't mention that the pictures of students doing clinical rotations are rarely taken at the school itself, but rather at U.S. or British hospitals, or, in at least one case, that "their" library was actually the town's municipal library.

This material also may be short on specifics—they generally don't include (or they misrepresent) the number of faculty members or books and computers in the library, the number and quality of associated teaching hospitals, the number of students who transfer to LCME- or AOA-approved schools, or how many recent graduates passed the USMLE and obtained U.S. or Canadian residency positions, particularly, *desirable* residency programs. (Getting into a pathology residency at East Nowhere Community Hospital, for example, is not too difficult if you can first get an ECFMG Certificate.)

FIGURE 17.2

Percentage of All Entering Medical Students Who Graduate

Country	Students Who Graduate	Country	Students Who Graduate
Argentina	15%	Mexico	54%
Canada	96	Norway	96
Dominican Republic	55	Poland	85
Finland	97	Spain	85
Germany	95	Sweden	85
Iceland	100	Switzerland	60
Ireland	98	United States	92
Israel	90		

Adapted from: Carlson CA. International medical education. *JAMA*. 1991;266(7):921-3.

They are also usually reluctant to divulge how many of their graduates are licensed to practice medicine in the United States and Canada, and how many, if any, have medical school appointments. Remember that anecdotal reports are much less helpful than solid information on the performance of entire recent graduating classes. Few foreign schools, however, will supply this information—it's generally too embarrassing.

As with all advertisers, foreign medical schools catering to U.S. and Canadian students try to sell potential applicants on their glitz. Much of it, however, is simply sizzle with no steak. Among the "great benefits" foreign schools tout (some even do it on their envelopes) are:

- *"Curricula identical to the best U.S. and Canadian medical schools."* If you are trying to attract U.S. and Canadian applicants by suggesting that graduates will be able to pass their country's medical licensing examinations, what curriculum would you use? Since all U.S. and Canadian medical schools have basically the same curricula, it is the pattern they must follow.
- *"Students are permitted to do clinical rotations in the United States."* Permitted? Students at Caribbean schools *must* do rotations in the United States, Canada, or the United Kingdom. The islands do not have adequate clinical teaching facilities. (A few schools have permission to send their students to New York or New Jersey for extended clinical rotations. Only those schools can rightfully make this claim, since state agencies have approved their educational quality.)
- *"The school is listed in the International Medical Education Directory (IMED)."* Available on the Web at http://imed.ecfmg.org, the directory provides accurate and up-to-date information about international medical schools that are recognized by the appropriate government agency in the countries where the medical schools are located. The list is produced and updated by an ECFMG subsidiary foundation. It doesn't take much to get on this list; it is only a little more stringent than the prior World Health Organization listing of medical schools.
- *"Graduates are eligible for ECFMG Certification."* Graduates of only one medical school in the world (San Juan Bautista in Puerto Rico) are *not* eligible for ECFMG certificates. Being eligible doesn't mean that graduates can actually pass the examinations necessary to get the certificate.
- *"U.S.-based education."* Just as with many ocean-going vessels, several schools began by being incorporated "under foreign flags," but were physically located in the United States. U.S. government officials quickly squashed this ploy. Occasionally, however, foreign schools will still try this.
- *"Students are eligible for U.S. Government educational loans."* This is now actually a big deal, since students at most non-U.S./Canadian medical schools no longer qualify. The situation is fluid, however, and if they say that you are eligible, get it confirmed in writing—and check with lenders (see Chapter 18: *Paying for Medical School*) to see if they are willing to make government-backed loans to students at that school.

The Schools

While the prior edition of *Get Into Medical School: A Guide for the Perplexed* described a selection of foreign medical schools, much of the information quickly became outdated. Since virtually everyone reading this book will have access to the Web, current contact information for selected medical schools is being provided, rather than a brief description that changes too quickly to be useful.

To read about students' experiences—good and very bad—in the international medical education system, go to the "International Medical" forum in the Student Doctor Network (http://forums.studentdoctor.net). It is worth your time not only for the valuable information provided, but also to get answers to your questions in a timely manner. You can also check the website of the American Association of International Medical Graduates (www.aaimg.com/words/index.html), which has detailed lists of the deficiencies present at many of the foreign medical schools considered by U.S. applicants.

Excellence Abroad

There are many excellent medical schools outside the United States and Canada. Most do not accept noncitizen students, preferring to educate their own nationals. The three schools listed below routinely take U.S. students and stand far above the rest. Each provides a medical education that is good enough for nearly all their American graduates to pass the USMLE, which is required for an ECFMG Certificate, residency training, and U.S. medical licensure. (Even so, graduates of these schools must still surmount the extra hurdles that residency programs and medical boards have established for IMGs.)

- **Sackler School of Medicine, Tel Aviv, Israel**
  Office of Admissions, Sackler School of Medicine
  17 East 62nd Street, New York, NY 10021
  (212) 688-8811; fax: (212) 223-0368; www.tau.ac.il/medicine/NYprog
- **Touro College/Faculty of Medicine of the Technion-Israel Institute of Technology, Haifa, Israel**
  Touro College School of Health Sciences
  1700 Union Boulevard, Bay Shore, NY 11706
  (516) 665-1600; fax: (516) 665-4986; www.technion.ac.il/medicine
- **Royal College of Surgeons, Dublin, Ireland**
  Admission Office, 123 St. Stephen's Green, Dublin 2, Ireland
  (353) 1-402-2228, fax: (353) 1-403-2451; e-mail: admissions@rcsi.ie/admissions

  U.S. and Canadian applicants can also contact:
  The Atlantic Bridge Program
  3419 Via Lido, PMB #629, Newport Beach, CA 92663, USA
  (949) 723-6318; fax: (949) 723-4436; e-mail: info@atlanticbridge.com

Australia

There are three programs in Australia that may be of interest to those considering foreign medical schools. They have only recently begun admitting U.S. and Canadian students using a U.S./Canadian teaching model, but they come with proven track records, government approval, and apparently sound programs based on problem-based learning. Primarily for Australians, these schools admit a small number of international students.

- **Flinders University School of Medicine**
  GPO Box 2100, Adelaide, Australia 5001
  tel: +61-8-8204-4162 (general); +61-8-8201-2421 (student/course related); fax: +61-8-8204-5845 (general); +61-8-8201-3905 (student/course related)
  e-mail: wwwperson@cal.fmc.flinders.edu.au; http://som.flinders.edu.au
- **Sydney University Medical School**
  Faculty Office and Medical Program Administration Unit
  Faculty of Medicine, Edward Ford Building (A27), The University of Sydney, NSW 2006 Australia
  tel: +61-2-9351-3132; fax: +61-2-9351-3196
  e-mail: admissions@med.usyd.edu.au; www.medfac.usyd.edu.au
- **Queensland University School of Medicine**
  University of Queensland, Mayne Medical School
  Herston Road, Herston QLD 4006, Australia
  tel: +61-7-3365-5278; fax: +61-7-3365-5433; e-mail: admissions@som.uq.edu.au
  www.som.uq.edu.au

Caribbean and Mexican Schools

The Caribbean, or "off-shore," medical schools primarily cater to medical school applicants rejected from U.S. and Canadian schools. Many schools have come and gone over the past few decades, leading to their generally poor reputation. Others have been involved in lawsuits over "dirty tricks," usually for trying to lure students from one school to another and for mailing deceptive advertising. But for candidates who carefully pick their school, the Caribbean may be a reasonable choice.

The non-U.S./Canadian school with the most graduates practicing in the United States is the Autonomous University of Guadalajara. It has a program for international students in English.

- **St. George's University, Grenada**
  Office of Admissions, c/o The North American Correspondent, University Services, Ltd.
  1 East Main St., Bay Shore, NY 11706-8399
  tel: (from US): (631) 665-8500 or (800) 899-6337; tel: (from United Kingdom): 08001-699061
  Grenada: (473) 444-4175; fax: (631) 665-5590; e-mail: sguinfo@sgu.edu; www.sgu.edu
- **Universidad Autónoma de Guadalajara, Mexico**
  San Antonio Office: 4715 Fredericksburg Rd., 3rd Floor, San Antonio, TX 78229
  tel: (210) 366-1611; (800) 531-5494; fax: (210) 377-2975; uagsat@uag.edu
  Albany Office: 20 Corporate Woods Blvd., Ste. 205, Albany, NY 12211-2370
  tel: (518) 434-7392, (866) 434-7392; fax: (518) 434-7393; uagny@uag.edu
  Puerto Rico Office: IBM Plaza, Ste. 1124, 654 Muñoz Rivera Ave., San Juan, Puerto Rico 00918-4133
  tel: (787) 763-2457, (800) 981-9925; fax: (787) 753-0760; uagpr@uag.edu
  www.uag.mx/medicine
- **Ross University, Dominica**
  Main U.S. Admission Office, 499 Thornall St., 10th Floor, Edison, NJ 08837
  tel: (732) 978-5300, (888) 404-7677; admissions@rossmed.edu; www.rossmed.edu
- **American University of the Caribbean, St. Maarten**
  Medical Education Information Office, Inc. (MEIO)
  901 Ponce de Leon Blvd., Ste. 401, Coral Gables, FL 33134-3036
  tel: (305) 446-0600; admissions@aucmed.edu; www.aucmed.edu

Western Europe

The great traditions of Western medicine began and continue to flourish in Western Europe. Until the late 1930s, it was not unusual for outstanding students to take part or all of their medical training in Europe. In the 1960s and 1970s, many Americans went to Europe, especially to Italy and Belgium, if they could not enter U.S. schools. Since then, Belgium has all but closed its doors to U.S. and Canadian students, and experience has shown that U.S. graduates of Italian schools often don't do well when they take the tests for their ECFMG Certification.

There are many great medical schools in Western Europe, but the best generally don't accept applications from U.S. or Canadian students (except for Dublin's Royal College) unless the applicant has a special language or cultural connection with the country. The most obvious connection is dual citizenship. Applicants must be proficient in the country's language, since the application materials and all instruction are in that language. If you do apply to European schools, excluding Dublin's Royal College, experts in the field say that the best schools are those in Scandinavia, Ireland, the United Kingdom, Holland, France, and Switzerland. Avoid schools in Germany (which was once the sine qua non of Western medical training), Spain, and Italy.

Dealing with the applications can be a burdensome process. It will usually be difficult to complete the process by mail and will be trying, at best, in person. (Remember that Europeans have honed bureaucracy to a fine art.)

Well-publicized among premeds and premed advisers is the "Cambridge Connection," which places students in one of several schools. For a picture of the dismal conditions you may encounter if you enroll (despite its prestigious name, this is not affiliated with Cambridge University's medical school), go to www.aaimg.com/list/cambridge.html.

For information, contact the individual country's consulate or the address listed in *Appendix E*. Be prepared for an immediate rejection at that level unless you clearly state your connection to that country and your language proficiency. (Writing your letter in their native language may help.)

Eastern Europe

Willie Sutton reportedly said he robbed banks "because that's where the money was." Short on hard currencies since the political changes in Eastern Europe, many old and distinguished schools in this region have tried to copy the Israeli model by developing U.S.-style medical curricula and teaching courses in English to attract tuition dollars. Some have U.S. representatives and advertise heavily.

Students need to learn the native language before beginning their clinical studies at these schools. Although students will be immersed in the language and culture during their first two years of study, I suggest taking a look at a language book for that country before you leap into this. Some of these languages (Hungarian, for example) may be virtually impossible for most native English speakers to learn with any facility.

Also of concern in Eastern Europe is that many of their medical systems and technologies have fallen far behind those of Western Europe, the United States, and Canada. If your medical training does not include the techniques, medications, and equipment typically used in Western medical settings, you will not have the necessary knowledge either to pass the USMLE or to obtain a residency. Also, Eastern European medical schools, including those in Russia, have been involved in scams such as taking money and either having no school or not providing the agreed-upon education.

For more information, contact the schools or their representatives directly. (See *Appendix E.*)

Philippines

Quite a few Americans trek to the Philippines for their medical education. Although there are many medical schools in the Philippines, U.S.-citizen graduates of two schools have had above-average results in the tests for an ECFMG Certificate.

- **University of the Philippines, Manila**
  (They annually accept up to two of their alumni's children, even if they were born in the United States)
  Chair, Admission Committee, College of Medicine, University of the Philippines Manila
  547 Pedro Gil St., Ermita, P.O. Box 593, Manila 1000, Philippines
  tel: +63-2-526-4170; fax: +63-2-526-0371; www.upm.edu.ph/upm-cm.html
- **University of the East, Quezon City, Santo Thomas**
  Office of the Registrar, University of the East, Ramon Magsaysay Memorial Medical Center
  College of Medicine, Aurora Blvd., Sta. Mesa, Quezon City 1105, Philippines
  tel: +63-2-715-0861; www.uerm.edu

Other Schools

Medical schools, of course, exist all over the world. There have, on occasion, been U.S. and Canadian students at most of these. However, the only students who should even remotely think about going to these schools are those who have definite ties to the local culture, know the language (of instruction and daily use) thoroughly, and are willing to undergo even more extraordinary difficulties to eventually get U.S. or Canadian residency training and licensure than do other IMGs. Even in industrialized nations, such as Japan, there are often medical systems, medications, and methods that are quite different from those normally used in North America. Although you may want to learn special techniques at these schools after you are licensed (acupuncture, for example), they are not places you should attend to get your primary medical education.

Scams

Fake and Temporary Schools

U.S. students who are desperate for slots in medical schools are good candidates for intentional and unintentional scams. In one instance, a fake European school was widely advertised and many students applied. When they were "accepted," the school required a $1,000 deposit to "hold their spot." When the students arrived to begin classes, they discovered that no such school existed.

In the Caribbean, several entrepreneurs have quickly opened, closed, reopened, and again closed schools, leaving hundreds of students out of money and bereft of their dreams. Sometimes these schools opened and closed under the same name on another (or even the same) island. They had great advertisements and brochures, but they weren't good enough to warrant spending the tens of thousands of dollars each student wasted on a bogus, partial medical education.

Other entrepreneurs have reportedly sold medical diplomas for cash. These, of course, are completely worthless except to paper the wall, as at least one of these medical school administrators supposedly did. He granted himself a medical degree several months after starting his school.

In the 1960s and 1970s, similar episodes occurred in Mexico. A number of private medical schools sprang up in small towns. These schools often had names very similar to those of well-respected and established Mexican medical schools. Some of these bogus schools were only two rooms in a private home, with one "professor" who had gotten a mail-order degree. They took students' tuition, taught for two years, and disappeared—often reappearing in another small town under a different (or even the same) school name. These "schools" disappeared in the 1980s when medical school applications plummeted, but they may return if there is a dramatic increase in rejected applicants.

Somewhat less egregious, but only because they did not plan it, were the for-profit (primarily Caribbean) medical schools that simply went broke and were forced to close their doors. This mainly happened during the 1980s when, believe it or not, few applicants needed to look outside the United States or Canada for a medical education. The foreign schools could not survive the lack of students and went belly up. This is why experts suggest that, if you are looking at foreign schools, you visit the campus first to see if it is legitimate and that you consider only those schools in existence for a decade or more. These are the least likely to evaporate after you pay your money.

Agencies

A 1970s scam that is now reappearing involves agencies that "help" you get into foreign—currently primarily Eastern European—medical schools. They come in two varieties. The first type, usually with a very prestigious name and located in the United States or Canada, is nothing more than a contractor or agent for a particular medical school attempting to lure U.S. and Canadian students. These contractors' addresses are just "fronts" for the schools' marketing services. Honest foreign schools state that their North American addresses are merely a convenient address for their school.

The second type of agency offers to submit applications for you to international medical schools—for a big fee. It's unclear what paying this fee accomplishes, since they don't guarantee admission to any of the schools, and many schools have open (or nearly open) admission policies. Furthermore, some of these agencies specifically encourage applicants to apply everywhere, although, as discussed above, applying to Canadian, British, and Western European schools is a waste of time unless you both have a cultural "in" and are a good student. (Canadian schools are as difficult or more difficult to enter than those in the United States.) The fees you pay to these agencies do not include the costs for transcripts and other paperwork, nor do they include the schools' individual application fees.

Online Medical Schools

Given the increasing popularity of online graduate education in other fields, it was inevitable that the trend (fad?) would find its way to medical education, and it has. Numerous medical schools are developing programs to provide distance learning for some or all of their medical students. Beware!

The first to get into the act were various island medical schools around the world. Not associated with any other medical facility, these are simply scams. However, some legitimate medical schools, and even consortia of medical schools, are now toying with the idea of providing online education. The danger is that there has been no indication that the state medical licensing boards will accept this type of medical education as legitimate. Until they do, spending money, time, and effort to complete these online courses is a fruitless effort. If you are considering doing this (it is expected that at least part of preclinical medical education will eventually be accepted), the primary question to ask is whether any medical board has yet agreed, in writing, to accept that type of education.

Language

All mainland-U.S. medical schools and all Canadian schools outside of Quebec (and McGill within Quebec) teach their classes in English.

Some schools in non-English-speaking countries also teach their courses in English or have special English tracks for English-speaking students. The following medical schools teach all their courses in English: St. George's University, American University of the Caribbean, Ross University, Spartan Health Sciences University, Medical University at Pecs, Touro College (NY/Technion University, Israel), and Saba University School of Medicine. Schools in England, Australia, New Zealand, and South Africa, of course, teach in English.

A number of schools around the world claim to teach courses in English. This may be true, but consider the unspoken (and often unwritten) fine print. While the classes may be taught in English, the quality of this English varies greatly, so understanding your professors may be difficult at times. In addition, even though the professors speak English, the patients you will see in the clinics do not. Therefore, you need to learn the native language(s) well enough to work in a clinical setting. This is not always an easy task, especially if you are trying to learn a new language while enrolled in a very daunting medical school curriculum.

Some schools require those students not fluent in the primary local language(s) to attend their intensive language course before beginning school or during the first few (and often the most difficult) semesters. The medical school in Pecs (Budapest), for example, includes Hungarian language lessons along with the basic sciences. Great! During my visit to Hungary, the Hungarians admitted that it is harder for a nonnative speaker to learn Hungarian than to become an astronaut. If you're a whiz at languages, fine; otherwise, watch out!

The same goes for two outstanding foreign medical schools—Sackler and Technion. At both schools, clinical work is in Hebrew, and some patients speak only Arabic or Russian. If you already know the languages, fine. Otherwise, it may be difficult to learn a language not related in any way (including the alphabet) to English.

Students going to foreign schools should also consider one other, not-so-obvious language/cultural problem. While pharmacology courses may be taught using the generic drug names used throughout the world, on clinical services, you will often use the drugs' brand names—which vary from country to country. In addition, some pharmaceuticals commonly used in other countries are not available in the United States, and vice versa. This also holds true for some medical equipment and procedures. Just because they speak English, does not mean they will use American medical terminology.

A Useful Algorithm

If you are confused by this wealth of information, perhaps the following algorithm can simplify your decision process. If you elect to go to a non-U.S./Canadian medical school, first consider going to the Australian or Irish medical schools listed below. Then, use the algorithm based on your language ability to select other possible medical schools.

Australian Four-year Programs (Flinders, Sydney, and Queensland Universities)
Royal College of Surgeons, Dublin, Ireland

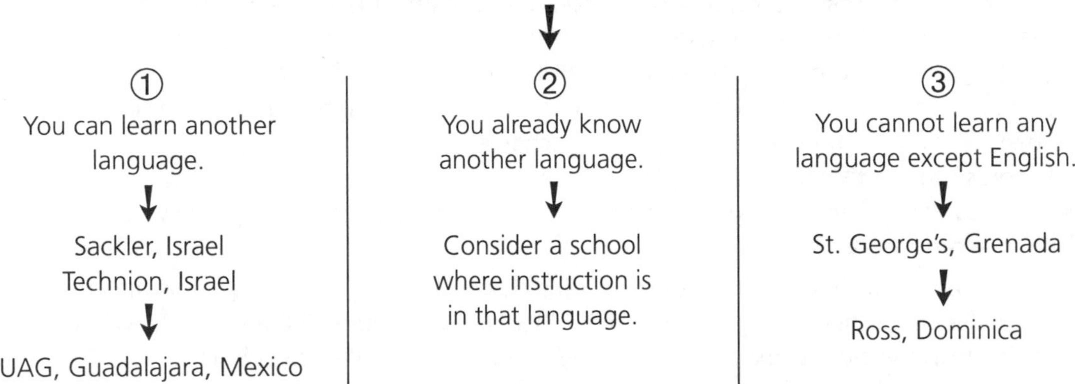

— Transferring into U.S. Medical Schools —

Don't go to a foreign medical school expecting to later transfer to a U.S. school. The odds are not in your favor—and they seem to be getting worse. Nevertheless, the best way to get into a U.S. residency is to transfer into a U.S. medical school prior to graduation. To accomplish this, you will have to do very well in your courses during the first two or three years of medical school. You will also have to perform well on Step 1, and possibly Step 2, of the USMLE as administered through the ECFMG. Doing well on the USMLE will be an impressive accomplishment, since U.S. citizen-IMGs have consistently done worse on licensing examinations than their foreign-born counterparts (Figure 17.1).

In 2002–03, only 88 students studying at foreign medical schools were accepted for transfer into U.S. M.D.-granting schools (down from 350 to 400 per year from 1970 to mid-1980, but nearly constant at 90 per year since then). Most had to repeat one or more years of medical school. Spots become available because a small number of students fail their classes, drop out, or take leaves of absence. About half of all U.S. medical schools simply leave these spots empty or offer them only to students from other LCME- or AOA-approved schools who must transfer for personal reasons.

Approximately 40 U.S. medical schools accept transfers from foreign medical schools and seek not only good students who can help rebuild the class size, but also students who can replace the tuition income lost when students leave. The M.D.-granting schools who accept students from non-U.S. medical schools can be found at http://services.aamc.org/tsp_reports. Some Osteopathic schools also accept such transfers, but each must be contacted to determine their current policy.

In recent years, most medical students who successfully transferred to U.S. schools had high GPAs after completing at least two years of medical school, did very well on the USMLE, and transferred to private schools or to schools in states where they were official residents. (Note that you cannot "transfer" once you have received your medical degree.) The implicit requirement to complete two years of school before transferring plays havoc with the system, since second-year classes at many off-shore schools don't finish until mid- to late-August, when it may be too late for students to transfer to a U.S. school. This leaves students with two options: To apply for a transfer while continuing at the original medical school or to drop out and hope to be accepted in transfer. This latter option is not a good idea, since the odds are even less favorable for foreign medical students who are not currently enrolled.

Students who have tried to transfer to U.S. schools say that some medical schools, particularly in the Caribbean and Mexico, are not pleased when their students transfer to U.S. schools and show that displeasure by delaying the transmission of transcripts to U.S. schools for months. (Some students try to bypass this problem by having their transcripts sent to them, but U.S. medical schools will usually accept only transcripts sent directly to them.) St. George's University, which encourages its students to transfer, is an exception.

U.S. and Canadian medical schools that say they accept transfers from foreign schools are listed in Figure 15.8. The Deans of Students at international schools with large numbers of U.S. citizens also keep lists of U.S. medical schools that have accepted their students. U.S. schools that, in recent years, have taken four or more such transfer students per year are: Drexel University, Finch UHS–Chicago Med, George Washington University, Marshall University–Edwards, Northeastern Ohio University, Ponce, SUNY–Upstate, and the University of Wisconsin. It is unclear how many international students have been allowed to transfer to D.O.-granting schools.

Records suggest that the relatively few students who transfer to U.S. medical schools do very well. They are, however, a very select group of students. The steps listed below may help you locate a school willing to accept you.

1. At least a year before you expect to transfer, contact U.S. medical schools directly to inquire about their willingness to take USIMGs. Look at Figure 15.8 and the AAMC website (http://services.aamc.org/tsp_reports) to see which are the "best bets."
2. Mail these inquiry letters to the admission offices of all U.S. medical schools that accept U.S. citizen-foreign medical students as transfers. For any school where you have any kind of "tie" (such as birthplace, undergraduate school, long residence, parents' residence, etc.), specifically mention the connection.
3. Contact Osteopathic medical schools if they are located in a state where you have strong ties to see if they accept transfers from foreign schools.
4. Do not be picky about where these schools are located, and be prepared to repeat one or more years of course work.

— Clerkships in the United States —

Most "off-shore" (mainly Caribbean) medical schools have no local clinical teaching facilities and, except for St. George's University, will not say where their students go for clinical rotations. As one AMA spokesman said, "Most of these schools have no clinical facilities to teach medical students, so they sort of cut them loose at the end of their basic science training and tell them to go to the mainland and find a clinical setting." This is not true for most medical schools located elsewhere in the world. They usually have substantial clinical facilities, although they are not always up to American and Canadian health care standards.

This situation leads to many U.S. students from foreign medical schools seeking sites on their own for their third- and fourth-year clinical clerkships. This search can be long and frustrating, since some states now restrict these students from doing clerkships. In addition, the AAMC has imposed its own limitations on them.

The scandal involving fake diplomas granted by some now-defunct medical schools led three jurisdictions (PA, PR, TX) to ban IMGs from taking clinical clerkships in their hospitals. Seventeen states (AL, AK, CA, CT, DE, DC, FL, GA, KY, MA, NJ, NY, OR, PA, PR, TX, VA) regulate IMGs in clinical clerkships. New York reportedly has the toughest regulations (and the most expensive process) to certify non-U.S. medical schools to send their students for clerkships: Currently there are only two schools whose students are allowed to spend more than 12 weeks in New York doing clerkships. In addition, AAMC rules preclude U.S. medical schools from "co-mingling" their students with the students from non-U.S. schools during required clerkships. (Some hospitals have gotten around this by using "separate-but-equal" ward teams.) These restrictions, however, attack the mechanism through which foreign-trained medical students demonstrate their clinical competence, and subsequently get residency slots and become licensed. (Twenty-one licensing boards evaluate the quality of a clinical clerkship in deciding whether to grant a license to an IMG.)

— Fifth Pathway Programs —

If you cannot transfer to a school in the United States, you may be eligible to enter a Fifth Pathway Program. The Fifth Pathway route allows students in countries that require a year of internship or of social service before granting the M.D. degree (primarily Mexico) to qualify for their M.D. and medical license by taking a year of supervised clinical training at a U.S. medical school. Finishing this program is a route to U.S. medical licensure without getting an ECFMG Certificate with its attendant requirements, such as the English-language test and CSA exam. More that 7,000 individuals have completed the Fifth Pathway Program since it was initiated in 1971. To qualify for the New York Medical College program (the primary Fifth Pathway course still operating), students must be U.S. citizens/permanent residents and meet all the following requirements:

1. Have completed their undergraduate premedical studies at a U.S. college or university with grades and scores acceptable for entrance into a U.S. medical school.
2. Within two years of beginning the Fifth Pathway Program, have completed all formal requirements except for internship and social service at a foreign medical school that is listed in the *World Directory of Medical Schools*.
3. Have an academic record acceptable to New York Medical College.
4. Have passed USMLE Step 1.
5. Have *not* completed their internship/social service requirement.
6. Have *not* received their M.D. degree.
7. Have *not* met the ECFMG's certification requirements.

Four U.S. medical schools list themselves as accepting Fifth Pathway students. However, only the New York Medical College (NYMC) in Valhala, New York, and Brown University in Rhode Island actually accept students for this program on a routine basis. (Brown University accepts only Rhode Island residents, so only a few people are eligible each year.) Contact NYMC at: (914) 594-4489 or (914) 594-3651; fax: (914) 594-4325; www.nymc.edu/depthome/fifth.asp.

The NYMC program charges a $100 application fee and a nonrefundable $500 reservation fee once the student has been accepted. To receive an application, complete the screening preapplication form on their website. If you qualify, they will send an application. Tuition varies—in 2003, it was $24,000. NYMC now has at least eight participating hospitals in New York, New Jersey, and Connecticut. Priority is given to students from Mexican medical schools, since the state of New York recognizes these schools. Students from the Simmelweiss Medical School in Hungary have also gone through NYMC's program, but must be placed in hospitals outside New York.

NYMC's Fifth Pathway program lasts 12 months, with starting dates in January and July. The clinical programs vary among the participating hospitals. From this springboard, USIMGs are usually able to leap into residency slots much more easily. During their Fifth Pathway year, they generally apply to residencies through the Match as Independent Candidates. The school assists students by allowing time to study for USMLE Step 2 and to go for residency interviews.

There is a problem, however. Five jurisdictions (Arkansas, Guam, Indiana, Michigan, Virgin Islands) accept Fifth Pathway graduates for licensure on a case-by-case basis. Two others (Utah and Vermont) do not accept a Fifth Pathway certificate as part of an application for licensure. Twenty-three other states and the District of Columbia require that the Fifth Pathway graduates either complete the USMLE or have an ECFMG Certificate. Mississippi and South Carolina accept Fifth Pathway only if the applicant also is certified by an ABMS Board (in other words, has completed both residency and Board certification). Louisiana may count the Fifth Pathway as one year of the three years that they require for IMG licensure. Other jurisdictions leave acceptance of the Fifth Pathway certificate to the licensing board's discretion; only 13 jurisdictions accept it unconditionally. This can lead to horror stories, as one physician related:

> I had been accepted in an Orthopedic Surgery residency in my home state after finishing the Fifth Pathway program. I was ecstatic! However, the residency was notified that the state's Board of Medical Examiners had decided not to accept the Fifth Pathway route to licensure. Since residents were required to be licensed, I could not take the position and had to sit out a year until I could reapply somewhere else.

For more information about the Fifth Pathway program, contact: the Licensure and Certification Section, American Medical Association, 515 N. State St., Chicago, IL 60610.

— Returning to the United States for Residency and Practice —

Before you jump into a foreign medical school experience, realize that completing medical school will only be the first (and usually least) of your headaches on the road to practicing medicine in the United States. USIMGs (USIMGs) are those individuals who are currently citizens or permanent residents of the United States but who have received their medical degrees outside the United States, Puerto Rico, or Canada.

Here, in a nutshell, is what USIMGs have to do to practice medicine in the United States. (Each step is described in further detail below.)

- Apply for and meet the requirements for an ECFMG Certificate.
- Once the ECFMG Certificate is received, apply for a residency position. No matter what training you may have had, you must complete at least one year of residency (and often more) in the United States.
- Apply for and pass the USMLE Step 3 given by State medical licensing boards. You must also fulfill any other requirements of the licensing boards. Once you do that, you can practice medicine.

In spite of this, by 2003, nearly 200,000 (or about 23% of) physicians practicing medicine in the United States were trained outside the United States, Puerto Rico, or Canada. Their practices are generally medical rather than surgical (Figure 17.3). In 2003, about 80% of IMGs worked in patient care, with 58% in office-based practices (nearly one-quarter of all office-based U.S. physicians). IMGs account for about 26% of physicians in residency training, and approximately 37% of PGY-1s. Nearly 50% of all IMGs train in internal medicine or a medicine specialty.

FIGURE 17.3

IMGs Practicing Medicine in Various Specialties

	Number of IMGs	% of All Physicians in Specialty	% of all IMGs
Nuclear Medicine	480	33%	0.2%
Pathology	6,003	33	3.0
Physical Med/Rehab	2,154	33	1.1
Internal Medicine	42,762	32	21.7
Psychiatry	12,009	30	6.1
Anesthesiology	10,842	30	5.5
Cardiovascular Disease	6,178	29	3.1
Neurology	3,606	29	1.8
Pulmonary Diseases	2,527	29	1.3
Pediatrics	17,115	27	8.7
Child & Adolescent Psych	1,630	26	0.8
Gastroenterology	2,735	26	1.4
Allergy & Immunology	999	25	0.5
Colon & Rectal Surgery	247	22	0.1
Thoracic Surgery	1,065	22	0.5
General/Family Practice	18,028	21	9.1
Medical Genetics	76	21	0.1
Radiation Oncology	833	21	0.4
General Surgery	7,343	20	3.7
Obstetrics/Gynecology	7,159	18	3.6
Urology	1,731	17	0.9
Gen Preventive Med	252	15	0.1
Radiology (All)	4,378	15	2.3
Neurological Surgery	722	14	0.4
Occupational Medicine	407	14	0.2
Plastic Surgery	816	13	0.4
Public Health	220	12	0.1
Otolaryngology	1,007	11	0.5
Emergency Medicine	2,296	10	1.7
Aerospace Medicine	43	9	0.1
Ophthalmology	1,493	8	0.8
Orthopedic Surgery	1,709	8	0.9
Dermatology	638	7	0.3

Adapted from: American Medical Association. *Physician Characteristics and Distribution in the U.S., 2002.* Chicago, IL: AMA, 2002, Tables 5.2, 5.6, 5.7.

USIMGs may have a greater image problem than do foreign nationals. While foreign-born physicians have a reason to train outside the United States, it is often assumed that USIMGs could not measure up to U.S. standards and thus had to leave the country. While this may be true for some, the fact remains that many qualified applicants are rejected from U.S. schools simply because there are not enough positions.

In 2003, 53% of IMGs in U.S. residency training programs were U.S. citizens or permanent U.S. residents. (Only 11%, however, were native U.S. citizens.) This is an increase from 1988, when USIMGs made up only 41% of IMGs in U.S. residencies. Of the 2,029 USIMGs who completed the NRMP PGY-1 Match process in 2002, only 1,092 (54%) obtained residency positions. This is slightly lower than the rate for foreign-born IMGs (52%).

— ECFMG Certification —

U.S. citizens who graduate from foreign medical schools must get ECFMG Certification to be eligible for: (1) acceptance into an ACGME-accredited residency or fellowship training position in the United States; (2) an application to take Step 3 of the USMLE; and (3) a medical license in most states. (Fifth Pathway students do not need an ECFMG Certificate, and Oklahoma does not require it for licensure.) The ECFMG issues fewer than 6,000 new Certificates each year—which is only about half the number of Certificates they issued in the 1990s, before the CSA Exam was required.

Note that 16 states have requirements in addition to obtaining an ECFMG Certificate for IMGs to be appointed to a residency position. Those states are Alaska, Arizona, California, Connecticut, Iowa, Kansas, Kentucky, Louisiana, Michigan, Minnesota, Nevada, New Jersey, New Mexico, Pennsylvania, Texas, and Vermont.

To qualify for an ECFMG Certificate (Figure 17.4), you must be either a student attending a medical school listed in the current edition of the *International Medical Education Directory* (http://imed.ecfmg.org), published by the Foundation for Advancement of International Medical Education and Research (FAIMER), or a graduate of a medical school that is listed in this directory, with your graduation date within the "Graduation Years" listed for the school.

You must submit your application to take the United States Medical Licensing Examination (USMLE) and the required documentation to the ECFMG. This documentation includes a copy (front and back) of every document (and English translations) relating to your medical education. They provide a list of what is required from schools in every country. Once they receive all the required documents, the ECFMG sends the papers back to the medical school for verification. This processing may take several months (or longer), especially at European and third-world medical schools. Schools that specifically cater to U.S. citizens usually do better. If you have graduated, you must also document completion of the educational requirements for your final medical diploma. This must include at least four years of medical study for which credit was received.

If you receive approval to take the USMLE, you must pass Step 1 and Step 2 for ECFMG certification at one of the 300 test centers in the United States and Canada.

To apply to take Step 3 (which you don't have to worry about until during or after residency training), an applicant must have obtained an M.D. degree or equivalent, successfully passed USMLE Steps 1 and 2, obtained an ECFMG Certificate or completed a Fifth Pathway program, and met any other specific requirements imposed by the state licensing board administering the test. Information about specific state requirements is available from individual state boards or from The Federation of State Medical Boards, 400 Fuller Wiser Rd., Ste. 300, Euless, TX 76039; (817) 868-4000; fax: (817) 868-4098; www.fsmb.org.

FIGURE 17.4

Requirements to Practice Medicine, Do Postgraduate Training, or Be a Clinical Research Fellow in the United States (Patient Contact)

	ECFMG English Test	USMLE	CSA Exam	ECFMG Certification	Applicable Visas
Foreign National: Graduate of LCME-accredited U.S., Canadian, or Puerto Rican Medical School (EVIMG)		✔			✔
U.S. Citizen: Graduate of Foreign Medical School (USIMG)*	✔	✔	✔	✔	
Foreign National: Graduate of Foreign Medical School (FNIMG)	✔	✔	✔	✔	✔

*An alternative for U.S. citizen/permanent resident IMGs is to enter the Fifth Pathway Program. Participants do not need to get an ECFMG Certificate, so do not need to take the English-language test or the CSA exam.

If history is any guide, those IMGs with the best chance of passing Steps 1 and 2 of the USMLE are younger than 30 years old, male, native English-speakers, foreign national IMGs (FNIMGs), or educated in countries with low infant mortality rates and high per capita income. Those with the least chance of passing the examination are over 40 years of age, female, nonnative English-speakers, taking the test more than ten years after medical school, USIMGs, or educated in countries with medium to high infant mortality rates and medium per capita income. Women comprise less than 40% of all IMGs in U.S. residencies.

ECFMG English Language Examinations

All IMGs must also pass an English proficiency examination for ECFMG certification, even if they are U.S. citizens or native English speakers. As of March 1999, the ECFMG is only using the Test of English as a Foreign Language™ (TOEFL®) developed by the Educational Testing Service. The test results are only good for two years (unless you get accepted into a residency). So if you pass TOEFL but don't get a residency position before it expires, you must retake the examination.

Clinical Skills Assessment (CSA)

Because of concerns raised by residency directors, state licensing boards, and the public, the ECFMG implemented a new exam to test the clinical and communication skills (especially proficiency in spoken English) that graduates of foreign medical schools are expected to have. The test, the Clinical Skills Assessment (CSA), is similar to the Objective Structured Clinical Examination (OSCE) given at many medical schools.

The CSA consists of 11 standardized patient (SP) encounters, 10 of which are scored (one case is used for research). The cases are similar to those that are commonly encountered in doctor's offices and emergency departments in the United States or Canada.

All 10 case scores are averaged. This test is standards-based (criterion-referenced), meaning that a specific score is required to pass—it is not graded on a curve. Examinees who meet the preset criteria, pass; those who don't, fail.

All applicants for an ECFMG Certificate must take the CSA *after* having passed both USMLE Step 1 and the English Language Test (TOEFL). A passing score on the CSA is valid for three years from the exam date. If the CSA date expires before a physician begins a residency in the United States, the applicant must pass the exam again. (Graduates of U.S. medical schools may soon have to take a similar test, the Clinical Skills Examination, to pass the USMLE.) In 2003, the CSA cost $1,200.

The CSA is currently given throughout the year, up to seven days a week, based on demand, at two centers: ECFMG CSA Center, 3624 Market St., 3rd Floor, Philadelphia, PA 19104; and at ECFMG CSA Center, Two Crown Center, 1745 Phoenix Blvd., Ste. 500, Atlanta, Georgia 30349-5585.

As of September 2002, 80% of those taking the CSA passed, while 89% of USIMGs passed compared to 80% of FMIMGs. The difference in failure rates is primarily due to communication difficulties. The relatively high pass rate is thought to be due to candidate self-selection.

— Getting a Residency Position —

Even if you get an ECFMG Certificate, you have just jumped one hurdle—more are ahead. As previously stated, IMGs have a difficult time getting residency positions, especially in the most competitive specialties and at the most desirable locations (nice geography or good university programs). U.S. and Canadian graduates sweat out the residency application and matching processes—and they are not IMGs. IMGs have a considerably more difficult and stressful time obtaining training positions. As one AMA spokesman said, "The two ways they most often find [good residency positions] is through family or political connections or at institutions in badly underserved areas, such as big city public hospitals."

For help with the entire process, and to see what you need to go through, check out *Iserson's Getting Into A Residency: A Guide For Medical Students,* Sixth Edition (Tucson, AZ: Galen Press, 2003). It's the same book that most U.S. medical students use to help them select their specialty, apply to and interview at programs, and complete the Match process.

Aside from their reluctance to take IMGs for other reasons, residency programs, especially those that train large numbers of international medical graduates, are now concerned about changes in Medicare laws that severely restrict programs' and hospitals' reimbursement for training non-U.S. medical school graduates. These residency programs often operate on a shoestring as it is. Threatening to restrict their funds even further has already had the desired effect of closing down many training opportunities for IMGs.

There is little question that many, if not most, residency programs discriminate against IMGs. Yet, Section 102 of the 1992 Federal Health Professions Education Extension Amendments (PL 102-408) states:

> *Graduates of Foreign Medical Schools.*—The Secretary [of Health and Human Services] may make an award of a grant, cooperative agreement, or contract under this title to an entity [including a medical school] that provides graduate training in the health professions only if the entity agrees that, in considering applications for admissions to a program of such training, the entity will not refuse to consider an application solely on the basis that the application is submitted by a graduate of a foreign medical school.

How much sway this holds over residency directors is unknown, since many are probably not aware of it. Studies show that some residency programs discriminate against IMGs as early in the process as when they send out application materials. As residency positions tighten, however, enterprising IMGs will certainly begin making them aware of the law.

What does sway residency directors is the past performance of IMGs in residency programs. IMGs, especially those that contract with residency programs outside a matching program, have a higher attrition rate than U.S. graduates. Also, IMGs pass some specialty Board examinations, such as internal medicine's, only about two-thirds as often on their first try as do U.S. graduates. Since residency programs are, in part, judged on their graduates' pass rates, this is important to residency directors.

Some IMGs are forced to take residency slots that are unfunded. In some cases these are called externships; in others, they actually count toward completion of a residency. It is not unusual to see offers of payment for a residency slot from either the applicants themselves or third parties acting on their behalf. Proposals of $25,000 or more per year (plus any cost for salary, benefits, and allowances) have been offered for competitive positions. It is possible, however, that many of the individuals filling these positions are not treated as equals, do not get similar responsibilities, or do not end up with training equivalent to that of other residents in the same program.

Despite all the unfavorable press and the tough requirements, the number of IMGs in U.S. residency positions increased from just over 12,000 in 1989 to nearly 25,000 in 2002. The number of IMGs in first-year residency positions increased over this same period from 2,689 to more than 3,500. USIMGs (U.S. citizens and permanent residents) make up about 6% of first-year residents, but more than one-third of all first-year IMG residents. In the 2002 NRMP Match, IMGs made up a large proportion of those entering some specialties (Figure 17.5).

The American Medical Association has formed an International Medical Graduates Section. It tackles licensure, discrimination, and visa issues on behalf of IMGs. For information, contact: AMA International Medical Graduate Section, 515 N. State St., Chicago, IL 60610, or go to the AMA website (www.ama-assn.org) and search for the Section by name. The website contains interesting, although not necessarily the most current, information.

— Obtaining a Medical License —

Each U.S. state and territory (and each province in Canada) has its own medical licensing board. Although licensing tests have become relatively uniform, each locale has its own specific rules and paperwork required to obtain a medical license.

There are thousands of IMGs in the United States who have not been able to obtain a license to practice medicine. In many cases this is because residency programs will not accept them for training, and *all jurisdictions in the United States require at least one year of postgraduate training in the United States or Canada for licensure* (Figure 17.6). Nineteen jurisdictions require IMGs to have at least two

FIGURE 17.5

Types of Applicants Filling PGY-1 and Advanced Positions in Specialties through NRMP Match[1]

Specialty	% Filled by U.S. Senior Students	% Filled by Osteopaths & U.S. Grad. Physicians	% Filled by IMGs, Fifth Pathway, & Can. Grads	% Total Positions Filled by NRMP
Anesthesiology	78%	5%	13%	96%
Emergency Medicine	81	12	54	98
Family Practice	47	11	21	79
Internal Medicine	59	7	29	94
Obstetrics/Gynecology	75	7	12	94
Orthopedic Surgery	93	5	1	99
Pathology[2]	50	9	28	84
Pediatrics	71	6	14	90
Psychiatry	59	9	27	95
Radiology, Diagnostic	81	8	5	95
Surgery, General[4]	75	6	13	91
Transitional	84	<1	1	92
Osteopaths Unmatched[3]	—	29	—	—
5th Pathway Unmatched[3]	—	—	41	—
U.S. IMGs Unmatched[3]	—	—	46	—
FNIMGs Unmatched[3]	—	—	49	—
Total Unmatched[3]	6	40	47	—

1: Numbers in the columns for percent of graduates matching within a specialty may not add up to total percentage matched due to rounding.

2: A significant number of entry-level positions (PGY-1 or above) are offered outside the Match.

3: The percentage is of those going through the entire NRMP process. Between 5% (U.S. Seniors) and 24% (U.S. and Foreign IMGs) of the candidates withdrew before the Match or did not submit a Rank Order List.

4: Categorical positions.

Derived from: National Residency Matching Program. *Results and Data 2002.* Washington, DC: NRMP, 2002 (April).

years of training for licensure and 27 require three years. This exceeds what most jurisdictions require from U.S. graduates. In addition, 26 licensing boards (AL, AR, CO, CT, DC, GA, GU, ID IA, KY, LA, MN, MS, MO, MT, NM, NC, ND, OK, OR, PR, RI, SD, TN, VT, WY) maintain lists of state-approved foreign medical schools whose graduates are eligible for a medical license.

Even with these additional requirements, state medical boards are very wary of IMGs. They have either been snookered or know of other boards that have been scammed by individuals with false medical credentials. These episodes often end up on a newspaper's front page. Boards don't want egg on their face. So, even though graduates from U.S. and Canadian schools don't have to appear in person before the medical board or submit all medical school, ECFMG, and residency paperwork (again translated by an official if not in English), you may have to do so.

It seems to be clear from their prior behavior that some medical boards simply don't want IMGs practicing in their states. However, they can raise the postgraduate educational barriers only so high. Another ploy that some have suggested (but no one has yet had the *cajones* to implement) is to require that most or all of a medical student's clinical training be in the country where the medical school is located. That will effectively eliminate the graduates of Caribbean schools, since none ot these schools have adequate facilities to meet this requirement.

Taking the foreign medical school route should not be done lightly. The colossal problems include personal and academic difficulties during preclinical courses, frequent problems with acquiring adequate clinical experiences, language differences, and problems reentering the United States to complete a residency and practice medicine. Take this route only if you have no other option—including waiting a year or two while you improve your credentials. You should only consider this route if you have the fortitude to overcome all of these difficulties, and also have the academic skills to complete the course of study and pass the USMLE.

FIGURE 17.6

Graduate Education Requirements for M.D. Licensure

Number of years of accredited U.S. or Canadian graduate medical education (residency) required for a medical license.

One Year

Alabama[1]	Hawaii[1]	Missouri[1]	South Carolina[1]
Arizona[1]	Idaho[1]	Nebraska[1]	Tennessee[1]
Arkansas	Indiana[1,4]	New Jersey[1]	Texas[1]
California[1,9]	Iowa	New York[1]	Vermont[1]
Colorado[1]	Kansas[1]	North Carolina[1]	Virgin Islands
Delaware[1]	Louisiana[1]	North Dakota[1]	Virginia[1]
District of Columbia	Maryland[1,4]	Ohio[1]	West Virginia[1]
Florida[1]	Massachusetts[1]	Oklahoma[1]	Wisconsin
Georgia[1]	Minnesota[1]	Oregon[1]	Wyoming[1]
Guam[1]	Mississippi[1]	Puerto Rico	

Two Years

Alaska[1]	Indiana[2]	Minnesota[2]	Rhode Island[7]
California[2]	Kansas[2]	Montana[1]	South Dakota[5]
Connecticut[8]	Kentucky	New Hampshire	Utah
Florida[2]	Maine[1]	New Mexico	Washington
Guam[3]	Maryland[2]	Ohio[2]	Wyoming[2]
Hawaii[2]	Massachusetts[2]	Oklahoma[2]	
Illinois	Michigan	Pennsylvania[1]	

Three Years

Alabama[2]	Louisiana[2,10]	New Jersey[2]	South Carolina[2]
Alaska	Maine[2,7,8]	New York[2,8]	Tennessee[2,8]
Arizona[2]	Mississippi[2]	North Carolina[2]	Texas[2]
Colorado[2]	Missouri[2]	North Dakota[2]	Vermont[2,6,8]
Delaware[2,8]	Montana[2]	Oregon[2]	Virginia[2]
Georgia[2]	Nebraska[2]	Pennsylvania[2,8]	West Virginia[2]
Idaho[2]	Nevada	Rhode Island[2]	

1: Graduates of U.S. medical schools only.
2: International medical graduates.
3: Canadian training not accepted.
4: An additional year of residency is required if the applicant failed any Step of their licensing exam three or more times.
5: Must complete a residency program.
6: Canadian training accepted only from Canadian medical school graduates.
7: May accept graduate medical education completed in England, Scotland, and Ireland for credit toward a license.
8: May accept specialty certificates granted by non-U.S. boards for credit toward a license.
9: Does not accept a single "straight" Psychiatry, Anesthesia, or Pathology year for licensure.
10: May count Fifth Pathway as one year for licensure.

Adapted from: *State Medical Licensure Requirements & Statistics: 2001–2002*. Chicago, IL: AMA, 2001, Tables 6 and 8.

18

Paying For Medical School

Forgive us our debts, as we forgive our debtors.

— Matthew, 6:12

A medical education can be very expensive. Costs include not only tuition and school fees, but also living expenses and the books, special clothes (lab coats, uniforms), and equipment required for school.

Since 1960, medical school tuition has increased by 500% for private schools and nearly 350% for public schools, even after being adjusted for inflation (see Figure 15.2). The actual tuition and fees (the University of California's schools pretend they have no tuition by calling their tuition a "fee") range from about $3,000 (Montréal) and $4,500 (Brody/East Carolina) to more than $65,000 a year (Colorado, out-of-state students), and vary depending upon whether the school is public or private and whether you are a state resident. (The Uniformed Services University is "free," but you owe them a service commitment.) On average, state residents pay an annual tuition of $10,000 at their state's public medical schools, while out-of-staters pay about $28,000. Tuition at private schools averages more than $29,000 a year (see Figure 15.2). Most schools also charge additional "academic fees," which can be substantial.

Medical textbooks are very expensive (up to $5,000 the first year). Lab coats and other equipment must be purchased or rented. The cost of living varies significantly across the country, but is generally lowest in the Deep South and in the Midwest. The farther northeast or west you go, the higher the average living costs.

Lest you think that tuition provides the financial support for medical schools, be aware that only 3.5% of the average medical school's budget comes from tuition and fees (it is slightly less at public schools and slightly more at private schools). The balance is generated from patient care revenues, research grants, and government sources.

You must pay for medical school with cash, scholarships, or loans, or by working for the federal or state government after you graduate. Loans constitute most of the financial aid available to pay for a medical education. However, everyone accepted to a U.S. medical school should be able to obtain all the financial assistance they need up to their "cost of education" as determined by the school's financial aid office—as long as they are U.S. citizens or permanent residents and *do not have a bad credit rating*.

In addition, to obtain a federal student loan, the individual must

- Not be in default on a federal student loan and not owe money on a federal student grant.
- Not have been convicted under federal or state law for sale or possession of illegal drugs.
- Be in compliance with the Selective Service registration requirements.
- Make satisfactory academic progress (to keep the loan).
- Keep the lender apprised of the borrower's address and telephone number.

In recent years, medical students received more than $1 billion in educational loans. In 2003, 82% of graduating medical students had borrowed money to pay for their education (including premed) and each owed, on average, nearly $109,457. Fifty-eight percent of all 2003 medical school graduates owed more than $100,000, and 25% of graduates owed $150,000 or more. This debt has increased 200% since 1982! (For perspective, the average graduating medical student's debt in 1971 was only $8,435.) Students at private medical schools have debts that are nearly 30% higher than those of students at public schools. The 94% of Osteopathic medical graduates who incurred debt had an average debt of nearly $130,000 in 2002.

Students will face even larger debts, given that at least 31 medical schools now have annual tuition/fee charges of more than $35,000, and four schools charge in excess of $48,000. In addition, nearly one in five spouses of medical school graduates have debt exceeding $50,000. The spouses and significant others of women medical graduates have significantly higher debts (about $80,000) than their male cohorts' partners (about $65,000).

About 16% of medical students take more than four years to complete medical school, which increases their debt. In addition, about 3% of students leave medical school without graduating, either for personal or for academic reasons. In most cases, they will end up with a large debt for the schooling they received.

Many medical schools provide basic financial aid information at their orientation session during the interview visit (see Figure 21.2). Those who don't may provide applicants with an opportunity to talk with their financial aid officer. If you have the chance, find out about the school's financial aid resources during your visit.

— Financial Planning/Debt Management —

The basic idea of financial planning is simple: Decide what you want to have and do in the future, and then make current financial decisions so that you can accomplish these goals. Easily said; hard to do.

Most medical students' financial planning includes determining how to repay their loans while maintaining the lifestyle they desire. Their debt may force them to adjust their spending habits. And the impact will depend on how large their debt becomes. That is where debt management becomes important. You need to determine how much debt you really need and then get loans at the lowest possible cost, stay on a budget so you will not borrow and spend excessively, and consolidate your loans when it is economically beneficial.

The three most important things students can do to get ready to finance their medical education are to:

1. Apply for scholarships (see "Scholarships," below).
2. Maintain good credit.
3. Learn to use credit cards responsibly.

Accrue Debt Carefully

How good is your credit? "Why does that matter?" you ask. "I'm going to medical school and will make a mint of money when I get out." Maybe. But you may not even get in if your current credit rating is poor. Medical schools have *rescinded some applicants' acceptances because they had dismal credit ratings* and could not get loans to pay for medical school!

To avoid this situation, a small but increasing number of medical schools require students to submit a credit history with their application to prove that they can get the loans that most students need to pay for medical school.

To find out about your own credit rating, contact one of the three major credit bureaus. The basic report is all you really need. It costs from $10 to $15 (in 2003), depending upon which service you use. (Except for applicants living in Colorado, Georgia, Maryland, Massachusetts, New Jersey, and Vermont; these states require credit bureaus to give consumers a free report each year). If you have been denied employment based on information in a credit report or have been a victim of fraud, federal law requires the bureaus to provide you with a free report.

Equifax Credit Information Services, Inc.
P.O. Box 740241
Atlanta, GA 30374
(800) 997-2493
www.equifax.com

Experian
475 Anton Blvd.
Costa Mesa, CA 92626
(888) 397-3742
www.experian.com

Transunion
P.O. Box 2000
Chester, PA 19022
(800) 888-4213
www.transunion.com

You've heard it before: Be careful when using those credit cards! The interest rates and fees can be astronomical; debts pile up quickly and soon can get out of control. Ask yourself, "Am I using my credit cards for credit or for convenience?" You should only use a credit card for convenience if you pay the bill in full each month. Otherwise, you are using it as a very expensive form of credit—and living beyond your means. Unfortunately, such behavior typifies more than 75% of the U.S. populace.

If you have trouble with overspending, you may want to investigate using a debit card. These cards immediately withdraw money from your account when you make a purchase. If you have no money, you cannot spend the money. Think of it as the"tough (credit) love" approach. All financial aid officers recommend that you pay off all your consumer debt before you enter medical school. Doing so will save you many headaches in the future.

To stay out of financial trouble during medical school, you will need to live within the budget that the financial aid office develops when they calculate your loans and scholarships. If you elect to live like a professional when you are a medical student, you may live like a student when you are a physician (or you may not even make it through medical school). Don't treat yourself to a new car to celebrate getting into medical school (unless you can afford to pay cash for that Lamborghini—in which case, you're not reading this section anyway).

— Obtaining Financial Aid —

More than 80% of all medical students require financial assistance to get through medical school. The only way to obtain this help (aside from family assistance and veterans' benefits) is to carefully complete the appropriate financial aid applications for each school—and to return them quickly! That way, once you are accepted, the school can immediately begin to process your financial application.

Financial aid is available in several forms:

- Scholarships without a service obligation as payback (i.e., "free" money)
- Scholarships with a service obligation in a uniformed service or an underserved area
- Loans subsidized by the government
- Loans not subsidized by the government
- Other funds (e.g., Veterans' educational benefits)
- Private money (e.g., family)

Except for the last two sources, the availability of these funds may be based on a student's financial need, background, willingness to provide future services, special achievements, or interests.

Most students use multiple sources of funds to finance their medical education.

Assess How Much You Will Need

Figure 18.1 is a simple guide to developing a budget for each year of medical school. When using it, remember to update the information as your situation and expenses change. This should give you a rough idea of how you stand financially. The amount by which "expenses" exceed "income" indicates approximately how much additional financial assistance you will need.

The financial aid you receive will be limited to the "Cost of Education."As determined by the financial aid office, the "Cost of Education" includes only educational expenses; therefore, attending a family wedding or taking a vacation are not justifiable expenses for federal aid. You will need to depend on personal savings or family assistance, or to reduce other expenses (sharing the expenses of an apartment, for example) to fit these "extras" into your budget.

It is best not to enter medical school with car payments and credit card debts. If it is unavoidable, discuss this with a financial aid counselor at the medical school(s) prior to getting yourself into a situation you can't afford. The feds frown on using federal financial aid to finance automobiles, so car payments are another "extra." If public transportation is insufficient to get you to the various hospitals, clinics, and doctors' offices required for your clinical training, discuss this with the medical school's financial aid counselor.

The school's financial aid office may add the child-care expenses required for you to attend school to the Cost of Education if you request that they reevaluate your budget. They may also add medical, dental, and optical expenses not covered by insurance. If these items apply to you, discuss this with the financial aid office. Since federal funds are involved, additions that can be made to the financial aid budget are subject to federal regulation and school policy.

The Forms

During the January before you plan to enter medical school, you should receive a packet of financial information (or an e-mail directing you to their financial aid website) from each school to which you have applied. If you do not, call the financial aid office and request the information. Schools vary widely in how and when they send out this information (see Figure 15.8). These are *big* packets—or websites—containing lots of information about the available financial aid, with numerous forms to complete. If you thought you saw mountains of paperwork before, you haven't seen anything until you get these packets.

It is wise to carefully complete the required application forms as soon as you can. *Students who get their financial forms back early, often before March 1, have priority in receiving assistance over others who apply later*. Since many programs quickly deplete their available funds, it's first come, first served. *DO NOT WAIT TO BE ACCEPTED TO MEDICAL SCHOOL TO APPLY FOR FINANCIAL AID*. Many first-time applicants make this extremely costly mistake.

The basic form is the Department of Education's *Free Application for Federal Student Aid* (FAFSA). Most students now use the web-based form, a better method for completing the FAFSA, which can be found at www.fafsa.ed.gov. Applicants complete the form by going through the steps in its three sections: (1) *Before Beginning a FAFSA*; (2) *Filling Out a FAFSA*; and (3) *FAFSA Followup*. The site has excellent instructions and contains built-in edit checks to catch simple errors.

FAFSA requests very personal and very detailed information. General rules for completing the FAFSA are:

1. For information about FAFSA, how to complete it, and how to answer specific questions on the form, go to the website at http://studentaid.ed.gov/students/publications/completing_fafsa/index.html.
2. Experienced counselors recommend that you complete your federal income tax forms before you complete FAFSA.
3. Make a copy of the form to use as a draft. You can submit only the original, however.
4. Be as accurate as possible. If you have to estimate to meet the priority deadline set by the schools, do so, but you will need to submit corrections later. If your answers are too far off, this might result in an adjustment of the amount of aid you are offered. You are responsible for the accuracy of the information you provide. If you intentionally give false or misleading information, you may be fined $20,000, sent to prison, or both.
5. You must include information about you, your spouse, and any dependents.
6. Federal law considers all medical students "independent students" for many financial aid programs. However, some federal loans and scholarships require you to provide information about your parents, including their signatures. In addition, many medical schools require parental information to be considered for their scholarships. Check with the schools you are interested in attending.

FIGURE 18.1

Personal Budget for One Year of Medical School

Income	Fall Semester	Spring Semester
Parents/family	$	$
Spouse's earnings (net)		
Savings/other assets		
Job while in school (net)		
Financial aid (approved)		
Other		
TOTAL Income	$	$

Expenses		
Tuition	$	$
Other fees		
Credit card payments		
Books/supplies/instruments		
Laptop computer/PDA		
Phone/internet connection		
Rent/mortgage		
Utilities (water, electric, gas)		
Household supplies/upkeep		
Food (at home/out of home)		
Medical insurance & expenses		
Clothing/laundry		
Car/transportation		
Parking/tolls		
Other insurance		
Dependent expenses		
Child-care		
Travel/vacations*		
Recreation/entertainment*		
Miscellaneous		
TOTAL Expenses	$	$
INCOME minus EXPENSES =	$	$

*These expenses, along with car payments and credit card interest, are not built into the calculations for financial aid.

7. Type or neatly print the information on the original forms after you complete your final draft. Not only does it have to be read, but it also may be scanned into computers.
8. Check the form carefully before submitting it.

While the size of the financial packets you receive can appear quite daunting, the best way to handle them is to:

- Remove the application from the packet (or print it from the website) and make a copy of the blank forms to use for your rough draft.
- Work through the application using the accompanying instruction booklet, one step at a time. Do this, even if you will use the web-based application.
- *Keep a copy of all paperwork related to your financial aid applications, including worksheets and your calculations!* Once you complete this paperwork, you don't want to do it again, especially since you may have to justify the numbers you entered.
- Get confirmation that the financial application was successfully transmitted. If you must mail a signature page, do it promptly. If the process is not complete within 45 days, the application is deleted from the federal system.

The government is ready to answer any questions you have via phone at (800) 433-3243, or you can write the Federal Student Aid Information Center, P.O. Box 84, Washington, DC 20044.

Federal Stafford Loans, on the other hand, require only some personal information; private lenders require only this plus limited credit information—so it's not quite as intimidating.

Useful Financial Terms

Although the following terms may sound like items from a *New York Times* crossword puzzle, you should become very familiar with them, since they are necessary for your financial well-being.

Accrediting Agency: An agency, such as the LCME, that certifies that medical schools have met specific educational standards.

Actual Interest Rate: The annual interest rate charged by a lender, which may be equal to or less than the "applicable" (statutory) interest rate for that loan.

Applicable (Statutory) Interest Rate: The maximum annual interest rate a lender may legally charge on a loan.

Assignment: A change in ownership of the loan (i.e., a change in the lending agency).

Award Letter: The school's notification to an applicant of the amount and type of financial aid that will be available to him or her. (Described more fully below.)

Base Year: The calendar year prior to the year for which financial aid is being sought.

Borrower: The individual taking out a loan. This person is responsible for repaying it.

Capitalization: An increase in the amount owed to the lender created by adding accrued (but unpaid) interest to the loan principal.

Capitalized Interest: The unpaid interest added to the principal. Interest is then calculated on the new balance that includes both the prior principal balance and the interest that has been added.

Consolidation: Federal loan programs in which a student can combine and refinance multiple educational loans and obtain a single new loan. This new loan has new terms, which can be to a borrower's advantage or disadvantage.

Credit Rating: An estimate of how likely an individual is to default on a loan.

Default: The failure of a borrower to repay a loan or to fulfill other portions of the contract.

Deferment: A period of time during which the borrower need not make payments on the loan principal. The borrower must meet specific requirements to be eligible for a deferment. Interest still accrues, however.

Delinquency: The period after a borrower fails to make a payment when it is due.

Disclosure Statement: The written description, provided by the lender to the borrower, of a loan's terms, the actual cost of the loan including all fees, and the consequences of defaulting.

Disability: A condition rendering an individual incapable of working, earning money, or attending school. A borrower is considered "totally and permanently disabled" if the condition is expected to continue for a long or indefinite time or to result in death.

Disadvantaged Background: A person whose background provided significantly fewer opportunities to be a successful medical school applicant than others or whose family income falls into the lower federal income brackets for families of comparable size.

Expected Family Contribution: The monetary amount a student or the student's family is expected to contribute to his or her education. This amount is used to calculate "Financial Need."

***FAFSA* (Free Application for Federal Student Aid Form):** All federal student aid programs and many private lenders, schools, and state agencies require completion of this form to determine eligibility for financial aid.

***FFELP* (Federal Family Education Loan Program):** The Federal Stafford loans that are financed through private lenders, but which the federal government guarantees against default.

***FDSLP* (Federal Direct Student Loan Program):** It provides loans from the federal government, through schools, directly to students and their parents.

Financial Aid Package: The total amount of financial aid given to a student.

Fixed Interest Rate: An interest rate that remains constant over the life of the loan.

Forbearance: A period of time, approved by the lender, during which the borrower need not make loan payments. Interest accrues and is capitalized.

Forgiveness: Reducing the loan amount due for "Special Service," as described in the contract.

Garnishment: Intercepting a portion of an individual's wages to repay the lender for a defaulted loan.

Grace Period: The period between graduation (or ceasing to be enrolled in school at least half-time) and when repayment of the loan must begin.

Guarantee Fee: A fee charged for guaranteeing the loan. It is usually deducted from the amount the borrower receives.

Holder: The organization that owns your promissory note. This may change over time.

Independent Student: Under current federal law, all medical students qualify for this status because they are graduate or professional students.

Interest: The amount of money that lenders charge for the privilege of providing funds to a borrower. Calculated as a percentage of the amount borrowed.

Loan Servicer: The organization that handles the billing, deferment, and forbearance requests, and other activities related to a loan. This may be a third-party rather than the "holder."

Loan Transfer: A change in the identity of the loan holder or of the agency that services the loans.

Need-based Funding: Funding given to "financially needy" students, determined by using criteria set by the funding agency. These loans usually have the most favorable terms.

Origination Fee: Similar to the Guarantee fee, this is also deducted from the amount received. This fee covers preparation of some loan documents and other unspecified items.

Principal Balance: The amount of the loan outstanding and on which the lender charges interest. A portion of each payment reduces the principal and a portion pays the accrued interest.

Principal: The amount originally borrowed, not including any accrued interest.

Promissory Note: The legal document with the conditions of the loan.

Repayment Period: The time during which the loan must be repaid, excluding any period of authorized deferment or forbearance.

Repayment Start Date: The date on which the repayment period begins.

Sallie Mae: This organization holds more than one-third of all educational loans, which they acquire from the original lender.

Special Service: Service in the military, in medically underserved areas, or to other groups or in areas described in the financial agreement. This service often counts toward repayment of all or part of the principal.

Subsidized Loan: A loan on which the federal government pays the interest that accrues during medical school, the grace period, authorized deferments, and, if applicable, postdeferment grace periods.

Unsubsidized Loan: A loan on which the borrower is responsible for paying all accrued interest.

Variable Interest Rate: An interest rate that changes at set periods of time (e.g., quarterly, annually) according to the terms described in the loan agreement.

How Schools Use Financial Aid Information

Most schools first evaluate a student's eligibility for need-based funding. They match the information a student provides against criteria set by the funding programs. If a student meets the criteria for need-based programs (which have more favorable terms), he or she may be offered need-based aid.

Most schools DO NOT consider students' financial needs when they decide whether to accept them. The admissions and financial assistance processes are separate. Most admission committees assume that every student will need financial assistance. Neither they nor the school's administration are concerned about where you will find the money to pay the tuition; they assume you can get it. The financial support offices exist to help you find the money you need.

While no medical student is dismissed because of lack of funds, poor personal financial management has forced some students to withdraw from medical school. And, since lenders are primarily concerned about an individual's credit rating, medical school financial aid officers are now checking the credit ratings of accepted applicants and suggesting that those with bad credit ratings work for a year to improve their credit rating prior to entering medical school. That way, they may qualify for the loans they need to pay for school.

Are You "Financially Needy"?

Since medical school is so expensive, most students are financially needy. The calculation used to determine a student's financial need is:

[Cost of Medical Education] minus [Expected Family Contribution] = FINANCIAL NEED

[Financial Need] minus [Financial Assistance] = UNMET FINANCIAL NEED

"Cost of Medical Education," as determined by the school, includes tuition, fees, books, equipment, supplies, housing, food, transportation, personal expenses, child-care, and miscellaneous expenses.

The "family" in "Expected Family Contribution" (EFC) consists of the student plus his spouse and dependent children. The EFC is determined by taking the family income and subtracting federal, state, and social security taxes. An employment allowance for working spouses, funds to support other family members, and funds for discretionary spending are also subtracted.

Financial aid officers evaluate a student's assets based on their cash, savings, investments, and the net worth of any business or farm. For older students (25 years old and above), they protect a graduated percentage of the assets for retirement. Finally, they consider how many family members are in college, and estimate how much the family can contribute to the applicant's educational expenses.

The FAFSA does not ask for parental income for students who are working on a graduate/professional degree, such as an M.D., so you do not need to include this information. However, voluntarily submitting your parents' financial information will give the school the data necessary to consider you for additional programs administered by the Department of Health and Human Services. Many schools require parental information before selecting scholarship recipients. The AAMC website (http://services.aamc.org/msar_reports?msar_report1.cfm) lists the financial aid forms and information required by each M.D.-granting U.S. school.

If sufficient financial aid is available, the "Unmet Financial Need" (the money you don't have and cannot get) will be zero. If it isn't, or if you feel that the aid awarded is not enough, contact the financial aid counselor for guidance.

The Award Letter

After your forms have been processed and you have been accepted to a medical school, the financial aid office will send you an "award letter" specifying the amount and type of aid the school can provide. Typically, it will list several loans and, perhaps, a scholarship. Funding from sources you must obtain on your own, such as from the military or National Health Service Corps, will not be listed in the letter. If you enter one of these programs, you are required to notify the school's financial aid office so that the information can be incorporated into your financial aid calculations.

You may accept some, all, or only part of the proffered funds. You may also discuss any data in the letter with the school's financial aid officer. In some instances, financial aid officers may modify the "Cost of Medical Education" or "Expected Family Contribution" used in the calculations. They might, for example, include the cost of child-care or take into account the changes to a family's financial situation that will result when the student leaves a well-paying job to enter medical school. Requesting such changes does not jeopardize the awards they have already offered you. Whether your appeal will succeed depends on how well you document your case, what the federal law allows, how much they want you as a student, and how much money they have for financial aid. The amounts available for financial assistance vary widely from school to school.

Accepting a financial aid package does not obligate you to attend that medical school. If a school you would prefer to attend subsequently offers you a position or a better financial aid package, you are free to accept its offer. If you decide to decline either all the financial aid a school offers or the acceptance to that school, you must return the award letter before their deadline. *Otherwise, the school assumes you accept all the offered aid.* If you do not want the entire amount of financial aid offered, ask the school's financial aid officer about the procedure to decrease your loan amount. (Loans are usually for the entire school year, so don't decrease the amount thinking that you can get more when you begin the second semester.)

To obtain loans, borrowers must sign a legal document that contains details about the loan, called a promissory note. Medical students applying for loans sign a Master Promissory Note (MPN) that lasts for 10 years if they don't change schools or lenders. This note obligates them to repay all the money they receive during that time. Therefore, it is vital for students to keep careful records of how much they borrow, because the details are not provided in a separate promissory note every time they get a new school loan.

The Best Strategy

When the ton of paperwork for loans and scholarships arrives at your door, you have two options: Pull out your hair in frustration or take two aspirins (or your favorite nonsteroidal anti-inflammatory agent) and get to work collecting the necessary information and completing the forms. Remember all those minimum-wage jobs you had? The time you spend completing these forms will earn you far more than they paid. In addition, the sooner you return these completed forms, the better your chance of receiving the most favorable financial aid terms. (Since some loans are renewable, if you do it right once, you're "in Fat City.")

Apply for All Types of Aid

Go for it all—scholarships and loans. See what the school's financial aid office can find for you. Also, check on the Web—especially for scholarships. Your reference librarian may be able to supply you with reference books and other sources that provide leads. Many medical school websites contain scholarship information—both specific to their school and more general.

One danger of accessing the myriad of scholarship sites on the Web is the dreaded spam. A suggestion is to set up a Hotmail account just for this search, abandoning it when you are done. That way, your personal mailbox will not be inundated with spam.

Contact organizations to which you, your spouse, your siblings, or your parents belong. They or their national bodies may offer little-known financial assistance. Because these funds usually are not well-publicized or are available to only a small group, they are often not disbursed. If you don't check, you won't know about them. Don't pay "application fees" to services that promise to find scholarships for you. They are rarely worth the expense: Millions of dollars are lost each year by students and their families paying fees to fraudulent scholarship search services.

In recent years, medical students received far more Federal Stafford Loans (nearly 70,000) than any other loan or scholarship—many individuals received more than one. (There are more than 80,000 medical students in the United States at any time, and more at non-U.S. medical schools.)

In decreasing order, the most common sources for student financial aid are:

1. Federal Subsidized Stafford Loan (36,000 loans)
2. Federal Unsubsidized Stafford Loan (31,000)
3. Scholarships from individual medical schools (29,000)
4. Federal Direct Student Loan—Subsidized and Unsubsidized (22,000)
5. Federal Perkins Loan (14,000)
6. Loans from individual medical schools (12,000)
7. Scholarship without a service commitment (12,000)
8. Privately insured loan (7,000)
9. Health Professions Student Loan (4,000)

Measuring financial aid in terms of the average annual amount per student, the largest amounts of aid came from these sources:

1. Medical Scientist Training Program ($26,400)
2. National Health Service Corps Scholarship ($25,000)
3. Health Professions Student Loan ($25,000)
4. Armed Forces Health Professions Scholarship ($25,000)
5. Financial Assistance for Disadvantaged Health Professions Students (FADHPS) Scholarship ($20,000) [Merged into the Scholarships for Disadvantaged Students Program and Primary Care Loans.]
6. Exceptional Financial Need (EFN) Scholarship ($18,000) [Merged into the Scholarships for Disadvantaged Students Program and Primary Care Loans.]
7. Federal Stafford Unsubsidized Loan (not through school) ($18,000)
8. Federal Stafford Unsubsidized Loan (through school) ($13,000)
9. Federal Direct Student Loan, Subsidized and Unsubsidized ($22,000)
10. Scholarship with a service commitment ($12,000)
11. State-funded scholarship ($10,000)
12. Privately insured loan ($9,000)

Only about 3,000 medical students receive funds from the six programs that provide the highest average amount per student. Several of the most commonly used financial aid programs are not listed above, because their annual amount per student is so low. These are: Stafford Subsidized Loan ($8,330), Scholarships from school funds ($7,000), Perkins Loan ($5,000), and other school scholarships without a service commitment ($4,000).

Understand Your Loan/Scholarship Terms and Obligations

Some financial aid programs are described below. Note that programs and their terms are subject to change, often based on the whims of the funding agencies. This is particularly true for the federal government's programs.

Each loan has different rules about when, and exactly how, you must pay back what you borrowed. Consider when interest begins accruing and whether you will be able to put off repaying the loan principal or interest until after your residency. Some loans and "scholarships" now also include service obligations. Read the fine print carefully and review the rules below before obligating yourself.

Since the information about loans and scholarships changes annually, an excellent source to update your information is the nonprofit, free website, *FinAid! The SmartStudent Guide to Financial Aid* (www.finaid.org). It contains links to current information about virtually all the financial aid available, as well as some nifty tools to calculate various aspects of your costs, savings, needs, loans, and insurance. There is also a free scholarship search, although signing up puts you on lenders' e-mail "hit lists." An affiliated website, *FastWeb!* (www.studentservices.com), provides a free scholarship search—albeit with the same constraints.

— Scholarships with No Payback Obligations —

School-Based

Most medical schools have special scholarship funds for their students. Each school's financial aid office will have the information about these funds.

State

Many states have scholarship programs (usually need-based) for medical students. Each school has information about what is available in its state. Many of these scholarships have service obligations attached. If you are from a state without a medical school, contact the premed adviser at the largest of your state's undergraduate schools to find out what is available.

You can also check out the Association of American Medical School's website under "State and Other Loan Repayment/Forgiveness and Scholarship Programs," which lists many of the scholarships each state provides. The website, www.aamc.org/students/financing/repayment/start.html, is searchable by state.

National

Health Professions Scholarships–Scholarships For Disadvantaged Students (SDS) is a need-based program administered through the Department of Health and Human Services. Participating schools are responsible for selecting scholarship recipients, making reasonable determinations of need, and providing scholarships that do not exceed the cost of attendance (tuition, and reasonable educational and living expenses).

U.S. citizens, permanent residents, and residents of the Marianas Islands, U.S. Virgin Islands, Guam, American Samoa, Trust Territory of the Pacific Islands, Republic of Palau, Republic of Marshall Islands, and Federated States of Micronesia are eligible.

Although the student will be the recipient of the funds, all applicants must supply information about their parents' finances to be eligible for this program. The amount of the scholarship varies. There is no payback obligation.

To apply for this scholarship, contact the student financial aid office at the school where you intend to apply for admission or where you are enrolled.

For Special Groups

Many special scholarships are available, but you may need to conduct your own search for them. Medical schools do not always have a complete list of such scholarships, since the available funds and the criteria change frequently, especially for the smaller programs. If you do get such funding, inform the school's financial aid office, since these amounts must be coordinated with other aid provided to you.

Groups for whom special scholarships may be available include:

- Underrepresented Minorities in Medicine (blacks, Chicanos, Mainland Puerto Ricans, Native Americans/Alaska Natives/Native Hawaiians)
- Women
- Members of other ethnic groups (through regional or national organizations)

— "Scholarships" with Payback Obligations —

Free lunches do exist, but they are rare. More commonly, medical students mortgage their future when they accept loans and some scholarships. Some financial aid officers now say it's not "strings" that are attached to some of these programs, but rather "shackles." Be aware of the obligations you incur before accepting the money.

Health Professions Scholarship Program (HPSP)

The HPSP scholarships are sponsored by the uniformed services, and pay for students' tuition, books, fees, and other required medical school expenses. In addition, they provide a (taxable) stipend at the O-1 (entry-level officer—a second lieutenant or ensign) level. In return, participants generally owe four years of military service when they get out of school (one year for each sponsored year).

Students in the program also must do a clinical rotation at a military facility during both their junior and senior years of medical school. They are paid at a higher level during this active duty and have base privileges. Participants are also required to apply for military residencies unless they get a waiver based on the specialty they want to enter. These waivers are hard to get, and are granted only when the service needs the specialty and there are too few military residency spots available in that specialty. With the downsizing of the military medical corps, few people qualify for this waiver.

To be eligible for any of the HPSP programs, the individual must:

- Be a U.S. citizen.
- Be enrolled in or have an acceptance letter (not a wait-list letter) from an accredited M.D.- or D.O.-granting medical school in the United States or Puerto Rico.
- Not be obligated to any other party (such as a state) after graduation.
- Meet all other requirements (including the physical examination and being "of good moral character") for a commissioned officer.

The HPSP programs are relatively competitive, accepting about half of all applicants. Military boards select recipients based on their GPA, MCAT scores, work experiences, extracurricular activities, letters of reference, and, often, essays. (Sounds a lot like applying to medical school again.) The Air Force says that it offers more scholarships to those attending less-expensive schools; few scholarships are awarded to students in schools that cost more than $30,000 per year. The other services use similar protocols.

A former military physician who went through this program gives this advice: "If you are thinking about taking an HPSP scholarship, don't do it for the money. There are other ways to get the money. Only do it if you really want to be a *military officer first* and a physician second. Otherwise, it will be an extremely onerous experience." Having been through this program myself, I agree and have an additional warning: Don't believe everything the recruiter says or the glossy brochures illustrate. Evaluate the plusses and minuses for yourself. It's unlikely that you are going to "pull a fast one" on Uncle Sam, but he may pull one on you. Tread carefully.

There are unique aspects to each service's program; the next three sections illustrate this.

U.S. Navy Scholarship Program

The Navy has the worst reputation concerning its treatment of young physicians. After they complete an internship, the Navy often assigns physicians to duty as general medical officers, which means that they are usually at sea for at least a year or two. As the Navy's recruiting brochure says, "Medical Corps officers typically serve as general medical officers between their internships and residencies." The Navy assigns some of its physicians to serve with Marine Corps units. Upon completing their tours as general medical officers, physicians may then apply for residencies.

As with the other programs, Navy HPSP students receive school-required fees and expenses (except room and board), reimbursement for microscope rental, required books and equipment, and a monthly stipend. Information about Navy scholarships can be obtained from Commander, Navy Recruiting Command, (Code 32), 801 North Randolph St., Arlington, VA 22203-1991; (800) 327-6289; www.navyjobs.com.

U.S. Army Scholarship Program

After participants are commissioned as reserve officers, the Army pays for their tuition, required books, rental of most nonexpendable equipment, and most academic fees. Participants also receive 10½ months of stipend each year as reserve officers. For the other six weeks each year, they receive the salary and allowances of a second lieutenant while they are on "Active Duty for Training." During this time, participants normally work at a major Army medical center in the United States or elsewhere. If school assignments do not permit this time away, students get the same pay but are on active duty at school.

Participants must apply for an Army internship. If they get a position, and most do, they must accept it. The Army has been better about allowing individuals to complete their residency training than the Navy. The active duty obligation varies, but is usually one year for each year of scholarship.

For more information about Army scholarships, contact U.S. Army Health Professions Support Agency SGPS-PD, Recruiting Command–RCHS-OP, 5109 Leesburg Pike, Falls Church, VA 22041-3258; http://healthcare.goarmy.com/flindex.htm.

U.S. Air Force Scholarship Program

After being commissioned as a reserve officer, each Air Force participant receives tuition, required educational fees, approved books, supplies, small equipment and microscope rental, plus 10½ months of stipend each year as a reserve officer. For the other six weeks each year, the Air Force pays participants the salary and allowances of a second lieutenant while they are on "Active Duty Tours." During the first two active duty stints, participants must attend courses whose names alone give you a sense of the military mind: "Health Professions Officer Indoctrination Course" (taken the summer before beginning school) and "Indoctrination to the Air Force Medical Service and Aerospace Medicine" (taken between the first and second years). The third- and fourth-year stints are at Air Force medical teaching facilities. If school assignments do not permit this time away, students get the same pay while on active duty at school.

Participants must apply for an Air Force internship. If they get a position, and most do, they must accept it. The Air Force also has been better than the Navy about allowing individuals to complete their residency training. They are not interested in those pursuing dual specialties, such as pediatrics–internal medicine. The Air Force also says that it is not interested in those students combining advanced degree programs, such as M.D.–Ph.D. The active duty obligation varies, but it is usually one year for each year of scholarship.

For more information about Air Force scholarships, contact USAF Medical Recruiting, Medical Recruiting Division HQ, USAFRS/RSOHM, 550 D Street West, Suite 1, Randolph AFB, TX 78150-4527.

National Health Service Corps (NHSC) Scholarship Programs

The National Health Service Corps (NHSC) is the component of the Public Health Service (PHS) Bureau of Primary Health Care that recruits physicians and other health professionals for underserved areas in the United States. Both M.D. and D.O. students are eligible for scholarships if they agree to train in and to practice general internal medicine, family practice, general pediatrics, general psychiatry, or obstetrics and gynecology in a federally designated underserved area. In return, the NHSC pays all medical school tuition and fees, a monthly stipend, and other "reasonable educational expenses." Program participants owe one year of service for each year of support, with a two-year minimum.

Qualified applicants must agree to complete a primary care residency. They also must exhibit the characteristics that suggest they will remain with the NHSC. These include:

- A strong motivation to practice primary care in a health-profession-shortage area after completing their commitment.
- Prior experience with indigent or underserved communities.
- An understanding and acceptance of the NHSC's mission.
- Availability during medical school to serve at rural or urban community-based health care facilities.

Individuals who meet these requirements and have documentation from their school that shows they are (or would have been) eligible to participate in the federal "Financial Assistance for Disadvantaged Health Professions Students" program will be given preference over other applicants.

Only about 350 NHSC scholarships have been awarded annually to medical students in recent years. Fewer than 10% of all applicants get scholarships. Although the NHSC is under the Public Health Service, most scholarship recipients do not become commissioned PHS officers.

Information about NHSC scholarships (and their loan-repayment programs) can be obtained from: National Health Services Corps Scholarship Program, U.S. Public Health Service, (800) 638-0824; http://nhsc.bhpr.hrsa.gov. For information about the NHSC's Commissioned Officer Student Training and Extern Program (COSTEP), go to www.usphs.gov/assets/applets/SRCInformation.PDF.

Indian Health Service Scholarship Program

This federally funded scholarship program is only for Native Americans or Alaskan Natives who are recognized as such under federal criteria and who are also members of their tribe. The program is similar to the National Health Service Corps Scholarship Program described above. (They also have a loan-repayment program for non-Native Americans.) For more information, see their website: www.ihs.gov/JobsCareerDevelop/DHPS/index.asp.

Osteopathic Medicine Programs

While Osteopathic medical students are eligible for the same scholarships and loans as other medical students, there are some programs specifically for them. Lists of school-based scholarships, other scholarships (generally larger amounts), general scholarship information, and search engines are available through the American Association of Colleges of Osteopathic Medicine's website at: www.aacom.org/financialaid/index.html.

State Programs

Many states have programs to assist state residents through medical school. Most require some type of service obligation, usually in primary care. Each state's programs are described on the Association of American Medical Colleges' website under "State and Other Loan Repayment/Forgiveness and Scholarship Programs" at: www.aamc.org/students/financing/repayment/start.htm. The database can be searched by state—and even by a few organization names. Each listing contains the source of funds, service requirements, eligibility, the number of recent applicants and recipients, unique features of the program, and contact information.

— Loans —

Getting loans to help pay for medical school makes most students feel pretty good: Don't get carried away. And don't forget these points about borrowing money:

- Every time you borrow, you obligate part of your future income.
- *You will pay back up to $3.50 for every $1.00 you borrow*. That extra DVD you rented for $3.00 (using part of the money you borrowed for living expenses) may end up costing you $10.50! Was it worth it?
- It is your responsibility to repay the loans, and to keep the lenders apprised of where you live, name changes, your phone number, and any special circumstances why you shouldn't be paying them back, such as deferments, forbearance, grace periods, special service, or disability. (See *Definitions*, above.)
- If you don't repay your loans or meet your required obligations, both private and government lenders can get nasty; they can mess up both your credit rating and your life. The federal government, for example, publishes a list of those who fail to repay student loans. They send this list to medical associations, state licensing agencies, and medical schools. Failure to repay a government loan may also bar you from accepting Medicare payments—which may preclude you from accepting many medical positions.

Compare Loan Costs and Lenders' Policies

All loans are not equal. If you have the option of taking one of two $15,000 loans, you need to carefully consider the costs of both, as well as the policies of each lending agency. Don't just compare the interest rates, although these are very important.

Compare the following attributes of each loan. For many medical school applicants, these financial concepts may be unfamiliar. For most students, federal loans are the best deal.

- Are there extra fees attached, such as "loan origination" or "guarantee" fees?
- Does interest accrue during medical school? If it does, can this interest be added to the principal (capitalized) so you don't have to pay it while in school? If so, do they add the interest to the principal every three months, at graduation, or on another schedule? The longer it takes to add the interest to the principal, the greater your savings.
- How and when do they calculate interest?
- Does the lender generally sell its loans (to other lenders) on the "secondary market"? The second lender (the one who buys your loan) may change the loan's terms; for example, by not honoring the first lender's liberal policy on capitalizing interest.
- When does the repayment period begin? Is there a "grace" period during which you don't have to pay the loan? Loan terms may allow students a one- to nine-month grace period following the completion of medical school.
- Are there provisions for deferments during residency, fellowship, military service, etc.? Are these deferments interest-free or does interest accrue?
- Once repayment begins, how often are the payments due?
- How long is the repayment period?
- Are there service obligations associated with the loan? If so, can you live with them? If you change your mind about fulfilling these obligations, how Draconian are the adjusted repayment rules?

Loan Repayment

Normally, loans do not have to be repaid until at least six months after graduating from medical school. Most do not have to be paid back until after you finish your internship and begin residency training. As described above, a "grace period" is the time between completing school (while going at least half-time) and beginning to repay the loan. Unsubsidized loans accrue interest during the grace period, while subsidized loans do not.

During part or all of their residencies, physicians generally have two options, depending on their overall financial situation: To avoid paying the loans while accruing interest on *some* of them (deferment), or to avoid paying the loans but still accrue interest on *all* of them (forbearance or deferment of unsubsidized loans). The requirements for implementing these options have become stricter in recent years, but most residents still qualify for an "Economic Hardship Deferment." This deferment has a three-year limit and the borrower must reapply each year. The rules will certainly continue to change, so check with your loan officer to find out the current regulations.

During forbearance and during deferments for unsubsidized loans, interest still accrues. It can either be paid as it accrues or be added to the principal, i.e., "capitalized." If the interest is capitalized on a quarterly basis (as some lenders do), the cost of the loan increases substantially, since after interest is capitalized, you then accrue interest on the original principal plus the capitalized interest. Some lenders capitalize the interest at the end of medical school—this practice makes these loans exceptionally attractive to borrowers.

Sometimes large portions of certain loans, or even the entire loan amount, will be "forgiven" (eliminated) if the recipient works in a particular field, usually doing primary care or research, or in a particular location, either a state or a designated "health-profession-shortage area" (HPSA), for a specified amount of time. Recipients enroll at or after graduation or during their last year of residency. Examples of these programs include:

- National Institutes of Health Loan Repayment Program (research)
  www.lrp.nih.gov
- National Health Service Corps Loan Repayment Program
  www.cfda.gov/public/viewprog.asp?progid=1169
- Disadvantaged Faculty Loan Repayment Program (FLRP)
  (301) 443-1700; http://bhpr.hrsa.gov/dsa/flrp

Loans sponsored by the federal government (most medical students' loans) may be canceled only if the recipient dies or is "permanently and totally disabled." Very few loans are canceled. *Most loans remain in effect, even if the recipient does not complete medical school.*

Sample Loan Costs

The following examples illustrate the relative amounts a typical medical student who qualifies as financially needy may have to repay. (Note that changing rules and using different lenders will alter the amounts.)

Federal Subsidized Stafford Loan: $34,000 borrowed

Terms: $8,500 borrowed per year for four years. No interest accrues during medical school. Interest rate is 7%. (Interest rates are now capped at 8.25%, but who knows what the future may bring.)

Repayment: $394.77 per month x 120 months = $47,372.20

Federal Unsubsidized Stafford Loan: $40,000 borrowed

Terms: $10,000 borrowed per year for four years. Interest rate is 9%. Interest is calculated once a year (simple interest). Interest accrues during four years of medical school, with the interest capitalized at graduation ($9,000).

Repayment: $620.72 per month x 120 months = $74,486.40

Federal Perkins Loan: $10,000 borrowed

Terms: $10,000 borrowed over two years with no interest accruing during medical school, and 5% interest during repayment.

Repayment: $106.00 per month x 120 months = $12,720.00

Loan Management

All borrowers, including medical students and residents, need two qualities to manage their loans: organization and calmness. Residents who are currently repaying their loans (or managing to stay in deferment or forbearance) report having to deal with constant hassles and rudeness from the lending institutions. (They weren't rude when you were applying, were they?) The best way to avoid hassles with lending agencies is to keep accurate records of all loan applications, agreements, payments, correspondence, other paperwork, and telephone conversations with these agencies.

First, create a filing system for your loan and scholarship paperwork—especially for scholarships with payback obligations. If you have more than one loan, create a file for each. This will help you avoid panic when you get a threatening letter from the lender. Keep a copy of all correspondence in your file. Also, keep a log of all telephone calls, with the time, date, subject, names of the people with whom you spoke, and what was said by whom. If you call the lender, stay calm. You will most likely be talking, at least initially, to folks with limited knowledge about loans and the specific rules governing your loan. Have your account or loan number (usually your Social Security number) and your file for that loan available.

Keep a copy of the master promissory note you sign and all the loan disclosure statements you receive. In addition, if the school sends any refunds to the lender, check after 30 to 90 days to be sure they credited it to your loan. Ask for written documentation from the lender and place a copy in your file. These records can save you a lot of money, as Maggie Gumble, the University of Arizona College of Medicine's Senior Financial Aid Counselor, observed:

One of our students refunded $5,000 of her loan to the lender; it was appropriately credited, leaving a balance borrowed of $5,000. Yet, when the lender sold the loan to another lender, they sold it for the original $10,000! Fortunately, the individual caught the error and we were able to provide documentation of the refund. Sallie Mae, who had purchased the loan, went back to the lender for their money!

If you mail material to the lender, send it certified, return-receipt requested. Although this costs more and you have to go to the post office, it's worth the trouble. An unbelievable amount of borrowers' correspondence gets "lost" on the way to lenders. If you request deferment or forbearance forms, inform the lender that you are in a medical residency training program, even if they don't ask for this information.

A good source to get data on some of your student loans is the U.S. Department of Education website (www.nslds.ed.gov) that is a central database for federal loans. This agency receives data from schools, agencies that guaranty loans, the Direct Loan program, the Pell Grant program, and other U.S. Department of Education programs. The database includes information on FFELP loans, Direct Loans, the old SLS loans, etc., but does not include information on federal Health Profession Loans or on private loans.

Loan Consolidation

Loan consolidation allows a borrower with several different loans to lump them together and only make one payment. Essentially, this is a new loan (for the total amount of the old ones) with new terms and a new—sometimes lower—interest rate. You may want to consider this option, because it streamlines the paperwork (and saves your sanity) to have only one loan payment per month, rather than several payments on different schedules to different lenders. However, if you are considering this option, carefully read the fine print. Be sure not to sacrifice favorable loan terms for the convenience of consolidating your loans. Note that loans from the Primary Care Loan Program cannot be consolidated due to its service commitment.

The government has two consolidation programs available. The Federal Loan Consolidation Program can consolidate loans made under the following programs: Federal Stafford Loans, Federal Perkins Loans, and Health Professional Student Loans (HPSL), including Loans for Disadvantaged Students (LDS). The government's webpage for educational loan consolidation is: http://loanconsolidation.ed.gov. Consolidation under the Sallie Mae programs allows borrowers to have up to 30 years to repay their loans, depending on the size of their debt. The interest on these loans is a weighted-average of the original interest rates, rounded up to the nearest one-eighth of one percent and fixed for the life of the loan. The Sallie Mae website, from which a variety of loan information can be accessed, is: www.salliemae.com.

There are a number of other loan consolidators you can use. One that many medical students find particularly attractive is the MEDLOANS Consolidation Loan Program offered to students from M.D. programs in the United States. Their information can be accessed at: (800) 858-5050 or www.aamc.org/students/medloans/start.htm. You can locate other consolidators through your financial aid officer or your lenders. As with any loan, shop around for the best deal you can get.

Loan Programs

The following descriptions of common medical student loan programs provide an overview of what is available. *The rules change each year*. Get the most current information from your medical school's financial aid office. Note that with some loans, you can elect to take only part of the funds initially and wait to see whether you need the balance, such as with the Unsubsidized Federal Stafford Loan. For others, such as the Federal Perkins loan, if you decline to take the money, it will be immediately offered to another student. Check with the school's financial aid officer for specific information about the type of loan you are offered.

Federal Stafford Loans

Stafford Loans are administered under the Federal Family Education Loan Program (FFELP). For information about these loans, the eligibility requirements, how financial need is determined, how to complete the forms, and additional federal student aid publications, see their "Student Guide" (available in English and Spanish). Contact (800) 443-3243; TTY: (800) 730-8913; http://studentaid.ed.gov/students/publications/student_guide.

Subsidized

This is a need-based program for citizens and permanent residents of the United States. Under this program, the federal government subsidizes interest payments. The maximum annual loan amount is $8,500. Students may borrow up to a total of $65,500 in subsidized loans for undergraduate and graduate schools. The maximum loan-origination fee is 3% and the maximum loan-guarantee fee is 1%. These are taken out of the loan amount. No interest accrues while the borrower is in school, and there is a six-month grace period following graduation. The interest rate varies, with a cap of 8.25%.

Most physicians will be eligible for a three-year deferment based on economic hardship during residency. The deferment rules require that the individual have either (1) a federal educational debt equal to or greater than 20% of their adjusted gross income or (2) an adjusted gross individual income minus federal education debt burden of less than 220% of the federal poverty level for a family of two. Given current resident salaries and typical debt levels, most residents qualify for the economic hardship deferment.

Unsubsidized

This is not a need-based program, but the maximum of all financial aid received cannot exceed the "Cost of Education" as determined by the school. The maximum annual loan amount is $38,500 (minus the amount of any Subsidized Federal Stafford Loan). Full-time medical students can borrow up to an aggregate limit of $189,125 from the Federal Stafford Loan Program. United States citizens and permanent residents are eligible.

The loan terms are the same as those for subsidized loans, except that borrowers must pay interest on the loan while in school, during the six-month grace period following school, and during any authorized deferment period. If it is not paid while a student is in school, the interest will be added to the principal amount of the loan (capitalized). Since lenders' policies vary concerning when interest is capitalized, it is wise to shop among the available lenders. Resident physicians are automatically eligible, but must apply for forbearance during residency and pay (or capitalize) interest during this period. It is wise to pay as much as possible during forbearance so the interest won't snowball.

William D. Ford Federal Direct Loan Program

In this program, eligible students borrow directly from the federal government through a Department of Education program at participating schools. Loan terms and amounts are similar to the Federal Stafford Loans. Information is available at: www.ed.gov/DirectLoan/index.html, or from your financial aid office.

Federal Perkins Loan

This program for the exceptionally financially needy was formerly called the National Direct Student Loan (NDSL) program. U.S. citizens and permanent residents are eligible. The maximum annual loan amount is $6,000. Students may borrow up to a total of $40,000 for undergraduate and graduate schools. The interest rate is 5% and there are no loan-origination or loan-guarantee fees. No interest accrues while in school or during the nine-month grace period following graduation. Recipients may qualify for up to three years of economic-hardship deferment. Loans must be repaid within 10 years after beginning repayment. Because this program has relatively limited funding, it is unusual for students to get a Federal Perkins Loan every year. Up to 70% of the debt can be canceled for Peace Corps or Vista service. For more information, see the "Student Guide" (in English and Spanish) at www.ed.gov/prog_info/SFA/StudentGuide, or fax: (800) 443-3243; TTY: (800) 730-8913.

Health Professions Loans

These are need-based programs. Although the medical student will be the official borrower, applicants must supply information about their parents' income and finances, since it is designed for the neediest students.

Loans for Disadvantaged Students (LDS)

This program provides long-term, low-interest loans to full-time, financially needy students from disadvantaged backgrounds. According to the federal government, an individual from a disadvantaged background is a person "who comes from an environment that has inhibited the individual from obtaining the knowledge, skill, and abilities required to enroll in and graduate from a health professions school . . . or comes from a family with an annual income below a level based on low-income thresholds according to family size published by the U.S. Bureau of Census, adjusted annually for changes in the Consumer Price Index, and adjusted by the Secretary, HHS, for use in health professions."

Recipients must be citizens or nationals of the United States, or lawful permanent residents of the United States, Commonwealth of Puerto Rico, Northern Mariana Islands, Virgin Islands, Guam, American Samoa, or Trust Territory of the Pacific. Students who remain in this country on a student or visitor's visa are not eligible.

Application for these loans is through the medical school, which selects loan recipients, determines need, and provides loans that do not exceed the cost of attendance (tuition and reasonable educational and living expenses).

The loans remain interest-free during medical school, residency, two years of fellowship, and three years in a uniformed service or the Peace Corps. The interest rate during repayment is 5%. The loan must be repaid within 10 years after completing school. There is no service obligation.

Primary Care Loan (PCL)

While this is a need-based loan, applicants do not have to be "disadvantaged." U.S. citizens and permanent residents attending accredited U.S. medical schools are eligible. The loans remain interest-free during medical school and during an eligible primary care residency. The interest rate during repayment is 5%. The loan must be repaid within 10 years after completing school.

Recipients must complete an ACGME- or AOA-approved primary care (family practice, general internal medicine, general pediatrics, combined medicine–pediatrics, or preventive medicine) residency no later than four years after graduating from medical school. They must also agree to practice medicine in primary care until the loan is repaid. If a borrower fails to comply with the agreement to train in and practice primary care, the loan will accrue interest continuously at an annual rate of 18% beginning on the date of noncompliance and ending when the loan is fully repaid. If you are considering this loan, be aware of this stiff penalty for changing your specialty choice.

Medical schools select loan recipients, determine financial need, and provide loans that do not exceed the cost of attendance (tuition and reasonable educational and living expenses). Loans to third- and fourth-year students may be increased to repay outstanding balances on other loans taken out while attending that school.

Recipients must be citizens or nationals of the United States, or lawful permanent residents of the United States, Commonwealth of Puerto Rico, Northern Mariana Islands, Virgin Islands, Guam, American Samoa or Trust Territory of the Pacific. Students who remain in this country on a student or visitor's visa are not eligible.

Other Loans

Private Loans

As long as you have good credit, there are many sources of private loans for medical education. The interest rates and terms are not generally as favorable as those provided by the government or professional organizations. However, medical students with good credit ratings generally do not have difficulty getting extra money, provided that they need it and they stay within their approved financial aid budget.

MEDLOANS

The AAMC sponsors this highly regarded private loan program for full-time students who are U.S. citizens or permanent residents accepted by an AAMC-member institution (M.D.-granting U.S. medical schools). MEDLOANS allows students to access two loan programs with favorable terms and conditions: The Federal Stafford Loan program and the Alternative Loan Program (ALP), which accesses private loan sources. For more information, go to: www.aamc.org/students/medloans/start.htm. (You can also apply for these programs through the AMCAS application.) They also offer the MEDEX loan for residency interviewing, as well as relocation expenses for graduating student borrowers.

AMWA

The American Medical Women's Association Foundation has a limited fund available for loans to its student members who are enrolled in M.D. or D.O. schools and are U.S. citizens or permanent residents. They loan $2,500 annually, up to a maximum of $5,000 per student, during medical school. The interest rate is 7% and repayment begins in December following graduation. The loan must be repaid within three years. Applications are available each January on the AMWA website at www.amwa-doc.org/Foundation.

— Other Funding Sources —

Veterans Benefits

Veterans who believe they are eligible for educational benefits should contact their local or regional VA office for an application (VA Form 22-1990v).

Foreign Medical Schools and Non-U.S. Citizens

Only U.S. citizens or permanent residents are eligible for most of the financial aid, including loans targeted at medical students. A few U.S. medical schools have some funding available for foreign students.

U.S. citizens or permanent residents attending foreign medical schools or unaccredited U.S. medical schools may be eligible for Unsubsidized Stafford Loans, although the federal government currently is enforcing very restrictive rules, so many of these schools' students (especially in the Caribbean) may no longer qualify. Private loans still may be available.

Working during Medical School

Some students can successfully work during medical school to supplement their income. *Very limited* part-time work, especially if it is related to medicine, may actually be beneficial. Such jobs give you time to think seriously about matters other than schoolwork. But many students with jobs overextend themselves and subsequently have to either take a leave of absence or withdraw from school. Be careful and be warned: Any outside work must be very limited for you to succeed as a medical student—which, by itself, is a strenuous and time-consuming job.

— Paying It Back —

Some students believe that no matter how much money they borrow, they will be able to easily pay it back once they are earning a physician's salary. However, completing a residency and fellowship can take up to seven years, and large loans can be burdensome, even to those who eventually earn high wages. At this point, you may be willing "to spend whatever it takes" to go to medical school, but the choices you make in your borrowing and spending will determine how much discretionary income you will have when you graduate and have to begin paying off your loans. Jeffrey E. Hanson, Ph.D., formerly of Northwestern University, has come up with a form (Figure 18.2) that you may want to use when considering how much you borrow and spend.

The last amount is what you will have left at the end of each month. If this is a negative number, you can spend less (and, therefore, borrow less) now or you can spend less (or continue borrowing) when you get out of medical school or residency. Remember that it is much cheaper to reduce your borrowing now. Also, note the items under "What I have to pay for." Unless you want to go directly to jail (in some cases), expect to pay these bills—even if paying them does not leave you much money to buy food.

FIGURE 18.2

How Far Will My Paycheck Go?

INCOME

My annual salary/wages	$ ____________
My spouse's annual salary/wages	$ ____________
Other annual income ____________	$ ____________
Total annual income (*sum of above*)	$ ____________
TOTAL MONTHLY INCOME (*total annual income ÷ 12*)	$ ____________(1)

WHAT I HAVE TO PAY FOR

Taxes (*assume 1/3 of Total Monthly Income*)	$ ____________
Employment benefits (*e.g., your share of medical insurance, etc.*)	$ ____________
My monthly student loan payment (*assume a monthly payment of $125 for every $10,000 you owe*)	$ ____________
My spouse's monthly student loan payment	$ ____________
My total monthly credit card payment (*assume monthly payment is 2% of total credit card balance and include all other personal debt payments*)	$ ____________
My spouse's total monthly credit card payment	$ ____________
TOTAL OF WHAT I HAVE TO PAY EACH MONTH (*sum of above*)	$ ____________(2)

DISCRETIONARY MONTHLY INCOME

Total monthly income ((1) *from Box 1*)	$ ____________
Total monthly required payments ((2) *from Box 2*)	$ ____________
TOTAL MONEY AVAILABLE FOR LIVING EXPENSES [*(1)–(2)*]	$ ____________(3)

WHAT I WANT TO PAY FOR

Housing (*e.g., rent, mortgage*)	$ ____________
Utilities/telephone	$ ____________
Food	$ ____________
Transportation (*e.g., car payment(s), parking fees, insurance, gas, upkeep, bus fare*)	$ ____________
Clothing	$ ____________
Insurance (*e.g., home, life, medical, dental*)	$ ____________
Retirement investments (*financial planners recommend saving 10% of gross monthly income*)	$ ____________
Other personal expenses (*e.g., entertainment, vacations, pet care, personal care*)	$ ____________
TOTAL OF WHAT I WANT TO PAY EACH MONTH (*sum of above*)	$ ____________(4)

AMOUNT OF MONEY I HAVE LEFT OVER EACH MONTH [*(3)–(4)*] $ ____________

This form reproduced with permission: Jeffrey E. Hanson, Ph.D. (formerly of Northwestern University).

Why NOT to Go into Medicine for Money

One aspect of entering medicine, which is rarely, if ever, spoken about except in a humorous fashion, is the expected financial remuneration. While it may be both noble and consistent with the values that bring people into the medical field to try to ignore financial considerations, it is unrealistic.

For physicians, it can be said that money is the root of all, or at least much, sadness. Certain aspects of medical practice make it extremely attractive to individuals who have experienced or who fear economic instability in their lives. Among these are the facts that:

- Medicine is one of the most consistently lucrative of all professions.
- Some specialists make extraordinary incomes.
- U.S.-trained physicians are rarely involuntarily unemployed.

Individuals who enter medicine for these reasons often are disappointed, depressed, and unhappy as physicians. The additional money does not make up for having to shoulder the responsibilities, work the long hours, or bear the stresses of being a physician. Those who choose high-paying specialties solely for the income usually become very discontented practitioners.

Physicians who remain happy in their work are those who derive satisfaction from their work, and not from the monetary rewards. Remember, being a medical professional is a lifelong commitment, not a short-term goal.

Residents'/Fellows' Salaries

Unlike nearly all other aspiring professionals, residents never negotiate their salary—it is fixed in advance. Generally, institutions give the same salary to all residents in the same postgraduate year of training. Yet, salaries can vary considerably among institutions and regions of the country. In general, PGY-1 residents will receive the highest average salary, about $38,000, in the Northeastern United States and the lowest, about $34,000, in the West. Salaries rise about 5% per year during training. Housestaff salaries have actually remained fairly constant over the last 35 years, if adjusted for inflation.

Residents' salaries should be compared to the cost of living in particular locales. Residents may have difficulty "making ends meet" in Washington, D.C.; San Francisco; Boston; New York City; and parts of Los Angeles, even with relatively high salaries. However, much lower salaries may allow for a nice lifestyle in many smaller, southern, or midwestern cities.

Practicing Physicians' Salaries

Many medical students seem to believe that their educational investment will pay off handsomely. More than one-third of graduating medical students expect to be earning more than $200,000 annually within 10 years of completing their postgraduate training. However, based on what it costs for a medical education, the "hours-adjusted net present value" of the money invested in education is $10.73 for attorneys, $10.40 for procedure-based physicians, $8.90 for dentists, $8.27 for businessmen, and only $5.97 for primary care physicians. After their mid-20s, lawyers, businessmen, and dentists also work fewer hours than do physicians.

In general, the surgical specialties are the most lucrative. And the differences between the income of a surgeon and his or her nonsurgical colleague can be truly amazing. This is because, at present, the insurance payment schemes reward *doing* (procedures) at a much higher level than *thinking* (cognition). While pediatricians have median annual incomes of about $126,000, orthopedic surgeons earn more than twice as much (Figure 18.3). Recent estimates are that new internists get only one-fourth to one-half the starting salary of those physicians trained in procedurally or technically oriented areas. Repeated attempts to rectify this have proved fruitless.

If the past is any indicator, the disparity between doers and thinkers will persist. For example, a major income realignment was to have occurred in the early 1990s with the implementation of the Resource Based Relative Value Scale (RBRVS). Despite predictions from the government, American Medical Association, and other reputable sources that primary care practitioners would benefit, they didn't. The changing health care environment, however, should eventually decrease the income of and need for many specialists. So far, this has not been widespread. In general, though, managed care

FIGURE 18.3

Physicians' Median Annual Income after Expenses and before Taxes

SPECIALTY	INCOME
Orthopedic Surgery	$ 280,000
Radiology	250,000
General Surgery	215,000
Anesthesiology	210,000
Obstetrics & Gynecology	200,000
Emergency Medicine	184,000
Pathology	184,000
Neurology	170,000
All Physicians	**160,000**
General Internal Medicine	140,000
Family Practice	130,000
Psychiatry	130,000
Pediatrics	126,000

Adapted from: American Medical Association. *Physician Socioeconomic Statistics 2000–2002.* Chicago, IL: AMA, 2002.

organizations try to keep their patients away from medical specialists who cost more than primary care practitioners.

Other changes may also affect the incomes of certain specialists. Recent rules concerning physician reimbursement have severely reduced the income of clinical pathologists. The government unilaterally disallowed payment for a large portion of their practice. This, as is usually the case, was followed by a similar move by all other insurers. The government is now seriously looking at making similar changes in reimbursement for other hospital-based specialists, such as anesthesiologists, radiologists, and emergency physicians. How this will affect their income is uncertain.

Then there is the malpractice insurance dilemma, cycling from merely being uncomfortable to a crisis level. It will continue to affect some specialties until broad tort reform is enacted. In some locales, obstetricians still find it difficult to deliver babies at a cost that new families can afford, while paying the ever-increasing premiums for their malpractice insurance. In many cases, family practitioners have completely stopped doing obstetrics, outpatient orthopedics, and surgery. Radiologists have recently joined the luckless group of the most frequently sued specialties, mainly because of the risks of inaccurately reading mammograms. Neurosurgeons, plastic surgeons, and many other specialists now face similar large increases in the already astronomical cost of malpractice insurance. While the highest-income specialties are still lucrative, even after subtracting the malpractice premium cost, the net remuneration is not quite as attractive as it would first appear.

Overall, physicians earning the highest net income live in metropolitan areas with fewer than one million people, are not in solo practice, are not linked to a managed care group, and are between 46 and 55 years old.

The Importance of Income

A final note is necessary concerning the importance of income at various career stages. For the entry-level physician, income is extremely important. This makes sense, since most new physicians have enormous debts, no money, and increasing financial responsibilities. At mid-career, however, income is of only medium importance, with job security being the most important factor keeping the physician in practice. At this stage of a physician's career, job satisfaction is equally as important as income. Job satisfaction becomes of overwhelming importance for physicians in the last third of their careers. Those

FIGURE 18.4

Influence of Indebtedness as It Relates to Medical Students' Career Choices*

	Minor/Moderate	Major
Debt <$50,000		
General specialty	24%	2%
Medical specialty	19	5
Surgical specialty	19	3
Support specialty	24	5
Debt $50–$75,000		
General specialty	18	5
Medical specialty	29	5
Surgical specialty	28	7
Support specialty	36	12
Debt >$75,000		
General specialty	33	8
Medical specialty	31	8
Surgical specialty	34	14
Support specialty	39	20

*The percentage of medical students who felt that the amount of their debt had played a "Minor/Moderate" or a "Major" role in their specialty choice. No row's percentages equal 100%, showing that for many students, this is not an important consideration.

Adapted from: Kassebaum DG, Szenas PL. Relationship between indebtedness and the specialty choices of graduating medical students. *Acad Med.* 1992;67:700-7.

who have high job satisfaction presumably keep working longer than those who do not, and have more fun while they are working.

Debt and Specialty Choice

No one has consistently shown that medical students make career choices based on their level of debt. However, some studies, such as that shown in Figure 18.4, suggest a trend in that direction. While this is the most recent detailed data available, a 2001 AAMC survey showed that as the level of their educational debt increased, more medical students found that it swayed their specialty choices. Most of the highest-paying specialties, though, have also been the most difficult to enter. Perhaps many medical students simply are attracted to those specialties, or by the promise of a nice income, whether or not they have large debts.

— Conclusion —

The bottom line is to:

- Make certain that your credit rating is good.
- Complete your income tax forms early for the year before you want to enter medical school.
- Get financial aid information from the medical schools to which you are applying.
- Complete the loan application forms and scholarship agreements (if any) and submit them as quickly as possible, but definitely before their "priority" deadline.
- Apply for any other programs that interest you (such as HPSP or NHSC schoslarships).
- Conduct your own search for additional funding sources.
- Carefully read the fine print on all loan and scholarship papers.
- Be prepared to live within the budget prescribed by the financial aid office.
- Be certain about your commitment to a medical career before signing any loan papers. Ask yourself if it is worth $100,000 or more. (Climbing Mt. Everest only costs $65,000.)

19

Combined-Degree Programs

Whenever men attempt, they seem driven to overdo.

— Bernard Baruch

As if medical school weren't difficult enough, some hardy folks decide to combine their medical education with training for other advanced degrees. Whether you are interested in pursuing such a program or simply want to find out what the "gunners" are doing, this chapter discusses the available options.

— Combined M.D./D.O.–Ph.D. —

Nearly all U.S. and Canadian M.D.-granting and six D.O.-granting schools offer students the option of combining their training for a medical degree with fulfilling the requirements for a Ph.D. About 2% of all medical students graduate from such combined-degree programs. The hope is that they will form the core of the physician–scientist community, practicing medicine while pursuing the studies that will advance medical practice. In reality, most of these individuals pursue either the practice of medicine or scientific research—in part, because each is a separate and distinct world with markedly different thought processes. Time constraints also influence most of their decisions to take one or the other path. A high percentage of physician–Ph.D.'s end up on medical school faculties.

Medical schools offer Ph.D.'s in many disciplines. Some only offer them in medically related sciences, while others also offer programs in other disciplines. For M.D.-granting schools, the AAMC's online *Curriculum Directory* (http://services.aamc.org/currdir/section3/start.cfm) lists some combined-degree programs, and can be searched either by the type of program or by the school. However, it is updated only periodically, does not list most non-Ph.D. programs, and does not list programs at Osteopathic medical schools. The AAMC's annual *Medical School Admission Requirements* also has a (more or less) up-to-date chart listing each school's Ph.D. science areas. Ph.D.'s in nonscience subjects should contact each school directly. If the school is part of or affiliated with a larger university, get the graduate school's catalog for a list of Ph.D. subject areas.

Applicants must inquire directly to find out which nonscience Ph.D.'s each medical school offers. In some cases, nonscience Ph.D.'s are awarded through adjacent campuses or schools, and are limited only by the degrees such schools offer and their faculty's flexibility. Those interested in combined D.O.–Ph.D. programs must directly contact the individual schools for more information. (See Figure 19.1 for a list of programs.)

The method of applying to combined medical degree–Ph.D. programs depends upon the individual school(s) and graduate programs involved. In some cases, applicants must take not only the MCAT, but also the General and Subject Graduate Record Examinations (GREs). In most cases, admission into both medical school and the Ph.D. program requires two different applications and two sets of interviews. Applicants may be accepted to one, both, or neither program. At some institutions, after combined-degree applicants are interviewed, they are removed from consideration for the medical degree-only program.

If you apply to a combined-degree program, do not accept a position until they guarantee your funding in writing. Once you accept a position, begin searching immediately for a faculty adviser. Don't wait until you get onto the medical campus. This will markedly speed your progress through the Ph.D. portion of the program. Select someone who is well-known in the field, personable, and available. It helps if they have no plans to leave the school anytime soon.

While the campus tour is of only moderate importance to typical medical school applicants, it is extremely important to those considering a combined medical degree–Ph.D. program. Are the library facilities, including the hours they are open, adequate? Do they have extensive online services? Are the laboratories (or other facilities you need if pursuing a nonscience Ph.D.) modern and up-to-date? While most medical students can complete their degree in any environment, Ph.D. candidates have a specific performance task (their dissertation) and must have the facilities to complete it.

Questions you should anticipate when interviewing for these programs are:

- What research have you done or are you doing now? This is the number one question. If you can't answer it adequately, forget about applying to these programs. An "adequate" answer includes being specific about your contribution to the research, why the research was done, what theories supported doing it, and the (potential) implications of the results.
- Why do you need or want both degrees?
- What are your research interests?
- How will you have enough time to pursue both careers? No one has yet discovered a truly adequate answer to this question.

Funding

Several methods exist for funding your medical degree–Ph.D. education. The two that usually provide the best funding are the Medical Scientist Training Program (MSTP) and Minority Access to Research Careers (MARC)—both oriented toward earning a science Ph.D.

Medical Scientist Training Program (MSTP)

Formal federal support for combined M.D.–Ph.D. programs is provided through the Medical Scientist Training Program (MSTP). The National Institute of General Medical Sciences supports programs, now at 40 medical schools, that provide both basic and clinical science training to highly motivated students with outstanding research and academic potential. A list of these schools, with links to their websites, is at www.nigms.nih.gov/funding/mstp.html. A 1998 study showing how successful previous MSTP graduates have been can be found online at www.nigms.nih.gov/news/reports/mstpstudy/mstpstudy.html.

If accepted, students receive tuition and approximately $20,000 each year for up to six years, although their course of study may be longer (as of 2003). There are about 150 new positions each year, and the competition for them is fierce. Applicants must be U.S. citizens or permanent residents. For further information regarding the MSTP and a current list of participating medical schools, contact: MSTP, Program Administrator, National Institute of General Medical Sciences, 45 Center Drive MSC 6200, Bethesda, MD 20892-6200; (301) 594-3830. Contact individual schools for their additional information.

Minority Access to Research Careers (MARC)

The Minority Access to Research Careers (MARC) program is similar to MTSP, except that it was created for underrepresented minority students. Grants are given to schools whose student body is primarily drawn from underrepresented minorities. The schools then distribute the money so that selected students can pursue studies leading to a Ph.D. and a research career. For a list of participating schools, go to www.nigms.nih.gov/funding/marc.html (note that not all schools offer combined medical degrees), or write: Director, MARC Program, National Institute of General Medical Sciences, 45 Center Drive MSC 6200, Bethesda, MD 20892-6200.

Other Programs

Don't limit your search to just federally funded programs. Many (if not most) schools with combined programs offer participants funding similar to that from the MSTP; the money just comes from other sources. If you find a program that otherwise meets your needs, contact the school to find out about available funding.

— Combined Medicine–Law Degrees —

Thirteen schools have official combined medicine–law programs, although other schools may be willing to consider this combination. In the latter case, applicants will need to go through the entire and separate admission procedures of the law and medical schools, and then arrange to have adequate blocks of time to complete each curriculum. This can be very difficult, but it has been done. A J.D. degree can normally be completed in three years, with the first year being the toughest.

See Figure 19.1 for a list of programs. Contact the schools' admission offices for more information (see *Appendix E*).

— Combined M.D.–Oral and Maxillofacial Surgery —

Two schools offer dentists an opportunity to simultaneously obtain their M.D. and credentials in oral and maxillofacial surgery (Figure 19.1). These six-year programs combine class work with the required specialty residency program.

— Combined Medical–Master's Degrees —

About 1% of all medical students graduate from programs combining master's and medical degrees. The two most common are medical degrees combined with either a Master of Business Administration (M.B.A.) or a Master of Public Health (M.P.H.). With the increasing involvement of physicians in medical management, some medical schools now offer a combined medical degree with a Master of Health Administration (M.H.A.).

Many schools offer the opportunity to obtain either an M.S. or an M.A. in a variety of disciplines while pursuing a medical degree. Students must usually arrange these on their own. Formalized combined programs include master's degrees in Management, Divinity, Geriatric Medicine, Engineering, and Informatics. The programs are listed in Figure 19.1.

Medical Degree–M.B.A./M.H.A.

With the marked changes in health care delivery systems, it has become evident that more physicians should be fluent in business terminology and techniques. Students often ask me whether it is worthwhile spending the extra time to also get an M.B.A. while going through medical school, and whether residency directors will see this as a positive or a negative factor. My advice has been that since physicians are, in general, poorly prepared to be leaders in health care systems, and since these systems run on business, not medical, principles, an M.B.A. is indeed worthwhile. Forward-looking residency directors, especially those who have had significant administrative experience or have dealt frequently with managed care organizations, will undoubtedly view this education in a very positive light.

Forty-six schools offer an official program leading to a combined medical degree–M.B.A. Each has different admission requirements and curricula. The differences in their M.B.A. curricula are much greater than among law school curricula. Investigate M.B.A. programs very carefully before applying to schools. The normal length of study for an M.B.A. degree is two years.

The Masters in Health Administration is a similar degree. How it differs from an M.B.A. will be unique to each program. In some cases, it will be essentially the same program, but oriented to medically related problems. Twelve medical schools now offer an M.H.A. or a similar combined-degree program.

See Figure 19.1 for a list of programs. Contact each school's admission office for more information (see *Appendix E*).

Medical Degree–M.P.H./M.S.P.H.

Physicians often get a Master of Public Health (M.P.H.) or Master of Science in Public Health (M.S.P.H.) degree to study epidemiology, to broaden their understanding of public health issues, or to fulfill the requirements of a residency in public health, aerospace medicine, or preventive medicine. Fifty-nine medical schools now offer M.P.H. or M.S.P.H. degrees in a formal combined program also leading to a medical degree (Figure 19.1).

— Pros and Cons of Combined-Degree Programs —

When considering a combined-degree program, first look at the positive and negative aspects of such a program. Also, ask yourself whether you are pursuing the second degree to enhance your medical career or to avoid it. (The latter reason is okay. But then you need to ask yourself: Why get a medical degree at all; why not simply get the degree that best meets your needs?)

Pros

- Prepares you for a career in academia, research, law, medical administration, or other endeavors, depending upon your second degree.
- M.D./Ph.D.'s often have an advantage when applying for grants.
- Prestige within academia.
- Affords more options and opportunities than simply having an M.D. or a D.O.

Cons

- Big (long) commitment.
- No guarantee that you will be able to use the skills gained from your other degree when you finish, since there is decreasing funding for research, too many lawyers and administrators, and a marked discrepancy between physicians' and most other professionals' salaries.
- You will be a different person when you finish. Seven or more years is a long time, and you may not want to do research, practice/teach law, or do medical administration when you finish. Or, you may not want to practice medicine.
- An M.D. or D.O. degree already provides a vast number of career options, including research and medical administration.
- You will be very poor for a long time.
- Using your combined degree often means residing in a relatively large city.

— Applying to a Combined-Degree Program —

"Other degree" interviews require special preparation. Do a database search using Medline, CancerLine, or a similar online tool to find publications by the faculty at the other program. You can access these databases through your local medical school and many university libraries. Use *Westlaw* or *Lexis* for the J.D. programs. These can be accessed through a local law school, some university libraries, or a friendly lawyer.

These searches allow you to identify specific faculty members sharing your interests. It looks very good on your application to say that you are applying to that school's program "because, like Professor Potatohead, I have a strong interest in investigating the mitochondrial activity of the spud." In addition, since some programs allow you to pick your interviewers for the "other" degree, you will have an idea about what the interviewers do, so you can intelligently converse with them.

This additional investigation is particularly useful for medical degree–Ph.D. programs. They want to see that an individual has a firm commitment to a life of research, not just to the $200,000 or more in tuition and stipends they will get while in the program.

Particularly at combined-degree programs, expect to have some interviews conducted by current students. These, as well as other nonmedical interviews, may be "blind" by design or because of the interviewer's own laziness. A "blind" interview is one in which the interviewer has not seen any of your application materials and must gather all information in the interview. (It is a very poor and sloppy interview method.) You may have to answer questions that you have already answered in your application materials.

In combined-degree interviews, you may have some questions of your own to ask. For example:

1. Can I begin my research or any required projects before I formally begin classes? (Implies you are a dynamo who can't wait to start.)
2. How much time do most students take to get both degrees? (Unlike the typical medical school program, many of these programs have more flexible timetables—although the funding is usually not flexible.)
3. How much leeway do I have about with whom I will work?
4. How flexible is the schedule?
5. How are the two programs integrated?

You will, of course, also want to ask the questions about the medical degree program that are listed in Chapter 24.

Combined-degree programs can offer you additional career choices, but you must consider the amount of time (and income) you sacrifice to get a second degree. Before you set out on this course, ask yourself whether you are interested enough to make the necessary sacrifices.

FIGURE 19.1

Schools Offering Formal Combined-Degree Programs

Ph.D.

- Nearly all U.S. and Canadian M.D.-granting medical schools
- D.O.-granting schools: Chicago COM; Michigan State University COM; Ohio University COM; Philadelphia COM; Texas COM; UMDNJ–School of Osteopathic Medicine

J.D.

Case Western Reserve SOM
Duke SOM
Nova Southeastern Univ. (Master of Health Law)
Southern Illinois Univ.
UMDNJ–NJ Med. Sch.
UMDNJ–Sch. Osteo. Med.
Univ. Chicago Pritzker SOM
Univ. Minnesota Med. Sch., Minneapolis
Univ. Pennsylvania SOM
Univ. Puerto Rico
Vanderbilt SOM
Yale Univ.

Oral and Maxillofacial Surgery

Univ. Texas Houston
Mayo Medical School

M.B.A.

Baylor Coll. of Med.
Boston Univ. SOM
Case Western Reserve Univ. SOM
Columbia Univ. Coll. Physicians and Surgeons
Dartmouth Medical School
Drexel Univ. Coll. of Med.
Duke Univ. SOM
East Carolina Univ. SOM
Georgetown Univ.
Howard Univ.
Indiana Univ. SOM
Jefferson Medical College
McGill Univ. Faculty of Med.
Medical College of Ohio
New York COM/NYIT
Northwestern Univ. Med. Sch.
Nova Southeastern Univ.
Ohio State Univ.
Ohio Univ. COM
Philadelphia COM
St. Louis Univ. SOM
SUNY–Buffalo
Temple Univ. SOM
Texas Tech Univ.
Tufts Univ. SOM
UMDNJ–NJ Med. Sch.
UMDNJ–Robert Wood Johnson Med. Sch.
Univ. Calgary
UC–Davis
UC–Irvine
UC–Los Angeles
UC–San Diego
Univ. Chicago Pritzker SOM
Univ. Cincinnati Coll. of Med.
Univ. Colorado
Univ. Connecticut
Univ. Health Sciences COM
Univ. Kentucky Coll. of Med.

(continued)

FIGURE 19.1 (continued)

M.B.A., cont'd.

Univ. Michigan Med. Sch. Univ.
Univ. Minnesota Med. Sch., Minneapolis
Univ. Pennsylvania SOM
Univ. Rochester
USC Keck SOM
Vanderbilt SOM
Wake Forest Univ. SOM
Yale Univ.

M.P.H./M.S.P.H.

Boston Univ. SOM
Case Western Reserve SOM
Columbia Univ. Coll. Physicians and Surgeons
Cornell Univ.
Des Moines Univ. COM
Drexel Univ. Coll. of Med.
Duke Univ. SOM
Eastern Virginia Med. Sch.
Emory Univ. SOM
George Washington Univ.
Harvard Medical School
Indiana Univ. SOM
Jefferson Medical College
Kirksville COM
LSU–New Orleans
Medical College of Ohio
Medical College of Virginia
Morehouse SOM
Mount Sinai
New York Medical College
Northwestern Univ. Med. Sch.
Nova Southeastern Univ.
Ohio State Univ.
Oregon Health & Science Univ.
Philadelphia COM
St. Louis Univ. SOM
SUNY–Buffalo
SUNY–Downstate
Temple Univ. SOM
Texas COM
Tufts Univ. SOM
Tulane Univ. SOM
UMDNJ–NJ Med. Sch.
UMDNJ–Sch. Osteo. Med.
Univ. Arizona Coll. of Med.
UC–Davis
UCLA
UC–San Diego
UC–San Francisco
Univ. Calgary
Univ. Connecticut
Univ. Illinois Coll. of Med.
Univ. Kansas SOM
Univ. Kentucky Coll. of Med.
Univ. Minnesota–Duluth
Univ. Minnesota Med. Sch., Minneapolis
Univ. Michigan Med. Sch.
Univ. North Carolina, Chapel Hill
Univ. North Dakota
Univ. Oklahoma
Univ. Pittsburgh SOM
Univ. Rochester
USC Keck SOM
Univ. South Carolina
Univ. Texas, Houston
Univ. Texas, Southwestern
Univ. Utah SOM
Vanderbilt SOM
Yale Univ.

M.S. or M.A.

Arizona COM
Case Western Reserve SOM
Duke Univ. SOM
Kirksville COM
Michigan State Univ. COM
Michigan State Univ.
Medical College of Ohio
New York COM/NYIT
Ohio Univ. COM
Tulane Univ. SOM
Tufts Univ. SOM
UMDNJ–NJ Med. Sch.
UMDNJ–Robert Wood Johnson Med. Sch.
Univ. Montréal
Univ. Calgary
UC–Davis
UC–San Francisco
Univ. Hawaii
Univ. Manitoba Faculty of Medicine
Univ. Maryland SOM
Univ. Missouri–Columbia
Univ. North Dakota
Univ. Oklahoma
Univ. Pittsburgh SOM
Univ. Rochester
Univ. Virginia
Vanderbilt SOM
Wake Forest Univ. SOM
Washington Univ. SOM (MO)
Western Univ of Hlth. Sci. COM of the Pacific

Master of Health Administration

Des Moines Univ. COM
Jefferson Medical College
Kirksville COM
Medical College of Virginia
Ohio State Univ.
Ohio Univ. COM
UMDNJ–Robert Wood Johnson Med. Sch.
UMDNJ–SOM (Master of Public Administration)
Univ. Calgary
Univ. Kansas SOM (M.H.S.A.)
Univ. Minnesota Med. Sch., Minneapolis
Univ. Oklahoma

Master of Biomedical Engineering
Tufts Univ.

Master of Public Policy
Duke Univ. SOM
Harvard Med. Sch.

Master of Management
Univ. Alabama SOM

Master of Divinity
Yale Univ.

Master of Education
Case Western Reserve SOM

Master of Geriatric Medicine
Kirksville COM

Master of Informatics
UMDNJ–NJ Medical School

COM = College of Osteopathic Medicine; SOM = School of Medicine.

20

Preparing For The Visit

When we are summoned from afar,
Ourselves, and not our words will count—
Not what we said, but what we are!

— William Winter, *George Fawcett Rowe*

Before going to a medical school interview, you must learn about the school, its curriculum, and any special programs it offers. If you don't, you might just as well not go to the interview, since the interviewers will not believe that you are a serious candidate. Two sources for this information are the "School Entries" section in the AAMC's annual *Medical School Admission Requirements* and each school's online catalog and the brochures and additional papers that many schools still send to applicants. If you know, or have an opportunity to talk with, a school's current students or graduates (who may be residents at a local hospital), you may obtain additional information. Also, if you have time the night before your interview, stop by the school's medical library and glance through some recent alumni bulletins. These can provide you with valuable insights into the workings of the medical school.

— The Interview —

No matter how irrational it may seem, the 10- to 30-minute medical school interviews count for at least as much, in most cases, toward your acceptance into the medical profession as do all of your accomplishments in the previous three and a half (or more) undergraduate years. That's not just my personal belief; several recent studies have shown this to be true. When you prepare to go for interviews, put your best effort toward doing a good job. This is where it all comes together!

The Mock Interview

How well will you do when you actually sit in the hot seat, interviewing for that medical school slot you want above all others? Don't wait until you are sitting in that chair to find out! When you think that you are prepared to go out on the interview circuit, arrange for a mock interview. Doing this will make you calmer and more organized, and help you to appear more polished during the real thing.

What is a mock interview? A mock interview is to an interview as near-drowning is to drowning. In both cases, you think you are going to die, but only one actually threatens your life. Your mock interview should closely imitate the actual interview process. You must prepare for it in exactly the same way that you prepare for your real interviews. Dress the same, carry identical materials with you, and go over your interview answers just as you would before actual interviews. The mock interview should be as realistic as possible so you will get the most accurate and useful feedback. If you don't feel anxiety, you're not doing it correctly.

Who should conduct the mock interview? Ideally, your mentor (if you have one) and the premed adviser. If they are not available, ask another faculty member with interviewing experience. Tell them that you want the mock interview to be as realistic as possible; they should ask you the "difficult" questions and treat you in the same manner they would treat any applicant—not as someone they know. Then ask for feedback about the way you presented yourself, your appearance and grooming, and how you handled the questions. This should yield an overall assessment of areas to be improved upon before you hit the interview trail.

Note that a premed committee interview is not a mock interview—it's the real thing! This interview may count as much as the interviews at some medical schools. Schools take premed committee evaluations very seriously. These interviews are *not* the place to practice.

One useful technique for self-critique is to audio- or videotape the interview. Would you select the person you hear or see? What seems wrong with the applicant (you)? How can you improve your interview performance next time? As with all other parts of the application process, this takes a little extra effort. Experience has shown that it pays off in a big way.

Besides the formal mock interview, it also helps to review interview elements in your mind during those odd times when you are commuting, awaiting others, or sitting through a really boring lecture. Review anticipated questions and situations, as well as those from previous interviews. Don't sweat over past interviews; just analyze how they could have gone better. This frequent review will keep you prepared to face the next interview without too much last-minute preparation.

Timing

Applicants often have little leeway when scheduling their interviews. The best way to get an early interview (and possibly an early acceptance) is to submit all your application materials as soon as possible. Then, if your schedule permits, accept the earliest interview dates that the schools offer you. (See Figure 21.2 for individual schools' interview schedules.)

When traveling to interviews, students will inevitably miss classes and, sometimes, laboratory sessions that are hard to make up. One way to avoid this is to try to carry a lighter schedule without laboratory courses during the time you will be interviewing. If you plan your schedule far enough in advance, this is often possible. Also, be sure to explain absences to your instructors if your classes are small enough so that you will be missed.

When I interviewed for a nearby medical school, I told the teaching assistant I was only going to miss one laboratory class. When he asked why I would be gone, I told him that I would be interviewing. He told me he also would be gone that day—interviewing at the same medical school. We ended up as classmates.

— Dressing the Part —

Some medical school applicants find it distasteful to "sell out" to the establishment and dress in the manner some have referred to as a "medi-clone." If you are one of those students, think of proper attire as camouflage to hide the rebellious you in a land of "straight arrows." This is the world you want to inhabit, so begin playing by its rules.

The key here is to do what others do—but better. Yes, there is a "uniform" to wear. It is conservative, tasteful, and neat. It looks like upper-middle-class success. And it works. Of course, you wear blue jeans and sweatshirts as an undergraduate. That's fine for weekends with your friends, but now it is time for you to shine—both literally and figuratively. While people in some areas of the country (e.g., Northwest) traditionally dress more casually than in other areas, don't assume that this applies to medical school interviews. If in doubt, before you go, ask the admission office what most applicants wear to the interview.

One interviewee, medical student Scott Fishman, described this uniform as "remarkably drab . . . a ridiculous costume . . . a rite of passage." He went on to say that "sitting there waiting for our turns outside the interviewer's office, we all look like we are going to a funeral." Perhaps. But better to wear the uniform and look as if you're going to a funeral, than to not wear it and attend your own.

No, you don't have to go out and spend lots of money you don't have on clothes you can't afford. Just do what you can to get into the uniform. Ideally, interviewers should not be aware of your clothes; you want them to remember you, not what you wore. The proper dress for medical school interviews is essentially identical, no matter where in the country you are applying. Appropriate dress can help you a little; the wrong outfit can destroy you.

Men

Clothing

A suit is the standard dress for an interview. It should be solid or pinstripe, navy or gray. "The men who run America," says John T. Molloy, author of *Dress for Success*, "run it blue, gray, and dull." Do not wear a suit with bright or avant-garde colors or designs. "If you try to spruce up the look," Mr. Molloy continues, "you're in trouble."

The suit doesn't have to be expensive nor in the latest style, but it should be tailored and well-cut. If you don't have or cannot afford a suit, wear a navy-blue sport jacket with matching pants. If you don't have these either, it is time you visited a clothing store. Charge the bill to your future. Serious and solid is the image you are looking for in your outfit. And *before* you show up at your first interview, make sure that your clothes fit. Few things distract an interviewer more than an applicant fidgeting with his tight collar.

Wear either a white or pale-blue solid-color shirt. Long sleeves are in order, if you plan to remove your jacket. Avoid stripes, loud colors, or any weird designs. Shirttails should be long enough to keep the shirt tucked in, even when you raise your arms. With the top button fastened, your collar should fit snugly, but not so tightly that your eyes bulge. A friend and former resident, Peter Brown (Vermont, '94), talks about an interesting experience he had on the interview circuit.

> **Having graduated some years before, I was working full-time at an exhausting and time-consuming job with the New York City Child Protective Services. I had little time to really prepare for my medical school interviews, especially in terms of my clothes. (Being a bachelor is not always that great.) I found that I did not have a clean shirt that was ironed, and my ironing skills are, at best, rudimentary. Needing a shirt, however, I picked a clean shirt that went with my suit and simply ironed the front of the shirt. "No problem," I thought, "I'll be wearing a jacket anyway." During my first interview, the room was extremely hot and the interviewer suggested that we both remove our jackets. My eyes must have bulged at the suggestion, judging from his facial expression. Then I burst out laughing. I explained the situation to him. He began laughing too, saying that, as a bachelor himself, his shirt was probably in worse shape than mine. It was a great way to establish instant rapport.**

Peter, of course, understands that he was very lucky to have pulled this one off. He says he always made sure that he had fully ironed shirts after that.

Wear a tie—even if you are a laid-back individual. An open-neck shirt and gold chain just won't cut it. Your tie should be solid, have repeating stripes (rep), small polka dots, or repeating small insignias (club). Avoid gaudy, bright colors, large patterns, and black. The "power colors" are red and navy. Knot the tie so its tip meets the belt and put the back of the tie through the label, so the ends stay together. Do not wear a bow tie. It gives the impression that you're odd, like showing the world that you're odd, and are out of touch with this decade.

Wear black or very dark brown conservatively designed shoes. Make sure that they are in good repair and shined. Dirty shoes are male applicants' most common clothing error. Also make sure that there are no holes in your soles; if there are, be sure to keep your feet flat on the floor. Wear calf-length plain socks that match your suit.

If you wear an undershirt, a crew neck looks best, since it doesn't show through a shirt. A plain, dark leather belt with a small square buckle works well. If you wear suspenders, be sure they button to your pants. If you carry a wallet, make sure that it does not bulge out of your pocket.

Accessories

The key here is sedate. Limit jewelry to a watch and wedding band (only if you are married). If you wear a watch, avoid anything unusual such as a dive watch or one with a picture of Mickey Mouse on the front. No lapel pins, no ID bracelets, no tie clasps, and—definitely—NO EARRINGS! No matter what the protestations, that little flash of gold will cost you big points. Save it for later. Inappropriate or too much jewelry will elicit very strong negative responses.

If you wear glasses, make sure that they are in standard frames. No initials on the lenses or unusual colors. It is best not to wear tinted or photo-gray lenses, since they tend to place a barrier between you and the interviewer. Also, keep the lenses clean.

The pen and pencil you carry should look classy. They should not look like they're leftovers from your last trip to the miniature golf course. And don't stick them in a shirt-pocket protector. A serious candidate will carry a small folding, zippered, leather-covered note pad with the materials to make notes and store papers, in addition to a PDA. If you have a cell phone, *turn it off during the interview*!

Grooming

As for personal grooming, be neat, squeaky clean, and conservative. Your hair should be short. If it's shorter than you like it, it's probably close to the right length. Ask your mentor (if he or she is over 35 years old), a parent, or close (older) friend to advise you on this. Definitely, no ponytails or punk or otherwise unusual haircuts. Your hair must also be something close to a natural color. One excellent student appeared to be a "shoe-in" at a fine medical school, both on paper and during the interview. The interviewers, however, said that they couldn't avoid concentrating on his purple hair. He did not get into any medical school. Assuming that your hair is a reasonable shade, also make sure it has been very recently trimmed and washed. Invest in a good haircut about one week before the interview; new haircuts look best after one week. If you wear facial hair, avoid goatees and handlebar mustaches which have strong negative connotations. Trim and manicure your nails. Remember, you want to be a physician, putting your hands on—and in—patients.

The odor the interviewer perceives should only be that of deodorant or nervousness. Avoid after-shave; you are not going on a date. If you are concerned about your breath, carry breath mints. If you smoke, quit! If you cannot quit in time for your interviews, do not smoke once you shower for the day. Few medical school faculty or physicians smoke; they will be able to smell the smoke on you and your clothes, and this will count heavily against you. And, above all, no alcohol within 24 hours of the interview. There are enough perceived and anticipated problems with drug and alcohol abuse in the medical field. You do not want to show the interviewers that you could be part of the problem.

The bottom line is that you want to look as much like a successful upper-middle-class physician as possible. That's the direction in which you wish to head. Wear the garments symbolizing the successful individual in our society. There is no need to flaunt your lifestyle in your dress. Leave your personal preferences out of this. They can only harm you.

Women

Clothing

Although styles are changing in the workplace, the standard dress for a woman going to an interview is still the suit. In this case, it is a skirted suit. A good skirted suit suggests that you are an upper-middle-class professional—just the image you want to project. Don't be led down the path to destruction by following fads or fashion. The classic suit is the uniform of success. Find out what woman accountants or lawyers who work for large firms wear. This will be the "classic" style.

In purchasing a suit, choose wool, linen, or a synthetic that simulates either. The fabric should be solid, tweed, or plaid. For solid suits, the three best colors are gray (a couple of shades lighter than charcoal), medium-range blue, and dark maroon. Stay away from bold, flashy patterns. The skirt should extend to just below the knee (no miniskirts!) and the matching jacket should be a blazer cut with long sleeves.

Two alternatives to the suit are a tailored dress or a skirt worn with a jacket. Neither is as powerful as the suit, but if you do not feel comfortable in a suit, these are two reasonable substitutes.

The blouse should be simply cut, not too frilly or lacy, and the neckline must not be too low. If it's equivalent to a man's shirt with one button open, it will be acceptable. The blouse should be cotton, silk, or a look-alike synthetic. Usually, it will be white, cream, or pastel—not red or fuchsia. In general, it should be in a solid color that complements the suit.

Shoes should be simple pumps, closed at the toe and heel, and not brand new. They should be in a dark or neutral color that is compatible with your suit. The heels should not be more than 1½ inches high. Do not wear boots. Most medical school applicants will be doing a lot of walking around the medical center; be sure that you will survive in the shoes you wear.

Accessories

Although a scarf is not as essential as a man's tie, it can be eye-catching if used properly. Wear silk or a look-alike synthetic and tie it in an ascot, necktie, or scout style. If worn, a scarf must have simple lines and no frills to detract from the center of attention—your face. Hosiery should be skin-colored.

As with men, the less jewelry that you wear the better. Aside from a simple watch (plain gold or silver) and wedding ring, be careful about what other ornaments you wear. While a brooch or a simple necklace with very simple earrings are often suitable, multiple rings, bracelets, or anything ornate or gaudy is not. The current fad of wearing multiple earrings may be looked at with some disfavor by conservative interviewers. NO NOSE RINGS! (The only exception is if you are an East Indian woman for whom a nose ring is generally accepted. Still, think twice about wearing it to interviews, especially in the South or Midwest.)

If you need to wear an overcoat, make sure that it is long enough to cover the bottom of your skirt. Many coat styles are acceptable—furs are not. If you wear gloves, make them leather. They should match your coat in color.

Do not carry a purse. Carry a leather zippered case or attaché case for any necessities, including a small leather-covered note pad. This connotes power and authority. Put everything that you need in it. But do not overstuff it or keep it sloppy—you may have to open it during an interview.

Grooming

As for the more personal items, such as hair, makeup, and perfume, just remember that you are going to a business interview, not on a date. (The important "business" is, of course, getting into medical school.) If the interviewer is aware that you are wearing perfume, you are wearing too much. Similarly with makeup—it works best when it is not obvious. Be especially careful to avoid obvious eye shadow, eyeliner, or gaudy lipstick. Nails should be manicured. Your hair should be clean and conservative in appearance. If it is long, it may be a good idea to put it up to keep it from looking sloppy. Many consultants recommend that women should avoid hairstyles that cover either eye, and that their hair should be pulled away from the jaw line and ears so they will look more serious.

The bottom line is that you dress for the interview in a uniform. Although there is considerable variation allowed, for maximum success, applicants should adhere to the standard style. As one woman who did very well in her interviews said about the wardrobe, "sophistication and maturity are the keys to success."

Clothing as Camouflage

Clothes can hide real or perceived problems. For those "Doogie Howser" types who think they look too young to be taken seriously, dressing conservatively will age you a bit. Wearing glasses, even if you normally wear contacts, also helps.

Some people are self-conscious about their weight. Clothes can help disguise those extra pounds. Both men and women can wear suit jackets slightly longer than normal, and women can wear a loose jacket over a business dress or flared skirt. The key is to be certain that your clothes fit well. Even thin people look heavy if their buttons are popping out or their collar is too tight.

Wear the "Uniform" Stylishly

Now that you have acquired the uniform, make sure that you get the most out of it. Your clothes must appear neat, clean, and pressed. Do *not* travel in your clothes and show up five minutes before the interview looking like a Raggedy Anne doll that has gone through the washer. If possible, arrive at the interview city the night before, having traveled in your normal attire. You will get a good night's sleep and put on your freshly pressed uniform the next morning to go to the interview. Take the appropriate garments, such as overcoat, umbrella, etc., to protect your uniform in case of inclement weather. When you get to the interview site, slip into the restroom for a last-minute inspection.

Once you dress correctly for your interview, forget about your clothes. They should be a natural part of you. Think of these clothes like new hiking boots. You don't want to go 20 miles in a new pair without breaking them in first. If you aren't comfortable in these fancy duds, wear them a few times before you hit the interview trail.

— Packing for the Interview Trip —

When packing for interviews, especially now with strict airport security, your motto should be "less is more." Sophisticated travelers decrease the amount they carry by making sure that all their clothes are coordinated, by packing clothes that can serve more than one function, and by avoiding the tendency to pack for every possible eventuality that could happen on the trip. Remember to include a small sewing kit for emergency repairs.

Packing lists ease pretrip anxieties. Once you decide what to take with you on one trip, analyze your list, modify it, and then use the same packing list for subsequent trips. That way you won't forget anything. Keep the list with you to serve as a record of your belongings in case your bags are lost.

Whether you use a large suitcase or a small carryon, your clothes should arrive intact and as pristine as possible. To accomplish this, place trousers, skirts, dresses, shirts, blouses, and jackets (all zipped or buttoned, and folded along their natural seams) in the suitcase, alternating side to side. Suits will stay at their best if they are first placed in a plastic dry cleaner's bag. Lay all items partially in the suitcase, and then fold the remainder inside, one garment over the other (Figure 20.1). Each item will then cushion the others and help prevent creases. Pack shoes, stuffed with toiletries, socks, etc., along the hinged side of the bag. Finally, stuff rolled T-shirts, undergarments, sleepwear, and sweaters in any available space to cushion the contents and keep them from shifting. The result should be neat and clean clothing. Pack any small items in plastic bags so security can easily see them without pawing through your bag.

Use Carryon, If Possible

One danger of flying is that your checked baggage won't show up—at least not in time to do you any good. The fact that it appears back at your home the day after the interview is little consolation for being forced to dress in "low camp" style for the interview at your most desired school. The solution, especially if you are only going to be away from home for one or two days, is to use a carryon suit bag and an under-the-seat bag. This saves you from having to retrieve your bags at the airport and alleviates any worry about losing your uniform.

It is *essential* to carry interview schedules, airline tickets, travelers' checks, credit cards, driver's license, jewelry, hotel and automobile confirmations, airline schedules, medications, and telephone numbers and addresses for your travel agent and your interviews with you. (I have seen more than one distraught applicant who had lost the suitcase containing their interview materials, not to mention their clothes.)

Be careful when choosing your carryon bags. Each airline, and even each plane or configuration of seats on a particular airline, has a different allowable space for carryons. These days, traveling with as little baggage as possible is the best bet. Most airlines now limit you to one carryon bag and a personal item, such as a purse or a briefcase/computer. It is wise to check with a travel agent or the airline to avoid bringing bags that won't fit in the overhead bin or under the seat. If possible, get a rolling carryon and a garment bag that attaches to it. That may save some strain on your back.

Honesty Works (The Sympathy and Uniqueness Votes)

Okay, so you weren't able to use the carryon method—and now your baggage is somewhere between here and Outer Mongolia. You have an interview in three hours and are wearing hand-me-downs from a backwoods orphanage. What should you do?

FIGURE 20.1

Packing a Suitcase

Before packing, every garment should be buttoned, zippered, belted, and folded along natural creases.

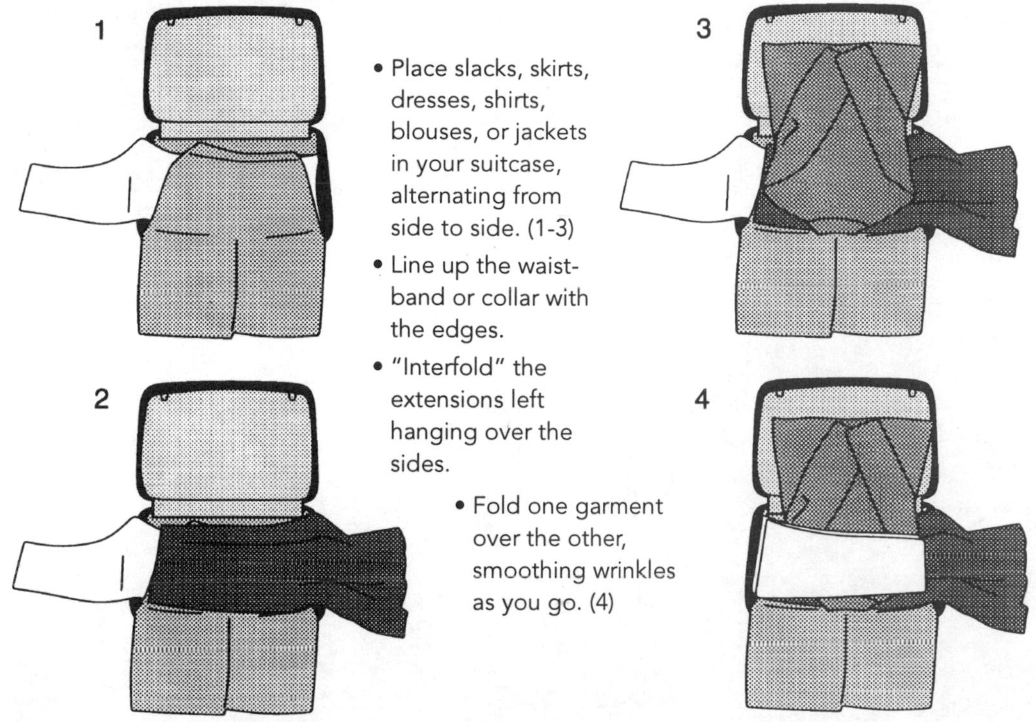

Each item will cushion the other, helping to prevent creases.

Try to stay calm. If your checked bags are damaged or lost, maximum reimbursement is only $1,250. Keep a list of what is in your bag, file a claim with the airline's baggage claim department, and keep your baggage claim receipts. They will normally get your bag to you (if you stay in the same city) by the next day, but it may not be in time for your interview. But, you do need to look presentable, so badger the airline representatives. If you present a good enough sob story, they might front you the money for a decent shirt and tie (or blouse and scarf). You will need at least this much.

Then, when you get to the interview, apologize to everyone you meet for your appearance. Any faculty member who will be interviewing you has undoubtedly had a great deal of travel experience, including having his or her bags misplaced by the airlines—probably more than once. The "airline-lost-my-luggage" story never fails to both get the sympathy (or empathy) vote and to keep you in the interviewers' minds. A good story and a good attitude may actually win you some points.

21

The Visit

The style is the man himself.

— Buffon, *Discourse*

— Travel —

The extensive traveling that you undertake during the interview process may be the most that you have ever done. It may be your first real chance to see many parts of the country. It can also be a rude introduction to the frequent delays, cancellations, and sardine-can-like accommodations of our nation's air-travel system.

Simply traveling to many parts of the country, packing and unpacking in hotels, and finding your way around strange cities will be very tiring—not to mention costly. There are, however, some ways you can decrease your fatigue and make traveling the interview circuit more tolerable, if not actually pleasant.

Clustering Interviews

The first method is to cluster your interviews. This can be done either chronologically (to effectively use available blocks of time) or geographically.

It is not unusual for some applicants to fly back and forth across the country several times for interviews. Clustering interviews geographically saves both time and the considerable effort necessary to travel great distances. It also, of course, saves money. Clustering reduces your costs by lessening your time away from home (usually spent in hotels) and the amount of traveling you do. These costs can run anywhere from nothing to $5,000 or more, depending upon the geographical range in which you evaluate schools, the level of your accommodations, and your savvy in clustering interviews to use available transportation in the least expensive manner possible.

To cluster interviews, it is essential that you have both luck and flexibility. The harder you work on the problem, the luckier you will become. Flexibility results from getting your materials to schools early. This will allow you a maximum number of interview dates to choose from. Luck is involved in being offered interviews at the right schools in time for you to arrange clusters. Work with the admission secretaries to try to arrange these clusters of interviews. Most of the time they will understand your situation and try to help you out.

There are limits to the number of interviews you should schedule in a short time period. Some obsessive-compulsive individuals will try to schedule multiple interviews day after day for a period of time. This is very dangerous. Not only will these individuals become stressed out, but they will also have very little flexibility if they encounter transportation delays. Remember, bad weather shuts down many of the nation's major airports during the interview season. As one medical student said, "The only problem I had doing my interviews was flight delays. For example, I had to reschedule my interview at Harvard Medical School when a blizzard hit. I had to pay an extra $50 plus the difference in the flight costs." In addition, these applicants will have too little time to digest the information obtained from one set of interviews before going on to the next school. They also won't be able to get a sense of the school's or the area's ambiance, an important factor if you will live there for four years or more.

One method some applicants have used to obtain additional insight into the school at which they have just interviewed is to informally drop by the school's teaching hospital that evening or the next morning to talk with students, and perhaps sit in on a class. This practice provides an opportunity to get a better perspective on the information gathered while in the midst of hectic interviewing. If you can stay, you can also get a feel for the surrounding community. But to do this, you need extra time. I advise that you take the time, even if you are clustering your interviews chronologically.

Special Fares

Another way to save money is by using special fares available from airlines, railroads, and bus companies. Often these allow you unlimited travel during a specified period or to a specific region of the country. However, the rates, rules, and special offers change with dizzying frequency.

While getting cheap airline fares has become more complicated in the past few years, you can use some specific strategies. Once you know which cities you will visit for interviews, learn what the standard 21-day advance-purchase fare costs and compare it with the other fares you find. To get cheaper rates, check for special "student" or weekend fares, book in advance, and try to include a Saturday night stay.

Compare prices and schedules at several discount travel websites; check back frequently for better deals. Then, if you find a fare that is 45% to 50% less than the 21-day advance-purchase rate, book it immediately. (But understand that "nonrefundable" tickets mean you will pay more if you need to change the schedule.) Discounts are usually available only for a limited time and there may be only a few seats available at that rate. You can also save by flying one of the no-frills, low-cost carriers. Remember, the only people who pay full fare for transportation, especially air travel, are those who have someone else pay for their trip. Frequent-flyer programs can also save you money by supplying you with discounted or free car rentals, airline tickets, and hotel accommodations.

Although not usually any cheaper than airline travel, trains may be a more convenient method of transportation, especially on both coasts. The primary benefit of this travel mode is that train stations are located inside cities, so less time and money are involved than in getting to the airport.

The National Association of Advisers for the Health Professions (to which your premed adviser probably belongs) occasionally offers airline discounts. The discounts and conditions change each year, so check to see what is currently available.

Ask the residency program you are visiting for the best and cheapest (they may be different) way to get from the airport to the hospital. Trains will usually be the cheapest and fastest transportation method—but may not be the safest method at certain times of the day. Also, you may have to lug your baggage a long distance to get to the train. A useful alternative is an airport shuttle. Remember to get the cheaper round-trip fare. Taxis are for those who don't have to watch their budget and rental cars are for special situations or if you plan additional sightseeing in the area.

If you must rent a car, the average daily rate in 2003 was $65, including mileage, gas, insurance, taxes, etc. You can often pay less by checking with different rental agencies for special rates. Local car rental agencies and those not based at the airport (but who will pick you up there) often have much lower rates than the major companies. You can get their phone numbers from the Web. Search for "rental car" + "cheap" + "[the name of the city where you want the car]". If you do drive to your interview, check ahead to find out where to park. At many medical schools, visitor parking is almost impossible to find.

Surviving Air Travel

Most medical school applicants fly to their interviews. As a business traveler, rather than a vacationer, you must do everything possible to save time and fly comfortably. Figure 21.1 lists suggestions gleaned from thousands of business travelers on how to do this.

FIGURE 21.1

Air Travel Made Easier

- Go a day before you must arrive—or at least not on the last flight of the day to your destination.
- Don't check luggage. Use a carryon bag with wheels.
- Dress comfortably, unless you will go directly to your interview.
- Pack a snack and a bottle of water. Airlines rarely offer meals, and flight schedules often prevent travelers from eating between flights.
- If meals are served on the flights, order special ones, such as vegetarian, weight-watcher, or kosher. They are usually fresher than other meals.
- Take early morning or late-night flights. Late in the afternoon, delays are common. (Late-night flights may also be less expensive.)
- If you arrive at the airport early, try to get on an earlier flight.
- Arrive at the airport early enough to get through the enhanced security procedures.
- Keep your booking agent's or website's toll-free telephone number handy. If your flight is canceled, call the agent to rebook you rather than standing in line with the angry masses.
- Have a current copy of the *Official Airline Guide* (the relevant pages) to help reschedule flights if necessary. Look for it in the library or on the Web.
- Board the plane as soon as possible. It is easier to find storage space for your carryon bags, as well as a pillow and a blanket.
- Sit in the front of the plane to be one of the first off the plane.
- Get an aisle seat. You can get to the bathroom easier and get off the plane faster. (You may be disturbed by the "inside" passengers climbing over you to get out.)
- If you are right-handed, sit on the right side of the plane, so people passing in the aisle won't jiggle your arm as you work or eat. To sleep, get a window seat so passengers won't crawl over you to get out. Get a seat in the exit row for more legroom. On some planes, though, those seats don't recline.
- Carry foam earplugs to sleep on the plane or if you fly on a small (usually commuter) plane. Also use eyeshades to sleep.
- Join the airlines' frequent flier programs. You may board earlier and get special perquisites. Use one airline and its affiliated hotel and car rental companies to maximize benefits.
- If you will fly a lot on one airline, join their airport club. The relaxation between flights may be worth the cost.
- Join hotel and car rental clubs if you will be using them frequently.
- Use the airplane restroom before landing. This may save up to 20 minutes on the ground if you are first to the taxis or car rental counters.
- Use a skycap to avoid taxi lines. A small tip can save you lots of time.

You may get "bumped" from your flight, meaning there is no room for you, even though you have a confirmed reservation. If you arrive on time and are bumped but the airline can get to your destination within an hour of the scheduled time, the airline must pay you the one-way cost of your ticket up to $200. If they cannot get you there within two hours of the scheduled time, the compensation is doubled, up to $400. In some cases, they also throw in free tickets—so getting bumped may be a good deal if you have some time to spare.

Do exercises on the airplane to loosen up and to avoid blood clots and swollen legs and feet.

- *Neck Stretches:* Flex and extend your neck 5 times anteriorly-posteriorly to and away from the chest and 5 times laterally toward the shoulders. Then rotate your head from side to side 5 times, holding it at full rotation for 3 to 5 seconds.
- *Shoulder Stretch:* Link fingers and hold them in front of your chest. Lift them above your head, breathing in while stretching toward the ceiling and hold your breath and position for 3 seconds. Bring your arms behind your head while breathing out. Hold your breath and position for 3 seconds.
- *Arm Isometrics:* Push down on the armrest for the count of 5 and then pull up on the armrest for the count of 5. Repeat 5 times.
- *Lower-Back Stretch:* Clasp your knee with both hands, pull it to your chest, and hold it there for the count of 5. Repeat with other leg.
- *Leg/Foot Stretch:* With your shoes off, press firmly with your palms on both knees. Dorsiflex your foot so your heels are touching the floor and your toes are raised as high as possible. Then plantar flex so that your toes touch the floor and the heels are raised. Repeat quickly 8 times.

Traveling by Car

Many applicants can drive to interviews, since they apply to schools within a reasonable distance from their homes. (What is considered a "reasonable" distance varies with the individual and the car's condition.)

While this may seem to be simple, be aware that parking at most medical schools is a nightmare. If you drive to the interview, allow plenty of time to find parking. In some cases, you may have to allow an extra hour, either to find a parking spot or to hike from your parking spot to the school.

One trick that may be worth the few extra dollars is to park in a commercial lot or garage in the general vicinity and then take a taxi to the school. It may save you time and aggravation, especially in large cities.

Cheap Lodging

One source of information about inexpensive lodging is the admission office for the medical school. If such information is not included in the material they send, call the secretary and ask about good, inexpensive, and *safe* lodging near the school. You will not be the first one to ask, so the school probably has a list of good places to stay. Some schools even offer accommodations in students' homes to applicants who request it (see Figure 21.2). If this is service available, use it, since this provides many benefits besides cheap lodging.

Sometimes you will need to use hotels. The average hotel room cost $135 per night in 2003. The rate is higher in major business and resort cities. Contact hotels directly or use discount-travel websites to get the best rates.

Simultaneous Vacationing

As mentioned, the interview circuit is no picnic. But in some situations, you can turn it into a real vacation. If you try to chronologically cluster interviews but there is a gap in your interview schedule, see if there are vacation spots in the surrounding area. A vacation can be a relaxing break in the action—a needed rest period at a relatively low cost, since you are already nearby. If you have a spouse or significant other, he or she might want to meet you at this spot. A friendly face will be a very welcome sight and may help to bolster your spirits. Having someone along to talk to and share your experiences with may add to the relief. Given the stresses of medical school, and the anticipated heavy work schedule, you and your spouse or significant other (if you have one) probably need a vacation anyway!

Schedule

It's vital that you not only know your schedule but also arrive on time, if not early. There are many applicants, so slip-ups, such as being late, will count against you. Most medical schools interview on a tight schedule. Everyone involved has a specific job to do at a specific time. If you don't arrive on time (Murphy's Law says that the only time faculty members will be on time is when you are not), you can botch the schedule. They won't be happy about it and if they're not happy . . .

Once you begin your interviews, things can go wrong that are beyond your control. Interviewers run late, don't show up, or keep you longer than they should. If this happens to you and you think that these events will be detrimental to your application, report the problem to the admission office. They may not be aware that this is occurring and may make special arrangements to rectify the situation.

One medical school applicant described his interview experience:

> **[It was] a disaster. I showed up early for my first interview, but the interviewer didn't show up until five minutes before it was supposed to end (for a 30-minute interview). He kept me late and the second interviewer was visibly upset that I was late. I explained, but that didn't seem to help. I guess I should have said something to the admission office staff, but I didn't. (He didn't get into that medical school.)**

Information Gathering

While at the school, you have many opportunities to find out more about it. Since you may spend four or more years there, find out if it will meet your needs. You need this information to complete your "Must/Want" Analysis for this school.

— A Typical Medical School Visit —

Typically, medical school visits are divided into the orientation (and description of financial aid), tour, and interviews (Figure 21.2). Some schools permit (and a few encourage) students to attend classes if they are in session. If you have the chance, this is always a great idea, since it helps you get the "flavor" of the school.

Not all schools have an orientation, even though this is an excellent way to give every applicant updated information about the school, as well as being a dynamic arena in which to "sell" the school to top-notch candidates.

Most schools provide a tour, usually led by a current student. You can classify medical school facilities as relatively new (or refurbished), old, or very old. That is less important than finding out whether the facilities are adequate to meet your educational needs, relatively comfortable (you will spend many hours in the lecture halls and laboratories), and safe (many of those hours will be late at night). Ignore the fancy multimillion-dollar "cyclohexojumbodubotron" they show you. How often do you think you will even go near it? That's just for public relations. Stick to the important basics. For example, is the library open 24 hours a day? Your schedule won't be 9 a.m. to 5 p.m. You need access to the library nearly around-the-clock and a way to tie in to their on-line teaching materials at any time. (You also need this access to the anatomy labs.)

The interviews are the third part of the visit. This is where the rubber meets the road—and where you have the possibility of going flat, blowing out, or speeding your way to victory. Since they are so important, interviews are discussed in their own chapters.

Occasionally, the "typical" interview visit has a twist that can influence which medical school you select, as this story shows.

> **At one school known for its research, a very good applicant who had done research as an undergraduate was initially interviewed by a member of the clinical faculty. While reviewing**

the student's résumé, the interviewer began asking about the applicant's research experiences and interest. Seeing that this was a major interest for the student, the interviewer called the admission office and arranged for the student's next interviewer to be changed to a researcher. This is the school where the applicant eventually went. He was impressed with their real interest and their flexibility.

Talk to Students

If you haven't talked to the current medical students, assume that you really do not know very much about a school. Be very wary of any school that either does not give you the opportunity or does not insist that you talk to some of its students. Students often see things quite differently than the faculty. Their perspectives, while not necessarily the same as those you might have in the same situation, may be much closer to yours than those of the school's administrators. Talks with students are usually informal and, because of limitations on their time, may occur in group settings. Nevertheless, the students' opinions, viewpoints, and insights about the school should strongly influence how you will rate it for each of the factors on your "Must/Want" Analysis.

Many schools have current medical students give tours to the applicants (see Figure 21.2). Most of these tours are rather boring. As they say, if you have seen one medical school, you have seen them all. The only exceptions are a few Eastern medical schools. One interesting tour is at the University of Maryland, where students walk through the original medical school building, now a National Historic Landmark. Boring or not, when you write a thank-you letter to the Dean of Admissions after your visit, be sure to mention the name of the student who gave you the tour, as well as any who may have housed you during your stay.

Besides giving you a view of the facilities and general information about the medical school, these tours give you a chance to talk with one or more students who are attending the school where you might want to go. Take this opportunity to ask them some questions. (See Chapter 24 for questions you may want to ask.) Get their phone numbers, snail-mail addresses, or e-mail addresses so you can contact them if you have additional questions. Some schools provide the phone numbers of current medical students who will answer applicant's questions. Ask for them.

If you have done your homework, you may have identified one or more students at that school who are from your hometown or your undergraduate school. Arrange in advance to meet with them while you are there. Even though they may be very busy, they *must* eat sometime, so perhaps you can join them and their colleagues for a meal. Even better, if you can arrange to stay with them while interviewing at their school, you should have lots of opportunities to talk with them about what is *really* going on at the school—and to see beyond the rose-colored picture the admission office paints.

Talk to Graduates Later

Another great source of information about a school is its graduates. While at the school, stop by the alumni office and get contact information for any of the school's recent graduates who live in or near your hometown. When you return home, contact these physicians for additional details about the school. Be considerate of their time, however, since they are now residents with very hectic schedules. It's often best to call and ask them if they would be willing to talk with you by phone or in person at a convenient time.

Exam Schedule

When talking with students and perusing a school's curriculum, consider whether that school's examination schedule fits your learning pattern. Are tests scheduled every two weeks, or only as midterms and finals? Individuals differ markedly in the way they learn, their comfort in taking examinations, and their need for feedback on their performance. If you do best in courses where you get frequent feedback, your work may suffer at schools with only two examinations in each course. Does this school's examination schedule work for you?

Learning Skills Specialist

For many medical students, one of the most important faculty members will be the Learning Skills Specialist. This individual may be the school's only faculty member with training in how to assess a student's learning and test-taking skills—and with the ability to help students improve those skills. Find out if such a specialist exists at the school. If the student giving the tour does not know, check with the medical school's "teaching" or "learning" center.

Minority Applicants

Aside from the information discussed above, minority applicants should also use other criteria and get additional information to evaluate the school. How knowledgeable and helpful is the minority affairs office? Did you get a chance to talk with current minority medical students or faculty, especially those from your culture? (In some cases, the minority affairs office can arrange for you to stay with these students during your visit.) Also, be aware of the school's locale, ambiance, and the attitude as you visit. How do you *feel* in these surroundings? The answer to that question alone may make or break your medical school career.

The Meal

Applicants may be asked to go to lunch (or sometimes dinner or breakfast) with students or faculty members (see Figure 21.2). Several rules apply to this experience, as with any business lunch—for that is exactly what it is.

Stay away from alcohol! You need to be on your toes, not under the table. Even if you don't lose your wits after imbibing alcohol, your afternoon interviewers may be teetotalers and, thus, discount you as a viable candidate if you have been drinking.

Do not eat too much. The postprandial tide is a very effective soporific. You don't want to sleep through the afternoon's activities, do you?

Be sure to use good table manners. If you have never learned them before, it is essential to do so now. You will need to know how to eat in a reasonably civilized manner throughout your medical career. Start at the interview lunch. Common errors in table manners that cost people medical school slots include: Holding your fork like a knife, talking with your mouth full, not putting the napkin in your lap, not breaking bread before you eat it, and pushing food onto the fork with your thumb. Even in the hospital cafeteria, some table manners are necessary. If you need help, ask a friend. The following real example from an interview meal suggests the poor level of social skills some people have.

> When one candidate went with some of us to a Chinese restaurant during her interview visit, everything seemed to go very well. But when she was served a fortune cookie, I saw her put the entire thing in her mouth, paper and all! Then she pulled the fortune out of her mouth and read it to us.

Finally, avoid foods that can cause accidents and embarrassment. Soups, creamy dressings, spaghetti, desserts, and greasy hand-held foods, such as tacos, can easily end up on your new clothes. Onions and garlic can make even the most stalwart interviewer want to avoid you. The best advice is to use lunch to ward off hypoglycemia. Do your real eating after you have left the school for the day.

Read Me First!

Figure 21.2 contains information gleaned from multiple sources, including questionnaires sent to the schools and the school's written and online material. Every attempt has been made to confirm the information prior to publication. *Always* contact the school to verify any information you consider vital.

FIGURE 21.2

Medical Schools: Interviews and Visits

School	Months	Days	Length	No.[1]	Open File?[2]	Type[3]	Meal/ Tour	Orien- tation[4]	Housing[5]
Alabama	Sept-Mar	Th	½ hr	3	P	U	Y/Y	Y/Y	NA
Alabama, South	Sept-Mar	W	½-¾ hr	3	O	U	Y/Y	Y/Y	S/$
Albany	Sept-Apr	WTh[6]	½-¾ hr	2	O	SS	Y/Y	Y/N	S/$
Albert Einstein	Sept-May	M-F	¾ hr	1	O	U	Y/Y	N/Y	S
Alberta[7]	Feb-May	M-S	¾ hr	1	P	U	N/Y	N/N	No
Arizona	Oct-Jan	MTW	50 min	2	CL	U	Y/Y	Y/N	No
Arizona Osteo.[8]	Nov-May	MF	½-¾ hr	1[9]	P	C	Y/Y	Y/Y	No
Arkansas	Aug-June	S	¾-1 hr	1	CL	SS	N/Y	Y/Y	No
Baylor	Sept-Feb	FS[6]	½ hr	2	P	C	Y/Y	Y/Y	S/$
Boston	Oct-Jan	MWF	¾ hr	1	O	U	Y/Y	N/N	$
British Columbia[7]	Jan-Mar	M-F	½-¾ hr	2	P	U	N/N	Y/N	No
Brown	No interviews; applicants may visit school								
Calgary[7]	March	FSSuM	1 hr	1	P	C	Y/Y	Y/Y	S
Calif.–Davis	Oct-Apr	M-F	1 hr	2	P	U	Y/Y	Y/Y	S/$
Calif.–Irvine	Oct-Apr	Th	1 hr	2	P	SS	Y/Y	Y/Y	S
Calif.–San Diego	Sept-Mar	MTTh	1 hr	2	P	C	Y/Y	Y/Y	S/$
Calif.–San Francisco	Oct-Mar	M-Th	¾-1 hr	2	CL	U	Y/Y	N/Y	S
Calif.–Los Angeles	Nov-Apr	M-F	½-1 hr	1-2	O	SS	Y/Y	N/N	S/$
Calif., Southern (Keck)	Oct-Apr	TWF	¾-1 hr	2	CL	C	Y/Y	Y/N	S/$
Caribe[S]	Nov-Apr	M-F	½ hr	1[9]	CL	S	N/Y	N/N	No
Case Western Res.	Sept-Mar	MTF	½-1 hr	1	O	SS	Y/Y	Y/Y	S/$
Chicago–Pritzker	Sept-Mar	MTTh	¾-1 hr	2	1 O/1 P	SS	Y/Y	Y/Y	S
Chicago Medical	Oct-May	Varies	½-¾ hr	2	O	SS	Y/Y	Y/N	$
Chicago Osteo.[8]	Nov-Apr	MF	NA	1[9]	P	SS	Y/Y	Y/Y	$
Cincinnati	Sept-Feb	MT	1 hr	1	O	U	Y/Y	N/N	S/$
Colorado	Sept-Apr	M-F	½ hr	2	P	C	Y/Y	Y/Y	$
Columbia	Sept-Mar	M-F	½ hr	1	O	U	Y/Y	N/N	S
Connecticut	Sept-Mar	MWF	¾ hr	2	NA	C	Y/Y	Y/N	S
Cornell	Sept-Mar	TWTh	½-¾ hr	2	O	U	Y/Y	Y/Y	S/$
Creighton	Nov-Mar	F	½ hr	2	CL	U	Y/Y	Y/Y	S
Dalhousie[7]	Feb-Apr	FS	½ hr	1	P	SS	N/Y	N/NA	No
Dartmouth	Oct-Apr	TTh	½ hr	2	O	C	Y/Y	N/Y	S
Des Moines Osteo.[8]	Oct-Apr	ThF	½ hr	1	O	S	Y/Y	Y/Y	$
Drew/UCLA	No information available								
Drexel[X]	Sept-Mar	MTW	½-¾ hr	2	O	U	Y/Y	Y/Y	S
Duke	Sept-Feb	M-F	½ hr	2	O	SS	Y/Y	Y/Y	S/$
East Carolina (Brody)	Aug-Apr	M-F	¾ hr	2	P	U	Y/Y	Y/Y	No
E.V. Virginia Osteo.[8]	No information available								
Emory	Oct-Feb	MWF	½-¾ hr	2[9,11]	P	U	Y/Y	Y/Y	S/$
Florida State	Sept-Mar	F	1 hr	2	O	U	Y/Y	Y/Y	S
Florida, South	Oct-Mar	M	¾ hr	2	NA	NA	Y/Y	Y/Y	S
Florida, Univ. of	Sept-Mar	F	1 hr	2	P	U	Y/Y	Y/Y	S/$
Geo. Washington	Sept-Apr	TThF	20 min	2	CL	SS	Y/Y	Y/Y	S/$
Georgetown	Oct-Apr	M-F	½-¾ hr	1	P	C	Y/Y	Y/Y	S/$
Georgia, Med. Coll.	Oct-Mar	MF	½ hr	2	CL	U	Y/Y	Y/Y	S

(continued)

FIGURE 21.2 (continued)

School	Months	Days	Length	No.[1]	Open File?[2]	Type[3]	Meal/ Tour	Orien- tation[4]	Housing[5]
Harvard	Sept-Jan	Not W	½-¾ hr	2	O	U	Y/Y	Y/Y	S
Hawaii	Sept-Mar	All	½-1½ hr	2	P	U/S	N/Y	Y/N	No
Howard	Oct-May	TW	40 min	1	O	U	Y/Y	Y/Y	No
Illinois, Southern	Aug-Mar	M-F	¼-1 hr	2-3	O/CL	S	N/Y	Y/Y	$
Illinois, Univ.	Sept-Apr	M-F	½ hr	1[9]	P	S	Y/Y	Y/Y	$
Indiana	Sept-Feb	W	¾ hr	1[9]	O	SS	Y/Y	Y/Y	$
Iowa	Oct-Jan	M-F	½ hr	1	CL	S/U	Y/Y	Y/Y	S/$
Jefferson	Sept-Apr	W	½-¾ hr	1	O	SS	Y/Y	Y/Y	S/$
Johns Hopkins	Sept-Mar	ThF	½ hr	2	O	C	Y/Y	Y/Y	S
Kansas	Sept-Jan	Varies	½ hr	2	O/P	SS	Y/Y	Y/Y	S
Kentucky	Aug-Apr	TS	¾ hr	2	O	SS	Y/Y	Y/N	S
Kirksville Osteo.[8]	Aug-Mar	MThF	1 hr	2	O	SS	Y/Y	Y/Y	S/$
Lake Erie Osteo.[8]	Oct-Mar	MThF	½ hr	1[9]	O	S	N/Y	Y/Y	No
Laval[7,F]	Apr-May	TWTh	3 hrs	1[11,12]	CL	S[NC]	Y/Y	Y/N	$
Loma Linda	Nov-Apr	M-F	½-1 hr	1-2	P	U	Y/Y	Y/Y	$
Louisville	Sept-Apr	WTh	½ hr	2	P	S	Y/Y	Y/N	S
Loyola–Stritch	Sept-Apr	M-F	¾-1 hr	2	O	SS	Y/Y	Y/Y	S/$
LSU–New Orleans	Oct-May	MTW	40 min	3	O/CL	S/U	Y/Y	Y/N	$
LSU–Shreveport	Oct-Mar	T	40 min	3	O/P	SS	N/Y	Y/Y	NA
Manitoba[7]	Feb-Mar	S	1 hr	1[9]	P	SS	N/Y	Y/Y	S
Marshall	Sept-Mar	MTW	½-¾ hr	2	O	U	N/Y	Y/N	No
Maryland	Oct-Mar	MW	¾-1 hr	2	O	U	Y/Y	Y/Y	S/$
Massachusetts	Oct-Mar	TW	½ hr	2	CL	SS	N/Y	Y/Y	No
Mayo	Sept-Feb	MThF	1 hr	2	P	U	Y/Y	N/N	S
McGill[7]	Jan-Mar[Q]	M-F	½ hr	2	P	U	Y/Y	Y/Y	S
McMaster[7]	Mar-Apr	M-F	½ hr	2[9,11]	P	S	N/Y	N/N	NA
Meharry	Oct-Apr	MTWF	½ hr	2	CL	U	Y/Y	Y/Y	NA
Mercer	Dec-Mar	TWTh	50 min	2	O	U	Y/Y	Y/Y	$
Miami	Oct-Apr	MF	1 hr	1	O	S	Y/Y	Y/Y	S/$
Michigan Osteo.[8]	Oct-Mar	MTThF	1 hr	2	P	S	Y/Y	N/Y	S
Michigan State	Sept-Apr	Th	½ hr	2	P	C	Y/Y	Y/Y	S/$
Michigan, Univ.	Sept-Mar	F	½ hr	3	O	U	Y/Y	Y/Y	S
Minnesota–Duluth	Oct-Mar	M-F	1 hr	2	O	U	Y/Y	N/Y	No
Minnesota–Minneap.	Sept-Apr	MF	1 hr	1	P	SS	Y/Y	N/Y	No
Mississippi	Aug-Jan	MTThF	½-1 hr	3	P	SS	Y/Y	N/N	No
Missouri–Columbia	Sept-Apr	M-F	¾ hr	2	O	U	N/Y	Y/Y	No
Missouri–KS City[13]	Dec-Mar	Not T	½-1 hr	2	O	SS	N/Y	Y/Y	$
Montréal[7,F]	Mar-May	MF	2 hrs	1[9]	CL	S	N/N	N/N	No
Morehouse	Oct-Mar	F	½-¾ hr	1	CL/P	S	Y/Y	Y/Y	S/$
Mount Sinai	Sept-Apr	M-F	½ hr	2	O	U	Y/Y	Y/N	S
Nebraska	Oct-Jan	F	½ hr	1	CL	NA	Y/Y	Y/N	No
Nevada	Sept-Dec	M-F	1 hr	2	CL	S	N/Y	N/Y	No
New England Osteo.[8]	Sept-Mar	TThS	½-¾ hr	1[9]	P	U	Y/Y	Y/N	S/$
New Mexico	Aug-Feb	M-F	½-1 hr	2	O	U	Y/Y	N/N	No
New York Osteo.[8]	Oct-May	M-F	½ hr	1	O	SS	Y/Y	Y/N	S/$

(continued)

FIGURE 21.2 (continued)

School	Months	Days	Length	No.[1]	Open File?[2]	Type[3]	Meal/ Tour	Orien-tation[4]	Housing[5]
New York Medical	Oct-Apr	M-Th	½ hr	1-2	CL	S	Y/Y	Y/Y	S
New York Univ.	Nov-Feb	M-S	½-¾ hr	1	O	U	Y/Y	N/N	$
Newfoundland[7]	Feb-Apr	WS	1 hr	1[9]	CL	SS	N/Y	Y/Y	$
North Carolina	Sept-Apr	MTWF	½ hr	2	O	SS	Y/Y	Y/Y	S
North Dakota	Dec-Jan	ThFS	1 hr	1[9,11]	O	SS	N/Y	N/N	S
Northwestern	Nov-Mar	T-F	⅓ &1 hr	2[9,11]	O/P	C/SS	Y/Y	N/Y	S/$
Nova Univ. Osteo.[8]	Sept-(F)	MF	½ hr	1[9]	O	U	Y/Y	Y/Y	$
Ohio Osteo.[8]	Oct-Apr	TW	½ hr	3	O	S/U	Y/Y	Y/Y	S
Ohio State	Sept-Mar	MW	½-¾ hr	1[9]	O	U	Y/Y	Y/Y	S
Ohio, Med. Coll.	Oct-Apr	M-Th	1 hr	2	O	S	Y/Y	Y/N	S/$
Ohio, Northeast[10]	Sept-Mar	M-F	¾ hr	1[9]	O	S	Y/Y	Y/Y	$
Oklahoma	Nov-Jan	Varies	¼-¾ hr	1[9]	O	SS	Y/Y	Y/Y	S
Oklahoma Osteo.[8]	Sept-Mar[14]	M-F	¾ hr	1	P	NA	Y/Y	Y/Y	S
Ontario, Western[7]	Mar-Apr	SSu	¾ hr	2[9]	CL	SS	Y/Y	Y/N	S
Oregon	Oct-Mar	TWTh	¾ hr	2	O	SS	Y/Y	N/Y	S/$
Ottawa[7]	Mar-Apr	M-S	¾ hr	1[9]	P	SS	Y/Y	Y/N	S
Pacific Osteo.[8]	Sept-Mar	TThF	½ hr	1[9]	O	S	Y/Y	Y/Y	S/$
Pennsylvania State	Sept-Mar	MWF	½ hr	1[9]	O	U	Y/Y	Y/Y	S/$
Pennsylvania, Univ.	Oct-Feb	M-S	½ hr	2	P	U	Y/Y	Y/Y	S/$
Philadelphia Osteo.[8]	Sept-May	M-Th	¾ hr	1[9]	O	SS	Y/Y	Y/Y	S/$
Pikeville Osteo.[8]	Oct-Jun	S	½-¾ hr	1[9]	O	U	Y/NA	Y/Y	No
Pittsburgh	Sept-Apr	MTF	1 hr	2	P	NA	Y/Y	Y/N	S/$
Ponce[S]	Oct-Apr	M-F	2 hrs	1[9,11]	CL	SS	N/Y	Y/Y	No
Puerto Rico[S]	Nov-Feb	M-F	1 hr	1[9]	CL	S	N/N	N/N	No
Queen's Univ.[7]	March	SSu	¾ hr	1[9]	P	SS	N/Y	Y/N	$
Rochester	Sept-Mar	MThF	½-1 hr	2	CL	U	Y/Y	Y/Y	S/$
Rush	Sept-May	MTh	¾-1 hr	2	O/CL	S	Y/Y	N/N	S
Saint Louis	Sept-May	T	1 hr	1	O/CL	SS	Y/Y	Y/Y	S
Saskatchewan[7]	Mar	SSu	¾ hr	1[9]	CL	SS	N/Y	N/N	No
Sherbrooke[7,F]			No information available						
South Carol., Med. U.	Sept-Mar	F	1 hr	3	P	SS	Y/Y	Y/Y	$
South Carol., Univ.	Sept-Mar	W	½ hr	2	O/CL	U	Y/Y	Y/Y	No
South Dakota	Oct-Mar	M-F	¾-1 hr	2	O	C	N/Y	N/Y	No
Stanford	Sept-Mar	M-Th	1 hr	2	O	SS	Y/Y	Y/Y	S
SUNY–Brooklyn	Sept-Mar	M-Th	1 hr	1	O	SS	Y/Y	Y/N	S/$
SUNY–Buffalo	Sept-Apr	W	¾ hr	2	O	SS	Y/Y	Y/N	S/$
SUNY–Stony Brook	Sept-Mar	TThF	¾-1 hr	1	O	S/U	Y/Y	Y/N	S
SUNY–Syracuse	Sept-Apr	MW	¾-1 hr	2	P	SS	Y/Y	Y/Y	S/$
Temple	Sept-Mar	M-Th	¾-1 hr	1	O	U	Y/Y	Y/Y	S/$
Tennessee State, E.	Sept-Mar	M-Th	½-1 hr	2	P	U	Y/Y	Y/Y	No
Tennessee, Univ.	Oct-Feb	MTW	½-1 hr	2	P	U	Y/Y	Y/Y	$
Texas A&M	Aug-Dec	Th	½ hr	2	P	S	Y/Y	Y/Y	S/$
Texas Coll. Osteo.[8]	Aug-Dec	TThF	¾-1½ hr	2	CL	U	Y/Y	Y/Y	S
Texas Tech	Aug-Jan	WF	¾ hr	2	O	U	Y/Y	Y/Y	S
Texas–Galveston	Aug-Dec	WF	½ hr	2	P	U	Y/Y	Y/Y	S

(continued)

FIGURE 21.2 (continued)

School	Months	Days	Length	No.[1]	Open File?[2]	Type[3]	Meal/ Tour	Orien-tation[4]	Housing[5]
Texas–Houston	Aug-Jan	F	½-1 hr	2	P	U	Y/Y	Y/Y	S
Texas–San Antonio	Sept-Dec	M	½ hr	2	P	U	Y/Y	Y/N	S/$
Texas–Southwest	Sept-Dec	S	½ hr	2	O	U	Y/Y	Y/Y	$
Toronto[7]	Mar-May	FSSu	1 hr	1[9]	P	SS	N/Y	Y/N	$
Touro Osteo.[8]	Oct.-Apr	MTW	1 hr	1	O	S	Y/NA	Y/NA	No
Tufts	Oct-Apr	T	½ hr	2	O	U	Y/Y	Y/Y	S/$
Tulane	Sept-Mar	Not T	½ hr	3	O/CL	S	N/Y	N/N	S
UMDNJ–Osteo.[8]	Sept-Apr	M-F	½ hr	5	O	SS	Y/Y	Y/Y	$
UMDNJ–NJ Med.	Aug-Mar	M-F	1 hr	1	O	SS	N/Y	Y/Y	No
UMDNJ–RWJ	Aug-Mar	M-F	¾-1 hr	1	O	U	Y/Y	Y/Y	S
Uniformed Serv. U.	Oct-Mar	Th	½ hr	2	P	U	N/Y	Y/Y	Yes
U. Health Sci. Osteo.[8]	Sept-May	MWF	¼-¾ hr	1[9]	O	U	Y/Y	Y/Y	S/$
Utah	Oct-Feb	MThF	½-¾ hr	1	P	S	Y/Y	Y/Y	No
Vanderbilt	Aug-Mar	Not W	½-1 hr	1	P	U	Y/Y	Y/Y	$
Vermont	Sept-Apr	TTh	¾ hr	1[9]	P	SS	Y/Y	Y/Y	$
Virginia, Eastern	Sept-Mar	WF	½-¾ hr	1[9]	O	NA	Y/Y	Y/Y	S
Virginia, Med. Coll.	Sept-Mar	M-Th	½-¾ hr	1	O/CL	S	Y/Y	Y/Y	S
Virginia, Univ. of	Sept-Mar	M-Th	½ hr	2	O	U	Y/Y	Y/Y	S
Wake Forest (B. Gray)	Oct-Mar	MTWF	¼-½ hr	3	P	U	Y/Y	Y/Y	S/$
Washington U. (MO)	Sept-Feb	M-F	½-¾ hr	1	P	U	Y/Y	Y/Y	S
Washington, Univ. of	Oct-Feb	M-F	½ hr	2-3	O	U	Y/Y	N/N	S
Wayne State	Sept-May	M-F	1 hr	1	O	S	N/Y	N/N	$
West Virginia	Sept-Mar	Not T	½ hr	4-6	O/CL	C	Y/Y	N/N	No
West Virginia Osteo.[8]	Aug-Apr	M-Th	½ hr	1	O	S	Y/Y	Y/Y	$
Wisconsin, Med. Coll.	Nov-May	F	½ hr	2	O/CL	S/U	Y/Y	Y	S/$
Wisconsin, Univ. of	Sept-Feb	F	1 hr	2	P	U	Y/Y	Y/Y	S
Wright State	Sept-Apr	TW	¾ hr	2	O	SS	Y/Y	Y/Y	S
Yale	Oct-Mar	MWF	½-¾ hr	2	O	SS	Y/Y	Y/Y	$

1: The number of interviews
2: Whether the interviewer has the entire student application file available. If they have the entire file, it is "Open" (O). If they have only a portion, it is "Part" (P), and if they do not have any of the file, it is "Closed" (CL)
3: The interview can be unstructured "U"; structured "S"; semistructured "SS"; or interviewer's choice "C"
4: Student orientation/Financial aid orientation is or is not offered
5: "S" indicates that housing with students is available, often only if requested; "$" indicates that information about inexpensive housing is available, often only on request
6: The interview process takes two days
7: Canadian medical school
8: College of Osteopathic Medicine
9: Applicants interviewed by more than one person at once
10: Information is primarily for those not applying through the eight-year program
11: Applicants interviewed in a group
12: Applicants are placed in "simulated situations" to test their reactions
13: Information refers to six-year program interviews
14: Interviews occur only in four weeks during this period
F: Classes taught in French
(F): Interviews until class is full
NA: Data not available
S: Classes taught in Spanish
Q: Quebec residents in March; non-Canadians in January; non-Quebec Canadians in February
X: Formerly Medical College of Pennsylvania/Hahnemann/Allegheny Univ. Health Sciences

22

Preparing For The Interview

Decisions are made in the first thirty seconds of the interview—
the rest of the time is used to justify the decision.

— An axiom in the personnel field

— Before You Go —

Understand the Requirements for a Medical Career

Ideally, before you began the application process you learned as much as you could about a medical career. If not, be certain you know what it means to be a physician before you arrive at the medical school interviews you've worked so hard to obtain. This does not mean amassing medical knowledge; you will acquire that during your training. Rather, you need to become acquainted with the *culture* of medicine. Find out what a physician's life is like (not the television or movie images). Know what type of educational experiences you can expect to have in medical school, during your residency, and, perhaps, during a fellowship. What do physicians really do? Of course, this will differ by specialty, but have at least some general knowledge about what a primary care physician does. (See Chapter 3: *Specialty Descriptions* for details about medical specialties.)

Faculty members want to be assured that you have fully thought out your decision about a medical career before you commit your entire professional life to it. Otherwise, you could become very unhappy later, a situation that they know leads to depression, anger, and poor performance. It can also cause a student to drop out before graduation, or, worst of all, to become a dissatisfied (and usually a bad) physician. Therefore, demonstrate that you have seriously thought about your career choice. Know about medicine. Read the medical student journals (see the *Annotated Bibliography*) to learn about the changes occurring within the profession and what current medical students think. The more you know about a medical career, the more committed to it you will appear. And commitment is one of the most important qualities interviewers seek.

Know School-Specific Information

Just as you must know basic information about a medical career, you also need to know about each school you visit.

You initially received a lot of information from the school's website and in the packet they send to applicants. If you were as careful as you should have been, you also received additional written or oral information that updated the packet. More complete information may be found in the AAMC's annual publication, *Medical School Admission Requirements*. AACOM has a similar publication—*Osteopathic Medical College Information*—on the internet (www.aacom.org/colleges) that has links to every Osteopathic medical school's website.

To get additional information about a school, run a Medline search (www.ncbi.nlm.nih.gov/pubmed) for recent articles by the school's faculty (you can get a list of the faculty on each school's website). Medline is the National Library of Medicine's primary online bibliographic service. Look particularly for articles dealing with medical education. These may describe innovations in the school's curriculum or teaching methods. Gathering this information may help you avoid going to a school whose teaching methods, such as small groups, are not compatible with your learning style. The articles may also provide insight into questions faculty might ask you or subjects they might like to discuss. In any case, the more you know about a specific school before going to the interview, the better the chance that you will leave well-remembered and highly regarded.

Many schools use more than one hospital for teaching. If possible, see all of the school's affiliated hospitals rather than just the primary one. They may not want to show you some institution(s) for a very good reason: You would not apply to the school if you saw them!

The Night Before the Interview

Review the school's information before going into your interview. No matter whether this is the first school at which you are interviewing or the twentieth, it is a major *faux pas* to confuse basic information about the school at which you are currently interviewing with that of another school. Have the relevant facts firmly in your mind before you set out in the morning. If you, like most people, have a little trouble keeping the details straight, make some notes for reference.

How do successful medical school applicants (current medical students) prepare the night before their interviews? The following list, from a survey of medical students, demonstrates the wide diversity in preparation methods. However, the four overwhelming responses were:

1. Reread all the application materials I sent to this school.
2. Reread all the information I had about this school.
3. Reviewed questions to ask the interviewers (see Chapter 24: *Your Questions*).
4. Thought about questions I might be asked (see Chapter 25: *The Questions—The Answers*).

Additional things these applicants did to prepare varied greatly, and depended upon each individual's personality, how stressed they felt, and how many interviews they already had done.

- Saw a great movie.
- Spoke to medical students attending the school.
- Prayed.
- Thought about the ethical issues in health care.
- Read the local newspaper and a national news magazine.
- Went through another mock interview session with a friend.
- Reviewed my résumé.
- Reexamined my motivations for why I wanted to be a physician.
- Ate a bowl of oatmeal (with chocolate chips).
- Drank coffee, coffee, coffee—too much coffee—and didn't sleep well.
- Reviewed my own research papers and my past research projects.
- Tried to relax a bit—very difficult to do.
- Cruised the Internet.
- Browsed through *JAMA.*
- Read a good (nonmedical) book.
- Got eight hours of sleep.
- Went shopping.
- Went to a nice restaurant with friends.
- Watched television.
- Listened to some great music.
- Played video games in my hotel room.
- Drank a couple beers while watching a basketball game.
- Listened to National Public Radio.

- Toured the city and had a good time.
- Read some recent journals on health policy.
- Exercised and jogged.
- Talked with friends on the telephone.

— Basic Interview Rules —

Once you actually get to the interview site, there are some very basic things that you need to do aside from answering questions in a satisfactory manner. In fact, questions and answers may be, in some cases, merely window-dressing for the actual interview process.

The "behavioral interview" is becoming more common as laws limit the questions that interviewers can ask. Behavioral interviewers are much more interested in whether you look and act like a medical student (and a physician) than in your answers to specific questions. They evaluate communication skills, physical presence, motivation, truthfulness, and how suited each applicant is to be a medical student at their school.

All good interviewers look for small but important details. Some of these are discussed below.

Know How to Pronounce Your Interviewers' Names

How do you say "Dr. Swnolwyg"? You don't know? How could that be when he will be interviewing you in five minutes? It may seem petty, especially considering some of the difficult or unique pronunciations of names in the world, to expect you to know how to pronounce, on the first try, all the names of the people that you will meet. Nevertheless, it is expected. So, you should know how. Remember that, above all else, a person's name is a unique part of him or her. Mispronouncing an interviewer's name can, even if subconsciously, leave a negative impression about you.

At the start of the day, ask the admission secretary how to pronounce any difficult or unusual names among those listed on your interview schedule. As he or she tells you, write each down phonetically, so you will be able to repeat it correctly when necessary. If this is not possible, listen carefully when the individual introduces him or herself to you. If it is a difficult name, repeat it and ask if you said it right. Don't slip up on this simple point of etiquette.

Enter and Depart in a Polite, Assured Manner

Look confident! Walk into the interview with your head up, shoulders squared, looking poised. Pause briefly as you enter the room to assert your strong presence. If you slink into an interview like a scared rabbit, how are you going to look to an interviewer? Certainly not like one of the people likely to get a spot at his school. Physicians are supposed to exude an air of confidence. Remember that initial impressions are very important. In the first minute, interviewers determine whether applicants meet their expectations. Send a message of confidence, calmness, and control.

Shake hands with interviewers using a firm, but not bone-crushing, grip. This goes for both men and women. The dainty "dead fish" handshake connotes meekness and a lack of authority; avoid it like the plague. Extend your hand to the other person with the thumb up and out. Make sure that the web between your thumb and index finger meets the other person's web. Try to shake hands from the elbow, not the shoulder or wrist. It is also desirable to have reasonably dry hands. If your palms sweat when you get nervous, dry them off just before meeting each interviewer. One solution to sweaty palms is to sit with your palms exposed to the air rather than stuffed in your pockets or lying palms down in your lap.

Greet the interviewer with an enthusiastic voice and manner. When you begin speaking to an individual, the actual words you say are much less important than the manner in which you say them. The first thing interviewers notice is your tone of voice. They will judge you by your enthusiasm, facial expressions, gestures, and posture. Therefore, try to act as if you are *really* pleased to have an opportunity to talk with the faculty and students. Practice this with some critical observers at home. You must not sound forced or pretentious. If you do, you will do yourself more harm than good. Sincere enthusiasm will greatly enhance your entire visit.

During the interview, sit comfortably straight, leaning slightly forward in the chair. This demonstrates your interest through nonverbal cues. You can prove this to yourself. Have a friend (trying to keep a neutral expression in both instances) face you sitting forward in a chair. Then have the individual lean back in a relaxed posture. If you were the interviewer, which applicant would interest you more?

Negative body language includes resting your head on your hand, tilting your head to one side (the coy look), and fiddling with your beard, hair, mustache, or earrings. Keep your head upright and your hands away from your head. Likewise, don't fiddle with your clothes, pen, or anything else. And don't cross your arms, perhaps the most negative nonverbal signal you can give—rest your hands in your lap or on your thighs.

Always try to look an interviewer in the eyes. Applicants who look away when they answer questions suggest either that their answers are less than honest or that they are afraid of the situation. Those who look away when the interviewer is talking (a true kiss of death) indicate that they do not care about what the interviewer has to say. Obviously, neither situation is favorable. Some experienced interviewers suggest looking at a person first in one eye, then the other. That way, the speaker gets the feeling that the listener is listening intently; and the listener avoids having the glazed look some people get when they look at a person only in one eye (a common behavior). If you plan to try this, practice ahead of time; the first few times you do it you may become distracted and miss what the speaker is saying.

Acknowledge what the interviewer is saying by nodding or with brief verbal phrases such as, "I see," "Of course," or "Yes." Try not to use expressions such as "wow," "yeah," or "cool," which connote something other than professionalism. Vary the expressions you use, so you don't sound wooden or monotonous.

If you are in the middle of answering a question and the interviewer cuts you off or moves the interview in another direction, don't get flustered. Often they do this so that they can ask all the required questions within the allotted time. Remember, they are the interviewers; you are the interviewee.

Your exit from the interview must also be graceful and enthusiastic. As speechwriters know, the last thing the audience (in this case, the interviewer) hears will be the thing best remembered. Shake your interviewer's hand and say, again, how glad you are to have had a chance to talk with him or her. Offer to provide any other information he or she might desire about you. You will rarely, if ever, be taken up on this offer. State that you look forward to being associated with him or her as a medical student. This should take less than 15 seconds and appear very smooth. Practice this one little segment ahead of time so you don't appear awkward. As you can see from some television interviews, even the best speakers and the most intelligent individuals often look like dolts if they do not know how to smoothly terminate an interview. Don't let this be your downfall.

Show Enthusiasm for *This* School

It is important to show your enthusiasm for a medical career. However, showing enthusiasm for the *school at which you are currently interviewing* makes interviewers rate you even more highly. Base your interest on the strong points that you gleaned from the school's own information. Generally, the areas of which the school is most proud are included in their packet. So basing your interest on these areas should get the best results.

An amazing number of applicants arrive at schools with the attitude that either (1) they are browsing and will not reveal that they really *want* a position at the school or (2) they don't need to be concerned about the attitude they demonstrate. Both approaches are wrong. Show enthusiasm! If you cannot work up any enthusiasm for a school, you should not be interviewing there.

You Are Not Selling a Medical Student, You Are Selling a Promise

Forget that you are not yet a medical student. During the interview visit, you are the promise of a bright future. You will be medicine's finest clinician, a noted researcher, a diligent healer of indigent patients, a solid member of the medical community. You will achieve this because you are an extremely hard worker who is compulsive, intelligent, responsive to teaching, happy in your work, and who will cause no trouble for the faculty. That is the promise you are selling.

To get into medical school, you must project the ability to make this promise a reality. You can contribute to this school and to the profession. You are the salesman. You are the product. Go forth and sell.

— Interview Materials —

Although it may seem silly to detail what you need to take with you to interviews, it is surprising how many applicants forget basic materials. In addition to the basics, two forms, *Interview Notes* and your *"Must/Want" Analysis* (each discussed below), are suggested as part of your standard interview equipment. These will aid you later when you evaluate each school and write your follow-up letters.

General Materials

The first two items that you need to bring with you are the *directions to the interview site* and the *telephone numbers* with which to contact the school if you either get lost or are delayed. Next, carry along *whatever information you have received from the school* (in hard copy or on your computer or PDA). Not only should you review it immediately before setting out for the interview in the morning, but you may also want to consult it during the interview day to refresh your memory or recheck questionable points brought up in conversation.

Of course, you should have a *list of questions* that you want to ask at each school (see Chapter 24: *Your Questions*), as well as a *pad of paper and pens* to record the answers—scribbling on a PDA won't cut it. Test your pens to make sure that they work. Bring a *photograph* of yourself to give to the admission secretary if your appearance has changed noticeably since you submitted your application photo or if the school has not yet received a photograph of you.

If you have any *additional credentials or vital paperwork*, such as information about additional clinical experience, major awards, or certificates of special training, be certain that you bring them with you. Finally, bring *something to read*, be it a textbook, news magazine, or newspaper. At most schools you will spend a lot of time waiting. If you have something to occupy your mind, it will make you more alert and less cranky.

Interview Notes

The Interview Notes form (Figure 22.1) is designed to give you an organized method for remembering key information obtained during interviews. It will also act as a reminder when you want to send follow-up notes or materials to individual interviewers. This form is also the one to use to note the phonetic spelling of the interviewers' names.

"Must/Want" Analysis as an Interview Checklist

The "Must/Want" Analysis you previously completed (see Figure 16.1) can now act as an interview checklist (see examples, Figures 16.2 and 16.3). Its use both simplifies your evaluation of each school and helps you discriminate among them. The factors listed on your personal "Must/Want" Analysis and the weights you assigned to each one will remain constant for all the schools you visit.

Immediately following your visit to each school, score each item on a 1 to 10 scale (10 is perfect). Even if you have previously given some items "Scores" based on written materials, you should consider those "Scores" tentative until confirmed during the site visit. Then multiply the "Weights" by the "Scores" for each factor to obtain that factor's "Total." Adding the values in the "Total" column will give you your personal ranking for the school ("School Evaluation Score").

This "School Evaluation Score" can later be compared to similar scores which you calculate after you visit other schools. In some cases, your ratings may suffer from the same problem that interviewers face; early ratings will tend to be lower because you are comparing the school to an ideal that probably doesn't exist. Later ratings will tend to be higher since they are being made in comparison to schools you have previously visited. If you take this into account, you should have no difficulty correctly interpreting the scores.

FIGURE 22.1

Interview Notes

School ____

Address ____

Secretary ____

Telephone ____

INTERVIEWER	NOTES
1.	
2.	
3.	
4.	
5.	

OTHER NOTES

23

The Interview

Questions are never indiscreet.
Answers sometimes are.

— Oscar Wilde, *An Ideal Husband, 1.*

Nearly everyone who gets invited for an interview has the "paper credentials" to get into medical school. Their GPAs are at least adequate, they did pretty well on their MCAT, they have some clinical or research experience, and their reference letters imply that they possess most of the qualities necessary to survive medical training and to be good physicians.

So the interview is a very important determinant as to whether an individual is accepted to medical school. Applicants must demonstrate to the interviewers that they are not complete social misfits—or at least that they can hide it well enough to survive the interview. (If you can hide your lack of socialization, you have demonstrated that you have "growth potential" and may eventually acquire better social skills. Some physicians, of course, never develop these skills and their careers are usually spent far from patient care.)

— Why Interview Applicants? —

Most, but not all, medical schools interview applicants. These interviews have two purposes: To assess applicants' characteristics and to "sell" students on their schools (see Figure 23.1). In general, interviewers want to be sure that candidates fit in with their school's culture and mission, aren't "off-the-wall," and have the maturity to make this important career decision.

Part of the purpose of assessing an applicant's *characteristics* is to predict the individual's success in medical school. Medical schools and interviewers both claim that they use interviews to assess "noncognitive" variables, such as people skills, friendliness, interpersonal skills, communication ability, and social skills. While this may be true, studies show that the characteristics medical school interviewers most commonly assess, in order of frequency, are:

1. Motivation for and interest in medical school
2. Interpersonal skills and character
3. Maturity
4. Evidence of extracurricular activities
5. Communication skills
6. Empathy and concern for others
7. Social awareness and self-awareness
8. Knowledge, judgment, and problem-solving abilities

At least one-third of all medical schools assess some or all of these qualities during the interview.

FIGURE 23.1
Typical Interview from the Interviewer's Viewpoint

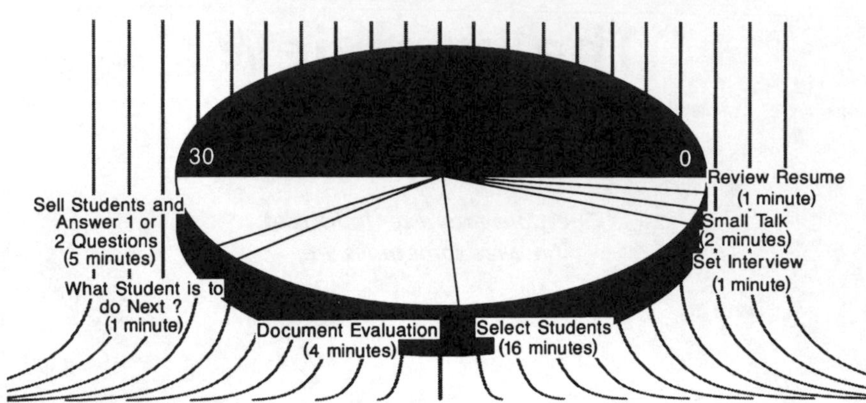

©2003 Kenneth V. Iserson. All rights reserved. Reprinted with permission from: Iserson KV. *Iserson's Getting Into A Residency: A Guide for Medical Students*, 6th ed. Tucson, AZ: Galen Press, Ltd., 2003.

Characteristics less frequently assessed include: emotional stability, integrity and responsibility, academic performance and ability, learning approach and study habits, health-related clinical research experience, coping skills and support, community service, leadership, work experience, deportment, and appearance.

Interviewers generally assess communication and language skills informally. However, extremely good or poor language skills affect most students' interview ratings. One-fifth of schools formally evaluate language skills by keeping track of the amount of time the applicant speaks, the vocabulary used, and their clarity and speech habits. (Most interviewers are not trained for this type of interview, however, so these evaluations may not be reliable.)

Medical schools also strive to *entice individuals* whom they see as the "best" applicants to come to their school by showing off the school's best points. They do this by demonstrating their academic strengths and most impressive facilities, and by emphasizing their community's benefits. Most urban schools emphasize their community's cultural attributes, while suburban or rural schools describe their lifestyles. (When you get to this part of the presentation, realize that it's mostly a public relations display.) An important part of the interview visit, however, is to allow applicants to see the reality of a particular medical school so that they aren't surprised when they arrive on their first day.

A number of studies suggest that interview scores (especially from structured interviews) seem to correlate well with the same student's subsequent Dean's letter—the summary of medical school performance sent to residency programs. Many of these letters contain an overall assessment of students compared to their classmates. Students with high interview scores most often have very favorable Dean's letters, while those with poor scores rarely have favorable letters.

How Important Is the Interview?

Very important! You may have spent four or more years achieving your GPA and several months studying for the MCAT, but most schools consider your interview evaluation to be the *most important admission factor*. On average, the interview evaluation counts 35% in the admission committee's decision!

The factors considered important for admission are, in order:

1. Interview evaluation
2. Undergraduate science GPA
3. Reference letters
4. MCAT scores
5. Undergraduate nonscience GPA

According to a Cornell University study, most students who were not accepted to medical school but who should have been accepted based on their GPAs and MCAT scores (GPA >3.5 and MCAT >30 total) were introverts. Nearly nine out of ten of these students with GPAs >3.7 were in this category. Introversion becomes painfully obvious in the interview setting. Since faculty use interviews to assess how well applicants might interact with patients, any shyness will be a detriment.

The following are typical characteristics of introverts and extroverts, taken from Paul D. Tieger and Barbara Barron-Tieger's book, *Do What You Are*:

Introverts

- Are energized by spending time alone.
- Avoid being the center of attention.
- Think, then act.
- Are private; prefer to share personal information with a select few.
- Think things through inside their heads.
- Listen more than talk.
- Keep their enthusiasm to themselves.
- Respond after taking the time to think things through.
- Prefer depth to breadth.

Extroverts

- Are energized by being with other people.
- Like being the center of attention.
- Act, then think.
- Tend to think out loud.
- Are easier to "read" and know; share personal information freely.
- Talk more than listen.
- Communicate with enthusiasm.
- Respond quickly; enjoy a fast pace.
- Prefer breadth to depth.

Consider which characteristics most describe you, and ask the opinion of your friends, family, teachers, and premed adviser. Many people exhibit mixed traits and there is no harm in this. But watch out during an interview; you don't want a medical school interviewer to describe you as "shy," "quiet," "private," or (horrors!) "introverted." The mock interview, described in Chapter 20, can help you overcome the most obvious flaws in your interview style, whatever your personality traits.

Regional Interviews

Some U.S. and Canadian schools—and many foreign schools—offer to interview applicants at regional locations convenient to the applicant. Domestic schools may employ this technique as a screening mechanism or to entice certain applicants to apply to their school. Often, these interviews will be with either an admission officer who travels to other parts of the country or the school's alumni who live nearby. The benefit is that applicants save time and money. The downside is that applicants do not get to see the school's facilities or interact with students and faculty. If you have such an interview and think you may want to attend the school, try to visit the campus before you "sign on," perhaps after you have been accepted. But be advised: Many of the schools that offer regional interviews suggest that "serious applicants" interview at the school, implying that regional interviews are viewed as a lesser option.

Seven U.S. and Canadian schools currently offer regional interviews: Duke, George Washington, Johns Hopkins, St. Louis University, UMDNJ–New Jersey Medical, University of Michigan, and Yale.

Most foreign medical schools offer interviews in the United States or Canada. While this is very convenient, the danger of not seeing what you are getting for your tuition is greatly magnified in the case of foreign schools (see Chapter 17). Except for the relatively few schools with stellar reputations and great track records, *do not accept any offer until you see the school*. In some cases, students have paid their money, traveled to the schools, and found that they didn't even exist!

— The Interview Day —

The medical school interview has changed little over the past half century, except that women and minorities now participate in significant numbers. This description of interviews in the late 1950s in the book, *Boys in White* (Univ. of Chicago Press, 1961), could well apply today.

> In the fall of the year, several thousand college seniors get out of their casual college clothing, put on the uniform of the young executive . . . and present themselves to be interviewed by the admission committees of medical schools. They are a picked lot. They have done well in college, and they have given good account of themselves in the standard tests taken by all students who apply to enter medical schools in this country.
>
> The interview is a serious affair. At stake is one's opportunity to enter one of the most honored and—at the present in America—most lucrative of the professions. They comport themselves on this solemn occasion not as boys but as men. The teachers of medicine who interview them look at them seriously and anxiously. They ask themselves and one another, "Will this bright boy really make a medical man?" (p. 3)

Okay, now it's your turn. You have your interviews scheduled, and you are ready to go and "knock their socks off." Remember that it is not only your interview performance, but also your conduct throughout your entire time at a school that will determine how the interviewers will rank you. So here are some last-minute tips to help you smooth out any remaining rough spots in your presentation.

Timeliness

To mangle an old saying, "Timeliness is next to Godliness." You will make a major impact on all interviewers, a significantly *negative* impact, if you are late for your appointments. Excuses are fine for your mother, your spouse, and sometimes your friends and teachers. But they work poorly on medical school faculty. Faculty members' time is valuable and they have set some of it aside to interview you. Don't waste their time, or yours, by being late. *The key to success is to show up on time, ready for action!*

Of course, unavoidable delays do occur. Unexpected bad weather and transportation breakdowns are the two most common causes (especially during part of the interview "season," which has some of the worst weather of the year). If you run into difficulties that will cause you to be late, have the courtesy to call ahead. Even if you only think that you might be delayed due to these or other valid reasons, let the school know early. They will then be able to reschedule people and, possibly, work you in at a later time or on a later date. Do not leave them wondering what happened to you. Even if you do not care about that school, leaving them hanging is extremely discourteous and unprofessional.

Confirm Your Interview

Although you are expected to be on time and at the correct location, either you or the school may have made a scheduling error. It is very embarrassing for an applicant to show up on the wrong day for a scheduled interview because of miscommunication.

Occasionally, there is a problem at the school requiring that interviews be postponed or rescheduled. Mistakes also happen, especially when there are dozens or hundreds of individuals interviewing at the same school during a short period of time. Moreover, since you may be on the road, they may have difficulty contacting you about such a situation. (That is one reason to give them your cell phone number and e-mail address. You should check your e-mail daily when you are on interview trips.) The professional way to avoid complications is to call to confirm your interview a day or two before traveling to the school. That way you stand little chance of making a wasted trip or being embarrassed by a scheduling mistake.

Know the Schedule

If you can get your interview day's schedule for each school before you arrive, so much the better. Have them fax or e-mail it to you. You will then know how to pace yourself throughout the visit. You will also be able to plan specific activities for any blocks of free time, such as visiting the library, wards, and other teaching hospitals and clinics (if they are nearby). You can also try out the cafeteria—this could be the food you eat for the next several years—to see how bad (or good) it is.

If you cannot get your entire schedule, at least find out what time you begin. Recheck your information the afternoon before to make certain that it is correct. You cannot afford to be late. It usually helps if you are *early*. Even if you have never been early for anything in your life, this is an excellent time to start.

Once your interviews have started, it is up to the interviewers themselves and the admission secretary to keep everyone on schedule. Many interviewers have a bad habit of running over their allotted times. Do not let this make you uncomfortable. However, when you get to the next appointment late, apologize immediately and explain that you just got out of your last interview with Dr. X. If it happens to you, it has happened to others—and faculty members will understand and not count it against you. They probably are already aware of their colleague's foibles.

Leave Some Time Flexible

Now that you have gotten the interview and have worked hard to make a good impression, don't ruin it by running out early. Would you leave a fancy dinner party before dessert? Of course not. Scheduling departing flights out of town without giving yourself enough flexibility to "eat dessert" is the same situation. Allow yourself some leeway in case your interviews run overtime. When they do, it will usually be because one or more of the faculty has an extra interest in your candidacy. This is a golden opportunity; don't blow it.

Also, you may find that you have a greater interest in a school than you initially thought you would. In that case, you may want to investigate that school's finer points while you are there. You will need some extra time to do this. Remain a little flexible.

Attitude

SMILE! It doesn't cost you anything. Of course you are prepared to be on your best footing with interviewers. But astute admission officers are just as interested in your attitude outside the formal interview setting. This indicates to them how you will behave during day-to-day activities, how you will interact with your peers, and whether you will get along with the faculty and the medical staff.

Be pleasant to everyone—all the time. This does not mean you must fawn over the students and bow down to the secretaries. It does mean, at the least, that you should treat them as the friendly individuals they probably are. Be pleasant and try to interact with them warmly. This also holds true for other applicants. If the other applicants like you, this is often seen as a point in your favor, since working well with a team is a key ingredient in being a successful physician. When applicants are observed as a group, those who get along with others can be clearly identified.

The bottom line is that input from sources other than the interviewers is often very important. You should consider yourself under observation the entire time you are at the school. The show doesn't stop when you walk out the door at the end of the day; it continues with every subsequent phone call and written communication you have with the school.

The Typical Interviewer

All schools use both physician and nonphysician faculty to interview applicants. About two-thirds also use current medical students, nearly half use alumni, and one-third use admission office staff. Only about one-fifth of medical schools use residents as interviewers, and those residents who interview generally went to that school (recent alumni). One-fifth also use community "representatives," including physicians in private practice and lay community leaders.

Some studies suggest that ratings given by women interviewers correlate better with subsequent medical school performance than do ratings by men. Only scores from physician interviewers significantly and consistently correlate with medical school performance. Therefore, if you think you will do well in medical school, hope for an interview with a woman physician.

Interviewers, like all individuals, receive only a small portion of the information sent to them. There is a great deal of "noise" between the encoded message you send and their decoding of that message (Figure 23.2). Interviewers take your information and change it to fit their preconceived ideas. As a medical school applicant, you battle three communication devils:

1. ***Selective exposure.*** People are constantly exposed to a tremendous amount of stimuli. They notice only exceptional deviations from normal patterns. These deviations can be either positive (beneficial to you) or negative (counterproductive to you). It is essential that you be noticed—and noticed positively.
2. ***Selective distortion.*** People tend to interpret data in ways that support, rather than challenge, their preconceptions. They will most likely base their preconceptions about you upon the written material that you have supplied to the school. It is your job to add to the positive feelings you have already worked hard to create.
3. ***Selective retention.*** People forget much of what they learn. Moreover, they forget it quickly. Your job is to make sure that they remember you.

Interviewer Training

Most medical school interviewers have little or no training for the job. While the clinicians may be gifted clinical interviewers, they are generally not prepared to interview medical school applicants, which is much more akin to a job interview than a clinical interview.

Many schools claim to train their interviewers, but the instruction is usually general and consists of reading materials. (Common sense tells you that most faculty interviewers won't read them.) Some schools provide lectures on interview techniques; others show videotaped interviews, role-play, or have new interviewers watch more experienced interviewers (with neophytes often learning their less-than-stellar interviewing techniques). Less than half of all medical schools provide interviewers with any training in questioning, recruiting, and rapport-building techniques. Few schools offer interviewers education about rater bias or structured interviewing.

Given the lack of training, how well do these interviewers do in selecting the best applicants for their medical school? A study using simulated applicants showed that interviewers can correctly identify whether an applicant is "good," "average," or "poor" about half the time. Experienced interviewers did better than novices, but how well an applicant interacts with the interviewer clearly plays a big role in his chance of getting accepted at many medical schools.

That is why, at many schools, applicants have a formal opportunity to evaluate their visit, including the interviews, before they leave. If anything egregious happens during an interview, be sure to notify

FIGURE 23.2

Elements in the Communication Process

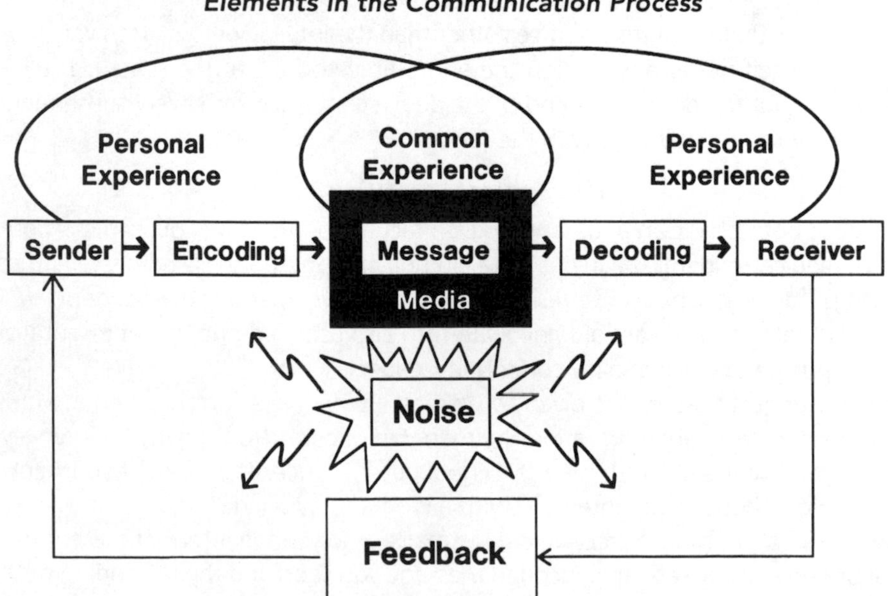

©2003 Kenneth V. Iserson. All rights reserved. Reprinted with permission from: Iserson KV. *Iserson's Getting Into A Residency: A Guide for Medical Students*, 6th ed. Tucson, AZ: Galen Press, Ltd., 2003.

the Dean of Admissions before you leave the school. In some cases, they can offer you another interview while you are there.

In sum, most medical school interviewers are essentially untrained to do the most important single evaluation that determines whether you will get into medical school.

Don't Worry about the "Competition"

One applicant wrote, "One would arrive at the waiting lounge and there in the crowd of applicants *he* would be—the guy with the perfect tan, athletic build, and air of quiet perfection—he even seemed to *smell* successful. . . . Speaking in dulcet tones, he would let slip that he'd already received two admission offers, including one from Harvard. And it was still only October." Okay, so what?

There are one or two Mr. or Ms. Perfects in each medical school class. Don't worry about them—and don't let them rattle you. Most of your medical school class will be composed of people just like you, trying hard, but with obvious flaws. In other words, real people. Ignore the "Perfects" and stick to your game plan.

— A Typical Interview —

The most common interview scenario is the one-on-one serial interview, in which you go from interviewer to interviewer, with each asking his or her own questions. Nearly two-thirds of medical schools have applicants do two interviews, nearly one-third require only one, and a small number require three or four (see Figure 21.2). The average medical school interview lasts 44 minutes.

Most experienced interviewers begin the interview, after suitable amenities, by gathering information, such as why the applicant wants to be a physician, how he or she got interested in medicine, what the applicant knows about a medical career, and what direct exposure he or she has had to medicine. Next, they will often inquire about the applicant's family, personal background, interests, education, and anything in the application packet that they need to clarify. Finally, most interviewers allow time for applicants' questions. If interviewers believe the applicant to be a "good catch" as a prospective student, they may also make a sales pitch for the school.

Most schools conduct relatively standard interviews, no matter who the applicant is. At about 20% of the schools, however, they modify interviews for individual applicants. Some schools add special recruitment (selling) efforts for highly desirable candidates, while others may probe the motivation of weaker candidates and even provide alternative-career counseling. Some schools pair minority candidates with minority interviewers.

Open- and Closed-file Interviews

Most schools supply their interviewers with at least the most important information from applicants' admission packets. This gives them the opportunity to review the packets in advance (see Figure 21.2), so interview time is not wasted rehashing information the applicant has already supplied to the school. This is an *open-file interview*.

Some schools do not supply the interviewers with anything other than the applicant's name. They believe that the absence of information allows the interviewer to form a more objective opinion of the applicant, without being influenced by an applicant's academic record. In other cases, interviewers simply have not reviewed the record, due to their laziness or to a misguided sense of fair play. In either case, they conduct *closed-file interviews*.

If you are faced with a closed-file interview, you will need to recite everything you put in your application to many interviewers. In this setting, some interviewers simply abandon the factual information and ask questions designed to demonstrate your personal characteristics. In any event, smile through the adversity and be gracious.

Structured Interviews

Most interviewers simply ask their favorite questions, being careful to steer away from illegal areas. There are some schools, however, that use a structured interview format, in which the interviewer asks standardized questions (see Figure 21.2). Studies show that this type of interview has a higher validity and reliability than a free-floating interview.

Generally, there are four types of structured interview questions.

1. ***Situations.*** Interviewers ask all applicants to discuss one or more standard situations. They may ask, for example, a hypothetical ethics question.
2. ***Knowledge.*** Interviewers may ask applicants to recall specific information from classes they took or inquire about activities listed in their application. Applicants for combined M.D.–Ph.D. programs encounter these questions most often.
3. ***Tasks.*** Interviewers may ask you to perform simple tasks, such as tying a knot. Often this is not meant to test you, but rather to have all applicants perform specific medically related tasks, so there does not seem to be discrimination against disabled applicants. In rare cases, the interviewer may ask you to take a short test, such as an abbreviated personality profile examination.
4. ***School requirements.*** The interviewer may ask whether you can you meet the school's entry and performance requirements. Again, they normally ask these questions to meet the legal requirement that the disabled must not be asked different questions than everyone else. In some cases, however, interviewers may ask because they question your prior performance or motivation.

You may not be aware that an interview is structured unless the interviewer tells you, you see him or her reading questions from a form, or you have found out from other applicants, medical students, or your premed adviser. There is no need to do anything special during this type of interview. Just be aware that the interviewer may feel a little more constrained than normal and that the conversation may not be as relaxed, since this type of interview limits his or her range of questions. After a structured interview, the interviewer and admissions committee will compare your answers to those of other applicants who have been asked the same questions.

Stressful Interviews

Stress interviews were very common at one time. Interviewers asked questions to purposely make applicants confused, fearful, and hostile. One of the apocryphal tales that continues to make the rounds of the interview circuit (akin to urban legends) is that of the interviewer who asked the applicant to open the window. No matter how much effort the applicant exerted, he could not open it. Of course, it had been nailed shut.

You will not encounter anything that obvious. However, some admission officers believe they can weed out applicants who cannot handle stress. Others treat applicants shabbily because that is how they treat their students. The applicants they actually eliminate this way are those individuals with enough self-esteem to determine that they do not want to work with people who treat potential students like dirt. While the business world stopped using this method long ago, some schools still use it.

Panel Interviews

Occasionally, you will be faced with an unusual scenario—the panel or group interview, in which several individuals interview you at the same time. Experts generally consider this a poor interview technique, both from an interviewer's and from an applicant's perspective. However, it is still in use, primarily because administrators think that it saves interviewers time. Some people also believe this technique is useful to assess the sophisticated communication skills that physicians need.

About 10% of medical schools use panel interviews and most premed committees use them. Most panels have only two interviewers, but some schools have up to 11 people on a panel. All panel members may question an applicant. Some schools use these panels to interview more than one student at a time (see next section).

They generally conduct these interviews using either a question or a scenario format. In the question format, each panel member asks his or her own questions. In the scenario format, candidates discuss one or more cases with the entire panel. At one large medical school, each member of a seven-person panel asks applicants the same question. (This must get boring.)

Your best approach in this type of interview is to look at the individual who asked the question when you answer. For a scenario, since it is a question from the entire group, look at all the members while answering. If an individual member asks you a follow-up question, address only that person when answering. Do *not* try to determine the most influential person on the panel so you can direct most of your attention to him or her. The others will feel slighted. When the panel members meet later to discuss the candidates, your implied insult will damage your chance of getting into that medical school.

For some reason, panel members may feel obliged to put stress on interviewees, as one candidate found to her dismay.

> **One interviewer, who was sitting across from me, looked at his watch as soon as I began answering his question. He must have looked at his watch 20 times during the 30-minute interview. I completely lost my train of thought and went into a blabber-blunder mode for about five minutes—complete stream-of-consciousness. By the time I left the interview, I was devastated, thinking that I had no chance of getting into that medical school. Only later did I learn that the group usually picked one person to be "rude," so they could see how the interviewee reacted under pressure. Actually, I got accepted to that school anyway.**

A particularly nasty variation used at some schools is to sit the applicant between the wings of a V-shaped table facing the interviewers seated on both outside wings. They then pepper interviewees with questions, alternating sides to make candidates swivel their heads back and forth to answer each question. One applicant quickly adjusted by simply slowing down and completely turning to face each questioner when she answered. Her solution was to avoid getting flustered. You could also get up and move your chair back so the angle to view the interviewers is not so acute.

Multiple-Interviewee Panels

Even worse is another technique employed, thankfully, by only a few, Gestapo-like schools. At the end of an interview day, they bring two or three students at a time into a roomful of faculty. They then rapidly ask the students the same questions at the same time. This is really an abuse of power. My suggestion, if this happens to you, is to stand up, thank them for their time, and leave without participating.

> **One school had three students being interviewed at once by a panel. A woman from an excellent Midwestern school was seated with two Ivy League men. One of the men dominated the discussion. When they were asked what they did in stressful situations and she answered that she talked it over with her twin sister, this other applicant guffawed. She became rather depressed by this episode. Another applicant in a similar situation stood up, walked out, and later received a written apology from the Dean of Admissions. This second applicant ended up going to that school. The obnoxious character did not.**

If you are faced with any type of panel interview, remember that it will be as unnerving an experience for everyone else as it is for you. So, keep cool and knock their socks off!

Silence

The most stressful time in any interview can be a period of silence. This is an occasion to reveal all your twitches, nervousness, and insecurity. It is also an opportunity to show self-assurance. Be strong!

Silence occurs for several reasons. Rarely are faculty interviewers disciplined enough, or nasty enough, to impose a period of silence simply to test an applicant. Rather, they may remain quiet while they contemplate a question or your answer. They also may suddenly have remembered that they did not turn off their headlights when they parked their car that morning. Don't feel that a period of silence is negatively directed at you. Sometimes the interviewer doesn't even know it's happening:

> **At one school, the interviewer fell asleep during the interview. He asked a simple question, and I had barely started my answer, when he started snoring. I just ended with a sigh, and said "And so that's what happened." I never did answer his question, but he never realized it. I got accepted to that school in spite (or because?) of this.**

Some people respond to silence during an interview by fidgeting. They brush their hair back, move around in their chair, straighten their clothes, or mutter to themselves. Others try to break the silence by repeating (or worse, contradicting) what they just said. Don't do it. Sit still, be calm, and be quiet—it, too, will end. One way experienced individuals combat periods of silence in interviews is to simply begin counting the time to see how long the period lasts. It will seem like days, but it rarely lasts more than 15 seconds. You should practice this during your mock interviews.

You, too, can occasionally use silence to demonstrate your contemplative side. If an interviewer asks a particularly deep or thoughtful question, you don't have to jump in immediately with an answer, even if you are prepared for it. Wait a few seconds as you "think" it through. Rather than appearing impulsive, you will now seem to be a deep thinker.

— Noninterview Visits —

The noninterview visit is still very rare; essentially, it is the same as a traditional interview visit, but without the interviews. At present, only Brown University, which is unique in many ways, invites students to its campus for optional medical school interviews. These visits are solely to provide applicants with information about the school. During the visit, applicants see the physical plant, the didactic program, and the school's social milieu. Without evaluating the applicant in person, the faculty screens applicants on the basis of their undergraduate performance, MCAT scores, and by using other written materials they feel are important. They then assume that students they admit to their school are acceptable. Their studies, based on medical school and residency performance, show that there appears to be no difference between medical school classes chosen based on interviews and those chosen without interviews.

Two other medical schools have also dabbled with eliminating interviews in the application process. The University of Iowa tried noninterview visits, but returned to the traditional application process in 1996. The Mayo Medical School investigated using structured telephone interviews, since they found that this predicts admission committee decisions better than undergraduate GPAs and MCAT scores. The problem for applicants was that they did not visit the school. (It comes as a very nasty surprise to learn just how cold Rochester, Minnesota, gets in the winter.) Mayo continues to have on-site admission interviews.

24

Your Questions

I keep six honest serving men
(They taught me all I know):
Their names are What and Why and When
And How and Where and Who.

— Kipling, *The Elephant's Child*

Judge a person not by his answers,
but by his questions.

— Voltaire

In addition to answering questions, you will need to ask your own. It is important to know not only what questions you want to ask, but also what you are searching for in the replies. You want to hear specific answers, e.g., the percentage of students that have passed the USMLE on the first try, and to observe your interviewers' attitude toward the subjects you raise. Notice as well their attitude toward you as a person and toward students in general. Are they friendly and open? Or haughty and cold? This could make a big difference in how you rank the school.

When you ask your own questions, do so in a courteous, diplomatic manner. More than one applicant has "gone down the tubes" by trying to cross-examine interviewers. Doing so is crass, and demonstrates immaturity. Ask your questions in a way that expresses enthusiasm for a positive answer. Rather than the question "What problems have students had adjusting to the curriculum changes?", you might inquire, "What kind of an impact have curriculum changes had on the students and faculty?" The first is accusatory, the second merely inquisitive. Get your information, but be nice about it.

Ask simple, straightforward, open-ended (requiring something other than a "yes" or "no" answer) questions. Do not ask questions with multiple parts or that are too long to follow easily. If you ask these types of questions, you may not get the information you want; and you will probably make a negative impression on the interviewer.

Know when to ask your questions. Most schools try to give applicants the opportunity to have their questions fully answered. They gain as much, or more, information about you from your questions as they do from your answers to their questions. But, wait until the proper time to ask them. Let the interviewers ask their questions first and wait for them to ask if you have any questions of your own.

Finally, ask the right people the right questions. At the start of your interview day, ask the admission secretary which individuals you will meet and what their positions are within the school. Ask full-time faculty (especially basic science faculty) about changes in the curriculum. Ask clinical faculty about their graduates. Do not ask faculty members about teaching quality or student esprit de corps. These are questions to ask students.

Prepare a typed list of your questions so that you can easily refer to it during your interviews. What are some of the questions you should ask, and what should you look for in the answers? The list below is divided into questions to ask the faculty and those to ask students. You may want to ask both groups some questions, especially question number 21, "Could you give me (show me) an example?"

— The List: To Ask Faculty —

1. *Where are your recent graduates?*

This question is actually a two-parter. The first part asks, "Where are your recent graduates geographically?" Are they only in local residency programs or are they spread throughout the United States? This gives you a realistic perspective about the school's orientation and its reputation among residency programs. The places where recent graduates have obtained training positions reflect the school's reputation and the quality of graduates they have produced.

The second part of the question asks, "What types of residencies do your graduates enter?" Have they primarily gone to community-based primary care residencies, or are they also at academic centers in "difficult-to-match-with" specialties and programs? How many have gone into clinical practice and how many have gone into research? (If more than 10% of any school's graduates are in research, the school is heavily weighted in that direction.)

Ask this question in a general manner. If either part is not answered, follow it up with a more specific question designed to get the missing information. If you cannot get adequate information, simply ask, "May I see a list of residency programs where your recent graduates went?" All schools have these lists, at least for their most recent class; some even post them on the school's website. You then can evaluate the answer at your leisure. Also, find out (from the student records or school's alumni office) if any recent graduate from the school lives near your home; you could gain valuable insight into the school by talking with this individual.

2. *For which special programs is this medical school well-known?*

If you have learned of any special programs the medical school offers, either from their brochure or from talking with students, you may want to ask for more details. You also want to know about any other special programs, some of which may be too new to list in the brochures or on the website, or which have not yet started. These programs will be bonuses of attending this medical school, and the interviewers will generally be thrilled that you asked about them. This allows them to show off their school to its best advantage.

When evaluating the interviewers' answers, remember that programs in which you do not plan to participate (such as an international electives program which won't fit in with caring for your three young children) are of no benefit to you. They may, however, demonstrate the medical school's educational direction, which is very useful to know.

3. *How many courses use Problem-based learning?*

Problem-based learning, or PBL, is the newest wrinkle in medical education. The concept stems from the need to teach physicians to independently solve many clinical problems and to stay current with medical changes throughout their careers. PBL is a logical method of introducing the physician's mindset into the teaching environment. Students receive problems (often clinical cases), which they must then solve (often with a study group) using appropriate resources from diverse sources. The process is similar to the method clinicians use to solve clinical problems on a daily basis. The difficulty with applying this method to basic science courses is that it works best in small groups and requires more faculty. When medical schools' budgets are being decreased, hiring more faculty for teaching becomes very difficult.

A few schools, such as Harvard, Hawaii, and Kentucky, have taken the PBL "bull" by the horns and run with it. Most of their courses, both preclinical and clinical, use this teaching method. The majority of schools, though, have applied the method to only a few preclinical courses or to parts of courses. In most cases, they also still rely on standard testing methods to evaluate students, rather than using their contributions in these small-group sessions.

If PBL-type instruction strikes you as useful and is compatible with your learning style, you may want to investigate it further.

4. *How much flexibility is there in the course work and the timing of the courses during the preclinical and clinical years?*

None of us can anticipate all the twists and turns our lives will take. Although you may plan to zip through medical school, family, health, or other reasons may make you slow down or take time off. How flexible is the school? If something untoward happens, do they have policies allowing students to make up lost time without harsh penalties? Will your loans and scholarships remain active even if you must take a decreased course load or a leave of absence? Will your tuition decrease if you take fewer (or no) courses for a period of time?

Or, you may wish to accelerate your medical school experience. Is that possible? Can you go straight through without breaks? Will the school give you any credit for advanced study that you completed before medical school? If so, can you take advanced classes to shorten your route to a medical degree? If you do finish early, will the school allow you to "graduate" early to start your residency training? Again, each school has its own rules, which may change over time. It's best to know them in advance.

5. *What changes do you anticipate in the school's curriculum?*

This is a question to ask a Dean or basic science faculty member. Clinical faculty are often not aware of curriculum changes until well after they have been implemented.

You should expect to hear about such changes. Most U.S. and Canadian medical schools are constantly implementing curriculum changes. In some cases, they have little impact on students—either because they are relatively minor or because the school can't seem to get its act together to structure and fully implement them. In other cases, the curriculum and teaching methods undergo dramatic changes over a short period.

Problem-based learning (PBL) is an example of such a change. (See Question 3, above.) If you learn that the school is going to implement PBL, ask how long they have been working on introducing it into the curriculum, which courses use it, how much of each course is taught in this way, and whether they have adequate facilities and faculty to use this method. Later, ask the students the same questions. Also ask the students how well PBL is working, and how well they think they are learning using this method. You might want to ask similar questions about the use of computers in teaching and testing.

6. *How much of an administrative, legal, and bioethics curriculum is there?*

Although academicians have been slow to recognize it, medicine is also a business—at times a dangerous business. How much training in the administrative and legal aspects of medical practice will you get at this school? Will you acquire at least a basic understanding of managed care and other health care delivery systems? Will you receive in-depth training about the legal pitfalls now so common in medicine, or will this come only after your first malpractice suit?

How about the ethical issues that now pervade medicine and society? Does the school offer a formal bioethics course, or are these topics addressed only when it is convenient or if there is extra time? Although these topics do not fall within the "hard science" component of medicine, they fall into the two, often-neglected, parts of medicine's tripod: Medicine as an art and medicine as a business. Schools that neglect these components do so at their own—and their students'—peril.

7. *How well have students done in their class work?*

Nearly all applicants want to ask this question. The answer you will get, however, is of little help in evaluating the schools. Nearly every medical school has the same percentage of students who get "Honors" and the same percentage who fail their courses. The difference, however, is the criteria schools use to determine these rankings, which are based on their student bodies and their educational expectations.

The question you *should* ask is: How do the school's students do on Step 1 and Step 2 of their licensing examinations (USMLE or COMLEX)? (See Question 14.) This is important, not only as a measure of the school itself, but also when residency directors assess applicants from many different medical schools. The licensing examination scores are the only "even playing field" on which they can compare applicants. It is also vital when assessing non-U.S./Canadian medical schools. Graduates who cannot pass Steps 1 and 2 of the USMLE, the Clinical Skills Assessment, and the Test of English as a Foreign Language (TOEFL) cannot do a U.S. residency and thus cannot be licensed to practice medicine in the Unites States.

8. *What are the clinical opportunities for students during the preclinical years?*

You will eventually be exposed to the clinical side of medicine, but, if you are like most students, you do not want to wait two more years to start working with patients while you vegetate in the classroom and laboratory. Are there early opportunities to work with clinicians?

The typical answer is that you will begin a physical diagnosis course sometime during your first year. This means that a resident or a "standardized patient" (a patient trained to teach you specific parts of the physical examination) will probably instruct you and a small cohort of your classmates in the basics of taking a history and doing a physical examination. That is fine. However, physical diagnosis is to clinical practice what the crust is to a pizza—it serves as a necessary foundation, but it lacks any zing on its own. Your real question is whether you will have an opportunity, be encouraged, or even be required to actively participate with clinicians while you learn the basic sciences.

This may be a personal bias, but if there was no opportunity for early clinical exposure, I would be reluctant to go to that medical school. I have found that most medical students learn best if they can relate their classroom work to the patients they see in the hospital and clinics. Clinical work also reminds them that patient care is why they are in medical, rather than graduate, school.

9. *What types of clinical sites are used for clerkships?*
How many students do rotations at other institutions or internationally?

Medical schools have a variety of clinical settings available for their students, including ambulatory clinics, private preceptors, private hospitals, and rural clinics. Which ones does this school offer? Is there a wide variety of both outpatient and inpatient facilities, and does each offer a large number of electives? Or are all the facilities generally the same, with little chance for electives? Do the types of clinical facilities mimic the medical practice you envision yourself having? (For example, if you think you want to do missionary or travel medicine, you will need to get some clinical experience at remote sites.)

Since you will spend more than half of medical school in clinical settings, this information is very important. Be aware that many older, poorly funded medical school-associated hospitals and clinics do not have enough staff (you do the "scut" work), enough up-to-date working equipment (you make do using available materials), or the necessary variety of clinicians (you must refer interesting patients to other facilities) to provide you with the quality experience you need.

Medical schools in the United States and Canada have an excellent reputation, specifically because of the superb clinical training they provide. Don't shortchange yourself. Investigate the clinical sites that are available at each school.

10. *How many students are involved in required or voluntary community service?*

Some medical schools have outreach programs for the aged, the poor, new immigrants, or children. These programs allow students to get excellent clinical experience while working within the local community, so find out if they exist. The type and extent of, and support for, these programs also gives you insight into how the school regards its community—and vice versa. (Some schools allow students to begin these patient-contact experiences in the first year.)

11. *How does the school deal with students who are exposed to infectious diseases?*
Is disability insurance provided?

Medical schools have become more aware of the dangers to medical students from infectious diseases. (Before the antibiotic era, it was not unusual for medical students or young house officers to die from contagious diseases such as tuberculosis.) Today each school has policies for dealing with medical students who acquire or who are exposed to serious infectious diseases. Some schools provide free immunizations, prophylactic medications, and disability insurance, while others believe that students can fend for themselves. For example, nearly all M.D.-granting U.S. medical schools require students to have health insurance, and about half require disability insurance.

Every medical student should be immunized against hepatitis B, tested for TB, and have their Rubella titer checked (necessary for obstetric work). Ask if the school pays for these. Of course, *you* don't plan to acquire a serious infectious disease or to be stuck by a needle that may be HIV- or hepatitis C-positive. However, for the sake of argument, what if something does happen? Will this school help you out? For peace of mind, find out before you need to know.

12. *What research opportunities are available?*

Some applicants may envision careers in academia or research. If you are one of them, look for a school that can provide you with the resources and guidance to do research.

Start with the question "On what research projects are current medical students working?" That will give you a range of interests and the levels of activity. Are faculty mentors available? Is funding for student projects easily obtained, or will you have to scrounge for it? Is research barely tolerated, or actively encouraged? How fairly have students been treated when working with faculty members on research projects in the past? (Have the students done the work and been given secondary, or no, credit?)

Also find out about facilities and time available to do research. Does the institution provide facilities? Can you take a leave of absence to pursue research or a research-oriented degree? In addition, if you do research and it is accepted for presentation at a national meeting, will the school pay for you to go? Will they give you the necessary time off? Ask now to avoid disappointment later.

13. *What types of student evaluations are used? How often are they given?*

Frequent feedback is essential for medical students' mental health, as well as to insure their best performance. At one time, a well-known medical school had no required examinations until the end of the second year, when students took the first part of the licensing examination. The suicide rate soared. This was because many of the students, rather than being calmed by their instructor's assurances that they were learning more than enough to pass the examination, were scared witless that they could not possibly know enough.

Much of a medical school's curriculum is "open-ended," meaning that there is no real limit to the knowledge encompassed within a subject area. An individual could study anatomy and biochemistry his entire career without knowing all there is to learn about the subjects. Yet, medical students must take a national examination covering all the subject areas they study. They do best if they get repeated feedback by taking examinations similar to the licensing examinations in each area. This pertains not only to the preclinical, but also to the clinical years.

Unfortunately, the tests most medical schools administer have not yet caught up with the changes the USMLE has made in its examination format. The new format contains many questions that integrate diverse subject areas, reflecting the way clinicians actually apply the basic science and clinical knowledge they have learned. These types of questions can be difficult to formulate, especially if faculty from different disciplines must work together to do so. More importantly for medical students, these questions can be difficult to answer if you first experience them when taking the licensing examinations. Therefore, it is useful to know if the school has changed its testing methods, including offering computerized tests, to mimic those used on the national exams.

You also want to know whether students get feedback during clinical rotations, or only after finishing each specialty's clinical work and taking the course's written test. The latter suggests sloppy teaching methods. As an applicant, you may ask to see a sample set of evaluations for a student's clinical rotation. Be careful, however. The evaluation and teaching methods usually vary among departments, even within the same school. In addition, although they are not supposed to vary within the rotation sites, they often do.

14. *How have your graduates done on the USMLE or COMLEX? How does the school assist students who do not pass?*

The primary goal of a medical school education is to prepare you to practice medicine. An important milepost in your career is passing the medical licensing examination (USMLE for M.D.'s or D.O.'s, and COMLEX for D.O.'s only), often referred to as "The Boards." (At many schools, passing individual parts of this examination is required before students can advance to their next academic year or graduate. Both exams have three parts, the first two of which are usually taken while in medical school.) Your score on "The Boards" may well determine the type and site of the residency you can obtain, so doing well is important. How have students from this school done on their licensing exams? How many passed on the first try? This can be asked tactfully, as in "How many students had to take their Boards more than once?" (Some schools have had failure rates of 10% or more above the national average on USMLE Step 1.) Also ask if there are programs to prepare students for these exams, as well as any special programs to help those who don't do well (fail) on their first attempt.

Some of the faculty interviewing you should know this information or could easily obtain it from the Dean of Students. If not, call, visit or write to the Dean of Students yourself. Be sure to say that you are interested because you are applying to the school. Although information on specific students is, of course, confidential, the cumulative data should be available to all applicants. If it isn't, there may be a problem.

15. *What does the student honor code cover? What is the policy on family (parental) leave? What is the policy on infections in medical students?*

If you are interested in a medical school's specific policies, determine how best to ask about them. You want to know about the honor code? Great question! This suggests, correctly or incorrectly, not only that you are aware of the profession's ethical norms, but also that you understand how medical schools operate. Interviewers are usually impressed that anyone even thinks to ask this question. Follow up by asking how well the code operates, and whether students are involved in its associated arbitration process.

Twenty-five years ago, just asking about a family or parental (at that time called "maternity") leave policy would have doomed an applicant's chances of getting into medical school. Today, parental leave policies are probably among the safest ones to discuss. Pregnancy among medical students and their partners is no longer a rare event, and most interviewers expect any married or engaged applicant to ask about these policies.

Asking about infections among medical students, however, may be near the "taboo zone." Simply asking this question suggests that you have a personal problem with which the school probably does not want to deal. While the Americans with Disabilities Act of 1990 supposedly prevents discrimination toward applicants with infectious diseases, few schools will accept applicants who could cost them money (increased premiums on health insurance policies) or adverse publicity, or subject them to legal actions from patients or other health care workers.

16. *How many students dropped out of school recently?*

With 400 or more students at most medical schools at any given time, some of them will inevitably leave school before graduating. This occurs for many reasons. Many take leaves of absence due to family or personal crises, expecting to return. Some transfer to other schools. A few decide that a medical career is just not for them. (For example, Michael Crichton, the well-known author, described how a faculty mentor kept encouraging him to stay in school, although he had already determined that he was not cut out to be a physician.) This information is not, however, what you are after. You are asking whether any students have left because they failed academically. This happens at every school, but how did this school's faculty try to help the student before he or she was forced to leave? Are there tutoring programs for those in academic "hot water"? Of course, *you* won't need these services. But it is nice to know that they are there if a friend of yours does.

17. *How does your mentor/adviser system function? Who are the advisers—faculty members, other students, or both?*

As mentioned elsewhere in this book, medical students do best if they have mentors. The definition of "adviser" varies widely among medical schools. While each medical school has a system to supply advisers and most medical students utilize these individuals (with varying intensity and success), it is useful to know in advance what the school offers. Do they assign individuals who will see you as a faceless number and "rubber stamp" your forms, or individuals who will help you over rough spots and offer career advice?

18. *What kinds of academic, personal, financial, and career counseling are available to students? Does the school offer any of these services to spouses and dependents/children? What support services or organizations are there for ethnic minorities and women?*

If the medical school has none of these services available, it indicates that they (1) have little regard for your future welfare and (2) have little understanding of what their mission as a school really entails. In either case, you've been warned.

Most students must finance their medical education with a complex arrangement of scholarships, loans, and grants. Even those who don't must balance personal and school finances. Personal financial management is not usually taught in the premed curricula, and the "school of hard knocks" is a terrible place to learn the ropes. Many medical schools offer special programs on personal financial management and provide counseling for students if they face personal or financial difficulties. Financial aid offices often provide assistance with personal finances, including evening courses on basic financial management. If these are available, they may save you many anguished hours trying to salvage your credit rating or making ends meet.

Schools with a large number of minority students often have special advisers and support groups for them. Women students also may have their own faculty- or student-run support groups, although these do not receive as much funding as those for minorities.

All schools help their students to find residency positions. What has this school done for its recent graduates? With the increasing difficulty of locating positions in some fields (e.g., general surgery, emergency medicine, orthopedic surgery), it is important to learn how much effort the staff expends on helping its students. Some schools hold seminars to educate students about the entire process, some provide specialty-specific counseling, and some even provide students with a copy of *Iserson's Getting Into A Residency: A Guide For Medical Students,* 6th ed. (Sorry about the plug, but I'm proud of this book's contribution to medical education. See *Annotated Bibliography*.) Some schools also use the faculty's contacts to advocate with residency programs for their students.

19. *How stable are the current tuition and fees? If they aren't fixed, at what rate will they increase?*

You will be paying a lot of money in tuition and fees (unless you go the Uniform School for Health Sciences). Fairness dictates that schools tell you how much they think these costs will increase over the next four years. Many schools plan tuition and fee increases that far ahead, so they can provide you with this information. Ask now so you won't have an unpleasant surprise halfway through medical school.

20. *What impact has health care reform had on this school's teaching and patient care?*

Far from an idle question, the past decade saw the most devastating and grievous insult to medical student education in this century. Medicare rules and punitive actions (fining a number of medical schools tens of millions of dollars each) have made most university teaching hospitals seriously restrict what medical students can do clinically. For example, third- and fourth-year medical students on their clinical rotations routinely wrote histories, physicals, progress notes, and orders in their patients' charts that were later countersigned by their supervising physicians; in most cases, they can no longer do that. The encroachment of managed care organizations has siphoned off many patients from teaching hospitals, their teaching services, and their clinics. How does this medical school ensure that medical students will continue to get a quality medical education and graduate with a good fund of clinical knowledge and skills? Or do they adhere to the "European" system of making students wait until after graduation to learn clinical medicine?

21. *Could you give me (show me) an example?*

This is one of the most important questions you can ask during interviews. Ask it to supplement information you get from faculty and students.

While trying to ascertain whether you and a medical school are compatible, you need to have specific information, not unsubstantiated statements. "Our students' on-call schedule is very benign," says the interviewer. "Could you show me the current students' night-call schedule for your service?" you ask. After you see the schedule, you will know if it really is as easy as he claims it is. Don't forget that the interviewer's interpretation of what "benign" means could be very different from your own interpretation. (If, as in some schools, the students don't stay all night, find out when they leave and when they must return.)

Many questions lend themselves to confirmation or explanation. Asking for examples is a safe, pleasant, and enlightening way to get further information about important points.

You can never ask this question too often.

— The List: To Ask Medical Students —

22. Tell me about the library, student housing, and extracurricular facilities.

The library is the bellwether of an institution's educational commitment. Is it stocked with useful and up-to-date materials, equipped with a sufficient number of modern computers with links to other medical resources, staffed with knowledgeable and helpful people, and open long (or all) hours? Note that many medical students need the library not only for its resources, but also for its tranquillity. Those who live in noisy surroundings need it as a place to study, and many medical libraries provide special rooms for group study. If so, the school has done its job.

Do you plan to live on your own, or would you like the option of a school-sponsored dorm or other housing? Many schools provide low-cost housing alternatives, generally in close proximity to the school. Given the time (and financial) pressures of the first and second years, these options can look very good.

Since, despite your best intentions, you really cannot study 24 hours a day, you may be interested in free or low-cost recreational facilities. If they are located near the school, they can provide an enormous boost to your mental and physical well-being, as well to the camaraderie among classmates.

23. What computer facilities are available to students? Are they integrated into the curriculum/learning?

Our new century is computerized and the medical field is no exception, although it currently lags behind other segments of society in its use of computers. All physicians will need to be computer literate, using information systems as readily as they do their stethoscopes. Does the school provide access to computers and use them for teaching? Are computer labs or specialists available to students? How about special computer courses? It's no longer enough to know how to take a medical history and do a physical examination. You also need to know how to access computerized medical records, lab results, bedside nurses' notes, clinic schedules, library materials, databases, and, eventually, billing records.

Somewhat beyond the call of duty, some schools also provide students with PDAs to use for class work. Others require them to purchase their own. Many, especially those associated with universities, also provide students with e-mail addresses—essential for communication with classmates, professors, mentors, and, eventually, residency programs.

24. Is there a note-taking service? If so, is it university- or student-run?

Note-taking services can be a wonderful boon to many medical students. However, there are differences in the way each service calculates the charges and in the finished products. So, if this service interests you, find out the details. Aside from the cost, begin by finding out how the service runs. Do faculty members provide the "notes" or, at least, correct those taken by students? If not, errors often creep into them—a major flaw in any such service. If taken by students, are the notes transcribed from lecture tapes or from notes taken during the class? In the latter case, note-takers can miss significant material. Do one or two excellent note-takers do the work, or does the job rotate among participants? As you know from viewing fellow students' notes, this latter method is not optimal, but it is usually cheaper. Some note-taking services also provide copies of old exams to use for studying. These can often be very helpful. One caveat, of course: Many students do much better when they take their own notes and use them for studying. If you are one of these, only use a note-taking service as a supplement.

25. *Do students regularly have an opportunity to formally evaluate the faculty? What recent changes has the school made due to this feedback?*

This question really asks, "How important is the educational mission?" Feedback on the faculty's performance is an essential part of all education. If the school is serious about educating medical students, it will have a good evaluation system. Virtually all schools, however, will say that they have an evaluation system, since their licensing body requires it. What tells you that they are serious about these evaluations is if they can recite substantive changes that have been made based on these evaluations. That means that they not only have the system, but also value their students' opinions.

26. *What contact will I have with the clinical faculty?*

The material that the school sent to you said that they have hundreds (or thousands, in some cases) of clinical faculty members. Did they happen to mention how often you will have contact with *any* of them? The faculty can only help you if you have direct contact with them. If faculty members hide in their offices or labs rather than attend in the clinics, wards, emergency departments, or operating rooms, they might as well not be there. Many of those listed as faculty may be on clinical services with which students have little or no contact, such as radiation oncology or nuclear medicine. Others may be located at remote sites where students don't go.

So the questions that you should ask are "How often are the faculty members present?" and "How often do students find that faculty input is not available when they want it?" You might want to specifically ask "How available are they on nights and weekends?" Of course, as a student, you will usually be taught by residents. Nevertheless, you will also want input from the faculty, who are supposedly in that position because of their knowledge and experience. Do members of this school's clinical faculty teach students on a regular basis?

27. *Is a car necessary to get to clinical rotations or to decent housing? Is parking a problem?*

Do you need or want another hassle in your life? Cars eat up money and cause unexpected difficulties when they break down, but offer you greater mobility than you might otherwise have. If a medical school is in a large city with excellent public transportation, you may be able to survive without a car—at least for the first two years. Your classes will generally be held on a regular schedule and any outside clinical work will normally be in the school's vicinity.

When you get on your clinical rotations, however, you will work bizarre schedules and will often be "farmed out" to many different hospitals, sometimes in other cities. Will you need a car then? If you won't (as in Chicago, New York, or Washington, DC), you may be able to save a lot of money and aggravation.

Finally, how about parking? Is it difficult to find (or expensive) at the medical school, hospital, and other clinical sites? If you drive to your medical school interview, you may get a taste of what the parking is like. Is this the norm for students, or just for visitors?

28. *What support staff are available?*

Medical students commonly feel overworked during clinical rotations because there are too few people to perform what are typically nonphysician tasks. You owe it to yourself to find out how much scutwork the school's medical students typically perform.

Who starts routine IV lines, draws blood, and does clerical work? Who pushes patients to x-ray or to radiation oncology for treatments? Does the institution provide an adequate level of nursing and ancillary support?

The opposite situation applies at some schools, and this can be even more dangerous to a student's education. If nurses or special technicians start most of the IVs, put in most of the catheters and nasogastric tubes, or draw most blood samples, students miss out on valuable opportunities to learn procedures they will perform throughout their careers. While some students may complain that they do these procedures so often "they can do them in their sleep," that is exactly when you will have to do most procedures during residency—so you had better know how to do them very well.

While faculty may be able to tell you about some of the available clinical support, ask the students and residents for the real answers. Don't complain after the fact. Find out in advance.

29. *What is the call schedule on third-year rotations?*

In general, the third year is when you will have your first real contact with the clinical side of medicine—including working nights and weekends. It is a very stressful time, second only to internship. (For most students, their excitement in learning new procedures, seeing new clinical environments, and the fact that they have finally found their way to clinical medicine outweighs the stress.)

Third-year schedules can affect your learning in two ways. The first is by providing too little time for learning. Students on some services work such long hours that they do not have enough time to read and absorb new information. In good clinical settings, however, the practical knowledge and skills they obtain make up for this. In addition, even though the hours may be long, most clinical rotations have "down times," during which the student's clinical duties are light or nonexistent. Those are fine opportunities to read (or to waste time).

The second way third-year schedules can affect your learning is by providing too much free time. This rarely occurs, but it can have an adverse effect on your clinical proficiency, such as when students do not spend the night with their hospital-based teams. While this may sound great, the result is that residents and faculty view students as frivolous attachments to the clinical team, since they are not around when their help is most needed. In addition, since students gain so much clinical experience after normal hours when fewer people remain in the hospital, they lose important educational opportunities by not being there.

At most schools, your fourth-year schedule will be your responsibility and will depend almost entirely on the rotations you select. Therefore, you should ask about the third-year rather than the fourth-year schedule.

30. *What is the patient population I will see?*

Patients (their numbers, ages, the nature of their diseases, and who cares for them in what settings) are the basic element of all medical training programs. The school's hospital and clinic rotations must provide an adequate number of patient encounters for a thorough education.

Find out about the patient population served and the distribution of disease processes. Some teaching hospitals have an overabundance of a few types of disease processes, such as penetrating trauma, tertiary oncology, or AIDS. A skewed distribution does not provide adequate training for students who will eventually serve a more diverse population with more common diseases. Today, as physicians deliver more medical care in outpatient settings, students should also see patients in the clinics and outpatient surgeries.

31. *On what medical school committees (e.g., curriculum, admissions) do students have representation?*

You may want to ask this question even if you have no plans to become active in your medical school's politics. Student representation, especially if it includes voting and other rights of full committee members, shows a school's commitment to medical student input and involvement. If students currently going through the curriculum don't have a ready conduit to the curriculum committee, for example, it demonstrates that the faculty (or at least the school's administration) wants a barrier between students and teachers. Do medical students have a significant voice in determining and changing school policy? If they do, there is probably more of collegial relationship between the faculty and the students. If not, the student body can become frustrated from banging their heads against the proverbial brick walls to get changes made in the school's education and management.

32. *Do the students socialize as a group?*

Group socialization demonstrates one element of esprit de corps. Social events help to relieve stress and cement personal friendships that can last a lifetime. Are social events classwide or institutionwide? You may also want to ask about the ratio of married to single students (in the current first-year class or the institution), how many students have children, and how often the social events involve spouses, significant others, or children. Does there seem to be any particular area of special interest among the students and faculty, or do their interests vary?

Is socializing related to educational activities, such as journal clubs? Or are there separate events, such as volleyball games or picnics? Note that if the activities are student-organized, they may vary considerably from year to year.

— Confirm Questionable Points —

A number of the questions that you raise may be critical. Which questions these are will depend, in part, upon your own "Must/Want" Analysis. Even though the questions are important, you may not get straight answers to some of them. This may be because no one you ask knows the answer. For example, in October no one may really know how many of the faculty will still be on-site next July. However, you may be getting the runaround for other, more nefarious reasons. If you ask a faculty interviewer about how much interaction the faculty has with students and she hems and haws, then you will need to search elsewhere for the real story. This is where the technique of crosschecking facts comes into play.

Whenever you have some doubt about the answer to an important question, repeat the question to another interviewer. Better yet, if it is appropriate, ask a student. In fact, if the issue is extremely important to you, ask everyone you talk to the same question. But be sure not to do so within earshot of others you have already asked or will ask that same question; it will be taken as a sign that you doubt their honesty, which, of course, you do. Remember that the school is trying to sell its product to you at the same time that you are selling yourself to it. Not all salesmen are honest. *Caveat emptor!*

— What Not to Ask —

There are specific questions that you must not ask during an interview, even though the answers are important. These questions involve two areas: vacation and competition. Let's discuss them individually, so you will know what information to get from *appropriate* sources.

If you don't think that *vacation* is important, wait until you have been up most of every night for a week studying for finals or Board exams. At that point, dreaming about an upcoming vacation may be all that keeps you going. Most students have 8 to 12 weeks of vacation between their first and second years, with an equivalent amount during their third and fourth years, although they have more choice as to when they schedule this time off. Usually, the school specifies the amount of vacation time in their material for applicants. If you don't have the information, either ask for a typical student's schedule (which will include vacation) or ask a noninterviewer student. Don't ask an official interviewer, since inquiring about vacation time during any interview is akin to asking whether you will actually have to do any work in medical school. While everyone understands that vacation—even a student's vacation—is important, interviewers assume that during the interview you will concentrate on the great educational experience that the school offers, rather than your time off.

Who is your *competition*? It doesn't matter! Asking about other applicants will serve no purpose and can only direct an interviewer's attention away from you. The key, as has been stressed throughout this book, is to put your own best efforts before the admission committee and let them select you based upon what they see. Forget the others. Concentrate on selling yourself.

— What Not to Do —

Just as there are certain questions that you should avoid, there are certain things that you should not do during the interview. The items below are attitudes or actions that will evoke negative responses from interviewers.

Show Discouragement

Be upbeat! This is your time to shine. One poor interview should not influence the rest of your visit. Remember that the interviewer may not have thought it was a poor interview at all. Looking "down in the dumps" will destroy any positive effect that your interview could possibly have made.

Stand up straight. *SMILE*—it won't break your face. If you cannot find the courage to smile through some adversity now, you are really going to be in trouble when you get into medical school and residency.

Disparage Other Schools, Faculty, or Applicants

You might very well be asked about the other schools that you have visited. The question could be phrased as "Tell me about the poorest schools that you have visited." Although this may be tempting—you may have interviewed at some places you really didn't like—back up a minute to redirect the question. Say that you are not in a position to determine which schools are poor, but there may be some that do not seem to meet your needs. Then you can describe specific aspects of schools that you feel did not fully meet your expectations. However, go easy. If you really berate a school that you have visited, the interviewer might wonder what you will say about his or her school when you go elsewhere.

It should go without saying that you should not say anything derogatory about faculty at another institution. Academic medicine is rather close-knit; there is a good chance that the person you describe will be well-known to the interviewer.

Falsify Background

Although it may appear that you could say almost anything about your background during the interview and get away with it, you do so only at great risk. The first danger is that your lies will immediately be discovered.

Not many years ago, an applicant was eloquently describing his activities in the Emergency Medical System. He stated that he frequently responded to calls even while in school. It was quite an impressive achievement. Yet, as he went on with his story, it became obvious to the interviewer that he was being less than honest. As the applicant described activities on the opposite side of the country, it just so happened that the interviewer was also from that area and noticed major factual errors in the story. A call to the student's adviser later confirmed his deceit.

The second danger is even worse. If information that you provide when you apply for any position, including that of medical student, is later found to be false, it is grounds for immediate dismissal. Thus, giving fraudulent information puts you in jeopardy throughout medical school. Stick to the truth. Make it appear as favorable as possible, but keep it honest.

> **A number of years ago, a Dean of Admissions at a U.S. medical school was talking with the premed adviser at a large university. The premed adviser was lauding the attributes of a particular student. The Dean replied that she hoped that this student was not the same (bad) caliber as a current student they had from that school, whose name the premed adviser recognized. After a moment of silence, the premed adviser said he would get back to the Dean—he had something to check. When he called back, he related that the medical student in question, now in his seventh year (having failed and repeated the first, second, and third years and who was now only weeks away from graduation), had never graduated from their school, much less gotten the glowing reference letters the student had submitted. After an investigation by officials, including the FBI, the student was dismissed, along with a number of individuals at other medical schools who had also used fraudulent application credentials.**

Use Inappropriate Humor

There is a place for humor in interviews. One medical student said,

> **I'm always ready with a joke. So when I was asked by an interviewer if I knew any good ones, I said, "Sure. A horse walks into a bar and sits down. The bartender says to the horse, 'Hey, what's with the long face?' I'm sure that swung it for me." [After asking that question, the interviewer got what he deserved.]**

While jokes can be stupid, they should not be offensive. Even if an interviewer laughs after you tell an off-color, sexist, or racist joke, you almost certainly will have lowered yourself in his or her eyes. In fact, a large number of administrators consider off-color or inappropriate humor to be the major breach of etiquette in the classroom and workplace. If you have an uncontrollable urge to tell these types of jokes, at least keep them out of the interview.

Drink Coffee, Smoke, Chew Gum, or Bite Nails

Four activities that you must not indulge in during an interview are drinking coffee, smoking, chewing gum, or biting your nails. You may be offered coffee by each interviewer. They mean well. However, do they also offer you a bathroom break in the middle of the interview? No! If you are concentrating on a full bladder instead of the interviewer's questions, you could end up in deep trouble.

There are four problems with smoking. The first is that it is unlikely that your interviewer smokes, since the habit is now rare among physicians and medical students. The second is that smoking looks bad during an interview. So, even if you are addicted, hold out until the interview is over—or you have left the school for the day. The smell that lingers on your clothes and breath if you smoke will not endear you to nonsmoking interviewers. Third, interviewers may be biased against hiring smokers. As of yet, no medical school has gone public with an explicit ban on accepting smokers, but it is likely that it would be legal. There is no protection under current civil rights legislation for smokers. This makes it legal for an interviewer to ask whether you are a smoker. Note, of course, that if they inquire, it can only be a (un-Lucky?) strike against you. Fourth, an old ploy, used to put an applicant in an awkward position, is to suggest that you smoke and then have no ashtray available. You can avoid this (rare) problem by not smoking.

Chewing gum is absolutely out. It evokes a fatuous, sophomoric image that will destroy everything that you have worked so hard to achieve. If blowing bubbles is your "thing," hold out until you leave the hospital. No one is physiologically addicted to chewing gum (except, perhaps, nicotine gums—use patches during interviews). One stick of gum at the wrong time can cancel your chance for a medical school slot that you really want.

Finally, even though you are nervous and your common response is to bite your nails (or fidget in your chair or play with things on the interviewer's desk), restrain yourself when at medical schools. It signals your neuroses to interviewers. To clinicians, it also demonstrates potentially dangerous, infection-producing behavior.

— Steering the Interview —

As you will see in the next chapter, it is often possible to steer an interview in a direction that is beneficial to you. You can mold your answers to interviewers' questions in such a way as to bring out your most favorable points. However, this must be done subtly. Some interviewers may view your pushing an interview in a specific direction as being impudent. This, of course, would be counterproductive. So, if you can, steer the interview in a beneficial direction—but do it so gently that the interviewer does not notice.

— Why Interviews Fail—

There are six main reasons why interviews fail.

The first is due to the applicant's *arrogance* or *cockiness*. You may be "hot stuff," having come from a high-powered undergraduate school where you achieved stellar grades, whipped the MCAT, and acquired research and clinical experience. So what! Unbelievably, there are plenty of others just like you who are being interviewed. The interviewer won't be impressed, since he or she was probably a

FIGURE 24.1

Guidelines for Effective Listening

- Demonstrate attentiveness.
- Listen for "what" and "why" questions.
- Listen for key issues.
- Keep your mind from drifting.
- Repeat the interviewer's message.
- Do not interrupt the interviewer.
- Ask clarifying questions.
- Identify the interviewer's feelings and attitudes.
- Do not let "trigger words" like "foolish," "immature," etc., provoke an emotional response.
- Do not waste time evaluating the interviewer.

similar "star" when applying to medical school. Those factors got you this far. The point during interviews is to see if you are personable and have the qualities we desire (but don't necessarily achieve) in the physician population. Eat a little humble pie before you begin your interviews. Think of how exalted you will feel if you don't get accepted. Save the strutting for your friends and family (most of whom also won't be too impressed).

The second reason interviews fail is due to *inadequate preparation* on the applicant's part. While this book helps you to prepare for the medical school interview, in the end, it is up to you to know about the medical field, the school, the faculty, your own ambitions and desires, and the questions that interviewers will probably ask. It takes hard work on your part to get ready for interviews, but, in the end, it is worth it.

The third reason that interviews fail is because the *applicant does not listen to the interviewer's questions*. This results in miscommunication, distorting the messages coming in and going out. It often happens when you let your mind wander during an interview—and it spells disaster. Remember that an interview is a battle of wits. If your thoughts stray, you lose!

Since many medical school interviews are conducted in busy offices, clinical settings, or even hallways, you may have to concentrate very hard on the interview to avoid the ever-present distractions, sometimes justifiably called "interview blockers" (Figure 23.2). This can be difficult, but your experience studying in noisy dorms and libraries should help you to concentrate on the task at hand. Moreover, don't just listen to the question; *listen to how the question is asked*. Many times an interviewer will give the astute listener clues to the answer he or she expects to hear. Figure 24.1, *Guidelines for Effective Listening*, should help you out.

Occasionally, your mind may go blank during an interview. It's okay. Just apologize to the interviewer and simply ask for a moment to think about the question or, second best, ask the interviewer to repeat the question. As Sam Donaldson, the television newsman, says, "Even the pros get tongue-tied."

One caveat. If you have carefully read the questions and answers in Chapter 25, you may be planning how to answer what you think will be the next question. Or, you may be analyzing how you might interact during your classes and clinical rotations with the faculty and students you have met. Stop! Turn off that mental audiotape and concentrate on what the interviewer is saying. By now, you should be able to answer questions without rehearsing, and there will be plenty of time later to analyze your visit.

If you really listen, and you still cannot understand what an interviewer is looking for, ask for clarification. This might also work (once) if you miss a question completely—but it would be unwise to use it repeatedly. Remember that the most ego-gratifying thing you can do for interviewers is to listen to them.

If you are asked a question that you just don't know how to answer, be honest and say so. Perhaps you can say, "I'll have to think about that. Can we come back to it later?" Normally, the interviewer will oblige. It is then your responsibility to return to the question before the end of the interview. At that point, if you still cannot come up with an answer, say that you will continue to think about it and get back to the interviewer by letter. Then, in your thank-you letter (which is much more impressive than an e-mail note), give that interviewer an answer to his or her question. In these cases, honesty (and thoughtfulness in later responding by letter), rather than bluffing your way through an answer, may be your ticket to success.

A fourth reason for interview failures is that interviewers may get annoyed by *answers to questions that were not asked.* Here, you are treading the fine line between guiding the interview and destroying it. For example, answering a question about your spare-time activities with a description of your undergraduate awards makes you sound like a politician: They routinely give answers that have no relation at all to the questions that they were asked. Rather, talk about the rock band you organized or the Internet bulletin board you established. These both answer the question and highlight your initiative and talents.

Similar applicant behavior that interviewers detest includes answering questions with questions, telling jokes to change the subject, and answering with gibberish. Like reporters, good interviewers will simply repeat their original question until they get a straight answer. In addition, because interviewers are human, many factors can influence their behavior, and answers that might work one day may not work on another (see Figure 24.2).

The fifth way to wreck your interview is to *ramble*, providing superfluous information. Interviewers are easily bored—not surprising given the number of applicants they often must see in one day. If you have a lot of information to impart in answer to a specific question, tell the interviewer the main points, and then ask if he or she would like you to continue. For example, if you are asked to describe your most interesting volunteer experience, give the highlights in several sentences and then ask if the interviewer would like to know more. Since you are watching the interviewer while you answer, you may note nonverbal cues indicating that you have said enough. In general, keep your answers brief, to the point, and interesting.

The sixth reason interviews fail is that the applicant inadvertently gives *warning signals* to the interviewer that there may be an unstable personality lurking behind a deceptive smile. Trained interviewers seek specific warning signs (Figure 24.3). Very few faculty interviewers are sophisticated enough in the techniques of employment interviewing to consciously recognize these signs. Being good clinicians, though, they unconsciously assimilate clues and will give the applicant a poor rating. It would be a good idea to review the warning signs and make certain that you do not demonstrate any unintentionally.

Interview Disasters

Interviewers see some unusual behavior during medical school interviews. (They understand that premeds are strange, but there are limits.) In general, interviewers eliminate applicants from consideration if they demonstrate arrogance, superficiality, egocentrism, over- or under-confidence, or incompetence.

FIGURE 24.2

Factors Influencing an Interviewer's Behavior

- Age & Stage in Life Cycle
- Cultural Background
- Interests
- Prior Experiences
- Goals/Aspirations
- Successes/Failures
- Mood
- Personality

FIGURE 24.3

Warning Signs for Interviewers

- Inconsistent answers during the interview
- Inconsistencies between what is said in the interview and past performance
- Abrasiveness or any other personality quirk that makes the interviewer uncomfortable
- Evasiveness
- A pattern of unhappiness in former jobs
- Blaming others for all the applicant's problems
- Dullness when responding to questions
- A pattern of taking advantage of, or of deceiving, other people

Adapted from: Perham JC. Spotting bad apples: the warning signals. *Dun's Business Month*. October 1986, pp. 54-56.

Life, however, is often stranger than fiction, and so are some interviews. An applicant's behavior often reveals her true nature. Below are some unusual, but real, interview moments.

- One applicant remained standing when offered a chair, so that he could maintain his "superior" position.
- On her arrival, one applicant put her overstuffed briefcase on the interviewer's already-full desk.
- Another applicant left the dry cleaning tag on his jacket, saying that he wanted to demonstrate just how neat and clean he was.
- Yet another arrived with his long hair tucked under his collar, thinking that no one would notice.
- When told to take his time answering questions, an applicant began writing out the answers before speaking.
- One applicant described his recent divorce—blow-by-blow.
- Another contradicted everything the interviewer said.
- After sneezing, one applicant asked for a tissue, and then another. She had neglected to bring any, although she had a cold.
- One applicant finished all the interviewer's sentences for her.
- Another suggested that he had friends in the administration who would get him admitted to the school.
- As the interviewer described the school's important features, one applicant yawned widely and stared at his watch.
- When an interviewer received a telephone call, the applicant sulked, taking it as a personal affront.
- In one instance, an applicant's mother called and asked that the interviewer strongly consider her son.
- Another brought his five children and the family cat to the interview.
- At the end of the interview, one applicant simply asked, "How did I do, Coach?"

Hopefully, you won't make any of these errors. Just think, if this is how other applicants behave, you don't have much to worry about. Of course, most applicants to medical school are smart enough to avoid such crass behavior.

FIGURE 24.4

Key Personality Traits Interviewers Seek

Personal

- Enthusiasm
- Motivation/Initiative
- Communication Skills
- Chemistry
- Energy
- Determination
- Confidence
- Humility

Professional

- Reliability
- Honesty/Integrity
- Pride
- Dedication
- Analytical Skills
- Listening Skills

— Evaluation of Applicants —

Nearly half of all medical schools simply have the interviewer rate the applicant using a narrative statement, without any formal rating scale. The balance use Likert-type scales with numbers or adjectives (1=poor to 5=excellent) to describe either end of the scale. A few schools have behavioral descriptions (e.g., works in medical area 20 hours per week) as their guide. Figure 24.5 is a typical interviewer rating form.

When, as is usual, there is more than one interviewer, the admission committee gives a final "interview score" at nearly half the schools. At another one-third, there is an automatic arithmetic addition or averaging of the scores. At the remaining schools, the interviewers reach a consensus by discussing the applicant interviews with each other.

— Sell Yourself —

The bottom line during an interview is that you must sell yourself. At the same time, you also need to elicit information. To have the best chance of being accepted by the schools that interest you, you must do a good job of showing your own wares. Interviewers look for specific attributes in applicants (Figure 24.4). When talking with individuals at each school, keep these attributes in mind. Remember that interviewers rate these elements in the applicants they interview. Although every school has a different rating form for interviewers to complete, the essential items will always be the same.

It is your job to demonstrate how closely you resemble the interviewer's ideal candidate by exhibiting the sought-after traits. Remember, if you don't sell yourself, no one else will do it for you!

FIGURE 24.5

Interviewer's Rating Form

Date____________________________

Applicant Name ____

- **General:** Physical appearance (dress, grooming), character (reliability, honesty, integrity), timeliness, energy

  1 = Poor *2* *3 = Average* *4* *5 = Excellent*

- **Knowledge:** About medicine, about this school, computer literacy

  1 = Poor *2* *3 = Average* *4* *5 = Excellent*

- **Intellect:** Mental ability, judgment, flexibility, communication ability

  1 = Poor *2* *3 = Average* *4* *5 = Excellent*

- **Emotions:** Work ethic, personality, motivation, teachable, attitude, sense of humor, stability, outside interests, self-confidence

  1 = Poor *2* *3 = Average* *4* *5 = Excellent*

- **Record:** MCAT score, class rank, undergraduate school, quality of reference letters, clinical experience, extracurricular activities, honors/awards, research

  1 = Poor *2* *3 = Average* *4* *5 = Excellent*

________ **Average of Scored Items**

Narrative Summary

Recommendation (circle one)

Reject *Conditional* *Accept*

25

The Questions—The Answers

Silence is the only good substitute for intelligence.

— Folk saying

As I walk'd by myself, I talk'd to myself,
And myself replied to me;
And the questions myself then put to myself,
With their answers, I give to thee.

— Bernard Barton, *Colloquy With Myself*

What must you remember in the process of preparing for, and participating in, the interview? Only two things: *Sell yourself by showing your best qualities* and *prepare in advance*.

Interviews generally start with some simple pleasantries and then move on to the skills/attitude evaluation (Figure 23.1). In this part of the interview, no matter what the format or the type of questions they use, most admission officers look for three qualities: *intellectual strength, energy*, and *personal compatibility* with faculty, staff, and current students. Interviewers don't really want "the truth." They want "correct" answers. If you believe there is no such thing as the correct answer to a typical interview question, you are sadly mistaken. Good interviewers know exactly what they are looking for in a medical student and they know how to extract the needed information in a way that is disarmingly benign. Their questions are simply tools with which to hammer out an impression of the applicant.

Intellectual Strength

Admission officers already know a great deal about your intellectual strength. Reference letters, MCAT scores, transcripts, and narratives of your undergraduate performance have gotten you the interview. Now it is time to see if you can think on your feet. Can you apply what you know to new situations? Are you really interested in learning, or just in getting through school so you can practice medicine? Do you know about anything other than your schoolwork? Was it your quick smile rather than a solid intellect that got you your good grades? Do you believe that you have very little left to learn? Basically, the interviewer tries to determine what you know, how well you are able to apply what you have learned, and if you really want to learn any more.

Energy

Medical students spend the majority of their time attending to their studies and memorizing vast amounts of information. No matter where a school is located or how well the curriculum is arranged, fatigue, stress, and depression can result. The less these factors afflict a school's students, the fewer problems the faculty must deal with and, consequently, the happier they are. Make them happy. Demonstrate that you have the good humor, self-confidence, and stamina to go the distance. However, don't just say the words—show them by your actions during your entire interview visit.

Personal Compatibility

Each medical school has its own "personality." Will you fit in? Will they be comfortable with you? A little thought and a lot of care are necessary here. A hyper-aggressive image may work in some schools, but fail in others. Modify the image you project to meet the situation. However, don't fool yourself. If you will not fit in with a group, it is better to find that out during the interview, rather than after you arrive for at least a four-year stint as a student.

— Presenting Yourself —

Show Your Best Qualities

As you answer the interviewers' questions, remember to highlight your best qualities.

Be careful not to sell yourself short! Know what your strengths are. Know what the school is looking for, and, if you don't have an obvious opportunity to let the interviewers know how well you meet their needs, make one. This may come through answering questions—all questions—with different strengths you want to emphasize. Alternatively, it may come in the form of a "question" at the end of the interview, such as: "Is it true that students have an opportunity to get involved clinically during their first year? I'm really excited about that possibility."

Prepare

When getting ready for the interview it is absolutely essential to *prepare, prepare, prepare!* How many hours have you spent studying, preparing for exams? One thousand? Five thousand? The interview is, perhaps, the single toughest exam of your life. Make sure that you spend enough time studying for it. The steps to preparing for an interview are very straightforward: Learn to talk about yourself easily. Also learn the types of questions interviewers ask and what they hope to learn from your answers. Then combine these and formulate your answers in advance.

Talking about Yourself

Blowing your own horn can be very difficult. Many people are loath to extol their own virtues. However, you must be ready to tell the interviewers about your positive qualities so that they hear them loud and clear.

First, put yourself in the position of the faculty and students where you will be interviewing. What work habits and personal characteristics would you want in an individual applying to *your* school? You should be able to get a good idea of what they are looking for from the material you have collected from medical student organizations, from the school's own information, and from conversations with medical students and physicians. Write these characteristics down. Then write out questions you would ask to discover if an applicant has those characteristics.

Next, list your strengths that match these characteristics. This step requires a good bit of objectivity. You may need some help from your adviser or a close friend. The following exercise will help you get into the habit of thinking and talking positively about yourself.

Exercise:

List *three accomplishments* of which you are proud and what each indicates about you:

1. ____

____

2. ____

____

3. ____

____

List *three attributes* you have that will make you an excellent medical student:

1. ____

____

2. ____

____

3. ____

____

List *three abilities* you have that will make you an excellent physician:

1. ____

____

2. ____

____

3. ____

____

Now, can you use these accomplishments and abilities in a short narrative that describes you? If you can, you have made a good start toward a successful interview.

Finally, write some great answers to the questions you developed. Be sure to incorporate your accomplishments and abilities into your answers. However, do not memorize them word for word—they will sound forced. Guests on television talk shows prepare by making a list of the ten questions they *don't* want to be asked and then developing answers for each of them. Note that this process may change a bit as you gain interview experience. However, it gets easier and easier each time you do it, and is well worth the effort.

— Types of Questions —

Typical interviewers use only five types of interview questions, although they can be phrased in many different ways. Recognizing the type of question being asked will help you determine what information the interviewer is seeking.

Closed Question

These questions ask for specific information and simple, definitive answers. "How many years did you go to undergraduate school?" for example, deserves a simple answer, such as "four years." Nothing deep here. Interviewers use closed questions to elicit information that is not included in the application materials.

Open-ended, Informal Question

These questions also ask for specific information, but require more in-depth answers. Such a question might be "What clinical experiences have you had so far?" or "What did you do during the year when you were not attending school?" While the question requires specific information, it allows the applicant a chance to speak and to become relaxed.

Open-ended, Attitudinal Question

These questions determine how well an applicant organizes his or her thoughts before speaking. An example is "What do you think of direct pharmaceutical company advertising to consumers?" Most interviewers want to see if the answer is concise, to the point, and shows that you have the ability to take a reasoned position.

Probing Question

Interviewers ask probing questions as a follow-up to open-ended questions. They are especially useful after the applicant has given an answer expressing an opinion. An example of this type of question is "Why do you feel that way?" This makes applicants defend and further explain their previous answer. It also allows an interviewer to control the direction of the interview.

Sometimes an interviewer will go back to an earlier answer, quote the applicant, and ask a probing question, such as "You said you felt this area of the country was more progressive medically than your undergraduate school's area. Why is that?"

Leading Question

Interviewers use leading questions to direct applicants' answers or to see if they have the gumption to express their own opinions. Unfortunately, it is not always easy to tell what is expected. Such a question might begin "Medical students should do night call just like residents," and be followed with "Don't you agree?" The interviewer may be serious or merely prodding the interviewee into an untenable position. If the intent is unclear, a way to find out *before answering* is simply to ask, "What makes you think that?" (In this case, interviewers often welcome a question in response to their own.)

Impossible Questions

Medical school applicants often encounter questions that they cannot answer—either because they lack the experience to answer them or because there simply is no answer to that particular question. Interviewers may ask, for example, about specific clinical scenarios or about how to solve the problems with health care delivery in the state. It's not only okay, but also prudent, to say "I don't know." Add, of course, that in the first case you don't (yet) have the knowledge and experience to answer the question and, in the second, that you would love to hear the interviewer's thoughts on the matter. (You would, wouldn't you?) The key is to admit that you do not have a clue when you are asked questions that you really should not be able to answer.

Helpful Sources

Many premed offices keep files containing the questions that their students have been asked at specific medical schools. They may also have information about the interview formats different schools use. Check with your adviser, since having some advance knowledge can be very helpful. Information about medical school applicants' experiences during interviews also shows up at various sites on the Web, although they are often short-lived. Contact your premed adviser or club for the current Web addresses for this information.

— Questions and Answers —

The following are questions that medical school interviewers have asked applicants over the past several years. Following the prototypical question and a discussion of possible answers, I have listed similar questions that may be more thoughtful or original than classics such as "Why do you want to be a physician?" Perhaps some interviewers will read this list and buff up their interviewing "act." Of course, it is impossible to predict every possible question. If you prepare for the questions listed below, you will have the confidence to answer anything an interviewer asks.

1. How are you today?

What a pleasant way for an interviewer to begin. A simple icebreaker, you think. Wrong! Sophisticated interviewers use this and similar questions as rapid and effective screening tools. "Gee, it's raining outside and I got soaked coming here," said one applicant. "I'm really frustrated that my plane was late and that I had trouble getting a cab," whined another. Even worse was the response, "Terrible! My last interviewer really raked me over the coals!"

Interviewers look for individuals whose demeanor stays upbeat even under adversity. The travails on the interview circuit are insignificant when compared to those of medical school, residency, and medical practice. Simple opening questions delivered in an off-hand manner often expose an applicant's true personality far better than the well-rehearsed "deep" questions that most applicants have come to expect. The point is that *there are no innocent questions*!

- Did you have any trouble finding us, or getting here?
- You're looking a little flustered. What's wrong?

2. Do you have any questions?

This is the "behavioral" interviewer's classic opening. The interviewee is expected to take the initiative right from the start. Many applicants respond by asking standard questions and, therefore, waste this opportunity.

When the "any questions" opportunity begins an interview, use it to show that you are achievement-oriented and really do know about medical school and the career on which you are embarking. An example might be, "I recently read in *American Medical News* that many schools now use computer-based teaching and examinations—especially in anatomy and pathology. Is that true here? I have a particular interest in computer programming. Would the instructors be interested in helping me to develop programs for their use?"

Get such information from reading recent issues of American Medical Student's Association's (AMSA) journal, *The New Physician*, or from the AMA's *American Medical News* (*AMNews*). Both publications contain a wealth of information about the current state of medical education and medical practice. Most college libraries subscribe to both. You can also get copies of *AMNews* from many physicians. In addition, the AMA's website (www.ama-assn.org) often highlights the newest medical information—both clinical and nonclinical—offering you some great discussion topics.

While some excellent interviewers ask this question, usually faculty members who are poor interviewers ask it because they do not know what other questions to ask. Since many applicants say this is the most common question they get, you may want to make a long list of your own questions to use as answers.

Never answer "No" to this question since, no matter what the situation, a negative answer indicates that you do not have a serious interest in that school.

- Do you know much about our medical school?
- If you were in my (the interviewer's) seat, what you would ask? . . . Okay, now answer those questions.

3. Tell me about yourself.

This is the granddaddy of open-ended queries. You have the opportunity to say almost anything you want. You can put your best foot forward or stick it right in your mouth. This question gives you, by design, no hint of how to answer it. You can go off on almost any tangent and, if the interviewer is any good, you will be able to talk for as long as you want. The longer you talk, however, the less chance you have of scoring high on that interviewer's list of candidates.

To answer this and similar open-ended questions, first respond briefly and succinctly to the single question, "What motivates you?" For example, you might cite your most applicable qualities by stating, "I am a hard worker with a longtime interest in medicine. My role models and my reading first got me interested, and my volunteer clinical experiences only solidified my desire to be a physician." Then stop.

Ask the interviewer if you should continue. This demonstrates that you understand the interactive nature of interviews and that you have consideration for the other person's role. When you ask whether you should continue, many interviewers will direct you to specific areas for further discussion. This will help both you and the interviewer a great deal by allowing you to answer the questions that the interviewer really wants to ask.

One applicant, anticipating this question, went into his interviews with confidence. He said that the secret to successful medical school interviews was "a story" that would intrigue interviewers and make him a memorable (in a positive way) applicant. He had had an adventurous year off after undergraduate school and was prepared to talk about it in a way that emphasized his strengths. As he said, "I know lots of folks with great grades and solid MCAT scores who never got in. Perhaps they just didn't have a good story to tell." This student, now a practicing physician, understood that he should be prepared for the questions and that his answers should be interesting.

- What three adjectives best describe you?
- What are your team-player/leadership qualities?
- What might give me a better picture of you than I can get from your résumé?

- Tell me a story about yourself that best describes you.
- If you were going to die in five minutes, what would you tell someone about yourself?
- Of which of your accomplishments are you most proud?
- Do you have any hidden achievements or qualities of which you are secretly proud?
- Tell me about your elementary school years.
- Tell me about your adolescence.
- How have you changed since high school?
- What was the most important event in your life?
- What shaped you and got you to where you are today?
- What was the most difficult thing you have ever done?
- You have lived in [region/state/city] for the past 20 years; why would you consider moving to the other end of the country (smaller city) now?
- What are you passionate about?
- What do you like to cook? To eat?
- If you died right now, what would you want on your tombstone?
- How would your best friend/roommates/relatives describe you? What negative things would they say?
- Why did you write . . . in your personal statement/essay?
- What one thing do you want conveyed to the admission committee?

4. *What are your strengths and weaknesses?*

This is the "Tell me about yourself" question phrased in the negative. It essentially asks, "Tell me what's wrong with you." Basically, the interviewer asks you to jump off a cliff of your own design. All you need to do is to redesign the cliff so you can climb rather than jump.

First, answer the question about your strengths concisely. Beware of talking too much. Then work on the other half of the question—the dangerous part.

At this point, you must turn your "weaknesses" into more strengths. Of which character flaws would interviewers at a medical school approve? Is your weakness that you are obsessive about completing your work in an exacting manner? Or is it intolerance for your compatriots who do not perform their assigned tasks with a professional attitude? Maybe it is an inability to go home at night until all of your work is completed. These are, undoubtedly, the types of "failings" that the faculty will be interested in encouraging rather than disparaging. However, in relating these faults, show at least a little remorse about having them. Don't be glib.

Nearly all medical schools report that their interviewers ask about strengths and weaknesses. How boring!

- Tell me about your "secret identity," the part of your personality that you don't ordinarily share with strangers.
- Are there any skeletons in your closet that you want to tell me about?
- How well do you take criticism?
- What is your pet peeve?
- Which of your qualities would you want to pass down to your children?
- What about yourself would you change if you could?
- What is an example of your contributing to a group effort?
- What is your number one accomplishment?
- How have you used your strengths to help others?
- What are your three strongest qualities?
- What are your two worst qualities?
- Have you demonstrated leadership in any extracurricular activities?

5. *If you could be any cell in the human body, which would you choose and why?*

This is not much different from the directive to "Tell me about yourself." It is, however, a bit more inventive and has been used by many interviewers, especially for biology/zoology majors, ever since it found its way into *The New England Journal of Medicine* (1990;323:838). Unfortunately, you may have a hard time not being reminded of *Saturday Night Live's* Baba WaWa's similar question, "If you could be any kind of twee . . . ?" (Don't laugh when you're asked this question!)

Many applicants say that they would want to be neurons "to be in control, to be stimulated and stimulating, and to be the center of all things." Since you are now prepared in advance for this question, try to be original. No matter how nerdy the question sounds to you, don't be surprised if it pops up along the interview route.

- Do you see yourself as more relaxed/casual/informal or as more serious/dedicated/committed?
- Which is more important, the ability to organize, structure, and prioritize, or the ability to be flexible, modify, change, and make do as needed?
- Which is more important, knowledge or imagination?
- If you could be any kitchen object, what would you be?
- What is the strangest Halloween costume you ever wore?
- What was your favorite book when you were 11 years old?

6. *If your house were burning, what three objects would you save?*

Some interviewers really believe Freudian analysis will help them choose the best medical students. While this may seem to be essentially the same type of question as above, think again. This question narrows the scope to a very concrete and personal level by asking, "What do you value in your own life?" How important are material objects to you? Are you "sensitive" enough to reach for your beloved's picture or are you "sensible" enough to grab the car keys and credit cards?

There is no one correct answer to this question; the best answer depends upon the nature of the person asking the question. Sometimes the questioner actually wants to know whether you have planned ahead or can think quickly, since a fire is a real possibility in our lives—unlike turning into a tree or a cell (see Question 5).

An alternative form of this question is "If you had to repack your belongings, what would you have left behind?" This question is even more concrete, at least for the majority of students traveling to interviews. The follow-up questions will certainly be "Why leave that behind?" and "Why did you bring it?" Pack carefully.

- If you had unlimited money and two free hours (one day, one week, one month), what would you do?
- If you had three wishes, what would they be? (Shades of *Aladdin*)
- If you have moved in the past several years, what haven't you unpacked yet? Why not?
- If you were stranded on an island, what three books would you want to have with you? Why?
- What three material objects are most important to you?

7. *What kinds of people are your friends?*

"Know my friends, know me," goes an old expression. People attract people similar to themselves as friends. Applicants' descriptions of their friends often give interviewers deep insights into their personalities. This question essentially asks you to talk about yourself in the third person.

Answer this question as if you were describing yourself. Interviewers often respond favorably when married applicants state that their spouses are their best friends. Describing a spouse's glowing personal attributes only serves to enhance the applicant, as long as these attributes are not used as a contrast to the candidate's own qualities.

- Describe your best friend/roommate/spouse and his life.
- How are you similar and dissimilar to your best friend?
- If you could dine with anyone from the past, present, or future, who would it be?

- How would your friends or coworkers describe you?
- How do you differ from your siblings?
- What is your relationship with your family?

8. *Who are your heroes?*

Related to the question "Tell me about yourself," this is a deep probe into your psyche. It evaluates your self-image, direction, and goals. How the interviewer interprets your answer may, to some degree, reflect his or her own personality, age, and background. This is perhaps the most difficult interview question to answer. In an age without obvious heroes, your choice will, by necessity, be very personal.

There are several possible responses to this question.

One answer you may have already thought of is that you have no heroes. However, you have just completed many years of schooling, during which you had many new experiences and met countless interesting people as teachers, friends, and coworkers. Viewed from that perspective, it would be an unusual, and perhaps very narrow-minded, individual who could not find someone to look up to as a role model.

Another possible answer is to cite a family member, friend, or personal acquaintance. The follow-up question, of course, will be "Why?" You should be able to identify attributes this person demonstrates that justify your distinguishing him or her as your hero. A parent, sibling, or spouse is usually a very good choice. It shows respect for your family and a firm commitment to your roots.

If you choose a physician as your hero, be prepared to explain how you are trying, or will try, to emulate that person's attributes in your personal and professional life, as well as how you interacted with him or her. This can get somewhat sticky since, if you only had a superficial interaction, it might suggest that you have only a superficial idea about what medicine is and what physicians do.

Historic or public figures are perfectly acceptable answers. You can draw these heroes from science, education, or many other fields. Indeed, discussing the attributes of a lesser-known historical figure may lead the interview into new and interesting areas. Be prepared, though, to discuss the individual's attributes in depth.

Tread lightly, however, if your hero is a contemporary religious or political figure. An interviewer's bias may affect his evaluation of you if your hero exemplifies major philosophical differences between the two of you.

The worst answer is to name a contemporary star of television, the movies, or popular music. In that case, the interviewer probably will view both you and your answer as very superficial.

- What is your favorite movie? Why?
- What is the last book you read?
- What do "success" and "failure" mean to you?
- What do you believe?
- Do you have any black, Hispanic, etc. role models in medicine?
- What physician characteristics do you admire most? least?
- How can you tell if someone is truly compassionate?
- Tell me about your father/mother.
- What cross-cultural experiences have you had?

9. *What do you do in your spare time?*

The primary danger here is to give too long an answer. Everyone likes to talk about him- or herself and this is an invitation to do just that. But keep it brief. If you collect rocks, for example, you might say, "I am an avid rock collector and have been for about five years. I have had the opportunity to travel across the United States and Canada pursuing my hobby and have a great museum-quality collection." Then stop. If the interviewer wants to know any more, she will ask.

Your answer should show that you are not a couch potato (although a computer aficionado is okay). Do not describe activities that may cause you injuries resulting in prolonged leaves of absence from school. Also, pick a noncontroversial activity; avoid discussing hunting, guns, and religion unless you are certain that you will not raise the interviewer's hackles. In general, speak about community-oriented and people-centered activities. The focus of the rock collector's description might be the people she meets at collector's conventions.

The questioner usually wants to learn three things from this query.

First, does the applicant have any interests outside of school and work? An interviewee with no outside interests sends a serious danger signal. Medical students and residents who have no outlet for their anxieties, stresses, and frustrations may decompensate—and become a problem for the faculty. If you have no overriding outside interests, simply mention what you do in your spare time. Yes, spending lots of time with your family, spouse, children, and friends is certainly an outside interest.

Second, is the applicant more enthusiastic about his or her avocation than about the prospect of going to medical school and practicing medicine? Show equal enthusiasm for both.

Third, the interviewer is screening out those applicants who are so wrapped up in themselves that they will not be able to pay any attention to their patients, peers, and faculty. How do they spot these individuals? They are the ones who go on and on and on about their other activities with no prompting—even after the interviewer gives negative cues, such as turning away from the applicant, coughing, or even standing up. Answer questions about your outside activities as you have answered the other questions—fully, briefly, and with enthusiasm.

- What are your favorite games and sports? Why?
- What do you do for fun?
- How and why did you choose your outside activities?
- If you had a completely free day, what would you do?
- What is the most bizarre thing you have ever done (or, did in high school or in college)?
- What was the most unusual occurrence in your life? in the past month?
- Do you think you can remain intensely focused on medicine for the next four (or more) years?
- Besides your future medical accomplishments, what do you wish to be known for by your peers, friends, and family?
- Where have you traveled? Why?
- What nonmedical magazines do you regularly read?
- What have you contributed to groups and activities in which you participated?
- What have you learned from your volunteer work?
- Do you plan to continue your hobbies through medical school?
- What is the last book you read for pleasure?

10. *What clinical experiences have you had?*

At most medical schools, interviewers won't ask about whether you have had clinical experiences, but rather what these experiences were. They do not expect applicants to appear for interviews without having had medical experiences. With the current glut of excellent applicants, most medical school admission committees view it as an extraordinary, and unacceptable, risk to train future physicians who do not know what they are getting themselves into.

Whether your clinical experiences were as paid staff or as a volunteer, whether you merely observed or actually participated in patient care, and whether they lasted over a period of years or were a concentrated experience, you should have gained some valuable insights from them.

Realize that interviewers want you to have had patient contact; you need to know what working with the ill and injured is like. That differs from just "shadowing" a physician; it means talking with patients, families, many types of clinicians, and, if possible, actually participating in their care. Premeds most commonly gain this experience in hospitals, nursing homes, hospices, physician offices, or on ambulances. It's not the hours; it's the valuable lessons you have learned. Now it's time to relate your experiences.

What did you learn? What did you see? Which of these experiences did you like? Which didn't you like? Why? Did they reinforce your desire to be a physician or tend to dissuade you? Interviewers want these details. Describe your experiences with one or two illustrative stories. Think about them before your interviews.

Nearly all medical schools report that their interviewers ask applicants about their experiences in health care and what they are proud of having done in the field.

- How long have you stood on your feet at one time?
- Has someone ever come to you for help with a major personal crisis? What have you done to alleviate their emotional pain?
- What are patients most afraid of when they visit a doctor?
- What would you find most difficult to deal with if you were a patient?
- How well do you know Dr. _______ who wrote a recommendation letter for you?
- Has anyone close to you been seriously ill or died?
- Have you ever been seriously ill or injured?
- Would you stop at an accident scene if there were injured people? (For EMTs/RNs: Do you carry first aid/medical equipment in your car?)

11. *To which organizations do you belong?*

People join organizations that further their own agendas, be they recreational, spiritual, political, or professional. The organizations you belong to reflect your goals, background, and interests. The relevant question here is, how much do you want to reveal?

The groups you join often loudly signal your religion, political or sexual orientation, and cultural heritage. Since prejudice exists in many guises, it may be best to simply discuss the school-based (and if applicable, the professional) organizations to which you belong. These should include the premedical club/honorary, any special organization associated with your major subject area, organizations associated with your volunteer activities or work (e.g., Boy Scouts, National Association of EMTs), or, if you are out of school and working, any related societies.

Most interviewers now understand that pressing you for information about other organizations might violate state and federal laws. Note, however, that anything you included in your application materials is fair game during interviews. If you list an organization on your application, résumé, or personal statement, the interviewer may ask you about it. Although the following questions are all illegal, you'll probably hear some variation of them anyway.

- Your name sounds Hispanic (Arabic, Italian, Vietnamese, etc.). Is it?
- How did you learn to speak (non-English language)?
- Would you have any trouble working with our predominantly Catholic (LDS, Jewish, etc.) patients?
- When was the last time you went back to (country of origin or family's origin)?
- Why do you think you are a minority?

12. *What are your plans for a family?*

You probably will be asked a variety of questions that are not only uncomfortable to answer, but also patently illegal under state or federal statutes. These questions also provide ammunition for discrimination-in-admission lawsuits. (These suits are rarely brought, however, because discrimination is hard to prove in court.)

To determine whether a question is legal, ask yourself, "Is the answer important in assessing how I will perform as a medical student?" If it is relevant, then the question is probably legitimate. (The law, however, can be convoluted. See Figure 25.2.)

Questions about family, child-care, and birth control are most often directed at women. Other candidates may hear inquiries about race, nationality, physical infirmities, religion, and other subjects that are illegal for interviewers to raise. (See also Chapter 10: *Unconventional Premed Students,* and "Illegal Questions," below.)

A legal way to ask such questions is "Is there anything about your personal life that may affect your performance in this demanding school and profession?" Your answer is "No."

The following are some additional illegal questions you may hear:

- How important is your family to you?
- How do you propose to juggle marriage (relationship) and medical practice?
- What do your parents do for a living?

13. *If you couldn't be a physician, what career would you choose?*

Once again, let's see who is really hiding beneath the polished applicant veneer. How deeply are you committed to medicine? Is it a whimsical interest, or is it a burning desire that forms the core of your existence? How easily can you come up with an answer that you find acceptable? How upset do you seem by such a prospect?

Very few people can fake a response to something this important. Interviewers, especially those who live and breathe medicine, use this question to find people who have their same level of commitment. Older interviewers use this question frequently, since many distrust the younger generation's resolve.

Informed interviewers also use this question because some studies suggest that there is a high correlation between alternate career interests and certain medical specialties. Applicants who ultimately go into anesthesiology or radiology, for example, usually cite highly technical professional fields, such as engineering, research, the "hard" sciences, law, architecture, or finance-related business as alternative choices. Those entering pediatrics tend to view teaching, other health-related professions, the humanities, the arts, or nonprofessional careers as acceptable alternatives.

Faculty may also use variations of this question to explore an applicant's life vision. The interviewer may ask, "What do you think you will do when you stop practicing medicine (at the end of a career)?"

- Why did you choose to be a physician?
- What will you do if you don't get accepted to medical school?
- If your brain were the only part of your body that worked, what would you do with your life?
- What will happen if you develop a debilitating disease while you are in medical school? Residency?

14. *You seem really interested in research. Why do you want a medical degree?*

Well, what do you *really* want to do with your life? The clinician–interviewer may be asking, "Are you going to medical school simply for another credential to use as a stepping-stone into research?" The Ph.D.–interviewer may be asking, "Why are you bothering with a medical degree when you can be a researcher?" Obviously, the answers to these two questions will be different—and will depend in large measure upon your background and interests.

At this stage, a "safe" answer is that you plan on having a career in clinical research, and you will vary the percentage of time spent in each area based on your funding and interests. A rather negative corollary to this question is "Are you another Michael Crichton?" This reference is to the well-known, high-profile author of *Jurassic Park* and the television series, *ER*, who has said he only went to medical school to gain a solid background for his writing. Medical faculty don't consider this a good use of their time or of valuable medical school spots. If you have this type of aspiration, keep it to yourself.

- If you have such an interest in research, why aren't you applying to our M.D./Ph.D. program?
- If you had to choose between getting an M.D. and a Ph.D., which would you select and why?
- How might acupuncture work? Do we know enough about physiology and biophysics to determine that?
- What are the most important traits for a clinician/researcher?
- How will the research you have done alter scientific thought? Help mankind?

- Let's discuss the details of the research you have done.
- How did the idea come to you for any research you initiated?
- What did you contribute to get your name on the published research papers?

15. *In what specialty would you like to practice?*

With medical schools' and legislatures' emphasis on primary care (general internal medicine, general pediatrics, family practice, obstetrics and gynecology), applicants who already think they would like to specialize in another area have a tough decision to make. Should they tell the truth or fudge their answer?

Consider two things. First, not only do most medical students change their minds (several times) about which specialty to enter, but many residents do also. Therefore, it is perfectly reasonable to say, "I'm really not sure where my talents or interests lie. I simply want to help people by practicing medicine."

Second, telling the truth during interviews is essential, because lying (and remembering which lie you told to whom) is very hard work, is difficult for most folks to pull off, demonstrates poor character, will make you feel badly about yourself, and is not necessary. Even if your past experience strongly suggests that you will enter a particular field (e.g., a decade of experience as a psychiatric social worker), you can honestly say that you are leaving your options open.

In my experience, many students who are "sure" that they will enter one specialty because of their past experiences often find their niche in a totally different area. Note that most students who think that they want to enter a primary care specialty do so, while few students who enter medical school believing they will enter a subspecialty end up in primary care.

- In light of the relatively poor salaries for most nonprocedure-oriented physicians, why would anyone go into primary care?
- Have you given any thought to being a [fill in the interviewer's specialty]?
- Where do you plan to practice?
- Would you practice in an inner city? How would you change in that environment?

16. *How do you make important decisions?*

As you discuss some very important life decisions you have made, the interviewer may wonder how you came to these decisions. Individuals vary in how they make important decisions. Their methods reflect their personality and thought processes. Are your decisions thoughtful, deliberate, and slow, or are they inattentive, impulsive, and quick? Or does your decision-making method vary appropriately with the situation?

Be prepared to discuss your own decision-making strategies with interviewers. Think carefully before you respond to this question, however. Interviewers may ask you if you used those strategies when you decided to enter medicine or to apply to their school. Or they may ask how your method affected your ability to perform in specific situations, such as when making other life decisions revealed by your application materials.

If you use the "Must/Want" Analysis (Chapter 16) to help decide on the qualities you seek in a medical school, take a copy (without the school's ratings) to your interview and show it to any interviewer who asks you this question. They will probably be impressed with your logical and deliberate decision-making process.

- Are you a "risk-taker" or "safety-minded"?
- How do you handle stress?
- What made you choose your undergraduate major/minor?
- How did you select your undergraduate school?
- What was the most difficult decision you have had to make in your life? How did you make it?

17. *What were the major deficiencies in your premed training?*

This is an opportunity to demonstrate some realistic insight into the past 3½ years (or more) of your life. How well has your undergraduate experience prepared you for medical school? What were the strongest educational elements? Which were the weakest? If you could repeat your undergraduate education, what would you change? No interviewer believes that any undergraduate school is perfect. (Sorry to disillusion you, Ivy Leaguers.)

Avoid taking major swipes at your school. Just as you are, or soon will be, an alumnus of your undergraduate school, in about five years you will be an alumnus of the medical school at which you train. While a rah-rah response is not appropriate, neither is downgrading the training that you have received. Remember, your undergraduate education has gotten you as far as this interview.

While mentioning any deficiencies in your education, you have the perfect opportunity to talk about your plans to remedy the deficit. These may include taking extra courses during the balance of your senior year, your independent study plans, or relevant experiences you have arranged for the balance of the year or for the summer before medical school.

- Why did you choose your undergraduate institution and major? How satisfied are you with your decision?
- What nonscience college courses interested you the most?
- Which science classes did you enjoy most? Why?
- What does your major (science or nonscience) have to do with being a physician?
- Which undergraduate course would you recommend that all students take (regardless of the grade you got in the course)?
- Did you enjoy your college classes? Why?

18. *How do you explain your low grades? Leaves of absence? Poor MCAT scores?*

Not everyone who reads this book has an unblemished, outstanding scholastic record. In fact, very few medical school applicants do. Most have some area of their records that requires an explanation. Perhaps you did poorly in a science course or on the MCAT, and had to repeat it. Maybe you had to take a semester off at some point in your schooling. You should expect interviewers with access to your records to ask about these deficiencies or variations from the norm—if the faculty members interviewing you are at all on the ball.

You already know what these issues are and you should be prepared to explain them. If there is a good justification for a questionable action, such as having to take time off due to a death in the family or a personal illness, explain. However, if the poor grade or poor MCAT performance was, as is usual, due to your failure to put forth your best effort, just say so. Do not give excuses; they will sound lame to almost everyone except you. Your answer should be a variation of the terse military response, "No excuse, sir!"

Say that you did not give the course, test, etc. your best effort. If you think you can get away with it, blame it on immaturity, ignorance, or youth. This works best if the problem occurred during your first year in school, especially if you can demonstrate that you have expended more effort in subsequent years. For applicants in graduate school or postbaccalaureate programs, you must demonstrate that you have done significantly better in your recent schooling than in undergraduate school. If you have any questionable areas hanging over your application, be prepared in advance to answer for your aberrant behavior.

- If you could begin your schooling again, what would you change?
- Have you ever dropped a class? Why?
- Have you ever quit or been fired from a job? Why?
- With your undergraduate grades in (college subject), how did you even get an interview here?
- Do you use drugs?
- Do you like to study? How do you study best? What motivates you to keep studying?
- What did you do during this (specified) period of time?

19. *Have you always done the best work of which you are capable?*

If you imagine that you can just answer yes or no to this question, you haven't gotten the drift of the interviewing business yet. The correct response to this question must show not only that you have put in a tremendous effort but also humility—by acknowledging that you could often have done a better job.

How to do this? Simply say that you have always striven to do the best job that you could, but the results did not always match your effort. This again stresses that you are a hard worker, you are humble, and you understand your limitations—all positive attributes, all nicely wrapped up in that one-sentence answer. Very elegant.

- What have been your biggest failures in life?
- What have you done to ensure that these failures won't happen again?

20. *With which types of people do you have trouble working?*

This question really asks, "Why won't you fit in well with your medical school class or with the clinical team that exists at our hospitals and clinics?" In essence, what personality problems do you have? Will Rogers said, "I never met a man I didn't like." Maybe so, but most people have some difficulty dealing with arbitrary, obnoxious, and loud individuals. This is not, however, what you want to say.

The correct answer, if you cannot honestly state that you usually get along with everyone, is that you generally have problems with those individuals who do not pull their own weight. This is also the answer to the parallel question, "What qualities drive you crazy in colleagues?" Again, this emphasizes your interest in, and ability to do, hard work. At the same time, it will normally hit a responsive chord in the interviewer, who probably also dislikes picking up the workload for lazy colleagues. No one, of course, ever recognizes this problem in him- or herself.

Are there certain types of people that you consistently prefer not to deal with? No one will expect you to be thrilled to deal with whining, abusive, demanding, alcoholic, or drug-seeking patients. Most physicians do not like to treat such patients. If, however, you really dislike dealing with certain racial, ethnic, or age groups or with people in general, you should probably reconsider your decision to pursue a medical career.

Some interviewers will attempt to get the names of negative references by asking, "Who didn't you get along with in undergraduate school, in the clubs or organizations to which you belonged, or in past jobs?" Luckily, this is an unusual request, if only because programs are besieged with too many applicants to follow up on such information. If interviewers ask for such references, your willingness to provide them and your ability to explain why you did not get along with certain individuals will say a lot about your self-confidence, honesty, and insight.

- Describe the best/worst teacher you ever had.
- Do you prefer to work under supervision or on your own?
- As a physician, how will you deal with noncompliant patients?
- Is there something about you that would make it difficult to get along with you?
- Describe the most exciting (scary, unusual, etc.) event of your life.
- How will you deal with "know-it-all" patients?

21. *How do you normally handle conflict?*

Hopefully, you can answer that your interactions with people rarely lead to conflict but, when there is a problem, you try to work it through to a reasonable and amicable settlement.

You may want to prepare an example of just such a situation that you faced and how it was resolved. Optimally, this example will demonstrate that you handled the conflict in a thoughtful and good-natured manner, with goodwill ultimately restored. When telling such a story, your attitude, facial expressions, and body language will reveal much about your personality and your real ability to harmoniously work with others.

- How do you respond when you have problems with a parent, peer, coworker, or teacher?

- Have you ever challenged a teacher in class or a supervisor at work? What were the circumstances?
- How do you handle criticism, whether fair or unfair, from a superior, subordinate, peer, or family member?
- What was the most useful criticism you ever received? Why?
- What would you do if your boss told you to do something you know is absolutely wrong (medically or morally)?
- What was your most difficult/stressful life experience? How did you handle it?
- What frustrates you the most?

22. *With what subject did you have the most difficulty?*

Similar to the question concerning your strengths and weaknesses, this one asks you to incriminate yourself. You cannot plead the Fifth Amendment, so you need to know how to work through it. If you had problems with a course, as evidenced by a poor grade or dismal narrative evaluations, you will have to address this. Do so in a direct manner. Otherwise, use the same strategy you used for the strength and weakness question. Pick "difficulties" that will exhibit some of the strengths that you want the interviewer to see.

For example, by stating that you found organic chemistry very difficult because of the vast amount of seemingly pointless information you spent countless hours memorizing by rote, you will impress the interviewer with both your insight and your hard work. (You will also strike a responsive chord in most clinician-interviewers, who detested organic chemistry and cannot understand why it is still part of the premed curriculum.) In general, emphasize that any trouble that you have had was the result of the long hours you spent—explanation, not a complaint—in the learning process. However, if you really did poorly in a course, the interviewer is probably asking you to explain why (Question 18).

Commonly, the interviewer will have already spotted your problem area and will also ask, "How will that affect your performance as a medical student?" Of course, your answer is that it won't affect your performance, since you already have (or have a plan to) overcome any problems through hard work or extra training.

- Tell me about the most difficult (subject) class you took as a college freshman.
- What has been your greatest challenge?
- Have you ever cheated or helped a friend cheat?

23. *Why do you want to be a physician?*

This is probably the question most often asked of medical school applicants. The question poses two dangers. The first lies in not having a good answer. If you have gone through the steps in this book, you will have no trouble answering it. You initially matched your personal goals to those that medical practice can fulfill. Then, you talked with multiple physicians, read as much as you could about medicine, and tested whether medicine really interested you by spending time working in a clinical area. With this background to support your answer, you should have little trouble convincing the interviewer that you have firm and valid reasons for becoming a physician.

The second danger is that you will be asked this question so often—sometimes two or three times at each school—that you will become bored with your own answer. This will be obvious in your response and will reflect poorly upon your candidacy. Since each interviewer tends to ask applicants similar questions, they will compare your response to those from other candidates. Be enthusiastic when replying to this question—every time. Try to take a new tack when answering the question with different interviewers—and maybe vary any stories you tell. This way you will avoid repeating the same phrases, which will sound stale and trite not only to you, but also to them. You have an excellent answer to this question; make certain that your delivery matches it.

- What will you contribute to the medical profession (your community) as a physician?
- How can you be sure that medicine is the right career for you?
- You said (quotes your statement) in your application essay. What did you mean?

- What would you want your patients to say about you?
- What can be done to ensure that medical students are in medicine for the "right" reasons?
- With all the computer skills you have, why do you want to be a physician?
- The future of medicine looks bleak. Why do you think so many people are still pursuing a medical career?
- How did your family life contribute to your decision to become a physician?
- Do you know what you are getting into? Have you talked with physicians about what a medical career is really like?
- Did anyone you know influence your career choice?
- Do you have family members who are doctors? How have their lives changed over the past few years? Do you want to follow in their footsteps?
- What qualities would you look for in a doctor? Which do you have?
- Why do you want to work with sick people?
- What do you hope to get out of medicine?
- Why are some doctors disappointed with their medical career?

24. *Why did you apply to our medical school?*

There are lots of medical schools: public and private, M.D.- and D.O.-granting, research- and clinically oriented. So why did you apply to this school? Since this question is so basic, it is not surprising that interviewers ask it quite often. Since you based your medical school selections on your personal "Must/Want" Analysis, you have some excellent answers to this question. Maybe the school is particularly strong in research, which is an area you value highly. Alternatively, perhaps the faculty is outstanding, especially in areas that interest you: Did their reputation for primary care or for turning out great clinicians attract you?

Your answer to this question should include whatever drew you to the school. In addition, it never hurts to say that the school also got a strong recommendation from your premed adviser or from clinicians you know.

Review all material you have about the school, as well as your personal evaluation of it, before beginning the day's interviews. If you remember to individualize your answer for each school, you should have no problem. Your knowledge of the school should include:

- Class size
- Academic mission
- Teaching methods (PBL, etc.)
- Research opportunities
- Grading system
- Student services
- Academic support services
- Early clinical exposure
- Sites for clinical clerkships
- Elective opportunities
- Community outreach programs
- USMLE or OSCE for promotion/graduation
- Quarter/semester program
- Percent of women and minorities admitted

If you lack some of this information, that's okay. Make sure you ask for it at your first opportunity.

A more personal way to ask this question is, "Why are you willing to leave the West (or Northeast, Midwest, etc.) to come here for your medical education?" Rather than obviously directing the question toward the school's educational elements, the interviewer appears to be asking a more personal question. Without thinking, you may blurt out, "Well, I don't really want to live anywhere but the Boston area, but I heard this was a good school and I thought I'd take a look." Bad move! You have fallen into the interviewer's trap. It is not even worthwhile considering you as a serious applicant now, since you just said you would be unhappy away from Boston. The better answer is to say (hopefully with some truth) that you are willing to move anywhere to get an excellent medical education. Then tell the interviewer what you consider to be the school's finest qualities.

- Is this school your top choice?
- What qualities are you looking for in a medical school?

- What interests you most about this medical school?
- Do you have any concerns about attending our school?
- What have you heard about our medical school that you don't like?
- Our school is about to [undergo a major change]. Does that concern you? Why? Why not?
- Are you applying here because it is a familiar environment?
- Why do you want to leave (city or state where you live)?
- What do you think will be the most difficult aspect of living in this city, coming as you do from__________?
- Would you go to our school if I gave you an acceptance letter now?
- Have you considered the advantages/disadvantages of living in this area?

25. *What will be the toughest aspect of medical education/practice for you?*

This is another way of asking you about your strengths and weaknesses. Only the most skilled interviewers ask the question this way.

Medicine clearly has complex areas to master, as well as onerous aspects. What do you foresee as difficult areas for you? You may discuss learning specific skills or to how deal with vexing areas of medical practice.

It would be unrealistic for you not to recognize some of the difficult personal or professional aspects of medical training and practice. Failure to cite any indicates that you know little about medical school, a physician's life, yourself, or all three. A good way to answer this question is to note one or more of the small or commonly recognized difficulties (such as the large amount of material students must memorize) and describe how you intend to overcome each one. The fact that you visualize only small or common problems will either placate the interviewer or lead to other questions designed to reassure him that you haven't missed the big picture.

If the interviewer questions you about the "most enjoyable" part of medicine for you, answer in the most specific terms you can. Cite examples of experiences that excited you while doing clinical work, stimulated you to read further, or suggested interesting research opportunities. The more specific you can be, the better your answer will be received, and the better the interviewer will remember you.

Two-thirds of medical schools report that their interviewers ask applicants about their willingness to live the life of a medical student, resident, or physician.

- What would you be willing to sacrifice to become a physician?
- What is the greatest sacrifice you have already made to get where you are?
- Will you work graveyard shifts and all weekends for a month or more at a time?
- How will you handle the least interesting or least pleasant parts of medical school/residency/medical practice?
- What qualities are most important in a physician?
- What makes you think you can memorize the mass of information needed to complete medical school?
- Have you noticed any negative aspects in the doctors with whom you have come in contact?
- What about our school (or going to medical school, or being a physician) scares you the most? Why?

26. *How will you finance your medical education?*

This question is one most prospective medical students must carefully consider—whether or not an interviewer asks about it. The only people exempt from this concern are the 20% of medical students who can finance their education without loans, grants, scholarships, or otherwise mortgaging their future by obligating themselves to working in specific locations or specialties. (For additional advice, see Chapter 18: *Paying for Medical School*.)

Unless you are one of these fortunate few, your medical education will be one of the biggest expenses you ever incur. For most students, it will certainly be the biggest expense they have had so far. Medical school faculty are well aware of this and want to be sure that you have carefully considered the amount and type of debt that may burden you for many years to come. Note, however, that admission committees accept applicants based on merit rather than on financial need. Interviewers may also be interested in how savvy you are about the complicated financial aid system, and may even want to give you a few tips—especially if they see you as an excellent candidate.

- Did you know that you will be over $150,000 in debt when you begin residency?
- What income do physicians have? Is that appropriate?

27. *Why should we take you in preference to the other applicants?*

Danger! This is one of those questions designed to quickly lead you down the garden path to disaster. What is your first response? Most students would attempt to defend themselves against attack by trying to compare themselves favorably with other applicants they either know or imagine. Wrong move!

Start by acknowledging that you do not make the decision about who gets into medical school. State that you are not qualified to make that type of decision. In addition, acknowledge that there are, undoubtedly, many good applicants applying to the school. Then state that you can really only describe your own qualities and ask the interviewer if he or she would like you to do just that.

If the answer is yes, you have an excellent opportunity to tout your best qualities and finest achievements. Obviously, to answer the interviewer's initial question, you should stress those qualities that distinguish you from other applicants. Concentrate on some of the areas mentioned previously—your *energy level*, your *desire to do and to learn*, and your *ability to get along with others* under all circumstances. Never disparage other applicants. Only stress your own excellence.

- What can you add to our medical school class?
- What computer experience do you have?
- What are some qualities a good physician should possess? Do you possess them?
- How will your background in (major or career) be of any use in medicine?
- If you were on our admission committee, what would you look for in a candidate?
- Why should I tell the admission committee to pick you?
- What makes you unique?
- Give me your sales pitch.

28. *I don't think you'd be right for this medical school/for a medical career.*

Medicine has some pretty crass folks populating its ranks, but very few would actually invite you for an interview and really mean it when they tell you that you would not be right for their school, much less a medical career. If you are told this, recognize it for the ploy that it is. The statement is meant to fluster and confuse an applicant. A rather nasty maneuver, you can easily sidestep it if you remain calm. You can only answer this statement successfully with the question: "Why do you say that?"

If you come out swinging to defend yourself, you lose. Put the interviewer on the defensive by asking your question in your nicest, most polite manner. This will throw him or her off guard, and you might even receive an apology.

- Describe the ideal medical school curriculum.
- With your obvious (musical, artistic, literary, etc.) talents, why are you pursuing a medical career?
- Montana . . . hmm . . . Isn't that where the Unabomber lived?
- I see that neither of your parents graduated from high school. What does that say about your genetic background?
- How could you contribute to this school's glorification?

29. *What is your energy level like?*

Although this may be an interviewer's standard question, watch out. Some only ask it of applicants who demonstrate diminished energy levels during their interview. This is the time to appear animated. If you feel yourself fading, pump out a little more adrenaline and beef up your act. If you can't do it now, what will your performance be like at 3 a.m. while you are on call with a ward team?

You must answer a question about your energy level with an enthusiastic "Very high." A very brief anecdote of just how high it is would be appropriate. An example might be, "I was able to work 30 hours a week while maintaining a full course load—including labs." Try to make your anecdote relate to work, school, volunteer activities, or all three.

- How many hours of sleep do you require each night?
- How well do you function without adequate sleep?
- Do you ever have to use stimulants to stay awake?
- Did you ever pull an "all-nighter"? Why?

30. *How well do you function under pressure?*

Every physician, at one time or another, has practiced medicine under pressure. Some specialties have frequent stressors, and the physicians in them seem to thrive under this stress. Asking you about your performance under stress is a natural question.

The interviewer wants to know two things. First, have you thought about the pressures inherent in medical education, residency training, and medical practice? Second, are you up to them?

The best way to answer is to cite specific examples of your past performance under stress. Personal (and poignant?) stories work well here. Be sure that the examples, however, do not show that the stress resulted from your negligence, procrastination, or obstinacy. Assure the interviewer that you are up to medicine's challenges.

A potential curve ball here may be a secondary question dealing with the administrative stressors brought on by government and third-party payer interference with medical practice. Interviewers may raise this question because it is constantly, and annoyingly, on many practitioners' minds. If this topic is introduced, either state that you are certain that you will learn to handle these problems during your training or respond by simply asking the interviewer "What are the biggest problems you are facing in this area?" In all likelihood, the interviewer will be pleased to speak about the subject at length. Be a good listener.

- How do you handle stress?
- Can you handle stress without the resources you are accustomed to relying on?
- When was the last time you cried?
- Have you ever faced death? How did you handle it?

31. *Tell me about the patient from whom you learned the most.*

If you have had any clinical experience involving patient contact, whether it was volunteer or paid, you can expect this question. This question is a favorite of elderly professors, as well as smarter young interviewers. It examines your medical knowledge, your insight into the patient's condition, your ability to think quickly, your attitude toward medicine and learning, and your compassion. If an interviewer asks this question, the balance of the interview will remain on the same topic. How, then, should you approach it?

To answer this question satisfactorily, you must prepare at least two patients' cases in advance. Try to choose examples in which you understood at least some of the issues, such as with patients in a great deal of pain or those at the end of their life. Select patients you cared for or with whom you spoke at length (or spoke with the family). If they had specific diseases or injuries, read about them in depth. If they presented specific issues, such as using an advance directive or refusing care, read something about that, too.

What did you learn from these patients? Was it just the nature of the disease? Normally, this will not be enough. Did you learn something about physicians' limitations, the patient's fears and perceptions of the medical system, or the workings of the health care system itself? If you did, be prepared to say so. Also, if you have an opportunity to get follow-up information on the patient, do so. Following up on interesting patients demonstrates both a concern for them and your excitement in learning.

If you have prepared for this question and have begun to answer it appropriately, the interviewer may interrupt you with his own "war story." Sit back, listen, and enjoy. You did just fine.

- What were your most memorable experiences in college?
- Tell me about the nonphysician health care provider who most influenced you.
- Have you ever seen someone die?
- Have you handled a corpse?

32. *What is your greatest fear about practicing medicine?*

If you don't have some fears about eventually taking responsibility for patients' welfare and lives, you're a fool and no one wants you practicing medicine. Certainly, you have trepidations! You are worried that four years (or in some cases less) of medical education may not be enough. Will you be good enough to take on this responsibility and do a great job? Will you be able to fulfill your role as a physician and as a spouse/parent?

All physicians have some of these fears. Expressing them only shows that you know something about a medical career and are exploring your role within the profession. It may be difficult to fill the shoes of the great clinicians about whom you have read and those you know and will get to know while in medical school and residency. Tell the interviewer your fears, and explain that you know every physician has questioned him- or herself the same way. Then, state that you are up to the challenge.

- How do you feel about treating AIDS patients? Patients with Ebola virus?
- Have you read about any great physicians? Will you be able to fill their shoes?
- You've read about or seen depictions of how rough the intern year is. Do you think you will be able to handle it?

33. *Where do you see yourself in five (ten) years?*

Some realism, in addition to reviewing the medical school's mission (in their catalog and other documents), is required to answer this question. The questioner is attempting to find out if you have some life goals—and if these are consistent with the training that the school offers.

Have you looked beyond your existence as a student? Do you envision a high-powered career in clinical research, or a family practice in a rural or remote location? Are you equipped intellectually and emotionally to do either of these? Is this medical school designed to prepare you for the career you desire?

Incongruent goals stem from your evaluation of either your own abilities or the medical school's goals and mission. Medical school deans (including the Dean of Admissions) and most of the faculty usually have at least a general vision of what they would like most of their graduates to do with their careers. They want your goals to be consistent with those of the school. This is beneficial to both you and them. If a school's curriculum has been designed to produce primary care physicians, students who hope to become academic or research gurus will be very disappointed, and so will the school's faculty.

You should have previously analyzed the school's written materials. Do they promote goals consistent with your personal goals? If the two widely diverge, perhaps you should look elsewhere. However, do not be too certain about your final career direction. Many, if not most, students significantly change their career orientation during or shortly after training. This should not upset you. It is a normal part of learning and maturation. So, answer this question by giving a general response while listening to the interviewer. Try to understand the diversity of learning experiences that exist within the school's curriculum. Leave enough latitude in your reply, however, to allow for other possibilities in your future. Also, always phrase your answer so that it illustrates that your decision may change with training, experience, and age.

- Ten years from now, in what specialty and under what circumstances will you be practicing? Who will be paying for your services?
- Draw a picture of yourself in ten years.

- Would you prefer to stay on the East or West coast?
- What hobbies will you take up or renew after medical school or residency?

34. *How do you see the delivery of health care evolving in the future?*

This can be a very tricky question. It tests your knowledge of current events and politics, as well as your humility in recognizing that you do not have the ultimate answer. The interviewer, though, may think that he or she does. Only people who already have definite opinions about the trends in health care will ask this question. They actually may want to use it as a jumping-off point from which to expostulate on their pet theory. People like to hear themselves talk. If you give an interviewer a chance to say what is on her mind while you appear interested, you will do just fine.

The strategy for you is to give a broad answer to the initial question, such as "I expect that there will be numerous changes, not only in the way medicine is practiced, but also in the way it is paid for." You can go on to add that you do not have any definitive answers. This will give the interviewer a chance to jump in and give you either the lecture that was lying in wait, or at least some definite hints as to what she is thinking. You do not want to stick your neck out without some guidance.

This question is probably the closest that you will get to a direct inquiry about your political views, which is illegal to ask of medical school applicants (and in preemployment questioning). Listen closely, nod your head a lot, and do not go out on a limb without some support. If you want some solid background, read the book *Crossing the Quality Chasm: A New Health System for the 21st Century* (available online, see the *Annotated Bibliography*).

- What do you think is the number one issue in medicine today?
- Is health care a right or a privilege?
- What are your thoughts on naturopaths and herbal medicine?
- How do you think a socialized medical system will affect medical progress?
- If you were made Health Care Czar of the United States, what one thing would you change about health care delivery? Why?
- What is managed care? HMOs? PPOs? Capitation?
- What is the biggest challenge facing health care delivery?
- How would you improve our medical care system?
- What does "a cross-cultural approach to healing" mean?
- What will you do, as a physician, to curb the rising costs of medicine?
- What is the nurse's role and how much responsibility should a nurse be given for patient care?
- What role will nurse practitioners and physician assistants have in the future?
- Where does the money go in a prepaid medical system?
- What will be medicine's next great advance?
- What recent newsworthy medical event or announcement would you like to discuss?
- What is your least healthy personal habit?

35. *If a patient just stabbed your best friend . . . ?*

A favorite question of many interviewers is the ethics scenario. In virtually all cases, it involves a situation in which there is no "correct" answer. However, as with all ethics questions, there are wrong answers.

The key to answering this question appropriately (the question itself is usually "What would you do?") is to tell the interviewer that you need a moment to think about it. Then formulate at least one answer that does not violate your personal values. Relate this to the interviewer. It is best if you do not give responses based upon your religion. Generalities such as protecting patient autonomy or avoiding paternalism work best. (If you don't understand these concepts, you may want to check out *Ethics in Emergency Medicine*, 2nd ed., which has both general discussions of these concepts and discussions of interesting illustrative cases. See *Annotated Bibliography*.)

Do not appear dogmatic; state that you are sure that there are other possible options. The interviewer may want to discuss the problem. If so, listen to the options presented and discuss them. Do not argue! Try to see the interviewer's point of view, but do not escalate the discussion into a religious debate or a shouting match. There's an old saying which suggests that one should never discuss religion or politics with friends, or you are bound to lose them. That applies just as well to medical school interviewers.

Nearly all medical schools report that their interviewers ask applicants "opinion-type" questions.

- What would you do if the housestaff at the medical school's hospital had a "job action" (strike)?
- What would you do if you saw another medical student, a resident, or a physician snorting cocaine at a nightclub? While doing clinical work?
- What do you think about using animals in medical research and teaching?
- Should physicians be involved in assisted suicide or active euthanasia?
- What ethical questions will the health care delivery system face in the future?
- Should applicants who say they don't want to treat (AIDS, hepatitis B, life-threatening plague, etc.) patients be admitted to medical school?
- What would you do if you knew that someone in your class was cheating on an exam?
- Is health care rationing ethical?
- If a colleague and a patient each came to you with an unwanted pregnancy, would you treat them differently?
- How would you respond if a resident or a colleague wanted to keep a therapeutic error a secret from a patient and the patient's family?
- What do you think of hospitals that refuse admission to patients without insurance?
- What would you say to a patient who is interested in visiting a chiropractor, acupuncturist, or naturopath?
- What do you think about medical advice being available on the Web?
- What is the role of religion/spirituality in healing?
- Do you think physicians should tell a patient that s/he has only eight months to live? How would you tell him or her?
- Would you prefer to provide less-effective medicine to more people or more-effective medicine to fewer people?
- What is suffering? How does it relate to pain?
- Should pharmaceutical companies be allowed to directly advertise prescription medications to potential patients?
- How do you help people who don't want to be helped?

36. *What do you think of what is happening in the (economy, Middle East, Congress)?*

This question examines whether you have pulled your head out of your textbooks in the past several years. It's wise to prepare for it by reading weekly news magazines for a month or two prior to the interview season. It is also prudent to read the newspaper and, if possible, watch the morning news on the day of your interview.

As for the question itself, hope that it is on a relatively innocuous subject. If not, don't antagonize the interviewer by giving a polarized viewpoint. Try to take a balanced view—looking at both sides of the issue, e.g., "on the one hand . . . , but on the other hand . . ." This shows that you are aware of the world situation and that you are a diplomat—both desirable qualities.

- What is the most important development in the past 25 years in the world?
- What do you think is the largest problem facing American society on a statewide or a national basis?
- What wars are currently ongoing in the world?
- Where do you expect the next war to break out?

- What do you think about global warming?
- Are physicians doing enough to improve public health policies?
- Are physicians doing enough for women's issues? Minority issues?

37. *Teach me something not related to your schoolwork in five minutes.*

This is now the "question" I use most often. It shows me a great deal about applicants, including how well many of them think on their feet. It is also more fun to start an interview this way rather than with the routine questions most interviewers ask.

With this directive, applicants have a marvelous opportunity to discuss something in which they are an expert—and the interviewer has guaranteed that he or she will pay rapt attention. Pick a topic that you know really well and that you can explain a small piece of to a novice in five minutes.

But which topic is best? Is it something about your hobby, something unique you learned in childhood, something from a previous job, or something truly different, such as a lesson you learned through a difficult experience? The solution here is to pick a topic that will interest listeners, that fascinates you, and that can be successfully taught in the allotted time.

Among the topics applicants have discussed are how to tie fishing lures, how to write a simple computer program, how to select a ripe melon, and how to load a packhorse. I didn't always understand them, but they were always interesting. Often this directive leads naturally to further questions about the topic, the circumstances in which the subject was learned, and about the applicant.

Many applicants and interviewers find this the best, and most productive, interview question. (I now add a caveat in my interviews—Nothing about golf!)

- Without using your hands, tell me how to tie a shoelace.
- How are art and medicine similar?
- What is "beauty"?
- Why are manhole covers round?
- Give an example of a problem you solved and describe how you went about solving it.

38. *Where else have you interviewed?*

This is many interviewers' favorite question. Don't become paranoid when you hear it. In most cases, they are not trying to test your interview choices. They are doing two things.

First, they are determining whether you have selected enough medical schools to have a reasonable shot at getting into one of them. (If you are an outstanding applicant and only apply to one or two state schools, this might be acceptable.)

Second, they may want to find out current information about other medical schools and their interview/application procedures. Often, you are the best available source of information about other medical schools. Interviewers will be interested in pumping you for facts. Give them what they want. Tell them about what is going on in the places you visited.

If you just do not remember some of the specifics about these schools, be honest enough to say so. The interviewer will appreciate this. Be enthusiastic. However, as mentioned before, under no circumstances should you say anything derogatory about another school. If you say negative things about other schools to this interviewer, what will you say about his school when you go elsewhere? Negative comments are a sign of immaturity. Avoid them.

39. *What if you don't get into medical school?*

Okay. Now let's see you sweat a little. This question has become more frequent as the number of applicants has increased. If you are not prepared for it, you may internalize it and consider that it is a backhanded way of suggesting that you had better make other plans, since you won't be getting into (at least this) medical school. Keep cool. That is not usually why interviewers ask applicants this question.

The interviewer is trying to determine whether you have had the foresight to plan for contingencies. Planning ahead says something about your personality. These days, not making alternative plans when applying to medical school is just plain foolish. And people who do foolish things with their lives are not the people these schools look for as students. Interviewers would like you to mention alternative plans that include what you will do for the next year if you don't get in this year.

- Would you consider going to a foreign medical school?

40. *Can you think of anything else you would like to add?*

The answer to this question should always be "Yes." If the interviewer has neglected any critical area that further explains your qualifications for medical school, mention it now. Even if everything was covered, use this opportunity to give a summary of your sales pitch.

This is an alternate form of the frequent query, "Do you have any (other) questions?" that can be positioned at either the beginning or the end of the interview. It can also be a disaster at the end of a long interview day when you are tired, hungry, and sleepy. The wimpy response, "No, I think all of my questions have been answered," is not likely to score very many points with an interviewer.

Even if prior interviewers have already answered all your questions, ask one of them again. It is very useful to take this opportunity to confirm or clarify information that you consider important. You might also raise a point that demonstrates your knowledge about the school. For example, ask "How will the school's new problem-based learning curriculum affect medical students' clinical abilities?" In any event, do not leave the interviewer in the lurch when he or she gives you an opportunity to ask a final question.

- Is there anything else I should know about you?

— Illegal Questions —

Interviewers continue to ask many applicants, especially women, blatantly illegal questions (see Figures 25.1 and 25.2). In a survey of medical students, one-third reported being asked illegal questions during their medical school interviews. One applicant even reported receiving a letter from a large medical school before she interviewed "apologizing for anything that might be said in the interview" and stressing that it did "not reflect the school's beliefs."

The most commonly asked illegal questions center on marriage and family plans. Indeed, asking women about childbearing and child-care is the most common gaffe interviewers make. Besides implicitly asking whether a woman has children, interviewers often assume that she must be the sole person responsible for making child-care arrangements. (A few "dinosaur" interviewers still believe that if a female applicant inquires about the provisions for maternity leave, she should be written off as a serious candidate.)

The physically disabled are also frequently asked illegal questions. While interviewers may legally ask applicants about their ability to satisfy essential requirements (as determined by the school and

FIGURE 25.1

Illegal Questions—Sex Discrimination

- What was your maiden name?
- Do you wish to be addressed as Miss, Mrs., or Ms.?
- Are you married? Single? Divorced? Separated? A single parent?
- I notice that you are wearing an engagement ring. When are you going to be married?
- What is your spouse's name? What does (s)he do for a living?
- How does your spouse feel about your having a medical career?
- Do you believe medical students should have to use birth control?
- Are you planning to have children? Anytime soon?
- How will you take care of your children while you are at school?

FIGURE 25.2

Other Questions—Legal & Illegal Forms

Legal Form	Illegal Form
1. How well can you handle stress?	1. Does stress ever affect your ability to be productive?
2. Are you currently using illegal drugs?	2. What medications do you currently use?
3. Do you drink alcohol?	3. How much alcohol do you drink per week?
4. Do you have 20/20 corrected vision?	4. What is your corrected vision?
5. Can you perform as a student with or without reasonable accommodations?	5. Would you need reasonable accommodations to perform your job as a student or physician?
6. How many days were you absent from school last year?	6. How many days were you sick last year?

Adapted from: Equal Employment Opportunity Commission. *Enforcement Guidance on Pre-Employment Disability-Related Inquiries.* Washington, DC: GPO, July 2000.

listed in their publications), the Americans with Disabilities Act allows interviewers to ask these questions of the disabled only if all applicants are asked the same questions. Also, even if an applicant has a visible disability, such as using a wheelchair, a cane, or a guide dog or has voluntarily disclosed his disability, interviewers may not ask about its nature or severity, the condition causing the disability, the prognosis, or treatments. Increasing numbers of disabled medical school applicants are filing lawsuits so, hopefully, interviewers will become better informed about what constitutes an illegal question.

Since applicants are apparently still being asked illegal questions (why this is allowed to continue is uncertain), it is important for you to be prepared for these questions.

How Should You React to Illegal Questions?

How *should* you respond to illegal questions? This can be very tricky. There are several possible ways to respond.

First, *answer* the question in the most favorable manner possible. This is the most politic thing to do and will not eliminate you from that school's pool of potential students. Most applicants take this tack, both in the medical field and in other situations. You can use either direct or indirect answers. For example, when asked about plans for a family and children, a candidate may answer, "I plan to have children near the end of my residency." If you find it distasteful to answer such questions directly, you could use an indirect answer, such as "My training comes first." If you already have children, you might directly address the interviewer's concerns by stating that your past performance demonstrates that your family responsibilities do not detract from your work. These answers should not jeopardize your chance of obtaining a medical school slot. Answering such questions, even if you do so in an indirect manner, is preferable to saying "I prefer not to answer," since listeners will often infer the most negative response, just as they do when someone invokes his Fifth Amendment rights. In addition, the interviewer probably does not even realize that he (or she) is being sexist and is violating both federal and state civil rights statutes.

You may, however, want to decline to answer such questions, either because of the nature of your response or because your principles will not allow it. You then have three choices. The first, which will still permit you to remain a viable applicant, is to *finesse* the question. One way to do this is to laughingly ask whether the answer to the question, or the question itself, is relevant to being a medical student. If you do this lightly, the interviewer, who has probably been poorly prepared to do this type of interviewing, will be able to back off and save face at the same time. However, finessing a question requires skill. Smile and be very pleasant while you parry pointed questions. If you handle it correctly, you will still be a viable candidate for the school. But if you derisively ask whether the question is relevant or *state that the question is illegal* (your second choice), you will be on the interviewer's black list. Don't plan on getting into that medical school—feistiness is fine, impertinence is not.

Another option is to *refuse to answer* the query, perhaps stating that it is illegal to ask it or that it is none of the interviewer's business. Such an answer, however, while it is perfectly correct and legitimate, may ensure that you will not be admitted to that medical school. You may also report such illegal questions to the admission office (while you are still at the school) and ask for an alternate interviewer. Nearly all schools have a provision for dealing with this.

But if, as a result of answering such questions, you do not get in and you still want to go to that school, you have the option of taking legal action against the institution for violating your civil rights (your third choice). Such action has been successful in the business world many times. It is only a matter of time until these suits become frequent in the medical community. In fact, they may become commonplace enough that there will be much tighter control over the entire interview process in order to avoid legal entanglements.

The best plan if you are confronted with these illegal and uncomfortable questions is to relax. This will yield the best results.

26

Waiting For, Choosing, And Accepting An Offer

When the gods wish to punish us, they answer our prayers.

— Oscar Wilde, *An Ideal Husband*

— Waiting: The Hardest Part —

Now, you must wait. Make sure that the medical schools you have applied to can contact you. If you must be away from the address, e-mail, and phone numbers you gave them, arrange for someone who knows how to reach you to pick up your mail and listen to your messages. If you can't access your own e-mail, have a trusted person check it on a regular basis. If this is impossible, contact the schools by telephone and in writing to give them your new contact information. I don't know of any students who have actually lost regular acceptances to a medical school because they couldn't be contacted, but some came awfully close. (I do, however, know of students who missed getting first-week-of-medical-school-replacement positions because the school could not find them.)

If you are on a school's waiting list, continue to communicate with their admission office so that they know that you are still interested. Carefully look through all their materials to find out how interested they are in receiving additional information, e-mails, calls, and letters about the current activities of students on their waiting list. Some schools are quite interested, but a minority say that they don't want to hear from these applicants. In some cases, your premed adviser can find out for you. Many schools keep track of these contacts. Even if you don't get accepted this time around, they may place you high on their list next year when you reapply.

Most medical students, and all individuals who were not accepted, have experienced the anguish of receiving rejection letters. Dr. Robert Marion eloquently described his own experience in his novel, *Learning to Play God*:

> **Rejection letters are easy to spot in the mail. Painfully thin, the envelopes contain just a single sheet of stationery: "After careful consideration of your application," the letters all read, "we regret to inform you that we cannot offer you a place in our medical school class." Regardless of the reasons listed for the rejection, my reaction to these letters was always the same: First a queasiness would develop in the pit of my stomach, then an ache would begin in the front of my head, followed finally by the feeling that I'd had the wind knocked out of me. It got so bad that by February the queasiness began almost as soon as I saw the mailman coming down the street. (p. 8)**

Another student said of the mailman, "I think that he got sick of my asking him to be sure there weren't College of Medicine letters for me that had fallen on the floor of his truck."

While you wait to hear if you have been chosen, be sure that you also investigate alternative activities you can do during the next year—in case you don't get accepted this time around.

A few students on the waiting list won't hear that they have been accepted until the first week of medical school. If a student just doesn't show up, school officials may contact the next person still on their list and offer them the position. This happens to probably only 20 or 30 students a year, but, if those students can be flexible and quickly join their classes, it's like striking gold.

— Early-Decision Programs (EDPs) —

Some students don't have to go through the agonizing spring ritual of waiting to hear from medical schools—they already have their acceptance letters. Most medical schools have programs to accept well-qualified applicants by October 1. These are called Early-Decision Programs (EDPs). In the 2001–02 academic cycle, 91 schools had such programs (see Figure 15.5). Each school's listing in the AAMC's *Medical School Admission Requirements* or the AACOM's *Osteopathic Medical College Information* states whether it offers an EDP.

Since participating medical schools accept only a small percentage of their students through EDPs, only the most highly qualified students should use this mechanism. If you fall into this category and are willing to accept the rules that govern the program, however, it can markedly reduce your anxiety.

The rules for participating in an EDP are straightforward.

1. The applicant may apply to only one U.S. medical school (AMCAS- or non-AMCAS-participating).
2. The EDP deadline for AMCAS-participating schools to receive all application materials and transcripts is August 1. Dates for non-AMCAS schools are listed in the AAMC's *Medical School Admission Requirements* or can be obtained by contacting individual Osteopathic medical schools.
3. The school notifies applicants whether they have been accepted by October 1.
4. If accepted into a school through the EDP, students agree to attend that school.
5. Students may apply to other medical schools if
    a. they receive an EDP rejection,
    b. they receive a formal (written) release from their EDP commitment, *or*
    c. the October 1 deadline for notification has passed.

About half of all students who apply through EDP get accepted into medical school through the program. If an EDP applicant fails to get accepted to the medical school to which he or she has applied, that applicant is automatically placed in the school's regular applicant pool and may then apply to other schools as well. Such applicants will still have time to apply to other schools; medical schools intentionally set their deadlines after October 1 to attract these very desirable applicants.

— Acceptance Letters —

Medical schools accept applicants on a variety of schedules. Some send initial acceptances following each batch of applicant interviews. Others have fixed dates when they send acceptances. Keep a log of information about the various schools' acceptance schedules in the file with your "Must/Want" Analyses. You can find these dates in the AAMC's and AACOM's websites.

The only constant is that May 15 is, for virtually all applicants, the "day of reckoning." All medical schools have agreed to have a final list of students on this date. Most conform to this schedule. Many schools use this date to send rejection letters and to notify students who are on their waiting lists that they still have a chance.

Prior to this, admission offices normally send letters only to students who have been offered a position but who have not yet made up their minds about where to go or, even, whether to go to medical school at all. Called the "fish-or-cut-bait" letter by some Deans, it informs the applicants that unless they notify the school that they accept the proffered position by a certain date, the slot will be given to someone else. (Many applicants don't realize that each M.D. school's admission office has a list of all the students the other schools have accepted. So they know what choices you have to make.)

Acceptance letters are nearly always sent with the U.S. Post Office's "return-requested" notice attached. If you see such a letter from one of "your" medical schools in the mailbox before mid-May, it probably contains good news. Congratulations! Rejoice!

Occasionally, the post office fails to deliver (literally). This can lead to some interesting interactions when an admission officer finally does contact the applicant.

> One student, who was applying for her second time, didn't respond to a letter of acceptance. The admission office knew this applicant well, since she had badgered them with questions about whether her material had arrived, when she should show up for interviews, and where she was on the waiting list. Yet, when they finally sent an acceptance letter, there was only silence. Rather than sending another letter, the staff did something they rarely do: They called the student's home. She answered the phone. When they asked why she hadn't responded to the acceptance letter, the staff only heard five minutes of screaming. When she finally calmed down, she gasped that she had never received it, but would be at the office within 30 minutes to get a copy and to personally respond. The staff thanked her, but said that her acceptance had to be in writing. Less than 20 minutes later, she appeared with a signed letter accepting the position.
>
> Another student, who did not receive his acceptance letter either, was so overjoyed when he heard (by phone) that he had been accepted that he rushed right down to the admission office with his entire family and had everyone pose with him and his family for some "candid" pictures.

You're Accepted. What Now?

You are overjoyed by your acceptance to medical school and you want to call the school. Fine, they'll appreciate basking in your bliss. Just calling, however, won't suffice. Sit down and write an acceptance letter to the Dean of Admissions. Specify that you accept the position, and also include contact addresses and phone numbers for the time remaining until you begin medical school. If they have asked for any additional information, send it with this letter or tell them when you will send it.

This is an important letter, but you *don't* have to send it overnight mail. If you are accepted before April 15, you generally have at least two weeks in which to notify the medical school whether you accept their offer. After April 15, they may ask you to respond to them more quickly. Do, however, send your response by certified mail, with a receipt requested. That way you'll know that they have received it. If you don't get the receipt card back within ten days, call them to find out if they got your letter.

The school may require a deposit to hold your place. According to the rules U.S. M.D.-granting schools have agreed to, this should not be more than $100 and, generally, it is far less. This deposit should be fully refundable, in case you change your mind about going to that school, until May 15, although some schools use cutoffs as early as March 1. Some schools, including those in Canada, generally refund the deposit even later. Schools requiring a nonrefundable payment before May 1 to hold a place include Howard ($150), Wayne State ($50), Ponce ($1,000), and the Medical University of South Carolina ($50). A number of others require large payments by May 15. Osteopathic medical schools require a deposit of up to $1,000 to hold a spot. Often, most or all of this is nonrefundable.

After you have written your letter to the school, take another look at the letter they sent to you. Now, read the fine print. Most acceptance letters say that you are admitted as long as you continue to perform as well as you have in the past. Unfortunately, each year, some students "blow off" the rest of their courses once they get accepted to medical school. They're in, right? *Wrong!*

If you fail a course, or otherwise show that you have done poorly in this last school term, the medical school can and will withdraw the acceptance. They don't like to do it and students don't like to receive this news. As one student who didn't understand this policy said,

> I applied and was accepted the spring before medical school started. I had previously gotten my degree, but, to remain intellectually stimulated, I had enrolled in a class as a non-degree graduate student. After I got accepted, I was no longer interested in going to school for the next few months, so I failed the class. As required, I had to report my grade to the medical school admission office. The Committee re-reviewed my application packet and withdrew my acceptance. I was appalled that I could have such a short medical school career—

> **accepted in February and kicked out in April—before I ever started class! This was amazingly stressful, disconcerting, and a very hard way to learn that admission committees are serious about passing all courses. [This student applied again several years later, was accepted, and actually matriculated into medical school.]**

The key is to keep on plugging along—in an acceptable manner—until you finish school.

How to Deal with Multiple Acceptances

Some applicants are in the enviable position of having to choose among several schools to which they have been accepted. If you have used the "Must/Want" Analysis to select schools, you have a good basis for choosing the school that's best for you. Additionally, you may want to consider the availability of financial assistance. (Each school will probably offer you a different amount and selection of financial aid, depending upon their resources and the class composition.)

Schools must give you at least two weeks to decide whether you will accept their offer. You are not obligated to accept a medical school slot just because it is offered to you (unless you are accepted in an Early-Decision Program). Under AAMC rules, medical schools may require applicants accepted after May 15 to decide whether they accept the school's offer within less than two weeks.

Since medical schools have different schedules, you may get your first acceptances from schools you find less appealing rather than from the one to which you would prefer to go. (Some well-known schools were, at least for a time, notorious for sending out acceptance letters very late, causing a flurry of withdrawals from other schools. Hopefully, this rather crass behavior is a thing of the past.)

It's always best to accept the "bird in the hand." *Accept the first offer you get, no matter how the school ranked on your list*. If you later also get accepted by a school higher on your list, quickly send polite and professional letters (1) withdrawing your acceptance from the first school, (2) withdrawing your application from schools lower on your list, and, of course, (3) accepting the second (higher-rated) school's offer. Continue this process until either you don't get any further acceptances or your first-choice school offers you a position. Don't procrastinate about making a decision while holding two or more acceptances. This isn't fair to the schools or to the other applicants hoping to get a position and, if you have used the "Must/Want" Analysis, it won't be necessary.

Deferred Acceptances

Some medical schools allow students are who are accepted to postpone their medical education. This is called a "deferred acceptance." Although students give a variety of reasons for postponing medical school, many admission officers believe that the primary reason is usually that the students are not sure they want to make the commitment. This is borne out by the relatively high percentage of these students who never do go to medical school.

Figure 15.3 lists the U.S. and Canadian medical schools that will consider requests for deferred admission. There is no uniform policy among schools regarding deferred acceptance; they generally grant deferrals on a case-by-case basis. Some schools, for example, will not allow deferrals for students who were accepted from their waiting list. Most schools that accept deferrals will defer students for only one year. Some schools, however, such as Yale, Johns Hopkins, University of Arkansas, New York University, Case Western Reserve, Pennsylvania State University, and Vanderbilt, have occasionally granted longer deferrals.

If you are interested in a deferral and have been accepted to a medical school that allows individuals to postpone their starting date, find out the specific rules involved. There are two types of deferrals granted, and students usually must specify, in writing, which method they intend to use. The first type is a deferral granted with the understanding that you will only "reapply" to that school and will automatically be accepted. "Reapplying" usually means resubmitting only the basic uniform application the school uses so that you are in the national computer system for that year. The schools may also want a summary of what you have done since you last applied. In general, however, this type of deferral allows the school to admit you with only a pro forma application procedure.

With the second type of deferral, you specify that you intend to repeat the entire application process at multiple schools, taking your chances as you did the first time you applied. Essentially, you decline the school's offer to accept you as a student. Only choose this method if you are sure you don't want to be a physician or if you have a solid reason to believe that you can be admitted to a "better" medical school next time around. This is a risky game to play if you want to go to medical school, although it sometimes succeeds, as this story from a current medical student shows.

> **I was accepted to the U of W medical school during my senior year of college. But my boyfriend of four years had been at the U of W as an undergraduate the whole time I was at Notre Dame. He wasn't graduating until a semester after me. So when I didn't get into U of W as a senior, I had to decide if I would go to the school that accepted me or risk reapplying to the U of W. I followed my heart and moved to be with him, worked for a year, and had to reapply to both schools. (I couldn't defer at the other one). It was a little scary, and people doubted me. But I was accepted at both schools the next year, and now we are engaged and get to stay together. Anyway, my adviser said that the school that let me in wouldn't let me in a second time. But, because I was honest and had really benefited from the year off, I was only a better candidate the next year and they realized that. So don't always trust the advice of those who say they know what they are doing. (I am sure you don't want to put that in the book.)**

The following story, now almost a decade old, is still instructive: In 1996, Cornell University Medical College made headlines when they "bumped" students because they had accepted too many. Of the 249 applicants they accepted into their first-year class, 119 said they would enter Cornell. This was a far higher percentage than in prior years. Unfortunately, they could only accommodate 104 students. Cornell began offering incentives to any 15 applicants who accepted their offer of admission, but were willing to wait a year to enter their first-year class. The students were offered one year's tuition, a guaranteed spot in the 1997 class, and inexpensive (for New York City) student housing immediately. Most students didn't think their offer was worth the delay. (Financially, it certainly wasn't.)

Changing Your Mind

It may be hard for those who are struggling to get into medical school to believe, but every year, more than 1,000 students who have been accepted to U.S. M.D.-granting schools never go. Some of these students go to Osteopathic medical schools, and a few have personal or medical tragedies that preclude their attendance. Most, however, after pursuing what they thought was their dream, simply realize that they do not want a medical career.

Although these students may get grief from their families and friends, they have undoubtedly saved themselves a great deal of anguish by choosing not to pursue a career in which they were not passionately interested. They also have saved patients the heartache of having a physician who simply "goes through the motions." These individuals might have second thoughts about their decision, but if they were not firmly and fully committed to a medical career and a physician's life, then the best time to jump ship was before they set out on the very long journey.

Their spots then become available for applicants who are committed to medicine and who desperately want to become physicians. This is truly a win-win situation for all parties.

— What Else Do You Need to Do? —

Your first responsibility is to keep the school informed about your telephone numbers and your contact addresses—"snail mail" and e-mail. They will need to send you information about your class's orientation, special summer programs, and curriculum changes. Make sure they can find you.

In addition, you must do two more things so that your school is ready for you: Complete the various forms they send you and arrange to pay for your tuition and other expenses. It is important to complete any forms the school sends you immediately. Imagine sitting in class your first day, nervous and hoping that you will do okay, when you are called to the front of the lecture hall to receive papers you didn't complete when they were first sent to you. Embarrassing? You bet! Moreover, it doesn't make a great first impression on your teachers.

Now that you have been accepted to medical school, the time has come for you to find out about loans, scholarships, and grants. Shouldn't you have done this before? Of course. But history shows that applicants, especially when applying for the second or third time, neglect the financial forms, believing they can complete them after they get accepted. Usually, they completed the forms the first time they applied, and they aren't interested in doing it again. Unfortunately, by the time they get accepted, there may be only a few funding options still available to them at many medical schools. Those avenues that are left will certainly not be the cheapest. If you are in this position, proceed to the school's financial aid counselor immediately, without passing "Go," to get the best help available.

— Have an Alternate Plan —

What are you going to do if you don't get into medical school? Every year, medical schools reject nearly two out of three applicants. Many of these individuals reapply in subsequent years and many of them are successful, having "learned the ropes" the first time around (see Chapter 10: *Unconventional Premed Students*). Others decide to apply to foreign medical schools, some of which have "rolling" admission policies, so students can be admitted at various times during the year. Most will eventually abandon the effort, however, and go on to other careers within or outside of medicine (see Chapter 28: *Alternatives to Medical School*).

You should think hard about the alternatives you have so that you are not "left in the lurch" if you don't get admitted. There are several options to consider.

- ***Go to graduate school***

  Do you know what it takes to get in?
  Are you interested in any particular area?
  If you do not get accepted to medical school (or don't want to reapply), is this a field that interests you as a career?
  Can you afford to go to graduate school?

- ***Get a job***

  Are you qualified for a job, especially one you would like?
  Are jobs available in your local area or would you have to move?
  Can you get a job in a health-related field if you plan to reapply?
  Can you afford (financially) to take the job you want?
  Will the job allow you enough time to reapply if you want to?
  Could this job be a steppingstone to permanent employment if you don't eventually go to medical school?

- ***Other (for the independently wealthy few)***

  Travel (especially while volunteering at a remote medical facility)
  Research ("Volunteer" research positions abound at medical centers, especially for those with science degrees. Most people are paid for this, but the pay is usually only the minimum wage unless you have special qualifications.)

— Rejection —

It is said that defeat is a temporary condition; quitting is what makes it permanent. Rejection is a part of most medical school applicants' admission process. Two out of every three medical school applicants fail to get into medical school, and nearly all applicants receive at least one rejection letter, even if they are eventually accepted. (One applicant was distraught when a medical school sent her two rejection letters—in one month! That's overkill.) As one Dean of Admissions told me,

> **Our class would be just as good if we took the first 125 students we ranked or the next 125. All of them have the qualities to be great doctors. I always hope that the rejected group goes to other medical schools or reapplies here.**

Some applicants who are on waiting lists keep their hopes alive only to realize, as the summer drags on, that they will not get in. Depressed, anxious about the future, and less confident about themselves, they often go through five stages of "grieving": initial shock, anger and blaming, rationalization, depression, and resolution.

When they experience the initial shock of rejection, it comes like "a hammer blow to the head." For years, they have dreamed of entering medical school, and for the past year, they have spent lots of time completing forms, taking tests, interviewing, and planning to enter medical school. Now, that dream is gone and they must seek another (at least temporary) path. Often, however, they fail to seek out the help and guidance they need, because they are immobilized by shock, shame, and fear.

In the second stage, applicants direct their anger at others, such as the medical school admission committees, their premed advisers, or indeterminate "others" who were "unfair," "out to get them," or "prejudiced against [ethnic/religious/racial/geographic group or males/females]." Unfortunately, focusing blame on outside forces only delays the student's examining personal reasons for rejection and makes him or her unwilling to make changes to try again.

Next, applicants rationalize, comparing their traits to those of peers who were accepted. These comparisons are often superficial and focus on only one or two traits in which the rejected applicant is clearly superior or inferior. Again, this only delays the day of reckoning that comes with the next stage, depression.

In this stage, applicants feel worthless, often wondering why they thought they could get into medical school. It's at this stage that many promising applicants give up the dream. If, however, they work through their self-doubts, they (with the help of a good premed adviser, if one is available, or with the support of family and friends) can reassess their strengths and weaknesses, develop an action plan to correct any deficiencies in their applications, and formulate a timeline for a reapplication. Whether they give up their dream or reapply, they have come to resolution. (See the personal statements in Chapter 13 to see that, while some "give up" their dream, it sometimes returns later in life.)

— Reapplication —

If you are not accepted into medical school the first time you apply, you may want to apply again. What makes you think that you will be any more successful the second time around? The answer is that you will know the system a little better, have feedback from some of the schools from which you were rejected to help strengthen your application, and demonstrate commitment to a medical career by reapplying.

Many students who have been accepted to medical school on their second try have commented that they only learned the system during their first application process. This is unfortunate. Often, these applicants did not seek out the necessary information or the people who could have helped guide them successfully through the process on their first try.

If medical schools reject your application the first time you apply, ask if they will give you feedback on any deficiencies they see and how you can improve your application. Some medical school admission committees specifically record this information to pass on to rejected applicants if they ask for it. Some medical school admission officers will even counsel rejected students after they complete that year's hectic admissions process. They may suggest improving grades and knowledge in certain areas, perhaps by taking graduate-level courses, or updating information from courses that applicants took many years before. They often suggest getting more recent or more intense clinical exposure. Occasionally, they may also counsel applicants to improve their interviewing skills and image. (If you got your application in late, you need time-management skills, whether they say so or not.) Sometimes, rejected applicants will be offered a deal—acceptance if they fulfill specific criteria, such as passing one or more specific science courses with an "A."

While some medical schools will counsel rejected applicants, the increasing number of applicants has overwhelmed other schools that previously offered this service. If their counsel is not available, seek out a premed adviser who is willing to help you. Since you want to show schools that you have improved one or more key aspects of your application, get assistance in assessing what factors they may have considered weak. Go through the entire checklist: Reasons to be a physician, motivation, MCAT scores, GPA, application process, knowledge about a medical career, and interview style (especially any tendency toward introversion). Examine each aspect for weaknesses, strengths, and areas in need of improvement. Simply taking graduate-level courses without a specific action plan has little value.

Many "second-timers" get accepted to medical schools, as do a few who are applying for the third time or more. This is, in part, not only because they have improved any deficiencies, but also that they have shown commitment to a medical career by sitting out a year or more and reapplying. Committees understand that reapplying after this delay can be a financial and personal hardship that also demonstrates your determination. One older applicant epitomized this attitude when she said, "I was bullheaded and stubborn. I wouldn't go away, so they finally let me in." Another applicant who (barely) got in on his second attempt said,

> **It takes persistence, tenacity, and an uncompromising desire to become a physician. It took me two tries to get in. The second time the door hit me in the butt on the way in—I was number 31 on the wait list, and they only took 31 students from the list. Once you've decided that medicine is what you want, never give up regardless of how hopeless it seems. The higher the fruit, the sweeter the taste.**

If you decide to reapply and have used a premed office to handle your file, be sure to tell them you are reapplying so that they move your packet to the file with active applicants. Otherwise, it may end up in storage, where it doesn't do you any good.

The large rise in medical school applications seems to be due to the increased number of rejected applicants who continue to apply to medical schools. Whether or not an applicant reapplies relates directly to the postrejection support received from family and friends. With this support, applicants will generally reapply. Since nearly two out of every three applicants is rejected, this is a large group of people.

So, how do these folks do if they are accepted? Studies show that there is no significant difference in the performance of those who are accepted and those who were initially rejected but eventually got into medical school. Differences between these two groups seemed to rest primarily on admission committee preferences. This reinforces many applicants' claims that getting in to medical school seems to be a "crap shoot." Applicants who don't get into medical school seem, for the most part, to go into nonmedical, high-status careers.

27

Getting Ready For Medical School

Thy word is a lamp unto my feet,
and a light unto my path.

— Psalms, 119:105

— Prerequisites —

Once they have been accepted to medical school, some applicants still must complete specific prerequisites. This often means successfully finishing the current year's course work or degree program. In some cases, it may also mean completing the medical school's special requirements. Many Canadian schools, for example, require admitted students to complete courses in first aid or cardiopulmonary resuscitation before starting. Check your acceptance letter and the additional materials the school sends you to see if you have any special requirements to fulfill before starting classes.

— Time Management —

To get as far as you have, you had to learn some time-management skills. Now you must hone them to a fine point. Medical students cite their lack of time-management skills as one of their biggest, most keenly felt deficiencies. To use your time effectively in medical school, you must learn to:

- Study effectively
- Do multiple activities simultaneously (multitask)
- Delegate
- Use "to do" lists
- Realistically prioritize your life activities

Study Effectively

While you certainly did well in school and on tests, do you really use your study time to maximum advantage? How often do you let "little things" interrupt you? While you are studying, do you suddenly think of that letter you have to write, the phone call you have to make, or a friend you have to visit? You may have gotten away with that behavior as an undergraduate because the workload is much lighter: Not in medical school. If you have not learned to concentrate on the task at hand without being distracted, you will spend many wasted hours at the books—not learning, not relaxing, and not doing anything else that is useful.

To study effectively, find a place where you will have few interruptions. Stick to a study schedule (a set amount of time or of material to cover) and, most of all, don't allow extraneous thoughts to interrupt your studies (don't daydream or worry). One common interruption is the telephone. Turn it off while you are studying (or sleeping). One medical student finally realized that it was okay to turn the telephone off for a while, "since you are not God and She is not likely to call."

Learn to Do Multiple Activities Simultaneously

"Type-A" people often claim that they accomplish so much because they can do several things simultaneously. Often they say that they *must* perform multiple tasks to keep from getting bored. Yet, these individuals don't actually perform two activities that require concentration at the same time. Instead, they skip back and forth between them. A typical example is reading and watching television (not recommended for medical students while studying). What people really do is to read during commercials or when shows run through predictable plot segments. These people become easily bored, and use these "slow" times in one activity to do another.

Another way people do multiple things simultaneously is to consciously interdigitate two or more activities. For example, when they go to the laundromat, they often bring along other things that can be done in a noisy, uncomfortable setting with frequent interruptions. Studying isn't normally one of these activities. Rather, use such time to write letters, pay bills, and read newspapers or journals. Think about how much time you will spend at the one activity (washing clothes) and what tasks you can effectively do during that time. Sometimes it means putting off some things (such as going through a pile of magazines) until you can pair activities. People who use time effectively would never just sit and watch as their clothes go through the spin cycle.

Learn to Delegate

Do you have to do everything yourself? No!

You may often feel that if you don't do it yourself, it won't be done right. Being a "control freak," in part, defines many medical students' obsessive-compulsive personality. The truth is that if you don't do a task yourself it may not be done exactly as you would have done it, but it usually gets done in an acceptable way. Lighten up and learn to let go a little! Your spouse, significant other, friends, peers, and others are perfectly capable of doing many of the activities you often do. Share the responsibility and let them help. This not only frees up some of your time, but also fosters a sense of community and solidifies relationships.

One caveat about delegating: Some people try to delegate too much. When you need something done only once, do it yourself if someone else's doing it will result in an unacceptable delay. It may take you at least as much time to explain what you want done as to do the job itself. Examples include typing short letters, faxing documents, or completing forms. However, it is worthwhile spending the time to instruct someone else if a job needs to be done frequently. Examples of this are balancing the checkbook, buying groceries, and cooking meals.

However, be sensitive to the time-pressures and hectic schedules of those around you. Spouses and significant others have their own responsibilities and may not appreciate having all your chores "dumped" on them. Ask gently; don't assume their compliance.

Use "To Do" Lists

People are most often distracted by all the little things that they must do in life. Although it may seem trite, keeping a "to do" list helps you remember, sort, and prioritize these activities. When you suddenly remember (while studying, of course) that you must do something the next day, simply write it down and continue your present task, rather than obsess about whether you will remember it.

The "to do" list also helps you to effectively use your time when performing multiple activities. By reviewing which activities you have to do and the places you must go, determine how to do them with the least amount of backtracking (even if they are all within a single complex, like the medical school). This allows you to maximize the activities you can interdigitate with others. This works especially well when running errands.

Lastly, to avoid worrying about losing all your "to-do" lists, either use a PDA or buy a pocket-sized spiral notebook in which to write them down. Cross out items as you do them, discard pages when completed, and occasionally consolidate your lists to a fresh page. This will save you a lot of time, not only by optimizing your schedule, but also by pointing out which activities you didn't have to do in the first place. (These are the items that you have successfully avoided so long that you have "consolidated" them onto your new lists several times.)

Realistically Prioritize Your Life

You only have 24 hours each day. (Even medical students suffer under this natural law.) Therefore, you never can do everything you want to do. You must decide which activities are most important. Prioritizing your life activities is the hardest part of time management. *Realistically, you will have to give up some things to succeed in medical school*. What will they be?

First, make a list of the things you do now and expect to continue doing while in medical school. Then add new things you expect to begin doing. An example of one student's list of activities (alphabetically) is shown in Figure 27.1.

Next, prioritize the items on your list, as our example student has done (Figure 27.2). One excellent rule for prioritization, which this student used, is to highly rank anything that cannot be easily replaced or that will not matter if you don't do or spend less time on, such as watching TV or family relationships.

This student eliminated some activities she enjoyed and had commonly done in the past. She loved to read novels and to travel. In high school, she described herself as a "party animal." However, medical school takes its toll on personal activities. She had the foresight to make a rational, proactive decision about what was most important to her. This helped her to effectively use her available time. (Yes, she attended a few parties with her class and family during medical school, but these were exceptions, rather than the rule.)

Once she finished medical school and finished her intern year, she added back an additional activity. Now in practice, she has been able to add back one or two more. Some, though, are gone forever. Being a physician is time-consuming.

— Other Considerations —

Learning Disabilities

If you have any reason to suspect that you have a reading or test-taking deficiency, get a professional evaluation. There often are resources available at your college's learning center. (See also Chapter 10: *Unconventional Premed Students*.)

How do you recognize such a problem? A key signal is that you do markedly worse on standardized tests (such as the MCAT) than would be expected considering your normal course performance. Not that you failed, or you wouldn't have been accepted into medical school. You just didn't score as high as you should have—and there was no obvious explanation, such as failing to study, an illness, or partying the night before the exam. If you couldn't finish most sections of the MCAT and had to leave many questions blank, you may have a reading problem.

The point is that if you have a learning disability (usually a problem with reading or test-taking—they are often interrelated), the problem won't fix itself. However, you can learn how to improve your performance by getting professional assistance.

FIGURE 27.1

Life Activities in Medical School (Example)

Attend class
Attend religious services
Exercise
Go to parties
Read magazines and newspapers
Read novels
Spend time with my children
Spend time with my friends
Spend time with my spouse
Study
Travel
Volunteer clinically
Watch television
Work, part-time

FIGURE 27.2

Prioritized Life Activities in Medical School (Example)

Activity	Priority
1. Attend class	
2. Study	
3. Volunteer clinically	HIGH
4. Spend time with my spouse	
5. Spend time with my children	
6. Work, part-time	
7. Spend time with my friends	
8. Read the newspaper	LOWER
9. Attend religious services	
10. Exercise	
11. Go to parties	
12. Read magazines	
13. Read novels	ELIMINATE
14. Travel	
15. Watch television	

Even if you have dyslexia, you can be helped to read (and write) better, but you won't have much time for this once you are in medical school. Do it now! The most important reason to get help, however, is that you may be required to get it to obtain a medical license. If you have a disability that necessitates your asking for special accommodations to take the USMLE or NBOME licensing exams, the testing agencies will require documentation of your disability and a personal statement describing the history of your disability. For example, if you have a reading problem, you must have a psychologist's evaluation and letter.

Children

If you have small children while you are in medical school, they will invariably get ill at exam time. Before you start school, it is essential to arrange for baby sitters who are qualified and able to care for sick children on short notice. (Always have back-ups on your list.) Also, find a family physician or pediatrician who can quickly work you into his or her schedule. As a medical student, you will not have time to wait in a doctor's office. (Remember that when you go into practice.) Single mothers most frequently have to deal with these problems alone, but even couples have these difficulties, since working spouses (and they probably will be working so you can eat) often have less flexibility than medical students do.

Summer Vacation

Now that you have taken care of the big stuff, it's time to enjoy yourself a bit. This may be your last summer of freedom. You may not even have an entire summer, since many schools start between June and August. So, use whatever time you have available to have some fun. You earned it!

For all the Type-A+ personalities reading this, that means YOU! Put down those textbooks, pick up a trashy novel, go to the beach or mountains with a friend or loved one, and simply enjoy life. You are about to embark on a very tough journey. Come prepared with memories of your wonderful summertime experiences.

— Locate Special Resources at School —

Dean of Students

The Dean of Students is your contact with the faculty and the medical school's administration. He or she "knows the rules" and will have the most up-to-date information about new school policies, changes in national policies affecting medical students, your professional licensing examinations, and residency matching programs. If you get into academic or other difficulties, this is also the person you will need to see. Find out where the Dean of Students' office is and, if possible, introduce yourself.

Medical Library

Locate the school's library and what see resources they have. Libraries function as learning resource centers and provide not only books and journals but also videotapes, audiotapes, CD-ROMs, computer programs, and online services (including medical database searches). If you don't know how to use these services, ask. The reference librarians will guide you through the learning process and the school's computer gurus will help you learn the vital computer (research and word-processing) skills you will need as a medical student, resident, and practicing physician.

Student Organizations

Every medical school has student organizations. Even though your time is limited, there are many good reasons, including those listed below, for you to participate in at least one of these groups.

- ***Make a difference in your community***. Many groups do community outreach, run clinics, or assist other agencies in their charity work.
- ***Network***. Most organizations provide an opportunity to meet other students, residents, and practicing physicians on both local and national levels. These are ties that can last your entire career.
- ***Political action***. Students do have a strong voice on the national medical scene—including at the American Medical Association. See your ideas become national policy and your programs expand far beyond your local area.
- ***Fun***. Working with other professionals can be fun. You will need some "down time," and this is a great opportunity to get it.

For a list of medical student organizations, see *Appendix B*.

— Getting Organized at School —

Finding a Place to Live

Some schools have dormitories or student housing. Most don't. If you ask, and usually even if you don't, your medical school will send you information about available housing. Schools will also normally include other information about their city and the surrounding communities. To supplement this information, simply contact that city's Chamber of Commerce, Visitors' Bureau, and any websites about the area.

Moving to a New City

If you have been accepted at a school far from where you now live, you need to move. Since this may be a new experience for you, and because many students have told me that they got "burned" when using movers, be careful when hiring professional movers.

According to the U.S. Department of Transportation (DOT), complaints against interstate movers have been increasing since the Interstate Commerce Commission was abolished in 1995. Learn your rights and responsibilities when contracting with a mover from an online government booklet at www.fmcsa.dot.gov/states/ny/moving.htm.

Also, before contracting with any mover, contact your local Better Business Bureau (www.bbb.org); the American Moving & Storage Association, which has an online consumer handbook (www.moving.org); and the DOT (www.safersys.org) to find out if any complaints have been lodged against the company you are considering. Beware of unreliable movers. The larger national movers have local branches that can help with long-distance, and sometimes even local, moves. You can contact their national office if things go wrong. In addition, the following are helpful tips for hiring movers:

- Get on-site written estimates from at least three national moving companies. These estimates come in three forms: *Binding*, in which the price remains fixed once the estimate is signed by both parties; *Nonbinding*, in which you can be charged almost any price; and *Not-to-exceed $X*, which sets an upper limit on how much the move will cost. Remember that cheaper doesn't always mean better. If it's too good to be true, it is.

- Get details about any charges not covered by the estimate. These may include packing and unpacking, extra distance from the house or apartment to the truck (on either end of the trip), packing materials, stairs at either end of the move, moving heavy objects, and insurance.
- Carry any irreplaceable items with you. Do not entrust diplomas and other legal documents, heirlooms, family photographs, jewelry, safe-deposit-box contents, or other highly valued or easily broken items to the movers.
- Get adequate insurance for the possessions you will move. If you have a homeowners' insurance policy, check to see if it covers your possessions while the mover has them. *Basic (interstate) moving insurance* comes free with the move, but only covers about *60 cents for each pound* of material lost. (They would pay you only $12.00 if they lost your new $2,500 computer that weighs only 20 pounds.) Other options are *full-replacement-value insurance*, which costs about 85 cents per $100 of declared value of your goods; *depreciated-value-of-goods insurance* (what the goods are worth today), which costs about 25 cents per $100 of declared value of your goods; or a *full-replacement less-a-deductible insurance* policy. This latter is relatively inexpensive, but you must cover the deductible.
- Make a detailed list of all goods moved, including a list of everything in each box. The mover will make his own list of items and note whether furniture is "scratched," "dented," etc. Go over this list with the mover and be certain he correctly stated the condition of the items on his list. Number the boxes so you can see quickly if any are missing. (While it may be a pain, be sure to account for each box or item at the end of the move—before the movers leave.)
- Take photographs of any large or expensive items you must entrust to the movers, such as electronic equipment. Carry these photographs with you.
- Carry contact numbers for your mover's dispatcher and, if they will give it to you, the driver's cell phone number, so you can locate your truck when it's delayed. (The frequent-mover's law: Never expect the moving truck to arrive when scheduled.)

Getting Settled

Once you are in a new city, here are some things you should do:

- Notify the Department of Motor Vehicles of your new address or get the information to obtain a driver's license and to register your car in the new state.
- Register to vote.
- Call the Sanitation Department to find out when the trash will be picked up.
- Transfer insurance policies to agents in your new community, and get new ones if needed.
- Find a new bank and open an account.
- Find baby-sitters and day care for children.
- Check out nearby grocery stores, dry cleaners, gas stations, and drug stores now. You probably won't have a lot of time after you start school. Check with the Dean of Students' office for information about local stores, schools, and services. Some may have special discounts for medical students.
- Find out where to park for school, or how to get there using public transportation.
- Transfer your medical and dental records to providers in your new community. Check first with the medical school to see if they have a medical or dental plan for students.

28

Alternatives To Medical School

If you can't do what you want, do what you can.

— Jewish Proverb

About half of all unsuccessful applicants to medical school eventually work in health-related occupations. While some of these fields require only bachelor's degrees, most demand additional training to be eligible. There are many positions in health care (Figure 28.1); some occupations that provide primary health care are discussed in detail below.

Many "premed" advisers will also counsel individuals about other health-related professions. They may do it themselves or have others in their offices or on campus to whom they refer students. If you are set on a health care career but either do not want to go to or cannot get into medical school, contact the premed adviser to obtain the information you need.

One caveat: You will be much happier in your career if you go *toward* a profession, rather than viewing it as a "consolation prize" when you cannot get into medical school. Most practitioners in any field do not think they are second-rate, and will dismiss those who do. Educators, especially, will not see you as a viable or valuable addition to their ranks if you exhibit these feelings. They want people who really desire to be one of them. Is that you?

— Physician Assistant —

Physician Assistants (PA's) practice medicine under the supervision (often remote) of a licensed physician. More than 46,000 PA's currently practice in the United States, and more than 4,000 new PA's graduate annually. They, like nurse practitioners, are considered "mid-level practitioners." In rural areas, they may be the only practitioners, with their supervising physicians many miles away. After their initial training, some PA's, especially those at major medical centers, may concentrate (specialize) in specific areas, such as emergency medicine or a surgical subspecialty.

The scope of a PA's responsibilities is generally limited only by the physicians for whom they work. Some areas of the country are more hospitable to PA's than are others, although PA's work everywhere in the United States. They have prescribing privileges in 47 states (not Indiana, Louisiana and Ohio). The average PA is 41 years old and 58% of them are women. As of 2003, there were 134 physician assistant programs in the United States that were accredited by the Accreditation Review Commission on Education for the Physician Assistant (ARC-PA). They are located at medical schools, universities, teaching hospitals, and within the armed forces.

Most programs last about two years (without breaks), and include both didactics and labs (essentially the same curricula as medical students take, although abbreviated). In addition, PA's do clinical rotations on the same services that most third-year medical students do (sometimes with these students) and in emergency medicine, ambulatory clinics, long-term health facilities, and physicians' offices. The focus is on primary care. Some programs give their graduates not only a certificate of completion, but also a Master of Health Science.

The total tuition for a PA education ranges from under $4,000 to about $70,000, with costs in the public sector much cheaper than at private institutions. Master's degree programs are more costly than those offering a bachelor's degree or certificate. PA students expect to emerge from school with an average debt of $44,000. Programs at private institutions averaged more students per class and lasted longer than did those at public institutions.

The average student admitted to a PA program already has a bachelor's degree and about two years of health care experience, usually as a nurse, EMT, or other allied health professional. More than half of PA programs expect applicants to complete the following courses before applying: biology, general chemistry, anatomy, physiology, English, psychology, and microbiology. Fewer than half require organic chemistry, statistics, sociology, algebra, or humanities courses. Some programs, however, admit students with few college credits and no health care experiences. Admission to a PA program can be as difficult or, in some cases, more difficult than to medical school.

In nearly all states, a PA must have graduated from an accredited PA program and have passed the exam given by the National Commission on Certification of Physician Assistants (NCCPA). As of 2003, the NCCPA had certified about 50,000 PA's. To remain certified, a PA must complete 100 hours of continuing medical education every two years and pass a recertification exam every six years.

The mean annual income for physician assistants working full time is over $70,000, with new graduates having a mean income of more than $60,000. Most work for individual physicians, group practices, HMOs, and outpatient clinics. The job market for PA's is excellent: The United States Bureau of Labor Statistics (BLS) projects a 53% increase in PA positions between 2000 and 2010.

While PA's practice in at least 61 specialty fields, 46% work in a primary care specialty: family/general practice (32.1%), general internal medicine (8.4%), obstetrics and gynecology (2.7%), and general pediatrics (2.6%). Other major areas of practice are general surgery/surgical subspecialties (21.7%), emergency medicine (10.2%), and internal medicine subspecialties (9.4%).

The Central Application Service for Physician Assistants (CASPA) is a clerical service for applicants to participating PA programs. It collects one set of materials from each applicant—an online (or optional paper) application, standardized test scores, transcripts, and references—then authenticates them and distributes them to each member school that the applicant designates. For information about CASPA, contact the Association of Physician Assistant Programs (APAP), 950 N. Washington St., Alexandria, VA 22314-1552; (703) 548-5538; apap@apap.org. CASPA information can be accessed directly at https://secure.caspaonline.org or through the APAP website.

For more information about the profession, contact the American Academy of Physician Assistants, 950 N. Washington St., Alexandria, VA 22314-1552; (703) 836-2272; e-mail: aapa@aapa.org; www.aapa.org.

— Advance-Practice Nursing —

Advance-practice nursing includes certified registered nurse anesthetists (CRNA), certified nurse midwives (CNM), and nurse practitioners (NP). All have independent patient-care responsibilities and begin with a nursing degree.

CRNAs give anesthesia. They must be under a physician's (although not necessarily an anesthesiologist's) direct supervision. The more than 30,000 CRNAs who currently practice in the United States provide more than half of all anesthesia administration. Training, often quite intense, lasts from 24 to 36 months. To be certified, graduates must pass a national examination. The average annual CRNA salary is about $100,000.

CNMs provide prenatal care, delivery, and postnatal care. There are about 10,000 CNMs in the United States, but only about half work in that capacity. CNM programs last about two years. There are also Certified Midwife (CM) programs that don't require a nursing degree. There are 41 accredited programs offering master's degrees and four offering bachelors' degrees. The annual salary averages about $60,000.

Similar to PA's, nurse practitioners (NP's) are considered "mid-level" medical caregivers. They often work independently to provide health care services. All hold at least a Bachelor of Nursing degree and are licensed as RN's. There are more than 100,000 NP's in the United States. While about 90% of them work in nursing, only about two-thirds work as an NP. Unlike PA's, who train using a medical model, NP's train using a nursing model. All NP's may prescribe medications, although in some states they must first consult with a physician. State laws define the nurse practitioner's scope of practice. Full-time NP's have an average annual salary of about $66,000.

Most NP programs last two years (if students go full-time) and grant master's degrees. The programs include both didactics and clinical practice. Special programs exist for training nurse practitioners in family practice, pediatrics, women's health, geriatrics, and adult medicine.

Four different bodies credential NP's: the American Nurses Credentialing Center; the National Certification Board of Pediatric Nurse Practitioners and Nurses; the American Academy of Nurse Practitioners; and the National Certification Corporation for the Obstetric, Gynecologic and Neonatal Nursing Specialties. Not all states require that NP's have national certification to practice.

Unlike PA's, nurse practitioners are independent practitioners who are licensed and can independently diagnose and treat patients. Many, however, work with physicians in offices and hospitals. Thirteen jurisdictions allow them to practice completely independently or with only a minimal relationship with physicians. These are Alaska, Arizona, Iowa, Maine, Montana, New Hampshire, New Mexico, Oregon, Utah, Washington, Wisconsin, Wyoming, and Washington, DC.

Many nurses struggle with the decision about whether to enter an NP or a PA program. Especially in the more generalist-oriented NP programs, some nurses have been "turned off" by the rehashing of care plans and similar debris from their undergraduate nursing curricula. The programs, however, vary tremendously in their admission criteria, curricula, and the quality of their graduates. *Caveat emptor.*

For more information, contact:

American Academy of Nurse Practitioners
P.O. Box 12846
Austin, TX 78711
(512) 442-4262; www.aanp.org

American College of Nurse Practitioners
1111 19th St. NW, Ste. 404
Washington, DC 20036
(202) 659-2190

American College of Nurse Midwives
818 Connecticut Ave. NW, Ste. 900
Washington, DC 20006
(202) 728-9860; www.acnm.org

American Association of Nurse Anesthetists
222 S. Prospect Ave.
Park Ridge, IL 60068
(847) 692-7050; www.aana.com

— Dentistry —

Unlike medicine, dentistry is still primarily comprised of private practitioners. Of the roughly 150,000 active dentists in the United States, more than 90% are in private practice and about 80% practice general dentistry; the balance practice dental specialties. Dentistry remains one of the most-respected professions. Dentists have flexible working hours, a variety of work settings, and many opportunities to be creative in their work. Dentists actually have a higher return on their educational investment than do primary care physicians.

Applicants must take the Dental Admission Test (DAT). The test is computerized, takes a little more than a half day, and consists of four sections:

1. **Survey of the Natural Sciences**
   - Biology
   - General Chemistry
   - Organic Chemistry
2. **Perceptual Ability**
   - Angle discrimination
   - Form development cubes
   - Orthographic projections
   - Apertures
   - Paper folding

3. **Reading Comprehension**
   Ability to read, organize, analyze, comprehend and remember new science information
4. **Quantitative Reasoning**
   Algebraic problems
   Arithmetic calculations and measurement conversions
   Statistics
   Geometry
   Trigonometry

Materials for the DAT include the *Dental Admission Test Preparation Materials* (comes with the written registration materials) and a disk that familiarizes applicants with taking the DAT online. They are available through the American Dental Association's website at www.ada.org/prof/ed/testing/index.html.

Nearly all the 55 accredited U.S. dental schools require one year each of: English or English literature, introductory chemistry, organic chemistry, physics, and general biology. About one-third of all dental schools require college-level mathematics (and half of those specify one year of calculus). The specific requirements are listed in the *ADEA Official Guide to Dental Schools* (for schools in the United States and Canada), published by the American Dental Education Association (ADEA). Many U.S. dental schools participate in the Dental Schools Application Service (AADSAS) at http://aadsas.adea.org.

Slightly more than half of all applicants to U.S. dental schools get accepted. More than 90% of those accepted have at least four years of undergraduate education, and more than 80% obtained undergraduate degrees before entering dental school. Following four years in dental school, graduates (with a D.D.S. or D.M.D.) may take specialty training in endodontics, orthodontics, pediatric dentistry, prosthodontics, oral surgery, periodontics, or other areas. These programs have very stiff entry requirements; only the best students get into them (often after a required minimum time practicing general dentistry). General dentists earn about $160,000 annually, while specialists average about $250,000.

For more information, contact the American Dental Association, 211 E. Chicago Ave., Chicago, IL 60611-2678; (312) 440-2500; www.ada.org; or the ADEA, 1625 Massachusetts Ave. NW, Ste. 600, Washington, DC 20036-2212; (202) 667-9433; www.adea.org.

— Podiatric Medicine —

Podiatric medicine, more commonly known as podiatry, is a separate medical area devoted to the care of the foot and ankle. Podiatrists use surgery, medications, and orthotic devices to treat foot ailments. Depending upon the state's regulations and the practitioner's training, podiatrists may be able to do surgery anywhere on the lower extremity. About 18,000 podiatrists work in the United States, with most being in solo practice. About 29% of all podiatrists are women and 31% are minorities. A podiatrist's annual salary averages $100,000.

Applicants to a college of podiatric medicine must take the MCAT and complete at least three years or 90 semester hours of college credit, including six hours of English. In addition, applicants must complete eight semester hours each of biology, general/inorganic chemistry, organic chemistry, and physics, all of which should be the same courses that premed students take. In general, the average GPA and MCAT scores for those entering podiatry school (GPA about 3.1; MCAT scores about 6.9) are lower than those required for medical school. MCAT scores have been shown to correlate better with performance during the first two years of podiatry school than the undergraduate GPA or science GPA. Slightly more than half of all applicants to podiatry school are accepted.

More than 90% of all first-year podiatry students have baccalaureate degrees, with the balance having advanced degrees. Applicants must take the MCAT, although some colleges accept the Graduate Record Examination (GRE) instead.

Each year, more than 1,000 individuals apply to podiatry schools; there are approximately 525 positions available. Podiatry schools use a centralized application service; the applications can be obtained from the American Association of Colleges of Podiatric Medicine (AACPM), 1350 Piccard Dr., Ste. 322, Rockville, MD 20850-4307; (800) 922-9266; www.aacpm.org/apply/apply.asp.

The podiatric medicine curriculum lasts four years and is similar to that at medical schools. The first two years are devoted to the basic sciences, including anatomy, biochemistry, physiology, microbiology, pathology, and pharmacology. Third- and fourth-year students do clinical rotations, where they learn how to take general and podiatric histories, perform routine physical examinations, interpret test results, make diagnoses, and perform therapeutic procedures.

After receiving their Doctor of Podiatric Medicine (DPM) degree, graduates usually must take a one- to two-year postgraduate surgical or nonsurgical residency to become licensed. These residencies must be in institutions that also have physicians-in-training, so that residents can get an interdisciplinary experience. Using a centralized matching service, they can obtain nonsurgical residencies, which include the interdisciplinary rotating podiatric residency (RPR), the primary care-oriented primary podiatric medical residency (PPMR), and the podiatric orthopedic residency (POR), which concentrates on preserving and restoring leg and foot function. Alternatively, the podiatric surgical residencies (PSR) last from one to three years and provide additional operative training.

Podiatric physicians are licensed in all 50 states, the District of Columbia, and Puerto Rico to treat the foot and, usually, the ankle, by medical, surgical, or other means.

There are certifying Boards for the podiatric specialties of orthopedics, primary medicine, or surgery. Certification means that the podiatrist has met higher standards than those required for licensure. Each board requires advanced training, completion of written and oral examinations, and experience as a practicing podiatrist. Most managed care organizations prefer board-certified podiatrists.

For more information, contact the American Podiatric Medical Association, 9312 Old Georgetown Rd., Bethesda, MD 20814-1621; (800) 275-2762; www.apma.org/CPME.

— Optometry —

Optometrists examine eyes, test for visual acuity, and prescribe eyeglasses, contact lenses, vision therapy, and, in most states, medications. Unlike ophthalmologists (physicians), they do not do surgery. They work with both ophthalmologists and the opticians who fit, supply, and adjust glasses and contact lenses. Optometrists have a mean annual income of more than $140,000, and most are self-employed.

There are 16 optometry schools in the mainland United States, one in Puerto Rico, and two in Canada. Annual tuition and fees vary widely.

Applicants to schools of optometry must fulfill the standard premed requirements, plus calculus, microbiology, statistics, and psychology. Each school has somewhat different requirements, so it is important to check with the schools. Most successful applicants have undergraduate degrees. About two-thirds of all applicants are accepted into optometry school. The average GPA of accepted students ranges from 3.0 to 3.5, depending upon the school. Students graduate with an O.D. degree after four years of study.

Optometry schools require that applicants take the Optometry Admission Test (OAT), which is offered in February and October. The OAT has four sections: Quantitative Reasoning, Natural Sciences (Biology, Chemistry, Organic Chemistry), Reading Comprehension, and Physics. Applications and the *Optometry Admission Testing Program Online Candidate Guide* can be obtained from the Optometry Admission Testing Program at www.ada.org/oat.

For more information, contact the American Optometric Association (AOA), 243 N. Lindbergh Blvd., St. Louis, MO 63141; (314) 991-4100; www.aoanet.org; or the Association of Schools and Colleges of Optometry, 6110 Executive Blvd., Ste. 510, Rockville, MD 20852; (301) 231-5944; www.opted.org.

— Naturopathic Medicine —

Naturopaths (N.D.) treat diseases using "alternative therapies," including nutrition, herbal medicine, homeopathy, exercise therapy, counseling, acupuncture and acupressure, physical medicine, and hydrotherapy. As of 2003, there are four accredited schools of naturopathy in North America

(Washington, Oregon, Arizona, Ontario) and one (Connecticut) that has applied. Naturopaths are licensed in nine states and two U.S. territories (Alaska, Arizona, Connecticut, Hawaii, Kansas, Maine, Montana, New Hampshire, Oregon, Puerto Rico, Virgin Islands, Utah, Vermont, and Washington). Washington, with the most liberal licensing laws for Naturopaths, considers them "general care providers," and allows students to get state-supported scholarships.

A number of programs now offer "mail order" naturopathic degrees. None of their graduates have been permitted to take any licensing examination.

Most students have bachelor's degrees and have completed the standard premed courses before entering naturopathic school. Most ND students are women, and most of them are pursuing a second career. Matriculants' average GPA was about 3.1. The majority of the schools' admission deadlines are February 1. The course of study is four years.

For more information, contact the American Association of Naturopathic Physicians, 3201 New Mexico Ave. NW, Ste. 350, Washington, DC 20016; (866) 538-2267; www.naturopathic.org.

— Chiropractic —

Chiropractors (D.C.) manipulate the spine to relieve pain. Some claim to be able to cure systemic diseases using this manipulation. Chiropractors are licensed in all states and the District of Columbia.

Applicants to chiropractic school must have at least two years of college including the usual pre-health courses. The average GPA of entering students is about 3.0. Of about 6,000 annual applicants, the schools accept more than half; about 80% of accepted applicants actually enroll.

The course of study is five years. Some schools now offer postgraduate residencies in various areas, including sports medicine, neurology, and radiology. There are also some programs available for Chiropractic Assistant.

For more information, contact the Council on Chiropractic Education (CCE), 8049 N. 85th Way, Scottsdale, AZ 85258-4321; (480) 443-8877; e-mail: cce@cce-usa.org; www.cce-usa.org; or the Association of Chiropractic Colleges, 4424 Montgomery Ave., Ste. 102, Bethesda, MD 20814; e-mail: Info@ChiroColleges.org; www.chirocolleges.org.

— Forensics —

The term "forensics" is a catchall for a wide variety of careers, and has probably generated more interest in recent years than any other medically related area. Undoubtedly, the high profile and apparent glamour given these jobs on television and in other media has greatly contributed to the interest. The problem is that the media portrays a less-than-accurate picture of what forensic folks actually do—most of it is far from glamourous.

Some typical jobs in forensics include evidence photographer (civil or law enforcement), civil or criminal investigator, fire and arson investigator, legal video specialist, and coroner's assistant. The following are descriptions of some other forensic professions.

- **Forensic Psychologist.** They examine defendants, testify in court, often treat patients, and earn $50,000 or more annually. Many have only a master's degree, although the highest paid usually are Ph.D.'s in clinical psychology.
- **Forensic Science Technician.** Their job is to collect, identify, classify, and analyze physical evidence related to criminal investigations. Most have a bachelor's degree in criminology or a science-related field and work for the police or a related agency. Many forensic science technicians specialize in a specific area, especially in larger departments. Some perform tests on weapons or substances such as fiber, hair, and tissue to determine their significance to an investigation. Occasionally, they may testify as expert witnesses on evidence or on crime laboratory techniques, including ballistics, fingerprinting, handwriting, and biochemical analysis. The salary varies widely with the job and their expertise.

- **Forensic Pathologist, Anthropologist, Dentist, etc.** These are the folks with the most interesting jobs in forensics. All require a doctorate degree and special advanced training. Their salaries are commensurate with all this education—and with the responsibility they take.
- **Polygraph Examiner.** Polygraph examiners use a polygraph machine during a suspect's interrogation to detect those who are lying. The results are not always accepted by police or the courts. If they work independently, they must buy their own equipment. Often they have only a high school degree. The annual salary for full-time examiners is about $40,000.
- **Forensic Sketch Artist.** These artists draw the likenesses of subjects according to a witness's observations or description to assist law enforcement agencies in identifying suspects, and they also sketch courtroom scenes.These individuals usually have a high school degree—and all have artistic talent. Depending upon their employer, they can earn up to $40,000 per year.

For more information about any of the jobs in forensics, contact your local police agency, medical examiner's office, or favorite forensic website (not one associated with a television show).

— Pharmacy, Veterinary Medicine, Nursing —

These three medical fields are unique, and those going into them generally have decided well in advance to enter that field. Pharmacy and nursing require specific undergraduate degrees tailored to their professions, while prevets have to survive the same science courses as premeds, often with less chance of getting into their professional school.

These are excellent careers with many opportunities. If you are considering one of them, check out the information from the groups listed:

American Association of Colleges of Pharmacy
1426 Prince St., Alexandria, VA 22314
(703) 739-2330; e-mail: mail@aacp.org; www.aacp.org

Association of American Veterinary Colleges
1101 Vermont Ave. NW, Ste. 710
Washington, DC 20005
(202) 371-9195; www.aavmc.org

American Nurses Association
600 Maryland Ave. SW, Ste. 100 West
Washington, DC 20024-2571
(800) 274-4262; www.ana.org

— Other Careers in Medicine —

Figure 28.1 contains an abbreviated list of other opportunities in health care. (This is not a complete list.) You can find out more about these careers, including sources for more in-depth information, on the numerous websites describing each area. The national organizations for these professionals can supply even more information.

Graduate School

Graduate school can be either an alternative to a health care career or preparation for another attempt at entering a health professions school. Entering graduate school simply for "something to do" until reapplying to medical school is generally pointless. Medical schools don't see that course of action as beneficial or "substantially improving credentials," which is what most schools ask for in reapplicants. Have a clear reason for entering graduate school.

If you have an interest in a particular area and want to pursue those studies, now is a good time to do it. In some cases, individuals who took this route found a career path they really enjoyed and

FIGURE 28.1
Health Care-Related Careers

Acupuncturist
Anatomist
Anesthesiology Assistant
Art Therapist
Athletic Trainer
Audiologist
Biomedical Engineer
Biophotographer
Biostatistician
Blood Bank Technologist
Cardiovascular Technologist
Clinical Chemistry Technologist
Clinical Microbiology Technologist
Coding Specialist
Cytotechnologist
Dance Therapist
Dental Assistant
Dental Hygienist
Dental Technician
Dietitian
Electroneurodiagnostic Technician
Emergency Medical Technician
Epidemiologist
Exercise Physiologist
Genetic Counselor
Health Educator
Health Information Management
Health Sciences Librarian
Histology Technician
Home Health Aide
Hospital/Nursing Home Administrator
Kinesiotherapist
Laboratory Assistant
Licensed Practical Nurse
Medical Assistant
Medical Illustrator
Medical Records Administrator
Medical Records Technician
Medical Sonographer
Medical Technologist
Medical Writer
Music Therapist
Nuclear Medicine Technician
Nutritionist
Occupational Therapist
Ophthalmic Laboratory Technician
Optician
Orthoptist
Orthotist
Paramedic
Perfusionist
Pharmacologist
Physical Therapist
Physical Therapy Assistant
Psychologist
Radiology Technologist
Research Scientist
Respiratory Therapist
Science Writer
Social Worker
Speech Pathologist
Surgical Technologist
Technical Writer
Therapeutic Recreation Specialist
Toxicologist
Visual Impairment Professions

stayed with it. Another reason to enter graduate school is to take course work toward a degree you planned to get anyway, such as a Master of Public Health or Master of Health Administration. If the degree pertains to medicine, so much the better.

Finally, you may want to do graduate-level studies if your GPA was not up to medical school standards. This gives you an opportunity to improve your grades while continuing to hone your study skills. For this to be of significance to medical schools, however, the courses you take must be science-related and "rigorous" (not underwater basket-weaving).

— Income —

In general, annual income in the health-related fields varies with the number of years required for training or education. A factor not often considered, however, is that with more years in school there is less time to earn money—and, at least with physicians, a huge educational debt to pay off once they begin to make money. If a large income is your goal, a law or business degree may be a much better bet.

Figure 28.2 gives a general overview of the annual salary for some health-related professions and the number of post-high school years of education these jobs generally require.

— Summary —

Many career opportunities exist within the health care field. Some may fulfill your needs as well as, or better than, being a physician. Consider these options before you decide to enter medical school. If you have been rejected from medical schools, consider these options before completely abandoning any thought of entering the healing professions.

FIGURE 28.2

The Freddy Kruger Principle: No Pain, No Gain

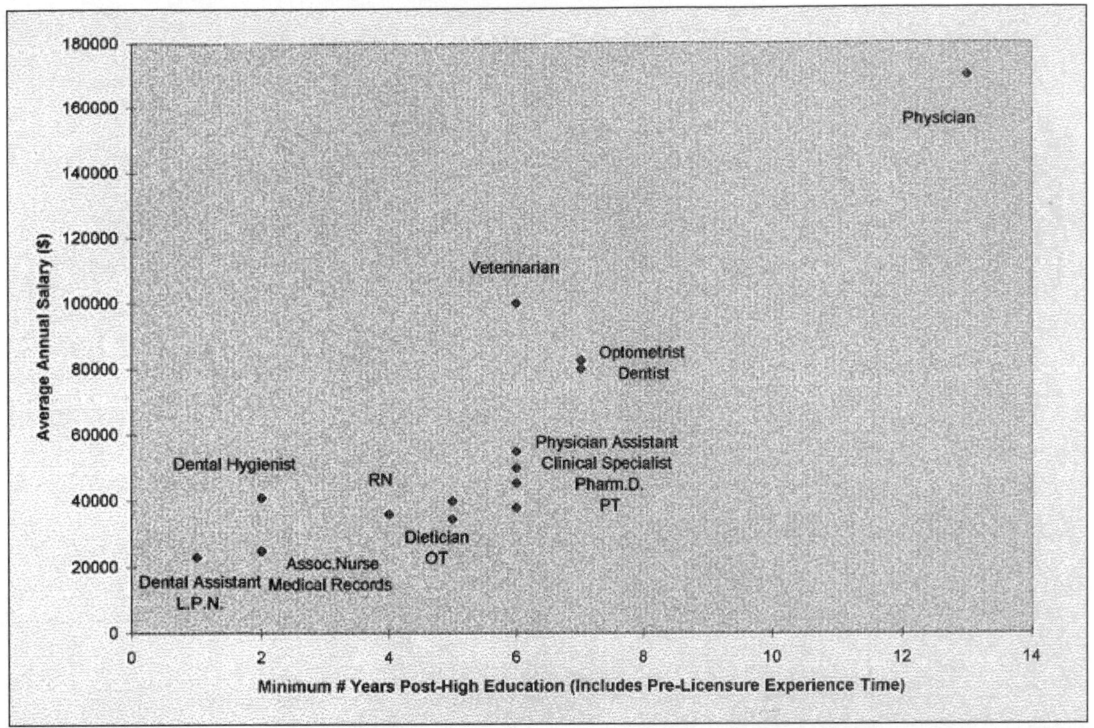

Used with permission of Dr. Stan Eisen, Director, Pre-Health Programs, Christian Brothers University, Memphis, TN (www.cbu.edu/~seisen/hc.html).

29

Now You Are A Medical Student

The master word in medicine is work . . .
Though a little one, it looms large in meaning.
It is the open sesame to every portal,
the great equalizer in the world, the true philosopher's stone
which transmutes all the base metal of humanity into gold.

— Sir William Osler

Now that you have started medical school, you have essentially received the profession's "secret handshake." You are one of "us," a physician (albeit a neophyte), rather than one of "them," the uninitiated. Make the most of this. Assertively seek out educational opportunities, especially those in clinical medicine. While these may have been difficult to obtain before, your only problem now will be not to put too much on your proverbial plate. Go forth—experience and learn!

Twelve Rules for Success in Medical School

1. **Your initial goal:** *Do well on the first set of exams.* This will give you confidence. It also helps you develop the study/work habits necessary to succeed throughout medical school. In addition, the first material taught is the foundation on which the balance of the course (and often other courses) rests. If you think of the first six weeks of medical school as a very tough survival course, you will have the right mindset. Study as you have never studied before. Take self-assessment tests and review exams that were previously used by current professors.
2. **Review your notes.** By the third or fourth day of school, begin spending between 10 to 15 minutes each day reviewing your notes from previous days. The more repetition, the better (and easier) you will learn the material for the exams and the longer you will retain it after the exams. Unlike undergraduate school, you will actually have to remember and apply much of what you learn.
3. **Consciously try to process new information on three levels.**
   - ***Rote learning.*** You have to memorize a lot of material. You proved you could do it by passing organic chemistry. Just suck it in (literally and figuratively).
   - ***Understanding.*** Okay, so you memorized how the drug works. Can you figure out what the side effects might be?
   - ***Application.*** If you have a patient with hypertension, which of the drugs you learned about would you dispense? Why would they be different for different patients? What side effects might make a patient stop using the medication? What are your alternatives?

   The examinations medical students take no longer require regurgitating memorized material (rote learning). Questions now test your understanding of and ability to apply information. This is true for all exams you take in medical school, as well as the licensing exams (USMLE, COMLEX).

4. **Join a study group early.** Study groups are essential. Not only do they help you study, but they also provide support and encouragement when things get rough.
5. **Decide early which classes you should attend.** If you spend five minutes in a class and are completely lost, leave. Read the material on your own and, if you have problems, go to your study group or the professor for extra help. Go back to the class for the next several sessions. If your experience is repeated and you seem to be doing well with self-study, keep with it. Just be sure that you follow the course syllabus and attend any lab sessions that are part of the class.
6. **Get the right books.** Books are expensive and you probably have limited funds to spend, so be careful what you buy. *Gray's Anatomy* and Goodman and Gilman's pharmacology text are expensive and of little use to most medical students. They have so many details that they often obscure the "big picture." Instead, use "review books" for various subjects early in your schooling. Condensed as they are, they emphasize the important details. They also have questions and answers that you can use for self-assessment, and are excellent for reviewing the subject before the USMLE and COMLEX. Your school will recommend texts and study aids for your regular courses. Some medical educators recommend the *Board Review Series* or the review books published by Lippincott and Williams & Wilkins. You also might want to look at the *First Aid for the USMLE* books, since they include students' ratings of various texts.
7. **Forget about "everyone for themselves."** Medical school is a team effort. Think of it as being in a lifeboat. In general, the better each person in the lifeboat does, the better everyone does. The same goes for a medical school class.
8. **Learn to ask for help.** It doesn't matter what undergraduate school you went to, how high your grades or MCAT scores were, or what your major was. Everyone starts medical school on an even footing—and nearly everyone needs help somewhere along the way. Ask for it early so that you don't "go under" so deep that no one can pull you out. Problems that medical students encounter include sudden financial crises (or longer-term problems), personal and family problems, and, naturally, difficult course work. Studies have shown that if you do poorly on the major tests in November of your first year, you will probably have difficulty for the balance of your first two years. Get help. Medical schools have qualified professionals ready to help you work through any or all of these problems. However, you have to tell them that you are having problems—and the sooner, the better. Asking for help does not mean that you are shirking your responsibilities. Rather, it demonstrates the level of maturity expected of a professional.
9. **Read every course syllabus** (the page on the front of the notes or a separate page handed out the first day of class). It describes how the class is graded. One student nearly failed pathology simply because he "blew off" watching a pathologist stain slides in the laboratory. He lost the "gimme" points the pathology faculty "donated" to the students—simply by not paying attention to the rules. (He passed, but barely. If he hadn't, it would have cost him an extra year while he repeated this major course.)
10. **Keep everything from your classes.** That includes syllabi, flash cards, textbooks, review books, lecture notes, tests, sample cases, other handouts, and bibliographies. These will be invaluable when taking other courses (since, unlike undergraduate school, most medical school courses build on information from prior courses) and when preparing for the USMLE. It is best to organize these materials in binders, expandable files, or banker's boxes—all clearly marked for easy retrieval.
11. **The *very* basic rules:** Listen carefully and accept all the help and support offered to you. Those medical students with good attitudes who are willing to be taught eventually succeed—no matter what.

12. **Find a mentor *early*.** Mentors were discussed earlier for undergraduate school. It is very important to find a mentor during medical school. Use the same technique of asking students in their junior and senior (clinical) years about the best clinical teachers. You can locate these students in the hospital cafeteria or emergency department any night. Once you have potential mentors' names, contact them to see if they are interested, compatible, and have the time to help you. It will be well worth your effort.

Go Be a Clinician: Start Clinical Work Early

Why are you in medical school? It's certainly not to sit in the same (albeit tougher) classes you took as an undergraduate or graduate student. It's to practice medicine. In that case, go forth and do some clinical work!

Did you say that your school doesn't offer any clinical experiences until the second, third, or fourth semesters? Then don't rely on it to get these experiences. You're a medical student now, and a member of the profession. Use this fact to get some clinical experience in the emergency department, with a member of the clinical faculty (your mentor, perhaps?), or with a clinician in the local community.

> **A medical student who knew that he wanted early clinical experience strolled into the brand-new Family Practice Clinic the week he started school. He said that he wanted to get as much clinical experience as possible and asked if they could accommodate him. The staff was astonished, and somewhat bewildered by the request. Nevertheless, they quickly conferred and agreed to the request. Minutes later, with the patient's laughing consent (she thought it was funny that she would be the first real patient for a new doctor-to-be), he participated in his first pelvic examination. Subsequently, he worked during the remainder of his medical schooling with a local family practitioner he met at the clinic. These are the clinical experiences he [actually, I] values most highly from medical school.**

Get your priorities straight. Early clinical experience enhances your classroom work, keeps you focused on why you are in medical school, and makes you that much more proficient when you begin your official clinical rotations. At most schools, it is up to you to seek out such experiences.

The Next Step: Preparing for Residency/Fellowship

Now that you are a medical student, you need to think about the next step. "The next step?" you ask. You've just been through the trying and often frustrating process of getting into medical school. Is there more? Yes, there is!

Making the decision to go into medicine was the easy part. ("Now you tell me!") It's like deciding to go out to eat. You know that you're hungry, but now you have to pick a restaurant. Medicine offers practitioners a myriad of opportunities, some well-known and some quite obscure. You need to begin investigating these early, so that you can make a reasonable career choice based on solid information and your own wants and needs.

For the basic information, review Chapter 3. Then look in the *Annotated Bibliography* for more information. Finally, go talk with practitioners in the various specialties to get a better idea of what they do and how each feels about the specialty.

30

So You Want To Go To A Different Medical School?

There are two tragedies in life.
One is not to get your heart's desire. The other is to get it.

— Bernard Shaw,
Man and Superman, IV

— Transferring between Medical Schools —

Once you are a medical student, you may be able to transfer between schools. Usually, students need to transfer for personal reasons. In recent years, students have found it increasingly difficult to transfer, since they must find a school with a similar curriculum that has space to accommodate them. For example, when they wish to transfer to be near their fiancé(e) or family, the limited options available at medical schools in the area may force them to repeat a school year. In some cases, schools will try to work with an individual who marries a student already in their school. Schools do not generally accept transfers into the final (usually fourth) year (see Figure 15.8). Special accommodations can often be made, however, to allow students to spend most or all of their senior year at another school, without officially "transferring."

To determine the most current transfer policies at M.D.-granting medical schools, go to www.aamc.org/students/medstudents. This site allows you to search by school, by region, or by specific transfer policy.

If you want or need to transfer between schools, contact the Dean's office at the school you want to transfer to as soon as you can. Also, be certain to contact your own Dean's office, since they will have to certify that you are a student in good standing at their school, that you have successfully completed the specified academic work, and that there are no other reasons for the new school not to accept you (e.g., the Feds don't have a warrant for your arrest).

Hundreds of students transfer from one U.S. M.D.-granting institution to another each year, but relatively few transfer from Canadian schools into U.S. schools or from Osteopathic medical schools into M.D.-granting schools. Transferring from a non-U.S./Canadian medical school into a U.S. M.D.- or D.O.-granting school is a difficult feat that requires jumping through quite a few hoops and having more than a bit of luck. (See Chapter 17 for details of the process.) Nevertheless, each year some students successfully make this leap.

— "Away" Electives —

The most common method medical students use to get experience at other medical schools is to do clinical (and sometimes research) clerkships there, usually in their final year of medical school. These clerkships vary in how easily they can be arranged, depending upon the specialty, the site, and the program.

Due to family, financial, or educational reasons, some students arrange to spend most of or all their senior year at another medical school. Although their final degree will come from their original medical school, these students get to see how medicine is practiced at two different sites.

There is no central registry or clearinghouse for "away" clerkships. Students must contact the programs where they wish to go for specific information. The best advice is to do this as far in advance as you can, since many schools have only limited positions for "visiting" students, especially in the most competitive specialties.

Students at many non-U.S./Canadian medical schools choose to do U.S.-based clerkships. (Some must do U.S.-based clerkships, because their medical school lacks the necessary clinical facilities.) This allows them to have clinical training similar to that of their U.S. medical school compatriots. Still, they must go through the ECFMG certification process before they can apply to U.S. residency programs. Students from non-LCME-accredited (U.S./Canadian M.D.-granting) schools should apply very early for "away" positions, since a number of institutions do not allow such students to rotate at their hospitals. So, leave yourself enough time to apply somewhere else, if necessary.

— Merged Medical Schools —

Some students enter one medical school but graduate from another—without ever transferring—after their medical schools merge. If medical schools merge, their existing students continue their education, albeit with some changes in the faculty and clinical education sites. Two Philadelphia medical schools merged about five years ago; more may do so in the future if the financial pressures on medical education keep mounting. The Medical College of Pennsylvania and Hahnemann University School of Medicine, both founded around 1850, now operate as one school called Drexel University College of Medicine. Drexel has more than 300 students in each class; this is the nation's largest medical school to operate on a single campus. New York University and Mt. Sinai Medical Schools also tried to merge in mid-1996. The resulting school would have had 1,177 M.D. and M.D./Ph.D. students, 1,775 residents and fellows, and 2,814 clinical faculty. That plan fell through. Unless you are interested in large classes, avoid schools that plan to merge.

— Closed Medical Schools —

Accredited U.S. medical schools rarely close these days. In the recent past, only the privately run Oral Roberts University Medical School has ceased to exist. Fortunately, the students at the school were not left to fend for themselves. They were either allowed to graduate (those in their clinical years) or allowed to transfer to other U.S. medical schools. National rules and agreements exist that allow medical students at accredited schools to complete their educations if their school should close.

Once you get into a U.S. medical school, the medical profession considers you a part of the team. And the profession looks out for its team members.

Appendix A

Abbreviations And Acronyms

Ask, and it shall be given you;
seek, and ye shall find;
knock, and it shall be opened unto you.

— Matthew, 7:7

AACOM: American Association of Colleges of Osteopathic Medicine

AACOMAS: American Association of Colleges of Osteopathic Medicine Application Service

AADSAS: American Association of Dental Schools Application Service

AAMC: Association of American Medical Colleges

ACGME: Accreditation Council for Graduate Medical Education

ADEA: American Dental Education Association

ALP: Alternative Loan Program

AMA: American Medical Association

AMCAS: American Medical Colleges Application Service

AMSA: American Medical Student Association

AMWA: American Medical Women's Association

AOA: American Optometric Association

AOA: American Osteopathic Association

AP: Advanced Placement credit

APAMSA: Asian Pacific American Medical Student Association

APAP: Association of Physician Assistant Programs

ARC–PA: Accreditation Review Commission on Education for the Physician Assistant

CACMS: Committee on Accreditation of Canadian Medical Schools

CASPA: Central Application Service for Physician Assistants

CLEP: College Level Examination Program

CNM: Certified Nurse Midwife

COMLEX: Comprehensive Osteopathic Medical Licensing Examination

CRNA: Certified Registered Nurse Anesthetist

CSA: Clinical Skills Assessment

DAT: Dental Admission Test

D.C.: Doctor of Chiropractic (Chiropractor)

DCAT: Developing Cognitive Abilities Test

D.D.S.: Doctor of Dental Surgery (Dentist)

D.M.D.: Doctor of Medical Dentistry (Dentist)

D.O.: Doctor of Osteopathic Medicine

D.P.M.: Doctor of Podiatric Medicine (Podiatrist)

D.V.M.: Doctor of Veterinary Medicine

ECFMG: Educational Commission for Foreign Medical Graduates

EDP: Early Decision Program

EFC: Expected Family (financial) Contribution

EFN: Exceptional Financial Need Scholarship

EMS: Emergency Medical System

EMT: Emergency Medical Technician

ENT: Ear, Nose, and Throat (Otolaryngology)

FADHPS: Financial Assistance for Disadvantaged Health Professions Students

FAFSA: Free Application for Federal Student Aid

FAP: Fee Assistance Program (AAMC)

FDSLP: Federal Direct Student Loan Program

FFELP: Federal Family Education Loan Program

FMG: Foreign Medical Graduate

FREIDA: Fellowship and Residency Electronic Interactive Database Access

FSLS: Federal Supplemental Loans for Students

FSMB: Federation of State Medical Boards

GPA: Grade Point Average

GRE: Graduate Record Examination

HCOE: Hispanic Centers of Excellence
HMO: Health Maintenance Organization
HPSA: Health Professions-Shortage Area
HPSL: Health Professional Student Loans
HPSP: Health Professions Scholarship Program
IMG: International Medical Graduate
INMED: Indians Into Medicine Program
IPA: Independent Practice Association
JAMA: *Journal of the American Medical Association*
JAOA: *Journal of the American Osteopathic Association*
J.D.: Juris Doctor (Law degree)
LCME: Liaison Committee on Medical Education
LDS: Loans for Disadvantaged Students
MARC: Minority Access to Research Careers
M.B.A.: Master of Business Administration
MCAT: Medical College Admission Test
M.D.: Doctor of Medicine
Med-MAR: Medical Minority Applicant Registry
M.H.A.: Master of Health Administration
MHSSRAP: Minority High School Summer Research Apprentice Program
M.M.: Master of Management
MMEP: Minority Medical Education Program
MMRN: Minority Mentor Recruitment Network
MPDB: Minority Physicians Database
M.P.H.: Master of Public Health
MPN: Master Promissory Note
MSAR: *Medical School Admission Requirements* (AAMC)
M.S.P.H.: Master of Science in Public Health
MSTP: Medical Scientist Training Program
NAAHP: National Association of Advisors for the Health Professions
NBME: National Board of Medical Examiners
NBOME: National Board of Osteopathic Medical Examiners
NCCPA: National Commission Certification of Physician Assistants
N.D.: Doctor of Naturopathy (Naturopath)
NDSL: National Direct Student Loan
NHMRN: National Hispanic Mentor Recruitment Network
NHSC: National Health Service Corps
NIH: National Institutes of Health
N.P.: Nurse Practitioner
NRMP: National Residency Matching Program
OAT: Optometry Admission Test
O.D.: Doctor of Optometry (Optometrist)
OMM: Osteopathic Manipulative Medicine
OMT: Osteopathic Manipulative Treatment
OMSAS: Ontario Medical Schools Application Service
OSCE: Objective Structured Clinical Examination
P.A.: Physician Assistant
PBL: Problem-Based Learning
PCL: Primary Care Loan
PGY: Postgraduate Year (of residency)
Ph.D.: Doctor of Philosophy
PHS: Public Health Service
PM&R: Physical Medicine and Rehabilitation
PPO: Preferred Provider Organization
R.N.: Registered Nurse
Sallie Mae: Student Loan Marketing Association
SAT: Scholastic Aptitude Test
SDS: Scholarship for Disadvantaged Students
SREB: Southern Regional Education Board
THx: Testing History (for MCAT)
TMDSAS: Texas Medical and Dental Schools Application Service
TOEFL: Test of English as a Foreign Language
URM: Underrepresented Minority
USIMG: U.S.-citizen International Medical Graduate
USMLE: United States Medical Licensing Examination
UTSMDAC: University of Texas System Medical and Dental Application Center
WICHE: Western Interstate Commission for Higher Education
WWAMI: Washington, Wyoming, Alaska, Montana, Idaho Cooperative Educational Program

Appendix B

Contact Information

Canadian Medical Schools
Association of Canadian Medical Colleges
774 Echo Drive
Ottawa, Canada K1S 5P2
(613) 730-0687; (613) 730-1196 (fax)
cjuneau@acmc.ca; www.acmc.ca

Health Professions Advisor
National Association of Advisors for the Health Professions, Inc. (NAAHP)
P.O. Box 1518
Champaign, IL 61824-1518
(217) 355-0063; (217) 355-1287 (fax)
staff@naahp.org; www.naahp.org

International Medical Schools and Graduates
Educational Commission for Foreign Medical Graduates (ECFMG)
3624 Market Street
Philadelphia, PA 19104-2685
(215) 386-5900; (215) 386-9196 (fax)
www.ecfmg.org

Foundation for Advancement of International Medical Education & Research (FAIMER)
3624 Market Street, 4th Floor
Philadelphia PA 19104
(215) 386-9767 (fax)
imed@ecfmg.org; http://imed.ecfmg.org

World Health Organization
525 23rd Street NW
Washington, DC 20037
(202) 974-3000; (202) 974-3663 (fax)
www.who.int/library/reference/query/faqs.html

MCAT Information and Applications
MCAT Program Office
P.O. Box 4056
Iowa City, IA 52243
(319) 337-1357; mcat_reg@act.org
www.aamc.org/students/mcat/start.htm

Medical School Applications (Ontario)
Ontario Medical School Application Service (OMSAS)
Ontario Universities' Application Centre
170 Research Lane
Guelph, Ontario, CANADA N1G 5E2
(519) 823-1940; (519) 823-5232 (fax)
www.ouac.on.ca/omsas

M.D. Medical School Applications (U.S.)
American Medical College Application Service (AMCAS)
Association of American Medical Colleges
Section for Student Services
2450 N Street NW
Washington, DC 20037-1130
(202) 828-0600; amcas@aamc.org
www.aamc.org/students/amcas/start.htm

M.D. Medicine (Canada)
Canadian Medical Association
1867 Alta Vista Drive
Ottawa, Ontario, CANADA K1G 3Y6
(800) 457-4205; (613) 236-8864 (fax)
www./cma.ca/cma/common/start.do?lang=2

M.D. Medicine (U.S.)
American Medical Association
515 N. State Street
Chicago, IL 60610
(312) 464-5000; www.ama-assn.org

National Medical Association
1010 10th Street NW
Washington DC 20002
(202) 347-1895; (202) 842-3293 (fax)
www.nmanet.org

Medical Student Organizations
Medical Student Section
American Medical Association
515 N. State Street
Chicago, IL 60610
(312) 464-4742
www.ama-assn.org/ama/pub/category/14.html

American Medical Student Association (AMSA)
1902 Association Drive
Reston, VA 20191
(703) 620-6600; (703) 620-5873 (fax)
amsa@www.amsa.org; www.amsa.org

AAMC–Organization of Student Representatives
2450 N Street NW
Washington, DC 20037-1127
(202) 828-0682
www.aamc.org/members/osr/start.htm

Association of Native American Medical Students
1225 Sovereign Row, Suite 103
Oklahoma City, OK 73108
(405) 946-7072; (405) 946-7651 (fax)
anams@aaip.com; www.aaip.com/anams

Latino Medical Student Association
P.O. Box 6215
Garden Grove, CA 92863
(714) 931-3323; (714) 891-1043 (fax)
info@lmsa.net; www.lmsa.net

Military Medical Students' Association
4301 Jones Bridge Road
Bethesda, MD 20814-4799
(301) 295-3101
ericdweber@militarymedicine.org
www.militarymedicine.org

Student National Medical Association (SNMA)
5113 Georgia Avenue NW
Washington, DC 20011
(202) 882-2881; (202) 882-2886 (fax)
snmamain@msn.com; www.snma.org

Student Osteopathic Medical Association (SOMA)
142 E. Ontario Street
Chicago, IL 60611
(800) 621-1773, ext. 8193; (312) 202-8200 (fax)
contact@studentdo.com; www.studentdo.com

Texas Association of Mexican-American Medical Students
8525 Floyd Curl Drive, #1005
San Antonio, TX 78240
(512) 590-4675

Osteopathic Medical Schools and Applications

American Association of Colleges of Osteopathic Medicine (AACOM)
5550 Friendship Boulevard, Suite 310
Chevy Chase, MD 20815-7231
(301) 968-4185; (301) 968-4101 (fax)
www.aacom.org

Application Service (AACOMAS)
(301) 968-4190; (301) 968-4191 (fax)
aacomas@aacom.org; aacomas.aacom.org

American Osteopathic Association (AOA)
142 E. Ontario Street
Chicago, IL 60611
(800) 621-1773; (312) 202-8000
(312) 202-8200 (fax)
info@aoa-net.org; www.aoa-net.org

Residency Programs

Accreditation Council for Graduate Medical Education (ACGME)
515 N. State Street, Suite 2000
Chicago, IL 60610-4322
(312) 755-5000; (312) 755-7498 (fax)
www.acgme.org

American Board of Medical Specialties
1007 Church Street, Suite 404
Evanston, IL 60201-5913
(847) 491-9091; (847) 328-3596 (fax)
www.abms.org

Council of Medical Specialty Societies
51 Sherwood Terrace, Suite M
Lake Bluff, IL 60044-2232
(847) 295-3456; (847) 295-3759 (fax)
mailbox@cmss.org; www.cmss.org

State Licensing Requirements

Federation of State Medical Boards of the United States, Inc. (FSMB)
P.O. Box 619850
Dallas, TX 75261-9850
(817) 868-4000; (817) 868-4098 (fax)
www.fsmb.org

Texas Medical & Dental Schools Application Service (TMDSAS)

702 Colorado, Suite 6.400
Austin, TX 78701
(512) 499-4785; (512) 499-4786 (fax)
TMDSAS@utsystem.edu
www.utsystem.edu/tmdsas

U.S. Medical Schools

Association of American Medical Colleges (AAMC)
2450 N Street NW
Washington, DC 20037-1126
(202) 828-0416
www.aamc.org/medicalschools.htm

USMLE Information

National Board of Medical Examiners
Department of Licensing Examination Services
3750 Market Street
Philadelphia, PA 19104-3102
(215) 590-9500; Webmail@nbme.org
www.nbme.org/programs/medsch.asp

Women in Medicine

American Association of University Women
1111 16th Street NW
Washington, DC 20036
(202) 728-7603
www.aauw.org/ef/index.cfm

American Medical Association
Women Physicians Congress
515 North State Street
Chicago, IL 60610
(312) 464-4392
www.ama-assn.org/ama/pub/category/172.html

American Medical Women's Association
801 N. Fairfax Street, Suite 400
Alexandria, VA 22314
(703) 838-0500; info@amwa-doc.org
www.amwa-doc.org/index.html

Association of American Medical Colleges
Women in Medicine
2540 N Street NW
Washington, DC 20037-1126
(202) 828-0521
www.aamc.org/members/wim/start.htm

Appendix C

Postbaccalaureate Premed Programs

READ ME FIRST! Considerable effort has gone into confirming the existence and correct contact information for the programs listed below. However, educational programs may come and go, change their contact information (especially their website URLs), or alter their program requirements and structure. This list should provide you with a starting point for locating postbaccalaureate premed programs. Ask your premed adviser and search the Web for the programs that best fit your needs.

Note: if the URL doesn't work, try incrementally chopping off pieces at the end until you get to a website that will allow you to locate or search for the postbaccalaureate information.

Minority Medical Education Program (MMEP)
This program is available at the following institutions for postbaccalaureate students who meet the acceptance criteria. Contact them at mmep@aamc.org or at (877) 310-MMEP (toll-free)
University of Alabama School of Medicine
Baylor College of Medicine and Rice University
Case Western Reserve University School of Medicine
Chicago Summer Science Enrichment Program
Columbia Univ. College of Physicians & Surgeons
Duke University School of Medicine
Fisk Univ. and Vanderbilt Univ. Medical Center (The College Fund/UNCF Summer Premedical Institute at Fisk Univ. and Vanderbilt Univ. Medical Center)
New Jersey Medical School
University of Virginia School of Medicine
Western Consortium (Univ. of Washington School of Med. and the Univ. of Arizona College of Med.)
Yale University School of Medicine

ALABAMA

Spring Hill College
David F. Dean, DVM, Ph.D.
Associate Professor, Department of Biology
4000 Dauphin Street
Mobile, AL 36608
(251) 380-3082; ddean@shc.edu

ARIZONA

Arizona State University Main Graduate College
P.O. Box 871003
Tempe, AZ 85287-1003
(602) 965-3521
www.asu.edu/graduate/admissions
Applicants apply to the graduate college as unclassified graduate students for the post-baccalaureate premedical program. A U.S. bachelor's degree or the equivalent from a regionally accredited institution is required.

Midwestern University
Biomedical Sciences Program
19555 N. 59th Avenue
Glendale, AZ 85308
(623) 572-3291; (623) 572-3261
www.midwestern.edu/az-biomed
Master of Biomedical Science.

CALIFORNIA

California State University–Fullerton
Health Professions Office, LH 203
800 N. State College Boulevard
Fullerton, CA 92834
(714) 278-3980; http://nsm.fullerton.edu/noflash/programs.asp?program=health
Accepts postbaccalaureate students who applied to medical school and were not admitted.

California State University–Dominguez Hills
College of Arts and Sciences Deans Office
Postbaccalaureate Premed Program
1000 E. Victoria Street
Carson, CA 90747
(310) 243-3389
www.cas.csudh.edu/specialprograms/premed/index.html

Loyola Marymount University
Dr. Anthony P. Smulders
One LMU Drive, MS 8220
Los Angeles, CA 90045-2659
(310) 338-5954; (310) 338-4479 (fax)
asmulders@lmu.edu; www.lmu.edu
Open to students who lack prerequisites basic to medicine, but who have completed bachelor's degrees with a minimum GPA of 3.40. Most undergraduate courses offered in the daytime only on a space-available basis; students may take a maximum of 18 semester-hours as non-degree students.

Mills College
Nancy Hutcheon
Postbaccalaureate Premedical Program
Office of Graduate Studies, MH Room 226
5000 MacArthur Boulevard
Oakland, CA 94613
(510) 430-2317; (510) 430-3314 (fax)
nhutcheo@mills.edu
www.mills.edu/GRST/gra.info.pmc.html
For those who have a bachelor's degree and want to pursue a health professions career, but lack the basic science courses. Not for applicants who have undergraduate degrees in biology or chemistry, have taken the MCAT, or have applied to and been rejected by medical schools.

Scripps College
Jodi Olson, Administrative Director
Postbaccalaureate Premedical Certificate Program
W.M. Keck Science Center
925 N. Mills Avenue
Claremont, CA 91711-5916
(909) 621-8764
Jolson@scrippscol.edu; www.scrippscol.edu
www.jsd.claremont.edu/postbac/postbac.html
Must have a bachelor's degree with a minimum 3.0 GPA; submit SAT, ACT, or GRE scores; and have experience in the medical field through paid or volunteer work.

University of California–Davis
Postbaccalaureate Re-Applicant Program
Office of Medical Education
UC–Davis School of Medicine
One Shields Avenue
Davis, CA 95616
(530) 752-8119; (530) 754-6252 (fax)
awblakely@ucdavis.edu; http://medome.ucdavis.edu/ome/diversity/pbprogram.htm
Open to underrepresented minorities or economically disadvantaged students who have been unsuccessful in gaining admission to medical school; CA residents only. A minimum GPA of 2.7 and a minimum MCAT average score of 6.0 is requried.

University of California–Irvine
Eileen Munoz, Director
Office of Admissions and Outreach
Postbaccalaureate Re-Applicant Program
P.O. Box 4089
Irvine, CA 92697-4089
(949) 824-5388 or (800) 824-5388
pbreapp@uci.edu; www.ucihs.uci.edu/admissions/index.html?top.html&menu.html&home.html
Open to economically, financially, or educationally disadvantaged students who have been unsuccessful in gaining admission to medical school. Must be a CA resident having a BS or BA, a GPA of 2.8 (both science and cumulative), and a minimum combined MCAT score of 21.

UCLA School of Medicine
Elizabeth Guerrero, MPH, Director
Re-Application Program (UCLA RAP)
Office of Academic Enrichment and Outreach
13-154 Center for Health Sciences
Los Angeles, CA 90095-6990
(310) 825-3575; www.medstudent.ucla.edu/osss
Must have been unsuccessful in gaining admission to any U.S. medical school, be considered disadvantaged or from an underserved community, have completed an undergraduate degree or higher from an accredited U.S. college or university, be a U.S. citizen or permanent resident, have a minimum GPA of 2.7, and have a minimum combined MCAT score of 15. Preference given to legal residents of CA.

University of California–San Diego School of Medicine
Loretta Lopez, Assistant Director
Student Outreach Services
Postbaccalaureate Program
9500 Gilman Drive, 0655
La Jolla, CA 92093-0655
(858) 534-4170; http://meded.ucsd.edu/postbac
Must be educationally or economically disadvantaged or be from an underserved community and have a baccalaureate degree; CA residents preferred. Must have applied and been rejected from a medical school no more than two times, with a minimum AMCAS science and nonscience GPA of 2.7 and a minimum MCAT score of 6 in each subtest.

University of Southern California
Admissions Coordinator
Postbaccalaureate Premedical Program
College Academic Services, CAS 120
Los Angeles, CA 90089-0151
(213) 740-2534; (213) 740-3664 (fax); CAS@usc.edu
http://chem.usc.edu/undergraduate/premed.html
Must have completed an undergraduate degree from an accredited U.S. college or university with a minimum GPA of 3.0 and submit scores from GRE, SAT, ACT, GMAT, or LSAT.

CONNECTICUT

Dr. Keat Sanford, Director
Postbaccalaureate Program
UConn Health Center–School of Medicine
263 Farmington Avenue
Farmington, CT 06030-3906
(203) 679-2152/3971
http://medicine.uchc.edu/departments/studentservices/admissions/postbac/index.shtml
Must have completed a baccalaureate degree program from an accredited college or university. Admitted students normally have at least a B- average. There are two programs: one for students with little science background and one for students who have completed science prerequisites.

DISTRICT OF COLUMBIA

American University
Dr. Frederick Carson
Premedical Programs Coordinator
Dept. of Chemistry
4400 Massachusetts Avenue NW
Washington, DC 20016-8014
(202) 885-1770; (202) 885-1752 (fax)
fcarson@american.edu
www.american.edu/cas/postbac.html
Open to students with a bachelor's degree and a cumulative GPA of 3.2 (on a 4.0 scale).

Georgetown University School of Medicine
Joy P. Williams, Program Coordinator
Office of Program for Minority Student Development
Georgetown Experimental Medical Studies Program
3900 Reservoir Road NW
Washington, DC 20007
(202) 687-1406

Accepts U.S. citizens from minority groups that traditionally have been underrepresented in medicine and others who meet all other criteria and show evidence of their ability to satisfy the social and educational goals of the program. Must have completed one year each of general chemistry, organic chemistry, biology, physics, and college mathematics; have a baccalaureate degree from an accredited college or university; be seeking admission to medical school; and submit MCAT scores.

Georgetown University
Dr. Adam Myers, Director, Special Masters Program
Dept. of Physiology & Biophysics
3900 Reservoir Road NW
Washington, DC 20007
(202) 687-1179
physio@georgetown.edu
www.georgetown.edu/departments/physiology/physios/index.htm
Admission is competitive. Selection of candidates is based on overall undergraduate college performance (3.0 or better) and MCAT scores (at least 26) or GRE results. An applicant who was rejected from medical school must include a copy of the unsuccessful AMCAS application.

Trinity College
Saundra Herndon Oyewole, Ph.D.
Dean of the Faculty
Postbaccalaureate Premedical Certificate Program
125 Michigan Avenue NE
Washington, DC 20017
(202) 939-5000; www.trinitydc.edu/academics/catalog/special.html#post-bac
Designed for students with baccalaureate degrees who wish to pursue a career in a health profession but have not taken the basic science and mathematics courses required for admission to medical school; women only.

FLORIDA

Barry University
Mr. Jocelyn Goulet
School of Natural & Health Sciences
11300 N.E. Second Avenue
Miami Shores, FL 33161
(305) 899-3541; (305) 899-3232 (fax)
healthsciences@mail.barry.edu; www.barry.edu
Special masters program.

Florida State University
College of Medicine
Health Professions Advisor
Postbaccalaureate Bridge Program
Tallahassee, FL 32306-4300
(904) 644-7678
www.med.fsu.edu/admissionsProcess.asp
Applicants from medically underserved populations of the state of Florida, rural, and inner city backgrounds that applied through the regular application process but were not accepted, are considered.

Nova Southeastern University
Attn: Medical Sciences Admissions
3200 S.University Drive
Fort Lauderdale, FL 33328
(954) 262-1101 or (800) 356-0026, ext. 1101
www.nova.edu
Must have a bachelor's degree from an accredited college with 8 semester hours each in biology, general chemistry, organic chemistry, and physics, all with labs. Selection based on academic qualifications (2.5 cumulative GPA and 2.0 science GPA); MCAT, OAT, PCAT, DAT, AHPAT, or GRE scores; and an evaluation of the candidate's qualifications, achievements, and commitment. Master of Biomedical Science.

University of Florida
Dean of the Graduate School
Box 115515
Gainesville, FL 32611-5515
(352) 392-1365
www.reg.ufl.edu/admission/baccapp-splash.html
Students who have received a bachelor's degree but who do not wish or who are not eligible to be admitted to graduate study.

University of Miami
Deborah Paris-Herbert, Coordinator, Prehealth Studies
Postbaccalaureate Program
College of Arts and Sciences
P.O. Box 248004
Coral Gables, FL 33124
(305) 284-5176; www.miami.edu
Program A is for those who have completed a baccalaureate program at an accredited college or university, but lack specific courses required for admission to medical school. Students must have a GPA of 3.3 for courses taken in their junior and senior years.
Program B is for those who have completed a baccalaureate program at an accredited college or university and have no premedical course deficiencies. Students must have a GPA of 3.3 for courses taken in their junior and senior years.

University of North Florida
Postbaccalaureate Premedical Program
Dr. Ray Bowman, Ph.D.
4567 St. Johns Bluff Road South
Jacksonville, FL 32224
(904) 620-2608
rbowman@unf.edu; www.unf.edu/dept/premed

GEORGIA

Agnes Scott College
Postbaccalaureate Premedical Program for Women
Amy Whitworth
Office of Graduate Studies
141 E. College Avenue
Decatur, GA 30030
(404) 471-6361
awhitworth@agnesscott.edu; www.agnesscott.edu
Must have a bachelor's degree in a nonscience field, a 2.8-3.0 minimum GPA, transcripts from all institutions, and standardized test scores.

HAWAII

Imi Ho`ola Postbaccalaureate Program
Nanette Kapulani Judd, MPH, Ph.D.
Program Director
1960 East-West Road, Biomed C-203
Honolulu, HI 96822
(808) 956-3466; (808) 956-3472
judd@hawaii.edu
Open to students who applied to the Univ. of Hawaii SOM from socially, educationally, or disadvantaged backgrounds who have a commitment to serve in areas of need in Hawaii and the U.S.-affiliated Pacific Islands.

ILLINOIS

Finch Univ. Health Sciences/Chicago Med. School
Kristine A. Jones, Director of Admissions and Registrar
Office of Graduate Admissions
Applied Physiology Program
3333 Green Bay Road
North Chicago, IL 60064
(847) 578-3209
www.finchcms.edu/sgpds/physiology/msapplied.cfm
Must have a bachelor's degree from an accredited college with courses in biological and physical sciences. Selection is based on academic qualifications and achievements, GRE and MCAT scores, letters of recommendation, and candidate's goals and commitment.

Illinois Institute of Technology
Reggie Jones, Ph.D., Executive Director
Chicago Area Health & Medical Careers Program
3200 S. Wabash Avenue
Chicago, IL 60616-3793
312-567-3890; www.iit.edu
Open to CAHMCP college graduates who have not been admitted to a health professional school. Must have completed all course prerequisites for admission. Current matriculants must have demonstrated capability to continue in health professions career pathway.

Dominican University
Rosary College
7900 W. Division Street
River Forest, IL 60305
(708) 524-6800; (708) 524-5990 (fax)
www.dom.edu/rcas/majors.asp?program_id=55&schnav_id=2109&tschnav_id=1025

Loyola University, Chicago
LaVerne Urich, Psy.D., Program Director (or)
Nadia Rausch, Administrative Assistant
Postbaccalaureate Premedical Program
Mundelein College, Sky 204, Water Tower Campus
6525 N. Sheridan Road
Chicago, IL 60626
Program Office: 773-508-6054
Application: 312-915-6501
mudelein@luc.edu; www.luc.edu/sps/index.html
For students who have completed a baccalaureate program at an accredited college or university but did not take the science courses needed to pursue a career in the health professions.

Midwestern University
Master of Biomedical Sciences
Fred D. Romano, Ph.D.
555 31st Street
Downers Grove, IL 60515
(630) 515-6392; (630) 971-6414 (fax)
froman@midwestern.edu
www.midwestern.edu/il-biomed
Master of Biomedical Science.

Roosevelt University
Dr. Jonathan Green, Ph.D., Chair
Dept. of Biology
430 S. Michigan
Chicago, IL 60605-1394
(312) 341-3676/3683; rcf@interaccess.com
Must have completed a baccalaureate program at an accredited college or university with a GPA of 3.0 for the last 60 semester hours of course work. Program A is for students with minimal or no science or mathematics college credits. Program B is for students with some mathematics and science.

Southern Illinois University
Vera Felts, Admissions Coordinator
Medical/Dental Education Preparatory Program
210 Wheeler Hall
Carbondale, IL 62901-4323
(618) 453-1554; (618) 453-1919 (fax)
vfelts@siumed.edu, medprep@siumed.edu
www.siumed.edu/medprep
Restricted to economically and educationally disadvantaged students who have completed most or all of the professional school prerequisites and have at least a 2.0 GPA in math/science. IL residents preferred.

INDIANA

Indiana University School of Medicine
Masters Degree Program Director
Dept. of Cellular & Integrative Physiology
635 Barnhill Drive, MS 446
Indianapolis, Indiana 46202-5120
(317) 274-7772; (317) 274-3318 (fax)
msphysio@iupui.edu
www.iupui.edu/~medphys/grad/ms.html
Must have a baccalaureate degree from an accredited college and have met medical school admissions requirements in biology, organic chemistry, and physics. Selection based on academic qualifications (3.2 GPA or better), MCAT scores (24 or better), or GRE results, and an evaluation of candidate's goals and commitment.

Indiana Univ.–Purdue Univ. at Indianapolis
Premedical Adviser, Biology Dept.
723 W. Michigan Street
Indianapolis, IN 46202-5132
(317) 274-0589; www.biology.iupui.edu/ms.html
Applicants should have a minimum of 16 credit hours in course work toward a biology major and chemistry course work up to and including organic chemistry.

IOWA

Iowa State University
Jennifer Owens
102 Carrie Chapman Catt Hall
Ames, IA 50011
(515) 294-4831; (515) 294-7446 (fax)
jowens@iastate.edu
www.las.iastate.edu/academics/healthprograms.shtml
Nondegree, undergraduate, noncertificate-granting program.

LOUISIANA

Tulane University
Kathleen Maier, Prehealth Adviser
106 Hebert Hall
New Orleans, LA 70118
(504) 865-5370; kmurphy@tulane.edu
www.tulane.edu/%7Eadvisor/premed/Default.htm
Should be enrolled as a regular premed student. Call for information.

MARYLAND

Goucher College
Postbaccalaureate Premedical Program
1201 Dulaney Valley Road
Baltimore, MD 21204-2794
(800) 414-3437; pbpm@goucher.edu
www.goucher.edu/postbac/index.cfm?page_id=175
Designed for those with a bachelor's degree from an accredited college or university and who have a favorable academic record, but lack the majority of science courses needed for medical school. Applicants should have at least pre-calculus, volunteer work in a medical setting, and SAT, ACT, or GRE scores.

The Johns Hopkins University
Postbaccalaureate Premedical Program Office
Wyman Park Building, Suite G1
3400 N. Charles Street
Baltimore, MD 21218-2685
(410) 516-7748
postbac@jhu.edu; www.jhu.edu/postbac
Must have a bachelor's degree and minimum GPA of 3.0; official transcripts from high school and all colleges attended; SAT, ACT, or GRE test scores; and have never applied to medical school.

National Institutes of Health
NIH Postbaccalaureate Training Program
Building 2, Room 2E6
2 Center Drive, MSC 0240
Bethesda, MD 20892-0240
(301) 402-1917; (301) 402-8975 (fax)
cohend@od.nih.gov; www.training.nih.gov

Coordinator of Student Programs
Predoctoral IRTA Fellowship
NIH Office of Education
Building 10, Room 1C129
Bethesda, MD 20892-1158
(800) 445-8283; www.training.nih.gov/student
Predoctoral IRTA program is open to students who have received their baccalaureate within the past 12 months. Must be U.S. citizen or permanent resident and supply 3 letters of recommendation from faculty emphasizing research potential.
Technical IRTA is open to students with a baccalaureate or M.S. degree. Must be U.S. citizen or permanent resident and supply 3 letters of recommendation from faculty emphasizing research potential.

Towson University
Dr. Caryl E. Peterson, Coordinator
Postbaccalaureate Premedical/Predental Committee
Dept. of Biological Sciences
8000 York Road
Towson, MD 21252
(410) 830-3042; cpeterson@towson.edu
http://pages.towson.edu/csm/postbac_home.html
Must have a bachelor's degree from an accredited college or university. Students preparing for admission to medical school should have a minimum undergraduate GPA of 3.4; for dental school admission, a 3.0 GPA. Most participants have not taken the MCAT or DAT.

University of Maryland, College of Life Sciences
Single Point of Contact (SPOC)
Mitchell Building, First Floor
College Park, MD 20742-7415
(301) 314-3572 or 1-877-989-SPOC
spoc-science@umail.umd.edu
www.life.umd.edu/evening
Must have a bachelor's degree from an accredited college or university.

MASSACHUSETTS

American International College
Dr. Alan C. Dickinson
1000 State Street
Springfield, MA 01109-3189
(413) 747-6379
adickins@acad.aic.edu; http://aic.map.com/dept_chemistry-preprofessional.html
Must have a bachelor's degree from an accredited college or university, and evidence of strong academic ability. Must register for a minimum of 8 credits per semester.

Assumption College
Dr. Allan Barnitt, Jr.
Division of Natural Sciences
500 Salisbury Street
P.O. Box 15005
Worcester, MA 01615-0005
(508) 767-7295; www.assumption.edu
Must have a bachelor's degree from an accredited college or university, with at least a B- average, or evidence of strong academic potential. Financial aid is available.

Boston University School of Medicine
Ruth R. Levine, Ph.D. Director
Medical Sciences Degree Program
Division of Graduate Medical Sciences
715 Albany Street
Boston, MA 02118-2394
617-638-5120; www.bumc.bu.edu
Must submit GRE or MCAT scores and have met the requirements for a baccalaureate degree, including general chemistry, organic chemistry, biology, and physics.

Brandeis University
Office of Undergraduate Academic Affairs
Postbaccalaureate Certificate Program
Kutz 108/MS 001
Waltham, MA 02454-9110
(781) 736-3470
jlewis@brandeis.edu; tschilling@brandeis.edu
www.brandeis.edu/uaafys/pb/index.html
www.brandeis.edu/academaffairs/postbac
Must have a bachelor's degree from an accredited university, some background in math, and volunteer experience in the medical field.

Bryn Mawr College
Office of Admissions, Postbaccalaureate Program
101 N. Merion Avenue
Bryn Mawr, PA 19010-2899
(610) 526-7350; postbac@brynmawr.edu
www.brynmawr.edu/postbac
Must have a strong academic record in both high school and college level, usually a B (3.0) average or better in college, and standardized test scores consistent with that level of performance.

Harvard University Extension School
William Fixsen, Director, Health Careers Program
51 Brattle Street
Cambridge, MA 02138-3722
(617) 495-2926; peterson@hudce.harvard.edu
www.extension.harvard.edu/hcp
Must have a bachelor's degree.

Mount Holyoke College
Kay Althoff, Director
Frances Perkins Postbaccalaureate Studies Program
6 Safford Hall
50 College Street
South Hadley, MA 01075
(413) 538-2077; (413) 538-3013 (fax)
frances-perkins@mtholyoke.edu
www.mtholyoke.edu/acad/programs/fp/postbac.shtml
Must have a baccalaureate degree with a strong academic record.

Tufts University
Liz Regan, Program Administrator
Postbac Premedical Program, Dowling Hall
419 Boston Avenue
Medford, MA 02155
(617) 627-2321
liz.regan@tufts.edu
http://studentservices.tufts.edu/postbac
Must have a bachelor's degree with a minimum GPA of 3.0 and SAT, ACT, or GRE scores. The program is not remedial and does not admit students who wish to retake their premedical requirements.

Tufts Univ. School of Veterinary Medicine
Admissions Office
200 Westboro Road
North Grafton, MA 01536
(508) 839-7920; vetadmissions@tufts.edu
www.tufts.edu/vet/cfa/index.html
Offers a Master of Science in Animals & Public Policy. Must have either a graduate or a bachelor's degree plus a history of experience in working with animals or on environmental or wildlife issues. Those without a Ph.D., M.D., D.V.M., or similar degree must submit GRE scores taken within the last five years.

University of Massachusetts–Amherst
W. Brian O'Connor, Karen F. O'Connor
Premed Office, N330 Morrill
Amherst, MA 01003
(413) 545-3674; www.umass.edu/ug_programguide/otheracadopp/premed.html
For students who lack prerequisites basic to medicine.

University of Massachusetts–Boston
Premedical Adviser, Career Services
McCormack Hall, 3rd Floor, Room 625
Boston, MA 02125
(617) 287-5519
grace.mcsorley@umb.edu; www.careers.umb.edu

Wellesley College
Continuing Education Coordinator
Office of the Dean of Continuing Education
106 Central Street
Wellesley, MA 02181-8201
(617) 283-2660
www.wellesley.edu/Admission/pdf/PostbacBro.pdf
Must have a bachelor's degree. Need work and volunteer experience, and recent course work that demonstrates intellectual ability and emotional maturity.

Worcester State College
Dr. Alan D. Cooper
Chairman, Premedical Advisory Committee
486 Chandler Street
Worcester, MA 01602
(508) 793-8000, ext. 8600
A bachelor's degree is required.

MICHIGAN

Michigan State University
College of Human Medicine
Advanced Baccalaureate Learning Experience (ABLE)
Prematriculation Programs
A254 Life Sciences Building
East Lansing, MI 44824-1317
(517) 355-2404
www.chm.msu.edu/chmhome/admissions/able.htm
Admits 7 to 12 students annually. Underrepresented minority and disadvantaged students who have applied for regular admission to CHM are interviewed and placed on hold by the CHM admissions committee. Upon successful completion of this program, they are guaranteed admission to Michigan State University's medical school.

Wayne State University School of Medicine
Director, Minority Recruitment
540 E. Canfield Avenue, Suite 1320
Detroit, MI 48201
(313) 577-1598
simmons@med.wayne.edu
www.med.wayne.edu/about_the_school/diversity.asp

MISSOURI

Avila University
Dr. C. Larry Sullivan
Postbaccalaureate Premedical Program
11901 Wornall Road
Kansas City, MO 64145
(816) 501-3655; (816) 501-2457 (fax)
sullivancl@mail.avila.edu
www.avila.edu/departments/biology/bioweb/premedical_program.htm
Must have a minimum 3.0 undergraduate GPA and be residents of MO.

Rockhurst University
Office of Graduate Admission
College of Arts and Sciences
1100 Rockhurst Road
Kansas City, MO 64110-2561
(816) 501-3590; 1-800-842-6776
graduate.admission@rockhurst.edu
www.rockhurst.edu/3.0/admission/graduate
Premedical postbaccalaureate program for students with a baccalaureate degree, usually in a nonscience area, who need the science requirements for medical school.

Saint Louis University School of Medicine
Office of Multicultural Affairs
Graduate Experience in Medical Education Program
1402 S. Grand Boulevard, C102
Saint Louis, MO 63104-9952
(314) 268-5398; (314) 268-5745 (fax); oma@slu.edu
http://medschool.slu.edu/oma/gemegrid.phtml

NEBRASKA

Creighton University School of Medicine
Office of Medical Admissions
Postbaccalaureate Program
2500 California Plaza
Omaha, NE 68178
(402) 280-2799; (800) 325-4405; (402) 280-1241 (fax)
medschadm@creighton.edu
http://medicine.creighton.edu/Postbac

NEW HAMPSHIRE

Dartmouth Medical School
Center for the Evaluative Clinical Sciences
Karen A. Tombs, M.Ed.
Hinman Box 7252
Hanover, NH 03755-3871
(603) 650-1782; (603) 650-1900 (fax)
karen.a.tombs@dartmouth.edu *or* Programs@dartmouth.edu
www.dartmouth.edu/dms/cecs
Applicants should have career goals that are commensurate with the educational goals of the program; interest in the evaluative clinical sciences; a strong academic background; and either advanced degrees or GRE or MCAT exam scores. Master's degree offered.

Saint Anselm College
Carolyn K. Weinreb, Ph.D.
Chief Health Professions Adviser, Dept. of Chemistry
100 Saint Anselm Dr.
Manchester, NH 03102
cweinreb@anselm.edu; www.anselm.edu

NEW JERSEY

Ramapo College of New Jersey
Rena Bacon, Director
Postbaccalaureate Program in the Health Sciences
School of Theoretical and Applied Science (TAS)
Building G, Third Floor, Room G-321
Mahwah, NJ 07430
(201) 684-7727; rbacon@ramapo.edu
www.ramapo.edu/catalog_03_04/academicPrograms/Pre-Med/healthSciences.html
Must have a bachelor's degree with a GPA of 3.0 (on a 4.0 scale), from an accredited undergraduate institution. Submit 3 letters of recommendation and official transcripts. An interview may be required. Postbaccalaureate students are "special students" in the School of Theoretical and Applied Science, and are awarded certificates upon the successful completion of the program. Full-time students must take a minimum of 12 credits per semester. Students may enroll on a part-time basis. Courses are offered day and evenings.

Richard Stockton College of New Jersey
Postbaccalaureate Certificate Program in the Health Professions
Jim Leeds Road
Pomona, NJ 08240
(609) 652-4462; ralph.werner@stockton.edu

Rutgers
Dr. Victoria Ukachukwu, Director
Postbaccalaureate Program for Pre-Health Professions Studies
Office of the Dean, University College
35 College Avenue
New Brunswick, NJ 08903
(732) 932-7683; vukachuk@rci.rutgers.edu
www.rutgers.edu/nbcampus/livingston
Must have a baccalaureate degree in any field from an accredited institution; official transcripts with a minimum 3.0 GPA; and a written autobiographical statement. Admission on a rolling basis.

UMDNJ–Graduate School of Biomedical Sciences
Office of Admissions
30 Bergen Street, ADMC 110
Newark, NJ 07107-3000
gsbsnadm@umdnj.edu; ingoglia@umdnj.edu
www.umdnj.edu/gsbsnweb
Applicants must submit GRE scores; have a baccalaureate degree with courses in biology, physics, general chemistry, and organic chemistry; and describe their goals. Nonrefundable $40 application fee. Master of Biomedical Sciences.

NEW MEXICO

New Mexico Health Sciences Center
Cultural & Ethnic Programs
Basic Medical Sciences Building, Room 106
915 Camino de Salud, NE
Albuquerque, NM 87131-5171
(505) 272-2728; (505) 272-6857 (fax)
http://hsc.unm.edu/ocep/index.html
Underrepresented or disadvantaged prospective medical students who were denied admission to the School of Medicine are eligible.

NEW YORK

Mr. Adrian L. Jones, Program Coordinator
Postbaccalaureate Program
Associated Medical Schools of New York
SUNY Buffalo School of Medicine & Biomedical Sciences
3435 Main Street, 40 CFS Building
Buffalo, NY 14214
(716) 829-2802
Educationally or economically disadvantaged students are eligible. Must have a bachelor's degree from an accredited institution, be a U.S. citizen or permanent resident, and be interviewed by and denied admission to one of the participating institutions.

Columbia University–School of General Studies
Postbaccalaureate Premedical Program
Admissions Office
408 Lewisohn Hall
2970 Broadway, Mail Code 4101
New York, NY 10027
(212) 854-2772; postbacc@columbia.edu
www.columbia.edu/cu/gs/postbacc
Must have a bachelor's degree from an accredited college or university in the U.S., or an equivalent degree from an institution outside of the U.S., and a GPA of 3.0. For those who have not applied to medical school.

The City College of New York / CUNY
Professor Robert P. Goode, Director
Program in Premedical Studies
Robert E. Marshak Science Building, Room 529
Convent Avenue at 138th Street
New York, NY 10031
(212) 650-6622/6623; (212) 650-7816 (fax)
www.sci.ccny.cuny.edu/pps/ppcp/index.html
Postbaccalaureate premedical certificate program is open to any student with a bachelor's degree from an accredited four-year college or university. A minimum GPA of 2.8 is required.

Hofstra University
University College for Continuing Education
Hempstead, NY 11549
(516) 463-5016; uccelibarts@hofstra.edu
www.hofstra.edu/Academics/UCCE/ContEd
Must have a bachelor's degree from an accredited college with a 3.0 GPA and SAT, GRE, or other standardized test scores.

Long Island University
Dr. A. A. Zavitsas, Director
Division of Science, University Plaza
Brooklyn, NY 11201
(718) 488-1209; www.liunet.edu
Minimum undergraduate GPA of 3.0 is required.

Manhattanville College
Pre-Health Professions Advisory (PHPA) Committee
2900 Purchase Street
Purchase, NY 10577
(914) 694-2200; (914) 694-2386 (fax)
www.mville.edu/academics/cooperative_prgs.html
Open to students who lack prerequisites basic to medicine.

New York College of Osteopathic Medicine
Office of Minority Affairs
P.O. Box 8000
Old Westbury, NY 11568
(516) 686-3800
Students must be applicants to the New York College of Osteopathic Medicine and submit a completed AACOMAS application indicating NYCOM, be interviewed by the NYCOM Admissions Committee, and comply with all admission requirements of the college.

New York Medical College
Graduate School of Basic Medical Sciences
Admissions Coordinator
Basic Sciences Building, Room A-41
Valhalla, NY 10595
(914) 594-4110; (914) 594-4944 (fax)
GSBMS_Apply@nymc.edu
www.nymc.edu/bms/basic_science.htm
Must have completed a baccalaureate degree and all the premedical requirements, and submit MCAT scores, the AMCAS application, letters of recommendation, and official transcripts.

New York University
Mr. James Montren
Preprofessional Advising Office, Main Building
100 Washington Square East, Room 901
New York, NY 10003
(212) 998-8160; (212) 995-4549 (fax)
Prehealth@nyu.edu
www.nyu.edu/cas/prehealth/postbaccs.htm
Must have a baccalaureate degree and a GPA of 3.0 or above, with no grade below a C. For students who have taken no science courses as undergraduates. Health-related work or volunteer experience is expected.

SUNY–Albany
Dept. of Health Policy, Management & Behavior
School of Public Health
One University Place, Room 175
Rensselaer, NY 12144-3456
(518) 402-0333; (518) 402-0414; lmg@albany.edu
www.albany.edu/sph/hpmb/hpmb_home.htm
Master of Health Policy and Management. Applicants must have a bachelor's degree from a recognized college or university, a GPA of 3.0 or better, and submit GRE scores. A college-level mathematics course (preferably statistics), minimum B grade, is recommended.

SUNY–Buffalo, Roswell Park Cancer Institute
Interdisciplinary Biomed/Oncology MS Program
Mr. Craig Johnson
408 Research Studies Center
Buffalo, NY 14263-0001
(716) 845-2339; (716) 845-8178 (fax)
gradapp@roswellpark.org
www.roswellpark.org/document_40.html

SUNY–Stony Brook
Faculty Committee on Health Professions
Office of Undergraduate Academic Affairs
Melville Library E2360
Stony Brook, NY 11794-3351
(516) 632-7082
http://ws.cc.stonybrook.edu/spd/graduate/premed.html
Students who do not have the requisite math and science courses may take undergraduate courses as nonmatriculating graduate students.

Syracuse University
Professor Sandy Bolanowski
Graduate Program Director
Dept. of Bioengineering & Neuroscience
Institute for Sensory Research
621 Skytop Road
Syracuse, NY 13244-5290
(315) 443-4164; Sandy_Bolanowski@isr.syr.edu
www.ecs.syr.edu/assetts/Documents/GradStudy_02.pdf
Must have a bachelor's degree with a minimum GPA of 3.0 and/or GRE scores in the 65th percentile. Transcripts and letters of recommendation also required.

Union College
Rhonda Sheehan, Coordinator of Admissions
Graduate Education
Lamont House Graduate Center
Schenectady, NY 12308
(518) 388-6239
postbacc@union.edu; www.union.edu
Must have a bachelor's degree from an accredited college or university and completed the majority of course work for medical school. Selection is based on the student's potential for admittance to medical school and MCAT or GMAT test scores. Master of Science in Clinical Leadership in Health Management.

NORTH CAROLINA

Fayetteville State University
Murthy V.L.N. Pinapaka
Dept. of Natural Sciences
1200 Murchison Road
Fayetteville, NC 28301
(910) 672-1691
www.uncfsu.edu/natsci/dptprog/index.htm

Wake Forest University School of Medicine
Postbaccalaureate Premedical Program
Student Services/Minority Affairs
Medical Center Boulevard
Winston-Salem, NC 27157-1037
(336) 716-4271; (336) 716-5807 (fax)
sdockery@wfubmc.edu
www.wfubmc.edu/school/MinorityAffairs/PostBac.htm
For underrepresented and disadvantaged individuals with bachelor's degrees. No cost to student. Must be willing to complete the program; have a minimum GPA of 2.5; a total MCAT score of 21 or more and N or above on the Writing Sample; and have 8 semester hours each of biology, chemistry, organic chemistry, and physics.

University of North Carolina–Greensboro
Robert Cannon
Dept. of Biology
P.O. Box 26170
Greensboro, NC 27402-6170
(336) 256-0071; (336) 334-5839 (fax)
recannon@uncg.edu; www.uncg.edu/bio/index.html

OHIO

Cleveland State University
Office of Graduate Admissions
Dept. of Health Sciences
2121 Euclid Avenue, FT1111
Cleveland, OH 44115
(216) 687-3567
www.csuohio.edu/healthsci/ms.html
Must have a baccalaureate or advanced degree from an accredited institution and be a health care professional. Submit transcripts and GRE scores (waived if GPA is above 3.0), and 3 letters of reference. Master of Science in Health Sciences

Ohio State University
College of Medicine
MEDPATH (Postbaccalaureate Program)
Office for Diversity and Cultural Affairs
370 W. 9th Avenue
Columbus, OH 43210
(614) 292-3161; yash.1@osu.edu
http://medicine.osu.edu/odca/medpath.cfm
Must have a bachelor's degree with minimum 2.5 GPA; be a U.S. citizen or permanent resident; be a member of group underrepresented in medicine; list Ohio State University College of Medicine as a school selection on the AMCAS application; and be recommended by OSU College of Medicine Admissions Committee to the MEDPATH Program.

Ohio University College of Osteopathic Medicine
Shannon Scott
Center of Excellence for Multicultural Medicine
030 Grosvenor Hall
Athens, OH 45701
(740) 593-0898; (740) 593-0892 (fax)
scotts1@ohio.edu
www.oucom.ohiou.edu/COE%20Excel/COEPostbacc.htm
Must have U.S. citizenship or permanent residency, a baccalaureate degree from an accredited college or university, a completed application to OU-COM, minimum course work required for admission to OU-COM, taken MCAT within the last three years, and have been interviewed by and denied admission to OU-COM.

University of Cincinnati College of Medicine
PATHWAYS Office
231 Albert Sabin Way
Cincinnati, OH 45267
(513) 558-7212; (513) 558-1165 (fax)
Roberta.Handwerger@uc.edu
www.med.uc.edu/admissions/summerenrich.cfm
Must be a U.S. citizen or permanent resident. No charge for the program; financial compensation is provided.

OREGON

Portland State University
College of Liberal Arts and Sciences
Premedical Postbaccalaureate Program
P.O. Box 751
Portland, OR 97207-0751
(503) 725 3514; (503) 725 3693 (fax)
www.clas.pdx.edu/advising/med-postbac.htm
Should have a GPA of 3.5 or better and an MCAT average of 30 (double digits in all numeric sections); participate in outside activities, such as hobbies and recreation; and have volunteer or paid experience with community service in church and related activities or experience in the health care field.

University of Oregon
Karen Cooper
Postbaccalaureate Premedical Program
Office of Academic Advising 5217
364 Oregon Hall
Eugene, OR 97403-5217
(541) 346-3211; (541) 346-6048 (fax)
karenc@oregon.uoregon.edu
http://advising.uoregon.edu/prof.html

PENNSYLVANIA

Beaver College
Melissa Keller
Office of Enrollment Management
Postbaccalaureate Certificate Programs
Glenside, PA 19038
(215) 572-2836; kellerm@arcadia.edu
www.beaver.edu/default.asp?t=1&m=71:3605&pmid=1&pid=945
Candidates should have a distinguished undergraduate record with at least a 3.0 GPA. Satisfactory performance on the MCAT or other health professions college admissions test is required.

Bryn Mawr College
Health Professions Advising Office
Canwyll Hall
101 N. Merion Avenue
Bryn Mawr, PA 19010-2899
(215) 526-7350; postbac@brynmawr.edu
www.brynmawr.edu/postbac/introduction.html
Open to students who have neither previously applied to medical school nor taken premed courses. A GPA of 3.0 is required.

Drexel University College of Medicine
Medical Science Preparatory Program
Room 4122 NCB
245 N. 15th Street, MS 344
Philadelphia, PA 19102
(215) 762-4692/7749; (215) 762-7434 (fax)
imsinfo@drexel.edu; www.drexel.edu/med/ims
There are three separate programs. Applicants must have a bachelor's degree from an accredited college or university, SAT scores of 1000 or an ACT score of 21, a GPA of 3.0, and understand algebra and trigonometry. Calculus is recommended. Offers a master's degree.

Drexel University College of Medicine
Biomedical Graduate Studies
Julian Mesina, D.V.M., Ph.D., Director
Master of Laboratory Animal Science Program
245 N. 15th Street, Mail Stop 436
Philadelphia, PA 19102-1192
(215) 762-8407; jmesina@drexel.edu *or* biograd@drexel.edu
www.drexel.edu/med/biograd/mlas
Must have a baccalaureate degree from an accredited institution, with a major in laboratory animal science, animal science, or a related field (such as biology, biochemistry, physiology, premedical studies, and preveterinary studies). Must also meet the admissions requirements of the graduate school and submit official scores from the GRE or the Veterinary College Admission Test (VCAT). Special consideration given to applicants with work experience or those currently employed in the field of laboratory animal science.

Duquesne University
Kenneth R. Boyd, Ph.D., Director (or)
Cathy Dvorak M.S.W./L.S.W., Assistant Director
Postbaccalaureate Premedical Program
B101 Bayer Learning Center
Pittsburgh, PA 15282
(412) 396-6335; (412) 396-5587 (fax)
selcer@duq.edu or postbacpremed@duq.edu
www.duq.edu/postbac
For those with a bachelor's degree who lack the sciences required for medical school. Both non-science and science backgrounds are accepted; however, students who majored in the sciences must have an overall GPA of 3.0, no "F" grades, a combined SAT score of 1100 or ACT of 26, and must not have taken the MCAT more than twice.

Immaculata University
S. Susan Cronin, Ph.D.
Biology Dept.
1145 King Road
Immaculata, PA 19345
(215) 647-4400; scronin@immaculata.edu
www.immaculata.edu/biology/postbac.htm
Must have a bachelor's degree from an accredited college or university, an undergraduate GPA of at least 3.0 (A=4.0) in the junior and senior years, and have not completed prerequisite courses for professional schools.

Lake Erie College of Osteopathic Medicine
Reza Nassiri, D.Sc., Director
Postbaccalaureate Program, Office of Admissions
1858 W. Grandview Boulevard
Erie, PA 16509-1025
(814) 866-8436; (814) 866-8411 (fax)
postbac@lecom.edu; rnassiri@lecom.edu
www.lecom.edu/academics/post.htm
Must have a bachelor's degree from an accredited college or university; 8 semester hours with at least a 2.0 GPA in each of the following: general biology, general chemistry, organic chemistry, and general physics; official reports of standardized test scores such as the MCAT, DAT, OAT, or GRE; and a cumulative GPA of 2.5.

LaSalle University
Geri Seitchick, Ph.D., Chair
Pre-Health Professions Programs
1900 W. Olney Avenue
Philadelphia, PA 19141-1199
(215) 951-1248; seitchik@lasalle.edu
www.lasalle.edu/academ/prehealth
Designed for students with a bachelor's degree from an accredited college or university, but who lack the majority of science courses needed for entrance into medical school.

The Pennsylvania State University
Mildred Rodriguez, Ph.D., Program Director
Postbaccalaureate Premedical Certificate Program
213 Whitmore Laboratory
University Park, PA 16802-6101
814-865-7620 or 1-800-778-8632; mxr22@.psu.edu
www.science.psu.edu/premed/postpm.html

Philadelphia College of Osteopathic Medicine
Biomedical Sciences Program
Office of Admissions
4170 City Avenue
Philadelphia, PA 19131
(800) 999-6998; (215) 871-6719
admissions@pcom.edu
www.pcom.edu/Academic_Programs/aca_biomed/aca_biomed.html
Must have a bachelor's degree with the undergraduate preprofessional science requirements completed; transcripts of standardized test scores such as the MCAT, DAT, OAT, or GRE; and a letter of recommendation from a faculty member or preprofessional advisory committee. Master's degree offered.

Temple University
Dr. William Nathan, Program Director
Pre-Health Professions Advising Center
Curtis Hall 113 (005-00)
1301 Montgomery Avenue
Philadelphia, PA 19122
(215) 204-8669/2500; wnathan@unix.temple.edu
www.temple.edu/healthadvising/postbac.html
GPA should be at least 3.0.

University of Pennsylvania
Lynne A. Hunter, Ph.D.
Assistant Dean, Pre-Health Programs
3440 Market Street, Suite 100
Philadelphia, PA 19104-3335
(215) 898-7326
prehealth@sas.upenn.edu; www.sas.upenn.edu/CGS
Applicants to the special science program should have an undergraduate GPA of 3.0 with substantial science course work and standardized test scores from MCAT, SAT, GRE, etc. Applicants for the postbaccalaurate program generally have been out of school for a least a year and have done excellent academic work.

West Chester University
Melissa Betz Cichowicz, Ph.D.
Director, Premedical Programs
117 Schmucker Science Center South
West Chester, PA 19383
(610) 436-2978; (610) 436-3277 (fax)
www.wcupa.edu/_information/official.documents/Undergrad.Catalog/PreMed.htm
Applicants should have a GPA of 3.2 and no previous MCAT. This program has agreements with Drexel University College of Medicine and Temple University School of Medicine.

RHODE ISLAND

Brown University
Brown Learning Community
Office of Special Studies
Box 1959
Providence, RI 02906
(401) 863-3452
www.brown.edu/Administration/BLC/specials/postbacs.html
Apply as a Special Student.

University of Rhode Island
Chair, Health Professions Advisory Committee
A-129, Biological Sciences Center
100 Flagg Road
Kingston, RI 02881
(401) 874-2670
healthpr@uri.edu; www.uri.edu/hpac/postbac.html
For some students, an unstructured, nondegree-granting plan of course work may be sufficient. For others, the Master of Biological Sciences (with a Non-Thesis option for Preprofessional Students) may be appropriate.

TENNESSEE

Carson-Newman College
Dr. Frank Pinkerton
Postbaccalaureate Program
CNC Box 71992
Russell Avenue
Jefferson City, TN 37760
(865) 471-3257; (865) 471-3578 (fax)
fpinkerton@cn.edu; www.cn.edu/CN.htm
Must have a minimum undergraduate GPA of 3.0.

Christian Brothers University
Biology Dept.
Dr. Stan Eisen, Director
Preprofessional Health Programs
650 E. Parkway South
Memphis, TN 38104
(901) 321-3447; (901) 321-4433 (fax)
seisen@cbu.edu; www.cbu.edu/%7Eseisen

East Tennessee State University
Dr. Lattie Collins
FasTrack Program
P.O. Box 70592-ETSU
Johnson City, TN 37614
(423) 439-6903; (423) 439-4840 (fax)
collinsl@mail.etsu.edu
www.etsu.edu/cas/premed/fastrack.htm

Fisk University
UNCF Premedical Summer Institute
Mary Welch
1000 17th Avenue North
Nashville, TN 37208-3051
(615) 329-8796; (615) 329-8636 (fax)
mckelvey@fisk.edu

TEXAS

Lamar University
Jim Westgate, Chair
Preprofessional Advisory Committee
Dept. of Biology
Beaumont, TX 77710
(409) 880-7970
http://dept.lamar.edu/artssciences/biology/index.html

Texas Christian University
Dr. Phil Hartman
Pre-Health Professions Program
Sid Richardson Building, Room 244
Fort Worth, TX 76129
(817) 257-6337
d.bennett@tcu.edu; www.tcu.edu
Open to students who lack prerequisites basic to medicine.

University of Houston
Health Professions Adviser
The University Studies Division
Student Service Center, Room 320
Houston, TX 77204
(713) 743-8982; alawrence@uh.edu
www.uh.edu/academics/usd/php/premed/index.htm

University of Texas–Arlington
Dean of Science
Life Science Building, Room 206
P.O. Box 19047
Arlington, TX 76019
(817) 273-2310
www.uta.edu/catalog/1999/Science.shtml
Postbaccalaureate premedical program for students with a bachelor's degree who wish to pursue admission to medical school. They also offer a 7-year B.S./M.D.+ program.

VERMONT

Bennington College
Rachel Emmons-Bradley
Postbaccalaureate Program for Premedical and Allied Health Sciences
Office of Admissions
Bennington, VT 05201
(800) 833-6845; (802) 440-4320 (fax)
rachel@bennington.edu; www.bennington.edu

University of Vermont
Continuing Education
Postbaccalaureate Premedical Program
322 S. Prospect Street
Burlington, VT 05405
800-639-3210/656-2085; learn@uvm.edu
http://learn.uvm.edu/?Page=ce/post_bac.html&SM=post_bac_submenu.html
Must have a bachelor's degree with a minimum GPA of 3.0 (Vermont residents) or 3.2 (nonresidents), and SAT, ACT, or GRE scores.

VIRGINIA

Eastern Virginia Medical School
Toni Dorn, Administrator
EVMS Biomedical Sciences Programs
Medical Masters Program
Fairfax Hall, Suite 512
721 Fairfax Avenue
Norfolk, VA 23507
(757) 446-8480; dornma@evms.edu
www.evms.edu/hlthprof/ms-biomed.html
Master of Science in Biomedical Sciences.

Old Dominion University
Sharon Melone-Orme
Prehealth Advisory Committee Assistant
OCNPS 133
Norfolk, VA 23529-0163
(757) 683-5200; smelone@odu.edu
www.odu.edu/oduprehealthclub

Virginia Commonwealth University
School of Graduate Studies
Ginter House B1
P.O. Box 843051
Richmond, VA 23298-3051
(804) 828-6916; gnielsen@vcu.edu
www.medschool.vcu.edu/gp/premed.html
Must have a baccalaureate degree with a 2.8 GPA and have completed organic chemistry. GRE or MCAT scores required. Applicants must complete the school of graduate studies admission forms, and indicate "Premedical BHS Certificate" as the curriculum, designating a preferred specialization of anatomy, biochemistry, human genetics, microbiology, pharmacology, or physiology.

WASHINGTON

Seattle University
Chief Premedical/Predental Adviser
Dept. of Biology
Seattle, WA 98122
(206) 296-5486; mhudson@seattleu.edu
www.seattleu.edu/scieng/biology

WEST VIRGINIA

Glenville State College
Division of Science and Mathematics
200 High Street
Glenville, WV 26351
(304) 462-4126
scimath@glenville.edu; www.glenville.edu

WISCONSIN

University of Wisconsin–Madison
School of Veterinary Medicine, Graduate Education
James W. Tracy, Ph.D.
1656 Linden Drive
Madison, WI 53706
(608) 263-1008; tracy@svm.vetmed.wisc.edu
www.ahabs.wisc.edu/gradprogram/introduction.html
www.ahabs.wisc.edu/gradprogram/fac_trainer.html
Must have either a graduate or bachelor's degree and a history of working with animals or on environmental or wildlife issues.

University of Wisconsin–Milwaukee
Certificate of Premedical Studies
Holton Hall 130
Milwaukee, WI 53201
(414) 229-3922; pacobb@uwm.edu
www.uwm.edu/letsci/services/premedcert.html

Appendix D

Medical School-Sponsored Summer Programs

READ ME FIRST! Considerable effort has gone into confirming the existence and correct contact information for the programs listed below. However, these programs may come and go, change their contact information (especially their website URLs), or alter their program requirements and structure. This list should provide you with a starting point, but check with your premed adviser and search the Web for the most up-to-date information on the programs that best fit your needs.

Note: Contact information can be found in *Appendix E* for each school. If the URL doesn't work, try incrementally chopping off pieces at the end until you get to a website that will allow you to locate or search for the information.

The duration of programs that last longer than the summer months is noted.

U.S. Medical Schools	Elementary/ Junior High School Program	High School Program	Under-graduate Program	Program for *their* Admitted Medical Students
ALABAMA				
University of Alabama School of Medicine		X	X	
University of South Alabama College of Medicine		X	X	
ARIZONA				
Arizona College of Osteopathic Medicine		X		
University of Arizona College of Medicine	X	X	X	X
ARKANSAS				
University of Arkansas College of Medicine	X	X		X
CALIFORNIA				
Loma Linda University School of Medicine			X	X
Stanford University		X	X	
UC–Davis School of Medicine	X	X	X	
UC–Irvine College of Medicine		X	X	X
UC–Los Angeles (David Geffen) School of Medicine		X	X	
UC–San Diego School of Medicine	X	X	X	X
UC–San Francisco School of Medicine	X	X	X	
University of Southern California (Keck) School of Medicine			X	X
Western University of Health Sciences College of Osteopathic Medicine of the Pacific				SR

(continued)

U.S. Medical Schools	Elementary/ Junior High School Program	High School Program	Under-graduate Program	Program for *their* Admitted Medical Students
COLORADO				
University of Colorado School of Medicine		X	X	
CONNECTICUT				
University of Connecticut Medical School	X	X	X	
Yale University School of Medicine		X	X	R, 6-12 mo
DISTRICT OF COLUMBIA				
Georgetown University School of Medicine	X	X	X, 1 yr	
Howard University College of Medicine				X
FLORIDA				
Florida State University College of Medicine	X	X	X	
Nova Southeastern University College of Osteopathic Medicine				R
University of Florida College of Medicine		X	X	
University of Miami School of Medicine		X	X, R	
University of South Florida College of Medicine		X	X	
GEORGIA				
Emory University School of Medicine		X	X	
Medical College of Georgia School of Medicine	X	X	X	X
Morehouse School of Medicine			X	X
HAWAII				
Univ. of Hawaii at Manoa, John A. Burns School of Medicine			X	
ILLINOIS				
FUHS/Chicago Medical School			X	R
Loyola Univ. of Chicago, Stritch School of Medicine			X	
Northwestern Univ., Feinberg School of Medicine			X, R	
Rush Medical College			X	
Southern Illinois University School of Medicine			X	R
University of Chicago Pritzker School of Medicine			X, R	
University of Illinois College of Medicine			R	X
INDIANA				
Indiana University School of Medicine		X	X, R	X
IOWA				
Univ. of Iowa, Carver College of Medicine	X	X[1]	X, R	R
KANSAS				
University of Kansas School of Medicine		X	X	
KENTUCKY				
Pikeville Coll. School of Osteopathic Medicine		X		
University of Louisville School of Medicine		X	X	X

(continued)

U.S. Medical Schools	Elementary/ Junior High School Program	High School Program	Under-graduate Program	Program for *their* Admitted Medical Students
LOUISIANA				
LSU–New Orleans School of Medicine				X
LSU–Shreveport School of Medicine	X	X	X	X
MARYLAND				
Johns Hopkins University School of Medicine	X[2]	X	X	
University of Maryland School of Medicine		X	X	X, R
MASSACHUSETTS				
Boston University School of Medicine		X	X	
Harvard Medical School		X	X	X
Tufts University School of Medicine				X
University of Massachusetts Medical School		X	X	
MICHIGAN				
Michigan State Univ. Coll. of Human Medicine			R	X
Michigan State Univ. Coll. of Osteopathic Medicine		X		
University of Michigan Medical School		X	X, R	
Wayne State University School of Medicine			R	X
MINNESOTA				
Mayo Medical School			R	
Univ. of Minnesota–Duluth School of Medicine		X	X, R	X
Univ. of Minnesota Medical School		X	X, R	R
MISSISSIPPI				
University of Mississippi School of Medicine		X	X	X
MISSOURI				
St. Louis University School of Medicine		X[4]		X
Univ. of Missouri–Columbia School of Medicine		X	X, R	X[3]
Univ. of Missouri–Kansas City School of Medicine		X	R	
Washington University School of Medicine		X	R	R
NEBRASKA				
Creighton University School of Medicine	X	X	X	X
University of Nebraska College of Medicine	X	X	X, R	
NEVADA				
University of Nevada School of Medicine	X	X		
NEW HAMPSHIRE				
Dartmouth Medical School			X, R	
NEW JERSEY				
UMDNJ–New Jersey Medical School	X	X	X, R	X
UMDNJ–Robert Wood Johnson Medical School			X	X
UMDNJ–School of Osteopathic Medicine			X, R	

(continued)

U.S. Medical Schools	Elementary/ Junior High School Program	High School Program	Under-graduate Program	Program for *their* Admitted Medical Students
NEW MEXICO				
University of New Mexico School of Medicine			X	
NEW YORK				
Albany Medical College		X		
Albert Einstein College of Medicine		X	X, R	
Columbia Univ. College of Physicians and Surgeons		X	X	
Cornell University			X	
Mount Sinai School of Medicine			X, R	X
New York College of Osteopathic Medicine of the New York Institute of Technology			X	
New York Medical College				X
New York University School of Medicine				R
SUNY–Buffalo School of Medicine			X, R	R
SUNY–Downstate College of Medicine		X, R		
SUNY–Stony Brook School of Medicine				R
SUNY–Upstate College of Medicine				X
University of Rochester School of Medicine		X, R	X, R	
NORTH CAROLINA				
Duke University School of Medicine			X	
East Carolina University Brody School of Medicine			X	
University of North Carolina at Chapel Hill School of Medicine			X, R	
Wake Forest University School of Medicine	X	X		X
NORTH DAKOTA				
University of North Dakota School of Medicine				X
OHIO				
Case Western Reserve University School of Medicine			X	
Medical College of Ohio			X, R	
Ohio State University College of Medicine			X (PB), R	
Ohio University College of Osteopathic Medicine	X		X	
University of Cincinnati College of Medicine	X	X	X, R	
Wright State University School of Medicine		X	X, R	X
OKLAHOMA				
Oklahoma State Univ. Coll. of Osteopathic Medicine		X		
University of Oklahoma Dotty Shaw Killam College of Medicine		X		
OREGON				
Oregon Health Science University School of Medicine	X	X, R	X, R	

(continued)

U.S. Medical Schools	Elementary/ Junior High School Program	High School Program	Under-graduate Program	Program for *their* Admitted Medical Students
PENNSYLVANIA				
Drexel University College of Medicine		R	R	
Jefferson Medical College			R	R
Lake Erie College of Osteopathic Medicine			X (PB)	
Pennsylvania State University College of Medicine			R	
Philadelphia College of Osteopathic Medicine				X
Temple University School of Medicine			X	
University of Pittsburgh School of Medicine		X	X	X
RHODE ISLAND				
Brown University School of Medicine		X	X, PB	
SOUTH CAROLINA				
Medical Univ. of South Carolina Coll. of Medicine	X		X, R	
SOUTH DAKOTA				
University of South Dakota School of Medicine	X	X	R	
TENNESSEE				
East Tennessee State University, James H. Quillen College of Medicine		X	X	
Meharry Medical College School of Medicine			X	
University of Tennessee College of Medicine		X	X	
Vanderbilt School of Medicine			X, R	
TEXAS				
Baylor College of Medicine		X, R	X, R	
Texas A&M University College of Medicine			X, R	
Texas Tech University School of Medicine			X	
University of North Texas Coll. of Osteopathic Medicine			X, R	
UT–Health Science Center at San Antonio			X	
UT–Galveston, Medical School		R	X, R	
UT–Houston, Medical School		X	X, R	
UT–Southwestern			X	
UTAH				
University of Utah School of Medicine	X, D	X, D		
VERMONT				
University of Vermont College of Medicine	X	X	PB, D Premed	
VIRGINIA				
Eastern Virginia Medical School			X	
Medical College of Virginia			X, PB	
University of Virginia School of Medicine			X	

(continued)

U.S. Medical Schools	Elementary/ Junior High School Program	High School Program	Under-graduate Program	Program for *their* Admitted Medical Students
WASHINGTON				
University of Washington School of Medicine		X	X	X
WEST VIRGINIA				
West Virginia School of Osteopathic Medicine				X
West Virginia University School of Medicine			X	
WISCONSIN				
Medical College of Wisconsin			X	X
University of Wisconsin Medical School			R	

1: Open only to American Indian high school students
2: Not specifically for medicine
3: After the first year has been completed
4: Open to high school minority students
D: Throughout the year
PB: Postbaccalaureate
R: Research available
SR: Summer research available
X: Available

Appendix E

Medical Schools

READ ME FIRST! Considerable effort has gone into confirming the contact information for the schools listed below. However, since schools may change this information (especially their website URLs), this list should be your starting point. Check with your premed adviser and search the Web for the most up-to-date information. If the URL doesn't work, try incrementally chopping off pieces at the end until you get to a website that will allow you to locate or search for the information.

Note that many medical schools fill their classes well before their "official" application deadlines. This is particularly true for those schools that have "rolling admissions" policies and deadlines after January 1 (such as all of the Osteopathic medical schools).

UNITED STATES

ALABAMA

University of Alabama School of Medicine
Office of Medical Student Services/Admissions
Volker Hall 100
1530 3rd Avenue South
Birmingham, AL 35294-0019
(205) 934-2330; (205) 934-8724 (fax)
e-mail: admissions@uasom.meis.uab.edu
http://main.uab.edu/uasom/show.asp?durki=2086
Application Deadline: Nov 1

Univ. of South Alabama College of Medicine
Office of Admissions, 241 CSAB
Mobile, AL 36688
(334) 460-7176; (334) 460-6278 (fax)
e-mail: mscott@usouthal.edu
http://southmed.usouthal.edu/com/same/admissions
Application Deadline: Nov 15

ARIZONA

Arizona College of Osteopathic Medicine
Office of Admissions
19555 N. 59th Avenue
Glendale, AZ 85308
(888) 247-9277; (623) 572-3229 (fax)
e-mail: admissaz@arizona.midwestern.edu
www.aacom.org/colleges/azcom.asp
Application Deadline: Jan 1

University of Arizona College of Medicine
Admission Office, Room 2209
P.O. Box 245075
Tucson, AZ 85724
(602) 626-6214; (602) 626-4884 (fax)
e-mail: admissions@medicine.arizona.edu
www.medicine.arizona.edu/student_info
Application Deadline: Nov 1

ARKANSAS

University of Arkansas College of Medicine
Office of Student Admissions
4301 West Markham Street, Slot 551
Little Rock, AR 72205-7199
(501) 686-5354; (501) 686-5873 (fax)
e-mail: SouthTomG@uams.edu
www.uams.edu/com/default.htm
Application Deadline: Nov 15

CALIFORNIA

Charles R. Drew Univ. College of Medicine and Science
Office of Medical Student Affairs, MP-48
1731 E. 120th Street
Los Angeles, CA 90059
(323) 563-5956; (323) 563-4957 (fax)
e-mail: wahall@cdrewu.edu
www.cdrewu.edu
Application Deadline: Nov 15

Loma Linda University School of Medicine
Associate Dean for Admissions
Loma Linda, CA 92350
(909) 558-4467; (800) 442-4558
(909) 824-4846 (fax)
e-mail: ledwards@som.llu.edu
www.llu.edu/llu/medicine
Application Deadline: Nov 15

Stanford University School of Medicine
M.D. Admissions
251 Campus Drive, MSOB 341
Stanford, CA 94305
(650) 723-6861; (650) 723-4599 (fax)
e-mail: admissions@med.stanford.edu
http://med-www.stanford.edu/school
Application Deadline: Nov 1

Touro Univ. College of Osteopathic Medicine
Director of Admissions
1310 Johnson Lane
Vallejo, CA 94592
(888) 880-7336 in CA; (888) 887-7336 outside CA
e-mail: haight@touro.edu
www.tucom.edu/admissions.htm
Application Deadline: Feb 15

Univ. of California–Davis, School of Medicine
Office of Admissions
Room 126, MS1-C
One Shields Avenue
Davis, CA 95616
(530) 752-2717; (530) 752-2376 (fax)
e-mail: medadmsinfo@ucdavis.edu
http://som.ucdavis.edu/Education_and_Admission
Application Deadline: Nov 1

Univ. of California–Irvine, College of Medicine
Office of Admissions and Outreach
Medical Education Building 802
Irvine, CA 92697-4089
(800) 824-5388; (949) 824-5388
(949) 824-2485 (fax)
e-mail: medadmit@uci.edu
www.ucihs.uci.edu/admissions
Application Deadline: Nov 1

Univ. of California–Los Angeles, (David Geffen) School of Medicine
Admissions Office
12-105 Center for Health Sciences
Box 957035
Los Angeles, CA 90095-7035
(310) 825-6081
e-mail: somadmiss@mednet.ucla.edu
www.medstudent.ucla.edu
Application Deadline: Nov 1

Univ. of California–San Diego, School of Medicine
Office of Admissions, 0621
Medical Teaching Facility
9500 Gilman Drive
La Jolla, CA 92093-0621
(858) 534-3880; (858) 534-5282 (fax)
e-mail: somadmissions@ucsd.edu
http://medicine.ucsd.edu
Application Deadline: Nov 1

Univ. of California–San Francisco, School of Medicine
Office of Admissions
C-200, Box 0408
San Francisco, CA 94143
(415) 476-4044
e-mail: admissions@medsch.ucsf.edu
www.som.ucsf.edu/som/education/admission
Application Deadline: Nov 1

Univ. of Southern California, Keck School of Medicine
Office of Admissions
1975 Zonal Avenue (KAM 100-C)
Los Angeles, CA 90033-1039
(323) 442-2552; (323) 442-2433 (fax)
e-mail: medadmit@hsc.usc.edu
www.usc.edu/schools/medicine/education/admissions
Application Deadline: Nov 1

Western University of Health Sciences, College of Osteopathic Medicine of the Pacific
Office of Admissions
309 E. Second Street
Pomona, CA 91766-1854
(909) 469-5261; (909) 469-5570 (fax)
e-mail: admissions@westernu.edu
www.aacom.org/colleges/western.asp
Application Deadline: Feb 1

COLORADO

University of Colorado School of Medicine
Medical School Admissions
4200 E. Ninth Avenue, C-297
Denver, CO 80262
(303) 315-7361
e-mail: Willa.Buswell@uchsc.edu
www.uchsc.edu/sm/sm
Application Deadline: Nov 15

CONNECTICUT

University of Connecticut Medical School
Admissions Center
263 Farmington Avenue, Room AG-036
Farmington, CT 06030-1905
(860) 679-4306; (860) 679-1282 (fax)
e-mail: robertson@nso2.uchc.edu
www9.uchc.edu/index.html
Application Deadline: Dec 15

Yale University School of Medicine
Office of Admissions
367 Cedar Street
New Haven, CT 06510
(203) 785-2643; (203) 785-3234 (fax)
e-mail: medical.admissions@yale.edu
http://info.med.yale.edu/ysm/index.html
Application Deadline: Oct 15

DISTRICT OF COLUMBIA

Georgetown University School of Medicine
Office of Admissions
Box 571421
Washington, DC 20007
(202) 687-1154
e-mail: medicaladmissions@georgetown.edu
www.dml.georgetown.edu/schmed
Application Deadline: Nov 1

George Washington Univ. School of Medicine
Office of Admissions
Walter G. Ross Hall, Room 716
2300 I Street NW
Washington, DC 20037
(202) 994-3506; (202) 994-1753 (fax)
e-mail: medadmit@gwu.edu
www.gwumc.edu/smhs
Application Deadline: Dec 1

Howard University College of Medicine
Admission Office
520 W Street NW
Washington, DC 20059
(202) 806-6270; (202) 806-7934 (fax)
e-mail: shumphrey@howard.edu
www.med.howard.edu/Admissions
Application Deadline: Dec 15

FLORIDA

Florida State University College of Medicine
Call Street at Stadium Drive
Tallahassee, FL 32306-4300
(904) 644-7904
e-mail: MedInformation@med.fsu.edu
www.med.fsu.edu/StudentAffairs.asp
Application Deadline: Dec 15

Nova Southeastern Univ., College of Osteopathic Medicine
Lynne Cawley, Assistant Director of Admissions & Student Affairs
3200 S. University Drive
Ft. Lauderdale, FL 33328
(800) 356-0026, ext. 1101; (954) 262-1101
(954) 262-2282 (fax)
e-mail: cawley@nova.edu; com@nova.edu
www.aacom.org/colleges/nsucom.asp
Application Deadline: Jan 15

University of Florida College of Medicine
Office of Admissions
J. Hillis Miller Health Center, Box 100216
Gainesville, FL 32610
(352) 392-4569; (352) 846-0622 (fax)
e-mail: admissions@mail.med.ufl.edu
www.med.ufl.edu/oea/admiss
Application Deadline: Jan 15

University of Miami School of Medicine
Office of Admissions
P.O. Box 248025
Coral Gables, Florida 33124
(305) 284-4323; (305) 243-6548 (fax)
e-mail: med.admissions@miami.edu
www.miami.edu/UMH/CDA/UMH_Main/1,1770,2600-1,00.html
Application Deadline: Dec 15

Univ. of South Florida, College of Medicine
Office of Admissions, MDC Box 3
12901 Bruce B. Downs Boulevard
Tampa, FL 33612-4799
(813) 974-2229; (813) 974-4990 (fax)
e-mail: md-admissions@lyris.hsc.usf.edu
www.med.usf.edu/MD/admis.htm
Application Deadline: Dec 1

GEORGIA

Emory University School of Medicine
Medical School Admissions Office
Woodruff Health Sciences Center
Administration Building
1440 Clifton Road, NE, Suite 115
Atlanta, GA 30322-4510
(404) 727-5660; (404) 727-5456 (fax)
e-mail: medadmiss@emory.edu
www.emory.edu/WHSC/MED/TEACHING
Application Deadline: Oct 15

Medical College of Georgia School of Medicine
Associate Dean for Admissions
Augusta, GA 30912-4760
(706) 721-3186; (706) 721-0959 (fax)
e-mail: stdadmin@mail.mcg.edu
www.mcg.edu/careers/medicine.htm
Application Deadline: Nov 1

Mercer University School of Medicine
Office of Admissions
1550 College Street
Macon, GA 31207
(478) 301-2542, (478) 301-2547 (fax)
e-mail: faust_ek@mercer.edu
http://medicine.mercer.edu/admin_services/admissions
Application Deadline: Dec 1

Morehouse School of Medicine
Admissions and Student Affairs
Hugh Gloster Building, Suite 104
720 Westview Drive, S.W.
Atlanta, GA 30310-1495
(404) 752-1500; (404) 752-1008 (fax)
www.msm.edu
Application Deadline: Dec 1

HAWAII

University of Hawaii at Manoa, John A. Burns School of Medicine
Office of Admissions
1960 East-West Road
Honolulu, HI 96822
(808) 956-8300; (808) 956-9547 (fax)
http://hawaiimed.hawaii.edu/student_affairs/admissions.html
Application Deadline: Dec 1

ILLINOIS

Chicago College of Osteopathic Medicine
Office of Admissions
555 Thirty-First Street
Downers Grove, IL 60515
(800) 458-6253; (630) 515-7200
(630) 971-6086 (fax)
e-mail: Admissil@midwestern.edu
www.aacom.org/colleges/ccom.asp
Application Deadline: Jan 1

Finch Univ. of Health Sciences/ Chicago Medical School
School of Medicine Admissions
3333 Green Bay Road
Chicago, IL 60064
(847) 578-3205/3206/3207
e-mail: jonesk@finchcms.edu
www.finchcms.edu/cms/admapp.cfm
Application Deadline: Nov 15

Loyola Univ. of Chicago, Stritch School of Medicine
Admissions Office, Room 1752
2160 S. First Avenue
Maywood, IL 60153
(708) 216-3229
www.meddean.luc.edu/ssom/studres
Application Deadline: Nov 15

Northwestern University, Feinberg School of Medicine
Associate Dean for Admissions
Morton Building 1-606
303 E. Chicago Avenue
Chicago, IL 60611-3008
(312) 503-8206
e-mail: med-admissions@northwestern.edu
http://med-admissions.northwestern.edu
Application Deadline: Nov 1

Rush Medical College
Office of Admissions, Suite 524-H
600 S. Paulina Street
Chicago, IL 60612-3832
(312) 942-6913; (312) 942-2333 (fax)
e-mail: medcol@rush.edu
www.rushu.rush.edu/medcol/admissions.html
Application Deadline: Nov 15

Southern Illinois Univ. School of Medicine
Office of Student Affairs
801 N. Rutledge, Room 3080
P.O. Box 19624
Springfield, IL 62794-9624
(217) 545-6013; (217) 545-5538 (fax)
e-mail: admissions@siumed.edu
www.siumed.edu/studentaffairs
Application Deadline: Nov 15

Univ. of Chicago, Pritzker School of Medicine
Office of Admissions
924 E. 57th Street, Suite 104
Chicago, IL 60637-5416
(773) 702-1937; (773) 702-2598 (fax)
e-mail: admissions@pritzker.bsd.uchicago.edu
http://pritzker.bsd.uchicago.edu/prospectiveStudents
Application Deadline: Oct 15

University of Illinois College of Medicine
Medical College Admissions
Room 165, CME M/C 783
808 S. Wood Street
Chicago, IL 60612-7302
(312) 996-5635; (312) 996-6693 (fax)
www.uic.edu/depts/mcam/admissions
Application Deadline: Dec 15

INDIANA

Indiana University School of Medicine
Medical School Admissions Office
1120 S. Drive, Fesler Hall 213
Indianapolis, IN 46202-5113
(317) 274-3772
e-mail: inmedadm@iupui.edu
www.medicine.iu.edu/admissions
Application Deadline: Dec 15

IOWA

Des Moines Univ., College of Osteopathic Medicine and Surgery
Office of Admissions
3200 Grand Avenue
Des Moines, Iowa 50312
(800) 240-2767, ext. 1450; (515) 271-1450
(515) 271-1578 (fax)
e-mail: DOADMIT@dsmu.edu
www.aacom.org/colleges/dmuomc.asp
Application Deadline: Feb 1

Univ. of Iowa, Carver College of Medicine
Office of Admissions
100 Medicine Administration Building
Iowa City, IA 52242-1101
(319) 335-8052; (319) 335-8049 (fax)
e-mail: medical-admission@uiowa.edu
www.medicine.uiowa.edu/osac/admissions
Application Deadline: Nov 1

KANSAS

University of Kansas School of Medicine
Office of Admissions
Mail Stop 1049
3901 Rainbow Boulevard
Kansas City, KS 66160-7301
(913) 588-5245; (913) 588-5259 (fax)
e-mail: premedinfo@kumc.edu
www.kumc.edu/som/som.html
Application Deadline: Oct 15

KENTUCKY

Pikeville College School of Osteopathic Medicine
Office of Admissions
147 Sycamore Street
Pikeville, KY 41501-1194
(606) 218-5406; (606) 218-5442 (fax)
e-mail: spayson@pc.edu; pcsom@pc.edu
http://pcsom.pc.edu
Application Deadline: Feb 1

University of Kentucky College of Medicine
Admissions Office
MN 102 UKMC
800 Rose Street
Lexington, KY 40536-0298
(859) 323-6161; (859) 323-2076 (fax)
e-mail: kstahlma@pop.uky.edu
www.mc.uky.edu/oaa/OAA/admissions
Application Deadline: Nov 1

University of Louisville School of Medicine
Admissions Office, Abell Administration Bldg.
323 E. Chestnut Street
Louisville, KY 40202
(502) 852-5193; (800) 334-8635, ext. 5193
e-mail: medadm@louisville.edu
www.louisville.edu/medschool/admissions.htm
Application Deadline: Nov 1

LOUISIANA

Louisiana State Univ.–New Orleans, School of Medicine
Admissions Office
1901 Perdido Street, Box P3-4
New Orleans, LA 70112-1593
(504) 568-6262; (504) 568-7701 (fax)
e-mail: ms-admissions@lsumc.edu
www.medschool.lsumc.edu/admissions
Application Deadline: Nov 15

LSU–Shreveport, School of Medicine
Office of Student Admissions
P.O. Box 33932
Shreveport, LA 71130-3932
(318) 675-5190; (318) 675-5244 (fax)
e-mail: shvadm@lsumc.edu
www.sh.lsuhsc.edu/academics/admission.html
Application Deadline: Nov 15

Tulane University School of Medicine
Office of Admissions
1430 Tulane Ave, SL-67
New Orleans, LA 70112-2699
(504) 588-5187; (504) 588-6462 (fax)
e-mail: medsch@tulane.edu
www1.omi.tulane.edu/departments/admissions
Application Deadline: Dec 15

MAINE

Univ. of New England, College of Osteopathic Medicine
Admissions Office
11 Hills Beach Road
Biddeford, ME 04005
(800) 477-4863
e-mail: admissions@une.edu
www.aacom.org/colleges/unecom.asp
Application Deadline: Jan 2

MARYLAND

Johns Hopkins University School of Medicine
Admission Office
720 Rutland Avenue
Baltimore, MD 21205-2196
(410) 955-3182
www.hopkinsmedicine.org/medicalschool/admissions.html
Application Deadline: Oct 15

Uniformed Services Univ. of the Health Sciences, F. Edward Hébert School of Medicine
Admission Office, Room A-1041
4301 Jones Bridge Road
Bethesda, MD 20814-4799
(800) 772-1743; (301) 295-3101
(301) 295-3545 (fax)
e-mail: admissions@mxa.usuhs.mil
www.usuhs.mil/medschool/fehsom.html
Application Deadline: Nov 1

University of Maryland School of Medicine
Committee on Admissions
655 West Baltimore Street, Room 1-005
Baltimore, MD 21201
(410) 706-7478; (410) 706-0467 (fax)
e-mail: mfoxwell@som.umaryland.edu
http://medschool.umaryland.edu/admissions
Application Deadline: Nov 1

MASSACHUSETTS

Boston University School of Medicine
Admissions Office
715 Albany Street, L-124
Boston, MA 02118
(617) 638-4630; (617) 638-4718 (fax)
e-mail: medadms@bu.edu
www.bumc.bu.edu/Departments/HomeMain.asp?DepartmentID=37
Application Deadline: Nov 15

Harvard Medical School
Office of the Committee on Admissions
25 Shattuck Street
Boston, MA 02115-6092
(617) 432-1550; (617) 432-3307 (fax)
e-mail: Admissions_Office@hms.harvard.edu
www.hms.harvard.edu/admissions
Application Deadline: Oct 15

Tufts University School of Medicine
Office of Admissions
136 Harrison Avenue
Boston, MA 02111
(617) 636-6571
e-mail: med-admissions@tufts.edu
www.tufts.edu/med/admissions
Application Deadline: Nov 1

University of Massachusetts Medical School
Office of Admissions
55 Lake Avenue, North
Worcester, MA 01655
(508) 856-2323; (508) 856-3629 (fax)
e-mail: admissions@umassmed.edu
www.umassmed.edu/som/admissions
Application Deadline: Nov 1

MICHIGAN

Michigan State Univ., College of Human Medicine
Office of Admissions
A-239 Life Sciences Building
East Lansing, MI 48824-1317
(517) 353-9620; (517) 432-0021 (fax)
e-mail: MDAdmissions@msu.edu
www.chm.msu.edu/chmhome/admissions
Application Deadline: Nov 15

Michigan State Univ., College of Osteopathic Medicine
Office of Admissions
C110 East Fee Hall
East Lansing, MI 48824-1316
(517) 353-7740; (517) 355-3296 (fax)
e-mail: comadm@com.msu.edu
www.aacom.org/colleges/msucom.asp
Application Deadline: Dec 6

University of Michigan Medical School
Admissions Office
M4130 Medical Sciences I Building
1301 Catherine Road
Ann Arbor, MI 48109-0624
(313) 764-6317; (313) 764-4542 (fax)
e-mail: kthorne@umich.edu
www.med.umich.edu/medschool
Application Deadline: Nov 15

Wayne State University School of Medicine
Office of Admissions
540 E. Canfield, Suite 1310
Detroit, MI 48201
(313) 577-1466; (313) 577-9420 (fax)
e-mail: admissions@med.wayne.edu
www.med.wayne.edu/admissions
Application Deadline: Dec 15

MINNESOTA

Mayo Medical School
Assistant Dean for Student Affairs
200 First Street, S.W.
Rochester, MN 55905
(507) 284-3671; (507) 284-2634 (fax)
e-mail: MedSchoolAdmissions@mayo.edu
www.mayo.edu/mms/md-admissions.html
Application Deadline: Nov 1

University of Minnesota–Duluth, School of Medicine
Office of Admissions
1035 University Drive
Duluth, MN 55812
(218) 726-8511; (218) 726-6235 (fax)
e-mail: medadmis@d.umn.edu
http://penguin.d.umn.edu/Admissions/default.asp
Application Deadline: Nov 15

University of Minnesota Medical School
Office of Admissions
Mayo Mail Code 293
420 Delaware Street, S.E.
Minneapolis, MN 55455-0310
(612) 624-1188; (612) 626-4200 (fax)
e-mail: meded@umn.edu
www.meded.umn.edu
Application Deadline: Nov 15

MISSISSIPPI

University of Mississippi School of Medicine
Associate Dean for Medical School Admissions
2500 N. State Street
Jackson, MS 39216-4505
(601) 984-5010; (601) 984-5008 (fax)
e-mail: AdmitMD@som.umsmed.edu
http://som.umc.edu/admissions.html
Application Deadline: Oct 15

MISSOURI

Kirksville College of Osteopathic Medicine
Office of Admissions
800 West Jefferson Street
Kirksville, MO 63501
(660) 626-2237; (660) 626-2969 (fax)
Outside of Missouri: (800) 626-5266, ext. 2237
e-mail: admissions@kcom.edu
www.aacom.org/colleges/kcom.asp
Application Deadline: Feb 1

Univ. of Health Sciences College of Osteopathic Medicine
Office of Admissions
1750 Independence Boulevard
Kansas City, MO 64106-1453
(800) 234-4847
e-mail: admissions@uhs.edu
www.aacom.org/colleges/uhscom.asp
Application Deadline: Feb 1

St. Louis University School of Medicine
Office of Admissions
1402 S. Grand Boulevard
St. Louis, MO 63104
(314) 577-8205; (314) 577-8214 (fax)
e-mail: medadmis@slu.edu
http://medschool.slu.edu/admissions
Application Deadline: Dec 15

Univ. of Missouri–Columbia, School of Medicine
Office of Admissions
MA215 Medical Sciences Building
One Hospital Drive
Columbia, MO 65212
(573) 882-9219; (573) 882-2988 (fax)
e-mail: nolkej@health.missouri.edu
www.muhealth.org/~medicine/admit.shtml
Application Deadline: Nov 1

Univ. of Missouri–Kansas City, School of Medicine
Council on Selection
120 Administrative Center
5100 Rockhill Road
Kansas City, MO 64110-2499
(816) 235-1870; (816) 235-5277 (fax)
e-mail: admit@umkc.edu
http://research.med.umkc.edu
Application Deadline: Dec 1

Washington University School of Medicine
Office of Admissions
660 S. Euclid Avenue, Campus Box 8107
St. Louis, MO 63110
(314) 362-6858; (314) 362-4658 (fax)
e-mail: wumscoa@msnotes.wustl.edu
http://medschool.wustl.edu/admissions
Application Deadline: Dec 1

NEBRASKA

Creighton University School of Medicine
Office of Admissions
2500 California Plaza
Omaha, NE 68178
(402) 280-2798; (402) 280-1241 (fax)
e-mail: medschadm@creighton.edu
http://medicine.creighton.edu
Application Deadline: Dec 1

Univ. of Nebraska College of Medicine
Office of Admissions and Students
986585 NE Medical Center
600 S. 42nd Street
Omaha, NE 68198
(402) 559-2259; (402) 559-6840 (fax)
e-mail: johara@unmc.edu
www.unmc.edu/student/colleges/medicine.htm
Application Deadline: Nov 1

NEVADA

University of Nevada School of Medicine
Office of Admissions and Student Affairs
Pennington Medical Education Building/357
Reno, NV 89557-0046
(702) 784-6063; (702) 784-6096 (fax)
e-mail: asa@med.unr.edu
www.unr.edu/med/dept/admissions
Application Deadline: Nov 1

NEW HAMPSHIRE

Dartmouth Medical School
Office of Admissions
3 Rope Ferry Road
Hanover, NH 03755-1404
(603) 650-1505; (603) 650-1560 (fax)
e-mail: dms.admissions@dartmouth.edu
www.dartmouth.edu/dms/admissions
Application Deadline: Nov 1

NEW JERSEY

UMDNJ–New Jersey Medical School
Associate Dean for Admissions
185 S. Orange Avenue
Newark, NJ 07103-2714
(973) 972-4631; (973) 972-7986 (fax)
e-mail: njmsadmiss@umdnj.edu
http://njms.umdnj.edu/od/educ/admis/index.htm
Application Deadline: Dec 15

UMDNJ–Robert Wood Johnson Medical School
Office of Admissions
675 Hoes Lane
Piscataway, NJ 08854-5635
(732) 235-4576; (732) 235-5078 (fax)
e-mail: rwjapadm@umdnj.edu
http://rwjms.umdnj.edu/admissions/index.html
Application Deadline: Dec 1

UMDNJ–School of Osteopathic Medicine
Admissions Office
One Medical Center Drive, Suite 162A
Stratford, NJ 08084
(856) 566-7050; (856) 566-6895 (fax)
e-mail: somadm@umdnj.edu
www.aacom.org/colleges/umdnjsom.asp
Application Deadline: Feb 1

NEW MEXICO

University of New Mexico School of Medicine
Office of Admissions and Student Affairs
Basic Medical Sciences Building, Room 107
Albuquerque, NM 87131-5166
(505) 272-4766; (505) 272-8239 (fax)
http://hsc.unm.edu/som/admissions
Application Deadline: Nov 15

NEW YORK

Albany Medical College
Office of Admissions
47 New Scotland Ave., Mail Code 3
Albany, NY 12208-3479
(518) 262-5521; (518) 262-5887 (fax)
e-mail: admissions@mail.amc.edu
www.amc.edu/academic/college/college_admissions.htm
Application Deadline: Nov 15

Albert Einstein College of Medicine
Office of Admissions
Jack and Pearl Resnick Campus
1300 Morris Park Avenue
Bronx, NY 10461
(718) 430-2106; (718) 430-8840 (fax)
e-mail: admissions@aecom.yu.edu
www.aecom.yu.edu/home/admissions
Application Deadline: Nov 1

Columbia Univ. College of Physicians and Surgeons
Admissions Office, Room 1-416
630 West 168th Street
New York, NY 10032
(212) 305-3595
e-mail: psadmissions@columbia.edu
http://t1.berlinprod.com/accounts/columbia/columbiasite8/home.html
Application Deadline: Oct 15

Cornell University, Weill Medical College
Office of Admissions, Room 104
445 E. 69th Street
New York, NY 10021
(212) 746-1067; (212) 746-8052 (fax)
e-mail: cumc-admissions@med.cornell.edu
www.med.cornell.edu/education
Application Deadline: Oct 15

Mount Sinai School of Medicine
Office of Admissions
Annenberg Building, Room 5-04
One Gustave L. Levy Place, Box 1002
New York, NY 10029-6574
(212) 241-6696
e-mail: Admissions@mssm.edu
www.mssm.edu/prospective.html
Application Deadline: Nov 1

New York College of Osteopathic Medicine of New York Institute of Technology
Office of Admissions
P.O. Box 8000
Old Westbury, NY 11568-8000
(516) 626-3747; (516) 686-3831 (fax)
e-mail: admissions@nyit.edu
www.aacom.org/colleges/nycom.asp
Application Deadline: Feb 1

New York Medical College
Office of Admissions
Administration Building
Sunshine Cottage, Room 127
Valhalla, NY 10595
(914) 594-4507; (914) 993-4976 (fax)
e-mail: mdadmit@nymc.edu
www.nymc.edu/admit/admt.htm
Application Deadline: Dec 15

New York University School of Medicine
Admissions Office
550 First Avenue
New York, NY 10016
(212) 263-5290
www.med.nyu.edu/som/medsch/index.html
Application Deadline: Nov 15

SUNY at Buffalo, School of Medicine and Biomedical Sciences
Office of Medical Admissions
131 Biomedical Education Building
Buffalo, NY 14214-3013
(716) 829-3466; (716) 829-3849 (fax)
e-mail: jjrosso@acsu.buffalo.edu
www.smbs.buffalo.edu/ome
Application Deadline: Nov 15

SUNY Downstate, College of Medicine
Office of Admissions
450 Clarkson Avenue, Box 60M
Brooklyn, NY 11203-2098
(718) 270-2446
e-mail: admissions@downstate.edu
www.hscbklyn.edu/college_of_medicine
Application Deadline: Dec 15

SUNY at Stony Brook, School of Medicine
Committee on Admissions
Health Sciences Center
Level 4, Room 147
Stony Brook, NY 11794-8434
(631) 444-2113; (631) 444-6032 (fax)
e-mail: somadmissions@stonybrook.edu
www.uhmc.sunysb.edu/som/students/cadaff/general.html
Application Deadline: Nov 15

SUNY Upstate Medical University College of Medicine
Admissions Office
Weiskotten Hall
766 Irving Ave, Room 1215
Syracuse, NY 13210
(315) 464-4570; (315) 464-8867 (fax)
e-mail: admiss@upstate.edu
www.upstate.edu/com/admissions.shtml
Application Deadline: Dec 1

Univ. of Rochester School of Medicine
Office of Admissions
601 Elmwood Ave, Box 601A
Rochester, NY 14642
(585) 275-4539; (585) 756-5479 (fax)
e-mail: mdadmish@urmc.rochester.edu
www.urmc.rochester.edu/smd/admiss
Application Deadline: Oct 15

NORTH CAROLINA

Duke University School of Medicine
Office of Medical School Admissions
DUMC 3710
Durham, NC 27710
(919) 684-2985; (919) 684-8893 (fax)
e-mail: medadm@mc.duke.edu
http://medschool.duke.edu
Application Deadline: Oct 15

East Carolina University Brody School of Medicine
Office of Admissions
600 Moye Boulevard
Greenville, NC 27858-4354
(252) 744-2202; (252) 744-1926 (fax)
e-mail: somadmissions@mail.ecu.edu
www.ecu.edu/bsomadmissions
Application Deadline: Nov 15

Univ. of North Carolina at Chapel Hill, School of Medicine
Admissions Office, CB# 7000
Room 121 MacNider Building
Chapel Hill, NC 27599-7000
(919) 962-8331; (919) 962-9930 (fax)
e-mail: randee_reid@med.unc.edu
www.med.unc.edu/ome_admit.htm
Application Deadline: Nov 15

Wake Forest Univ., School of Medicine
The Bowman Gray Campus
Office of Medical School Admissions
Medical Center Boulevard
Winston-Salem, NC 27157-1090
(336) 716-4264; (336) 716-5807 (fax)
www.wfubmc.edu/school
Application Deadline: Nov 1

NORTH DAKOTA

Univ. of North Dakota, School of Medicine
Secretary, Committee on Admissions
Office of Student Affairs and Admissions
P.O. Box 9037
Grand Forks, ND 58202-9037
(701) 777-4221; (701) 777-4942 (fax)
e-mail: jdheit@medicine.nodak.edu
www.med.und.nodak.edu/admissions.html
Application Deadline: Nov 1

OHIO

Case Western Reserve Univ. School of Medicine
Associate Dean for Admissions and Student Affairs
Office of Admissions
10900 Euclid Avenue
Cleveland, OH 44106-4920
(216) 368-3450; (216) 368-4621 (fax)
e-mail: ack@po.cwru.edu
http://mediswww.cwru.edu/admissions/index.htm
Application Deadline: Dec 15

Medical College of Ohio
Admissions Office
3045 Arlington Avenue
Toledo, OH 43614
(419) 381-4229; (419) 381-4005 (fax)
e-mail: admissions@mco.edu
www.mco.edu/smed/index.html
Application Deadline: Nov 1

Northeastern Ohio Univ. College of Medicine
Office of Admissions and Educational Research
P.O. Box 95, State Route 44
Rootstown, OH 44272-0095
(330) 325-6270; (330) 325-8372 (fax)
e-mail: admission@neoucom.edu
www.neoucom.edu/Students/ADMI/index.html
Application Deadline: Nov 1

Ohio Univ., College of Osteopathic Medicine
Office of Admissions
102 Grosvenor Hall
Athens, OH 45701-2979
(800) 345-1560; (740) 593-4313; (740) 593-2256 (fax)
e-mail: Admissions@exchange.oucom.ohiou.edu
www.aacom.org/colleges/oucom.asp
Application Deadline: Jan 2

Ohio State Univ., College of Medicine
Admissions Committee, 209 Meiling Hall
370 West Ninth Avenue
Columbus, OH 43210-1238
(614) 292-7137; (614) 292-1544 (fax)
e-mail: medicine@osu.edu
http://medicine.osu.edu/futurestudents/index.cfm
Application Deadline: Nov 1

University of Cincinnati College of Medicine
Office of Student Affairs/Admissions
P.O. Box 670552
Cincinnati, OH 45267-0552
(513) 558-7314; (513) 558-1165 (fax)
e-mail: comadmis@uc.edu
www.med.uc.edu/admissions
Application Deadline: Nov 15

Wright State University School of Medicine
Office of Admissions
P.O. Box 1751
Dayton, OH 45401
(937) 775-2934; (937) 775-3322 (fax)
e-mail: som_saa@wright.edu
www.med.wright.edu/admiss
Application Deadline: Nov 15

OKLAHOMA

Oklahoma State Univ. Center for Health Sciences College of Osteopathic Medicine
Admissions Office
1111 West 17th Street
Tulsa, OK 74107
(800) 677-1972; (918) 561-8421
(918) 561-8243 (fax)
e-mail: admissions@chs.okstate.edu
www.aacom.org/colleges/osucom.asp
Application Deadline: Feb 1

University of Oklahoma College of Medicine
P.O. Box 26901
Oklahoma City, OK 73190
(405) 271-2331; (405) 271-3032 (fax)
e-mail: adminmed@ouhsc.edu
www.medicine.ouhsc.edu
Application Deadline: Oct 15

OREGON

Oregon Health & Science Univ., School of Medicine
Office of Education Student Affairs, L102
3181 S.W. Sam Jackson Park Road
Portland, OR 97201
(503) 494-2998; (503) 494-3400 (fax)
www.ohsu.edu/som/dean/md/admissions
Application Deadline: Oct 15

PENNSYLVANIA

Drexel University College of Medicine
Admission Office
2900 Queen Lane Avenue
Philadelphia, PA 19129
(215) 991-8202; (215) 843-1766 (fax)
e-mail: medadmis@drexel.edu
www.drexel.edu/med/students
Application Deadline: Dec 1

Jefferson Medical College
Associate Director for Admissions
1015 Walnut Street, 110 Curtis Building
Philadelphia, PA 19107-5083
(215) 955-6983; (215) 955-5151 (fax)
e-mail: JMC.admissions@mail.tju.edu
www.tju.edu/jmc/admissions/home/index.cfm
Application Deadline: Nov 15

Lake Erie College of Osteopathic Medicine
Office of Admissions
1858 West Grandview Boulevard
Erie, PA 16509-1025
(814) 866-6641; (814) 866-8123 (fax)
e-mail: admissions@lecom.edu
www.aacom.org/colleges/lecom.asp
Application Deadline: Feb 1

Pennsylvania State Univ., College of Medicine
Office of Student Affairs, H060
500 University Dr., P.O. Box 850
Hershey, PA 17033
(717) 531-8755; (717) 531-6225 (fax)
e-mail: StudentAffairs@hmc.psu.edu
www.hmc.psu.edu/md/admissions
Application Deadline: Nov 15

Philadelphia College of Osteopathic Medicine
Office of Admissions
Associate Vice President for Enrollment Management
4170 City Avenue
Philadelphia, PA 19131
(800) 999-6998; (215) 871-6719 (fax)
e-mail: admissions@pcom.edu
www.aacom.org/colleges/pcom.asp
Application Deadline: Feb 1

Temple University School of Medicine
Office of Admission
Suite 305, Student Faculty Center
3340 N. Broad Street
Philadelphia, PA 19140
(215) 707-3656; (215) 707-6932 (fax)
e-mail: tusadm@blue.temple.edu
www.medschool.temple.edu/Main/Prospective_Students.html
Application Deadline: Dec 15

University of Pennsylvania School of Medicine
Office of Admissions and Financial Aid
Edward J. Stemmler Hall, Suite 100
Philadelphia, PA 19104-6056
(215) 898-8001; (215) 573-6645 (fax)
e-mail: admiss@mail.med.upenn.edu
www.med.upenn.edu/admiss
Application Deadline: Oct 15

University of Pittsburgh School of Medicine
Office of Admissions
518 Scaife Hall
3550 Terrace Street
Pittsburgh, PA 15261
(412) 648-9891; (412) 648-8768 (fax)
e-mail: linda@medschool.pitt.edu
www.dean-med.pitt.edu/bulletin/tableofcontent.html
Application Deadline: Dec 1

PUERTO RICO

Ponce School of Medicine
Admissions Office
P.O. Box 7004
Ponce, PR 00732
(809) 840-2511; (809) 844-3685 (fax)
e-mail: admissions@psm.edu
www.psm.edu
Application Deadline: Dec 15

Universidad Central Del Caribe School of Medicine
Office of Admissions
P.O. Box 60-327
Bayamón, PR 00960-6032
(787) 740-1611, ext. 210/211
(787) 269-7550 (fax)
e-mail: icordero@uccaribe.edu
www.uccaribe.edu
Application Deadline: Dec 15

University of Puerto Rico School of Medicine
Central Office of Admissions–Medicine
Medical Sciences Campus
P.O. Box 365067
San Juan, PR 00936-5067
(809) 758-2525, ext. 5213/5211/5215
(809) 282-7117 (fax)
e-mail: marrivera@rcm.upr.edu
http://medweb.rcm.upr.edu/admissions.php
Application Deadline: Dec 1

RHODE ISLAND

Brown University School of Medicine
Office of Admissions and Financial Aid
97 Waterman Street, Box G-A 212
Providence, RI 02912-9706
(401) 863-2149; (401) 863-3801 (fax)
e-mail: MedSchool_Admissions@brown.edu
http://bms.brown.edu/admissions
Application Deadline: Mar 18 (B.S.-M.D. program)

SOUTH CAROLINA

Medical Univ. of South Carolina, College of Medicine
Office of Enrollment Services
41 Bee Street
P.O. Box 250203
Charleston, SC 29425-0203
(843) 792-3281; (843) 792-3764 (fax)
e-mail: vanpeltd@musc.edu
www2.musc.edu/COM/Med_Student_Edu_Head.htm
Application Deadline: Dec 1

Univ. of South Carolina School of Medicine
Office of Admissions
Columbia, SC 29208
(803) 733-3325; (803) 733-3328 (fax)
e-mail: mills@med.sc.edu
www.med.sc.edu
Application Deadline: Dec 1

SOUTH DAKOTA

University of South Dakota School of Medicine
Office of Student Affairs, Room 105
414 E. Clark Street
Vermillion, SD 57069-2390
(605) 677-5233; (605) 677-5109 (fax)
e-mail: usdsmsa@usd.edu
http://med.usd.edu/md
Application Deadline: Nov 15

TENNESSEE

East Tennessee State University, James H. Quillen College of Medicine
Office of Student Affairs
P.O. Box 70580
Johnson City, TN 37614-1780
(423) 439-2033; (423) 439-2110 (fax)
e-mail: sacom@etsu.edu
http://qcom.etsu.edu/sacom
Application Deadline: Dec 1

Meharry Medical College School of Medicine
Director of Admissions
1005 Dr. D. B. Todd Jr. Boulevard
Nashville, TN 37208-3599
(615) 327-6223; (615) 327-6228 (fax)
e-mail: admissions@mmc.edu
www.mmc.edu/medschool/Admin/Admission.htm
Application Deadline: Dec 15

University of Tennessee College of Medicine
790 Madison Avenue
Randolph Hall, 3rd Floor
Memphis, TN 38163-2166
(901) 448-5559; (901) 448-1740 (fax)
e-mail: diharris@utmem.edu
www.utmem.edu/com_admissions
Application Deadline: Nov 15

Vanderbilt School of Medicine
Office of Admissions
215 Light Hall
Nashville, TN 37232-0685
(615) 322-2145; (615) 343-8397 (fax)
e-mail: medsch.admis@mcmail.vanderbilt.edu
www.mc.vanderbilt.edu/medschool/admissions/index.php
Application Deadline: Oct 15

TEXAS

Baylor College of Medicine
Office of Admissions
One Baylor Plaza, Room N104
Houston, TX 77030
(713) 798-4841
e-mail: melodym@bcm.tmc.edu
www.bcm.tmc.edu/education-admissions.html
Application Deadline: Nov 1

Texas A&M University College of Medicine
Assistant Dean for Admissions
Office of Student Affairs and Admissions
159 Joe H. Reynolds Medical Building
College Station, TX 77843-1114
(409) 845-7743; (409) 847-8663 (fax)
e-mail: Med-Stu-Aff@tamu.edu
http://medicine.tamu.edu
Application Deadline: Nov 1

Texas Tech University School of Medicine
Office of Admissions
Health Sciences Center
Lubbock, TX 79430
(806) 743-2297
e-mail: amanda.mcsween@ttuhsc.edu
www.ttuhsc.edu/SOM/Admissions/default.htm
Application Deadline: Nov 1

Univ. of North Texas College of Osteopathic Medicine
Office of Medical Student Admissions
3500 Camp Bowie Boulevard
Fort Worth, TX 76107-2699
(800) 535-8266; (817) 735-2204
(817) 735-2225 (fax)
e-mail: TCOMAdmissions@hsc.unt.edu
www.hsc.unt.edu/education/tcom/Admissions.cfm
Application Deadline: Nov 1

Univ. of Texas Health Science Center at San Antonio
Mail Code 7702
Medical Admissions/Registrar's Office
7703 Floyd Curl Drive
San Antonio, TX 78229-3900
(210) 567-6080; (210) 567-2685 (fax)
e-mail: msprospect@uthscsa.edu
http://som.uthscsa.edu/Information.html
Application Deadline: Oct 15

Univ. of Texas Medical School at Galveston
Office of Admissions
301 University Boulevard
Galveston, TX 77555-1317
(409) 772-3517; (409) 747-2909 (fax)
e-mail: smcarrol@utmb.edu
www.som.utmb.edu/Newcomers.htm
Application Deadline: Nov 1

Univ. of Texas Medical School at Houston
Office of Admissions
6431 Fannin, MSB 1.126
Houston, TX 77030
(713) 500-5116; (713) 500-0604 (fax)
e-mail: msadmissions@uth.tmc.edu
www.med.uth.tmc.edu
Application Deadline: Nov 1

University of Texas, Southwestern
Admissions Office
5323 Harry Hines Boulevard
Dallas, TX 75390-9162
(214) 648-5617; (214) 648-3289 (fax)
e-mail: admissions@utsouthwester.edu
www8.utsouthwestern.edu/utsw/ada/dept21170
Application Deadline: Nov 1

UTAH

University of Utah School of Medicine
Office of Admissions
30 N. 1900 E. #1C029
Salt Lake City, UT 84132-2101
(801) 581-7498; (801) 581-2931 (fax)
e-mail: deans.admissions@hsc.utah.edu
www.med.utah.edu/som
Application Deadline: Oct 15

VERMONT

University of Vermont College of Medicine
Office of Admissions
E-215 Given Building
89 Beaumont Avenue
Burlington, VT 05405
(802) 656-2154; (802) 656-8577 (fax)
e-mail: MedAdmissions@uvm.edu
www.med.uvm.edu/TB1+BL+I+C.asp?SiteAreaID=198
Application Deadline: Nov 1

VIRGINIA

Eastern Virginia Medical School
Office of Admissions
721 Fairfax Avenue
Norfolk, VA 23507-2000
(757) 446-5812; (757) 446-5896 (fax)
e-mail: reedtp@evms.edu
www.evms.edu/education/index.html
Application Deadline: Nov 15

Edward Via Virginia College of Osteopathic Medicine
Office of Admissions
2265 Kraft Drive
Blacksburg, VA 24060
(888) 818-5203; (540) 443-9106
e-mail: admissions@evvcom
www.aacom.org/colleges/vcom.asp
Application Deadline: Mar 1

Medical College of Virginia
Medical School Admissions
MCV Station Box 980565
Richmond, VA 23298-0565
(804) 828-9629; (804) 828-1246 (fax)
e-mail: awalker@vcu.edu
www.medschool.vcu.edu
Application Deadline: Nov 15

University of Virginia School of Medicine
Admissions Office, UVA Health System
P.O. Box 800725
Charlottesville, VA 22908
(434) 924-5571; (434) 982-2586 (fax)
e-mail: medsch-adm@virginia.edu
www.healthsystem.virginia.edu/internet/admissions
Application Deadline: Nov 1

WASHINGTON

University of Washington School of Medicine
Office of Admissions
A-300 Health Sciences Center, Box 356340
Seattle, WA 98195-6340
(206) 543-7212
e-mail: askuwsom@u.washington.edu
www.washington.edu/medicine/som
Application Deadline: Nov 1

WEST VIRGINIA

Marshall University Joan C. Edwards School of Medicine
Admissions Office, Suite 3400
1600 Medical Center Drive
Huntington, WV 25701
(800) 544-8514; (304) 691-1738
(304) 691-1744 (fax)
e-mail: warren@marshall.edu
http://musom.marshall.edu/admiss
Application Deadline: Nov 15

West Virginia School of Osteopathic Medicine
Office of Admissions
400 N. Lee Street
Lewisburg, WV 24901
(800) 356-7836; (304) 645-6270
(304) 645-4859 (fax)
e-mail: admissions@wvsom.edu
www.aacom.org/colleges/wvsom.asp
Application Deadline: Feb 15

West Virginia University School of Medicine
Office of Admissions and Records
Health Sciences Center
P.O. Box 9815
Morgantown, WV 26506
(304) 293-3521; (304) 293-7968 (fax)
e-mail: Medadmissions@hsc.wvu.edu
www.hsc.wvu.edu/som/NewSOM/mddegree.asp
Application Deadline: Nov 15

WISCONSIN

Medical College of Wisconsin
Office of Admissions
8701 Watertown Plank Road
Milwaukee, WI 53226
(414) 456-8246
e-mail: medschool@mcw.edu
www.mcw.edu/acad/admission
Application Deadline: Nov 1

University of Wisconsin Medical School
Admission Committee
Medical Sciences Center, Room 1250
1300 University Avenue
Madison, WI 53706
(608) 263-4925; (608) 262-2327 (fax)
e-mail: jwaisman@facstaff.wisc.edu
www.med.wisc.edu/Education/Programs/MD/Admissions
Application Deadline: Nov 15

CANADA

ALBERTA

University of Alberta Faculty of Medicine
Admissions Officer
2-45 Medical Sciences Building
Edmonton, Alberta, CANADA T6G 2H7
(780) 492-6350; (780) 492-9531 (fax)
e-mail: admissions@med.ualberta.ca
www.med.ualberta.ca/ugme
Application Deadline: Nov 1

University of Calgary Faculty of Medicine
Office of Admissions
G302 Health Sciences Centre
3330 Hospital Drive, N.W.
Calgary, Alberta, CANADA T2N 4N1
(403) 220-4262; (403) 270-2681 (fax)
e-mail: staylor@ucalgary.ca
www.med.ucalgary.ca/admissions
Application Deadline: Nov 15

BRITISH COLUMBIA

Univ. of British Columbia Faculty of Medicine
Office of the Dean, Admissions Office
317-2194 Health Sciences Mall
Vancouver, British Columbia, CANADA V6T 1Z3
(604) 822-4482; (604) 822-6061 (fax)
e-mail: admissions.md@ubc.ca
www.med.ubc.ca/md
Application Deadline: Oct 1

MANITOBA

University of Manitoba Faculty of Medicine
Assistant Dean for Admissions
753 McDermot Avenue, Room S-204
Winnipeg, Manitoba, CANADA R3E 0W3
(204) 789-3499; (204) 789-3929 (fax)
e-mail: registrar_med@umanitoba.ca
www.umanitoba.ca/faculties/medicine/admissions
Application Deadline: Nov 15

NEWFOUNDLAND

Memorial Univ. of Newfoundland Faculty of Medicine
Admissions Office
Room 1751, Health Sciences Centre
St. John's, Newfoundland, CANADA A1B 3V6
(709) 737-6615; (709) 737-8422 (fax)
e-mail: munmed@mun.ca
www.med.mun.ca/admissions/welcome.asp
Application Deadline: Oct 15

NOVA SCOTIA

Dalhousie University Faculty of Medicine
Director of Admissions and Student Affairs
Room C-132, Clinical Research Centre
5849 University Avenue
Halifax, Nova Scotia, CANADA B3H 4H7
(902) 494-1874; (902) 494-6369 (fax)
e-mail: medicine.admissions@dal.ca
www.medicine.dal.ca/admissions/application.htm
Application Deadline: Nov 31

ONTARIO

McMaster University School of Medicine
M.D. Admissions Office, HSC 1M7
1200 Main Street West
Hamilton, Ontario, CANADA L8N 3Z5
(905) 525-9140, ext. 22235; (905) 546-0349 (fax)
e-mail: mdadmit@mcmaster.ca
www-fhs.mcmaster.ca/education
Application Deadline: Oct 15

Queen's University School of Medicine
Admission Office
68 Barrie Street
Kingston, Ontario, CANADA K7L 3N6
(613) 545-2542; (613) 545-3190 (fax)
e-mail: jeb8@post.queensu.ca
http://meds-ss10.meds.queensu.ca/medicine
Application Deadline: Oct 15

University of Ottawa Faculty of Medicine
Admissions
451 Smyth Road
Ottawa, Ontario, CANADA K1H 8M5
(613) 562-5700; (613) 562-5323 (fax)
e-mail: admissio@uottawa.ca
www.uottawa.ca/academic/med
Application Deadline: Oct 15

University of Toronto Faculty of Medicine
Admissions
Medical Sciences Building, Room 2135
1 King's College Circle
Toronto, Ontario, CANADA M5S 1A8
(416) 978-2717; (416) 971-2163 (fax)
e-mail: ld.taylor@utoronto.ca
www.library.utoronto.ca/medicine
Application Deadline: Oct 15

Univ. of Western Ontario Faculty of Medicine & Dentistry
Admissions/Student & Equity Affairs
Medical Sciences Building
London, Ontario, CANADA N6A 5C1
(519) 661-3744; (519) 661-3797 (fax)
e-mail: admissions@fmd.uwo.ca
www.med.uwo.ca/admissions/index.asp
Application Deadline: Oct 15

QUEBEC

Université Laval Faculty of Medicine
Secretary, Admission Committee
Ste-Foy, Quebec, CANADA G1K 7P4
(418) 646-2492; (418) 646-2733 (fax)
e-mail: admission@fmed.ulaval.ca
www.fmed.ulaval.ca/fmed/fmed.html
Application Deadlines: Mar 1 (Canadians), Feb 1 (non-Canadians)

McGill University Faculty of Medicine
Admissions Office
3655 Promenade Sir William Osler, Room 633
Montreal, Quebec, CANADA H3G 1Y6
(514) 398-3517; (514) 398-4631 (fax)
e-mail: admissions.med@mcgill.ca
www.medicine.mcgill.ca/admissions
Application Deadlines: Nov 15 (out of province), Jan 15 (Quebec-resident applicants to 4-year program), Mar 1 (Quebec-resident applicants to 5-year program)

Université de Montréal Faculty of Medicine
Committee on Admission
P.O. Box 6128, Station Centre-Ville
Montreal, Quebec, CANADA H3C 3J7
(514) 343-6265; (514) 343-6629 (fax)
e-mail: admmed@ere.umontreal.ca
www.med.umontreal.ca/contenu/etudes/admission.html
Application Deadline: Mar 1

University of Sherbrooke Faculty of Medicine
Admission Office
Sherbrooke, Quebec, CANADA J1H 5N4
(819) 564-5208; (819) 564-5378 (fax)
e-mail: Admission.medicine@USherbrooke.ca
www.usherbrooke.ca
Application Deadline: Mar 1

SASKATCHEWAN

University of Saskatchewan College of Medicine
Admissions, Health Sciences Building
107 Wiggins Road
Saskatoon, Saskatchewan, CANADA S7N 5E5
(306) 966-8554; (306) 966-6164 (fax)
e-mail: med.admissions@usask.ca
www.usask.ca/medicine
Application Deadlines: Dec 1 (out of province), Jan 15 (in province)

Annotated Bibliography*

Some books are to be tasted, others to be swallowed,
and some few to be chewed and digested . . .

— Sir Francis Bacon, *Essays: Of Studies*

History (and Future) of Medicine

Committee on Quality of Health Care in America, Institute of Medicine. *Crossing the Quality Chasm: A New Health System for the 21st Century.* Washington, D.C.: National Academies Press, 2001. This book recommends a sweeping redesign of the American health care system and provides overarching principles for policymakers, health care leaders, clinicians, and others. Includes a set of performance expectations for the 21st-century health care system, ten rules to guide patient-clinician relationships, and steps to promote evidence-based practice. Available for purchase; also downloadable for free at www.nap.edu/books/0309072808/html.

Conrad LI, Neve M, Nutton V, et al. *The Western Medical Tradition: 800 BC to AD 1800.* Cambridge: Cambridge Univ. Press, 1995. The quintessential survey of Western medicine from the Greeks through the 1800s. Century by century, it describes once-common diseases, medical theories and therapies, religious and alternative healing, and the major scientific advances in medicine, surgery, and pharmacology. One of the most extensively researched and well-written medical histories available. (+)

Gevitz N. *Other Healers: Unorthodox Medicine in America.* Baltimore, MD: Johns Hopkins Univ. Press, 1988. Who else practices medicine? Botanists, chiropractors, Christian Scientists, folk healers, homeopaths, divine healers, and naturopaths, among others—that's who. This book describes what they do and how they affect patient care, and opens the door to the "other side" of medicine—a door that traditional physicians wonder about, but rarely enter. (+)

Kaiser Family Foundation. *National Survey of Physicians. Part III: Doctors' Opinions about Their Profession.* March 2002. (www.kff.org/content/2002/20020426c/PhysicianSurveypartIII.pdf) This survey of physicians' morale reveals what doctors today really think about their calling, how attitudes have changed over the past two decades, and whether they would recommend medicine as a profession. The short survey (3 pages plus 9 pages of charts) also reviews what physicians think about the health care system.

Nuland SB. *Doctors: The Biography of Medicine.* New York: Vintage, 1989. Medicine's great men were neither all perfect nor all men. This "warts and all" account of medicine's pioneers demonstrates their insightfulness and leadership, as well as their fears and failings. Was Semmelweis a genius or an egomaniac? And how did Taussig beat down resistance to her findings? This book rubs the patina off the schoolbook histories, demonstrating that real people were behind medicine's most important advances. (+)

Rothman DJ, Marcus S, Kiceluk SA, eds. *Medicine and Western Civilization.* New Brunswick, NJ: Rutgers Univ. Press, 1995. This comprehensive anthology depicts medicine's effect on society. Among the selections are excerpts from the Old Testament, classical Greek texts, eyewitness accounts of public anatomies (dissections), medieval treatises on witchcraft, and modern debates over brain death. Authors include Hippocrates, Galen, Vesalius, Pasteur, Koch, Freud, Plato, Frances Burney, and George Orwell. (+)

Thomas L. *The Youngest Science: Notes of a Medicine-Watcher.* New York: Penguin, 1995. A second-generation physician and former director of the Sloan Kettering Cancer Institute, Dr. Thomas poetically describes the basis for the changes in medicine from the time when his father made house calls, but had little to offer in the way of cures or effective therapy, to the technological present.

Weisse AB. *Medical Odysseys: The Different & Sometimes Unexpected Pathways to Twentieth-Century Medical Discoveries.* New Brunswick, NJ: Rutgers Univ. Press, 1991. This intriguing book looks at the stories and personalities of the researchers and patients who stumbled upon some of modern medicine's miraculous cures. Learn how a sausage manufacturer and a Ford dealer helped create the first successful artificial kidney machine,

*References marked with a plus (+) can be obtained through *The Galen Press Catalog*, at www.galenpress.com, or at P.O. Box 64400, Tucson, AZ 85728-4400; (800) 442-5369; fax: (520) 529-6459.

and how a Renaissance alchemist's fascination with mercury and a physician's concern with syphilis led to the first effective treatment for congestive heart failure. (+)

Medicine in Fiction

Lewis S. *Arrowsmith*. New York: Penguin, 1924. The tale of Martin Arrowsmith illustrates how a young doctor's devotion to science can allow medicine to become his life. Forced to give up successive sinecures—instructor in medicine, small-town doctor, research pathologist—by obstacles ranging from public ignorance to the publicity-mindedness of a great foundation, Arrowsmith becomes virtually isolated as a seeker-after-truth. Although written in the preantibiotic era, the issues remain as current today as they were then. (+)

Reynolds R, Stone J, eds. *On Doctoring: Stories, Poems, Essays*. New York: Simon & Schuster, 1995. The humanity of medicine has inspired countless writers. The selections in this anthology range from John Donne's classic "Death Be Not Proud" to Linda Pastan's delightfully wry account of giving birth in "Notes from the Delivery Room." At a time when medicine is becoming more technical and institutionalized, this book captures the breadth and wonder of the medical profession, reminding us what it is really all about. (+)

Schiedermayer D. *House Calls, Rounds, and Healings: A Poetry Casebook*. Tucson, AZ: Galen Press, 1996. A poignant look at how physicians treat patients in many settings. Written by a practicing internist with worldwide experiences, each poem is a case study of a patient or colleague. This book captures the insights and feelings that many physicians experience but cannot express. (+)

Selzer R. *Letters to a Young Doctor*. New York: Touchstone Books, 1982. Written by modern medicine's principal essayist, this book leads the reader on an amazing journey through the world of patients, physicians, and families, with an insight and sensitivity rarely found in medical literature. Contains "Imelda," the best medical essay by any current writer.

Periodicals, Journals, and Websites

Academic Medicine. The Association of American Medical College's journal contains articles about medical education, including entry into medical school, MCAT examinations, medical school curricular changes, and residency training. Offers some of the most up-to-date information available. All medical school libraries subscribe to it.

AOA Yearbook and Directory of Members. (www.aoa-net.org/Publications/yearbooktoc.htm) An online directory of Osteopathic physicians run by the American Osteopathic Association, and searchable by state. Also has information on specialty societies; a glossary of terms; training, licensure, and certification requirements; and more.

Caduceus Newsletter. (www.cbu.edu/~seisen/Caduceus.html) Created by a director of a preprofessional health program, this free, web-based newsletter is sent weekly during the academic year to students interested in health-related careers and their advisers. It contains information on scholarships, internships, summer programs, and health-related news updates. Back issues are archived on the website.

JAMA (Journal of the American Medical Association). The most widely read of all medical journals, this magazine contains not only research articles, but also information on medical student and resident education, governmental interactions with medical practice, and other articles that will give you an insight into how physicians think and feel. Available at most public libraries and all medical libraries.

Journal of the American Osteopathic Association. Similar to *JAMA*, this journal is produced by the Osteopathic side of the profession. A little more difficult to obtain, it is often easier to understand than some of the other medical journals. Available in libraries in areas where Osteopathic physicians practice, and in all medical libraries.

MedConnect. (www.medconnect.com) A free online monthly newspaper that includes articles describing both the science and the business of all fields in medicine. It also includes clinical cases. An excellent source to get an overview of the profession, hear about the latest developments, and find out what is coming in the next few years.

New England Journal of Medicine. The *New York Times* of clinical medicine, it contains "everything that's fit to print" for the clinician. Other clinical journals get the leftovers. Many of the research articles will be beyond most people's understanding or interest, but the case discussions are often fascinating. Reading the topic reviews is great practice for the Verbal Reasoning section of the MCAT. Available in nearly every library.

The New Physician. Published monthly and free with membership in the American Medical Student Association. This journal has frequent articles about medical specialties, interviewing, the Match, international medical graduates, medical practice, and other topics of vital interest to medical students.

Physician's Weekly. (www.physweekly.com) Another free online newspaper that includes articles describing both the science and business of all fields in medicine. An excellent source to get an overview of the profession, hear about the latest developments, and get a picture of what is coming in the next few years.

Selecting a Specialty

American Board of Internal Medicine's website (www.abim.org/info/dynamic.htm) contains a wealth of statistics about internists and internal medicine. From the folks that bring you the specialty examination for Internists, the site contains ABIM examination data, ABIM diplomates by state and worldwide, and workforce trends. Definitely worth looking over if you are considering internal medicine or one of its subspecialties

American Medical Association. "The future of . . ." series, developed by experts in each field, ran in *JAMA* in the late 1980s and in 1990. The articles still contain valuable information about some of the anticipated changes in the specialties. The citation for each specialty is listed below.

Adult Cardiology. *JAMA*. 1989;262(20):2874-8.
Family Practice. *JAMA*. 1988;260(9):1272-9.
General Internal Medicine. *JAMA*. 1989;262(15):2119-24.
General Surgery. *JAMA*. 1989;262(22):3178-83.
Obstetrics & Gynecology. *JAMA*. 1987;258(24):3547-53.
Pathology. *JAMA*. 1987;258(3):370-7.
Pediatrics. *JAMA*. 1989;261(19):2874-5.
Psychiatry. *JAMA*. 1990;264(19):2542-8.

Association of American Medical Schools' Careers in Medicine website (www.aamc.org/students/cim/specialties .htm) offers basic information about a variety of specialties, with links to webpages for further information.

Bosk CL. *Forgive and Remember: Managing Medical Failure*. 2nd ed. Chicago: Univ. of Chicago Press, 2003. Students and residents make mistakes, some serious and some even fatal. Which mistakes do professors "forgive" but remember? Which cannot be passed over? This classic book still provides the most important description available of surgical education. Bosk, who followed two surgical teams at one of the nation's leading medical schools, describes the surgical culture and mores that students and residents must understand to succeed. (+)

Burack JH, Irby DM, Carline JD, et al. A study of medical students' specialty-choice pathways: trying on possible selves. *Acad Med*. 1997;72(6):534-41. Are you thinking about a primary care specialty? This paper describes factors that previous students considered important when either entering or rejecting a primary care career. No doubt you will recognize yourself in some of these vignettes.

Colen BD. *O.R.: The True Story of 24 Hours in a Hospital Operating Room*. New York: Signet, 1994. So, what is the O.R. really like? In this minute-by-minute true account of 24 hours in a busy hospital, Pulitzer Prize-winner B. D. Colen vividly portrays the mysterious world of the operating room from multiple perspectives, where specialized teams perform scores of medical procedures. Read this fascinating book if you are considering a career in the O.R. (+)

Companion Disk for Iserson's Getting Into A Residency. Tucson, AZ: Galen Press, Ltd., 1996. This software makes *Iserson's Getting Into A Residency* easier to use. The program customizes, prints, and does the necessary calculations for the "Personal Trait Analysis, Synthesis, and Correlation of Traits," "Must/Want" Analysis, "Requirements for Application to Programs," and "Interview Notes." (+)

DeLisa JA, Leonard JA Jr, Smith BS, Kirshblum S. Common questions asked by medical students about Physiatry. *Am J Phys Med Rehabil*. 1995;74(2):145-54. The authors answer all common questions and correct the misunderstandings about Physical Medicine and Rehabilitation. Well worth reading.

Gabram SGA; Hoenig J; Schroeder JW, Jr; Mansour A; Gamelli R. What are the primary concerns of recently graduated surgeons and how do they differ from those of the residency training years? *Arch Surg*. 2001;136:1109-14. This article details the frustrations and concerns you are likely face if you enter a Surgical residency. The authors suggest that residents should receive greater assistance and mentoring during the residency years so that concerns with career planning, financial issues, job selection, and the availability of role models after graduation would be diminished.

Iserson KV. *Iserson's Getting Into A Residency: A Guide for Medical Students*. 6th ed. Tucson, AZ: Galen Press, Ltd., 2003. This book is the standard for selecting a specialty, picking your ideal residency programs, going through the residency matching process, and having the best chance of getting the residency position you want. It includes everything you need to know about the process, beginning with entry into medical school through the preclinical and clinical years, and culminating with the all-important interviews and matching programs. (+)

JAMA. Contempo Issue. This annual issue, usually available in July, contains articles describing the latest issues and developments in many medical specialties. Written by leaders in their fields, the articles provide insights into changes that will occur within the specialties and within the entire medical profession. Individual copies can be purchased from Customer Services at the American Medical Association.

National Medicine–Pediatric Residents' Association (NMPRA) (www.medpeds.org). A resident-driven organization dedicated to providing information, listing job opportunities, and providing links to combined Internal Medicine–Pediatrics programs for current and future med-peds residents.

Saketkhoo DD, Sunshine JH, Covey AM, Forman HP. Findings in 2002 from a help wanted index of job advertisements: is the job-market shortage of diagnostic radiologists easing? *Am J Roentgenol.* 2003;181(2):351-7. The demand for diagnostic radiologists nationwide appears to have stabilized during 2002, albeit at a level much higher than in previous years, and may be decreasing.

Scherger JE, Beasley JW, Rodney WM, et al. Responses to questions by medical students about family practice. *J Fam Prac.* 1988;26(2):169-76. A list of the most commonly asked questions about the specialty of Family Practice, with somewhat optimistic answers. The list of questions itself should stimulate a lot of thought, and is enough to recommend the article to anyone with an interest in this field.

Wiest FC, Ferris TG, Gokhale M, et al. Preparedness of internal medicine and family practice residents for treating common conditions. *JAMA* 2002;288:2609-14. A comparison of Internal Medicine and Family Practice residents' self-perceived preparedness to manage common adult conditions. The reported differences are consistent with the trainings' emphasis on an inpatient setting for IM residents and on office-based care for FP residents.

MCAT Preparation

Association of American Medical Colleges. *MCAT Student Manual.* Washington, DC: AAMC 2003. (www.aamc.org/students/mcat/studentmanual/start.htm) This basic study-guide for the MCAT is free and can be downloaded or read in sections on the AAMC website. It contains outlines of each section's topics, hints on how to prepare, and sample questions.

—*MCAT Practice Tests.* (www.aamc.org/students/mcat) Invaluable study aids for the MCAT, these practice tests are available online or in paper versions. One full-length test is free online; the rest can be purchased through the AAMC. The tests are updated to reflect all content, format, and scoring changes to the 2003 MCAT.

Flowers JL, Silver T. *The Princeton Review: Flowers & Silver MCAT with CD-ROM.* (latest edition) New York: Random House. A review of the required topics in the physical and biological sciences presented through sample problems, labeled illustrations, charts, and diagrams

—*The Princeton Review Flowers & Silver Practice MCATs.* (latest edition) New York: Random House. Two simulated tests with answer explanations. Also included is an introductory section that orients you to the MCAT and teaches you ways to approach all types of test questions.

McGaghie WC. Assessing readiness for medical education. Evolution of the Medical College Admission Test. *JAMA.* 2002;288(9):1085-90. Describes the history of the test from its inception, and the various iterations that led to the present version of the MCAT. Read this and fascinate your fellow premeds with great trivia.

Schaffzin NR. *The Princeton Review Reading Smart: Advanced Techniques for Improved Reading.* New York: Random House, 1994. The key to doing well on the MCAT (as well as in medical school) is to read quickly and understand what you read. Learn techniques such as prereading, pen-marking, and clustering to read faster with better comprehension. Diagnostic exercises let you measure your progress as you speed (hopefully) through the book. An excellent preparation for the MCAT Verbal Reasoning section. (+)

Veloski JJ, Callahan CA, Hojat M, Nash DB. Prediction of students' performance on licensing examinations using age, race, sex, undergraduate GPAs, and MCAT scores. *Acad Med.* 2000;75(10):S28-S30. MCAT scores do correlate nicely with medical school performance. It varies, however, by ethnic background, science and non-science GPAs, and the specific MCAT scores being correlated against various hurdles in a medical career.

Wiley A, Koenig JA. The validity of the Medical College Admission Test for predicting performance in the first two years of medical school. *Acad Med.* 1996;71(10):S83-S85. Surprise! The MCAT really does predict how well medical students will do, both in their grades and on Step 1 of the USMLE. This is a study of the graduating class of 1995 at 14 medical schools.

Résumés and Personal Statements

Jablonski S, ed. *Dictionary of Medical Acronyms & Abbreviations.* 2nd ed. New York: Hanley Belfus, 1993. If you don't know your MDF from your MDE, you need this complete desktop source to decipher medical abbreviations. The pocket-sized book becomes invaluable when misreading an abbreviation might be embarrassing or even dangerous. (+)

Tysinger JW. *Résumés and Personal Statements for Health Professionals.* 2nd ed. Tucson, AZ: Galen Press, Ltd., 1999. An in-depth guide to developing résumés and personal statements that reflect who you really are. This book provides step-by-step instructions to identify and describe your accomplishments to emphasize your strengths. Numerous examples of actual résumés and personal statements designed to impress admission officers. Also details how to write those important cover and thank-you letters. (+)

Venolia J. *Write Right! A Desktop Digest of Punctuation, Grammar, and Style*. 3rd ed. Berkeley, CA: Ten Speed Press, 1995. Do you appear as smart as you really are in your written communication? This book addresses such perennial questions as: Who or whom? That or which? Colon or semicolon? The easy-to-understand format provides a review of punctuation and grammar (with cartoons that help you understand why a sentence is wrong), as well as pointers to improve your writing style. (+)

Medical School

Association of American Medical Colleges. *Curriculum Directory*. (services.aamc.org/currdir) This online directory allows you to search for 125 medical schools and 16 Canadian medical schools by a particular course, educational innovation, whether they require passing the Boards to advance or graduate, research opportunities, grading intervals, required courses, combined-degree programs, and much more. Definitely worth a look as you try to determine to which schools you should apply.

JAMA. Education Issue. This annual issue, usually available in early September, contains the latest information and statistics on medical school and residency education. Besides the statistics, there are many valuable articles describing the latest trends in medical education. Individual copies can be purchased from Customer Services at the American Medical Association.

Klass P. *A Not Entirely Benign Procedure: Four Years as a Medical Student*. New York: Plume, 1987. Perri Klass not only graduated from Harvard Medical School, she wrote about it. This provocative book shows how doctors are really trained. Written from the perspective of a woman and mother in a field dominated by men and masculine sensibilities, Klass describes how she learned to deal with patients, blood, and hospital politics during her clinical years, addressing the fears that medical students feel, yet may be afraid to admit. (+)

Konner M. *Becoming a Doctor: A Journey of Initiation in Medical School*. New York: Penguin, 1987. Not sure what to expect during required clinical rotations? While taking the reader on his "rounds," Dr. Konner candidly and eloquently portrays his hectic, life-changing third year of medical school, when book knowledge comes face-to-face with disease. He asks, "Does this experience adequately train doctors to address medicine's human side?" (+)

Meador CK. *A Little Book of Doctors' Rules*. New York: Hanley Belfus, 1992. Medical school doesn't teach you everything you need to know to be a great doctor. Real life is a better instructor. Dr. Meador's sound advice and truisms such as "Never tell a patient 'Don't worry'," and "The higher the technology, the greater the need for human contact," apply to medical students throughout their careers. (+)

Financial Aid

American Medical Association. *Medical Student Financial Aid Resource Guide*. This free booklet is an excellent source to use to review the financing options available for your medical education. It has a wealth of information, including how to directly contact the agencies responsible for loans and scholarships. Go to www.ama-assn.org and use their search engine with the booklet's title to download this 22-page resource.

Association of American Medical Colleges. *Financial Planning and Management Manual for U.S. Medical Students*. Washington, DC: AAMC, 1994, 45 pp. This easy-to-read booklet explains how to plan a budget for your medical school expenses, manage debt, and go through the financial aid application process, and includes a glossary of terms, suggested reading, and tear-out worksheets. It does not, however, contain information about specific loan or scholarship programs. To order a copy, access the webpage: www.aamc.org/publications/fpm.htm.

—*Financing Your Medical Education.* (www.aamc.org/students/financing/start.htm) Comprehensive financial information for premedical and medical students with links to and information about the major scholarship and loan programs, a searchable database of the financial forms required by each (M.D.) medical school in the United States, a database of some service-based state loans, and a link to the excellent *Monetary Decisions for Medical Doctors* (see below). Nearly all information you need on financing your medical education can be found here.

—*Monetary Decisions for Medical Doctors (MD^2)* (www.aamc.org/students/financing/md2). One of the best sources to use for planning the financial aspects of medical education, this comprehensive program has three sections: (1) Premedical School Years, (2) The Medical School Years, and (3) Residency and Early Practice Years. Unlike many other financial sources, this site has specifically tailored the information to students at each level of their medical education. It includes information about making a successful transition to medical school, credit and consumer debt, types of financial aid, the financial aid application process, and relevant reference materials.

—*State and Other Loan Repayment/Forgiveness and Scholarship Programs*. (www.aamc.org/students/financing/repayment/start.htm). A searchable, state-by-state listing of programs that allow you to repay your student loans, or have them "forgiven," through service. Also includes programs offered by some national organizations and the federal government.

FinAid! (www.finaid.org) An excellent site through which you can access the online FAFSA application and information about completing the form, search for other scholarships and loans, and use their free financial calculators.

Office of Statewide Health Planning and Development, Health Professions Career Opportunity Program (HPCOP). *Financial Advice and Health Careers Resource Directory for Students*. A free 22-page booklet, available online, filled with a lot of good information and practical tips for navigating the financial aid process. An excellent place to get an overview of what will be required, and many ways to simplify the process. Download the document at: www.oshpd.cahwnet.gov/pcrcd/professions/hpcop.htm#publications.

Ramsey PG, Coombs JB, Hunt D, Marshall SG. From concept to culture: the WWAMI program at the University of Washington School of Medicine. *Acad Med*. 2001;76(8):765-75. This program offers selected applicants in the Northwestern United States an excellent method of both financing a medical education and entering a very good medical school. The paper describes the WWAMI program's history, success, and workings.

U.S. Department of Education. *Financial Aid*. (www.ed.gov/finaid.html) This website is an excellent entryway to nationally recognized resources for locating scholarships and loans, the latest information on federal educational financing, answers to common financing questions, and information about managing and consolidating loans. While not specifically geared toward medical students, its frequent updates and comprehensive information make it worth a visit.

—*The Student Guide*. Washington, DC: Federal Student Aid Information Center. Free. Revised annually. (studentaid.ed.gov/students/publications/student_guide/index.html) While not all of the listed programs apply to medical students, the booklet does contain up-to-date information about some federal aid programs, including Pell Grants, Federal Direct Loans, Federal Family Education Loans (FFEL), Federal Supplemental Educational Opportunity Grants (FSEOG), Federal Work-Study (FWS), and Federal Perkins Loans. Download for free or, for a paper copy, call 1-800-4FED-AID (1-800-433-3243) or write to U.S. Government Printing Office, Washington, DC 20402, or Federal Student Aid Information Center, P.O. Box 84, Washington, DC 20044-0084.

Osteopathic Medicine

American Association of Colleges of Osteopathic Medicine. *Osteopathic Medical College Information Book*. Rockville, MD: AACOM. (Annual; free) The official list of approved U.S. Osteopathic (D.O.-granting) medical schools. It describes each school's facilities, affiliations, entrance requirements, curriculum, special programs, admission procedures, class size, tuition and fees, and contact information. The same information is available on the Web (www.aacom.org) and on the "AACOMAS By Computer" program.

American Osteopathic Association, Division of Postdoctoral Training. Osteopathic graduate medical education. *J Am Osteopath Assoc*. (each November) This annual article provides an overview of the number of available AOA-approved and funded residency positions, the number of graduates, how many D.O.'s are taking ACGME-approved training, and new rules for specialty certification.

Gevitz N. *The D.O.'s: Osteopathic Medicine in America*. Baltimore, MD: Johns Hopkins Univ. Press, 1982. Where did Osteopathic medicine, "the other" medical degree, come from? Who are Osteopathic physicians? What is their training, history, and culture? This book must be read by anyone considering this field. (+)

Johnson SM, Kurtz ME. Diminished use of Osteopathic manipulative treatment and its impact on the uniqueness of the Osteopathic profession. *Acad Med*. 2001;76(8):821-828. Is OMT still being used? By whom and to what extent? This paper lays it all out.

Singer AM. *Debt, Career Plans, and Opinions of Osteopathic Medical Students in 2001*. Rockville, MD: AACOM, 2001. One of the few sources for this type of hard data on Osteopathic medical schools, students, and finances. Also includes the seniors' evaluations and comments on the quality of training they received. Well worth a look. Download or order a paper copy of this report at www.aacom.org/data/studentreport.

Admission and Applications

American Association of Colleges of Osteopathic Medicine. *Osteopathic Medical College Information Book*. Rockville, MD: AACOM. (Annual, free) The official list of approved U.S. Osteopathic (D.O.-granting) medical schools. Available on the Web (www.aacom.org) and on the "AACOMAS By Computer" program.

Association of American Medical Colleges. *Medical School Admission Requirements, United States and Canada*. (Annual) The most up-to-date information on application procedures and deadlines, tuition and student fees, and acceptance rates from every accredited medical school in the United States and Canada. For people who are just thinking about medicine as a career, there is an overview of the entire application and medical school process, with a timeline to help you get started. Order online at www.aamc.org/publications/ar04.htm.

Association of Canadian Medical Colleges. *Admission Requirements of Canadian Faculties of Medicine*. (Annual) This publication is similar to the AAMC's book, but smaller—since it only includes Canadian medical schools. Order online at www.acmc.ca/forms/order.html or at (613) 730-0687; fax: (613) 730-1196.

High School Students

Cassidy DJ. *The Scholarship Book 2003: The Complete Guide to Private-Sector Scholarships, Grants, and Loans for Undergraduates*. Paramus, NJ: Prentice-Hall, 2002. Describes scholarships awarded by foundations, associations, corporations, unions, and fraternal organizations. Includes indexes by major fields of study and scholarship name, and a Quick Find index for state of residence, ethnic background, physical handicap, and state of intended study.

Office of Statewide Health Planning and Development. Health Professions Career Opportunity Program (HPCOP). *Time Management for Students*. A free 43-page booklet, available online and filled with practical time-management skills. Includes a bibliography of time-management books. Download the document at: www.oshpd.cahwnet.gov/pcrcd/professions/hpcop.htm#publications.

Minorities

Association of American Medical Colleges. *Minority Students in Medical Education: Facts and Figures XII*. Washington, DC: AAMC, 2002, 174 pp. (www.aamc.org/publications/factsandfigures.htm) Virtually all the "hard data" you could want about how well underrepresented minorities are doing as medical school applicants, students, practitioners, and academicians. This book is updated periodically. Order this free publication by contacting: facts&figures@aamc.org, or download the entire publication from the AAMC website.

Basco, WT, Jr., Gilbert, GE, Blue AV. Determining the consequences for rural applicants when additional consideration is discontinued in a medical school admission process. *Acad Med*. 2002;77:S20-S22. This study shows that there has been a marked reduction in the proportion of rural applicants offered admission interviews when additional consideration and score adjustments were not applied.

Journal for Minority Medical Students. This journal focuses on the needs and concerns of minority medical students. Its annual *Keepsake* edition (see below) is a distillation of great information for minority premeds. Copies of the Journal can be obtained from medical school minority affairs offices and some premed offices.

Journal of the National Medical Association. Focusing on topics vital to black physicians and those serving black patients, this monthly journal has a wide variety of articles that should be interesting to black premed and medical students. The articles dealing with the Association's activities and the news relating to minority practitioners will be of particular interest. A free copy can be obtained online at www.slackinc.com/general/jnma/jnmahome.htm.

Keepsake: A Guide for Minority Premed Students. (Annual) Produced by the *Journal for Minority Medical Students*, it provides a good overview of the premed and medical school experience from the minority student's viewpoint. It also contains current addresses for summer and other special programs. Obtain a copy from your premed or minority affairs adviser.

Minority Student Opportunities in United States Medical Schools. Washington, DC: AAMC. (Biannual; even-numbered years) This book lists the minority affairs contact person at each U.S. medical school, and information about each school's programs for minority students, including recruitment, admission requirements, academic and financial aid, and summer enrichment programs. It also contains detailed, school-specific numbers of underrepresented minority students who applied, were accepted, began classes, and are in each class. These numbers are further broken down by gender and state of residence. To order a copy, go to the website: www.aamc.org/publications/ms02.htm.

Office of Statewide Health Planning and Development, Health Professions Career Opportunity Program (HPCOP). *Minority Students: A Guide for Premedical Students*. A free 36-page booklet, available online, filled with practical advice aimed at getting minority students accepted into medical school. The booklet is produced by HPCOP, an organization that aims to increase underrepresented minority student participation in the health professions in California. Download the document at www.oshpd.cahwnet.gov/pcrcd/professions/hpcop.htm#publications.

Disabled Students

Association of Academic Physiatrists. Recommended guidelines for admission of candidates with disabilities to medical school. *Am J Phy Med Rehabil*. 1993;72(1):45-7. This association acts as an advocate within the medical profession for disabled applicants and practitioners. The article presents guidelines for schools to use to determine if otherwise-qualified medical school applicants can perform a physician's functions.

Essex-Sorlie D. The Americans with Disabilities Act: I. History, summary, and key components. *Acad Med*. 1994;69(7):519-24. An excellent overview of the Americans with Disabilities Act and how it relates to medical schools. While it does not address the specific question of application to medical school directly, the article gives enough information from which to extrapolate. Clear, concise, and free of legal mumbo-jumbo.

Faigel HC. Changes in services for students with learning disabilities in U.S. and Canadian medical schools, 1991 to 1997. *Acad Med*. 1998 Dec;73(12):1290-3. This survey of U.S. and Canadian medical schools suggests that medical schools have improved their services for learning-disabled students over the past decade in response to the Americans with Disabilities Act.

Reichgott MJ. "Without handicap": issues of medical schools and physically disabled students. *Acad Med.* 1996; 71(7):724-9. A discussion of medical schools' roles in providing acceptable accommodations for physically handicapped students. He condemns the concept of the "undifferentiated graduate"—a common reason for rejecting physically disabled applicants—suggesting that this is no longer possible, or possibly even necessary.

Steinberg AG, Iezzoni LI, Conill A, Stineman M. Reasonable accommodations for medical faculty with disabilities. *JAMA*. 2002;288(24):3147-54. Although discussing disabled faculty members, this paper presents a thoughtful review of disability among medical practitioners and a scathing condemnation of medical school cultures that barely tolerate disabled clinicians.

Wu SS, Tsang P, Wainapel SF. Physical disability among American medical students. *Am J Phys Med Rehab.* 1996;75(3):183-7. A survey and review of the nature of, accommodations for, and success of disabled medical students in mainland United States and Puerto Rican medical schools.

Older and Younger Applicants

Baffi-Dugan C, Lang G. A postbac primer. *The Advisor*. 2001;22(1):6-10. An excellent description of the differences between the various types of postbaccalaureate programs. (Most premed advisers probably have copies of this journal.)

Lang G: Key questions to ask about postbac programs. *The Advisor*. 2001;22(1):11-3. A great set of questions to ask about potential postbaccalaureate programs. The set of questions is designed to help assess which programs will fit your needs. (Your premed adviser should have copies of this journal.)

International Medical Students and Graduates

American Medical Association. State licensure board requirements for IMGs. (www.ama-assn.org/ama/pub/category/1555.html) This webpage provides an overview of the hard-to-find state licensure requirements for IMGs, including Fifth Pathway requirements, taken from the AMA publication, *U.S. Medical Licensure Statistics and Requirements by State*.

Foundation for Advancement of International Medical Education and Research (FAIMER). *The International Medical Education Directory (IMED).* (http://imed.ecfmg.org) This online directory provides an up-to-date resource about international medical schools that are recognized by the appropriate government agency, usually the Ministry of Health, in the countries where the schools are located. Graduates of the listed medical schools are allowed to obtain ECFMG certification. If you are considering going to a foreign medical school, check to make sure it is listed. Unless the foreign school is still listed when you graduate, you cannot apply to practice medicine in the United States.

Spears RA. *Essential American Idioms*. Lincolnwood, IL: National Textbook, 1992. If you think that "a fine kettle of fish" is a gourmet meal, you need this book. A complete guide to the common idioms and quaintness found in American English, this book will help both those for whom English is a second language and those for whom American "lingo" is an impossible corruption of the Queen's English. (+)

World Health Organization. *World Directory of Medical Schools.* (Published intermittently.) This is no longer used for ECFMG certification. See FAMIR's *Directory*, above.

Women in Medicine

American Medical Association. *AMA Women In Medicine Data Source, 2003 Edition*. (www.ama-assn.org/ama/pub/article/171-194.html) A series of online tables filled with statistics and information about the status of women in medicine, from medical school through residency and into practice.

Davis C. Called by God, led by men: women face the masculinization of American medicine at the College of Medical Evangelists, 1909-1922. *Bull Hist Med.* 1993;67(1):119-48. A detailed description of the tribulations women faculty members endured at the precursor to the Loma Linda School of Medicine, an experience typical of all co-educational medical schools at that time.

Dobkin R, Sippy S. *The College Woman's Handbook*. New York: Workman, 1995. A peer-to-peer guide to everything a woman ought to know about college. From eleventh-hour cramming tips to safer partying to getting into grad school, this book is packed with tips, and the sidebar format allows for skimming and light reading. Subjects include classes, housing, relationships, studying, nutrition, health, and much more. (+)

Durso C. The long and winding road. *New Physician*. 1995;44:24-9. An excellent review of the tortuous path women's medical training has taken in the United States. A sidebar to the article looks at how women are faring in medicine around the globe.

Harrison M. *A Woman in Residence*. New York: Fawcett Crest, 1982. After a Psychiatry residency, Dr. Harrison entered Family Practice. In middle age, she began a rigorous Obstetric and Gynecology residency at a major U.S. hospital, but quickly became disillusioned after realizing that hospitals and medical staffs often compromise the care women need, want, and deserve, for their own convenience. The book, based on her diaries, describes her patients, her colleagues, the excitement of learning new procedures, and the pressures that never let up.(+)

Langelan MJ. *Back Off! How to Confront and Stop Sexual Harassment and Harassers*. New York: Simon & Schuster, 1993. This book examines the dynamics of sex and power in sexual harassment, the motives behind harassers' actions, and why traditional responses, such as appeasement or aggression, don't work. Most important, the author describes successful, nonviolent resistance strategies—including personal and group confrontation techniques, administrative remedies, and formal lawsuits. (+)

Nora LM. Sexual harassment in medical education: a review of the literature with comments from the law. *Acad Med*. 1996;71(1):S113-8. An excellent comprehensive review of the prevalence of sexual harassment in medical education, including a balanced and insightful look at the legal status of harassment claims.

Shrager JB. Three women at Johns Hopkins: private perspectives on medical coeducation in the 1890s. *Ann Int Med*. 1991;115(7):564-9. A fascinating and detailed look at the lives of three women who successfully faced the onslaught of a male-dominated profession by entering a co-educational medical school and graduating.

Interviews

Biegeleisen JI. *Make Your Job Interview a Success*. 4th ed. New York: Macmillan, 1994. This authoritative, advice-packed guide provides inside information and easy-to-use techniques to help you project the best image, respond with the right answers, and get the position you want. Contents include an interview checklist, job-interview scenarios, "63 Guaranteed Ways to Muff a Job Interview," suggestions for improving your appearance and speech, and your rights under the Americans with Disabilities Act. (+)

Zielinski R: *The Medical School Interview*. Champaign, IL: NAAHP, 1986. This publication details the interview process, including the admission committee's task, the screening levels, the review procedures, and the actual interview. Presents the opinions of medical school admission officers, interviewers, and a successful medical school candidate. Students will be able to evaluate their motivation, goals, strengths and weaknesses to effectively present their qualifications during interviews. To order, contact: Membership, NAAHP, Inc., P.O. Box 1518, Champaign, IL 61824-1518.

Licensing Examinations

American Medical Association. *U.S. Medical Licensure Requirements and Statistics*. Chicago, IL: AMA. (Annual) The basic information about medical/Osteopathic licensure requirements in every state and territory of the United States. All the permutations and combinations of licensing are included in easy-to-read charts. It includes contact information for individual state boards, as well as hard-to-get information on IMG licensure requirements. To obtain a copy, call (800) 621-8335, or order online at www.ama-assn.org.

The Federation of State Medical Boards of the U.S., Inc. *Exchange, Vol. 1: Physician Licensing Boards and Discipline*. Euless, TX: FSMB. (Triennial) Contains the USMLE Step 3 eligibility requirements and administrative rules. Also has the requirements for initial licensure, licensure by endorsement, reregistration of one's license, licenses for postgraduate education, and other special licenses. Order online at www.fsmb.org.

—*Exchange, Vol. 2: USMLE M.D. and D.O. Licensing Requirements*. Euless, TX: FSMB. (Triennial) Describes the basic structure and operation of each state medical board, their review and disciplinary functions, and contacts for both of these functions. Order online at www.fsmb.org.

National Board of Medical Examiners, The Federation of State Medical Boards of the U.S., Inc. *USMLE Step 1 (or 2, or 3) General Instructions, Content Outline, and Sample Items*. (www.nbme.org/programs/usmle.asp) This valuable website lists the current examination dates and eligibility requirements for all three Steps, as well as certification and registration procedures. Most important, there are subject/content outlines for all three Steps of the exam. The Step 3 information can be obtained from the state licensing board through which you will take the examination.

Internship and Residency

Marion R. *Learning to Play God*. New York: Fawcett Crest, 1991. We enter medical school filled with idealism and compassion, and what happens? Dr. Marion draws on his experiences to recreate the dehumanizing, slightly insane, and often brutal process of medical training. He leads readers on a tour of a modern teaching hospital: sleep deprivation while on call as an intern, the hysteria of the ER, and patients such as the "Turtle Man." More important, he offers suggestions on how to assure that humanity and idealism survive the grueling path to technical competency. (+)

—*The Intern Blues: The Private Ordeals of Three Young Doctors*. New York: Fawcett Crest, 1989. Taken from the actual diaries of three pediatric interns as they wend their way through a tumultuous year of discovery, sleepiness, and heartbreak, this book has become a classic. In addition to being a great read, you can use this book to learn medical terminology—an editor has explained all the medical terms right in the text. (+)

Moreno M. Diary of my intern year. *New Physician*. 2001;50(7):28-32. Describing one woman's year as a Pediatric intern, this short article offers some honest insights about what is often the toughest year in a physician's life. Well worth reading.

Shem S. *The House of God*. New York: Dell, 1978. This classic tale of one harrowing year in the life of six interns is still quoted on hospital wards, often in the dead of night in the ICU. The tongue-in-cheek, brutally honest, and hilarious (but only for physicians) book strips the cover off the white coats, and pompous attitudes to reveal how many physicians really feel about their patients. It is a thinly disguised description of the author's true-life experiences. (+)

Medical Ethics

Beauchamp TL, Childress JF. *Principles of Biomedical Ethics*. 4th ed. New York: Oxford Univ. Press, 1994. The book begins with a down-to-earth discussion of terms and philosophical principles (Utilitarianism, Kantianism, etc.), then discusses issues particular to biomedical ethics, such as autonomy, nonmaleficence, and beneficence. This classic of bioethical writing will help you to better understand some of medicine's most important debates—and maybe answer some of those sticky interview questions.(+)

Belkin L. *First, Do No Harm*. New York: Fawcett Crest, 1993. This book examines real patients and real ethical decisions in a big city hospital. From the very old to the young and fragile, the traumatized and those with disease—who should live and who should be allowed to die? A microcosm of the dilemmas facing everyone in America's health care system. (+)

Iserson KV. *Death to Dust: What Happens to Dead Bodies?* 2nd ed. Tucson, AZ: Galen Press, Ltd., 2001. So you plan to dissect a human body in medical school? This book describes, in a question-and-answer format, everything that happens, has happened, or may happen to corpses. Interesting stories and humor pepper the reader friendly text. Included are detailed explanations of organ and tissue donation, brain death, embalming, cremation, cryogenics, cannibalism, forensic investigations, autopsies, burials, funeral practices and, of course, anatomical dissection. (+)

Iserson KV, Sanders AB, Mathieu D. *Ethics in Emergency Medicine*. 2nd ed. Tucson, AZ: Galen Press, Ltd., 1995. How do clinicians decide whether a patient is "competent"? What do they do when a patient refuses necessary care? This book has the answers to the stickiest ethical situations. Discussions of actual cases from emergency medicine and prehospital care provide a straightforward approach to a wide range of ethical matters. Contributors include the country's best-known emergency clinicians and medical ethicists. (+)

La Puma J, Schiedermayer D. *Ethics Consultation: A Practical Guide*. Boston: Jones & Bartlett, 1994. What is an "ethics consultation"? How is it done? When do clinicians ask for one? Whether you have an interest in medical ethics or simply want to know some of clinical medicine's inner workings, this book provides information in simple, direct, and very practical terms. (+)

Pence GE. *Classic Cases in Medical Ethics: Accounts of Cases that have Shaped Medical Ethics, with Philosophical, Legal, and Historical Background*. 3rd ed. New York: McGraw Hill, 2000. Quinlan, Clark, Cruzan, Baby Doe, Kevorkian. Focusing on the cases that have shaped the field of medical ethics, the book presents the ethical issues, legal decisions, and historical backgrounds you need to know to understand this evolving field. The landmark cases include coma, physician-assisted suicide, in vitro fertilization, surrogacy, organ transplants and artificial organs, fetal tissue research, genetic testing, mandatory HIV testing, and health care reform. (+)

Zussman R. *Intensive Care: Medical Ethics and the Medical Profession*. Chicago: Univ. of Chicago Press, 1992. How are medical and ethical decisions made in the real world? In riveting case studies, Dr. Zussman describes how ethical decisions in ICUs are interpreted, negotiated, and renegotiated by physicians, nurses, patients, and families. A fascinating resource for anyone who anticipates working in an ICU. (+)

Other Health-Related Careers

American Chiropractic Association. *The Chiropractic College Directory*. (Biennial) This book contains information about Chiropractic and about the individual schools. Contact: KM Enterprises, P.O. Box 25978, Los Angeles, CA 90025; (818) 710-6868; fax: (818) 710-6855.

American Association of Colleges of Pharmacy. *Pharmacy School Admission Requirements*. (Annual) Similar to the book on medical school requirements. Contact: AACP, 1426 Prince St., Alexandria, VA 22314-2841; (703) 739-2330.

American Dental Education Association. *ADEA Official Guide to Dental Schools*. Similar to the book on medical school requirements. Contact: ADEA, 1625 Massachusetts Ave. NW, Suite 600, Washington, DC 20036-2212; (202) 667-9433.

American Medical Association. *Health Professions Career and Education Directory*. (Annual) A listing of nonphysician opportunities in medicine. Contact: AMA, P.O. Box 109050, Chicago, IL 60610-9050.

American Physical Therapy Association. *Directory of Accredited Physical Therapy Education Programs*. (Annual) A listing and description of all approved Physical Therapy programs. Contact: APTA, 1111 N. Fairfax St., Alexandria, VA 22314-1488; (703) 684-2782.

Corder BW, ed. *Medical Professions Admission Guide: Strategy for Success.* 5th ed. Champaign, IL: National Association of Advisors for the Health Professions. A thorough overview of the path to various careers in the health professions. It includes Dentistry, Medicine, Nursing, Nurse Practitioners, Occupational Therapy, Optometry, Pharmacy, Physical Therapy, Physician Assistants, Podiatry, and Veterinary Medicine. Written by undergraduate advisers to these health professions. Contact: NAAHP, P.O. Box 1518, Champaign, Il 61824-1518; (217) 355-0063.

National Health Council. *300 Ways to Put Your Talent to Work in the Health Field.* (June 2002) This resource includes career descriptions, plus information on work setting, education, and salary for more than 300 health careers. Also listed is the contact information for more than 150 organizations offering additional information. An excellent overview of the many careers within medicine and the related biomedical fields. Download an order form at www.nationalhealthcouncil.org/pubs/pub_list.htm or contact: NHC, 1730 M Street NW, Suite 500, Washington, DC 20036; (202) 785-3910.

Survival: Thinking, Eating, Doing

Archer J, Jr. *Managing Anxiety & Stress.* 2nd ed. Munice, IN: Accelerated Development, 1991. Premeds and medical students are under a lot of stress. Adjust your habits and your thinking to cope with stress before it is too late. Each chapter includes written activities to determine your own stress level and appropriate stress reduction methods to lower it. The book presents a simple stress interaction model to help explain the effects of stress and anxiety on relationships, values, transitions, time use, and spirituality. (+)

Cohen GD, Gladstone W. *How to Test & Improve Your Own Mental Health.* Rocklin, CA: Prima, 1995. Are you just stressed, or are you beginning to wonder if it might be something more serious? This book allows you to test your personal mental health and your ability to adapt to and cope with life's stresses. It includes over 120 questions covering every area of your life, with a complete analysis of what your answers mean. (+)

Edwards P. *Cheap Eating: How to Feed Your Family Well and Spend Less.* Hinesburg, VT: Upper Access, 1993. Understanding the pressures of a small budget, the authors provide many cheap-but-tasty meals, tell you how to shop, and even how to grow your own vegetables. Learn to feed a family of four for $30 a week, buy in bulk, use leftovers, control your weight without counting calories, and improve your nutrition while cutting costs. (+)

Fitzgerald M. *On Campus Cookbook: For the Non-Kitchen Cook!* New York: Workman, 1984. This book is the no-hassle answer to having no kitchen—food for any occasion, from all-nighters to a picnic date. It contains more than 70 easy recipes to make in your dorm room, using only hot-pots, blenders, and toaster ovens. The recipes take advantage of what is readily available, some even including food items from the cafeteria line. (+)

Fobes R. *The Creative Problem Solver's Toolbox.* Corvalis, OR: Solutions through Innovation, 1993. Too often we tell ourselves (or are told by others) that our ideas won't work before we even try them. The author provides the inspiration to listen to yourself more often and teaches you how to maximize your problem-solving potential. This book shows you how to recognize useful new applications for "useless" ideas, think in creative ways that schools neglect to teach, identify easily overlooked alternatives, and handle criticisms of your creative ideas. (+)

Frandsen BR., Frandsen KJ, Fransden KP. *Where's Dad Now That I Need Him?* Sandy, UT: Aspen West, 1995. What type of oil do you need for your car? Do you know the best way to start charcoal? This book provides the information that Dads often know best. Chapter topics include: using good consumer sense, managing your money and credit cards, succeeding on the job, travel and vacation tips, dad's recipes (sandwiches, eggs, barbecue, chili, popcorn, etc.), maintaining your car and home, buying and selling a car, crime prevention, and holiday safety. It even tells you how to hold a yard sale. (+)

Frandsen BR, Frandsen KJ, Fransden KP. *Where's Mom Now That I Need Her?* Sandy, UT: Aspen West, 1983. Quick! How long does it take to hard boil an egg? Does the red stripe on your sweat sock mean you should sort it with the whites or the colored laundry? If you're not sure about the answers to these questions, this book is for you. It contains all the essential household trivia that only Moms seem to know. Learn how to make household cleaners, buy a cantaloupe, and cook "comfort" foods, such as pancakes, meatloaf, and cheesy potatoes. (+)

Messner E. *Resilience Enhancement for the Resident Physician.* Durant, OK: EMIS, 1993. The ravages of internship and residency have concerned the medical profession for decades, including the deterioration in patient care that may result from sleep deprivation, physical exhaustion, clinical depression and substance abuse. This book describes the common warning signals of stress and burnout, and offers methods for self-treatment. Prepare yourself by reading this book. (+)

Michalko M. *Thinkpak: A Brainstorming Card Deck.* Berkeley, CA: Ten Speed Press, 1994. Stumped? These idea-stimulating cards help you generate new ideas, turn negatives into positives, and find solutions for "impossible" problems. Drawing on his own premise that "everything new is really an addition to or a modification of something that already existed," the author combines a deck of cards with a book on creative thinking to produce a method for jump-starting ideas. Excellent for brainstorming. (+)

Minninger J. *Total Recall: How to Boost Your Memory Power*. New York: Pocket Books, 1993. This book teaches you how to remember 20 things in less than two minutes using simple memory improvement techniques. Besides providing you with invaluable memory aids, it asks you to rethink your "inability" to learn certain subjects by explaining why emotions can block recall. You might find that you really can memorize mundane material, such as organic chemistry (if you want to). (+)

Ruchlis H, Oddo S. *Clear Thinking: A Practical Introduction*. Buffalo, NY: Prometheus, 1990. The ability to think critically is imperative in the Information Age, with its networked computers, global communications, and cleverly packaged ideas. This introduction to basic critical analysis shows how to evaluate evidence, isolate facts, and use sound reasoning skills in everyday situations. (+)

Tannen D. *Talking From 9 to 5—Women and Men in the Workplace: Language, Sex and Power*. New York: Avon, 1995. Workplace conversations are not idle chatter—they are the social cement that determines success and failure. How do women's and men's conversational styles affect who gets heard, who gets credit, and what gets done? This world-famous linguist answers those questions about miscommunication between the sexes. (+)

Marriage and Relationships

Carter J, Carter JD. *He Works/She Works: Successful Strategies for Working Couples*. New York: AMACOM, 1995. Marriage isn't easy, and it becomes much more difficult when both partners work at difficult, time-consuming jobs with hectic schedules. Both partners want to make it work; both harbor unspoken anger at themselves and their partner. This book helps you identify the problems, and suggests workable solutions. (+)

Pregnancy and Parenting

Eisenberg A, Murkoff HE, Hathaway SE. *What to Expect When You're Expecting*. Berkeley, CA: Ten Speed Press, 1991. This is the bible of pregnancy—the book that answers the concerns of mothers- and fathers-to-be, from the planning stage through postpartum, in a comprehensive month-by-month guide. This book answers virtually every pregnancy-related question or fear. (+)

Eisenberg A, Murkoff HE, Hathaway SE. *What to Eat When You're Expecting*. Berkeley, CA: Ten Speed Press, 1986. The book includes tips for maintaining proper weight gain; recipes for high-protein meatless entrées, nonalcoholic cocktails, naturally sweetened cakes and desserts; vitamin information; and nutrition charts. (+)

Eisenberg A, Murkoff HE, Hathaway SE. *What to Expect the First Year*. Berkeley, CA: Ten Speed Press, 1989. This month-by-month guide explains everything new parents need to know about the first year with their baby. It includes information on the infant's growth and development, feeding, sleeping habits, illnesses, child safety and first aid, traveling with your baby, and handling older siblings. (+)

National Library of Medicine. MEDLINEplus (www.nlm.nih.gov/medlineplus/childdaycare.html) This website from the U.S. National Library of Medicine and National Institutes of Health has many online articles related to child daycare, drawn from the American Academy of Pediatrics and other sources.

Sale JS, Kollengberg K. *The Working Parents' Handbook*. New York: Simon & Schuster, 1996. All working parents struggle with the same anxiety, guilt, and questions. This book presents workable solutions to such questions as how to deal with separation anxiety, find good child-care, simplify meal preparation and bedtime, and set up a baby-sitting co-op. (+)

Wiebe C. From here to maternity. *New Physician*. 1995;44:40-4. A good description of some problems pregnant women physicians faced during medical school and residency. They also offer some helpful suggestions.

The Lighter Side

Bennett H, ed. *The Best of Medical Humor*. 2nd ed. New York: Hanley Belfus, 1997. This anthology of humorous articles, quotes, poems, and cartoons will make you laugh out loud at medicine's funny side. Selections include, "Real Interns Don't Have Time to Eat Quiche," "The Fine Art of Disappearing from Meetings," and "How to Write Nifty Titles for Your Papers."(+)

Brilliant A. *I May Not Be Totally Perfect, But Parts of Me Are Excellent*. Santa Barbara, CA: Woodbridge, 1979. Once you are introduced to Mr. Brilliant's zany world-view, you may never want to return to your own again. This book contains nearly 300 illustrated Brilliant Thoughts® to provoke, amuse, energize, tranquilize, captivate, and liberate you. (+)

London O. *Kill as Few Patients as Possible, and Fifty-six Other Essays on How To Be the World's Best Doctor*. Berkeley, CA: Ten Speed Press, 1987. Funny short essays illustrate this practicing physician's rules about how to be successful and compassionate. Learn how to become the world's second-best doctor from lessons (many tongue-in-cheek) such as, "If you think you're indispensable, check your appointment book a week after you drop dead." (+)

Index

—A—

— Q —

About the Author

Kenneth V. Iserson, M.D., M.B.A., FACEP, is a noted medical teacher, clinician, and researcher. A past president of the Society of Teachers of Emergency Medicine and a Professor of Emergency Medicine, he directed the Residency Program in Emergency Medicine at the University of Arizona College of Medicine in Tucson for a decade. He frequently speaks to premedical students and advisers throughout the country on the complex process of selecting a medical school, applying to, interviewing for, and obtaining a desired medical school slot. He also speaks to medical students, advisers, and residency director groups about selecting a medical specialty and the residency selection process.

Dr. Iserson is also the author of the following books, all published by Galen Press, LTD., Tucson, Arizona:

- *Death to Dust: What Happens to Dead Bodies?, 2nd ed.* (2000)
- *Dying to Know: A Compendium of the Morbid, Mortal, and Macabre* (Fall 2004)
- *Ethics in Emergency Medicine, 2nd ed.* (1995)
- *Grave Words: Notifying Survivors about Sudden, Unexpected Deaths* (1999)
- *Iserson's Getting Into A Residency, 6th ed.* (2003)
- *Non-Standard Medical Electives in the U.S. and Canada* (1998)
- *Pocket Protocols: Notifying Survivors about Sudden, Unexpected Deaths* (1999)

Galen

Galen of Pergamum (A.D. 130–201), the Greek physician whose writings guided medicine for more than a millennium after his death, inspired the name, Galen Press. As the father of modern anatomy and physiology, Galen wrote more than 100 treatises while attempting to change medicine from an art form into a science. As a practicing physician, Galen first ministered to gladiators and then to Roman Emperor Marcus Aurelius. Far more than Hippocrates, Galen's work influenced Western physicians, and was the "truth" until the late Middle Ages when physicians and scientists challenged his teachings.

Galen Press, LTD., which publishes non-clinical, health-related books, follows Galen's advice that "the chief merit of language is clearness . . . nothing detracts so much from this as unfamiliar terms."

Also by Galen Press, Ltd.

After-Death Planning Guide
Kenneth V. Iserson, M.D.

Civil War Medicine: Challenges and Triumphs
Alfred Jay Bollet, M.D.

Death Investigation: The Basics
Brad Randall, M.D.

Death to Dust: What Happens to Dead Bodies?, 2nd ed.
Kenneth V. Iserson, M.D.

Dying to Know: A Compendium of the Morbid, Mortal, and Macabre*
Kenneth V. Iserson, M.D.

Ethics in Emergency Medicine, 2nd ed.
Edited by Kenneth V. Iserson, M.D.; Arthur B. Sanders, M.D.; and Deborah Mathieu, Ph.D.

Grave Words: Notifying Survivors about Sudden, Unexpected Deaths
Kenneth V. Iserson, M.D.

House Calls, Rounds, and Healings: A Poetry Casebook
David Schiedermayer, M.D.

Iserson's Getting Into A Residency: A Guide For Medical Students, 6th ed.
Kenneth V. Iserson, M.D.

Pocket Protocols: Notifying Survivors about Sudden, Unexpected Deaths
Kenneth V. Iserson, M.D.

Résumés and Personal Statements for Health Professionals, 2nd ed.
James W. Tysinger, Ph.D.

The Cost-Effective Use of Leeches and Other Musings of a Medical School Survivor
Jeffrey A. Drayer, M.D.

For more information, please contact:

Customer Service, Galen Press, Ltd.
P.O. Box 64400, Tucson, AZ 85728-4400 USA
Tel: (520) 577-8363 Fax: (520) 529-6459
www.galenpress.com

*Call for information

Pocket Protocols

Notifying Survivors about Sudden, Unexpected Deaths

Pocket-sized booklet containing the protocols from *Grave Words*

ISBN: 1-883620-05-8 $ 6.95 (bulk discounts available)

Slides for *Grave Words*

- Slide sets of the protocols and other tables from *Grave Words*
- Build your own Death Notification or Death & Dying Course using the specialized slide sets

Slide Set	Number of Slides
A. Main Protocol for Death Notification	65
B. General Set: Sudden Death/Nurse Interactions/Grief/ Communication/Survivors' Questions	50
C. Chaplains/Religions	42
D. Emergency Medicine/Trauma	35
E. Phrases: Helping and Hurtful	23
F. Telephone Notification Protocol	22
G. Students' Deaths	17
H. Emergency Medical Services	16
I. Telling Friends	16
J. Children: Telling & Grieving	13
K. Obstetrics	14
L. Disaster Survivors' Protocol	10
M. Organ Donation	10

Prices:

Item 1:	Complete set of 333 slides	$ 395.00
Item 2:	Main Protocol + Any three other sets	$ 345.00
Item 3:	Main Protocol + Any two other sets	$ 295.00
Item 4:	Main Protocol + Any one other set	$ 250.00
Item 5:	Individual set	$3.00/slide

Items 1-4: Includes one copy each of ***Grave Words*** and ***Pocket Protocols***. Shipping $15.
Item 5: Add shipping of $12 for first set and $2 for each additional set.

Educational Video: *The Gravest Words*

25 minutes long / $295.00 plus $12 shipping

Four scenarios dealing with sudden death notifications:

1. Preparation for the notification.
2. Notifying family and friends.
3. Survivor-clinician interactions during resuscitation attempts.
4. Telephone notifications.

Viewers learn how to:

- Prepare for the notification.
- Tell survivors.
- Build a Memory Box.
- Interact with family during a resuscitation attempt.
- Do telephone notifications.

Designed for instructor-student interactions, this video can be used alone or as part of resuscitation courses (ACLS, ATLS, PALS).

To order, and for more information, please contact Galen Press, Ltd., at:

P.O. Box 64400, Tucson, AZ 85728-4400 USA / Tel: (520) 577-8363 / Fax: (520) 529-6459

www.galenpress.com

Previews: We keep our prices low by not offering previews. See our 30-Day Guarantee.

30-Day Money Back Guarantee: You may return your purchase *within 30 days*

Order Form

Yes! . . . Please send me:

_____ copies of ***Get Into Medical School! A Guide for the Perplexed, 2nd ed.*** @ $36.95 each $ __________

_____ copies of ***Résumés and Personal Statements for Health Professionals, 2nd ed.*** @ $18.95 each $ __________

_____ copies of ***Iserson's Getting Into A Residency: A Guide for Medical Students, 6th ed.*** @ $38.95 each $ __________

_____ copies of ***The Companion Disk*** @ $12.00 $ __________

_____ copies of ***Grave Words: Notifying Survivors about Sudden, Unexpected Deaths*** @ $38.95 each $ __________

_____ copies of ***Pocket Protocols*** @ $6.95 each $ __________

_____ copies of ***Death to Dust: What Happens to Dead Bodies?, 2nd ed.*** @ $48.95 each $ __________

_____ copies of ***After-Death Planning Guide*** @ $3.00 each $ __________

_____ copies of ***Ethics In Emergency Medicine, 2nd ed.*** @ $39.95 each $ __________

_____ copies of ***Death Investigation: The Basics*** @ $24.95 each $ __________

_____ copies of ***Civil War Medicine: Challenges and Triumphs*** @ $44.95 each $ __________

_____ copies of ***House Calls, Rounds, and Healings: A Poetry Casebook*** @ $12.95 each $ __________

_____ copies of ***The Cost-Effective Use of Leeches and Other Musings of a Medical School Survivor*** @ $14.95 each $ __________

AZ Residents – Add 7.6% sales tax $ __________

Shipping: $3.95 for 1st Book, $1.50 / each additional $ __________

Priority Mail: ***ADD*** $3.00 for 1st Book, $2.00 / each additional $ __________

TOTAL ENCLOSED (U.S. funds only) $ __________

❒ Check ❒ VISA ❒ MasterCard ❒ Institutional Purchase Order

SHIP TO: Name ______________________________

Address ______________________________

____

City/State/Zip ______________________________

Phone *(required)* ______________________________

CREDIT CARD Number ______________________________

Expiration date ____________ Signature ______________________________

Send completed form and payment to:

Galen Press, Ltd.
PO Box 64400-GM2
Tucson, AZ 85728-4400 USA

Tel (520) 577-8363
Fax (520) 529-6459
Orders: 1-800-442-5369 (US/Canada)

www.galenpress.com

Also available through your local bookstore.
Bulk Discounts Available

Pocket Protocols

Notifying Survivors about Sudden, Unexpected Deaths

Pocket-sized booklet containing the protocols from *Grave Words*

ISBN: 1-883620-05-8 $ 6.95 (bulk discounts available)

Slides for *Grave Words*

- Slide sets of the protocols and other tables from *Grave Words*
- Build your own Death Notification or Death & Dying Course using the specialized slide sets

Slide Set	Number of Slides
A. Main Protocol for Death Notification	65
B. General Set: Sudden Death/Nurse Interactions/Grief/ Communication/Survivors' Questions	50
C. Chaplains/Religions	42
D. Emergency Medicine/Trauma	35
E. Phrases: Helping and Hurtful	23
F. Telephone Notification Protocol	22
G. Students' Deaths	17
H. Emergency Medical Services	16
I. Telling Friends	16
J. Children: Telling & Grieving	13
K. Obstetrics	14
L. Disaster Survivors' Protocol	10
M. Organ Donation	10

Prices:

Item 1:	Complete set of 333 slides	$ 395.00
Item 2:	Main Protocol + Any three other sets	$ 345.00
Item 3:	Main Protocol + Any two other sets	$ 295.00
Item 4:	Main Protocol + Any one other set	$ 250.00
Item 5:	Individual set	$3.00/slide

Items 1-4: Includes one copy each of ***Grave Words*** and ***Pocket Protocols***. Shipping $15.
Item 5: Add shipping of $12 for first set and $2 for each additional set.

Educational Video: *The Gravest Words*

25 minutes long / $295.00 plus $12 shipping

Four scenarios dealing with sudden death notifications:

1. Preparation for the notification.
2. Notifying family and friends.
3. Survivor-clinician interactions during resuscitation attempts.
4. Telephone notifications.

Viewers learn how to:

- Prepare for the notification.
- Tell survivors.
- Build a Memory Box.
- Interact with family during a resuscitation attempt.
- Do telephone notifications.

Designed for instructor-student interactions, this video can be used alone or as part of resuscitation courses (ACLS, ATLS, PALS).

To order, and for more information, please contact Galen Press, Ltd., at:

P.O. Box 64400, Tucson, AZ 85728-4400 USA / Tel: (520) 577-8363 / Fax: (520) 529-6459

www.galenpress.com

Previews: We keep our prices low by not offering previews. See our 30-Day Guarantee.

30-Day Money Back Guarantee: You may return your purchase *within 30 days*

Order Form

Yes! . . . Please send me:

_____ copies of ***Get Into Medical School! A Guide for the Perplexed, 2nd ed.*** @ $36.95 each $ ________

_____ copies of ***Résumés and Personal Statements for Health Professionals, 2nd ed.*** @ $18.95 each $ ________

_____ copies of ***Iserson's Getting Into A Residency: A Guide for Medical Students, 6th ed.*** @ $38.95 each $ ________

_____ copies of ***The Companion Disk*** @ $12.00 $ ________

_____ copies of ***Grave Words: Notifying Survivors about Sudden, Unexpected Deaths*** @ $38.95 each $ ________

_____ copies of ***Pocket Protocols*** @ $6.95 each $ ________

_____ copies of ***Death to Dust: What Happens to Dead Bodies?, 2nd ed.*** @ $48.95 each $ ________

_____ copies of ***After-Death Planning Guide*** @ $3.00 each $ ________

_____ copies of ***Ethics In Emergency Medicine, 2nd ed.*** @ $39.95 each $ ________

_____ copies of ***Death Investigation: The Basics*** @ $24.95 each $ ________

_____ copies of ***Civil War Medicine: Challenges and Triumphs*** @ $44.95 each $ ________

_____ copies of ***House Calls, Rounds, and Healings: A Poetry Casebook*** @ $12.95 each $ ________

_____ copies of ***The Cost-Effective Use of Leeches and Other Musings of a Medical School Survivor*** @ $14.95 each $ ________

AZ Residents – Add 7.6% sales tax $ ________

Shipping: $3.95 for 1st Book, $1.50 / each additional $ ________

Priority Mail: ***ADD*** $3.00 for 1st Book, $2.00 / each additional $ ________

TOTAL ENCLOSED (U.S. funds only) $ ________

❒ Check ❒ VISA ❒ MasterCard ❒ Institutional Purchase Order

SHIP TO: Name ________________________________

Address ________________________________

____

City/State/Zip ________________________________

Phone *(required)* ________________________________

CREDIT CARD Number ________________________________

Expiration date ____________ Signature ________________________________

Send completed form and payment to:

Galen Press, Ltd.
PO Box 64400-GM2
Tucson, AZ 85728-4400 USA

Tel (520) 577-8363
Fax (520) 529-6459
Orders: 1-800-442-5369 (US/Canada)

www.galenpress.com

Also available through your local bookstore.
Bulk Discounts Available